TITLE 17—COPYRIGHTS

This title was enacted by act July 30, 1947, ch. 391, 61 Stat. 652, and was revised in its entirety by Pub. L. 94–553, title I, § 101, Oct. 19, 1976, 90 Stat. 2541

AMENDMENTS

2010—Pub. L. 111–295, § 4(b)(1)(B), Dec. 9, 2010, 124 Stat. 3180, substituted "Importation and Exportation" for "Manufacturing Requirements, Importation, and Exportation" in item relating to chapter 6.

2008—Pub. L. 110–403, title I, § 105(c)(3), Oct. 13, 2008, 122 Stat. 4260, substituted "Manufacturing Requirements, Importation, and Exportation" for "Manufacturing Requirements and Importation" in item relating to chapter 6.

2004—Pub. L. 108–419, § 3(b), Nov. 30, 2004, 118 Stat. 2361, substituted "Proceedings by Copyright Royalty Judges" for "Copyright Arbitration Royalty Panels" in item relating to chapter 8.

1998—Pub. L. 105–304, title I, § 103(b), title V, § 503(a), Oct. 28, 1998, 112 Stat. 2876, 2916, added items relating to chapters 12 and 13.

1997—Pub. L. 105–80, § 12(a)(1), Nov. 13, 1997, 111 Stat. 1534, substituted "Requirements" for "Requirement" in item relating to chapter 6, "Arbitration Royalty Panels" for "Royalty Tribunal" in item relating to chapter 8, and "Semiconductor Chip Products" for "semiconductor chip products" in item relating to chapter 9, and added item relating to chapter 10.

1994—Pub. L. 103–465, title V, § 512(b), Dec. 8, 1994, 108 Stat. 4974, added item relating to chapter 11.

1984—Pub. L. 98–620, title III, § 303, Nov. 8, 1984, 98 Stat. 3356, added item relating to chapter 9.

TABLE I

This Table lists the sections of former Title 17, Copyrights, and indicates the sections of Title 17, as enacted in 1947, which covered similar and related subject matter.

Title 17 Former Sections	Title 17 1947 Revision Sections
1	1

TABLE I—CONTINUED

Title 17 Former Sections	Title 17 1947 Revision Sections
2	2
3	3
4	4
5	5
6	7
7	8
8	9
9	10
10	11
11	12
12	13
13	14
14	15
15	16
16	17
17	18
18	19
19	20
20	21
21	22
22	23
23	24
24	Rep.
25	101
26	102
27	103
28	104
29	105
30	106
31	107
32	108
33	109
34	110
35	111
36	112
37	113
38	114
39	115
40	116
41	27
42	28
43	29
44	30
45	31
46	32
47	201
48	202
49	203
50	204
51	205
52	206
53	207
54	208
55	209
56	210
57	211
58	212
59	213
60	214
61	215
62	26
63	6
64	6
65	25

TABLE II

This Table lists the sections of former Title 17, Copyrights, and indicates the sections of Title 17, as revised in 1976, which cover similar and related subject matter.

Title 17 1947 Revision Sections	Title 17 New Sections
1	106, 116
2	301

TABLE II—CONTINUED

Title 17 1947 Revision Sections	Title 17 New Sections
3	102, 103
4	102
5	102
6	102
7	103
8	104, 105, 303
9	104
10	401
11	410
12	408
13	407, 411
14	407
15	407
16	601
17	407
18	407, 506
19	401
20	401, 402
21	405
22	601
23	601
24	203, 301 et seq.
25	301 et seq.
26	101
27	109, 202
28	201, 204
29	204
30	205
31	205
32	201
101	412, 501–504
102	Rep. See T. 28 §1338
103	Rep. See F.R. Civ. Proc.
104	110, 506
105	506
106	602
107	602
108	603
109	603
110	Rep. See T. 28 §1338
111	Rep. See T. 28 §1400
112	502
113	502
114	502
115	507
116	505
201	701(a)
202	701(a)
203	708(c)
204	Rep.
205	701(c)
206	701(b)
207	702
208	705
209	407, 410
210	707
211	707
212	705
213	704
214	704
215	708(a), (b)
216	703

PRIOR PROVISIONS

Title 17, as enacted by act July 30, 1947, ch. 391, 61 Stat. 652, consisting of sections 1 to 32, 101 to 116, and 201 to 216, as amended through 1976, and section 203, as amended by Pub. L. 95–94, title IV, §406(a), Aug. 5, 1977, 91 Stat. 682, terminated Jan. 1, 1978.

EFFECTIVE DATE

Section 102 of Pub. L. 94–553, Oct. 19, 1976, 90 Stat. 2598, provided that: "This Act [enacting this title and section 170 of Title 2, The Congress, amending section 131 of Title 2, section 290e of Title 15, Commerce and Trade, section 2318 of Title 18, Crimes and Criminal Procedure, section 543 of Title 26, Internal Revenue Code, section 1498 of Title 28, Judiciary and Judicial Procedure, sections 3203 and 3206 of Title 39, Postal Service, and sections 505 and 2117 of Title 44, Public Printing and Documents, and enacting provisions set out as notes below and under sections 104, 115, 304, 401, 407, 410, and 501 of this title] becomes effective on January 1, 1978, except as otherwise expressly provided by this Act, including provisions of the first section of this Act. The provisions of sections 118, 304(b), and chapter 8 of title 17, as amended by the first section of this Act, take effect upon enactment of this Act [Oct. 19, 1976]."

SEPARABILITY

Section 115 of Pub. L. 94–553, Oct. 19, 1976, 90 Stat. 2602, provided that: "If any provision of title 17 [this title], as amended by the first section of this Act, is declared unconstitutional, the validity of the remainder of this title is not affected."

AUTHORIZATION OF APPROPRIATIONS

Section 114 of Pub. L. 94–553, Oct. 19, 1976, 90 Stat. 2602, provided that: "There are hereby authorized to be appropriated such funds as may be necessary to carry out the purposes of this Act [this title]."

LOST AND EXPIRED COPYRIGHTS; RECORDING RIGHTS

Section 103 of Pub. L. 94–553, Oct. 19, 1976, 90 Stat. 2599, provided that: "This Act [enacting this title] does not provide copyright protection for any work that goes into the public domain before January 1, 1978. The exclusive rights, as provided by section 106 of title 17 as amended by the first section of this Act, to reproduce a work in phonorecords and to distribute phonorecords of the work, do not extend to any nondramatic musical work copyrighted before July 1, 1909."

CHAPTER 1—SUBJECT MATTER AND SCOPE OF COPYRIGHT

AMENDMENTS

2010—Pub. L. 111–175, title I, §§102(a)(2), 103(a)(2), 104(a)(2), May 27, 2010, 124 Stat. 1219, 1227, 1231, added items 111, 119, and 122 and struck out former items 111

"Limitations on exclusive rights: Secondary transmissions", 119 "Limitations on exclusive rights: Secondary transmissions of superstations and network stations for private home viewing", and 122 "Limitations on exclusive rights: Secondary transmissions by satellite carriers within local markets".

2002—Pub. L. 107–273, div. C, title III, § 13210(2)(B), (3)(B), Nov. 2, 2002, 116 Stat. 1909, substituted "Reproduction" for "reproduction" in item 121 and "Limitations on exclusive rights: Secondary transmissions by satellite carriers within local markets" for "Limitations on exclusive rights; secondary transmissions by satellite carriers within local market" in item 122.

1999—Pub. L. 106–113, div. B, § 1000(a)(9) [title I, § 1002(c)], Nov. 29, 1999, 113 Stat. 1536, 1501A–527, added item 122.

1997—Pub. L. 105–80, § 12(a)(2), Nov. 13, 1997, 111 Stat. 1534, substituted "Limitations on exclusive rights: Computer programs" for "Scope of exclusive rights: Use in conjunction with computers and similar information systems" in item 117.

1996—Pub. L. 104–197, title III, § 316(b), Sept. 16, 1996, 110 Stat. 2417, added item 121.

1994—Pub. L. 103–465, title V, § 514(c), Dec. 8, 1994, 108 Stat. 4981, substituted "Copyright in restored works" for "Copyright in certain motion pictures" in item 104A.

1993—Pub. L. 103–198, § 3(a), (b)(2), Dec. 17, 1993, 107 Stat. 2309, renumbered item 116A as 116 and struck out former item 116 "Scope of exclusive rights in nondramatic musical works: Compulsory licenses for public performances by means of coin-operated phonorecord players."

Pub. L. 103–182, title III, § 334(b), Dec. 8, 1993, 107 Stat. 2115, added item 104A.

1990—Pub. L. 101–650, title VI, § 603(b), title VII, § 704(b)(1), Dec. 1, 1990, 104 Stat. 5130, 5134, added items 106A and 120.

1988—Pub. L. 100–667, title II, § 202(6), Nov. 16, 1988, 102 Stat. 3958, added item 119.

Pub. L. 100–568, § 4(b)(2), Oct. 31, 1988, 102 Stat. 2857, substituted "Compulsory licenses for public performances" for "Public performances" in item 116 and added item 116A.

§ 101. Definitions

Except as otherwise provided in this title, as used in this title, the following terms and their variant forms mean the following:

An "anonymous work" is a work on the copies or phonorecords of which no natural person is identified as author.

An "architectural work" is the design of a building as embodied in any tangible medium of expression, including a building, architectural plans, or drawings. The work includes the overall form as well as the arrangement and composition of spaces and elements in the design, but does not include individual standard features.

"Audiovisual works" are works that consist of a series of related images which are intrinsically intended to be shown by the use of machines, or devices such as projectors, viewers, or electronic equipment, together with accompanying sounds, if any, regardless of the nature of the material objects, such as films or tapes, in which the works are embodied.

The "Berne Convention" is the Convention for the Protection of Literary and Artistic Works, signed at Berne, Switzerland, on September 9, 1886, and all acts, protocols, and revisions thereto.

The "best edition" of a work is the edition, published in the United States at any time before the date of deposit, that the Library of Congress determines to be most suitable for its purposes.

A person's "children" are that person's immediate offspring, whether legitimate or not, and any children legally adopted by that person.

A "collective work" is a work, such as a periodical issue, anthology, or encyclopedia, in which a number of contributions, constituting separate and independent works in themselves, are assembled into a collective whole.

A "compilation" is a work formed by the collection and assembling of preexisting materials or of data that are selected, coordinated, or arranged in such a way that the resulting work as a whole constitutes an original work of authorship. The term "compilation" includes collective works.

A "computer program" is a set of statements or instructions to be used directly or indirectly in a computer in order to bring about a certain result.

"Copies" are material objects, other than phonorecords, in which a work is fixed by any method now known or later developed, and from which the work can be perceived, reproduced, or otherwise communicated, either directly or with the aid of a machine or device. The term "copies" includes the material object, other than a phonorecord, in which the work is first fixed.

"Copyright owner", with respect to any one of the exclusive rights comprised in a copyright, refers to the owner of that particular right.

A "Copyright Royalty Judge" is a Copyright Royalty Judge appointed under section 802 of this title, and includes any individual serving as an interim Copyright Royalty Judge under such section.

A work is "created" when it is fixed in a copy or phonorecord for the first time; where a work is prepared over a period of time, the portion of it that has been fixed at any particular time constitutes the work as of that time, and where the work has been prepared in different versions, each version constitutes a separate work.

A "derivative work" is a work based upon one or more preexisting works, such as a translation, musical arrangement, dramatization, fictionalization, motion picture version, sound recording, art reproduction, abridgment, condensation, or any other form in which a work may be recast, transformed, or adapted. A work consisting of editorial revisions, annotations, elaborations, or other modifications which, as a whole, represent an original work of authorship, is a "derivative work".

A "device", "machine", or "process" is one now known or later developed.

A "digital transmission" is a transmission in whole or in part in a digital or other nonanalog format.

To "display" a work means to show a copy of it, either directly or by means of a film, slide, television image, or any other device or process or, in the case of a motion picture or other audiovisual work, to show individual images nonsequentially.

An "establishment" is a store, shop, or any similar place of business open to the general public for the primary purpose of selling goods or services in which the majority of the gross square feet of space that is nonresidential is used for that purpose, and in which nondramatic musical works are performed publicly.

The term "financial gain" includes receipt, or expectation of receipt, of anything of value, including the receipt of other copyrighted works.

A work is "fixed" in a tangible medium of expression when its embodiment in a copy or phonorecord, by or under the authority of the author, is sufficiently permanent or stable to permit it to be perceived, reproduced, or otherwise communicated for a period of more than transitory duration. A work consisting of sounds, images, or both, that are being transmitted, is "fixed" for purposes of this title if a fixation of the work is being made simultaneously with its transmission.

A "food service or drinking establishment" is a restaurant, inn, bar, tavern, or any other similar place of business in which the public or patrons assemble for the primary purpose of being served food or drink, in which the majority of the gross square feet of space that is nonresidential is used for that purpose, and in which nondramatic musical works are performed publicly.

The "Geneva Phonograms Convention" is the Convention for the Protection of Producers of Phonograms Against Unauthorized Duplication of Their Phonograms, concluded at Geneva, Switzerland, on October 29, 1971.

The "gross square feet of space" of an establishment means the entire interior space of that establishment, and any adjoining outdoor space used to serve patrons, whether on a seasonal basis or otherwise.

The terms "including" and "such as" are illustrative and not limitative.

An "international agreement" is—

　(1) the Universal Copyright Convention;
　(2) the Geneva Phonograms Convention;
　(3) the Berne Convention;
　(4) the WTO Agreement;
　(5) the WIPO Copyright Treaty;
　(6) the WIPO Performances and Phonograms Treaty; and
　(7) any other copyright treaty to which the United States is a party.

A "joint work" is a work prepared by two or more authors with the intention that their contributions be merged into inseparable or interdependent parts of a unitary whole.

"Literary works" are works, other than audiovisual works, expressed in words, numbers, or other verbal or numerical symbols or indicia, regardless of the nature of the material objects, such as books, periodicals, manuscripts, phonorecords, film, tapes, disks, or cards, in which they are embodied.

The term "motion picture exhibition facility" means a movie theater, screening room, or other venue that is being used primarily for the exhibition of a copyrighted motion picture, if such exhibition is open to the public or is made to an assembled group of viewers outside of a normal circle of a family and its social acquaintances.

"Motion pictures" are audiovisual works consisting of a series of related images which, when shown in succession, impart an impression of motion, together with accompanying sounds, if any.

To "perform" a work means to recite, render, play, dance, or act it, either directly or by means of any device or process or, in the case of a motion picture or other audiovisual work, to show its images in any sequence or to make the sounds accompanying it audible.

A "performing rights society" is an association, corporation, or other entity that licenses the public performance of nondramatic musical works on behalf of copyright owners of such works, such as the American Society of Composers, Authors and Publishers (ASCAP), Broadcast Music, Inc. (BMI), and SESAC, Inc.

"Phonorecords" are material objects in which sounds, other than those accompanying a motion picture or other audiovisual work, are fixed by any method now known or later developed, and from which the sounds can be perceived, reproduced, or otherwise communicated, either directly or with the aid of a machine or device. The term "phonorecords" includes the material object in which the sounds are first fixed.

"Pictorial, graphic, and sculptural works" include two-dimensional and three-dimensional works of fine, graphic, and applied art, photographs, prints and art reproductions, maps, globes, charts, diagrams, models, and technical drawings, including architectural plans. Such works shall include works of artistic craftsmanship insofar as their form but not their mechanical or utilitarian aspects are concerned; the design of a useful article, as defined in this section, shall be considered a pictorial, graphic, or sculptural work only if, and only to the extent that, such design incorporates pictorial, graphic, or sculptural features that can be identified separately from, and are capable of existing independently of, the utilitarian aspects of the article.

For purposes of section 513, a "proprietor" is an individual, corporation, partnership, or other entity, as the case may be, that owns an establishment or a food service or drinking establishment, except that no owner or operator of a radio or television station licensed by the Federal Communications Commission, cable system or satellite carrier, cable or satellite carrier service or programmer, provider of online services or network access or the operator of facilities therefor, telecommunications company, or any other such audio or audiovisual service or programmer now known or as may be developed in the future, commercial subscription music service, or owner or operator of any other transmission service, shall under any circumstances be deemed to be a proprietor.

A "pseudonymous work" is a work on the copies or phonorecords of which the author is identified under a fictitious name.

"Publication" is the distribution of copies or phonorecords of a work to the public by sale or other transfer of ownership, or by rental, lease, or lending. The offering to distribute copies or phonorecords to a group of persons for purposes of further distribution, public performance, or public display, constitutes publication. A public performance or display of a work does not of itself constitute publication.

To perform or display a work "publicly" means—

(1) to perform or display it at a place open to the public or at any place where a substantial number of persons outside of a normal circle of a family and its social acquaintances is gathered; or

(2) to transmit or otherwise communicate a performance or display of the work to a place specified by clause (1) or to the public, by means of any device or process, whether the members of the public capable of receiving the performance or display receive it in the same place or in separate places and at the same time or at different times.

"Registration", for purposes of sections 205(c)(2), 405, 406, 410(d), 411, 412, and 506(e), means a registration of a claim in the original or the renewed and extended term of copyright.

"Sound recordings" are works that result from the fixation of a series of musical, spoken, or other sounds, but not including the sounds accompanying a motion picture or other audiovisual work, regardless of the nature of the material objects, such as disks, tapes, or other phonorecords, in which they are embodied.

"State" includes the District of Columbia and the Commonwealth of Puerto Rico, and any territories to which this title is made applicable by an Act of Congress.

A "transfer of copyright ownership" is an assignment, mortgage, exclusive license, or any other conveyance, alienation, or hypothecation of a copyright or of any of the exclusive rights comprised in a copyright, whether or not it is limited in time or place of effect, but not including a nonexclusive license.

A "transmission program" is a body of material that, as an aggregate, has been produced for the sole purpose of transmission to the public in sequence and as a unit.

To "transmit" a performance or display is to communicate it by any device or process whereby images or sounds are received beyond the place from which they are sent.

A "treaty party" is a country or intergovernmental organization other than the United States that is a party to an international agreement.

The "United States", when used in a geographical sense, comprises the several States, the District of Columbia and the Commonwealth of Puerto Rico, and the organized territories under the jurisdiction of the United States Government.

For purposes of section 411, a work is a "United States work" only if—

(1) in the case of a published work, the work is first published—

(A) in the United States;

(B) simultaneously in the United States and another treaty party or parties, whose law grants a term of copyright protection that is the same as or longer than the term provided in the United States;

(C) simultaneously in the United States and a foreign nation that is not a treaty party; or

(D) in a foreign nation that is not a treaty party, and all of the authors of the work are nationals, domiciliaries, or habitual residents of, or in the case of an audiovisual work legal entities with headquarters in, the United States;

(2) in the case of an unpublished work, all the authors of the work are nationals, domiciliaries, or habitual residents of the United States, or, in the case of an unpublished audiovisual work, all the authors are legal entities with headquarters in the United States; or

(3) in the case of a pictorial, graphic, or sculptural work incorporated in a building or structure, the building or structure is located in the United States.

A "useful article" is an article having an intrinsic utilitarian function that is not merely to portray the appearance of the article or to convey information. An article that is normally a part of a useful article is considered a "useful article".

The author's "widow" or "widower" is the author's surviving spouse under the law of the author's domicile at the time of his or her death, whether or not the spouse has later remarried.

The "WIPO Copyright Treaty" is the WIPO Copyright Treaty concluded at Geneva, Switzerland, on December 20, 1996.

The "WIPO Performances and Phonograms Treaty" is the WIPO Performances and Phonograms Treaty concluded at Geneva, Switzerland, on December 20, 1996.

A "work of visual art" is—

(1) a painting, drawing, print, or sculpture, existing in a single copy, in a limited edition of 200 copies or fewer that are signed and consecutively numbered by the author, or, in the case of a sculpture, in multiple cast, carved, or fabricated sculptures of 200 or fewer that are consecutively numbered by the author and bear the signature or other identifying mark of the author; or

(2) a still photographic image produced for exhibition purposes only, existing in a single copy that is signed by the author, or in a limited edition of 200 copies or fewer that are signed and consecutively numbered by the author.

A work of visual art does not include—

(A)(i) any poster, map, globe, chart, technical drawing, diagram, model, applied art, motion picture or other audiovisual work, book, magazine, newspaper, periodical, data base, electronic information service, electronic publication, or similar publication;

(ii) any merchandising item or advertising, promotional, descriptive, covering, or packaging material or container;

(iii) any portion or part of any item described in clause (i) or (ii);

(B) any work made for hire; or

(C) any work not subject to copyright protection under this title.

A "work of the United States Government" is a work prepared by an officer or employee of the United States Government as part of that person's official duties.

A "work made for hire" is—

(1) a work prepared by an employee within the scope of his or her employment; or

(2) a work specially ordered or commissioned for use as a contribution to a collective work, as a part of a motion picture or other audiovisual work, as a translation, as a supplementary work, as a compilation, as an instructional text, as a test, as answer material for a test, or as an atlas, if the parties expressly agree in a written instrument signed by them that the work shall be considered a work made for hire. For the purpose of the foregoing sentence, a "supplementary work" is a work prepared for publication as a secondary adjunct to a work by another author for the purpose of introducing, concluding, illustrating, explaining, revising, commenting upon, or assisting in the use of the other work, such as forewords, afterwords, pictorial illustrations, maps, charts, tables, editorial notes, musical arrangements, answer material for tests, bibliographies, appendixes, and indexes, and an "instructional text" is a literary, pictorial, or graphic work prepared for publication and with the purpose of use in systematic instructional activities.

In determining whether any work is eligible to be considered a work made for hire under paragraph (2), neither the amendment contained in section 1011(d) of the Intellectual Property and Communications Omnibus Reform Act of 1999, as enacted by section 1000(a)(9) of Public Law 106–113, nor the deletion of the words added by that amendment—

(A) shall be considered or otherwise given any legal significance, or

(B) shall be interpreted to indicate congressional approval or disapproval of, or acquiescence in, any judicial determination,

by the courts or the Copyright Office. Paragraph (2) shall be interpreted as if both section 2(a)(1) of the Work Made For Hire and Copyright Corrections Act of 2000 and section 1011(d) of the Intellectual Property and Communications Omnibus Reform Act of 1999, as enacted by section 1000(a)(9) of Public Law 106–113, were never enacted, and without regard to any inaction or awareness by the Congress at any time of any judicial determinations.

The terms "WTO Agreement" and "WTO member country" have the meanings given those terms in paragraphs (9) and (10), respectively, of section 2 of the Uruguay Round Agreements Act.

(Pub. L. 94–553, title I, § 101, Oct. 19, 1976, 90 Stat. 2541; Pub. L. 96–517, § 10(a), Dec. 12, 1980, 94 Stat. 3028; Pub. L. 100–568, § 4(a)(1), Oct. 31, 1988, 102 Stat. 2854; Pub. L. 101–650, title VI, § 602, title VII, § 702, Dec. 1, 1990, 104 Stat. 5128, 5133; Pub. L. 102–307, title I, § 102(b)(2), June 26, 1992, 106 Stat. 266; Pub. L. 102–563, § 3(b), Oct. 28, 1992, 106 Stat. 4248; Pub. L. 104–39, § 5(a), Nov. 1, 1995, 109 Stat. 348; Pub. L. 105–80, § 12(a)(3), Nov. 13, 1997, 111 Stat. 1534; Pub. L. 105–147, § 2(a), Dec. 16, 1997, 111 Stat. 2678; Pub. L. 105–298, title II, § 205, Oct. 27, 1998, 112 Stat. 2833; Pub. L. 105–304, title I, § 102(a), Oct. 28, 1998, 112 Stat. 2861; Pub. L. 106–44, § 1(g)(1), Aug. 5, 1999, 113 Stat. 222; Pub. L. 106–113, div. B, § 1000(a)(9) [title I, § 1011(d)], Nov. 29, 1999, 113 Stat. 1536, 1501A–544; Pub. L. 106–379, § 2(a), Oct. 27, 2000, 114 Stat. 1444; Pub. L. 107–273, div. C, title III, § 13210(5), Nov. 2, 2002, 116 Stat. 1909; Pub. L. 108–419, § 4, Nov. 30, 2004, 118 Stat. 2361; Pub. L. 109–9, title I, § 102(c), Apr. 27, 2005, 119 Stat. 220; Pub. L. 111–295, § 6(a), Dec. 9, 2010, 124 Stat. 3181.)

HISTORICAL AND REVISION NOTES

HOUSE REPORT NO. 94–1476

The significant definitions in this section will be mentioned or summarized in connection with the provisions to which they are most relevant.

REFERENCES IN TEXT

Section 1011(d) of the Intellectual Property and Communications Omnibus Reform Act of 1999, referred to in definition of "work made for hire", is section 1000(a)(9) [title I, § 1011(d)] of Pub. L. 106–113, which amended par. (2) of that definition. See 1999 Amendment note below.

Section 2(a)(1) of the Work Made For Hire and Copyright Corrections Act of 2000, referred to in definition of "work made for hire", is section 2(a)(1) of Pub. L. 106—379, which amended par. (2) of that definition. See 2000 Amendment note below.

Section 2 of the Uruguay Round Agreements Act, referred to in definitions of "WTO Agreement" and "WTO member country", is classified to section 3501 of Title 19, Customs Duties.

AMENDMENTS

2010—Pub. L. 111–295, § 6(a)(3), transferred the definition of "food service or drinking establishment" to appear after the definition of "fixed".

Pub. L. 111–295, § 6(a)(2), transferred the definition of "motion picture exhibition facility" to appear after the definition of "Literary works".

Pub. L. 111–295, § 6(a)(1), which directed transfer of the definition of "Copyright Royalty Judges" to appear after the definition of "Copyright owner", was executed by so transferring the definition of "Copyright Royalty Judge", to reflect the probable intent of Congress.

2005—Pub. L. 109–9 inserted definition of "motion picture exhibition facility" after definition of "Motion pictures".

2004—Pub. L. 108–419 inserted definition of "Copyright Royalty Judge" after definition of "Copies".

2002—Pub. L. 107–273, § 13210(5)(B), transferred definition of "Registration" to appear after definition of "publicly".

Pub. L. 107–273, § 13210(5)(A), transferred definition of "computer program" to appear after definition of "compilation".

2000—Pub. L. 106–379, § 2(a)(2), in definition of "work made for hire", inserted after par. (2) provisions relating to considerations and interpretations to be used in determining whether any work is eligible to be considered a work made for hire under par. (2).

Pub. L. 106–379, § 2(a)(1), in definition of "work made for hire", struck out "as a sound recording," after "motion picture or other audiovisual work," in par. (2).

1999—Pub. L. 106–113, which directed the insertion of "as a sound recording," after "audiovisual work" in par. (2) of definition relating to work made for hire, was executed by making the insertion after "audiovisual work," to reflect the probable intent of Congress.

Pub. L. 106–44, § 1(g)(1)(B), in definition of "proprietor", substituted "For purposes of section 513, a 'proprietor'" for "A 'proprietor'".

Pub. L. 106–44, § 1(g)(1)(A), transferred definition of "United States work" to appear after definition of "United States".

1998—Pub. L. 105–304, § 102(a)(1), struck out definition of "Berne Convention work".

Pub. L. 105–304, § 102(a)(2), in definition of "country of origin", substituted "For purposes of section 411, a work is a 'United States work' only if" for "The 'country of origin' of a Berne Convention work, for purposes of section 411, is the United States if" in introductory provisions, substituted "treaty party or parties" for "nation or nations adhering to the Berne Convention" in par. (1)(B) and "is not a treaty party" for "does not adhere to the Berne Convention" in par. (1)(C), (D), and struck out at end "For the purposes of section 411, the 'country of origin' of any other Berne Convention work is not the United States."

Pub. L. 105–298, § 205(1), inserted definitions of "establishment" and "food service or drinking establishment".

Pub. L. 105–304, § 102(a)(3), inserted definition of "Geneva Phonograms Convention".

Pub. L. 105–298, § 205(2), inserted definition of "gross square feet of space".

Pub. L. 105–304, § 102(a)(4), inserted definition of "international agreement".

Pub. L. 105–298, § 205(3), (4), inserted definitions of "performing rights society" and "proprietor".

Pub. L. 105–304, § 102(a)(5), inserted definition of term "treaty party".

Pub. L. 105–304, § 102(a)(6), inserted definition of term "WIPO Copyright Treaty".

Pub. L. 105–304, § 102(a)(7), inserted definition of term "WIPO Performances and Phonograms Treaty".

Pub. L. 105–304, § 102(a)(8), inserted definitions of terms "WTO Agreement" and "WTO member country".

1997—Pub. L. 105–147 inserted definition of "financial gain".

Pub. L. 105–80, in definition of to perform or to display a work "publicly", substituted "process" for "processs" in par. (2).

1995—Pub. L. 104–39 inserted definition of "digital transmission".

1992—Pub. L. 102–563 substituted "Except as otherwise provided in this title, as used" for "As used" in introductory provisions.

Pub. L. 102–307 inserted definition of "registration".

1990—Pub. L. 101–650, § 702(a), inserted definition of "architectural work".

Pub. L. 101–650, § 702(b), in definition of "Berne Convention work" added par. (5).

Pub. L. 101–650, § 602, inserted definition of "work of visual art".

1988—Pub. L. 100–568, § 4(a)(1)(B), inserted definitions of "The Berne Convention" and "Berne Convention work".

Pub. L. 100–568, § 4(a)(1)(C), inserted definition of "country of origin".

Pub. L. 100–568, § 4(a)(1)(A), in definition of "Pictorial, graphic, and sculptural works" substituted "diagrams, models, and technical drawings, including architectural plans" for "technical drawings, diagrams, and models".

1980—Pub. L. 96–517 inserted definition of "computer program".

EFFECTIVE DATE OF 2004 AMENDMENT

Amendment by Pub. L. 108–419 effective 6 months after Nov. 30, 2004, subject to transition provisions, see section 6 of Pub. L. 108–419, set out as an Effective Date; Transition Provisions note under section 801 of this title.

EFFECTIVE DATE OF 2000 AMENDMENT

Pub. L. 106–379, § 2(b)(1), Oct. 27, 2000, 114 Stat. 1444, provided that: "The amendments made by this section [amending this section] shall be effective as of November 29, 1999."

EFFECTIVE DATE OF 1999 AMENDMENT

Pub. L. 106–113, div. B, § 1000(a)(9) [title I, § 1012], Nov. 29, 1999, 113 Stat. 1536, 1501A–544, provided that: "Sec-

tions 1001, 1003, 1005, 1007, 1008, 1009, 1010, and 1011 [enacting sections 338 and 339 of Title 47, Telegraphs, Telephones, and Radiotelegraphs, amending this section, sections 111, 119, 501, and 510 of this title, and section 325 of Title 47, enacting provisions set out as a note under this section and section 325 of Title 47, and amending provisions set out as a note under section 119 of this title] (and the amendments made by such sections) shall take effect on the date of the enactment of this Act [Nov. 29, 1999]. The amendments made by sections 1002, 1004, and 1006 [enacting section 122 of this title and amending sections 119 and 501 of this title] shall be effective as of July 1, 1999."

EFFECTIVE DATE OF 1998 AMENDMENTS

Pub. L. 105–304, title I, § 105, Oct. 28, 1998, 112 Stat. 2877, provided that:

"(a) IN GENERAL.—Except as otherwise provided in this title [see section 101 of Pub. L. 105–304, set out as a Short Title of 1998 Amendments note below], this title and the amendments made by this title shall take effect on the date of the enactment of this Act [Oct. 28, 1998].

"(b) AMENDMENTS RELATING TO CERTAIN INTERNATIONAL AGREEMENTS.—(1) The following shall take effect upon the entry into force of the WIPO Copyright Treaty with respect to the United States [Mar. 6, 2002]:

"(A) Paragraph (5) of the definition of 'international agreement' contained in section 101 of title 17, United States Code, as amended by section 102(a)(4) of this Act.

"(B) The amendment made by section 102(a)(6) of this Act [amending this section].

"(C) Subparagraph (C) of section 104A(h)(1) of title 17, United States Code, as amended by section 102(c)(1) of this Act.

"(D) Subparagraph (C) of section 104A(h)(3) of title 17, United States Code, as amended by section 102(c)(2) of this Act.

"(2) The following shall take effect upon the entry into force of the WIPO Performances and Phonograms Treaty with respect to the United States [May 20, 2002]:

"(A) Paragraph (6) of the definition of 'international agreement' contained in section 101 of title 17, United States Code, as amended by section 102(a)(4) of this Act.

"(B) The amendment made by section 102(a)(7) of this Act [amending this section].

"(C) The amendment made by section 102(b)(2) of this Act [amending section 104 of this title].

"(D) Subparagraph (D) of section 104A(h)(1) of title 17, United States Code, as amended by section 102(c)(1) of this Act.

"(E) Subparagraph (D) of section 104A(h)(3) of title 17, United States Code, as amended by section 102(c)(2) of this Act.

"(F) The amendments made by section 102(c)(3) of this Act [amending section 104A of this title]."

Pub. L. 105–298, title II, § 207, Oct. 27, 1998, 112 Stat. 2834, provided that: "This title [enacting section 512 of this title, amending this section and sections 110 and 504 of this title, and enacting provisions set out as notes under this section] and the amendments made by this title shall take effect 90 days after the date of the enactment of this Act [Oct. 27, 1998]."

EFFECTIVE DATE OF 1995 AMENDMENT

Section 6 of Pub. L. 104–39 provided that: "This Act [see Short Title of 1995 Amendment note below] and the amendments made by this Act shall take effect 3 months after the date of enactment of this Act [Nov. 1, 1995], except that the provisions of sections 114(e) and 114(f) of title 17, United States Code (as added by section 3 of this Act) shall take effect immediately upon the date of enactment of this Act."

EFFECTIVE DATE OF 1992 AMENDMENT

Section 102(g) of Pub. L. 102–307, as amended by Pub. L. 105–298, title I, § 102(d)(2)(B), Oct. 27, 1998, 112 Stat. 2828, provided that:

"(1) Subject to paragraphs (2) and (3), this section [amending this section and sections 304, 408, 409, and 708 of this title and enacting provisions set out as a note under section 304 of this title] and the amendments made by this section shall take effect on the date of the enactment of this Act [June 26, 1992].

"(2) The amendments made by this section shall apply only to those copyrights secured between January 1, 1964, and December 31, 1977. Copyrights secured before January 1, 1964, shall be governed by the provisions of section 304(a) of title 17, United States Code, as in effect on the day before the effective date of this section [June 26, 1992], except each reference to forty-seven years in such provisions shall be deemed to be 67 years.

"(3) This section and the amendments made by this section shall not affect any court proceedings pending on the effective date of this section."

EFFECTIVE DATE OF 1990 AMENDMENT

Amendment by section 602 of Pub. L. 101–650 effective 6 months after Dec. 1, 1990, see section 610 of Pub. L. 101–650, set out as an Effective Date note under section 106A of this title.

Section 706 of title VII of Pub. L. 101–650 provided that: "The amendments made by this title [enacting section 120 of this title and amending this section and sections 102, 106, and 301 of this title], apply to—

"(1) any architectural work created on or after the date of the enactment of this Act [Dec. 1, 1990]; and

"(2) any architectural work that, on the date of the enactment of this Act, is unconstructed and embodied in unpublished plans or drawings, except that protection for such architectural work under title 17, United States Code, by virtue of the amendments made by this title, shall terminate on December 31, 2002, unless the work is constructed by that date."

EFFECTIVE DATE OF 1988 AMENDMENT

Section 13 of Pub. L. 100–568 provided that:

"(a) EFFECTIVE DATE.—This Act and the amendments made by this Act [enacting section 116A of this title, amending this section and sections 104, 116, 205, 301, 401 to 408, 411, 501, 504, 801, and 804 of this title, and enacting provisions set out as notes under this section] take effect on the date on which the Berne Convention (as defined in section 101 of title 17, United States Code) enters into force with respect to the United States [Mar. 1, 1989]. [The Berne Convention entered into force with respect to the United States on Mar. 1, 1989.]

"(b) EFFECT ON PENDING CASES.—Any cause of action arising under title 17, United States Code, before the effective date of this Act shall be governed by the provisions of such title as in effect when the cause of action arose."

SHORT TITLE OF 2010 AMENDMENT

Pub. L. 111–295, § 1, Dec. 9, 2010, 124 Stat. 3180, provided that: "This Act [amending this section and sections 114, 115, 119, 205, 303, 409, 503, 504, 512, 602, 704, 803, 1203, and 1204 of this title and section 2318 of Title 18, Crimes and Criminal Procedure, and repealing section 601 of this title] may be cited as the 'Copyright Cleanup, Clarification, and Corrections Act of 2010'."

Pub. L. 111–175, § 1(a), May 27, 2010, 124 Stat. 1218, provided that: "This Act [enacting section 342 of Title 47, Telegraphs, Telephones, and Radiotelegraphs, amending sections 111, 119, 122, 708, and 804 of this title and sections 325, 335, and 338 to 340 of Title 47, enacting provisions set out as notes under sections 111 and 119 of this title and sections 325, 338, and 340 of Title 47, and repealing provisions set out as a note under section 119 of this title] may be cited as the 'Satellite Television Extension and Localism Act of 2010'."

Pub. L. 111–151, § 1, Mar. 26, 2010, 124 Stat. 1027, provided that: "This Act [amending section 119 of this title and section 325 of Title 47, Telegraphs, Telephones, and Radiotelegraphs, and amending provisions set out as a note under section 119 of this title] may be cited as the 'Satellite Televison [sic] Extension Act of 2010'."

SHORT TITLE OF 2009 AMENDMENT

Pub. L. 111–36, § 1, June 30, 2009, 123 Stat. 1926, provided that: "This Act [amending section 114 of this title] may be cited as the 'Webcaster Settlement Act of 2009'."

SHORT TITLE OF 2008 AMENDMENT

Pub. L. 110–435, § 1, Oct. 16, 2008, 122 Stat. 4974, provided that: "This Act [amending section 114 of this title] may be cited as the 'Webcaster Settlement Act of 2008'."

Pub. L. 110–434, § 1(a), Oct. 16, 2008, 122 Stat. 4972, provided that: "This Act [amending section 1301 of this title] may be cited as the 'Vessel Hull Design Protection Amendments of 2008'."

SHORT TITLE OF 2006 AMENDMENT

Pub. L. 109–303, § 1, Oct. 6, 2006, 120 Stat. 1478, provided that: "This Act [amending sections 111, 114, 115, 118, 119, 801 to 804, and 1007 of this title, enacting provisions set out as notes under sections 111 and 119 of this title, and amending provisions set out as a note under section 801 of this title] may be cited as the 'Copyright Royalty Judges Program Technical Corrections Act'."

SHORT TITLE OF 2005 AMENDMENT

Pub. L. 109–9, § 1, Apr. 27, 2005, 119 Stat. 218, provided that: "This Act [enacting section 2319B of Title 18, Crimes and Criminal Procedure, amending this section and sections 108, 110, 408, 411, 412, and 506 of this title, sections 179m, 179n, 179p, 179q, and 179w of Title 2, The Congress, section 1114 of Title 15, Commerce and Trade, section 2319 of Title 18, and sections 151703, 151705, 151706, and 151711 of Title 36, Patriotic and National Observances, Ceremonies, and Organizations, enacting provisions set out as notes under this section, section 179*l* of Title 2, and section 101 of Title 36, and provisions listed in a table relating to sentencing guidelines set out as a note under section 994 of Title 28, Judiciary and Judicial Procedure] may be cited as the 'Family Entertainment and Copyright Act of 2005'."

Pub. L. 109–9, title I, § 101, Apr. 27, 2005, 119 Stat. 218, provided that: "This title [enacting section 2319B of Title 18, Crimes and Criminal Procedure, amending this section, sections 408, 411, 412, and 506 of this title, and section 2319 of Title 18, and enacting provisions listed in a table relating to sentencing guidelines set out as a note under section 994 of Title 28, Judiciary and Judicial Procedure] may be cited as the 'Artists' Rights and Theft Prevention Act of 2005' or the 'ART Act'."

Pub. L. 109–9, title II, § 201, Apr. 27, 2005, 119 Stat. 223, provided that: "This title [amending section 110 of this title and section 1114 of Title 15, Commerce and Trade] may be cited as the 'Family Movie Act of 2005'."

Pub. L. 109–9, title IV, § 401, Apr. 27, 2005, 119 Stat. 226, provided that: "This title [amending section 108 of this title] may be cited as the 'Preservation of Orphan Works Act'."

SHORT TITLE OF 2004 AMENDMENTS

Pub. L. 108–447, div. J, title IX, § 1(a), Dec. 8, 2004, 118 Stat. 3393, provided that: "This title [enacting sections 340 and 341 of Title 47, Telegraphs, Telephones, and Radiotelegraphs, amending sections 111, 119, 122, and 803 of this title and sections 307, 312, 325, 338, and 339 of Title 47, enacting provisions set out as notes under section 119 of this title and sections 325 and 338 of Title 47, and amending provisions set out as a note under section 119 of this title] may be cited as the 'Satellite Home Viewer Extension and Reauthorization Act of 2004' or the 'W. J. (Billy) Tauzin Satellite Television Act of 2004'."

Pub. L. 108–419, § 1, Nov. 30, 2004, 118 Stat. 2341, provided that: "This Act [enacting chapter 8 of this title, amending this section and sections 111, 112, 114 to 116, 118, 119, 1004, 1006, 1007, and 1010 of this title, and enacting provisions set out as a note under section 801 of this title] may be cited as the 'Copyright Royalty and Distribution Reform Act of 2004'."

SHORT TITLE OF 2002 AMENDMENTS

Pub. L. 107–321, §1, Dec. 4, 2002, 116 Stat. 2780, provided that: "This Act [amending section 114 of this title and enacting provisions set out as notes under section 114 of this title] may be cited as the 'Small Webcaster Settlement Act of 2002'."

Pub. L. 107–273, div. C, title III, §13301(a), Nov. 2, 2002, 116 Stat. 1910, provided that: "This subtitle [subtitle C (§13301) of title III of div. C of Pub. L. 107–273, amending sections 110, 112, and 802 of this title] may be cited as the 'Technology, Education, and Copyright Harmonization Act of 2002'."

SHORT TITLE OF 2000 AMENDMENT

Pub. L. 106–379, §1, Oct. 27, 2000, 114 Stat. 1444, provided that: "This Act [amending this section and sections 121, 705, and 708 of this title, repealing section 710 of this title, and enacting provisions set out as notes under this section and section 708 of this title] may be cited as the 'Work Made For Hire and Copyright Corrections Act of 2000'."

SHORT TITLE OF 1999 AMENDMENTS

Pub. L. 106–160, §1, Dec. 9, 1999, 113 Stat. 1774, provided that: "This Act [amending section 504 of this title and enacting provisions set out as notes under section 504 of this title and section 994 of Title 28, Judiciary and Judicial Procedure] may be cited as the 'Digital Theft Deterrence and Copyright Damages Improvement Act of 1999'."

Pub. L. 106–113, div. B, §1000(a)(9) [title I, §1001], Nov. 29, 1999, 113 Stat. 1536, 1501A–523, provided that: "This title [enacting section 122 of this title and sections 338 and 339 of Title 47, Telegraphs, Telephones, and Radiotelegraphs, amending this section, sections 111, 119, 501, and 510 of this title, and section 325 of Title 47, enacting provisions set out as notes under this section and section 325 of Title 47, and amending provisions set out as a note under section 119 of this title] may be cited as the 'Satellite Home Viewer Improvement Act of 1999'."

SHORT TITLE OF 1998 AMENDMENTS

Pub. L. 105–304, §1, Oct. 28, 1998, 112 Stat. 2860, provided that: "This Act [enacting section 512 and chapters 12 and 13 of this title and section 4001 of Title 28, Judiciary and Judicial Procedure, amending this section, sections 104, 104A, 108, 112, 114, 117, 411, 507, 701, and 801 to 803 of this title, section 5314 of Title 5, Government Organization and Employees, sections 1338, 1400, and 1498 of Title 28, and section 3 of Title 35, Patents, and enacting provisions set out as notes under this section and sections 108, 109, 112, 114, 512, and 1301 of this title] may be cited as the 'Digital Millennium Copyright Act'."

Pub. L. 105–304, title I, §101, Oct. 28, 1998, 112 Stat. 2861, provided that: "This title [enacting chapter 12 of this title, amending this section and sections 104, 104A, 411, and 507 of this title, and enacting provisions set out as notes under this section and section 109 of this title] may be cited as the 'WIPO Copyright and Performances and Phonograms Treaties Implementation Act of 1998'."

Pub. L. 105–304, title II, §201, Oct. 28, 1998, 112 Stat. 2877, provided that: "This title [enacting section 512 of this title and provisions set out as a note under section 512 of this title] may be cited as the 'Online Copyright Infringement Liability Limitation Act'."

Pub. L. 105–304, title III, §301, Oct. 28, 1998, 112 Stat. 2886, provided that: "This title [amending section 117 of this title] may be cited as the 'Computer Maintenance Competition Assurance Act'."

Pub. L. 105–304, title V, §501, Oct. 28, 1998, 112 Stat. 2905, provided that: "This Act [probably means "this title", enacting chapter 13 of this title and amending sections 1338, 1400, and 1498 of Title 28, Judiciary and Judicial Procedure] may be referred to as the 'Vessel Hull Design Protection Act'."

Pub. L. 105–298, title I, §101, Oct. 27, 1998, 112 Stat. 2827, provided that: "This title [amending sections 108, 203, and 301 to 304 of this title, enacting provisions set out as a note under section 108 of this title, and amending provisions set out as notes under this section and section 304 of this title] may be referred to as the 'Sonny Bono Copyright Term Extension Act'."

Pub. L. 105–298, title II, §201, Oct. 27, 1998, 112 Stat. 2830, provided that: "This title [enacting section 512 of this title, amending this section and sections 110 and 504 of this title, and enacting provisions set out as notes under this section] may be cited as the 'Fairness In Music Licensing Act of 1998'."

SHORT TITLE OF 1995 AMENDMENT

Section 1 of Pub. L. 104–39 provided that: "This Act [amending this section and sections 106, 111, 114, 115, 119, and 801 to 803 of this title and enacting provisions set out as a note above] may be cited as the 'Digital Performance Right in Sound Recordings Act of 1995'."

SHORT TITLE OF 1994 AMENDMENT

Pub. L. 103–369, §1, Oct. 18, 1994, 108 Stat. 3477, provided that: "This Act [amending sections 111 and 119 of this title and enacting and repealing provisions set out as notes under section 119 of this title] may be cited as the 'Satellite Home Viewer Act of 1994'."

SHORT TITLE OF 1993 AMENDMENT

Pub. L. 103–198, §1, Dec. 17, 1993, 107 Stat. 2304, provided that: "This Act [amending sections 111, 116, 118, 119, 801 to 803, 1004 to 1007, and 1010 of this title and section 1288 of Title 8, Aliens and Nationality, renumbering sections 116A and 804 of this title as sections 116 and 803, respectively, of this title, repealing sections 116, 803, and 805 to 810 of this title, and enacting provisions set out as notes under section 801 of this title and section 1288 of Title 8] may be cited as the 'Copyright Royalty Tribunal Reform Act of 1993'."

SHORT TITLE OF 1992 AMENDMENTS

Pub. L. 102–563, §1, Oct. 28, 1992, 106 Stat. 4237, provided that: "This Act [enacting chapter 10 of this title, amending this section, sections 801, 804, and 912 of this title, and section 1337 of Title 19, Customs Duties, and enacting provisions set out as a note under section 1001 of this title] may be cited as the 'Audio Home Recording Act of 1992'."

Section 101 of title I of Pub. L. 102–307 provided that: "This title [amending this section and sections 304, 408, 409, and 708 of this title and enacting provisions set out as notes under this section and section 304 of this title] may be referred to as the 'Copyright Renewal Act of 1992'."

SHORT TITLE OF 1991 AMENDMENT

Pub. L. 102–64, §1, June 28, 1991, 105 Stat. 320, provided that: "This Act [amending section 914 of this title and enacting provisions set out as a note under section 914 of this title] may be cited as the 'Semiconductor International Protection Extension Act of 1991'."

SHORT TITLE OF 1990 AMENDMENTS

Section 601 of title VI of Pub. L. 101–650 provided that: "This title [enacting section 106A of this title, amending this section and sections 107, 113, 301, 411, 412, 501, and 506 of this title, and enacting provisions set out as notes under this section and section 106A of this title] may be cited as the 'Visual Artists Rights Act of 1990'."

Section 701 of title VII of Pub. L. 101–650 provided that: "This title [enacting section 120 of this title, amending this section and sections 102, 106, and 301 of this title, and enacting provisions set out as a note above] may be cited as the 'Architectural Works Copyright Protection Act'."

Section 801 of title VIII of Pub. L. 101–650 provided that: "This title [amending section 109 of this title and enacting provisions set out as notes under sections 109 and 205 of this title] may be cited as the 'Computer Software Rental Amendments Act of 1990'."

Pub. L. 101–553, § 1, Nov. 15, 1990, 104 Stat. 2749, provided that: "This Act [enacting section 511 of this title, amending sections 501, 910, and 911 of this title, and enacting provisions set out as a note under section 501 of this title] may be cited as the 'Copyright Remedy Clarification Act'."

Pub. L. 101–319, § 1, July 3, 1990, 104 Stat. 290, provided that: "This Act [amending sections 701 and 802 of this title and sections 5315 and 5316 of Title 5, Government Organization and Employees, and enacting provisions set out as a note under section 701 of this title] may be cited as the 'Copyright Royalty Tribunal Reform and Miscellaneous Pay Act of 1989'."

Pub. L. 101–318, § 1, July 3, 1990, 104 Stat. 287, provided that: "This Act [amending sections 106, 111, 704, 708, 801, and 804 of this title and enacting provisions set out as notes under sections 106, 111, 708, and 804 of this title] may be cited as the 'Copyright Fees and Technical Amendments Act of 1989'."

SHORT TITLE OF 1988 AMENDMENTS

Pub. L. 100–667, title II, § 201, Nov. 16, 1988, 102 Stat. 3949, provided that: "This title [enacting section 119 of this title and sections 612 and 613 of Title 47, Telegraphs, Telephones, and Radiotelegraphs, amending sections 111, 501, 801, and 804 of this title and section 605 of Title 47, and enacting provisions set out as notes under section 119 of this title] may be cited as the 'Satellite Home Viewer Act of 1988'." [Section ceases to be effective Dec. 31, 1994, see section 207 of Pub. L. 100–667, set out as an Effective and Termination Dates note under section 119 of this title.]

Section 1(a) of Pub. L. 100–568 provided that: "This Act [enacting section 116A of this title, amending this section and sections 104, 116, 205, 301, 401 to 408, 411, 501, 504, 801, and 804 of this title, and enacting provisions set out as notes under this section] may be cited as the 'Berne Convention Implementation Act of 1988'."

SHORT TITLE OF 1984 AMENDMENTS

Pub. L. 98–620, title III, § 301, Nov. 8, 1984, 98 Stat. 3347, provided that: "This title [enacting chapter 9 of this title] may be cited as the 'Semiconductor Chip Protection Act of 1984'."

Pub. L. 98–450, § 1, Oct. 4, 1984, 98 Stat. 1727, provided that: "This Act [amending sections 109 and 115 of this title and enacting provisions set out as a note under section 109 of this title] may be cited as the 'Record Rental Amendment of 1984'."

SHORT TITLE OF 1976 ACT

Pub. L. 94–553, Oct. 19, 1976, 90 Stat. 2541, which enacted this title and section 170 of Title 2, The Congress, amended section 131 of Title 2, section 290e of Title 15, Commerce and Trade, section 2318 of Title 18, Crimes and Criminal Procedure, section 543 of Title 26, Internal Revenue Code, section 1498 of Title 28, Judiciary and Judicial Procedure, sections 3202 and 3206 of Title 39, Postal Service, and sections 505 and 2117 of Title 44, Public Printing and Documents, and enacted provisions set out as notes preceding this section and under sections 104, 115, 304, 401, 407, 410, and 501 of this title, is popularly known as the "Copyright Act of 1976".

SEVERABILITY

Pub. L. 106–379, § 2(b)(2), Oct. 27, 2000, 114 Stat. 1444, provided that: "If the provisions of paragraph (1) [see Effective Date of 2000 Amendment note above], or any application of such provisions to any person or circumstance, is held to be invalid, the remainder of this section [amending this section and enacting provisions set out as a note above], the amendments made by this section, and the application of this section to any other person or circumstance shall not be affected by such invalidation."

CONSTRUCTION OF 1998 AMENDMENT

Pub. L. 105–298, title II, § 206, Oct. 27, 1998, 112 Stat. 2834, provided that: "Except as otherwise provided in this title [enacting section 512 of this title, amending this section and sections 110 and 504 of this title, and enacting provisions set out as notes under this section], nothing in this title shall be construed to relieve any performing rights society of any obligation under any State or local statute, ordinance, or law, or consent decree or other court order governing its operation, as such statute, ordinance, law, decree, or order is in effect on the date of the enactment of this Act [Oct. 27, 1998], as it may be amended after such date, or as it may be issued or agreed to after such date."

FIRST AMENDMENT APPLICATION

Section 609 of title VI of Pub. L. 101–650 provided that: "This title [see Short Title of 1990 Amendments note above] does not authorize any governmental entity to take any action or enforce restrictions prohibited by the First Amendment to the United States Constitution."

BERNE CONVENTION; CONGRESSIONAL DECLARATIONS

Section 2 of Pub. L. 100–568 provided that: "The Congress makes the following declarations:

"(1) The Convention for the Protection of Literary and Artistic Works, signed at Berne, Switzerland, on September 9, 1886, and all acts, protocols, and revisions thereto (hereafter in this Act [see Short Title of 1988 Amendment note above] referred to as the 'Berne Convention') are not self-executing under the Constitution and laws of the United States.

"(2) The obligations of the United States under the Berne Convention may be performed only pursuant to appropriate domestic law.

"(3) The amendments made by this Act, together with the law as it exists on the date of the enactment of this Act [Oct. 31, 1988], satisfy the obligations of the United States in adhering to the Berne Convention and no further rights or interests shall be recognized or created for that purpose."

BERNE CONVENTION; CONSTRUCTION

Section 3 of Pub. L. 100–568 provided that:

"(a) RELATIONSHIP WITH DOMESTIC LAW.—The provisions of the Berne Convention—

"(1) shall be given effect under title 17, as amended by this Act [see Short Title of 1988 Amendment note above], and any other relevant provision of Federal or State law, including the common law; and

"(2) shall not be enforceable in any action brought pursuant to the provisions of the Berne Convention itself.

"(b) CERTAIN RIGHTS NOT AFFECTED.—The provisions of the Berne Convention, the adherence of the United States thereto, and satisfaction of United States obligations thereunder, do not expand or reduce any right of an author of a work, whether claimed under Federal, State, or the common law—

"(1) to claim authorship of the work; or

"(2) to object to any distortion, mutilation, or other modification of, or other derogatory action in relation to, the work, that would prejudice the author's honor or reputation."

WORKS IN PUBLIC DOMAIN WITHOUT COPYRIGHT PROTECTION

Section 12 of Pub. L. 100–568 provided that: "Title 17, United States Code, as amended by this Act [see Short Title of 1988 Amendment note above], does not provide copyright protection for any work that is in the public domain in the United States."

DEFINITIONS

Pub. L. 103–465, title V, § 501, Dec. 8, 1994, 108 Stat. 4973, provided that: "For purposes of this title [enacting section 1101 of this title and section 2319A of Title 18, Crimes and Criminal Procedure, amending sections 104A and 109 of this title, sections 1052 and 1127 of Title 15, Commerce and Trade, and sections 41, 104, 111, 119, 154, 156, 172, 173, 252, 262, 271, 272, 287, 292, 295, 307, 365, and 373 of Title 35, Patents, enacting provisions set out as notes under section 1052 of Title 15 and sections 104 and 154 of Title 35, and amending provisions set out as a note under section 109 of this title]—

"(1) the term 'WTO Agreement' has the meaning given that term in section 2(9) of the Uruguay Round Agreements Act [19 U.S.C. 3501(9)]; and

"(2) the term 'WTO member country' has the meaning given that term in section 2(10) of the Uruguay Round Agreements Act.''

§ 102. Subject matter of copyright: In general

(a) Copyright protection subsists, in accordance with this title, in original works of authorship fixed in any tangible medium of expression, now known or later developed, from which they can be perceived, reproduced, or otherwise communicated, either directly or with the aid of a machine or device. Works of authorship include the following categories:

(1) literary works;

(2) musical works, including any accompanying words;

(3) dramatic works, including any accompanying music;

(4) pantomimes and choreographic works;

(5) pictorial, graphic, and sculptural works;

(6) motion pictures and other audiovisual works;

(7) sound recordings; and

(8) architectural works.

(b) In no case does copyright protection for an original work of authorship extend to any idea, procedure, process, system, method of operation, concept, principle, or discovery, regardless of the form in which it is described, explained, illustrated, or embodied in such work.

(Pub. L. 94–553, title I, § 101, Oct. 19, 1976, 90 Stat. 2544; Pub. L. 101–650, title VII, § 703, Dec. 1, 1990, 104 Stat. 5133.)

HISTORICAL AND REVISION NOTES

HOUSE REPORT NO. 94–1476

Original Works of Authorship. The two fundamental criteria of copyright protection—originality and fixation in tangible form are restated in the first sentence of this cornerstone provision. The phrase "original works or authorship," which is purposely left undefined, is intended to incorporate without change the standard of originality established by the courts under the present copyright statute. This standard does not include requirements of novelty, ingenuity, or esthetic merit, and there is no intention to enlarge the standard of copyright protection to require them.

In using the phrase "original works of authorship," rather than "all the writings of an author" now in section 4 of the statute [section 4 of former title 17], the committee's purpose is to avoid exhausting the constitutional power of Congress to legislate in this field, and to eliminate the uncertainties arising from the latter phrase. Since the present statutory language is substantially the same as the empowering language of the Constitution [Const. Art. I, § 8, cl. 8], a recurring question has been whether the statutory and the constitutional provisions are coextensive. If so, the courts would be faced with the alternative of holding copyrightable something that Congress clearly did not intend to protect, or of holding constitutionally incapable of copyright something that Congress might one day want to protect. To avoid these equally undesirable results, the courts have indicated that "all the writings of an author" under the present statute is narrower in scope than the "writings" of "authors" referred to in the Constitution. The bill avoids this dilemma by using

a different phrase—"original works of authorship"—in characterizing the general subject matter of statutory copyright protection.

The history of copyright law has been one of gradual expansion in the types of works accorded protection, and the subject matter affected by this expansion has fallen into two general categories. In the first, scientific discoveries and technological developments have made possible new forms of creative expression that never existed before. In some of these cases the new expressive forms—electronic music, filmstrips, and computer programs, for example—could be regarded as an extension of copyrightable subject matter Congress had already intended to protect, and were thus considered copyrightable from the outset without the need of new legislation. In other cases, such as photographs, sound recordings, and motion pictures, statutory enactment was deemed necessary to give them full recognition as copyrightable works.

Authors are continually finding new ways of expressing themselves, but it is impossible to foresee the forms that these new expressive methods will take. The bill does not intend either to freeze the scope of copyrightable subject matter at the present stage of communications technology or to allow unlimited expansion into areas completely outside the present congressional intent. Section 102 implies neither that that subject matter is unlimited nor that new forms of expression within that general area of subject matter would necessarily be unprotected.

The historic expansion of copyright has also applied to forms of expression which, although in existence for generations or centuries, have only gradually come to be recognized as creative and worthy of protection. The first copyright statute in this country, enacted in 1790, designated only "maps, charts, and books"; major forms of expression such as music, drama, and works of art achieved specific statutory recognition only in later enactments. Although the coverage of the present statute is very broad, and would be broadened further by the explicit recognition of all forms of choreography, there are unquestionably other areas of existing subject matter that this bill does not propose to protect but that future Congresses may want to.

Fixation in Tangible Form. As a basic condition of copyright protection, the bill perpetuates the existing requirement that a work be fixed in a "tangible medium of expression," and adds that this medium may be one "now known or later developed," and that the fixation is sufficient if the work "can be perceived, reproduced, or otherwise communicated, either directly or with the aid of a machine or device." This broad language is intended to avoid the artificial and largely unjustifiable distinctions, derived from cases such as *White-Smith Publishing Co. v. Apollo Co.*, 209 U.S. 1 (1908) [28 S.Ct. 319, 52 L.Ed. 655], under which statutory copyrightability in certain cases has been made to depend upon the form or medium in which the work is fixed. Under the bill it makes no difference what the form, manner, or medium of fixation may be—whether it is in words, numbers, notes, sounds, pictures, or any other graphic or symbolic indicia, whether embodied in a physical object in written, printed, photographic, sculptural, punched, magnetic, or any other stable form, and whether it is capable of perception directly or by means of any machine or device "now known or later developed."

Under the bill, the concept of fixation is important since it not only determines whether the provisions of the statute apply to a work, but it also represents the dividing line between common law and statutory protection. As will be noted in more detail in connection with section 301, an unfixed work of authorship, such as an improvisation or an unrecorded choreographic work, performance, or broadcast, would continue to be subject to protection under State common law or statute, but would not be eligible for Federal statutory protection under section 102.

The bill seeks to resolve, through the definition of "fixation" in section 101, the status of live broadcasts—

sports, news coverage, live performances of music, etc.—that are reaching the public in unfixed form but that are simultaneously being recorded. When a football game is being covered by four television cameras, with a director guiding the activities of the four cameramen and choosing which of their electronic images are sent out to the public and in what order, there is little doubt that what the cameramen and the director are doing constitutes "authorship." The further question to be considered is whether there has been a fixation. If the images and sounds to be broadcast are first recorded (on a video tape, film, etc.) and then transmitted, the recorded work would be considered a "motion picture" subject to statutory protection against unauthorized reproduction or retransmission of the broadcast. If the program content is transmitted live to the public while being recorded at the same time, the case would be treated the same; the copyright owner would not be forced to rely on common law rather than statutory rights in proceeding against an infringing user of the live broadcast.

Thus, assuming it is copyrightable—as a "motion picture" or "sound recording," for example—the content of a live transmission should be regarded as fixed and should be accorded statutory protection if it is being recorded simultaneously with its transmission. On the other hand, the definition of "fixation" would exclude from the concept purely evanescent or transient reproductions such as those projected briefly on a screen, shown electronically on a television or other cathode ray tube, or captured momentarily in the "memory" of a computer.

Under the first sentence of the definition of "fixed" in section 101, a work would be considered "fixed in a tangible medium of expression" if there has been an authorized embodiment in a copy or phonorecord and if that embodiment "is sufficiently permanent or stable" to permit the work "to be perceived, reproduced, or otherwise communicated for a period of more than transitory duration." The second sentence makes clear that, in the case of "a work consisting of sounds, images, or both, that are being transmitted," the work is regarded as "fixed" if a fixation is being made at the same time as the transmission.

Under this definition "copies" and "phonorecords" together will comprise all of the material objects in which copyrightable works are capable of being fixed. The definitions of these terms in section 101, together with their usage in section 102 and throughout the bill, reflect a fundamental distinction between the "original work" which is the product of "authorship" and the multitude of material objects in which it can be embodied. Thus, in the sense of the bill, a "book" is not a work of authorship, but is a particular kind of "copy." Instead, the author may write a "literary work," which in turn can be embodied in a wide range of "copies" and "phonorecords," including books, periodicals, computer punch cards, microfilm, tape recordings, and so forth. It is possible to have an "original work of authorship" without having a "copy" or "phonorecord" embodying it, and it is also possible to have a "copy" or "phonorecord" embodying something that does not qualify as an "original work of authorship." The two essential elements—original work and tangible object—must merge through fixation in order to produce subject matter copyrightable under the statute.

Categories of Copyrightable Works. The second sentence of section 102 lists seven broad categories which the concept of "works of authorship" is said to "include". The use of the word "include," as defined in section 101, makes clear that the listing is "illustrative and not limitative," and that the seven categories do not necessarily exhaust the scope of "original works of authorship" that the bill is intended to protect. Rather, the list sets out the general area of copyrightable subject matter, but with sufficient flexibility to free the courts from rigid or outmoded concepts of the scope of particular categories. The items are also overlapping in the sense that a work falling within one class may encompass works coming within some or all of the other categories. In the aggregate, the list covers all classes of works now specified in section 5 of title 17 [section 5 of former title 17]; in addition, it specifically enumerates "pantomimes and choreographic works".

Of the seven items listed, four are defined in section 101. The three undefined categories—"musical works," "dramatic works," and "pantomimes and choreographic works"—have fairly settled meanings. There is no need, for example, to specify the copyrightability of electronic or concrete music in the statute since the form of a work would no longer be of any importance, nor is it necessary to specify that "choreographic works" do not include social dance steps and simple routines.

The four items defined in section 101 are "literary works," "pictorial, graphic, and sculptural works," "motion pictures and audiovisual works", and "sound recordings". In each of these cases, definitions are needed not only because the meaning of the term itself is unsettled but also because the distinction between "work" and "material object" requires clarification. The term "literary works" does not connote any criterion of literary merit or qualitative value: it includes catalogs, directories, and similar factual, reference, or instructional works and compilations of data. It also includes computer data bases, and computer programs to the extent that they incorporate authorship in the programmer's expression of original ideas, as distinguished from the ideas themselves.

Correspondingly, the definition of "pictorial, graphic, and sculptural works" carries with it no implied criterion of artistic taste, aesthetic value, or intrinsic quality. The term is intended to comprise not only "works of art" in the traditional sense but also works of graphic art and illustration, art reproductions, plans and drawings, photographs and reproductions of them, maps, charts, globes, and other cartographic works, works of these kinds intended for use in advertising and commerce, and works of "applied art." There is no intention whatever to narrow the scope of the subject matter now characterized in section 5(k) [section 5(k) of former title 17] as "prints or labels used for articles of merchandise." However, since this terminology suggests the material object in which a work is embodied rather than the work itself, the bill does not mention this category separately.

In accordance with the Supreme Court's decision in *Mazer v. Stein*, 347 U.S. 201 (1954) [74 S.Ct. 460, 98 L. Ed. 630, rehearing denied 74 S.Ct. 637, 347 U.S. 949, 98 L.Ed. 1096], works of "applied art" encompass all original pictorial, graphic, and sculptural works that are intended to be or have been embodied in useful articles, regardless of factors such as mass production, commercial exploitation, and the potential availability of design patent protection. The scope of exclusive rights in these works is given special treatment in section 113, to be discussed below.

The Committee has added language to the definition of "pictorial, graphic, and sculptural works" in an effort to make clearer the distinction between works of applied art protectable under the bill and industrial designs not subject to copyright protection. The declaration that "pictorial, graphic, and sculptural works" include "works of artistic craftsmanship insofar as their form but not their mechanical or utilitarian aspects are concerned" is classic language; it is drawn from Copyright Office regulations promulgated in the 1940's and expressly endorsed by the Supreme Court in the *Mazer* case.

The second part of the amendment states that "the design of a useful article * * * shall be considered a pictorial, graphic, or sculptural work only if, and only to the extent that, such design incorporates pictorial, graphic, or sculptural features that can be identified separately from, and are capable of existing independently of, the utilitarian aspects of the article." A "useful article" is defined as "an article having an intrinsic utilitarian function that is not merely to portray the appearance of the article or to convey information."

This part of the amendment is an adaptation of language added to the Copyright Office Regulations in the mid-1950's in an effort to implement the Supreme Court's decision in the *Mazer* case.

In adopting this amendatory language, the Committee is seeking to draw as clear a line as possible between copyrightable works of applied art and uncopyrighted works of industrial design. A two-dimensional painting, drawing, or graphic work is still capable of being identified as such when it is printed on or applied to utilitarian articles such as textile fabrics, wallpaper, containers, and the like. The same is true when a statue or carving is used to embellish an industrial product or, as in the *Mazer* case, is incorporated into a product without losing its ability to exist independently as a work of art. On the other hand, although the shape of an industrial product may be aesthetically satisfying and valuable, the Committee's intention is not to offer it copyright protection under the bill. Unless the shape of an automobile, airplane, ladies' dress, food processor, television set, or any other industrial product contains some element that, physically or conceptually, can be identified as separable from the utilitarian aspects of that article, the design would not be copyrighted under the bill. The test of separability and independence from "the utilitarian aspects of the article" does not depend upon the nature of the design—that is, even if the appearance of an article is determined by aesthetic (as opposed to functional) considerations, only elements, if any, which can be identified separately from the useful article as such are copyrightable. And, even if the three-dimensional design contains some such element (for example, a carving on the back of a chair or a floral relief design on silver flatware), copyright protection would extend only to that element, and would not cover the over-all configuration of the utilitarian article as such.

A special situation is presented by architectural works. An architect's plans and drawings would, of course, be protected by copyright, but the extent to which that protection would extend to the structure depicted would depend on the circumstances. Purely nonfunctional or monumental structures would be subject to full copyright protection under the bill, and the same would be true of artistic sculpture or decorative ornamentation or embellishment added to a structure. On the other hand, where the only elements of shape in an architectural design are conceptually inseparable from the utilitarian aspects of the structure, copyright protection for the design would not be available.

The Committee has considered, but chosen to defer, the possibility of protecting the design of typefaces. A "typeface" can be defined as a set of letters, numbers, or other symbolic characters, whose forms are related by repeating design elements consistently applied in a notational system and are intended to be embodied in articles whose intrinsic utilitarian function is for use in composing text or other cognizable combinations of characters. The Committee does not regard the design of typeface, as thus defined, to be a copyrightable "pictorial, graphic, or sculptural work" within the meaning of this bill and the application of the dividing line in section 101.

Enactment of Public Law 92–140 in 1971 [Pub. L. 92–140, Oct. 15, 1971, 85 Stat. 391, which amended sections 1, 5, 19, 20, 26, and 101 of former title 17, and enacted provisions set out as a note under section 1 of former title 17] marked the first recognition in American copyright law of sound recordings as copyrightable works. As defined in section 101, copyrightable "sound recordings" are original works of authorship comprising an aggregate of musical, spoken, or other sounds that have been fixed in tangible form. The copyrightable work comprises the aggregation of sounds and not the tangible medium of fixation. Thus, "sound recordings" as copyrightable subject matter are distinguished from "phonorecords," the latter being physical objects in which sounds are fixed. They are also distinguished from any copyrighted literary, dramatic, or musical works that may be reproduced on a "phonorecord."

As a class of subject matter, sound recordings are clearly within the scope of the "writings of an author" capable of protection under the Constitution [Const. Art. I, §8, cl. 8], and the extension of limited statutory protection to them was too long delayed. Aside from cases in which sounds are fixed by some purely mechanical means without originality of any kind, the copyright protection that would prevent the reproduction and distribution of unauthorized phonorecords of sound recordings is clearly justified.

The copyrightable elements in a sound recording will usually, though not always, involve "authorship" both on the part of the performers whose performance is captured and on the part of the record producer responsible for setting up the recording session, capturing and electronically processing the sounds, and compiling and editing them to make the final sound recording. There may, however, be cases where the record producer's contribution is so minimal that the performance is the only copyrightable element in the work, and there may be cases (for example, recordings of birdcalls, sounds of racing cars, et cetera) where only the record producer's contribution is copyrightable.

Sound tracks of motion pictures, long a nebulous area in American copyright law, are specifically included in the definition of "motion pictures," and excluded in the definition of "sound recordings." To be a "motion picture," as defined, requires three elements: (1) a series of images, (2) the capability of showing the images in certain successive order, and (3) an impression of motion when the images are thus shown. Coupled with the basic requirements of original authorship and fixation in tangible form, this definition encompasses a wide range of cinematographic works embodied in films, tapes, video disks, and other media. However, it would not include: (1) unauthorized fixations of live performances or telecasts, (2) live telecasts that are not fixed simultaneously with their transmission, or (3) filmstrips and slide sets which, although consisting of a series of images intended to be shown in succession, are not capable of conveying an impression of motion.

On the other hand, the bill equates audiovisual materials such as filmstrips, slide sets, and sets of transparencies with "motion pictures" rather than with "pictorial, graphic, and sculptural works." Their sequential showing is closer to a "performance" than to a "display," and the definition of "audiovisual works," which applies also to "motion pictures," embraces works consisting of a series of related images that are by their nature, intended for showing by means of projectors or other devices.

Nature of Copyright. Copyright does not preclude others from using the ideas or information revealed by the author's work. It pertains to the literary, musical, graphic, or artistic form in which the author expressed intellectual concepts. Section 102(b) makes clear that copyright protection does not extend to any idea, procedure, process, system, method of operation, concept, principle, or discovery, regardless of the form in which it is described, explained, illustrated, or embodied in such work.

Some concern has been expressed lest copyright in computer programs should extend protection to the methodology or processes adopted by the programmer, rather than merely to the "writing" expressing his ideas. Section 102(b) is intended, among other things, to make clear that the expression adopted by the programmer is the copyrightable element in a computer program, and that the actual processes or methods embodied in the program are not within the scope of the copyright law.

Section 102(b) in no way enlarges or contracts the scope of copyright protection under the present law. Its purpose is to restate, in the context of the new single Federal system of copyright, that the basic dichotomy between expression and idea remains unchanged.

AMENDMENTS

1990—Subsec. (a)(8). Pub. L. 101–650 added par. (8).

EFFECTIVE DATE OF 1990 AMENDMENT

Amendment by Pub. L. 101–650 applicable to any architectural work created on or after Dec. 1, 1990, and any architectural work, that, on Dec. 1, 1990, is unconstructed and embodied in unpublished plans or drawings, except that protection for such architectural work under this title terminates on Dec. 31, 2002, unless the work is constructed by that date, see section 706 of Pub. L. 101–650, set out as a note under section 101 of this title.

§ 103. Subject matter of copyright: Compilations and derivative works

(a) The subject matter of copyright as specified by section 102 includes compilations and derivative works, but protection for a work employing preexisting material in which copyright subsists does not extend to any part of the work in which such material has been used unlawfully.

(b) The copyright in a compilation or derivative work extends only to the material contributed by the author of such work, as distinguished from the preexisting material employed in the work, and does not imply any exclusive right in the preexisting material. The copyright in such work is independent of, and does not affect or enlarge the scope, duration, ownership, or subsistence of, any copyright protection in the preexisting material.

(Pub. L. 94–553, title I, § 101, Oct. 19, 1976, 90 Stat. 2545.)

HISTORICAL AND REVISION NOTES

HOUSE REPORT NO. 94–1476

Section 103 complements section 102: A compilation or derivative work is copyrightable if it represents an "original work of authorship" and falls within one or more of the categories listed in section 102. Read together, the two sections make plain that the criteria of copyrightable subject matter stated in section 102 apply with full force to works that are entirely original and to those containing preexisting material. Section 103(b) is also intended to define, more sharply and clearly than does section 7 of the present law [section 7 of former title 17], the important interrelationship and correlation between protection of preexisting and of "new" material in a particular work. The most important point here is one that is commonly misunderstood today: copyright in a "new version" covers only the material added by the later author, and has no effect one way or the other on the copyright or public domain status of the preexisting material.

Between them the terms "compilations" and "derivative works" which are defined in section 101 comprehend every copyrightable work that employs preexisting material or data of any kind. There is necessarily some overlapping between the two, but they basically represent different concepts. A "compilation" results from a process of selecting, bringing together, organizing, and arranging previously existing material of all kinds, regardless of whether the individual items in the material have been or ever could have been subject to copyright. A "derivative work," on the other hand, requires a process of recasting, transforming, or adapting "one or more preexisting works"; the "preexisting work" must come within the general subject matter of copyright set forth in section 102, regardless of whether it is or was ever copyrighted.

The second part of the sentence that makes up section 103(a) deals with the status of a compilation or derivative work unlawfully employing preexisting copyrighted material. In providing that protection does not extend to "any part of the work in which such material has been used unlawfully," the bill prevents an infringer from benefiting, through copyright protection, from committing an unlawful act, but preserves protection for those parts of the work that do not employ the preexisting work. Thus, an unauthorized translation of a novel could not be copyrighted at all, but the owner of copyright in an anthology of poetry could sue someone who infringed the whole anthology, even though the infringer proves that publication of one of the poems was unauthorized. Under this provision, copyright could be obtained as long as the use of the preexisting work was not "unlawful," even though the consent of the copyright owner had not been obtained. For instance, the unauthorized reproduction of a work might be "lawful" under the doctrine of fair use or an applicable foreign law, and if so the work incorporating it could be copyrighted.

§ 104. Subject matter of copyright: National origin

(a) UNPUBLISHED WORKS.—The works specified by sections 102 and 103, while unpublished, are subject to protection under this title without regard to the nationality or domicile of the author.

(b) PUBLISHED WORKS.—The works specified by sections 102 and 103, when published, are subject to protection under this title if—

(1) on the date of first publication, one or more of the authors is a national or domiciliary of the United States, or is a national, domiciliary, or sovereign authority of a treaty party, or is a stateless person, wherever that person may be domiciled; or

(2) the work is first published in the United States or in a foreign nation that, on the date of first publication, is a treaty party; or

(3) the work is a sound recording that was first fixed in a treaty party; or

(4) the work is a pictorial, graphic, or sculptural work that is incorporated in a building or other structure, or an architectural work that is embodied in a building and the building or structure is located in the United States or a treaty party; or

(5) the work is first published by the United Nations or any of its specialized agencies, or by the Organization of American States; or

(6) the work comes within the scope of a Presidential proclamation. Whenever the President finds that a particular foreign nation extends, to works by authors who are nationals or domiciliaries of the United States or to works that are first published in the United States, copyright protection on substantially the same basis as that on which the foreign nation extends protection to works of its own nationals and domiciliaries and works first published in that nation, the President may by proclamation extend protection under this title to works of which one or more of the authors is, on the date of first publication, a national, domiciliary, or sovereign authority of that nation, or which was first published in that nation. The President may revise, suspend, or revoke any such proclamation or impose any conditions or limitations on protection under a proclamation.

For purposes of paragraph (2), a work that is published in the United States or a treaty party within 30 days after publication in a foreign nation that is not a treaty party shall be considered to be first published in the United States or such treaty party, as the case may be.

(c) EFFECT OF BERNE CONVENTION.—No right or interest in a work eligible for protection under this title may be claimed by virtue of, or in reliance upon, the provisions of the Berne Convention, or the adherence of the United States thereto. Any rights in a work eligible for protection under this title that derive from this title, other Federal or State statutes, or the common law, shall not be expanded or reduced by virtue of, or in reliance upon, the provisions of the Berne Convention, or the adherence of the United States thereto.

(d) EFFECT OF PHONOGRAMS TREATIES.—Notwithstanding the provisions of subsection (b), no works other than sound recordings shall be eligible for protection under this title solely by virtue of the adherence of the United States to the Geneva Phonograms Convention or the WIPO Performances and Phonograms Treaty.

(Pub. L. 94–553, title I, § 101, Oct. 19, 1976, 90 Stat. 2545; Pub. L. 100–568, § 4(a)(2), (3), Oct. 31, 1988, 102 Stat. 2855; Pub. L. 105–304, title I, § 102(b), Oct. 28, 1998, 112 Stat. 2862.)

HISTORICAL AND REVISION NOTES

HOUSE REPORT NO. 94–1476

Section 104 of the bill [this section], which sets forth the basic criteria under which works of foreign origin can be protected under the U.S. copyright law, divides all works coming within the scope of sections 102 and 103 into two categories: unpublished and published. Subsection (a) imposes no qualifications of nationality and domicile with respect to unpublished works. Subsection (b) would make published works subject to protection under any one of four conditions:

(1) The author is a national or domiciliary of the United States or of a country with which the United States has copyright relations under a treaty, or is a stateless person;

(2) The work is first published in the United States or in a country that is a party to the Universal Copyright Convention;

(3) The work is first published by the United Nations, by any of its specialized agencies, or by the Organization of American States; or

(4) The work is covered by a Presidential proclamation extending protection to works originating in a specified country which extends protection to U.S. works "on substantially the same basis" as to its own works.

The third of these conditions represents a treaty obligation of the United States. Under the Second Protocol of the Universal Copyright Convention, protection under U.S. Copyright law is expressly required for works published by the United Nations, by U.N. specialized agencies and by the Organization of American States.

AMENDMENTS

1998—Subsec. (b). Pub. L. 105–304, § 102(b)(1)(G), inserted concluding provisions.

Subsec. (b)(1). Pub. L. 105–304, § 102(b)(1)(A), substituted "treaty party" for "foreign nation that is a party to a copyright treaty to which the United States is also a party".

Subsec. (b)(2). Pub. L. 105–304, § 102(b)(1)(B), substituted "treaty party" for "party to the Universal Copyright Convention".

Subsec. (b)(3). Pub. L. 105–304, § 102(b)(1)(E), added par. (3). Former par. (3) redesignated (5).

Subsec. (b)(4). Pub. L. 105–304, § 102(b)(1)(F), substituted "pictorial, graphic, or sculptural work that is incorporated in a building or other structure, or an architectural work that is embodied in a building and the building or structure is located in the United States or a treaty party" for "Berne Convention work".

Subsec. (b)(5), (6). Pub. L. 105–304, § 102(b)(1)(C), (D), redesignated par. (3) as (5) and transferred it to appear after par. (4) and redesignated former par. (5) as (6).

Subsec. (d). Pub. L. 105–304, § 102(b)(2), added subsec. (d).

1988—Subsec. (b)(4), (5). Pub. L. 100–568, § 4(a)(2), added par. (4) and redesignated former par. (4) as (5).

Subsec. (c). Pub. L. 100–568, § 4(a)(3), added subsec. (c).

EFFECTIVE DATE OF 1998 AMENDMENT

Amendment by section 102(b)(1) of Pub. L. 105–304 effective Oct. 28, 1998, except as otherwise provided, and amendment by section 102(b)(2) of Pub. L. 105–304 effective May 20, 2002, see section 105(a), (b)(2)(C) of Pub. L. 105–304, set out as a note under section 101 of this title.

EFFECTIVE DATE OF 1988 AMENDMENT

Amendment by Pub. L. 100–568 effective Mar. 1, 1989, with any cause of action arising under this title before such date being governed by provisions in effect when cause of action arose, see section 13 of Pub. L. 100–568, set out as a note under section 101 of this title.

PROC. NO. 3792. COPYRIGHT EXTENSION: GERMANY

Proc. No. 3792, July 12, 1967, 32 F.R. 10341, provided:

WHEREAS the President is authorized, in accordance with the conditions prescribed in Section 9 of Title 17 of the United States Code which includes the provisions of the act of Congress approved March 4, 1909, 35 Stat. 1075, as amended by the act of September 25, 1941, 55 Stat. 732, to grant an extension of time for fulfillment of the conditions and formalities prescribed by the copyright laws of the United States of America, with respect to works first produced or published outside the United States of America and subject to copyright or to renewal of copyright under the laws of the United States of America, by nationals of countries which accord substantially equal treatment to citizens of the United States of America; and

WHEREAS satisfactory official assurances have been received that, since April 15, 1892, citizens of the United States have been entitled to obtain copyright in Germany for their works on substantially the same basis as German citizens without the need of complying with any formalities, provided such works secured protection in the United States; and

WHEREAS, pursuant to Article 2 of the Law No. 8, Industrial, Literary and Artistic Property Rights of Foreign Nations and Nationals, promulgated by the Allied High Commission for Germany on October 20, 1949, literary or artistic property rights in Germany owned by United States nationals at the commencement of or during the state of war between Germany and the United States of America which were transferred, seized, requisitioned, revoked or otherwise impaired by war measures, whether legislative, judicial or administrative, were, upon request made prior to October 3, 1950, restored to such United States nationals or their legal successors; and

WHEREAS, pursuant to Article 5 of the aforesaid law, any literary or artistic property right in Germany owned by a United States national at the commencement of or during the state of war between Germany and the United States of America was, upon request made prior to October 3, 1950, extended in term for a period corresponding to the inclusive time from the date of the commencement of the state of war, or such later date on which such right came in existence, to September 30, 1949; and

WHEREAS, by virtue of a proclamation by the President of the United States of America dated May 25, 1922, 42 Stat. 2271, German citizens are and have been entitled to the benefits of the act of Congress approved March 4, 1909, 35 Stat. 1075, as amended, including the benefits of Section 1(e) of the aforementioned Title 17 of the United States Code [section 1(e) of former Title 17]; and

WHEREAS, a letter of February 6, 1950, from the Chancellor of the Federal Republic of Germany to the

Chairman of the Allied High Commission for Germany established the mutual understanding that reciprocal copyright relations continued in effect between the Federal Republic of Germany and the United States of America:

NOW, THEREFORE, I, LYNDON B. JOHNSON, President of the United States of America, by virtue of the authority vested in me by Section 9 of Title 17 of the United States Code [section 9 of former Title 17], do declare and proclaim:

(1) That, with respect to works first produced or published outside the United States of America: (a) where the work was subject to copyright under the laws of the United States of America on or after September 3, 1939, and on or before May 5, 1956, by an author or other owner who was then a German citizen; or (b) where the work was subject to renewal of copyright under the laws of the United States of America on or after September 3, 1939, and on or before May 5, 1956, by an author or other person specified in Sections 24 and 25 of the aforesaid Title 17 [sections 24 and 25 of former Title 17], who was then a German citizen, there has existed during several years of the aforementioned period such disruption and suspension of facilities essential to compliance with conditions and formalities prescribed with respect to such works by the copyright law of the United States of America as to bring such works within the terms of Section 9(b) of the aforesaid Title 17 [section 9(b) of former Title 17]; and

(2) That, in view of the reciprocal treatment accorded to citizens of the United States by the Federal Republic of Germany, the time within which persons who are presently German citizens may comply with such conditions and formalities with respect to such works is hereby extended for one year after the date of this proclamation.

It shall be understood that the term of copyright in any case is not and cannot be altered or affected by this proclamation. It shall also be understood that, as provided by Section 9(b) of Title 17, United States Code [section 9(b) of former Title 17], no liability shall attach under that title for lawful uses made or acts done prior to the effective date of this proclamation in connection with the above-described works, or with respect to the continuance for one year subsequent to such date of any business undertaking or enterprise lawfully undertaken prior to such date involving expenditure or contractual obligation in connection with the exploitation, production, reproduction, circulation or performance of any such works.

IN WITNESS WHEREOF, I have hereunto set my hand this twelfth day of July in the year of our Lord nineteen hundred and sixty-seven, and of the Independence of the United States of America the one hundred and ninety-second.

LYNDON B. JOHNSON.

PRESIDENTIAL PROCLAMATIONS ISSUED UNDER
PREDECESSOR PROVISIONS

Section 104 of Pub. L. 94–553 provided that: "All proclamations issued by the President under section 1(e) or 9(b) of title 17 as it existed on December 31, 1977, or under previous copyright statutes of the United States, shall continue in force until terminated, suspended, or revised by the President."

§ 104A. Copyright in restored works

(a) AUTOMATIC PROTECTION AND TERM.—

(1) TERM.—

(A) Copyright subsists, in accordance with this section, in restored works, and vests automatically on the date of restoration.

(B) Any work in which copyright is restored under this section shall subsist for the remainder of the term of copyright that the work would have otherwise been granted in the United States if the work never entered the public domain in the United States.

(2) EXCEPTION.—Any work in which the copyright was ever owned or administered by the Alien Property Custodian and in which the restored copyright would be owned by a government or instrumentality thereof, is not a restored work.

(b) OWNERSHIP OF RESTORED COPYRIGHT.—A restored work vests initially in the author or initial rightholder of the work as determined by the law of the source country of the work.

(c) FILING OF NOTICE OF INTENT TO ENFORCE RESTORED COPYRIGHT AGAINST RELIANCE PARTIES.—On or after the date of restoration, any person who owns a copyright in a restored work or an exclusive right therein may file with the Copyright Office a notice of intent to enforce that person's copyright or exclusive right or may serve such a notice directly on a reliance party. Acceptance of a notice by the Copyright Office is effective as to any reliance parties but shall not create a presumption of the validity of any of the facts stated therein. Service on a reliance party is effective as to that reliance party and any other reliance parties with actual knowledge of such service and of the contents of that notice.

(d) REMEDIES FOR INFRINGEMENT OF RESTORED COPYRIGHTS.—

(1) ENFORCEMENT OF COPYRIGHT IN RESTORED WORKS IN THE ABSENCE OF A RELIANCE PARTY.—As against any party who is not a reliance party, the remedies provided in chapter 5 of this title shall be available on or after the date of restoration of a restored copyright with respect to an act of infringement of the restored copyright that is commenced on or after the date of restoration.

(2) ENFORCEMENT OF COPYRIGHT IN RESTORED WORKS AS AGAINST RELIANCE PARTIES.—As against a reliance party, except to the extent provided in paragraphs (3) and (4), the remedies provided in chapter 5 of this title shall be available, with respect to an act of infringement of a restored copyright, on or after the date of restoration of the restored copyright if the requirements of either of the following subparagraphs are met:

(A)(i) The owner of the restored copyright (or such owner's agent) or the owner of an exclusive right therein (or such owner's agent) files with the Copyright Office, during the 24-month period beginning on the date of restoration, a notice of intent to enforce the restored copyright; and

(ii)(I) the act of infringement commenced after the end of the 12-month period beginning on the date of publication of the notice in the Federal Register;

(II) the act of infringement commenced before the end of the 12-month period described in subclause (I) and continued after the end of that 12-month period, in which case remedies shall be available only for infringement occurring after the end of that 12-month period; or

(III) copies or phonorecords of a work in which copyright has been restored under this section are made after publication of the notice of intent in the Federal Register.

(B)(i) The owner of the restored copyright (or such owner's agent) or the owner of an exclusive right therein (or such owner's agent) serves upon a reliance party a notice of intent to enforce a restored copyright; and

(ii)(I) the act of infringement commenced after the end of the 12-month period beginning on the date the notice of intent is received;

(II) the act of infringement commenced before the end of the 12-month period described in subclause (I) and continued after the end of that 12-month period, in which case remedies shall be available only for the infringement occurring after the end of that 12-month period; or

(III) copies or phonorecords of a work in which copyright has been restored under this section are made after receipt of the notice of intent.

In the event that notice is provided under both subparagraphs (A) and (B), the 12-month period referred to in such subparagraphs shall run from the earlier of publication or service of notice.

(3) EXISTING DERIVATIVE WORKS.—(A) In the case of a derivative work that is based upon a restored work and is created—

(i) before the date of the enactment of the Uruguay Round Agreements Act, if the source country of the restored work is an eligible country on such date, or

(ii) before the date on which the source country of the restored work becomes an eligible country, if that country is not an eligible country on such date of enactment,

a reliance party may continue to exploit that derivative work for the duration of the restored copyright if the reliance party pays to the owner of the restored copyright reasonable compensation for conduct which would be subject to a remedy for infringement but for the provisions of this paragraph.

(B) In the absence of an agreement between the parties, the amount of such compensation shall be determined by an action in United States district court, and shall reflect any harm to the actual or potential market for or value of the restored work from the reliance party's continued exploitation of the work, as well as compensation for the relative contributions of expression of the author of the restored work and the reliance party to the derivative work.

(4) COMMENCEMENT OF INFRINGEMENT FOR RELIANCE PARTIES.—For purposes of section 412, in the case of reliance parties, infringement shall be deemed to have commenced before registration when acts which would have constituted infringement had the restored work been subject to copyright were commenced before the date of restoration.

(e) NOTICES OF INTENT TO ENFORCE A RESTORED COPYRIGHT.—

(1) NOTICES OF INTENT FILED WITH THE COPYRIGHT OFFICE.—(A)(i) A notice of intent filed with the Copyright Office to enforce a restored copyright shall be signed by the owner of the restored copyright or the owner of an exclusive right therein, who files the notice under subsection (d)(2)(A)(i) (hereafter in this paragraph referred to as the "owner"), or by the owner's agent, shall identify the title of the restored work, and shall include an English translation of the title and any other alternative titles known to the owner by which the restored work may be identified, and an address and telephone number at which the owner may be contacted. If the notice is signed by an agent, the agency relationship must have been constituted in a writing signed by the owner before the filing of the notice. The Copyright Office may specifically require in regulations other information to be included in the notice, but failure to provide such other information shall not invalidate the notice or be a basis for refusal to list the restored work in the Federal Register.

(ii) If a work in which copyright is restored has no formal title, it shall be described in the notice of intent in detail sufficient to identify it.

(iii) Minor errors or omissions may be corrected by further notice at any time after the notice of intent is filed. Notices of corrections for such minor errors or omissions shall be accepted after the period established in subsection (d)(2)(A)(i). Notices shall be published in the Federal Register pursuant to subparagraph (B).

(B)(i) The Register of Copyrights shall publish in the Federal Register, commencing not later than 4 months after the date of restoration for a particular nation and every 4 months thereafter for a period of 2 years, lists identifying restored works and the ownership thereof if a notice of intent to enforce a restored copyright has been filed.

(ii) Not less than 1 list containing all notices of intent to enforce shall be maintained in the Public Information Office of the Copyright Office and shall be available for public inspection and copying during regular business hours pursuant to sections 705 and 708.

(C) The Register of Copyrights is authorized to fix reasonable fees based on the costs of receipt, processing, recording, and publication of notices of intent to enforce a restored copyright and corrections thereto.

(D)(i) Not later than 90 days before the date the Agreement on Trade-Related Aspects of Intellectual Property referred to in section 101(d)(15) of the Uruguay Round Agreements Act enters into force with respect to the United States, the Copyright Office shall issue and publish in the Federal Register regulations governing the filing under this subsection of notices of intent to enforce a restored copyright.

(ii) Such regulations shall permit owners of restored copyrights to file simultaneously for registration of the restored copyright.

(2) NOTICES OF INTENT SERVED ON A RELIANCE PARTY.—(A) Notices of intent to enforce a restored copyright may be served on a reliance party at any time after the date of restoration of the restored copyright.

(B) Notices of intent to enforce a restored copyright served on a reliance party shall be signed by the owner or the owner's agent, shall identify the restored work and the work in which the restored work is used, if any, in detail sufficient to identify them, and shall include an English translation of the title, any other alternative titles known to the owner by which the work may be identified, the use or uses to which the owner objects, and an address and telephone number at which the reliance party may contact the owner. If the notice is signed by an agent, the agency relationship must have been constituted in writing and signed by the owner before service of the notice.

(3) EFFECT OF MATERIAL FALSE STATEMENTS.—Any material false statement knowingly made with respect to any restored copyright identified in any notice of intent shall make void all claims and assertions made with respect to such restored copyright.

(f) IMMUNITY FROM WARRANTY AND RELATED LIABILITY.—

(1) IN GENERAL.—Any person who warrants, promises, or guarantees that a work does not violate an exclusive right granted in section 106 shall not be liable for legal, equitable, arbitral, or administrative relief if the warranty, promise, or guarantee is breached by virtue of the restoration of copyright under this section, if such warranty, promise, or guarantee is made before January 1, 1995.

(2) PERFORMANCES.—No person shall be required to perform any act if such performance is made infringing by virtue of the restoration of copyright under the provisions of this section, if the obligation to perform was undertaken before January 1, 1995.

(g) PROCLAMATION OF COPYRIGHT RESTORATION.—Whenever the President finds that a particular foreign nation extends, to works by authors who are nationals or domiciliaries of the United States, restored copyright protection on substantially the same basis as provided under this section, the President may by proclamation extend restored protection provided under this section to any work—

(1) of which one or more of the authors is, on the date of first publication, a national, domiciliary, or sovereign authority of that nation; or

(2) which was first published in that nation.

The President may revise, suspend, or revoke any such proclamation or impose any conditions or limitations on protection under such a proclamation.

(h) DEFINITIONS.—For purposes of this section and section 109(a):

(1) The term "date of adherence or proclamation" means the earlier of the date on which a foreign nation which, as of the date the WTO Agreement enters into force with respect to the United States, is not a nation adhering to the Berne Convention or a WTO member country, becomes—

(A) a nation adhering to the Berne Convention;

(B) a WTO member country;

(C) a nation adhering to the WIPO Copyright Treaty;

(D) a nation adhering to the WIPO Performances and Phonograms Treaty; or

(E) subject to a Presidential proclamation under subsection (g).

(2) The "date of restoration" of a restored copyright is—

(A) January 1, 1996, if the source country of the restored work is a nation adhering to the Berne Convention or a WTO member country on such date, or

(B) the date of adherence or proclamation, in the case of any other source country of the restored work.

(3) The term "eligible country" means a nation, other than the United States, that—

(A) becomes a WTO member country after the date of the enactment of the Uruguay Round Agreements Act;

(B) on such date of enactment is, or after such date of enactment becomes, a nation adhering to the Berne Convention;

(C) adheres to the WIPO Copyright Treaty;

(D) adheres to the WIPO Performances and Phonograms Treaty; or

(E) after such date of enactment becomes subject to a proclamation under subsection (g).

(4) The term "reliance party" means any person who—

(A) with respect to a particular work, engages in acts, before the source country of that work becomes an eligible country, which would have violated section 106 if the restored work had been subject to copyright protection, and who, after the source country becomes an eligible country, continues to engage in such acts;

(B) before the source country of a particular work becomes an eligible country, makes or acquires 1 or more copies or phonorecords of that work; or

(C) as the result of the sale or other disposition of a derivative work covered under subsection (d)(3), or significant assets of a person described in subparagraph (A) or (B), is a successor, assignee, or licensee of that person.

(5) The term "restored copyright" means copyright in a restored work under this section.

(6) The term "restored work" means an original work of authorship that—

(A) is protected under subsection (a);

(B) is not in the public domain in its source country through expiration of term of protection;

(C) is in the public domain in the United States due to—

(i) noncompliance with formalities imposed at any time by United States copyright law, including failure of renewal, lack of proper notice, or failure to comply with any manufacturing requirements;

(ii) lack of subject matter protection in the case of sound recordings fixed before February 15, 1972; or

(iii) lack of national eligibility;

(D) has at least one author or rightholder who was, at the time the work was created, a national or domiciliary of an eligible country, and if published, was first published in an eligible country and not published in the United States during the 30-day period following publication in such eligible country; and

(E) if the source country for the work is an eligible country solely by virtue of its adherence to the WIPO Performances and Phonograms Treaty, is a sound recording.

(7) The term "rightholder" means the person—

(A) who, with respect to a sound recording, first fixes a sound recording with authorization, or

(B) who has acquired rights from the person described in subparagraph (A) by means of any conveyance or by operation of law.

(8) The "source country" of a restored work is—

(A) a nation other than the United States;

(B) in the case of an unpublished work—

(i) the eligible country in which the author or rightholder is a national or domiciliary, or, if a restored work has more than 1 author or rightholder, of which the majority of foreign authors or rightholders are nationals or domiciliaries; or

(ii) if the majority of authors or rightholders are not foreign, the nation other than the United States which has the most significant contacts with the work; and

(C) in the case of a published work—

(i) the eligible country in which the work is first published, or

(ii) if the restored work is published on the same day in 2 or more eligible countries, the eligible country which has the most significant contacts with the work.

(Added Pub. L. 103–182, title III, § 334(a), Dec. 8, 1993, 107 Stat. 2115; amended Pub. L. 103–465, title V, § 514(a), Dec. 8, 1994, 108 Stat. 4976; Pub. L. 104–295, § 20(e)(2), Oct. 11, 1996, 110 Stat. 3529; Pub. L. 105–80, § 2, Nov. 13, 1997, 111 Stat. 1530; Pub. L. 105–304, title I, § 102(c), Oct. 28, 1998, 112 Stat. 2862.)

References in Text

The date of the enactment of the Uruguay Round Agreements Act, referred to in subsecs. (d)(3)(A) and (h)(3), is the date of enactment of Pub. L. 103–465, which was approved Dec. 8, 1994.

Section 101(d)(15) of the Uruguay Round Agreements Act, referred to in subsec. (e)(1)(D)(i), is classified to section 3511(d)(15) of Title 19, Customs Duties.

Amendments

1998—Subsec. (h)(1)(A) to (E). Pub. L. 105–304, § 102(c)(1), added subpars. (A) to (E) and struck out former subpars. (A) and (B) which read as follows:

"(A) a nation adhering to the Berne Convention or a WTO member country; or

"(B) subject to a Presidential proclamation under subsection (g)."

Subsec. (h)(3). Pub. L. 105–304, § 102(c)(2), amended par. (3) generally. Prior to amendment, par. (3) read as follows: "The term 'eligible country' means a nation, other than the United States, that—

"(A) becomes a WTO member country after the date of the enactment of the Uruguay Round Agreements Act;

"(B) on such date of enactment is, or after such date of enactment becomes, a member of the Berne Convention; or

"(C) after such date of enactment becomes subject to a proclamation under subsection (g).

For purposes of this section, a nation that is a member of the Berne Convention on the date of the enactment of the Uruguay Round Agreements Act shall be construed to become an eligible country on such date of enactment."

Subsec. (h)(6)(E). Pub. L. 105–304, § 102(c)(3), added subpar. (E).

Subsec. (h)(8)(B)(i). Pub. L. 105–304, § 102(c)(4), inserted "of which" before "the majority" and struck out "of eligible countries" after "domiciliaries".

Subsec. (h)(9). Pub. L. 105–304, § 102(c)(5), struck out par. (9) which read as follows: "The terms 'WTO Agreement' and 'WTO member country' have the meanings given those terms in paragraphs (9) and (10), respectively, of section 2 of the Uruguay Round Agreements Act."

1997—Subsec. (d)(3)(A). Pub. L. 105–80, § 2(1), amended subpar. (A) generally. Prior to amendment, subpar. (A) read as follows: "In the case of a derivative work that is based upon a restored work and is created—

"(i) before the date of the enactment of the Uruguay Round Agreements Act, if the source country of the derivative work is an eligible country on such date, or

"(ii) before the date of adherence or proclamation, if the source country of the derivative work is not an eligible country on such date of enactment,

a reliance party may continue to exploit that work for the duration of the restored copyright if the reliance party pays to the owner of the restored copyright reasonable compensation for conduct which would be subject to a remedy for infringement but for the provisions of this paragraph."

Subsec. (e)(1)(B)(ii). Pub. L. 105–80, § 2(2), struck out at end "Such list shall also be published in the Federal Register on an annual basis for the first 2 years after the applicable date of restoration."

Subsec. (h)(2), (3). Pub. L. 105–80, § 2(3), (4), amended pars. (2) and (3) generally. Prior to amendment, pars. (2) and (3) read as follows:

"(2) The 'date of restoration' of a restored copyright is the later of—

"(A) the date on which the Agreement on Trade-Related Aspects of Intellectual Property referred to in section 101(d)(15) of the Uruguay Round Agreements Act enters into force with respect to the United States, if the source country of the restored work is a nation adhering to the Berne Convention or a WTO member country on such date; or

"(B) the date of adherence or proclamation, in the case of any other source country of the restored work.

"(3) The term 'eligible country' means a nation, other than the United States, that is a WTO member country, adheres to the Berne Convention, or is subject to a proclamation under subsection (g)."

1996—Subsec. (h)(3). Pub. L. 104–295 substituted "subsection (g)" for "section 104A(g)".

1994—Pub. L. 103–465 substituted "Copyright in restored works" for "Copyright in certain motion pictures" as section catchline and amended text generally, substituting present provisions for provisions restoring copyright in certain motion pictures and providing for effective date of protection as well as use of previously owned copies.

Effective Date of 1998 Amendment

Subsec. (h)(1)(A), (B), (E), (3)(A), (B), (E) of this section and amendment by section 102(c)(4), (5) of Pub. L. 105–304 effective Oct. 28, 1998, except as otherwise provided, subsec. (h)(1)(C), (3)(C) of this section effective Mar. 6, 2002, and subsec. (h)(1)(D), (3)(D) of this section and amendment by section 102(c)(3) of Pub. L. 105–304 effective May 20, 2002, see section 105(a), (b)(1)(C), (D), (2)(D)–(F) of Pub. L. 105–304, set out as a note under section 101 of this title.

Effective Date

Section effective on the date the North American Free Trade Agreement enters into force with respect to the United States [Jan. 1, 1994], see section 335(a) of Pub. L. 103–182, set out in an Effective Date of 1993 Amendment note under section 1052 of Title 15, Commerce and Trade.

URUGUAY ROUND AGREEMENTS: ENTRY INTO FORCE

The Uruguay Round Agreements, including the World Trade Organization Agreement and agreements annexed to that Agreement, as referred to in section 3511(d) of Title 19, Customs Duties, entered into force with respect to the United States on Jan. 1, 1995. See note set out under section 3511 of Title 19.

§ 105. Subject matter of copyright: United States Government works

Copyright protection under this title is not available for any work of the United States Government, but the United States Government is not precluded from receiving and holding copyrights transferred to it by assignment, bequest, or otherwise.

(Pub. L. 94–553, title I, § 101, Oct. 19, 1976, 90 Stat. 2546.)

HISTORICAL AND REVISION NOTES

HOUSE REPORT NO. 94–1476

Scope of the Prohibition. The basic premise of section 105 of the bill is the same as that of section 8 of the present law [section 8 of former title 17]—that works produced for the U.S. Government by its officers and employees should not be subject to copyright. The provision applies the principle equally to unpublished and published works.

The general prohibition against copyright in section 105 applies to "any work of the United States Government," which is defined in section 101 as "a work prepared by an officer or employee of the United States Government as part of that person's official duties." Under this definition a Government official or employee would not be prevented from securing copyright in a work written at that person's own volition and outside his or her duties, even though the subject matter involves the Government work or professional field of the official or employee. Although the wording of the definition of "work of the United States Government" differs somewhat from that of the definition of "work made for hire," the concepts are intended to be construed in the same way.

A more difficult and far-reaching problem is whether the definition should be broadened to prohibit copyright in works prepared under U.S. Government contract or grant. As the bill is written, the Government agency concerned could determine in each case whether to allow an independent contractor or grantee, to secure copyright in works prepared in whole or in part with the use of Government funds. The argument that has been made against allowing copyright in this situation is that the public should not be required to pay a "double subsidy," and that it is inconsistent to prohibit copyright in works by Government employees while permitting private copyrights in a growing body of works created by persons who are paid with Government funds. Those arguing in favor of potential copyright protection have stressed the importance of copyright as an incentive to creation and dissemination in this situation, and the basically different policy considerations, applicable to works written by Government employees and those applicable to works prepared by private organizations with the use of Federal funds.

The bill deliberately avoids making any sort of outright, unqualified prohibition against copyright in works prepared under Government contract or grant. There may well be cases where it would be in the public interest to deny copyright in the writings generated by Government research contracts and the like; it can be assumed that, where a Government agency commis-

sions a work for its own use merely as an alternative to having one of its own employees prepare the work, the right to secure a private copyright would be withheld. However, there are almost certainly many other cases where the denial of copyright protection would be unfair or would hamper the production and publication of important works. Where, under the particular circumstances, Congress or the agency involved finds that the need to have a work freely available outweighs the need of the private author to secure copyright, the problem can be dealt with by specific legislation, agency regulations, or contractual restrictions.

The prohibition on copyright protection for United States Government works is not intended to have any effect on protection of these works abroad. Works of the governments of most other countries are copyrighted. There are no valid policy reasons for denying such protection to United States Government works in foreign countries, or for precluding the Government from making licenses for the use of its works abroad.

The effect of section 105 is intended to place all works of the United States Government, published or unpublished, in the public domain. This means that the individual Government official or employee who wrote the work could not secure copyright in it or restrain its dissemination by the Government or anyone else, but it also means that, as far as the copyright law is concerned, the Government could not restrain the employee or official from disseminating the work if he or she chooses to do so. The use of the term "work of the United States Government" does not mean that a work falling within the definition of that term is the property of the U.S. Government.

LIMITED EXCEPTION FOR NATIONAL TECHNICAL INFORMATION SERVICE

At the House hearings in 1975 the U.S. Department of Commerce called attention to its National Technical Information Service (NTIS), which has a statutory mandate, under Chapter 23 [§ 1151 et seq.] of Title 15 of the U.S. Code, to operate a clearinghouse for the collection and dissemination of scientific, technical and engineering information. Under its statute, NTIS is required to be as self-sustaining as possible, and not to force the general public to bear publishing costs that are for private benefit. The Department urged an amendment to section 105 that would allow it to secure copyright in NTIS publications both in the United States and abroad, noting that a precedent exists in the Standard Reference Data Act (15 U.S.C. § 290(e) [§ 290e]).

In response to this request the Committee adopted a limited exception to the general prohibition in section 105, permitting the Secretary of Commerce to "secure copyright for a limited term not to exceed five years, on behalf of the United States as author or copyright owner" in any NTIS publication disseminated pursuant to 15 U.S.C. Chapter 23 [§ 1151 et seq.]. In order to "secure copyright" in a work under this amendment the Secretary would be required to publish the work with a copyright notice, and the five-year term would begin upon the date of first publication.

Proposed Saving Clause. Section 8 of the statute now in effect [section 8 of former title 17] includes a saving clause intended to make clear that the copyright protection of a private work is not affected if the work is published by the Government. This provision serves a real purpose in the present law because of the ambiguity of the undefined term "any publication of the United States Government." Section 105 of the bill, however, uses the operative term "work of the United States Government" and defines it in such a way that privately written works are clearly excluded from the prohibition; accordingly, a saving clause becomes superfluous.

Retention of a saving clause has been urged on the ground that the present statutory provision is frequently cited, and that having the provision expressly stated in the law would avoid questions and explanations. The committee here observes: (1) there is nothing in section 105 that would relieve the Government of its obligation to secure permission in order to publish a copyrighted work; and (2) publication or other use by the Government of a private work would not affect its copyright protection in any way. The question of use of copyrighted material in documents published by the Congress and its Committees is discussed below in connection with section 107.

Works of the United States Postal Service. The intent of section 105 [this section] is to restrict the prohibition against Government copyright to works written by employees of the United States Government within the scope of their official duties. In accordance with the objectives of the Postal Reorganization Act of 1970 [Pub. L. 91–375, which enacted title 39, Postal Service], this section does not apply to works created by employees of the United States Postal Service. In addition to enforcing the criminal statutes proscribing the forgery or counterfeiting of postage stamps, the Postal Service could, if it chooses, use the copyright law to prevent the reproduction of postage stamp designs for private or commercial non-postal services (for example, in philatelic publications and catalogs, in general advertising, in art reproductions, in textile designs, and so forth). However, any copyright claimed by the Postal Service in its works, including postage stamp designs, would be subject to the same conditions, formalities, and time limits as other copyrightable works.

§ 106. Exclusive rights in copyrighted works

Subject to sections 107 through 122, the owner of copyright under this title has the exclusive rights to do and to authorize any of the following:

(1) to reproduce the copyrighted work in copies or phonorecords;

(2) to prepare derivative works based upon the copyrighted work;

(3) to distribute copies or phonorecords of the copyrighted work to the public by sale or other transfer of ownership, or by rental, lease, or lending;

(4) in the case of literary, musical, dramatic, and choreographic works, pantomimes, and motion pictures and other audiovisual works, to perform the copyrighted work publicly;

(5) in the case of literary, musical, dramatic, and choreographic works, pantomimes, and pictorial, graphic, or sculptural works, including the individual images of a motion picture or other audiovisual work, to display the copyrighted work publicly; and

(6) in the case of sound recordings, to perform the copyrighted work publicly by means of a digital audio transmission.

(Pub. L. 94–553, title I, § 101, Oct. 19, 1976, 90 Stat. 2546; Pub. L. 101–318, § 3(d), July 3, 1990, 104 Stat. 288; Pub. L. 101–650, title VII, § 704(b)(2), Dec. 1, 1990, 104 Stat. 5134; Pub. L. 104–39, § 2, Nov. 1, 1995, 109 Stat. 336; Pub. L. 106–44, § 1(g)(2), Aug. 5, 1999, 113 Stat. 222; Pub. L. 107–273, div. C, title III, § 13210(4)(A), Nov. 2, 2002, 116 Stat. 1909.)

HISTORICAL AND REVISION NOTES

HOUSE REPORT NO. 94–1476

General Scope of Copyright. The five fundamental rights that the bill gives to copyright owners—the exclusive rights of reproduction, adaptation, publication, performance, and display—are stated generally in section 106. These exclusive rights, which comprise the so-called "bundle of rights" that is a copyright, are cumulative and may overlap in some cases. Each of the five enumerated rights may be subdivided indefinitely and, as discussed below in connection with section 201, each subdivision of an exclusive right may be owned and enforced separately.

The approach of the bill is to set forth the copyright owner's exclusive rights in broad terms in section 106, and then to provide various limitations, qualifications, or exemptions in the 12 sections that follow. Thus, everything in section 106 is made "subject to sections 107 through 118", and must be read in conjunction with those provisions.

The exclusive rights accorded to a copyright owner under section 106 are "to do and to authorize" any of the activities specified in the five numbered clauses. Use of the phrase "to authorize" is intended to avoid any questions as to the liability of contributory infringers. For example, a person who lawfully acquires an authorized copy of a motion picture would be an infringer if he or she engages in the business of renting it to others for purposes of unauthorized public performance.

Rights of Reproduction, Adaptation, and Publication. The first three clauses of section 106, which cover all rights under a copyright except those of performance and display, extend to every kind of copyrighted work. The exclusive rights encompassed by these clauses, though closely related, are independent; they can generally be characterized as rights of copying, recording, adaptation, and publishing. A single act of infringement may violate all of these rights at once, as where a publisher reproduces, adapts, and sells copies of a person's copyrighted work as part of a publishing venture. Infringement takes place when any one of the rights is violated: where, for example, a printer reproduces copies without selling them or a retailer sells copies without having anything to do with their reproduction. The references to "copies or phonorecords," although in the plural, are intended here and throughout the bill to include the singular (1 U.S.C. § 1).

Reproduction.—Read together with the relevant definitions in section 101, the right "to reproduce the copyrighted work in copies or phonorecords" means the right to produce a material object in which the work is duplicated, transcribed, imitated, or simulated in a fixed form from which it can be "perceived, reproduced, or otherwise communicated, either directly or with the aid of a machine or device." As under the present law, a copyrighted work would be infringed by reproducing it in whole or in any substantial part, and by duplicating it exactly or by imitation or simulation. Wide departures or variations from the copyrighted work would still be an infringement as long as the author's "expression" rather than merely the author's "ideas" are taken. An exception to this general principle, applicable to the reproduction of copyrighted sound recordings, is specified in section 114.

"Reproduction" under clause (1) of section 106 is to be distinguished from "display" under clause (5). For a work to be "reproduced," its fixation in tangible form must be "sufficiently permanent or stable to permit it to be perceived, reproduced, or otherwise communicated for a period of more than transitory duration." Thus, the showing of images on a screen or tube would not be a violation of clause (1), although it might come within the scope of clause (5).

Preparation of Derivative Works.—The exclusive right to prepare derivative works, specified separately in clause (2) of section 106, overlaps the exclusive right of reproduction to some extent. It is broader than that right, however, in the sense that reproduction requires fixation in copies or phonorecords, whereas the preparation of a derivative work, such as a ballet, pantomime, or improvised performance, may be an infringement even though nothing is ever fixed in tangible form.

To be an infringement the "derivative work" must be "based upon the copyrighted work," and the definition in section 101 refers to "a translation, musical arrangement, dramatization, fictionalization, motion picture version, sound recording, art reproduction, abridgment, condensation, or any other form in which a work may be recast, transformed, or adapted." Thus, to constitute a violation of section 106(2), the infringing work must incorporate a portion of the copyrighted work in some form; for example, a detailed commentary on a work or a programmatic musical composition inspired by a novel would not normally constitute infringements under this clause.

Use in Information Storage and Retrieval Systems.—As section 117 declares explicitly, the bill is not intended to alter the present law with respect to the use of copyrighted works in computer systems.

Public Distribution.—Clause (3) of section 106 establishes the exclusive right of publication: The right "to distribute copies or phonorecords of the copyrighted work to the public by sale or other transfer of ownership, or by rental, lease, or lending." Under this provision the copyright owner would have the right to control the first public distribution of an authorized copy or phonorecord of his work, whether by sale, gift, loan, or some rental or lease arrangement. Likewise, any unauthorized public distribution of copies or phonorecords that were unlawfully made would be an infringement. As section 109 makes clear, however, the copyright owner's rights under section 106(3) cease with respect to a particular copy or phonorecord once he has parted with ownership of it.

Rights of Public Performance and Display. *Performing Rights and the "For Profit" Limitation.*—The right of public performance under section 106(4) extends to "literary, musical, dramatic, and choreographic works, pantomimes, and motion pictures and other audiovisual works and sound recordings" and, unlike the equivalent provisions now in effect, is not limited by any "for profit" requirement. The approach of the bill, as in many foreign laws, is first to state the public performance right in broad terms, and then to provide specific exemptions for educational and other nonprofit uses.

This approach is more reasonable than the outright exemption of the 1909 statute. The line between commercial and "nonprofit" organizations is increasingly difficult to draw. Many "non-profit" organizations are highly subsidized and capable of paying royalties, and the widespread public exploitation of copyrighted works by public broadcasters and other noncommercial organizations is likely to grow. In addition to these trends, it is worth noting that performances and displays are continuing to supplant markets for printed copies and that in the future a broad "not for profit" exemption could not only hurt authors but could dry up their incentive to write.

The exclusive right of public performance is expanded to include not only motion pictures, including works recorded on film, video tape, and video disks, but also audiovisual works such as filmstrips and sets of slides. This provision of section 106(4), which is consistent with the assimilation of motion pictures to audiovisual works throughout the bill, is also related to amendments of the definitions of "display" and "perform" discussed below. The important issue of performing rights in sound recordings is discussed in connection with section 114.

Right of Public Display.—Clause (5) of section 106 represents the first explicit statutory recognition in American copyright law of an exclusive right to show a copyrighted work, or an image of it, to the public. The existence or extent of this right under the present statute is uncertain and subject to challenge. The bill would give the owners of copyright in "literary, musical, dramatic, and choreographic works, pantomimes, and pictorial, graphic, or sculptural works", including the individual images of a motion picture or other audiovisual work, the exclusive right "to display the copyrighted work publicly."

Definitions. Under the definitions of "perform," "display," "publicly," and "transmit" in section 101, the concepts of public performance and public display cover not only the initial rendition or showing, but also any further act by which that rendition or showing is transmitted or communicated to the public. Thus, for example: a singer is performing when he or she sings a song; a broadcasting network is performing when it transmits his or her performance (whether simultaneously or from records); a local broadcaster is performing when it transmits the network broadcast; a cable television system is performing when it retransmits the broadcast to its subscribers; and any individual is performing whenever he or she plays a phonorecord embodying the performance or communicates the performance by turning on a receiving set. Although any act by which the initial performance or display is transmitted, repeated, or made to recur would itself be a "performance" or "display" under the bill, it would not be actionable as an infringement unless it were done "publicly," as defined in section 101. Certain other performances and displays, in addition to those that are "private," are exempted or given qualified copyright control under sections 107 through 118.

To "perform" a work, under the definition in section 101, includes reading a literary work aloud, singing or playing music, dancing a ballet or other choreographic work, and acting out a dramatic work or pantomime. A performance may be accomplished "either directly or by means of any device or process," including all kinds of equipment for reproducing or amplifying sounds or visual images, any sort of transmitting apparatus, any type of electronic retrieval system, and any other techniques and systems not yet in use or even invented.

The definition of "perform" in relation to "a motion picture or other audiovisual work" is "to show its images in any sequence or to make the sounds accompanying it audible." The showing of portions of a motion picture, filmstrip, or slide set must therefore be sequential to constitute a "performance" rather than a "display", but no particular order need be maintained. The purely aural performance of a motion picture sound track, or of the sound portions of an audiovisual work, would constitute a performance of the "motion picture or other audiovisual work"; but, where some of the sounds have been reproduced separately on phonorecords, a performance from the phonorecord would not constitute performance of the motion picture or audiovisual work.

The corresponding definition of "display" covers any showing of a "copy" of the work, "either directly or by means of a film, slide, television image, or any other device or process." Since "copies" are defined as including the material object "in which the work is first fixed," the right of public display applies to original works of art as well as to reproductions of them. With respect to motion pictures and other audiovisual works, it is a "display" (rather than a "performance") to show their "individual images nonsequentially." In addition to the direct showings of a copy of a work, "display" would include the projection of an image on a screen or other surface by any method, the transmission of an image by electronic or other means, and the showing of an image on a cathode ray tube, or similar viewing apparatus connected with any sort of information storage and retrieval system.

Under clause (1) of the definition of "publicly" in section 101, a performance or display is "public" if it takes place "at a place open to the public or at any place where a substantial number of persons outside of a normal circle of a family and its social acquaintances is gathered." One of the principal purposes of the definition was to make clear that, contrary to the decision in *Metro-Goldwyn-Mayer Distributing Corp. v. Wyatt*, 21 C.O.Bull. 203 (D.Md.1932), performances in "semipublic" places such as clubs, lodges, factories, summer camps, and schools are "public performances" subject to copyright control. The term "a family" in this context would include an individual living alone, so that a gathering confined to the individual's social acquaintances would normally be regarded as private. Routine meetings of businesses and governmental personnel would be excluded because they do not represent the gathering of a "substantial number of persons."

Clause (2) of the definition of "publicly" in section 101 makes clear that the concepts of public performance and public display include not only performances and displays that occur initially in a public place, but also acts that transmit or otherwise communicate a performance or display of the work to the public by means of any device or process. The definition of "transmit"—to communicate a performance or display "by any device or process whereby images or sound are received beyond the place from which they are sent"— is broad enough to include all conceivable forms and combinations of wired or wireless communications media, including but by no means limited to radio and television broadcasting as we know them. Each and every method by which the images or sounds comprising a performance or display are picked up and conveyed is a "transmission," and if the transmission reaches the public in my [any] form, the case comes within the scope of clauses (4) or (5) of section 106.

Under the bill, as under the present law, a performance made available by transmission to the public at large is "public" even though the recipients are not gathered in a single place, and even if there is no proof that any of the potential recipients was operating his receiving apparatus at the time of the transmission. The same principles apply whenever the potential recipients of the transmission represent a limited segment of the public, such as the occupants of hotel rooms or the subscribers of a cable television service. Clause (2) of the definition of "publicly" is applicable "whether the members of the public capable of receiving the performance or display receive it in the same place or in separate places and at the same time or at different times."

AMENDMENTS

2002—Pub. L. 107–273 substituted "122" for "121" in introductory provisions.

1999—Pub. L. 106–44 substituted "121" for "120" in introductory provisions.

1995—Par. (6). Pub. L. 104–39 added par. (6).

1990—Pub. L. 101–650 substituted "120" for "119" in introductory provisions.

Pub. L. 101–318 substituted "119" for "118" in introductory provisions.

EFFECTIVE DATE OF 1995 AMENDMENT

Amendment by Pub. L. 104–39 effective 3 months after Nov. 1, 1995, see section 6 of Pub. L. 104–39, set out as a note under section 101 of this title.

EFFECTIVE DATE OF 1990 AMENDMENTS

Amendment by Pub. L. 101–650 applicable to any architectural work created on or after Dec. 1, 1990, and any architectural work, that, on Dec. 1, 1990, is unconstructed and embodied in unpublished plans or drawings, except that protection for such architectural work under this title terminates on Dec. 31, 2002, unless the work is constructed by that date, see section 706 of Pub. L. 101–650, set out as a note under section 101 of this title.

Section 3(e)(3) of Pub. L. 101–318 provided that: "The amendment made by subsection (d) [amending this section] shall be effective as of November 16, 1988."

§ 106A. Rights of certain authors to attribution and integrity

(a) RIGHTS OF ATTRIBUTION AND INTEGRITY.— Subject to section 107 and independent of the exclusive rights provided in section 106, the author of a work of visual art—

(1) shall have the right—

(A) to claim authorship of that work, and

(B) to prevent the use of his or her name as the author of any work of visual art which he or she did not create;

(2) shall have the right to prevent the use of his or her name as the author of the work of visual art in the event of a distortion, mutilation, or other modification of the work which would be prejudicial to his or her honor or reputation; and

(3) subject to the limitations set forth in section 113(d), shall have the right—

(A) to prevent any intentional distortion, mutilation, or other modification of that work which would be prejudicial to his or her honor or reputation, and any intentional distortion, mutilation, or modification of that work is a violation of that right, and

(B) to prevent any destruction of a work of recognized stature, and any intentional or grossly negligent destruction of that work is a violation of that right.

(b) SCOPE AND EXERCISE OF RIGHTS.—Only the author of a work of visual art has the rights conferred by subsection (a) in that work, whether or not the author is the copyright owner. The authors of a joint work of visual art are coowners of the rights conferred by subsection (a) in that work.

(c) EXCEPTIONS.—(1) The modification of a work of visual art which is a result of the passage of time or the inherent nature of the materials is not a distortion, mutilation, or other modification described in subsection (a)(3)(A).

(2) The modification of a work of visual art which is the result of conservation, or of the public presentation, including lighting and placement, of the work is not a destruction, distortion, mutilation, or other modification described in subsection (a)(3) unless the modification is caused by gross negligence.

(3) The rights described in paragraphs (1) and (2) of subsection (a) shall not apply to any reproduction, depiction, portrayal, or other use of a work in, upon, or in any connection with any item described in subparagraph (A) or (B) of the definition of "work of visual art" in section 101, and any such reproduction, depiction, portrayal, or other use of a work is not a destruction, distortion, mutilation, or other modification described in paragraph (3) of subsection (a).

(d) DURATION OF RIGHTS.—(1) With respect to works of visual art created on or after the effective date set forth in section 610(a) of the Visual Artists Rights Act of 1990, the rights conferred by subsection (a) shall endure for a term consisting of the life of the author.

(2) With respect to works of visual art created before the effective date set forth in section 610(a) of the Visual Artists Rights Act of 1990, but title to which has not, as of such effective date, been transferred from the author, the rights conferred by subsection (a) shall be coextensive with, and shall expire at the same time as, the rights conferred by section 106.

(3) In the case of a joint work prepared by two or more authors, the rights conferred by subsection (a) shall endure for a term consisting of the life of the last surviving author.

(4) All terms of the rights conferred by subsection (a) run to the end of the calendar year in which they would otherwise expire.

(e) TRANSFER AND WAIVER.—(1) The rights conferred by subsection (a) may not be transferred, but those rights may be waived if the author expressly agrees to such waiver in a written instrument signed by the author. Such instrument shall specifically identify the work, and uses of that work, to which the waiver applies, and the waiver shall apply only to the work and uses so identified. In the case of a joint work prepared by two or more authors, a waiver of rights under this paragraph made by one such author waives such rights for all such authors.

(2) Ownership of the rights conferred by subsection (a) with respect to a work of visual art is distinct from ownership of any copy of that work, or of a copyright or any exclusive right under a copyright in that work. Transfer of ownership of any copy of a work of visual art, or of a copyright or any exclusive right under a copyright, shall not constitute a waiver of the rights conferred by subsection (a). Except as may otherwise be agreed by the author in a written instrument signed by the author, a waiver of the rights conferred by subsection (a) with respect to a work of visual art shall not constitute a transfer of ownership of any copy of that work, or of ownership of a copyright or of any exclusive right under a copyright in that work.

(Added Pub. L. 101–650, title VI, §603(a), Dec. 1, 1990, 104 Stat. 5128.)

REFERENCES IN TEXT

Section 610(a) of the Visual Artists Rights Act of 1990 [Pub. L. 101–650], referred to in subsec. (d), is set out as an Effective Date note below.

EFFECTIVE DATE

Section 610 of title VI of Pub. L. 101–650 provided that:

"(a) IN GENERAL.—Subject to subsection (b) and except as provided in subsection (c), this title [enacting this section, amending sections 101, 107, 113, 301, 411, 412, 501, and 506 of this title, and enacting provisions set out as notes under this section and section 101 of this title] and the amendments made by this title take effect 6 months after the date of the enactment of this Act [Dec. 1, 1990].

"(b) APPLICABILITY.—The rights created by section 106A of title 17, United States Code, shall apply to—

"(1) works created before the effective date set forth in subsection (a) but title to which has not, as of such effective date, been transferred from the author, and

"(2) works created on or after such effective date, but shall not apply to any destruction, distortion, mutilation, or other modification (as described in section 106A(a)(3) of such title) of any work which occurred before such effective date.

"(c) SECTION 608.—Section 608 [set out below] takes effect on the date of the enactment of this Act."

STUDIES BY COPYRIGHT OFFICE

Section 608 of Pub. L. 101–650 provided that:

"(a) STUDY ON WAIVER OF RIGHTS PROVISION.—

"(1) STUDY.—The Register of Copyrights shall conduct a study on the extent to which rights conferred by subsection (a) of section 106A of title 17, United States Code, have been waived under subsection (e)(1) of such section.

"(2) REPORT TO CONGRESS.—Not later than 2 years after the date of the enactment of this Act [Dec. 1, 1990], the Register of Copyrights shall submit to the Congress a report on the progress of the study conducted under paragraph (1). Not later than 5 years after such date of enactment, the Register of Copyrights shall submit to the Congress a final report on the results of the study conducted under paragraph (1), and any recommendations that the Register may have as a result of the study.

"(b) STUDY ON RESALE ROYALTIES.—

"(1) NATURE OF STUDY.—The Register of Copyrights, in consultation with the Chair of the National Endowment for the Arts, shall conduct a study on the feasibility of implementing—

"(A) a requirement that, after the first sale of a work of art, a royalty on any resale of the work, consisting of a percentage of the price, be paid to the author of the work; and

"(B) other possible requirements that would achieve the objective of allowing an author of a work of art to share monetarily in the enhanced value of that work.

"(2) GROUPS TO BE CONSULTED.—The study under paragraph (1) shall be conducted in consultation with other appropriate departments and agencies of the United States, foreign governments, and groups involved in the creation, exhibition, dissemination, and preservation of works of art, including artists, art dealers, collectors of fine art, and curators of art museums.

"(3) REPORT TO CONGRESS.—Not later than 18 months after the date of the enactment of this Act [Dec. 1, 1990], the Register of Copyrights shall submit to the Congress a report containing the results of the study conducted under this subsection."

§ 107. Limitations on exclusive rights: Fair use

Notwithstanding the provisions of sections 106 and 106A, the fair use of a copyrighted work, including such use by reproduction in copies or phonorecords or by any other means specified by that section, for purposes such as criticism, comment, news reporting, teaching (including multiple copies for classroom use), scholarship, or research, is not an infringement of copyright. In determining whether the use made of a work in any particular case is a fair use the factors to be considered shall include—

(1) the purpose and character of the use, including whether such use is of a commercial nature or is for nonprofit educational purposes;

(2) the nature of the copyrighted work;

(3) the amount and substantiality of the portion used in relation to the copyrighted work as a whole; and

(4) the effect of the use upon the potential market for or value of the copyrighted work.

The fact that a work is unpublished shall not itself bar a finding of fair use if such finding is made upon consideration of all the above factors.

(Pub. L. 94–553, title I, §101, Oct. 19, 1976, 90 Stat. 2546; Pub. L. 101–650, title VI, §607, Dec. 1, 1990, 104 Stat. 5132; Pub. L. 102–492, Oct. 24, 1992, 106 Stat. 3145.)

HISTORICAL AND REVISION NOTES

HOUSE REPORT NO. 94–1476

General Background of the Problem. The judicial doctrine of fair use, one of the most important and well-established limitations on the exclusive right of copyright owners, would be given express statutory recognition for the first time in section 107. The claim that a defendant's acts constituted a fair use rather than an infringement has been raised as a defense in innumerable copyright actions over the years, and there is ample case law recognizing the existence of the doctrine and applying it. The examples enumerated at page 24 of the Register's 1961 Report, while by no means exhaustive, give some idea of the sort of activities the courts might regard as fair use under the circumstances: "quotation of excerpts in a review or criticism for purposes of illustration or comment; quotation of short passages in a scholarly or technical work, for illustration or clarification of the author's observations; use in a parody of some of the content of the work parodied; summary of an address or article, with brief quotations, in a news report; reproduction by a library of a portion of a work to replace part of a damaged copy; reproduction by a teacher or student of a small part of a work to illustrate a lesson; reproduction of a work in legislative or judicial proceedings or reports; incidental and fortuitous reproduction, in a newsreel or broadcast, of a work located in the scene of an event being reported."

Although the courts have considered and ruled upon the fair use doctrine over and over again, no real definition of the concept has ever emerged. Indeed, since the doctrine is an equitable rule of reason, no generally applicable definition is possible, and each case raising the question must be decided on its own facts. On the other hand, the courts have evolved a set of criteria which, though in no case definitive or determinative, provide some gauge for balancing the equities. These criteria have been stated in various ways, but essentially they can all be reduced to the four standards which have been adopted in section 107: "(1) the purpose and character of the use, including whether such use is of a commercial nature or is for nonprofit educational purposes; (2) the nature of the copyrighted work; (3) the amount and substantiality of the portion used in relation to the copyrighted work as a whole; and (4) the effect of the use upon the potential market for or value of the copyrighted work."

These criteria are relevant in determining whether the basic doctrine of fair use, as stated in the first sentence of section 107, applies in a particular case: "Notwithstanding the provisions of section 106, the fair use of a copyrighted work, including such use by reproduction in copies or phonorecords or by any other means specified by that section, for purposes such as criticism, comment, news reporting, teaching (including multiple copies for classroom use), scholarship, or research, is not an infringement of copyright."

The specific wording of section 107 as it now stands is the result of a process of accretion, resulting from the long controversy over the related problems of fair use and the reproduction (mostly by photocopying) of copyrighted material for educational and scholarly purposes. For example, the reference to fair use "by reproduction in copies or phonorecords or by any other means" is mainly intended to make clear that the doctrine has as much application to photocopying and taping as to older forms of use; it is not intended to give these kinds of reproduction any special status under the fair use provision or to sanction any reproduction beyond the normal and reasonable limits of fair use. Similarly, the newly-added reference to "multiple copies for classroom use" is a recognition that, under the proper circumstances of fairness, the doctrine can be applied to reproductions of multiple copies for the members of a class.

The Committee has amended the first of the criteria to be considered—"the purpose and character of the use"—to state explicitly that this factor includes a consideration of "whether such use is of a commercial nature or is for non-profit educational purposes." This amendment is not intended to be interpreted as any sort of not-for-profit limitation on educational uses of copyrighted works. It is an express recognition that, as under the present law, the commercial or non-profit character of an activity, while not conclusive with respect to fair use, can and should be weighed along with other factors in fair use decisions.

General Intention Behind the Provision. The statement of the fair use doctrine in section 107 offers some guidance to users in determining when the principles of the doctrine apply. However, the endless variety of situations and combinations of circumstances that can rise in particular cases precludes the formulation of exact rules in the statute. The bill endorses the purpose and general scope of the judicial doctrine of fair use, but there is no disposition to freeze the doctrine in the statute, especially during a period of rapid technological change. Beyond a very broad statutory explanation of what fair use is and some of the criteria applicable to it, the courts must be free to adapt the doctrine to particular situations on a case-by-case basis. Section 107 is intended to restate the present judicial doctrine of fair use, not to change, narrow, or enlarge it in any way.

Intention as to Classroom Reproduction. Although the works and uses to which the doctrine of fair use is applicable are as broad as the copyright law itself, most of the discussion of section 107 has centered around questions of classroom reproduction, particularly photocopying. The arguments on the question are summarized at pp. 30–31 of this Committee's 1967 report (H.R. Rep. No. 83, 90th Cong., 1st Sess.), and have not changed materially in the intervening years.

The Committee also adheres to its earlier conclusion, that "a specific exemption freeing certain reproductions of copyrighted works for educational and scholarly purposes from copyright control is not justified." At the same time the Committee recognizes, as it did in 1967, that there is a "need for greater certainty and protection for teachers." In an effort to meet this need the Committee has not only adopted further amendments to section 107, but has also amended section 504(c) to provide innocent teachers and other non-profit users of copyrighted material with broad insulation against unwarranted liability for infringement. The latter amendments are discussed below in connection with Chapter 5 of the bill [§ 501 et seq. of this title].

In 1967 the Committee also sought to approach this problem by including, in its report, a very thorough discussion of "the considerations lying behind the four criteria listed in the amended section 107, in the context of typical classroom situations arising today." This discussion appeared on pp. 32–35 of the 1967 report, and with some changes has been retained in the Senate report on S. 22 (S. Rep. No. 94–473, pp. 63–65). The Committee has reviewed this discussion, and considers that it still has value as an analysis of various aspects of the problem.

At the Judiciary Subcommittee hearings in June 1975, Chairman Kastenmeier and other members urged the parties to meet together independently in an effort to achieve a meeting of the minds as to permissible educational uses of copyrighted material. The response to these suggestions was positive, and a number of meetings of three groups, dealing respectively with classroom reproduction of printed material, music, and audio-visual material, were held beginning in September 1975.

In a joint letter to Chairman Kastenmeier, dated March 19, 1976, the representatives of the Ad Hoc Committee of Educational Institutions and Organizations on Copyright Law Revision, and of the Authors League of America, Inc., and the Association of American Publishers, Inc., stated:

You may remember that in our letter of March 8, 1976 we told you that the negotiating teams representing authors and publishers and the Ad Hoc Group had reached tentative agreement on guidelines to insert in the Committee Report covering educational copying from books and periodicals under Section 107 of H.R. 2223 and S. 22 [this section], and that as part of that tentative agreement each side would accept the amendments to Sections 107 and 504 [this section and section 504 of this title] which were adopted by your Subcommittee on March 3, 1976.

We are now happy to tell you that the agreement has been approved by the principals and we enclose a copy herewith. We had originally intended to translate the agreement into language suitable for inclusion in the legislative report dealing with Section 107 [this section], but we have since been advised by committee staff that this will not be necessary.

As stated above, the agreement refers only to copying from books and periodicals, and it is not intended to apply to musical or audiovisual works.

The full text of the agreement is as follows:

AGREEMENT ON GUIDELINES FOR CLASSROOM COPYING IN NOT-FOR-PROFIT EDUCATIONAL INSTITUTIONS

WITH RESPECT TO BOOKS AND PERIODICALS

The purpose of the following guidelines is to state the minimum and not the maximum standards of educational fair use under Section 107 of H.R. 2223 [this section]. The parties agree that the conditions determining the extent of permissible copying for educational purposes may change in the future; that certain types of copying permitted under these guidelines may not be permissible in the future; and conversely that in the future other types of copying not permitted under these guidelines may be permissible under revised guidelines.

Moreover, the following statement of guidelines is not intended to limit the types of copying permitted under the standards of fair use under judicial decision and which are stated in Section 107 of the Copyright Revision Bill [this section]. There may be instances in which copying which does not fall within the guidelines stated below may nonetheless be permitted under the criteria of fair use.

GUIDELINES

I. *Single Copying for Teachers*

A single copy may be made of any of the following by or for a teacher at his or her individual request for his or her scholarly research or use in teaching or preparation to teach a class:

A. A chapter from a book;

B. An article from a periodical or newspaper;

C. A short story, short essay or short poem, whether or not from a collective work;

D. A chart, graph, diagram, drawing, cartoon or picture from a book, periodical, or newspaper;

II. *Multiple Copies for Classroom Use*

Multiple copies (not to exceed in any event more than one copy per pupil in a course) may be made by or for the teacher giving the course for classroom use or discussion; *provided that:*

A. The copying meets the tests of brevity and spontaneity as defined below; *and,*

B. Meets the cumulative effect test as defined below; *and*

C. Each copy includes a notice of copyright.

Definitions

Brevity

(*i*) Poetry: (a) A complete poem if less than 250 words and if printed on not more than two pages or, (b) from a longer poem, an excerpt of not more than 250 words.

(*ii*) Prose: (a) Either a complete article, story or essay of less than 2,500 words, or (b) an excerpt from any prose work of not more than 1,000 words or 10% of the work, whichever is less, but in any event a minimum of 500 words.

[Each of the numerical limits stated in "i" and "ii" above may be expanded to permit the completion of an unfinished line of a poem or of an unfinished prose paragraph.]

(*iii*) Illustration: One chart, graph, diagram, drawing, cartoon or picture per book or per periodical issue.

(*iv*) "Special" works: Certain works in poetry, prose or in "poetic prose" which often combine language with illustrations and which are intended sometimes for children and at other times for a more general audience fall short of 2,500 words in their entirety. Paragraph "ii" above notwithstanding such "special works" may not be reproduced in their entirety; however, an excerpt comprising not more than two of the published pages of such special work and containing not more than 10% of the words found in the text thereof, may be reproduced.

Spontaneity

(*i*) The copying is at the instance and inspiration of the individual teacher, and

(*ii*) The inspiration and decision to use the work and the moment of its use for maximum teaching effectiveness are so close in time that it would be unreasonable to expect a timely reply to a request for permission.

Cumulative Effect

(*i*) The copying of the material is for only one course in the school in which the copies are made.

(*ii*) Not more than one short poem, article, story, essay or two excerpts may be copied from the same author, nor more than three from the same collective work or periodical volume during one class term.

(*iii*) There shall not be more than nine instances of such multiple copying for one course during one class term.

[The limitations stated in "ii" and "iii" above shall not apply to current news periodicals and newspapers and current news sections of other periodicals.]

III. *Prohibitions as to I and II Above*

Notwithstanding any of the above, the following shall be prohibited:

(A) Copying shall not be used to create or to replace or substitute for anthologies, compilations or collective works. Such replacement or substitution may occur whether copies of various works or excerpts therefrom are accumulated or reproduced and used separately.

(B) There shall be no copying of or from works intended to be "consumable" in the course of study or of teaching. These include workbooks, exercises, standardized tests and test booklets and answer sheets and like consumable material.

(C) Copying shall not:

(a) substitute for the purchase of books, publishers' reprints or periodicals;

(b) be directed by higher authority;

(c) be repeated with respect to the same item by the same teacher from term to term.

(D) No charge shall be made to the student beyond the actual cost of the photocopying.

Agreed March 19, 1976.

Ad Hoc Committee on Copyright Law Revision:

By SHELDON ELLIOTT STEINBACH.

Author-Publisher Group:

Authors League of America:

By IRWIN KARP, *Counsel.*

Association of American Publishers, Inc.:

By ALEXANDER C. HOFFMAN.

Chairman, Copyright Committee.

In a joint letter dated April 30, 1976, representatives of the Music Publishers' Association of the United States, Inc., the National Music Publishers' Association, Inc., the Music Teachers National Association, the Music Educators National Conference, the National Association of Schools of Music, and the Ad Hoc Committee on Copyright Law Revision, wrote to Chairman Kastenmeier as follows:

During the hearings on H.R. 2223 in June 1975, you and several of your subcommittee members suggested that concerned groups should work together in developing guidelines which would be helpful to clarify Section 107 of the bill [this section].

Representatives of music educators and music publishers delayed their meetings until guidelines had been developed relative to books and periodicals. Shortly after that work was completed and those guidelines were forwarded to your subcommittee, representatives of the undersigned music organizations met together with representatives of the Ad Hoc Committee on Copyright Law Revision to draft guidelines relative to music.

We are very pleased to inform you that the discussions thus have been fruitful on the guidelines which have been developed. Since private music teachers are an important factor in music education, due consideration has been given to the concerns of that group.

We trust that this will be helpful in the report on the bill to clarify Fair Use as it applies to music.

The text of the guidelines accompanying this letter is as follows:

GUIDELINES FOR EDUCATIONAL USES OF MUSIC

The purpose of the following guidelines is to state the minimum and not the maximum standards of educational fair use under Section 107 of H.R. 2223 [this section]. The parties agree that the conditions determining the extent of permissible copying for educational purposes may change in the future; that certain types of copying permitted under these guidelines may not be permissible in the future, and conversely that in the future other types of copying not permitted under these guidelines may be permissible under revised guidelines.

Moreover, the following statement of guidelines is not intended to limit the types of copying permitted under the standards of fair use under judicial decision and which are stated in Section 107 of the Copyright Revision Bill [this section]. There may be instances in which copying which does not fall within the guidelines stated below may nonetheless be permitted under the criteria of fair use.

A. *Permissible Uses*

1. Emergency copying to replace purchased copies which for any reason are not available for an imminent performance provided purchased replacement copies shall be substituted in due course.

2. (a) For academic purposes other than performance, multiple copies of excerpts of works may be made, provided that the excerpts do not comprise a part of the whole which would constitute a performable unit such as a section, movement or aria, but in no case more than 10% of the whole work. The number of copies shall not exceed one copy per pupil.

(b) For academic purposes other than performance, a single copy of an entire performable unit (section, movement, aria, etc.) that is, (1) confirmed by the copyright proprietor to be out of print or (2) unavailable except in a larger work, may be made by or for a teacher solely for the purpose of his or her scholarly research or in preparation to teach a class.

3. Printed copies which have been purchased may be edited or simplified provided that the fundamental character of the work is not distorted or the lyrics, if any, altered or lyrics added if none exist.

4. A single copy of recordings of performances by students may be made for evaluation or rehearsal purposes and may be retained by the educational institution or individual teacher.

5. A single copy of a sound recording (such as a tape, disc or cassette) of copyrighted music may be made from sound recordings owned by an educational institution or an individual teacher for the purpose of constructing aural exercises or examinations and may be retained by the educational institution or individual teacher. (This pertains only to the copyright of the music itself and not to any copyright which may exist in the sound recording.)

B. *Prohibitions*

1. Copying to create or replace or substitute for anthologies, compilations or collective works.

2. Copying of or from works intended to be "consumable" in the course of study or of teaching such as workbooks, exercises, standardized tests and answer sheets and like material.

3. Copying for the purpose of performance, except as in A(1) above.

4. Copying for the purpose of substituting for the purchase of music, except as in A(1) and A(2) above.

5. Copying without inclusion of the copyright notice which appears on the printed copy.

The problem of off-the-air taping for nonprofit classroom use of copyrighted audiovisual works incorporated in radio and television broadcasts has proved to be difficult to resolve. The Committee believes that the fair use doctrine has some limited application in this area, but it appears that the development of detailed guidelines will require a more thorough exploration than has so far been possible of the needs and problems of a number of different interests affected, and of the various legal problems presented. Nothing in section 107 or elsewhere in the bill is intended to change or prejudge the law on the point. On the other hand, the Committee is sensitive to the importance of the problem, and urges the representatives of the various interests, if possible under the leadership of the Register of Copyrights, to continue their discussions actively and in a constructive spirit. If it would be helpful to a solution, the Committee is receptive to undertaking further consideration of the problem in a future Congress.

The Committee appreciates and commends the efforts and the cooperative and reasonable spirit of the parties who achieved the agreed guidelines on books and periodicals and on music. Representatives of the American Association of University Professors and of the Association of American Law Schools have written to the Committee strongly criticizing the guidelines, particularly with respect to multiple copying, as being too restrictive with respect to classroom situations at the university and graduate level. However, the Committee notes that the Ad Hoc group did include representatives of higher education, that the stated "purpose of the * * * guidelines is to state the minimum and not the maximum standards of educational fair use" and that the agreement acknowledges "there may be instances in which copying which does not fall within the guidelines * * * may nonetheless be permitted under the criteria of fair use."

The Committee believes the guidelines are a reasonable interpretation of the minimum standards of fair use. Teachers will know that copying within the guidelines is fair use. Thus, the guidelines serve the purpose of fulfilling the need for greater certainty and protection for teachers. The Committee expresses the hope that if there are areas where standards other than these guidelines may be appropriate, the parties will continue their efforts to provide additional specific guidelines in the same spirit of good will and give and take that has marked the discussion of this subject in recent months.

Reproduction and Uses for Other Purposes. The concentrated attention given the fair use provision in the context of classroom teaching activities should not obscure its application in other areas. It must be emphasized again that the same general standards of fair use are applicable to all kinds of uses of copyrighted material, although the relative weight to be given them will differ from case to case.

The fair use doctrine would be relevant to the use of excerpts from copyrighted works in educational broadcasting activities not exempted under section 110(2) or 112, and not covered by the licensing provisions of section 118. In these cases the factors to be weighed in applying the criteria of this section would include whether the performers, producers, directors, and others responsible for the broadcast were paid, the size and nature of the audience, the size and number of excerpts taken and, in the case of recordings made for broadcast, the number of copies reproduced and the extent of their reuse or exchange. The availability of the fair use doctrine to educational broadcasters would be narrowly circumscribed in the case of motion pictures and other audiovisual works, but under appropriate circumstances it could apply to the nonsequential showing of an individual still or slide, or to the performance of a short excerpt from a motion picture for criticism or comment.

Another special instance illustrating the application of the fair use doctrine pertains to the making of copies or phonorecords of works in the special forms needed for the use of blind persons. These special forms, such as copies in Braille and phonorecords of oral readings (talking books), are not usually made by the publishers for commercial distribution. For the most part, such copies and phonorecords are made by the Library of Congress' Division for the Blind and Physically Handicapped with permission obtained from the copyright owners, and are circulated to blind persons through regional libraries covering the nation. In addition, such copies and phonorecords are made locally by individual volunteers for the use of blind persons in their communities, and the Library of Congress conducts a program for training such volunteers. While the making of multiple copies or phonorecords of a work for general circulation requires the permission of the copyright owner, a problem addressed in section 710 of the bill, the making of a single copy or phonorecord by an individual as a free service for blind persons would properly be considered a fair use under section 107.

A problem of particular urgency is that of preserving for posterity prints of motion pictures made before 1942. Aside from the deplorable fact that in a great many cases the only existing copy of a film has been deliberately destroyed, those that remain are in immediate danger of disintegration; they were printed on film stock with a nitrate base that will inevitably decompose in time. The efforts of the Library of Congress, the American Film Institute, and other organizations to rescue and preserve this irreplaceable contribution to our cultural life are to be applauded, and the making of duplicate copies for purposes of archival preservation certainly falls within the scope of "fair use."

When a copyrighted work contains unfair, inaccurate, or derogatory information concerning an individual or institution, the individual or institution may copy and reproduce such parts of the work as are necessary to permit understandable comment on the statements made in the work.

The Committee has considered the question of publication, in Congressional hearings and documents, of copyrighted material. Where the length of the work or excerpt published and the number of copies authorized are reasonable under the circumstances, and the work itself is directly relevant to a matter of legitimate legislative concern, the Committee believes that the publication would constitute fair use.

During the consideration of the revision bill in the 94th Congress it was proposed that independent newsletters, as distinguished from house organs and publicity or advertising publications, be given separate treatment. It is argued that newsletters are particularly vulnerable to mass photocopying, and that most newsletters have fairly modest circulations. Whether the copying of portions of a newsletter is an act of infringement or a fair use will necessarily turn on the facts of the individual case. However, as a general principle, it seems clear that the scope of the fair use doctrine should be considerably narrower in the case of newsletters than in that of either mass-circulation periodicals or scientific journals. The commercial nature of the user is a significant factor in such cases: Copying by a profit-making user of even a small portion of a newsletter may have a significant impact on the commercial market for the work.

The Committee has examined the use of excerpts from copyrighted works in the art work of calligraphers. The committee believes that a single copy reproduction of an excerpt from a copyrighted work by a calligrapher for a single client does not represent an infringement of copyright. Likewise, a single reproduction of excerpts from a copyrighted work by a student calligrapher or teacher in a learning situation would be a fair use of the copyrighted work.

The Register of Copyrights has recommended that the committee report describe the relationship between this section and the provisions of section 108 relating to reproduction by libraries and archives. The doctrine of fair use applies to library photocopying, and nothing contained in section 108 "in any way affects the right of fair use." No provision of section 108 is intended to take away any rights existing under the fair use doctrine. To the contrary, section 108 authorizes certain photocopying practices which may not qualify as a fair use.

The criteria of fair use are necessarily set forth in general terms. In the application of the criteria of fair use to specific photocopying practices of libraries, it is the intent of this legislation to provide an appropriate balancing of the rights of creators, and the needs of users.

AMENDMENTS

1992—Pub. L. 102–492 inserted at end "The fact that a work is unpublished shall not itself bar a finding of fair use if such finding is made upon consideration of all the above factors."

1990—Pub. L. 101–650 substituted "sections 106 and 106A" for "section 106" in introductory provisions.

EFFECTIVE DATE OF 1990 AMENDMENT

Amendment by Pub. L. 101–650 effective 6 months after Dec. 1, 1990, see section 610 of Pub. L. 101–650, set out as an Effective Date note under section 106A of this title.

§ 108. Limitations on exclusive rights: Reproduction by libraries and archives

(a) Except as otherwise provided in this title and notwithstanding the provisions of section 106, it is not an infringement of copyright for a library or archives, or any of its employees acting within the scope of their employment, to reproduce no more than one copy or phonorecord of a work, except as provided in subsections (b) and (c), or to distribute such copy or phonorecord, under the conditions specified by this section, if—

(1) the reproduction or distribution is made without any purpose of direct or indirect commercial advantage;

(2) the collections of the library or archives are (i) open to the public, or (ii) available not only to researchers affiliated with the library or archives or with the institution of which it is a part, but also to other persons doing research in a specialized field; and

(3) the reproduction or distribution of the work includes a notice of copyright that appears on the copy or phonorecord that is reproduced under the provisions of this section, or includes a legend stating that the work may be protected by copyright if no such notice can be found on the copy or phonorecord that is reproduced under the provisions of this section.

(b) The rights of reproduction and distribution under this section apply to three copies or phonorecords of an unpublished work duplicated solely for purposes of preservation and security or for deposit for research use in another library or archives of the type described by clause (2) of subsection (a), if—

(1) the copy or phonorecord reproduced is currently in the collections of the library or archives; and

(2) any such copy or phonorecord that is reproduced in digital format is not otherwise distributed in that format and is not made available to the public in that format outside the premises of the library or archives.

(c) The right of reproduction under this section applies to three copies or phonorecords of a published work duplicated solely for the purpose of replacement of a copy or phonorecord that is damaged, deteriorating, lost, or stolen, or if the existing format in which the work is stored has become obsolete, if—

(1) the library or archives has, after a reasonable effort, determined that an unused replacement cannot be obtained at a fair price; and

(2) any such copy or phonorecord that is reproduced in digital format is not made avail-

able to the public in that format outside the premises of the library or archives in lawful possession of such copy.

For purposes of this subsection, a format shall be considered obsolete if the machine or device necessary to render perceptible a work stored in that format is no longer manufactured or is no longer reasonably available in the commercial marketplace.

(d) The rights of reproduction and distribution under this section apply to a copy, made from the collection of a library or archives where the user makes his or her request or from that of another library or archives, of no more than one article or other contribution to a copyrighted collection or periodical issue, or to a copy or phonorecord of a small part of any other copyrighted work, if—

(1) the copy or phonorecord becomes the property of the user, and the library or archives has had no notice that the copy or phonorecord would be used for any purpose other than private study, scholarship, or research; and

(2) the library or archives displays prominently, at the place where orders are accepted, and includes on its order form, a warning of copyright in accordance with requirements that the Register of Copyrights shall prescribe by regulation.

(e) The rights of reproduction and distribution under this section apply to the entire work, or to a substantial part of it, made from the collection of a library or archives where the user makes his or her request or from that of another library or archives, if the library or archives has first determined, on the basis of a reasonable investigation, that a copy or phonorecord of the copyrighted work cannot be obtained at a fair price, if—

(1) the copy or phonorecord becomes the property of the user, and the library or archives has had no notice that the copy or phonorecord would be used for any purpose other than private study, scholarship, or research; and

(2) the library or archives displays prominently, at the place where orders are accepted, and includes on its order form, a warning of copyright in accordance with requirements that the Register of Copyrights shall prescribe by regulation.

(f) Nothing in this section—

(1) shall be construed to impose liability for copyright infringement upon a library or archives or its employees for the unsupervised use of reproducing equipment located on its premises: *Provided*, That such equipment displays a notice that the making of a copy may be subject to the copyright law;

(2) excuses a person who uses such reproducing equipment or who requests a copy or phonorecord under subsection (d) from liability for copyright infringement for any such act, or for any later use of such copy or phonorecord, if it exceeds fair use as provided by section 107;

(3) shall be construed to limit the reproduction and distribution by lending of a limited number of copies and excerpts by a library or

archives of an audiovisual news program, subject to clauses (1), (2), and (3) of subsection (a); or

(4) in any way affects the right of fair use as provided by section 107, or any contractual obligations assumed at any time by the library or archives when it obtained a copy or phonorecord of a work in its collections.

(g) The rights of reproduction and distribution under this section extend to the isolated and unrelated reproduction or distribution of a single copy or phonorecord of the same material on separate occasions, but do not extend to cases where the library or archives, or its employee—

(1) is aware or has substantial reason to believe that it is engaging in the related or concerted reproduction or distribution of multiple copies or phonorecords of the same material, whether made on one occasion or over a period of time, and whether intended for aggregate use by one or more individuals or for separate use by the individual members of a group; or

(2) engages in the systematic reproduction or distribution of single or multiple copies or phonorecords of material described in subsection (d): *Provided*, That nothing in this clause prevents a library or archives from participating in interlibrary arrangements that do not have, as their purpose or effect, that the library or archives receiving such copies or phonorecords for distribution does so in such aggregate quantities as to substitute for a subscription to or purchase of such work.

(h)(1) For purposes of this section, during the last 20 years of any term of copyright of a published work, a library or archives, including a nonprofit educational institution that functions as such, may reproduce, distribute, display, or perform in facsimile or digital form a copy or phonorecord of such work, or portions thereof, for purposes of preservation, scholarship, or research, if such library or archives has first determined, on the basis of a reasonable investigation, that none of the conditions set forth in subparagraphs (A), (B), and (C) of paragraph (2) apply.

(2) No reproduction, distribution, display, or performance is authorized under this subsection if—

(A) the work is subject to normal commercial exploitation;

(B) a copy or phonorecord of the work can be obtained at a reasonable price; or

(C) the copyright owner or its agent provides notice pursuant to regulations promulgated by the Register of Copyrights that either of the conditions set forth in subparagraphs (A) and (B) applies.

(3) The exemption provided in this subsection does not apply to any subsequent uses by users other than such library or archives.

(i) The rights of reproduction and distribution under this section do not apply to a musical work, a pictorial, graphic or sculptural work, or a motion picture or other audiovisual work other than an audiovisual work dealing with news, except that no such limitation shall apply with respect to rights granted by subsections (b), (c), and (h), or with respect to pictorial or graphic works published as illustrations, diagrams, or similar adjuncts to works of which copies are reproduced or distributed in accordance with subsections (d) and (e).

(Pub. L. 94–553, title I, § 101, Oct. 19, 1976, 90 Stat. 2546; Pub. L. 102–307, title III, § 301, June 26, 1992, 106 Stat. 272; Pub. L. 105–80, § 12(a)(4), Nov. 13, 1997, 111 Stat. 1534; Pub. L. 105–298, title I, § 104, Oct. 27, 1998, 112 Stat. 2829; Pub. L. 105–304, title IV, § 404, Oct. 28, 1998, 112 Stat. 2889; Pub. L. 109–9, title IV, § 402, Apr. 27, 2005, 119 Stat. 227.)

HISTORICAL AND REVISION NOTES

HOUSE REPORT NO. 94–1476

Notwithstanding the exclusive rights of the owners of copyright, section 108 provides that under certain conditions it is not an infringement of copyright for a library or archives, or any of its employees acting within the scope of their employment, to reproduce or distribute not more than one copy or phonorecord of a work, provided (1) the reproduction or distribution is made without any purpose of direct or indirect commercial advantage and (2) the collections of the library or archives are open to the public or available not only to researchers affiliated with the library or archives, but also to other persons doing research in a specialized field, and (3) the reproduction or distribution of the work includes a notice of copyright.

Under this provision, a purely commercial enterprise could not establish a collection of copyrighted works, call itself a library or archive, and engage in for-profit reproduction and distribution of photocopies. Similarly, it would not be possible for a non-profit institution, by means of contractual arrangements with a commercial copying enterprise, to authorize the enterprise to carry out copying and distribution functions that would be exempt if conducted by the non-profit institution itself.

The reference to "indirect commercial advantage" has raised questions as to the status of photocopying done by or for libraries or archival collections within industrial, profit-making, or proprietary institutions (such as the research and development departments of chemical, pharmaceutical, automobile, and oil corporations, the library of a proprietary hospital, the collections owned by a law or medical partnership, etc.).

There is a direct interrelationship between this problem and the prohibitions against "multiple" and "systematic" photocopying in section 108(g)(1) and (2). Under section 108, a library in a profitmaking organization would not be authorized to:

(a) use a single subscription or copy to supply its employees with multiple copies of material relevant to their work; or

(b) use a single subscription or copy to supply its employees, on request, with single copies of material relevant to their work, where the arrangement is "systematic" in the sense of deliberately substituting photocopying for subscription or purchase; or

(c) use "interlibrary loan" arrangements for obtaining photocopies in such aggregate quantities as to substitute for subscriptions or purchase of material needed by employees in their work.

Moreover, a library in a profit-making organization could not evade these obligations by installing reproducing equipment on its premises for unsupervised use by the organization's staff.

Isolated, spontaneous making of single photocopies by a library in a for-profit organization, without any systematic effort to substitute photocopying for subscriptions or purchases, would be covered by section 108, even though the copies are furnished to the employees of the organization for use in their work. Similarly, for-profit libraries could participate in interlibrary arrangements for exchange of photocopies, as long as the reproduction or distribution was not "systematic." These activities, by themselves, would ordinarily not be considered "for direct or indirect commercial advantage," since the "advantage" referred to in this clause must attach to the immediate commercial motivation behind the reproduction or distribution itself, rather than to the ultimate profit-making motivation behind the enterprise in which the library is located. On the other hand, section 108 would not excuse reproduction or distribution if there were a commercial motive behind the actual making or distributing of the copies, if multiple copies were made or distributed, or if the photocopying activities were "systematic" in the sense that their aim was to substitute for subscriptions or purchases.

The rights of reproduction and distribution under section 108 apply in the following circumstances:

Archival Reproduction. Subsection (b) authorizes the reproduction and distribution of a copy or phonorecord of an unpublished work duplicated in facsimile form solely for purposes of preservation and security, or for deposit for research use in another library or archives, if the copy or phonorecord reproduced is currently in the collections of the first library or archives. Only unpublished works could be reproduced under this exemption, but the right would extend to any type of work, including photographs, motion pictures and sound recordings. Under this exemption, for example, a repository could make photocopies of manuscripts by microfilm or electrostatic process, but could not reproduce the work in "machine-readable" language for storage in an information system.

Replacement of Damaged Copy. Subsection (c) authorizes the reproduction of a published work duplicated in facsimile form solely for the purpose of replacement of a copy or phonorecord that is damaged, deteriorating, lost or stolen, if the library or archives has, after a reasonable effort, determined that an unused replacement cannot be obtained at a fair price. The scope and nature of a reasonable investigation to determine that an unused replacement cannot be obtained will vary according to the circumstances of a particular situation. It will always require recourse to commonly-known trade sources in the United States, and in the normal situation also to the publisher or other copyright owner (if such owner can be located at the address listed in the copyright registration), or an authorized reproducing service.

Articles and Small Excerpts. Subsection (d) authorizes the reproduction and distribution of a copy of not more than one article or other contribution to a copyrighted collection or periodical issue, or of a copy or phonorecord of a small part of any other copyrighted work. The copy or phonorecord may be made by the library where the user makes his request or by another library pursuant to an interlibrary loan. It is further required that the copy become the property of the user, that the library or archives have no notice that the copy would be used for any purposes other than private study, scholarship or research, and that the library or archives display prominently at the place where reproduction requests are accepted, and includes in its order form, a warning of copyright in accordance with requirements that the Register of Copyrights shall prescribe by regulation.

Out-of-Print Works. Subsection (e) authorizes the reproduction and distribution of a copy or phonorecord of an entire work under certain circumstances, if it has been established that a copy cannot be obtained at a fair price. The copy may be made by the library where the user makes his request or by another library pursuant to an interlibrary loan. The scope and nature of a reasonable investigation to determine that an unused copy cannot be obtained will vary according to the circumstances of a particular situation. It will always require recourse to commonly-known trade sources in the United States, and in the normal situation also to the publisher or other copyright owner (if the owner can be located at the address listed in the copyright registration), or an authorized reproducing service. It is further required that the copy become the property of the user, that the library or archives have no notice that the copy would be used for any purpose other than private study, scholarship, or research, and that the library or archives display prominently at the place where reproduction requests are accepted, and include on its order form, a warning of copyright in accordance with requirements that the Register of Copyrights shall prescribe by regulation.

General Exemptions. Clause (1) of subsection (f) specifically exempts a library or archives or its employees from liability for the unsupervised use of reproducing equipment located on its premises, provided that the reproducing equipment displays a notice that the making of a copy may be subject to the copyright law. Clause (2) of subsection (f) makes clear that this exemption of the library or archives does not extend to the person using such equipment or requesting such copy if the use exceeds fair use. Insofar as such person is concerned the copy or phonorecord made is not considered "lawfully" made for purposes of sections 109, 110 or other provisions of the title.

Clause (3) provides that nothing in section 108 is intended to limit the reproduction and distribution by lending of a limited number of copies and excerpts of an audiovisual news program. This exemption is intended to apply to the daily newscasts of the national television networks, which report the major events of the day. It does not apply to documentary (except documentary programs involving news reporting as that term is used in section 107), magazine-format or other public affairs broadcasts dealing with subjects of general interest to the viewing public.

The clause was first added to the revision bill in 1974 by the adoption of an amendment proposed by Senator Baker. It is intended to permit libraries and archives, subject to the general conditions of this section, to make off-the-air videotape recordings of daily network news casts for limited distribution to scholars and researchers for use in research purposes. As such, it is an adjunct to the American Television and Radio Archive established in Section 113 of the Act [2 U.S.C. 170] which will be the principal repository for television broadcast material, including news broadcasts, the inclusion of language indicating that such material may only be distributed by lending by the library or archive is intended to preclude performance, copying, or sale, whether or not for profit, by the recipient of a copy of a television broadcast taped off-the-air pursuant to this clause.

Clause (4), in addition to asserting that nothing contained in section 108 "affects the right of fair use as provided by section 107", also provides that the right of reproduction granted by this section does not override any contractual arrangements assumed by a library or archives when it obtained a work for its collections: For example, if there is an express contractual prohibition against reproduction for any purpose, this legislation shall not be construed as justifying a violation of the contract. This clause is intended to encompass the situation where an individual makes papers, manuscripts or other works available to a library with the understanding that they will not be reproduced.

It is the intent of this legislation that a subsequent unlawful use by a user of a copy or phonorecord of a work lawfully made by a library, shall not make the library liable for such improper use.

Multiple Copies and Systematic Reproduction. Subsection (g) provides that the rights granted by this section extend only to the "isolated and unrelated reproduction of a single copy or phonorecord of the same material on separate occasions." However, this section does not authorize the related or concerted reproduction of multiple copies or phonorecords of the same material, whether made on one occasion or over a period of time, and whether intended for aggregate use by one individual or for separate use by the individual members of a group.

With respect to material described in subsection (d)—articles or other contributions to periodicals or collections, and small parts of other copyrighted works—subsection (g)(2) provides that the exemptions of section 108 do not apply if the library or archive engages in "systematic reproduction or distribution of single or multiple copies or phonorecords." This provision in S. 22 provoked a storm of controversy, centering around the extent to which the restrictions on "systematic" activities would prevent the continuation and development of interlibrary networks and other arrangements involving the exchange of photocopies. After thorough consideration, the Committee amended section 108(g)(2) to add the following proviso:

> *Provided*, that nothing in this clause prevents a library or archives from participating in interlibrary arrangements that do not have, as their purpose or effect, that the library or archives receiving such copies or phonorecords for distribution does so in such aggregate quantities as to substitute for a subscription to or purchase of such work.

In addition, the Committee added a new subsection (i) to section 108 [this section], requiring the Register of Copyrights, five years from the effective date of the new Act and at five-year intervals thereafter, to report to Congress upon "the extent to which this section has achieved the intended statutory balancing of the rights of creators, and the needs of users," and to make appropriate legislative or other recommendations. As noted in connection with section 107, the Committee also amended section 504(c) in a way that would insulate librarians from unwarranted liability for copyright infringement; this amendment is discussed below.

The key phrases in the Committee's amendment of section 108(g)(2) are "aggregate quantities" and "substitute for a subscription to or purchase of" a work. To be implemented effectively in practice, these provisions will require the development and implementation of more-or-less specific guidelines establishing criteria to govern various situations.

The National Commission on New Technological Uses of Copyrighted Works (CONTU) offered to provide good offices in helping to develop these guidelines. This offer was accepted and, although the final text of guidelines has not yet been achieved, the Committee has reason to hope that, within the next month, some agreement can be reached on an initial set of guidelines covering practices under section 108(g)(2).

Works Excluded. Subsection (h) provides that the rights of reproduction and distribution under this section do not apply to a musical work, a pictorial, graphic or sculptural work, or a motion picture or other audiovisual work other than "an audiovisual work dealing with news." The latter term is intended as the equivalent in meaning of the phrase "audiovisual news program" in section 108(f)(3). The exclusions under subsection (h) do not apply to archival reproduction under subsection (b), to replacement of damaged or lost copies or phonorecords under subsection (c), or to "pictorial or graphic works published as illustrations, diagrams, or similar adjuncts to works of which copies are reproduced or distributed in accordance with subsections (d) and (e)."

Although subsection (h) generally removes musical, graphic, and audiovisual works from the specific exemptions of section 108, it is important to recognize that the doctrine of fair use under section 107 remains fully applicable to the photocopying or other reproduction of such works. In the case of music, for example, it would be fair use for a scholar doing musicological research to have a library supply a copy of a portion of a score or to reproduce portions of a phonorecord of a work. Nothing in section 108 impairs the applicability of the fair use doctrine to a wide variety of situations involving photocopying or other reproduction by a library of copyrighted material in its collections, where the user requests the reproduction for legitimate scholarly or research purposes.

AMENDMENTS

2005—Subsec. (i). Pub. L. 109–9 substituted "(b), (c), and (h)" for "(b) and (c)".

1998—Subsec. (a). Pub. L. 105–304, § 404(1)(A), (B), in introductory provisions, substituted "Except as otherwise provided in this title and notwithstanding" for "Notwithstanding" and inserted ", except as provided in subsections (b) and (c)" after "of a work".

Subsec. (a)(3). Pub. L. 105–304, § 404(1)(C), inserted before period at end "that appears on the copy or phonorecord that is reproduced under the provisions of this section, or includes a legend stating that the work may be protected by copyright if no such notice can be found on the copy or phonorecord that is reproduced under the provisions of this section".

Subsec. (b). Pub. L. 105–304, § 404(2), substituted "three copies or phonorecords" for "a copy or phonorecord", struck out "in facsimile form" after "duplicated", and substituted "if—

"(1) the copy or phonorecord reproduced is currently in the collections of the library or archives; and

"(2) any such copy or phonorecord that is reproduced in digital format is not otherwise distributed in that format and is not made available to the public in that format outside the premises of the library or archives."

for "if the copy or phonorecord reproduced is currently in the collections of the library or archives."

Subsec. (c). Pub. L. 105–304, § 404(3), substituted "three copies or phonorecords" for "a copy or phonorecord", struck out "in facsimile form" after "duplicated", inserted "or if the existing format in which the work is stored has become obsolete," after "stolen,", substituted "if—

"(1) the library or archives has, after a reasonable effort, determined that an unused replacement cannot be obtained at a fair price; and

"(2) any such copy or phonorecord that is reproduced in digital format is not made available to the public in that format outside the premises of the library or archives in lawful possession of such copy."

for "if the library or archives has, after a reasonable effort, determined that an unused replacement cannot be obtained at a fair price.", and inserted concluding provisions.

Subsecs. (h), (i). Pub. L. 105–298 added subsec. (h) and redesignated former subsec. (h) as (i).

1997—Subsec. (e). Pub. L. 105–80 substituted "fair price" for "pair price" in introductory provisions.

1992—Subsec. (i). Pub. L. 102–307 struck out subsec. (i), which read as follows: "Five years from the effective date of this Act, and at five-year intervals thereafter, the Register of Copyrights, after consulting with representatives of authors, book and periodical publishers, and other owners of copyrighted materials, and with representatives of library users and librarians, shall submit to the Congress a report setting forth the extent to which this section has achieved the intended statutory balancing of the rights of creators, and the needs of users. The report should also describe any problems that may have arisen, and present legislative or other recommendations, if warranted."

EFFECTIVE DATE OF 1998 AMENDMENTS

Pub. L. 105–304, title IV, § 407, Oct. 28, 1998, 112 Stat. 2905, provided that: "Except as otherwise provided in this title [enacting section 4001 of Title 28, Judiciary and Judicial Procedure, amending this section, sections 112, 114, 701, and 801 to 803 of this title, section 5314 of Title 5, Government Organization and Employees, and section 3 of Title 35, Patents, and enacting provisions set out as notes under sections 112 and 114 of this title], this title and the amendments made by this title shall take effect on the date of the enactment of this Act [Oct. 28, 1998]."

Pub. L. 105–298, title I, § 106, Oct. 27, 1998, 112 Stat. 2829, provided that: "This title [amending this section and sections 203 and 301 to 304 of this title, enacting provisions set out as a note under section 101 of this title, and amending provisions set out as notes under sections 101 and 304 of this title] and the amendments made by this title shall take effect on the date of the enactment of this Act [Oct. 27, 1998]."

§ 109. Limitations on exclusive rights: Effect of transfer of particular copy or phonorecord

(a) Notwithstanding the provisions of section 106(3), the owner of a particular copy or phonorecord lawfully made under this title, or any person authorized by such owner, is entitled, without the authority of the copyright owner, to sell or otherwise dispose of the possession of that copy or phonorecord. Notwithstanding the preceding sentence, copies or phonorecords of works subject to restored copyright under section 104A that are manufactured before the date of restoration of copyright or, with respect to reliance parties, before publication or service of notice under section 104A(e), may be sold or otherwise disposed of without the authorization of the owner of the restored copyright for purposes of direct or indirect commercial advantage only during the 12-month period beginning on—

(1) the date of the publication in the Federal Register of the notice of intent filed with the Copyright Office under section 104A(d)(2)(A), or

(2) the date of the receipt of actual notice served under section 104A(d)(2)(B),

whichever occurs first.

(b)(1)(A) Notwithstanding the provisions of subsection (a), unless authorized by the owners of copyright in the sound recording or the owner of copyright in a computer program (including any tape, disk, or other medium embodying such program), and in the case of a sound recording in the musical works embodied therein, neither the owner of a particular phonorecord nor any person in possession of a particular copy of a computer program (including any tape, disk, or other medium embodying such program), may, for the purposes of direct or indirect commercial advantage, dispose of, or authorize the disposal of, the possession of that phonorecord or computer program (including any tape, disk, or other medium embodying such program) by rental, lease, or lending, or by any other act or practice in the nature of rental, lease, or lending. Nothing in the preceding sentence shall apply to the rental, lease, or lending of a phonorecord for nonprofit purposes by a nonprofit library or nonprofit educational institution. The transfer of possession of a lawfully made copy of a computer program by a nonprofit educational institution to another nonprofit educational institution or to faculty, staff, and students does not constitute rental, lease, or lending for direct or indirect commercial purposes under this subsection.

(B) This subsection does not apply to—

(i) a computer program which is embodied in a machine or product and which cannot be copied during the ordinary operation or use of the machine or product; or

(ii) a computer program embodied in or used in conjunction with a limited purpose computer that is designed for playing video games and may be designed for other purposes.

(C) Nothing in this subsection affects any provision of chapter 9 of this title.

(2)(A) Nothing in this subsection shall apply to the lending of a computer program for nonprofit purposes by a nonprofit library, if each copy of a computer program which is lent by such library has affixed to the packaging containing the program a warning of copyright in accordance with requirements that the Register of Copyrights shall prescribe by regulation.

(B) Not later than three years after the date of the enactment of the Computer Software Rental Amendments Act of 1990, and at such times thereafter as the Register of Copyrights considers appropriate, the Register of Copyrights, after consultation with representatives of copyright owners and librarians, shall submit to the Congress a report stating whether this paragraph has achieved its intended purpose of maintaining the integrity of the copyright system while providing nonprofit libraries the capability to fulfill their function. Such report shall advise the Congress as to any information or recommendations that the Register of Copyrights considers necessary to carry out the purposes of this subsection.

(3) Nothing in this subsection shall affect any provision of the antitrust laws. For purposes of the preceding sentence, "antitrust laws" has the meaning given that term in the first section of the Clayton Act and includes section 5 of the Federal Trade Commission Act to the extent that section relates to unfair methods of competition.

(4) Any person who distributes a phonorecord or a copy of a computer program (including any tape, disk, or other medium embodying such program) in violation of paragraph (1) is an infringer of copyright under section 501 of this title and is subject to the remedies set forth in sections 502, 503, 504, and 505. Such violation shall not be a criminal offense under section 506 or cause such person to be subject to the criminal penalties set forth in section 2319 of title 18.

(c) Notwithstanding the provisions of section 106(5), the owner of a particular copy lawfully made under this title, or any person authorized by such owner, is entitled, without the authority of the copyright owner, to display that copy publicly, either directly or by the projection of no more than one image at a time, to viewers present at the place where the copy is located.

(d) The privileges prescribed by subsections (a) and (c) do not, unless authorized by the copyright owner, extend to any person who has acquired possession of the copy or phonorecord from the copyright owner, by rental, lease, loan, or otherwise, without acquiring ownership of it.

(e) Notwithstanding the provisions of sections 106(4) and 106(5), in the case of an electronic audiovisual game intended for use in coin-operated equipment, the owner of a particular copy of such a game lawfully made under this title, is entitled, without the authority of the copyright owner of the game, to publicly perform or display that game in coin-operated equipment, except that this subsection shall not apply to any work of authorship embodied in the audiovisual game if the copyright owner of the electronic audiovisual game is not also the copyright owner of the work of authorship.

(Pub. L. 94–553, title I, § 101, Oct. 19, 1976, 90 Stat. 2548; Pub. L. 98–450, § 2, Oct. 4, 1984, 98 Stat. 1727; Pub. L. 100–617, § 2, Nov. 5, 1988, 102 Stat. 3194; Pub. L. 101–650, title VIII, §§ 802, 803, Dec. 1, 1990, 104 Stat. 5134, 5135; Pub. L. 103–465, title V, § 514(b), Dec. 8, 1994, 108 Stat. 4981; Pub. L. 105–80, § 12(a)(5), Nov. 13, 1997, 111 Stat. 1534; Pub. L. 110–403, title II, § 209(a)(1), Oct. 13, 2008, 122 Stat. 4264.)

HISTORICAL AND REVISION NOTES

HOUSE REPORT NO. 94–1476

Effect on Further Disposition of Copy or Phonorecord. Section 109(a) restates and confirms the principle that, where the copyright owner has transferred ownership of a particular copy or phonorecord of a work, the person to whom the copy or phonorecord is transferred is entitled to dispose of it by sale, rental, or any other means. Under this principle, which has been established by the court decisions and section 27 of the present law [section 27 of former title 17], the copyright owner's exclusive right of public distribution would have no effect upon anyone who owns "a particular copy or phonorecord lawfully made under this title" and who wishes to transfer it to someone else or to destroy it.

Thus, for example, the outright sale of an authorized copy of a book frees it from any copyright control over its resale price or other conditions of its future disposition. A library that has acquired ownership of a copy is entitled to lend it under any conditions it chooses to impose. This does not mean that conditions on future disposition of copies or phonorecords, imposed by a contract between their buyer and seller, would be unenforceable between the parties as a breach of contract, but it does mean that they could not be enforced by an action for infringement of copyright. Under section 202 however, the owner of the physical copy or phonorecord cannot reproduce or perform the copyrighted work publicly without the copyright owner's consent.

To come within the scope of section 109(a), a copy or phonorecord must have been "lawfully made under this title," though not necessarily with the copyright owner's authorization. For example, any resale of an illegally "pirated" phonorecord would be an infringement, but the disposition of a phonorecord legally made under the compulsory licensing provisions of section 115 would not.

Effect on Display of Copy. Subsection (b) of section 109 deals with the scope of the copyright owner's exclusive right to control the public display of a particular "copy" of a work (including the original or prototype copy in which the work was first fixed). Assuming, for example, that a painter has sold the only copy of an original work of art without restrictions, would it be possible for him to restrain the new owner from displaying it publicly in galleries, shop windows, on a projector, or on television?

Section 109(b) adopts the general principle that the lawful owner of a copy of a work should be able to put his copy on public display without the consent of the copyright owner. As in cases arising under section 109(a), this does not mean that contractual restrictions on display between a buyer and seller would be unenforceable as a matter of contract law.

The exclusive right of public display granted by section 106(5) would not apply where the owner of a copy wishes to show it directly to the public, as in a gallery or display case, or indirectly, as through an opaque projector. Where the copy itself is intended for projection, as in the case of a photographic slide, negative, or transparency, the public projection of a single image would be permitted as long as the viewers are "present at the place where the copy is located."

On the other hand, section 109(b) takes account of the potentialities of the new communications media, notably television, cable and optical transmission devices, and information storage and retrieval devices, for replacing printed copies with visual images. First of all, the public display of an image of a copyrighted work would not be exempted from copyright control if the copy from which the image was derived were outside the presence of the viewers. In other words, the display of a visual image of a copyrighted work would be an infringement if the image were transmitted by any method (by closed or open circuit television, for example, or by a computer system) from one place to members of the public located elsewhere.

Moreover, the exemption would extend only to public displays that are made "either directly or by the projection of no more than one image at a time." Thus, even where the copy and the viewers are located at the same place, the simultaneous projection of multiple images of the work would not be exempted. For example, where each person in a lecture hall is supplied with a separate viewing apparatus, the copyright owner's permission would generally be required in order to project an image of a work on each individual screen at the same time.

The committee's intention is to preserve the traditional privilege of the owner of a copy to display it directly, but to place reasonable restrictions on the ability to display it indirectly in such a way that the copyright owner's market for reproduction and distribution of copies would be affected. Unless it constitutes a fair use under section 107, or unless one of the special provisions of section 110 or 111 is applicable, projection of more than one image at a time, or transmission of an image to the public over television or other communication channels, would be an infringement for the same reasons that reproduction in copies would be. The concept of "the place where the copy is located" is generally intended to refer to a situation in which the viewers are present in the same physical surroundings as the copy, even though they cannot see the copy directly.

Effect of Mere Possession of Copy or Phonorecord. Subsection (c) of section 109 qualifies the privileges specified in subsections (a) and (b) by making clear that they do not apply to someone who merely possesses a copy or phonorecord without having acquired ownership of it. Acquisition of an object embodying a copyrighted work by rental, lease, loan, or bailment carries with it no privilege to dispose of the copy under section 109(a) or to display it publicly under section 109(b). To cite a familiar example, a person who has rented a print of a motion picture from the copyright owner would have no right to rent it to someone else without the owner's permission.

Burden of Proof in Infringement Actions. During the course of its deliberations on this section, the Committee's attention was directed to a recent court decision holding that the plaintiff in an infringement action had the burden of establishing that the allegedly infringing copies in the defendant's possession were not lawfully made or acquired under section 27 of the present law [section 27 of former title 17]. *American International Pictures, Inc. v. Foreman*, 400 F.Supp. 928 (S.D.Alabama 1975). The Committee believes that the court's decision, if followed, would place a virtually impossible burden on copyright owners. The decision is also inconsistent with the established legal principle that the burden of proof should not be placed upon a litigant to establish facts particularly within the knowledge of his adversary. The defendant in such actions clearly has the particular knowledge of how possession of the particular copy was acquired, and should have the burden of providing this evidence to the court. It is the intent of the Committee, therefore, that in an action to determine whether a defendant is entitled to the privilege established by section 109(a) and (b), the burden of proving whether a particular copy was lawfully made or acquired should rest on the defendant.

REFERENCES IN TEXT

The date of the enactment of the Computer Software Rental Amendments Act of 1990, referred to in subsec. (b)(2)(B), is the date of enactment of Pub. L. 101–650, which was approved Dec. 1, 1990.

The first section of the Clayton Act, referred to in subsec. (b)(3), is classified to section 12 of Title 15, Commerce and Trade, and section 53 of Title 29, Labor. The term "antitrust laws" is defined in section 12 of Title 15.

Section 5 of the Federal Trade Commission Act, referred to in subsec. (b)(3), is classified to section 45 of Title 15.

AMENDMENTS

2008—Subsec. (b)(4). Pub. L. 110–403 substituted "and 505" for "505, and 509".

1997—Subsec. (b)(2)(B). Pub. L. 105–80 substituted "Register of Copyrights considers appropriate" for "Register of Copyright considers appropriate".

1994—Subsec. (a). Pub. L. 103–465 inserted at end "Notwithstanding the preceding sentence, copies or phonorecords of works subject to restored copyright under section 104A that are manufactured before the date of restoration of copyright or, with respect to reliance parties, before publication or service of notice under section 104A(e), may be sold or otherwise disposed of without the authorization of the owner of the restored copyright for purposes of direct or indirect commercial advantage only during the 12-month period beginning on—

"(1) the date of the publication in the Federal Register of the notice of intent filed with the Copyright Office under section 104A(d)(2)(A), or

"(2) the date of the receipt of actual notice served under section 104A(d)(2)(B),

whichever occurs first."

1990—Subsec. (b)(1). Pub. L. 101–650, § 802(2), added par. (1) and struck out former par. (1) which read as follows: "Notwithstanding the provisions of subsection (a), unless authorized by the owners of copyright in the sound recording and in the musical works embodied therein, the owner of a particular phonorecord may not, for purposes of direct or indirect commercial advantage, dispose of, or authorize the disposal of, the possession of that phonorecord by rental, lease, or lending, or by any other act or practice in the nature of rental, lease, or lending. Nothing in the preceding sentence shall apply to the rental, lease, or lending of a phonorecord for nonprofit purposes by a nonprofit library or nonprofit educational institution."

Subsec. (b)(2), (3). Pub. L. 101–650, § 802(1), (2), added par. (2) and redesignated former pars. (2) and (3) as (3) and (4), respectively.

Subsec. (b)(4). Pub. L. 101–650, § 802(3), added par. (4) and struck out former par. (4) which read as follows: "Any person who distributes a phonorecord in violation of clause (1) is an infringer of copyright under section 501 of this title and is subject to the remedies set forth in sections 502, 503, 504, 505, and 509. Such violation shall not be a criminal offense under section 506 or cause such person to be subject to the criminal penalties set forth in section 2319 of title 18."

Pub. L. 101–650, § 802(1), redesignated par. (3) as (4).

Subsec. (e). Pub. L. 101–650, § 803, added subsec. (e).

1988—Subsec. (d). Pub. L. 100–617 substituted "(a) and (c)" for "(a) and (b)" and "copyright" for "coyright".

1984—Subsecs. (b) to (d). Pub. L. 98–450 added subsec. (b) and redesignated existing subsecs. (b) and (c) as (c) and (d), respectively.

EFFECTIVE DATE OF 1990 AMENDMENT

Section 804 of title VIII of Pub. L. 101–650, as amended by Pub. L. 103–465, title V, § 511, Dec. 8, 1994, 108 Stat. 4974, provided that:

"(a) IN GENERAL.—Subject to subsection (b), this title [amending this section and enacting provisions set out as notes under sections 101 and 205 of this title] and the amendments made in section 802 [amending this section] shall take effect on the date of the enactment of this Act [Dec. 1, 1990]. The amendment made by section 803 [amending this section] shall take effect one year after such date of enactment.

"(b) PROSPECTIVE APPLICATION.—Section 109(b) of title 17, United States Code, as amended by section 802 of this Act, shall not affect the right of a person in possession of a particular copy of a computer program, who acquired such copy before the date of the enactment of this Act [Dec. 1, 1990], to dispose of the possession of that copy on or after such date of enactment in any manner permitted by section 109 of title 17, United States Code, as in effect on the day before such date of enactment.

"(c) TERMINATION.—The amendments made by section 803 shall not apply to public performances or displays that occur on or after October 1, 1995."

EFFECTIVE DATE OF 1984 AMENDMENT

Section 4 of Pub. L. 98–450, as amended by Pub. L. 100–617, §1, Nov. 5, 1988, 102 Stat. 3194; Pub. L. 103–182, title III, §332, Dec. 8, 1993, 107 Stat. 2114, provided that:

"(a) The amendments made by this Act [amending this section and section 115 of this title and enacting provisions set out as a note under section 101 of this title] shall take effect on the date of the enactment of this Act [Oct. 4, 1984].

"(b) The provisions of section 109(b) of title 17, United States Code, as added by section 2 of this Act, shall not affect the right of an owner of a particular phonorecord of a sound recording, who acquired such ownership before the date of the enactment of this Act [Oct. 4, 1984], to dispose of the possession of that particular phonorecord on or after such date of enactment in any manner permitted by section 109 of title 17, United States Code, as in effect on the day before the date of the enactment of this Act."

[Amendment by Pub. L. 103–182 to section 4 of Pub. L. 98–450, set out above, effective on the date the North American Free Trade Agreement enters into force with respect to the United States [Jan. 1, 1994], see section 335 of Pub. L. 103–182, set out as an Effective Date of 1993 Amendment note under section 1052 of Title 15, Commerce and Trade.]

EVALUATION OF IMPACT OF COPYRIGHT LAW AND AMENDMENTS ON ELECTRONIC COMMERCE AND TECHNOLOGICAL DEVELOPMENT

Pub. L. 105–304, title I, §104, Oct. 28, 1998, 112 Stat. 2876, provided that:

"(a) EVALUATION BY THE REGISTER OF COPYRIGHTS AND THE ASSISTANT SECRETARY FOR COMMUNICATIONS AND INFORMATION.—The Register of Copyrights and the Assistant Secretary for Communications and Information of the Department of Commerce shall jointly evaluate—

"(1) the effects of the amendments made by this title [enacting chapter 12 of this title and amending sections 101, 104, 104A, 411, and 507 of this title] and the development of electronic commerce and associated technology on the operation of sections 109 and 117 of title 17, United States Code; and

"(2) the relationship between existing and emergent technology and the operation of sections 109 and 117 of title 17, United States Code.

"(b) REPORT TO CONGRESS.—The Register of Copyrights and the Assistant Secretary for Communications and Information of the Department of Commerce shall, not later than 24 months after the date of the enactment of this Act [Oct. 28, 1998], submit to the Congress a joint report on the evaluation conducted under subsection (a), including any legislative recommendations the Register and the Assistant Secretary may have."

§110. Limitations on exclusive rights: Exemption of certain performances and displays

Notwithstanding the provisions of section 106, the following are not infringements of copyright:

(1) performance or display of a work by instructors or pupils in the course of face-to-face teaching activities of a nonprofit educational institution, in a classroom or similar place devoted to instruction, unless, in the case of a motion picture or other audiovisual work, the performance, or the display of individual images, is given by means of a copy that was not lawfully made under this title, and that the person responsible for the performance knew or had reason to believe was not lawfully made;

(2) except with respect to a work produced or marketed primarily for performance or display as part of mediated instructional activities transmitted via digital networks, or a performance or display that is given by means of a copy or phonorecord that is not lawfully made and acquired under this title, and the transmitting government body or accredited nonprofit educational institution knew or had reason to believe was not lawfully made and acquired, the performance of a nondramatic literary or musical work or reasonable and limited portions of any other work, or display of a work in an amount comparable to that which is typically displayed in the course of a live classroom session, by or in the course of a transmission, if—

(A) the performance or display is made by, at the direction of, or under the actual supervision of an instructor as an integral part of a class session offered as a regular part of the systematic mediated instructional activities of a governmental body or an accredited nonprofit educational institution;

(B) the performance or display is directly related and of material assistance to the teaching content of the transmission;

(C) the transmission is made solely for, and, to the extent technologically feasible, the reception of such transmission is limited to—

(i) students officially enrolled in the course for which the transmission is made; or

(ii) officers or employees of governmental bodies as a part of their official duties or employment; and

(D) the transmitting body or institution—

(i) institutes policies regarding copyright, provides informational materials to faculty, students, and relevant staff members that accurately describe, and promote compliance with, the laws of the United States relating to copyright, and provides notice to students that materials used in connection with the course may be subject to copyright protection; and

(ii) in the case of digital transmissions—

(I) applies technological measures that reasonably prevent—

(aa) retention of the work in accessible form by recipients of the transmission from the transmitting body or institution for longer than the class session; and

(bb) unauthorized further dissemination of the work in accessible form by such recipients to others; and

(II) does not engage in conduct that could reasonably be expected to interfere with technological measures used by copyright owners to prevent such retention or unauthorized further dissemination;

(3) performance of a nondramatic literary or musical work or of a dramatico-musical work of a religious nature, or display of a work, in

the course of services at a place of worship or other religious assembly;

(4) performance of a nondramatic literary or musical work otherwise than in a transmission to the public, without any purpose of direct or indirect commercial advantage and without payment of any fee or other compensation for the performance to any of its performers, promoters, or organizers, if—

(A) there is no direct or indirect admission charge; or

(B) the proceeds, after deducting the reasonable costs of producing the performance, are used exclusively for educational, religious, or charitable purposes and not for private financial gain, except where the copyright owner has served notice of objection to the performance under the following conditions:

(i) the notice shall be in writing and signed by the copyright owner or such owner's duly authorized agent; and

(ii) the notice shall be served on the person responsible for the performance at least seven days before the date of the performance, and shall state the reasons for the objection; and

(iii) the notice shall comply, in form, content, and manner of service, with requirements that the Register of Copyrights shall prescribe by regulation;

(5)(A) except as provided in subparagraph (B), communication of a transmission embodying a performance or display of a work by the public reception of the transmission on a single receiving apparatus of a kind commonly used in private homes, unless—

(i) a direct charge is made to see or hear the transmission; or

(ii) the transmission thus received is further transmitted to the public;

(B) communication by an establishment of a transmission or retransmission embodying a performance or display of a nondramatic musical work intended to be received by the general public, originated by a radio or television broadcast station licensed as such by the Federal Communications Commission, or, if an audiovisual transmission, by a cable system or satellite carrier, if—

(i) in the case of an establishment other than a food service or drinking establishment, either the establishment in which the communication occurs has less than 2,000 gross square feet of space (excluding space used for customer parking and for no other purpose), or the establishment in which the communication occurs has 2,000 or more gross square feet of space (excluding space used for customer parking and for no other purpose) and—

(I) if the performance is by audio means only, the performance is communicated by means of a total of not more than 6 loudspeakers, of which not more than 4 loudspeakers are located in any 1 room or adjoining outdoor space; or

(II) if the performance or display is by audiovisual means, any visual portion of the performance or display is communicated by means of a total of not more than 4 audiovisual devices, of which not more than 1 audiovisual device is located in any 1 room, and no such audiovisual device has a diagonal screen size greater than 55 inches, and any audio portion of the performance or display is communicated by means of a total of not more than 6 loudspeakers, of which not more than 4 loudspeakers are located in any 1 room or adjoining outdoor space;

(ii) in the case of a food service or drinking establishment, either the establishment in which the communication occurs has less than 3,750 gross square feet of space (excluding space used for customer parking and for no other purpose), or the establishment in which the communication occurs has 3,750 gross square feet of space or more (excluding space used for customer parking and for no other purpose) and—

(I) if the performance is by audio means only, the performance is communicated by means of a total of not more than 6 loudspeakers, of which not more than 4 loudspeakers are located in any 1 room or adjoining outdoor space; or

(II) if the performance or display is by audiovisual means, any visual portion of the performance or display is communicated by means of a total of not more than 4 audiovisual devices, of which not more than one audiovisual device is located in any 1 room, and no such audiovisual device has a diagonal screen size greater than 55 inches, and any audio portion of the performance or display is communicated by means of a total of not more than 6 loudspeakers, of which not more than 4 loudspeakers are located in any 1 room or adjoining outdoor space;

(iii) no direct charge is made to see or hear the transmission or retransmission;

(iv) the transmission or retransmission is not further transmitted beyond the establishment where it is received; and

(v) the transmission or retransmission is licensed by the copyright owner of the work so publicly performed or displayed;

(6) performance of a nondramatic musical work by a governmental body or a nonprofit agricultural or horticultural organization, in the course of an annual agricultural or horticultural fair or exhibition conducted by such body or organization; the exemption provided by this clause shall extend to any liability for copyright infringement that would otherwise be imposed on such body or organization, under doctrines of vicarious liability or related infringement, for a performance by a concessionnaire,[1] business establishment, or other person at such fair or exhibition, but shall not excuse any such person from liability for the performance;

(7) performance of a nondramatic musical work by a vending establishment open to the public at large without any direct or indirect admission charge, where the sole purpose of

---

[1] So in original. Probably should be "concessionaire".

the performance is to promote the retail sale of copies or phonorecords of the work, or of the audiovisual or other devices utilized in such performance, and the performance is not transmitted beyond the place where the establishment is located and is within the immediate area where the sale is occurring;

(8) performance of a nondramatic literary work, by or in the course of a transmission specifically designed for and primarily directed to blind or other handicapped persons who are unable to read normal printed material as a result of their handicap, or deaf or other handicapped persons who are unable to hear the aural signals accompanying a transmission of visual signals, if the performance is made without any purpose of direct or indirect commercial advantage and its transmission is made through the facilities of: (i) a governmental body; or (ii) a noncommercial educational broadcast station (as defined in section 397 of title 47); or (iii) a radio subcarrier authorization (as defined in 47 CFR 73.293–73.295 and 73.593–73.595); or (iv) a cable system (as defined in section 111(f));

(9) performance on a single occasion of a dramatic literary work published at least ten years before the date of the performance, by or in the course of a transmission specifically designed for and primarily directed to blind or other handicapped persons who are unable to read normal printed material as a result of their handicap, if the performance is made without any purpose of direct or indirect commercial advantage and its transmission is made through the facilities of a radio subcarrier authorization referred to in clause (8)(iii), *Provided*, That the provisions of this clause shall not be applicable to more than one performance of the same work by the same performers or under the auspices of the same organization;

(10) notwithstanding paragraph (4), the following is not an infringement of copyright: performance of a nondramatic literary or musical work in the course of a social function which is organized and promoted by a nonprofit veterans' organization or a nonprofit fraternal organization to which the general public is not invited, but not including the invitees of the organizations, if the proceeds from the performance, after deducting the reasonable costs of producing the performance, are used exclusively for charitable purposes and not for financial gain. For purposes of this section the social functions of any college or university fraternity or sorority shall not be included unless the social function is held solely to raise funds for a specific charitable purpose; and

(11) the making imperceptible, by or at the direction of a member of a private household, of limited portions of audio or video content of a motion picture, during a performance in or transmitted to that household for private home viewing, from an authorized copy of the motion picture, or the creation or provision of a computer program or other technology that enables such making imperceptible and that is designed and marketed to be used, at the direction of a member of a private household,

for such making imperceptible, if no fixed copy of the altered version of the motion picture is created by such computer program or other technology.

The exemptions provided under paragraph (5) shall not be taken into account in any administrative, judicial, or other governmental proceeding to set or adjust the royalties payable to copyright owners for the public performance or display of their works. Royalties payable to copyright owners for any public performance or display of their works other than such performances or displays as are exempted under paragraph (5) shall not be diminished in any respect as a result of such exemption.

In paragraph (2), the term "mediated instructional activities" with respect to the performance or display of a work by digital transmission under this section refers to activities that use such work as an integral part of the class experience, controlled by or under the actual supervision of the instructor and analogous to the type of performance or display that would take place in a live classroom setting. The term does not refer to activities that use, in 1 or more class sessions of a single course, such works as textbooks, course packs, or other material in any media, copies or phonorecords of which are typically purchased or acquired by the students in higher education for their independent use and retention or are typically purchased or acquired for elementary and secondary students for their possession and independent use.

For purposes of paragraph (2), accreditation—

(A) with respect to an institution providing post-secondary education, shall be as determined by a regional or national accrediting agency recognized by the Council on Higher Education Accreditation or the United States Department of Education; and

(B) with respect to an institution providing elementary or secondary education, shall be as recognized by the applicable state certification or licensing procedures.

For purposes of paragraph (2), no governmental body or accredited nonprofit educational institution shall be liable for infringement by reason of the transient or temporary storage of material carried out through the automatic technical process of a digital transmission of the performance or display of that material as authorized under paragraph (2). No such material stored on the system or network controlled or operated by the transmitting body or institution under this paragraph shall be maintained on such system or network in a manner ordinarily accessible to anyone other than anticipated recipients. No such copy shall be maintained on the system or network in a manner ordinarily accessible to such anticipated recipients for a longer period than is reasonably necessary to facilitate the transmissions for which it was made.

For purposes of paragraph (11), the term "making imperceptible" does not include the addition of audio or video content that is performed or displayed over or in place of existing content in a motion picture.

Nothing in paragraph (11) shall be construed to imply further rights under section 106 of this title, or to have any effect on defenses or limitations on rights granted under any other section of this title or under any other paragraph of this section.

(Pub. L. 94–553, title I, § 101, Oct. 19, 1976, 90 Stat. 2549; Pub. L. 97–366, § 3, Oct. 25, 1982, 96 Stat. 1759; Pub. L. 105–80, § 12(a)(6), Nov. 13, 1997, 111 Stat. 1534; Pub. L. 105–298, title II, § 202, Oct. 27, 1998, 112 Stat. 2830; Pub. L. 106–44, § 1(a), Aug. 5, 1999, 113 Stat. 221; Pub. L. 107–273, div. C, title III, §§ 13210(6), 13301(b), Nov. 2, 2002, 116 Stat. 1909, 1910; Pub. L. 109–9, title II, § 202(a), Apr. 27, 2005, 119 Stat. 223.)

HISTORICAL AND REVISION NOTES

HOUSE REPORT NO. 94–1476

Clauses (1) through (4) of section 110 deal with performances and exhibitions that are now generally exempt under the "for profit" limitation or other provisions of the copyright law, and that are specifically exempted from copyright liability under this legislation. Clauses (1) and (2) between them are intended to cover all of the various methods by which performances or displays in the course of systematic instruction take place.

Face-to-Face Teaching Activities. Clause (1) of section 110 is generally intended to set out the conditions under which performances or displays, in the course of instructional activities other than educational broadcasting, are to be exempted from copyright control. The clause covers all types of copyrighted works, and exempts their performance or display "by instructors or pupils in the course of face-to-face teaching activities of a nonprofit educational institution," where the activities take place "in a classroom or similar place devoted to instruction."

There appears to be no need for a statutory definition of "face-to-face" teaching activities to clarify the scope of the provision. "Face-to-face teaching activities" under clause (1) embrace instructional performances and displays that are not "transmitted." The concept does not require that the teacher and students be able to see each other, although it does require their simultaneous presence in the same general place. Use of the phrase "in the course of face-to-face teaching activities" is intended to exclude broadcasting or other transmissions from an outside location into classrooms, whether radio or television and whether open or closed circuit. However, as long as the instructor and pupils are in the same building or general area, the exemption would extend to the use of devices for amplifying or reproducing sound and for projecting visual images. The "teaching activities" exempted by the clause encompass systematic instruction of a very wide variety of subjects, but they do not include performances or displays, whatever their cultural value or intellectual appeal, that are given for the recreation or entertainment of any part of their audience.

Works Affected.—Since there is no limitation on the types of works covered by the exemption, teachers or students would be free to perform or display anything in class as long as the other conditions of the clause are met. They could read aloud from copyrighted text material, act out a drama, play or sing a musical work, perform a motion picture or filmstrip, or display text or pictorial material to the class by means of a projector. However, nothing in this provision is intended to sanction the unauthorized reproduction of copies or phonorecords for the purpose of classroom performance or display, and the clause contains a special exception dealing with performances from unlawfully made copies of motion pictures and other audiovisual works, to be discussed below.

Instructors or Pupils.—To come within clause (1), the performance or display must be "by instructors or pupils," thus ruling out performances by actors, singers, or instrumentalists brought in from outside the school to put on a program. However, the term "instructors" would be broad enough to include guest lecturers if their instructional activities remain confined to classroom situations. In general, the term "pupils" refers to the enrolled members of a class.

Nonprofit Educational Institution.—Clause (1) makes clear that it applies only to the teaching activities "of a nonprofit educational institution," thus excluding from the exemption performances or displays in profit-making institutions such as dance studios and language schools.

Classroom or Similar Place.—The teaching activities exempted by the clause must take place "in a classroom or similar place devoted to instruction." For example, performances in an auditorium or stadium during a school assembly, graduation ceremony, class play, or sporting event, where the audience is not confined to the members of a particular class, would fall outside the scope of clause (1), although in some cases they might be exempted by clause (4) of section 110. The "similar place" referred to in clause (1) is a place which is "devoted to instruction" in the same way a classroom is; common examples would include a studio, a workshop, a gymnasium, a training field, a library, the stage of an auditorium, or the auditorium itself, if it is actually used as a classroom for systematic instructional activities.

Motion Pictures and Other Audiovisual Works.—The final provision of clause (1) deals with the special problem of performances from unlawfully-made copies of motion pictures and other audiovisual works. The exemption is lost where the copy being used for a classroom performance was "not lawfully made under this title" and the person responsible for the performance knew or had reason to suspect as much. This special exception to the exemption would not apply to performances from lawfully-made copies, even if the copies were acquired from someone who had stolen or converted them, or if the performances were in violation of an agreement. However, though the performance would be exempt under section 110(1) in such cases, the copyright owner might have a cause of action against the unauthorized distributor under section 106(3), or against the person responsible for the performance, for breach of contract.

Projection Devices.—As long as there is no transmission beyond the place where the copy is located, both section 109(b) and section 110(1) would permit the classroom display of a work by means of any sort of projection device or process.

Instructional Broadcasting. *Works Affected.*—The exemption for instructional broadcasting provided by section 110(2) would apply only to "performance of a nondramatic literary or musical work or display of a work." Thus, the copyright owner's permission would be required for the performance on educational television or radio of a dramatic work, of a dramatico-musical work such as an opera or musical comedy, or of a motion picture. Since, as already explained, audiovisual works such as filmstrips are equated with motion pictures, their sequential showing would be regarded as a performance rather than a display and would not be exempt under section 110(2). The clause is not intended to limit in any way the copyright owner's exclusive right to make dramatizations, adaptations, or other derivative works under section 106(2). Thus, for example, a performer could read a nondramatic literary work aloud under section 110(2), but the copyright owner's permission would be required for him to act it out in dramatic form.

Systematic Instructional Activities.—Under section 110(2) a transmission must meet three specified conditions in order to be exempted from copyright liability. The first of these, as provided by subclause (A), is that the performance or display must be "a regular part of the systematic instructional activities of a governmental body or a nonprofit educational institution." The concept of "systematic instructional activities" is intended as the general equivalent of "curriculums," but it could be broader in a case such as that of an institution using systematic teaching methods not related to specific course work. A transmission would be a regular part of these activities if it is in accordance with the pattern of teaching established by the governmental body or institution. The use of commercial facilities, such as those of a cable service, to transmit the performance or display, would not affect the exemption as long as the actual performance or display was for nonprofit purposes.

Content of Transmission.—Subclause (B) requires that the performance or display be directly related and of material assistance to the teaching content of the transmission.

Intended Recipients.—Subclause (C) requires that the transmission is made primarily for:

(i) Reception in classrooms or similar places normally devoted to instruction, or

(ii) Reception by persons to whom the transmission is directed because their disabilities or other special circumstances prevent their attendance in classrooms or similar places normally devoted to instruction, or

(iii) Reception by officers or employees of governmental bodies as a part of their official duties or employment.

In all three cases, the instructional transmission need only be made "primarily" rather than "solely" to the specified recipients to be exempt. Thus, the transmission could still be exempt even though it is capable of reception by the public at large. Conversely, it would not be regarded as made "primarily" for one of the required groups of recipients if the principal purpose behind the transmission is reception by the public at large, even if it is cast in the form of instruction and is also received in classrooms. Factors to consider in determining the "primary" purpose of a program would include its subject matter, content, and the time of its transmission.

Paragraph (i) of subclause (C) generally covers what are known as "in-school" broadcasts, whether open- or closed-circuit. The reference to "classrooms or similar places" here is intended to have the same meaning as that of the phrase as used in section 110(1). The exemption in paragraph (ii) is intended to exempt transmissions providing systematic instruction to individuals who cannot be reached in classrooms because of "their disabilities or other special circumstances." Accordingly, the exemption is confined to instructional broadcasting that is an adjunct to the actual classwork of nonprofit schools or is primarily for people who cannot be brought together in classrooms such as preschool children, displaced workers, illiterates, and shut-ins.

There has been some question as to whether or not the language in this section of the bill is intended to include instructional television college credit courses. These telecourses are aimed at undergraduate and graduate students in earnest pursuit of higher educational degrees who are unable to attend daytime classes because of daytime employment, distance from campus, or some other intervening reason. So long as these broadcasts are aimed at regularly enrolled students and conducted by recognized higher educational institutions, the committee believes that they are clearly within the language of section 110(2)(C)(ii). Like night school and correspondence courses before them, these telecourses are fast becoming a valuable adjunct of the normal college curriculum.

The third exemption in subclause (C) is intended to permit the use of copyrighted material, in accordance with the other conditions of section 110(2), in the course of instructional transmissions for Government personnel who are receiving training "as a part of their official duties or employment."

Religious Services. The exemption in clause (3) of section 110 covers performances of a nondramatic literary or musical work, and also performances "of dramatico-musical works of a religious nature"; in addition, it extends to displays of works of all kinds. The exemption applies where the performance or display is "in the course of services at a place of worship or other religious assembly." The scope of the clause does not cover the sequential showing of motion pictures and other audiovisual works.

The exemption, which to some extent has its counterpart in sections 1 and 104 of the present law [sections 1 and 104 of former title 17], applies to dramatico-musical works "of a religious nature." The purpose here is to exempt certain performances of sacred music that might be regarded as "dramatic" in nature, such as oratorios, cantatas, musical settings of the mass, choral services, and the like. The exemption is not intended to cover performances of secular operas, musical plays, motion pictures, and the like, even if they have an underlying religious or philosophical theme and take place "in the course of [religious] services."

To be exempted under section 110(3) a performance or display must be "in the course of services," thus excluding activities at a place of worship that are for social, educational, fund raising, or entertainment purposes. Some performances of these kinds could be covered by the exemption in section 110(4), discussed next. Since the performance or display must also occur "at a place of worship or other religious assembly," the exemption would not extend to religious broadcasts or other transmissions to the public at large, even where the transmissions were sent from the place of worship. On the other hand, as long as services are being conducted before a religious gathering, the exemption would apply if they were conducted in places such as auditoriums, outdoor theaters, and the like.

Certain Other Nonprofit Performances. In addition to the educational and religious exemptions provided by clauses (1) through (3) of section 110, clause (4) contains a general exception to the exclusive right of public performance that would cover some, though not all, of the same ground as the present "for profit" limitation.

Scope of Exemption.—The exemption in clause (4) applies to the same general activities and subject matter as those covered by the "for profit" limitation today: public performances of nondramatic literary and musical works. However, the exemption would be limited to public performances given directly in the presence of an audience whether by means of living performers, the playing of phonorecords, or the operation of a receiving apparatus, and would not include a "transmission to the public." Unlike the clauses (1) through (3) and (5) of section 110, but like clauses (6) through (8), clause (4) applies only to performing rights in certain works, and does not affect the exclusive right to display a work in public.

No Profit Motive.—In addition to the other conditions specified by the clause, the performance must be "without any purpose of direct or indirect commercial advantage." This provision expressly adopts the principle established by the court decisions construing the "for profit" limitation: that public performances given or sponsored in connection with any commercial or profit-making enterprises are subject to the exclusive rights of the copyright owner even though the public is not charged for seeing or hearing the performance.

No Payment for Performance.—An important condition for this exemption is that the performance be given "without payment of any fee or other compensation for the performance to any of its performers, promoters, or organizers." The basic purpose of this requirement is to prevent the free use of copyrighted material under the guise of charity where fees or percentages are paid to performers, promoters, producers, and the like. However, the exemption would not be lost if the performers, directors, or producers of the performance, instead of being paid directly "for the performance," are paid a salary for duties encompassing the performance. Examples are performances by a school orchestra conducted by a music teacher who receives an annual salary, or by a service band whose members and conductors perform as part of their assigned duties and who receive military pay. The committee believes that performances of this type should be exempt, assuming the other conditions in clause (4) are met, and has not adopted the suggestion that the word "salary" be added to the phrase referring to the "payment of any fee or other compensation."

Admission Charge.—Assuming that the performance involves no profit motive and no one responsible for it gets paid a fee, it must still meet one of two alternative conditions to be exempt. As specified in subclauses (A) and (B) of section 110(4), these conditions are: (1) that no direct or indirect admission charge is made, or (2) that the net proceeds are "used exclusively for educational, religious, or charitable purposes and not for private financial gain."

Under the second of these conditions, a performance meeting the other conditions of clause (4) would be exempt even if an admission fee is charged, provided any amounts left "after deducting the reasonable costs of producing the performance" are used solely for bona fide educational, religious, or charitable purposes. In cases arising under this second condition and as provided in subclause (B), where there is an admission charge, the copyright owner is given an opportunity to decide whether and under what conditions the copyrighted work should be performed; otherwise, owners could be compelled to make involuntary donations to the fund-raising activities of causes to which they are opposed. The subclause would thus permit copyright owners to prevent public performances of their works under section 110(4)(B) by serving notice of objection, with the reasons therefor, at least seven days in advance.

Mere Reception in Public. Unlike the first four clauses of section 110, clause (5) is not to any extent a counterpart of the "for profit" limitation of the present statute. It applies to performances and displays of all types of works, and its purpose is to exempt from copyright liability anyone who merely turns on, in a public place, an ordinary radio or television receiving apparatus of a kind commonly sold to members of the public for private use.

The basic rationale of this clause is that the secondary use of the transmission by turning on an ordinary receiver in public is so remote and minimal that no further liability should be imposed. In the vast majority of these cases no royalties are collected today, and the exemption should be made explicit in the statute. This clause has nothing to do with cable television systems and the exemptions would be denied in any case where the audience is charged directly to see or hear the transmission.

With respect to section 110(5), the conference substitute conforms to the language in the Senate bill. It is the intent of the conferees that a small commercial establishment of the type involved in *Twentieth Century Music Corp. v. Aiken*, 422 U.S. 151 (1975), [95 S.Ct. 2040, 45 L.Ed.2d 84], which merely augmented a home-type receiver and which was not of sufficient size to justify, as a practical matter, a subscription to a commercial background music service, would be exempt. However, where the public communication was by means of something other than a home-type receiving apparatus, or where the establishment actually makes a further transmission to the public, the exemption would not apply.

On June 17, 1975, the Supreme Court handed down a decision in *Twentieth Century Music Corp. v. Aiken*, 95 S.Ct. 2040 [422 U.S. 151, 45 L.Ed.2d 84], that raised fundamental questions about the proper interpretation of section 110(5). The defendant, owner and operator of a fast-service food shop in downtown Pittsburgh, had "a radio with outlets to four speakers in the ceiling," which he apparently turned on and left on throughout the business day. Lacking any performing license, he was sued for copyright infringement by two ASCAP members. He lost in the District Court, won a reversal in the Third Circuit Court of Appeals, and finally prevailed, by a margin of 7–2, in the Supreme Court.

The *Aiken* decision is based squarely on the two Supreme Court decisions dealing with cable television. In *Fortnightly Corp. v. United Artists*, 392 U.S. 390 [88 S.Ct. 2084, 20 L.Ed.2d 1176, rehearing denied 89 S.Ct. 65, 393 U.S. 902, 21 L.Ed.2d 190], and again in *Teleprompter Corp. v. CBS*, 415 U.S. 394 [94 S.Ct. 1129, 39 L.Ed.2d 415], the Supreme Court has held that a CATV operator was not "performing" within the meaning of the 1909 statute, when it picked up broadcast signals off the air and retransmitted them to subscribers by cable. The *Aiken* decision extends this interpretation of the scope of the 1909 statute's right of "public performance for profit" to a situation outside the CATV context and, without expressly overruling the decision in *Buck v. Jewell-La-Salle Realty Co.*, 283 U.S. 191 (1931) [51 S.Ct. 410, 75 L.Ed. 971], effectively deprives it of much meaning under the present law. For more than forty years the *Jewell-La-Salle* rule was thought to require a business establishment to obtain copyright licenses before it could legally pick up any broadcasts off the air and retransmit them to its guests and patrons. As reinterpreted by the *Aiken* decision, the rule of *Jewell-LaSalle* applies only if the broadcast being retransmitted was itself unlicensed.

The majority of the Supreme Court in the *Aiken* case based its decision on a narrow construction of the word "perform" in the 1909 statute. This basis for the decision is completely overturned by the present bill and its broad definition of "perform" in section 101. The Committee has adopted the language of section 110(5) with an amendment expressly denying the exemption in situations where "the performance or display is further transmitted beyond the place where the receiving apparatus is located"; in doing so, it accepts the traditional, pre-*Aiken*, interpretation of the *Jewell-LaSalle* decision, under which public communication by means other than a home receiving set, or further transmission of a broadcast to the public, is considered an infringing act.

Under the particular fact situation in the *Aiken* case, assuming a small commercial establishment and the use of a home receiver with four ordinary loudspeakers grouped within a relatively narrow circumference from the set, it is intended that the performances would be exempt under clause (5). However, the Committee considers this fact situation to represent the outer limit of the exemption, and believes that the line should be drawn at that point. Thus, the clause would exempt small commercial establishments whose proprietors merely bring onto their premises standard radio or television equipment and turn it on for their customers' enjoyment, but it would impose liability where the proprietor has a commercial "sound system" installed or converts a standard home receiving apparatus (by augmenting it with sophisticated or extensive amplification equipment) into the equivalent of a commercial sound system. Factors to consider in particular cases would include the size, physical arrangement, and noise level of the areas within the establishment where the transmissions are made audible or visible, and the extent to which the receiving apparatus is altered or augmented for the purpose of improving the aural or visual quality of the performance for individual members of the public using those areas.

Agricultural Fairs. The Committee also amended clause (6) of section 110 of S. 22 as adopted by the Senate. As amended, the provision would exempt "performance of a nondramatic musical work by a governmental body or a nonprofit agricultural or horticultural organization, in the course of an annual agricultural or horticultural fair or exhibition conducted by such body or organization." The exemption extends only to the governmental body or nonprofit organization sponsoring the fair; the amendment makes clear that, while such a body or organization cannot itself be held vicariously liable for infringements by concessionaires at the fair, the concessionaires themselves enjoy no exemption under the clause.

Retail Sale of Phonorecords. Clause (7) provides that the performance of a nondramatic musical work or of a sound recording by a vending establishment open to the public at large without any direct or indirect admission charge, where the sole purpose of the performance is to promote the retail sale of copies or phonorecords of the work, is not an infringement of copyright. This exemption applies only if the performance is not transmitted beyond the place where the establishment is located and is within the immediate area where the sale is occurring.

Transmission to Handicapped Audiences. The new clause (8) of subsection 110, which had been added to S. 22 by the Senate Judiciary Committee when it reported the bill on November 20, 1975, and had been adopted by the Senate on February 19, 1976, was substantially amended by the Committee. Under the amendment, the exemption would apply only to performances of "nondramatic literary works" by means of "a transmission specifically designed for and primarily directed to" one or the other of two defined classes of handicapped persons: (1) "blind or other handicapped persons who are unable to read normal printed material as a result of their handicap" or (2) "deaf or other handicapped persons who are unable to hear the aural signals accompanying a transmission." Moreover, the exemption would be applicable only if the performance is "without any purpose of direct or indirect commercial advantage," and if the transmission takes place through government facilities or through the facilities of a noncommercial educational broadcast station, a radio subcarrier authorization (SCA), or a cable system.

Amendments

2005—Pub. L. 109–9, §202(a)(4), inserted two pars. relating to par. (11) at end of concluding provisions.

Par. (11). Pub. L. 109–9, §202(a)(1)–(3), added par. (11).

2002—Pub. L. 107–273, §13301(b)(2), inserted concluding provisions relating to par. (2).

Par. (2). Pub. L. 107–273, §13301(b)(1), added par. (2) and struck out former par. (2) which read as follows: "performance of a nondramatic literary or musical work or display of a work, by or in the course of a transmission, if—

"(A) the performance or display is a regular part of the systematic instructional activities of a governmental body or a nonprofit educational institution; and

"(B) the performance or display is directly related and of material assistance to the teaching content of the transmission; and

"(C) the transmission is made primarily for—

"(i) reception in classrooms or similar places normally devoted to instruction, or

"(ii) reception by persons to whom the transmission is directed because their disabilities or other special circumstances prevent their attendance in classrooms or similar places normally devoted to instruction, or

"(iii) reception by officers or employees of governmental bodies as a part of their official duties or employment;".

Par. (4)(B). Pub. L. 107–273, §13210(6), substituted colon for semicolon at end of introductory provisions.

1999—Par. (5)(A). Pub. L. 106–44 redesignated cls. (A) and (B) as (i) and (ii), respectively.

1998—Pub. L. 105–298, §202(a)(2), inserted concluding provisions relating to par. (5).

Par. (5). Pub. L. 105–298, §202(a)(1), designated existing provisions as subpar. (A), inserted "except as provided in subparagraph (B)," after "(A)", and added subpar. (B).

Par. (7). Pub. L. 105–298, §202(b), inserted "or of the audiovisual or other devices utilized in such performance," after "phonorecords of the work,".

1997—Par. (8). Pub. L. 105–80, §12(a)(6)(A), substituted semicolon for period at end.

Par. (9). Pub. L. 105–80, §12(a)(6)(B), substituted "; and" for period at end.

Par. (10). Pub. L. 105–80, §12(a)(6)(C), substituted "paragraph (4)" for "paragraph 4 above".

1982—Par. (10). Pub. L. 97–366 added par. (10).

Effective Date of 1998 Amendment

Amendment by Pub. L. 105–298 effective 90 days after Oct. 27, 1998, see section 207 of Pub. L. 105–298, set out as a note under section 101 of this title.

Effective Date of 1982 Amendment

Amendment by Pub. L. 97–366 effective 30 days after Oct. 25, 1982, see section 2 of Pub. L. 97–366, set out as a note under section 708 of this title.

§ 111. Limitations on exclusive rights: Secondary transmissions of broadcast programming by cable

(a) Certain Secondary Transmissions Exempted.—The secondary transmission of a performance or display of a work embodied in a primary transmission is not an infringement of copyright if—

(1) the secondary transmission is not made by a cable system, and consists entirely of the relaying, by the management of a hotel, apartment house, or similar establishment, of signals transmitted by a broadcast station licensed by the Federal Communications Commission, within the local service area of such station, to the private lodgings of guests or residents of such establishment, and no direct charge is made to see or hear the secondary transmission; or

(2) the secondary transmission is made solely for the purpose and under the conditions specified by paragraph (2) of section 110; or

(3) the secondary transmission is made by any carrier who has no direct or indirect control over the content or selection of the primary transmission or over the particular recipients of the secondary transmission, and whose activities with respect to the secondary transmission consist solely of providing wires, cables, or other communications channels for the use of others: *Provided,* That the provisions of this paragraph extend only to the activities of said carrier with respect to secondary transmissions and do not exempt from liability the activities of others with respect to their own primary or secondary transmissions;

(4) the secondary transmission is made by a satellite carrier pursuant to a statutory license under section 119 or section 122;

(5) the secondary transmission is not made by a cable system but is made by a governmental body, or other nonprofit organization, without any purpose of direct or indirect commercial advantage, and without charge to the recipients of the secondary transmission other than assessments necessary to defray the actual and reasonable costs of maintaining and operating the secondary transmission service.

(b) Secondary Transmission of Primary Transmission to Controlled Group.—Notwithstanding the provisions of subsections (a) and (c), the secondary transmission to the public of a performance or display of a work embodied in a primary transmission is actionable as an act of infringement under section 501, and is fully subject to the remedies provided by sections 502 through 506, if the primary transmission is not made for reception by the public at large but is controlled and limited to reception by particular members of the public: *Provided, however,* That such secondary transmission is not actionable as an act of infringement if—

(1) the primary transmission is made by a broadcast station licensed by the Federal Communications Commission; and

(2) the carriage of the signals comprising the secondary transmission is required under the rules, regulations, or authorizations of the Federal Communications Commission; and

(3) the signal of the primary transmitter is not altered or changed in any way by the secondary transmitter.

(c) SECONDARY TRANSMISSIONS BY CABLE SYSTEMS.—

(1) Subject to the provisions of paragraphs (2), (3), and (4) of this subsection and section 114(d), secondary transmissions to the public by a cable system of a performance or display of a work embodied in a primary transmission made by a broadcast station licensed by the Federal Communications Commission or by an appropriate governmental authority of Canada or Mexico shall be subject to statutory licensing upon compliance with the requirements of subsection (d) where the carriage of the signals comprising the secondary transmission is permissible under the rules, regulations, or authorizations of the Federal Communications Commission.

(2) Notwithstanding the provisions of paragraph (1) of this subsection, the willful or repeated secondary transmission to the public by a cable system of a primary transmission made by a broadcast station licensed by the Federal Communications Commission or by an appropriate governmental authority of Canada or Mexico and embodying a performance or display of a work is actionable as an act of infringement under section 501, and is fully subject to the remedies provided by sections 502 through 506, in the following cases:

(A) where the carriage of the signals comprising the secondary transmission is not permissible under the rules, regulations, or authorizations of the Federal Communications Commission; or

(B) where the cable system has not deposited the statement of account and royalty fee required by subsection (d).

(3) Notwithstanding the provisions of paragraph (1) of this subsection and subject to the provisions of subsection (e) of this section, the secondary transmission to the public by a cable system of a performance or display of a work embodied in a primary transmission made by a broadcast station licensed by the Federal Communications Commission or by an appropriate governmental authority of Canada or Mexico is actionable as an act of infringement under section 501, and is fully subject to the remedies provided by sections 502 through 506 and section 510, if the content of the particular program in which the performance or display is embodied, or any commercial advertising or station announcements transmitted by the primary transmitter during, or immediately before or after, the transmission of such program, is in any way willfully altered by the cable system through changes, deletions, or additions, except for the alteration, deletion, or substitution of commercial advertisements performed by those engaged in tele-

vision commercial advertising market research: *Provided*, That the research company has obtained the prior consent of the advertiser who has purchased the original commercial advertisement, the television station broadcasting that commercial advertisement, and the cable system performing the secondary transmission: *And provided further*, That such commercial alteration, deletion, or substitution is not performed for the purpose of deriving income from the sale of that commercial time.

(4) Notwithstanding the provisions of paragraph (1) of this subsection, the secondary transmission to the public by a cable system of a performance or display of a work embodied in a primary transmission made by a broadcast station licensed by an appropriate governmental authority of Canada or Mexico is actionable as an act of infringement under section 501, and is fully subject to the remedies provided by sections 502 through 506, if (A) with respect to Canadian signals, the community of the cable system is located more than 150 miles from the United States-Canadian border and is also located south of the forty-second parallel of latitude, or (B) with respect to Mexican signals, the secondary transmission is made by a cable system which received the primary transmission by means other than direct interception of a free space radio wave emitted by such broadcast television station, unless prior to April 15, 1976, such cable system was actually carrying, or was specifically authorized to carry, the signal of such foreign station on the system pursuant to the rules, regulations, or authorizations of the Federal Communications Commission.

(d) STATUTORY LICENSE FOR SECONDARY TRANSMISSIONS BY CABLE SYSTEMS.—

(1) STATEMENT OF ACCOUNT AND ROYALTY FEES.—Subject to paragraph (5), a cable system whose secondary transmissions have been subject to statutory licensing under subsection (c) shall, on a semiannual basis, deposit with the Register of Copyrights, in accordance with requirements that the Register shall prescribe by regulation the following:

(A) A statement of account, covering the six months next preceding, specifying the number of channels on which the cable system made secondary transmissions to its subscribers, the names and locations of all primary transmitters whose transmissions were further transmitted by the cable system, the total number of subscribers, the gross amounts paid to the cable system for the basic service of providing secondary transmissions of primary broadcast transmitters, and such other data as the Register of Copyrights may from time to time prescribe by regulation. In determining the total number of subscribers and the gross amounts paid to the cable system for the basic service of providing secondary transmissions of primary broadcast transmitters, the system shall not include subscribers and amounts collected from subscribers receiving secondary transmissions pursuant to section 119. Such statement shall also include a special statement of account covering any non-network television programming that was carried by the cable system in whole or in part beyond the local service area of the primary transmitter, under rules, regulations, or authorizations of the Federal Communications Commission permitting the substitution or addition of signals under certain circumstances, together with logs showing the times, dates, stations, and programs involved in such substituted or added carriage.

(B) Except in the case of a cable system whose royalty fee is specified in subparagraph (E) or (F), a total royalty fee payable to copyright owners pursuant to paragraph (3) for the period covered by the statement, computed on the basis of specified percentages of the gross receipts from subscribers to the cable service during such period for the basic service of providing secondary transmissions of primary broadcast transmitters, as follows:

(i) 1.064 percent of such gross receipts for the privilege of further transmitting, beyond the local service area of such primary transmitter, any non-network programming of a primary transmitter in whole or in part, such amount to be applied against the fee, if any, payable pursuant to clauses (ii) through (iv);

(ii) 1.064 percent of such gross receipts for the first distant signal equivalent;

(iii) 0.701 percent of such gross receipts for each of the second, third, and fourth distant signal equivalents; and

(iv) 0.330 percent of such gross receipts for the fifth distant signal equivalent and each distant signal equivalent thereafter.

(C) In computing amounts under clauses (ii) through (iv) of subparagraph (B)—

(i) any fraction of a distant signal equivalent shall be computed at its fractional value;

(ii) in the case of any cable system located partly within and partly outside of the local service area of a primary transmitter, gross receipts shall be limited to those gross receipts derived from subscribers located outside of the local service area of such primary transmitter; and

(iii) if a cable system provides a secondary transmission of a primary transmitter to some but not all communities served by that cable system—

(I) the gross receipts and the distant signal equivalent values for such secondary transmission shall be derived solely on the basis of the subscribers in those communities where the cable system provides such secondary transmission; and

(II) the total royalty fee for the period paid by such system shall not be less than the royalty fee calculated under subparagraph (B)(i) multiplied by the gross receipts from all subscribers to the system.

(D) A cable system that, on a statement submitted before the date of the enactment of the Satellite Television Extension and Lo-

calism Act of 2010, computed its royalty fee consistent with the methodology under subparagraph (C)(iii), or that amends a statement filed before such date of enactment to compute the royalty fee due using such methodology, shall not be subject to an action for infringement, or eligible for any royalty refund or offset, arising out of its use of such methodology on such statement.

(E) If the actual gross receipts paid by subscribers to a cable system for the period covered by the statement for the basic service of providing secondary transmissions of primary broadcast transmitters are $263,800 or less—

(i) gross receipts of the cable system for the purpose of this paragraph shall be computed by subtracting from such actual gross receipts the amount by which $263,800 exceeds such actual gross receipts, except that in no case shall a cable system's gross receipts be reduced to less than $10,400; and

(ii) the royalty fee payable under this paragraph to copyright owners pursuant to paragraph (3) shall be 0.5 percent, regardless of the number of distant signal equivalents, if any.

(F) If the actual gross receipts paid by subscribers to a cable system for the period covered by the statement for the basic service of providing secondary transmissions of primary broadcast transmitters are more than $263,800 but less than $527,600, the royalty fee payable under this paragraph to copyright owners pursuant to paragraph (3) shall be—

(i) 0.5 percent of any gross receipts up to $263,800, regardless of the number of distant signal equivalents, if any; and

(ii) 1 percent of any gross receipts in excess of $263,800, but less than $527,600, regardless of the number of distant signal equivalents, if any.

(G) A filing fee, as determined by the Register of Copyrights pursuant to section 708(a).

(2) HANDLING OF FEES.—The Register of Copyrights shall receive all fees (including the filing fee specified in paragraph (1)(G)) deposited under this section and, after deducting the reasonable costs incurred by the Copyright Office under this section, shall deposit the balance in the Treasury of the United States, in such manner as the Secretary of the Treasury directs. All funds held by the Secretary of the Treasury shall be invested in interest-bearing United States securities for later distribution with interest by the Librarian of Congress upon authorization by the Copyright Royalty Judges.

(3) DISTRIBUTION OF ROYALTY FEES TO COPYRIGHT OWNERS.—The royalty fees thus deposited shall, in accordance with the procedures provided by clause (4), be distributed to those among the following copyright owners who claim that their works were the subject of secondary transmissions by cable systems during the relevant semiannual period:

(A) Any such owner whose work was included in a secondary transmission made by a cable system of a non-network television program in whole or in part beyond the local service area of the primary transmitter.

(B) Any such owner whose work was included in a secondary transmission identified in a special statement of account deposited under clause (1)(A).

(C) Any such owner whose work was included in non-network programming consisting exclusively of aural signals carried by a cable system in whole or in part beyond the local service area of the primary transmitter of such programs.

(4) PROCEDURES FOR ROYALTY FEE DISTRIBUTION.—The royalty fees thus deposited shall be distributed in accordance with the following procedures:

(A) During the month of July in each year, every person claiming to be entitled to statutory license fees for secondary transmissions shall file a claim with the Copyright Royalty Judges, in accordance with requirements that the Copyright Royalty Judges shall prescribe by regulation. Notwithstanding any provisions of the antitrust laws, for purposes of this clause any claimants may agree among themselves as to the proportionate division of statutory licensing fees among them, may lump their claims together and file them jointly or as a single claim, or may designate a common agent to receive payment on their behalf.

(B) After the first day of August of each year, the Copyright Royalty Judges shall determine whether there exists a controversy concerning the distribution of royalty fees. If the Copyright Royalty Judges determine that no such controversy exists, the Copyright Royalty Judges shall authorize the Librarian of Congress to proceed to distribute such fees to the copyright owners entitled to receive them, or to their designated agents, subject to the deduction of reasonable administrative costs under this section. If the Copyright Royalty Judges find the existence of a controversy, the Copyright Royalty Judges shall, pursuant to chapter 8 of this title, conduct a proceeding to determine the distribution of royalty fees.

(C) During the pendency of any proceeding under this subsection, the Copyright Royalty Judges shall have the discretion to authorize the Librarian of Congress to proceed to distribute any amounts that are not in controversy.

(5) 3.75 PERCENT RATE AND SYNDICATED EXCLUSIVITY SURCHARGE NOT APPLICABLE TO MULTICAST STREAMS.—The royalty rates specified in sections 256.2(c) and 256.2(d) of title 37, Code of Federal Regulations (commonly referred to as the "3.75 percent rate" and the "syndicated exclusivity surcharge", respectively), as in effect on the date of the enactment of the Satellite Television Extension and Localism Act of 2010, as such rates may be adjusted, or such sections redesignated, thereafter by the Copyright Royalty Judges, shall not apply to the secondary transmission of a multicast stream.

(6) VERIFICATION OF ACCOUNTS AND FEE PAYMENTS.—The Register of Copyrights shall issue regulations to provide for the confidential verification by copyright owners whose works were embodied in the secondary transmissions of primary transmissions pursuant to this section of the information reported on the semiannual statements of account filed under this subsection for accounting periods beginning on or after January 1, 2010, in order that the auditor designated under subparagraph (A) is able to confirm the correctness of the calculations and royalty payments reported therein. The regulations shall—

(A) establish procedures for the designation of a qualified independent auditor—

(i) with exclusive authority to request verification of such a statement of account on behalf of all copyright owners whose works were the subject of secondary transmissions of primary transmissions by the cable system (that deposited the statement) during the accounting period covered by the statement; and

(ii) who is not an officer, employee, or agent of any such copyright owner for any purpose other than such audit;

(B) establish procedures for safeguarding all non-public financial and business information provided under this paragraph;

(C)(i) require a consultation period for the independent auditor to review its conclusions with a designee of the cable system;

(ii) establish a mechanism for the cable system to remedy any errors identified in the auditor's report and to cure any underpayment identified; and

(iii) provide an opportunity to remedy any disputed facts or conclusions;

(D) limit the frequency of requests for verification for a particular cable system and the number of audits that a multiple system operator can be required to undergo in a single year; and

(E) permit requests for verification of a statement of account to be made only within 3 years after the last day of the year in which the statement of account is filed.

(7) ACCEPTANCE OF ADDITIONAL DEPOSITS.— Any royalty fee payments received by the Copyright Office from cable systems for the secondary transmission of primary transmissions that are in addition to the payments calculated and deposited in accordance with this subsection shall be deemed to have been deposited for the particular accounting period for which they are received and shall be distributed as specified under this subsection.

(e) NONSIMULTANEOUS SECONDARY TRANSMISSIONS BY CABLE SYSTEMS.—

(1) Notwithstanding those provisions of the[1] subsection (f)(2) relating to nonsimultaneous secondary transmissions by a cable system, any such transmissions are actionable as an act of infringement under section 501, and are fully subject to the remedies provided by sections 502 through 506 and section 510, unless—

(A) the program on the videotape is transmitted no more than one time to the cable system's subscribers;

---

[1] So in original. The word "the" probably should not appear.

(B) the copyrighted program, episode, or motion picture videotape, including the commercials contained within such program, episode, or picture, is transmitted without deletion or editing;

(C) an owner or officer of the cable system (i) prevents the duplication of the videotape while in the possession of the system, (ii) prevents unauthorized duplication while in the possession of the facility making the videotape for the system if the system owns or controls the facility, or takes reasonable precautions to prevent such duplication if it does not own or control the facility, (iii) takes adequate precautions to prevent duplication while the tape is being transported, and (iv) subject to paragraph (2), erases or destroys, or causes the erasure or destruction of, the videotape;

(D) within forty-five days after the end of each calendar quarter, an owner or officer of the cable system executes an affidavit attesting (i) to the steps and precautions taken to prevent duplication of the videotape, and (ii) subject to paragraph (2), to the erasure or destruction of all videotapes made or used during such quarter;

(E) such owner or officer places or causes each such affidavit, and affidavits received pursuant to paragraph (2)(C), to be placed in a file, open to public inspection, at such system's main office in the community where the transmission is made or in the nearest community where such system maintains an office; and

(F) the nonsimultaneous transmission is one that the cable system would be authorized to transmit under the rules, regulations, and authorizations of the Federal Communications Commission in effect at the time of the nonsimultaneous transmission if the transmission had been made simultaneously, except that this subparagraph shall not apply to inadvertent or accidental transmissions.

(2) If a cable system transfers to any person a videotape of a program nonsimultaneously transmitted by it, such transfer is actionable as an act of infringement under section 501, and is fully subject to the remedies provided by sections 502 through 506, except that, pursuant to a written, nonprofit contract providing for the equitable sharing of the costs of such videotape and its transfer, a videotape nonsimultaneously transmitted by it, in accordance with paragraph (1), may be transferred by one cable system in Alaska to another system in Alaska, by one cable system in Hawaii permitted to make such nonsimultaneous transmissions to another such cable system in Hawaii, or by one cable system in Guam, the Northern Mariana Islands, the Federated States of Micronesia, the Republic of Palau, or the Republic of the Marshall Islands, to another cable system in any of those five entities, if—

(A) each such contract is available for public inspection in the offices of the cable systems involved, and a copy of such contract is filed, within thirty days after such contract is entered into, with the Copyright Office (which Office shall make each such contract available for public inspection);

(B) the cable system to which the videotape is transferred complies with paragraph (1)(A), (B), (C)(i), (iii), and (iv), and (D) through (F); and

(C) such system provides a copy of the affidavit required to be made in accordance with paragraph (1)(D) to each cable system making a previous nonsimultaneous transmission of the same videotape.

(3) This subsection shall not be construed to supersede the exclusivity protection provisions of any existing agreement, or any such agreement hereafter entered into, between a cable system and a television broadcast station in the area in which the cable system is located, or a network with which such station is affiliated.

(4) As used in this subsection, the term "videotape" means the reproduction of the images and sounds of a program or programs broadcast by a television broadcast station licensed by the Federal Communications Commission, regardless of the nature of the material objects, such as tapes or films, in which the reproduction is embodied.

(f) DEFINITIONS.—As used in this section, the following terms mean the following:

(1) PRIMARY TRANSMISSION.—A "primary transmission" is a transmission made to the public by a transmitting facility whose signals are being received and further transmitted by a secondary transmission service, regardless of where or when the performance or display was first transmitted. In the case of a television broadcast station, the primary stream and any multicast streams transmitted by the station constitute primary transmissions.

(2) SECONDARY TRANSMISSION.—A "secondary transmission" is the further transmitting of a primary transmission simultaneously with the primary transmission, or nonsimultaneously with the primary transmission if by a cable system not located in whole or in part within the boundary of the forty-eight contiguous States, Hawaii, or Puerto Rico: *Provided, however*, That a nonsimultaneous further transmission by a cable system located in Hawaii of a primary transmission shall be deemed to be a secondary transmission if the carriage of the television broadcast signal comprising such further transmission is permissible under the rules, regulations, or authorizations of the Federal Communications Commission.

(3) CABLE SYSTEM.—A "cable system" is a facility, located in any State, territory, trust territory, or possession of the United States, that in whole or in part receives signals transmitted or programs broadcast by one or more television broadcast stations licensed by the Federal Communications Commission, and makes secondary transmissions of such signals or programs by wires, cables, microwave, or other communications channels to subscribing members of the public who pay for such service. For purposes of determining the royalty fee under subsection (d)(1), two or more cable systems in contiguous communities under common ownership or control or operating

from one headend shall be considered as one system.

(4) LOCAL SERVICE AREA OF A PRIMARY TRANSMITTER.—The "local service area of a primary transmitter", in the case of both the primary stream and any multicast streams transmitted by a primary transmitter that is a television broadcast station, comprises the area where such primary transmitter could have insisted upon its signal being retransmitted by a cable system pursuant to the rules, regulations, and authorizations of the Federal Communications Commission in effect on April 15, 1976, or such station's television market as defined in section 76.55(e) of title 47, Code of Federal Regulations (as in effect on September 18, 1993), or any modifications to such television market made, on or after September 18, 1993, pursuant to section 76.55(e) or 76.59 of title 47, Code of Federal Regulations, or within the noise-limited contour as defined in 73.622(e)(1) of title 47, Code of Federal Regulations, or in the case of a television broadcast station licensed by an appropriate governmental authority of Canada or Mexico, the area in which it would be entitled to insist upon its signal being retransmitted if it were a television broadcast station subject to such rules, regulations, and authorizations. In the case of a low power television station, the "local service area of a primary transmitter" comprises the area within 35 miles of the transmitter site, except that in the case of such a station located in a standard metropolitan statistical area which has one of the 50 largest populations of all standard metropolitan statistical areas (based on the 1980 decennial census of population taken by the Secretary of Commerce), the number of miles shall be 20 miles. The "local service area of a primary transmitter", in the case of a radio broadcast station, comprises the primary service area of such station, pursuant to the rules and regulations of the Federal Communications Commission.

(5) DISTANT SIGNAL EQUIVALENT.—

(A) IN GENERAL.—Except as provided under subparagraph (B), a "distant signal equivalent"—

(i) is the value assigned to the secondary transmission of any non-network television programming carried by a cable system in whole or in part beyond the local service area of the primary transmitter of such programming; and

(ii) is computed by assigning a value of one to each primary stream and to each multicast stream (other than a simulcast) that is an independent station, and by assigning a value of one-quarter to each primary stream and to each multicast stream (other than a simulcast) that is a network station or a noncommercial educational station.

(B) EXCEPTIONS.—The values for independent, network, and noncommercial educational stations specified in subparagraph (A) are subject to the following:

(i) Where the rules and regulations of the Federal Communications Commission require a cable system to omit the further transmission of a particular program and such rules and regulations also permit the substitution of another program embodying a performance or display of a work in place of the omitted transmission, or where such rules and regulations in effect on the date of the enactment of the Copyright Act of 1976[2] permit a cable system, at its election, to effect such omission and substitution of a nonlive program or to carry additional programs not transmitted by primary transmitters within whose local service area the cable system is located, no value shall be assigned for the substituted or additional program.

(ii) Where the rules, regulations, or authorizations of the Federal Communications Commission in effect on the date of the enactment of the Copyright Act of 1976[2] permit a cable system, at its election, to omit the further transmission of a particular program and such rules, regulations, or authorizations also permit the substitution of another program embodying a performance or display of a work in place of the omitted transmission, the value assigned for the substituted or additional program shall be, in the case of a live program, the value of one full distant signal equivalent multiplied by a fraction that has as its numerator the number of days in the year in which such substitution occurs and as its denominator the number of days in the year.

(iii) In the case of the secondary transmission of a primary transmitter that is a television broadcast station pursuant to the late-night or specialty programming rules of the Federal Communications Commission, or the secondary transmission of a primary transmitter that is a television broadcast station on a part-time basis where full-time carriage is not possible because the cable system lacks the activated channel capacity to retransmit on a full-time basis all signals that it is authorized to carry, the values for independent, network, and noncommercial educational stations set forth in subparagraph (A), as the case may be, shall be multiplied by a fraction that is equal to the ratio of the broadcast hours of such primary transmitter retransmitted by the cable system to the total broadcast hours of the primary transmitter.

(iv) No value shall be assigned for the secondary transmission of the primary stream or any multicast streams of a primary transmitter that is a television broadcast station in any community that is within the local service area of the primary transmitter.

(6) NETWORK STATION.—

(A) TREATMENT OF PRIMARY STREAM.—The term "network station" shall be applied to a primary stream of a television broadcast station that is owned or operated by, or affiliated with, one or more of the television networks in the United States providing na-

---

[2] See References in Text note below.

tionwide transmissions, and that transmits a substantial part of the programming supplied by such networks for a substantial part of the primary stream's typical broadcast day.

(B) TREATMENT OF MULTICAST STREAMS.—The term "network station" shall be applied to a multicast stream on which a television broadcast station transmits all or substantially all of the programming of an interconnected program service that—

(i) is owned or operated by, or affiliated with, one or more of the television networks described in subparagraph (A); and

(ii) offers programming on a regular basis for 15 or more hours per week to at least 25 of the affiliated television licensees of the interconnected program service in 10 or more States.

(7) INDEPENDENT STATION.—The term "independent station" shall be applied to the primary stream or a multicast stream of a television broadcast station that is not a network station or a noncommercial educational station.

(8) NONCOMMERCIAL EDUCATIONAL STATION.—The term "noncommercial educational station" shall be applied to the primary stream or a multicast stream of a television broadcast station that is a noncommercial educational broadcast station as defined in section 397 of the Communications Act of 1934, as in effect on the date of the enactment of the Satellite Television Extension and Localism Act of 2010.

(9) PRIMARY STREAM.—A "primary stream" is—

(A) the single digital stream of programming that, before June 12, 2009, was substantially duplicating the programming transmitted by the television broadcast station as an analog signal; or

(B) if there is no stream described in subparagraph (A), then the single digital stream of programming transmitted by the television broadcast station for the longest period of time.

(10) PRIMARY TRANSMITTER.—A "primary transmitter" is a television or radio broadcast station licensed by the Federal Communications Commission, or by an appropriate governmental authority of Canada or Mexico, that makes primary transmissions to the public.

(11) MULTICAST STREAM.—A "multicast stream" is a digital stream of programming that is transmitted by a television broadcast station and is not the station's primary stream.

(12) SIMULCAST.—A "simulcast" is a multicast stream of a television broadcast station that duplicates the programming transmitted by the primary stream or another multicast stream of such station.

(13) SUBSCRIBER; SUBSCRIBE.—

(A) SUBSCRIBER.—The term "subscriber" means a person or entity that receives a secondary transmission service from a cable system and pays a fee for the service, directly or indirectly, to the cable system.

(B) SUBSCRIBE.—The term "subscribe" means to elect to become a subscriber.

(Pub. L. 94–553, title I, § 101, Oct. 19, 1976, 90 Stat. 2550; Pub. L. 99–397, §§ 1, 2(a), (b), Aug. 27, 1986, 100 Stat. 848; Pub. L. 100–667, title II, § 202(1), Nov. 16, 1988, 102 Stat. 3949; Pub. L. 101–318, § 3(a), July 3, 1990, 104 Stat. 288; Pub. L. 103–198, § 6(a), Dec. 17, 1993, 107 Stat. 2311; Pub. L. 103–369, § 3, Oct. 18, 1994, 108 Stat. 3480; Pub. L. 104–39, § 5(b), Nov. 1, 1995, 109 Stat. 348; Pub. L. 106–113, div. B, § 1000(a)(9) [title I, § 1011(a)(1), (2), (b)(1)], Nov. 29, 1999, 113 Stat. 1536, 1501A–543; Pub. L. 108–419, § 5(a), Nov. 30, 2004, 118 Stat. 2361; Pub. L. 108–447, div. J, title IX [title I, § 107(b)], Dec. 8, 2004, 118 Stat. 3406; Pub. L. 109–303, § 4(a), Oct. 6, 2006, 120 Stat. 1481; Pub. L. 110–229, title VIII, § 807, May 8, 2008, 122 Stat. 874; Pub. L. 110–403, title II, § 209(a)(2), Oct. 13, 2008, 122 Stat. 4264; Pub. L. 111–175, title I, § 104(a)(1), (b), (c), (e), (g), May 27, 2010, 124 Stat. 1231, 1235, 1238.)

HISTORICAL AND REVISION NOTES

HOUSE REPORT NO. 94–1476

Introduction and General Summary. The complex and economically important problem of "secondary transmissions" is considered in section 111. For the most part, the section is directed at the operation of cable television systems and the terms and conditions of their liability for the retransmission of copyrighted works. However, other forms of secondary transmissions are also considered, including apartment house and hotel systems, wired instructional systems, common carriers, nonprofit "boosters" and translators, and secondary transmissions of primary transmissions to controlled groups.

Cable television systems are commercial subscription services that pick up broadcasts of programs originated by others and retransmit them to paying subscribers. A typical system consists of a central antenna which receives and amplifies television signals and a network of cables through which the signals are transmitted to the receiving sets of individual subscribers. In addition to an installation charge, the subscribers pay a monthly charge for the basic service averaging about six dollars. A large number of these systems provide automated programing. A growing number of CATV systems also originate programs, such as movies and sports, and charge additional fees for this service (pay-cable).

The number of cable systems has grown very rapidly since their introduction in 1950, and now total about 3,450 operating systems, servicing 7,700 communities. Systems currently in operation reach about 10.8 million homes. It is reported that the 1975 total subscriber revenues of the cable industry were approximately $770 million.

Pursuant to two decisions of the Supreme Court (*Fortnightly Corp. v. United Artist Television, Inc.*, 392 U.S. 390 (1968) [88 S.Ct. 2084, 20 L.Ed.2d 1176, rehearing denied 89 S.Ct. 65, 393 U.S. 902, 21 L.Ed.2d 190], and *Teleprompter Corp. v. CBS, Inc.*, 415 U.S. 394 (1974)) [94 S.Ct. 1129, 39 L.Ed.2d 415], under the 1909 copyright law, the cable television industry has not been paying copyright royalties for its retransmission of over-the-air broadcast signals. Both decisions urged the Congress, however, to consider and determine the scope and extent of such liability in the pending revision bill.

The difficult problem of determining the copyright liability of cable television systems has been before the Congress since 1965. In 1967, this Committee sought to address and resolve the issues in H.R. 2512, an early version of the general revision bill (see H.R. Rep. No. 83, 90th Cong., 1st Sess.). However, largely because of the cable-copyright impasse, the bill died in the Senate.

The history of the attempts to find a solution to the problem since 1967 has been explored thoroughly in the voluminous hearings and testimony on the general revision bill, and has also been succinctly summarized by the Register of Copyrights in her Second Supplementary Report, Chapter V.

The Committee now has before it the Senate bill which contains a series of detailed and complex provisions which attempt to resolve the question of the copyright liability of cable television systems. After extensive consideration of the Senate bill, the arguments made during and after the hearings, and of the issues involved, this Committee has also concluded that there is no simple answer to the cable-copyright controversy. In particular, any statutory scheme that imposes copyright liability on cable television systems must take account of the intricate and complicated rules and regulations adopted by the Federal Communications Commission to govern the cable television industry. While the Committee has carefully avoided including in the bill any provisions which would interfere with the FCC's rules or which might be characterized as affecting "communications policy", the Committee has been cognizant of the interplay between the copyright and the communications elements of the legislation.

We would, therefore, caution the Federal Communications Commission, and others who make determinations concerning communications policy, not to rely upon any action of this Committee as a basis for any significant changes in the delicate balance of regulation in areas where the Congress has not resolved the issue. Specifically, we would urge the Federal Communications Commission to understand that it was not the intent of this bill to touch on issues such as pay cable regulation or increased use of imported distant signals. These matters are ones of communications policy and should be left to the appropriate committees in the Congress for resolution.

In general, the Committee believes that cable systems are commercial enterprises whose basic retransmission operations are based on the carriage of copyrighted program material and that copyright royalties should be paid by cable operators to the creators of such programs. The Committee recognizes, however, that it would be impractical and unduly burdensome to require every cable system to negotiate with every copyright owner whose work was retransmitted by a cable system. Accordingly, the Committee has determined to maintain the basic principle of the Senate bill to establish a compulsory copyright license for the retransmission of those over-the-air broadcast signals that a cable system is authorized to carry pursuant to the rules and regulations of the FCC.

The compulsory license is conditioned, however, on certain requirements and limitations. These include compliance with reporting requirements, payment of the royalty fees established in the bill, a ban on the substitution or deletion of commercial advertising, and geographic limits on the compulsory license for copyrighted programs broadcast by Canadian or Mexican stations. Failure to comply with these requirements and limitations subjects a cable system to a suit for copyright infringement and the remedies provided under the bill for such actions.

In setting a royalty fee schedule for the compulsory license, the Committee determined that the initial schedule should be established in the bill. It recognized, however, that adjustments to the schedule would be required from time to time. Accordingly, the Copyright Royalty Commission, established in chapter 8 [§ 801 et seq. of this title], is empowered to make the adjustments in the initial rates, at specified times, based on standards and conditions set forth in the bill.

In setting an initial fee schedule, the Senate bill based the royalty fee on a sliding scale related to the gross receipts of a cable system for providing the basic retransmission service and rejected a statutory scheme that would distinguish between "local" and "distant" signals. The Committee determined, however, that there was no evidence that the retransmission of "local" broadcast signals by a cable operator threatens the existing market for copyright program owners. Similarly, the retransmission of network programing, including network programing which is broadcast in "distant" markets, does not injure the copyright

owner. The copyright owner contracts with the network on the basis of his programing reaching all markets served by the network and is compensated accordingly.

By contrast, their retransmission of distant non-network programing by cable systems causes damage to the copyright owner by distributing the program in an area beyond which it has been licensed. Such retransmission adversely affects the ability of the copyright owner to exploit the work in the distant market. It is also of direct benefit to the cable system by enhancing its ability to attract subscribers and increase revenues. For these reasons, the Committee has concluded that the copyright liability of cable television systems under the compulsory license should be limited to the retransmission of distant non-network programing.

In implementing this conclusion, the Committee generally followed a proposal submitted by the cable and motion picture industries, the two industries most directly affected by the establishment of copyright royalties for cable television systems. Under the proposal, the royalty fee is determined by a two step computation. First, a value called a "distant signal equivalent" is assigned to all "distant" signals. Distant signals are defined as signals retransmitted by a cable system, in whole or in part, outside the local service area of the primary transmitter. Different values are assigned to independent, network, and educational stations because of the different amounts of viewing of non-network programing carried by such stations. For example, the viewing of non-network programs on network stations is considered to approximate 25 percent. These values are then combined and a scale of percentages is applied to the cumulative total.

The Committee also considered various proposals to exempt certain categories of cable systems from royalty payments altogether. The Committee determined that the approach of the Senate bill to require some payment by every cable system is sound, but established separate fee schedules for cable systems whose gross receipts for the basic retransmission service do not exceed either $80,000 or $160,000 semiannually. It is the Committee's view that the fee schedules adopted for these systems are now appropriate, based on their relative size and the services performed.

All the royalty payments required under the bill are paid on a semiannual basis to the Register of Copyrights. Each year they are distributed by the Copyright Royalty Commission to those copyright owners who may validly claim that their works were the subject of distant non-network retransmissions by cable systems.

Based on current estimates supplied to the Committee, the total royalty fees paid under the initial schedule established in the bill should approximate $8.7 million. Compared with the present number of cable television subscribers, calculated at 10.8 million, copyright payments under the bill would therefore approximate 81 cents per subscriber per year. The Committee believes that such payments are modest and will not retard the orderly development of the cable television industry or the service it provides to its subscribers.

Analysis of Provisions. Throughout section 111, the operative terms are "primary transmission" and "secondary transmission." These terms are defined in subsection (f) entirely in relation to each other. In any particular case, the "primary" transmitter is the one whose signals are being picked up and further transmitted by a "secondary" transmitter which in turn, is someone engaged in "the further transmitting of a primary transmission simultaneously with the primary transmission." With one exception provided in subsection (f) and limited by subsection (e), the section does not cover or permit a cable system, or indeed any person, to tape or otherwise record a program off-the-air and later to transmit the program from the tape or record to the public. The one exception involves cable systems located outside the continental United States, but not including cable systems in Puerto Rico, or, with limited exceptions, Hawaii. These systems are permitted to record and retransmit programs under the compulsory license, subject to the restrictive conditions of subsection (e), because off-the-air signals are generally not available in the offshore areas.

General Exemptions. Certain secondary transmissions are given a general exemption under clause (1) of section 111(a). The first of these applies to secondary transmissions consisting "entirely of the relaying, by the management of a hotel, apartment house, or similar establishment" of a transmission to the private lodgings of guests or residents and provided "no direct charge is made to see or hear the secondary transmission."

The exemption would not apply if the secondary transmission consists of anything other than the mere relay of ordinary broadcasts. The cutting out of advertising, the running in of new commercials, or any other change in the signal relayed would subject the secondary transmitter to full liability. Moreover, the term "private lodgings" is limited to rooms used as living quarters or for private parties, and does not include dining rooms, meeting halls, theatres, ballrooms, or similar places that are outside of a normal circle of a family and its social acquaintances. No special exception is needed to make clear that the mere placing of an ordinary radio or television set in a private hotel room does not constitute an infringement.

Secondary Transmissions of Instructional Broadcasts. Clause (2) of section 111(a) is intended to make clear that an instructional transmission within the scope of section 110(2) is exempt whether it is a "primary transmission" or a "secondary transmission."

Carriers. The general exemption under section 111 extends to secondary transmitters that act solely as passive carriers. Under clause (3), a carrier is exempt if it "has no direct or indirect control over the content or selection of the primary transmission or over the particular recipients of the secondary transmission." For this purpose its activities must "consist solely of providing wires, cables, or other communications channels for the use of others."

Clause (4) would exempt the activities of secondary transmitters that operate on a completely nonprofit basis. The operations of nonprofit "translators" or "boosters," which do nothing more than amplify broadcast signals and retransmit them to everyone in an area for free reception, would be exempt if there is no "purpose of direct or indirect commercial advantage," and if there is no charge to the recipients "other than assessments necessary to defray the actual and reasonable costs of maintaining and operating the secondary transmission service." This exemption does not apply to a cable television system.

Secondary Transmissions of Primary Transmissions to Controlled Group. Notwithstanding the provisions of subsections (a) and (c), the secondary transmission to the public of a primary transmission embodying a performance or display is actionable as an act of infringement if the primary transmission is not made for reception by the public at large but is controlled and limited to reception by particular members of the public. Examples of transmissions not intended for the general public are background music services such as MUZAK, closed circuit broadcasts to theatres, pay television (STV) or pay-cable.

The Senate bill contains a provision, however, stating that the secondary transmission does not constitute an act of infringement if the carriage of the signals comprising the secondary transmission is required under the rules and regulations of the FCC. The exclusive purpose of this provision is to exempt a cable system from copyright liability if the FCC should require cable systems to carry to their subscribers a "scrambled" pay signal of a subscription television station.

The Committee is concerned, however, that the Senate bill is not clearly limited to the situation where a cable system is required by the FCC to carry a "scrambled" pay television signal. The Committee believes that the provision should not include any authority or permission to "unscramble" the signal. Further, the Senate bill does not make clear that the exception would not apply if the primary transmission is made by a cable system or cable system network transmitting its own originated program, e.g., pay-cable. For these reasons, the subsection was amended to provide that the exception would only apply if (1) the primary transmission to a controlled group is made by a broadcast station licensed by the FCC; (2) the carriage of the signal is required by FCC rules and regulations; and (3) the signal of the primary transmitter is not altered or changed in any way by the secondary transmitter.

Compulsory License. Section 111(c) establishes the compulsory license for cable systems generally. It provides that, subject to the provisions of clauses (2), (3) and (4), the secondary transmission to the public by a cable system of a primary transmission made by a broadcast station licensed by the FCC or by an appropriate governmental authority of Canada or Mexico is subject to compulsory licensing upon compliance with the provisions of subsection (d) where the carriage of the signals comprising the secondary transmission is permissible under the rules and regulations of the FCC. The compulsory license applies, therefore, to the carriage of over-the-air broadcast signals and is inapplicable to the secondary transmission of any nonbroadcast primary transmission such as a program originated by a cable system or a cable network. The latter would be subject to full copyright liability under other sections of the legislation.

Limitations on the Compulsory License. Sections 111(c)(2), (3) and (4) establish limitations on the scope of the compulsory license, and provide that failure to comply with these limitations subjects a cable system to a suit for infringement and all the remedies provided in the legislation for such actions.

Section 111(c)(2) provides that the "willful or repeated" carriage of signals not permissible under the rules and regulations of the FCC subjects a cable system to full copyright liability. The words "willful or repeated" are used to prevent a cable system from being subjected to severe penalties for innocent or casual acts ("Repeated" does not mean merely "more than once," of course; rather, it denotes a degree of aggravated negligence which borders on willfulness. Such a condition would not exist in the case of an innocent mistake as to what signals or programs may properly be carried under the FCC's complicated rules). Section 111(c)(2) also provides that a cable system is subject to full copyright liability where the cable system has not recorded the notice, deposited the statement of account, or paid the royalty fee required by subsection (d). The Committee does not intend, however, that a good faith error by the cable system in computing the amount due would subject it to full liability as an infringer. The Committee expects that in most instances of this type the parties would be able to work out the problem without resort to the courts.

Commercial Substitution. Section 111(c)(3) provides that a cable system is fully subject to the remedies provided in this legislation for copyright infringement if the cable system willfully alters, through changes, deletions, or additions, the content of a particular program or any commercial advertising or station announcements transmitted by the primary transmitter during, or immediately before or after, the transmission of the program. In the Committee's view, any willful deletion, substitution, or insertion of commercial advertisements of any nature by a cable system or changes in the program content of the primary transmission, significantly alters the basic nature of the cable retransmission service, and makes its function similar to that of a broadcaster. Further, the placement of substitute advertising in a program by a cable system on a "local" signal harms the advertiser and, in turn, the copyright owner, whose compensation for the work is directly related to the size of the audience that the advertiser's message is calculated to reach. On a "distant" signal, the placement of substitute advertising harms the local broadcaster in the distant market because the cable system is then competing for local advertising dollars without having comparable program costs. The Committee has therefore attempted broadly to proscribe the availability of the compulsory license if a cable system substitutes commercial messages. Included in the prohibition are commercial messages and station announcements not only during, but also immediately before or after the program, so as to insure a continuous ban on commercial substitution from one program to another. In one situation, however, the Committee has permitted such substitution when the commercials are inserted by those engaged in television commercial advertising market research. This exception is limited to those situations where the research company has obtained the consent of the advertiser who purchased the original commercial advertisement, the television station whose signal is retransmitted, and the cable system, and provided further that no income is derived from the sale of such commercial time.

Canadian and Mexican Signals. Section 111(c)(4) provides limitations on the compulsory license with respect to foreign signals carried by cable systems from Canada or Mexico. Under the Senate bill, the carriage of any foreign signals by a cable system would have been subject to full copyright liability, because the compulsory license was limited to the retransmission of broadcast stations licensed by the FCC. The Committee recognized, however, that cable systems primarily along the northern and southern border have received authorization from the FCC to carry broadcast signals of certain Canadian and Mexican stations.

In the Committee's view, the authorization by the FCC to a cable system to carry a foreign signal does not resolve the copyright question of the royalty payment that should be made for copyrighted programs originating in the foreign country. The latter raises important international questions of the protection to be accorded foreign copyrighted works in the United States. While the Committee has established a general compulsory licensing scheme for the retransmission of copyrighted works of U.S. nationals, a broad compulsory license scheme for all foreign works does not appear warranted or justified. Thus, for example, if in the future the signal of a British, French, or Japanese station were retransmitted in the United States by a cable system, full copyright liability would apply.

With respect to Canadian and Mexican signals, the Committee found that a special situation exists regarding the carriage of these signals by U.S. cable systems on the northern and southern borders, respectively. The Committee determined, therefore, that with respect to Canadian signals the compulsory license would apply in an area located 150 miles from the U.S.-Canadian border, or south from the border to the 42nd parallel of latitude, whichever distance is greater. Thus the cities of Detroit, Pittsburgh, Cleveland, Green Bay and Seattle would be included within the compulsory license area, while cities such as New York, Philadelphia, Chicago, and San Francisco would be located outside the area.

With respect to Mexican signals, the Commission determined that the compulsory license would apply only in the area in which such signals may be received by a U.S. cable system by means of direct interception of a free space radio wave. Thus, full copyright liability would apply if a cable system were required to use any equipment or device other than a receiving antenna to bring the signal to the community of the cable system.

Further, to take account of those cable systems that are presently carrying or are specifically authorized to carry Canadian or Mexican signals, pursuant to FCC rules and regulations, and whether or not within the zones established, the Committee determined to grant a compulsory license for the carriage of those specific signals on those cable systems as in effect on April 15, 1976.

The Committee wishes to stress that cable systems operating within these zones are fully subject to the payment of royalty fees under the compulsory license for those foreign signals retransmitted. The copyright owners of the works transmitted may appear before the Copyright Royalty Commission and, pursuant to the provisions of this legislation, file claims to their fair share of the royalties collected. Outside the zones, however, full copyright liability would apply as would all the remedies of the legislation for any act of infringement.

Requirements for a Compulsory License. The compulsory license provided for in section 111(c) is contingent upon fulfillment of the requirements set forth in section 111(d). Subsection (d)(1) directs that at least one month before the commencement of operations, or within 180 days after the enactment of this act [Oct. 19, 1976], whichever is later, a cable system must record in the Copyright Office a notice, including a statement giving the identity and address of the person who owns or operates the secondary transmission service or who has power to exercise primary control over it, together with the name and location of the primary transmitter whose signals are regularly carried by the cable system. Signals "regularly carried" by the system mean those signals which the Federal Communications Commission has specifically authorized the cable system to carry, and which are actually carried by the system on a regular basis. It is also required that whenever the ownership or control or regular signal carriage complement of the system changes, the cable system must within 30 days record any such changes in the Copyright Office. Cable systems must also record such further information as the Register of Copyrights shall prescribe by regulation.

Subsection (d)(2) directs cable systems whose secondary transmissions have been subject to compulsory licensing under subsection (c) to deposit with the Register of Copyrights a semi-annual statement of account. The dates for filing such statements of account and the six-month period which they are to cover are to be determined by the Register of Copyrights after consultation with the Copyright Royalty Commission. In addition to other such information that the Register may prescribe by regulation, the statements of account are to specify the number of channels on which the cable system made secondary transmissions to its subscribers, the names and locations of all primary transmitters whose transmissions were carried by the system, the total number of subscribers to the system, and the gross amounts paid to the system for the basic service of providing secondary transmissions. If any non-network television programming was retransmitted by the cable system beyond the local service area of the primary transmitter, pursuant to the rules of the Federal Communications Commission, which under certain circumstances permit the substitution or addition of television signals not regularly carried, the cable system must deposit a special statement of account listing the times, dates, stations and programs involved in such substituted or added carriage.

Copyright Royalty Payments. Subsection (d)(2)(B), (C) and (D) require cable systems to deposit royalty fee payments for the period covered by the statements of account. These payments are to be computed on the basis of specified percentages of the gross receipts from cable subscribers during the period covered by the statement. For purposes of computing royalty payments, only receipts for the basic service of providing secondary transmissions of primary broadcast transmitters are to be considered. Other receipts from subscribers, such as those for pay-cable services or installation charges, are not included in gross receipts.

Subsection (d)(2)(B) provides that, except in the case of a cable system that comes within the gross receipts limitations of subclauses (C) and (D), the royalty fee is computed in the following manner:

Every cable system pays .675 of 1 percent of its gross receipts for the privilege of retransmitting distant non-network programming, such amount to be applied against the fee, if any, payable under the computation for "distant signal equivalents." The latter are determined by adding together the values assigned to the actual number of distant television stations carried by a cable system. The purpose of this initial rate, applicable to all cable systems in this class, is to establish a basic payment, whether or not a particular cable system elects to transmit distant non-network programming. It is not a payment for the retransmission of purely "local" signals, as is evident from the provision that it applies to and is deductible from the fee payable for any "distant signal equivalents."

The remaining provisions of subclause (B) establish the following rates for "distant signal equivalents:"

The rate from zero to one distant signal equivalent is .675 of 1 percent of gross subscriber revenues. An additional .425 of 1 percent of gross subscriber revenues is to be paid for each of the second, third and fourth distant signal equivalents that are carried. A further payment of .2 of 1 percent of gross subscriber revenues is to be made for each distant signal equivalent after the fourth. Any fraction of a distant signal equivalent is to be computed at its fractional value and where a cable system is located partly within and partly without the local service area of a primary transmitter, the gross receipts subject to the percentage payment are limited to those gross receipts derived from subscribers located without the local service area of such primary transmitter.

Pursuant to the foregoing formula, copyright payments as a percentage of gross receipts increase as the number of distant television signals carried by a cable system increases. Because many smaller cable systems carry a large number of distant signals, especially those located in areas where over-the-air television service is sparse, and because smaller cable systems may be less able to shoulder the burden of copyright payments than larger systems, the Committee decided to give special consideration to cable systems with semi-annual gross subscriber receipts of less than $160,000 ($320,000 annually). The royalty fee schedules for cable systems in this category are specified in subclauses (C) and (D).

In lieu of the payments required in subclause (B), systems earning less than $80,000, semi-annually, are to pay a royalty fee of .5 of 1 percent of gross receipts. Gross receipts under this provision are computed, however, by subtracting from actual gross receipts collected during the payment period the amount by which $80,000 exceeds such actual gross receipts. Thus, if the actual gross receipts of the cable system for the period covered are $60,000, the fee is determined by subtracting $20,000 (the amount by which $80,000 exceeds actual gross receipts) from $60,000 and applying .5 of 1 percent to the $40,000 result. However, gross receipts in no case are to be reduced to less than $3,000.

Under subclause (D), cable systems with semi-annual gross subscriber receipts of between $80,000 and $160,000 are to pay royalty fees of .5 of 1 percent of such actual gross receipts up to $80,000, and 1 percent of any actual gross receipts in excess of $80,000. The royalty fee payments under both subclauses (C) and (D) are to be determined without regard to the number of distant signal equivalents, if any, carried by the subject cable systems.

Copyright Royalty Distribution. Section 111(d)(3) provides that the royalty fees paid by cable systems under the compulsory license shall be received by the Register of Copyrights and, after deducting the reasonable costs incurred by the Copyright Office, deposited in the Treasury of the United States. The fees are distributed subsequently, pursuant to the determination of the Copyright Royalty Commission under chapter 8 [§ 801 et seq. of this title].

The copyright owners entitled to participate in the distribution of the royalty fees paid by cable systems under the compulsory license are specified in section 111(d)(4). Consistent with the Committee's view that copyright royalty fees should be made only for the retransmission of distant non-network programming, the claimants are limited to (1) copyright owners whose works were included in a secondary transmission made by a cable system of a distant non-network television program; (2) any copyright owner whose work is included in a secondary transmission identified in a spe-

cial statement of account deposited under section 111(d)(2)(A); and (3) any copyright owner whose work was included in distant non-network programming consisting exclusively of aural signals. Thus, no royalty fees may be claimed or distributed to copyright owners for the retransmission of either "local" or "network" programs.

The Committee recognizes that the bill does not include specific provisions to guide the Copyright Royalty Commission in determining the appropriate division among competing copyright owners of the royalty fees collected from cable systems under Section 111. The Committee concluded that it would not be appropriate to specify particular, limiting standards for distribution. Rather, the Committee believes that the Copyright Royalty Commission should consider all pertinent data and considerations presented by the claimants.

Should disputes arise, however, between the different classes of copyright claimants, the Committee believes that the Copyright Royalty Commission should consider that with respect to the copyright owners of "live" programs identified by the special statement of account deposited under Section 111(d)(2)(A), a special payment is provided in Section 111(f).

Section 111(d)(5) sets forth the procedure for the distribution of the royalty fees paid by cable systems. During the month of July of each year, every person claiming to be entitled to compulsory license fees must file a claim with the Copyright Royalty Commission, in accordance with such provisions as the Commission shall establish. In particular, the Commission may establish the relevant period covered by such claims after giving adequate time for copyright owners to review and consider the statements of account filed by cable systems. Notwithstanding any provisions of the antitrust laws, the claimants may agree among themselves as to the division and distribution of such fees. After the first day of August of each year, the Copyright Royalty Commission shall determine whether a controversy exists concerning the distribution of royalty fees. If no controversy exists, the Commission, after deducting its reasonable administrative costs, shall distribute the fees to the copyright owners entitled or their agents. If the Commission finds the existence of a controversy, it shall, pursuant to the provisions of chapter 8 [§ 801 et seq. of this title], conduct a proceeding to determine the distribution of royalty fees.

Off-Shore Taping by Cable Systems. Section 111(e) establishes the conditions and limitation upon which certain cable systems located outside the continental United States, and specified in subsection (f), may make tapes of copyrighted programs and retransmit the taped programs to their subscribers upon payment of the compulsory license fee. These conditions and limitations include compliance with detailed transmission, record keeping, and other requirements. Their purpose is to control carefully the use of any tapes made pursuant to the limited recording and retransmission authority established in subsection (f), and to insure that the limited objective of assimilating off-shore cable systems to systems within the United States for purposes of the compulsory license is not exceeded. Any secondary transmission by a cable system entitled to the benefits of the taping authorization that does not comply with the requirements of section 111(e) is an act of infringement and is fully subject to all the remedies provided in the legislation for such actions.

Definitions. Section 111(f) contains a series of definitions. These definitions are found in subsection (f) rather than in section 101 because of their particular application to secondary transmissions by cable systems.

Primary and Secondary Transmissions. The definitions of "primary transmission" and "secondary transmission" have been discussed above. The definition of "secondary transmission" also contains a provision permitting the nonsimultaneous retransmission of a primary transmission if by a cable system "not located in whole or in part within the boundary of the forty-eight contiguous states, Hawaii or Puerto Rico." Under a proviso, however, a cable system in Hawaii may make a nonsimultaneous retransmission of a primary transmission if the carriage of the television broadcast signal comprising such further transmission is permissible under the rules, regulations or authorizations of the FCC.

The effect of this definition is to permit certain cable systems in offshore areas, but not including cable systems in the offshore area of Puerto Rico and to a limited extent only in Hawaii, to tape programs and retransmit them to subscribers under the compulsory license. Puerto Rico was excluded based upon a communication the Committee received from the Governor of Puerto Rico stating that the particular television broadcasting problems which the definition seeks to solve for cable systems in other noncontiguous areas do not exist in Puerto Rico. He therefore requested that Puerto Rico be excluded from the scope of the definition. All cable systems covered by the definition are subject to the conditions and limitations for non-simultaneous transmissions established in section 111(e).

Cable System. The definition of a "cable system" establishes that it is a facility that in whole or in part receives signals of one or more television broadcast stations licensed by the FCC and makes secondary transmissions of such signals to subscribing members of the public who pay for such service. A closed circuit wire system that only originates programs and does not carry television broadcast signals would not come within the definition. Further, the definition provides that, in determining the applicable royalty fee and system classification under subsection (d)(2)(B), (C), or (D) cable systems in contiguous communities under common ownership or control or operating from one head-end are considered as one system.

Local Service Area of a Primary Transmitter. The definition of "local service area of a primary transmitter" establishes the difference between "local" and "distant" signals and therefore the line between signals which are subject to payment under the compulsory license and those that are not. It provides that the local service area of a television broadcast station is the area in which the station is entitled to insist upon its signal being retransmitted by a cable system pursuant to FCC rules and regulations. Under FCC rules and regulations this so-called "must carry" area is defined based on the market size and position of cable systems in 47 C.F.R. §§ 76.57, 76.59, 76.61 and 76.63. The definition is limited, however, to the FCC rules in effect on April 15, 1976. The purpose of this limitation is to insure that any subsequent rule amendments by the FCC that either increase or decrease the size of the local service area for its purposes do not change the definition for copyright purposes. The Committee believes that any such change for copyright purposes, which would materially affect the royalty fee payments provided in the legislation, should only be made by an amendment to the statute.

The "local service area of a primary transmitter" of a Canadian or Mexican television station is defined as the area in which such station would be entitled to insist upon its signals being retransmitted if it were a television broadcast station subject to FCC rules and regulations. Since the FCC does not permit a television station licensed in a foreign country to assert a claim to carriage by a U.S. cable system, the local service area of such foreign station is considered to be the same area as if it were a U.S. station.

The local service area for a radio broadcast station is defined to mean "the primary service area of such station pursuant to the rules and regulations of the Federal Communications Commission." The term "primary service area" is defined precisely by the FCC with regard to AM stations in Section 73.11(a) of the FCC's rules. In the case of FM stations, "primary service area" is regarded by the FCC as the area included within the field strength contours specified in Section 73.311 of its rules.

Distant Signal Equivalent. The definition of a "distant signal equivalent" is central to the computation of the royalty fees payable under the compulsory license. It is the value assigned to the secondary transmission of any non-network television programming carried by a cable system, in whole or in part, beyond the local service area of the primary transmitter of such programming. It is computed by assigning a value of one (1) to each distant independent station and a value of one-quarter (¼) to each distant network station and distant noncommercial educational station carried by a cable system, pursuant to the rules and regulations of the FCC. Thus, a cable system carrying two distant independent stations, two distant network stations and one distant noncommercial educational station would have a total of 2.75 distant signal equivalents.

The values assigned to independent, network and noncommercial educational stations are subject, however, to certain exceptions and limitations. Two of these relate to the mandatory and discretionary program deletion and substitution rules of the FCC. Where the FCC rules require a cable system to omit certain programs (e.g., the syndicated program exclusivity rules) and also permit the substitution of another program in place of the omitted program, no additional value is assigned for the substituted or additional program. Further, where the FCC rules on the date of enactment of this legislation permit a cable system, at its discretion, to make such deletions or substitutions or to carry additional programs not transmitted by primary transmitters within whose local service area the cable system is located, no additional value is assigned for the substituted or additional programs. However, the latter discretionary exception is subject to a condition that if the substituted or additional program is a "live" program (e.g., a sports event), then an additional value is assigned to the carriage of the distant signal computed as a fraction of one distant signal equivalent. The fraction is determined by assigning to the numerator the number of days in the year on which the "live" substitution occurs, and by assigning to the denominator the number of days in the year. Further, the discretionary exception is limited to those FCC rules in effect on the date of enactment of this legislation [Oct. 19, 1976]. If subsequent FCC rule amendments or individual authorizations enlarge the discretionary ability of cable systems to delete and substitute programs, such deletions and substitutions would be counted at the full value assigned the particular type of station provided above.

Two further exceptions pertain to the late-night or specialty programming rules of the FCC or to a station carried on a part-time basis where full-time carriage is not possible because the cable system lacks the activated channel capacity to retransmit on a full-time basis all signals which it is authorized to carry. In this event, the values for independent, network and non-commercial, educational stations set forth above, as the case may be, are determined by multiplying each by a fraction which is equal to the ratio of the broadcast hours of such station carried by the cable system to the total broadcast hours of the station.

Network Station. A "network station" is defined as a television broadcast station that is owned or operated by, or affiliated with, one or more of the U.S. television networks providing nationwide transmissions and that transmits a substantial part of the programming supplied by such networks for a substantial part of that station's typical broadcast day. To qualify as a network station, all the conditions of the definition must be met. Thus, the retransmission of a Canadian station affiliated with a Canadian network would not qualify under the definition. Further, a station affiliated with a regional network would not qualify, since a regional network would not provide nationwide transmissions. However, a station affiliated with a network providing nationwide transmissions that also occasionally carries regional programs would qualify as a "network station," if the station transmits a substantial part of the programming supplied by the network for a substantial part of the station's typical broadcast day.

Independent Station. An "independent station" is defined as a commercial television broadcast station other than a network station. Any commercial station that does not fall within the definition of "network station" is classified as an "independent station."

Noncommercial Educational Station. A "noncommercial educational station" is defined as a television station that is a noncommercial educational broadcast station within the meaning of section 397 of title 47 [47 U.S.C. 397].

REFERENCES IN TEXT

The date of the enactment of the Satellite Television Extension and Localism Act of 2010, referred to in subsecs. (d)(1)(D), (5) and (f)(8), is the date of the enactment of Pub. L. 111–175, which shall be deemed to refer to Feb. 27, 2010, see section 307(a) of Pub. L. 111–175, set out as an Effective Date of 2010 Amendment note below.

The date of the enactment of the Copyright Act of 1976, referred to in subsec. (f)(5)(B)(i), (ii), probably means the date of the enactment of Pub. L. 94–553, which was approved Oct. 19, 1976.

Section 397 of the Communications Act of 1934, referred to in subsec. (f)(8), is classified to section 397 of Title 47, Telegraphs, Telephones, and Radiotelegraphs.

AMENDMENTS

2010—Pub. L. 111–175, §104(a)(1), inserted "of broadcast programming by cable" after "transmissions" in section catchline.

Subsec. (a)(2), (3). Pub. L. 111–175, §104(g)(1)(A), substituted "paragraph" for "clause".

Subsec. (a)(4). Pub. L. 111–175, §104(b), substituted "or section 122;" for "; or".

Subsec. (c)(1). Pub. L. 111–175, §104(g)(1)(B), substituted "paragraphs" for "clauses".

Subsec. (c)(2) to (4). Pub. L. 111–175, §104(g)(1)(A), substituted "paragraph" for "clause".

Subsec. (d)(1). Pub. L. 111–175, §104(c)(1)(A), inserted heading and, in introductory provisions, substituted "Subject to paragraph (5), a cable system whose secondary" for "A cable system whose secondary" and "by regulation the following:" for "by regulation—".

Subsec. (d)(1)(A). Pub. L. 111–175, §104(c)(1)(B), (g)(2), substituted "A statement of account" for "a statement of account", "non-network" for "nonnetwork", and "carriage." for "carriage; and" at end.

Subsec. (d)(1)(B) to (G). Pub. L. 111–175, §104(c)(1)(C), added subpars. (B) to (G) and struck out former subpars. (B) to (D) which established fee schedules for certain royalty fees to be paid by cable systems based upon the gross receipts received from subscribers.

Subsec. (d)(2). Pub. L. 111–175, §104(c)(2), inserted heading and inserted "(including the filing fee specified in paragraph (1)(G))" after "shall receive all fees".

Subsec. (d)(3). Pub. L. 111–175, §104(c)(3)(A), inserted heading.

Subsec. (d)(3)(A). Pub. L. 111–175, §104(c)(3)(B), (g)(2), substituted "Any such" for "any such", "non-network" for "nonnetwork", and a period for "; and".

Subsec. (d)(3)(B). Pub. L. 111–175, §104(c)(3)(C), substituted "Any such" for "any such" and a period for the semicolon at end.

Subsec. (d)(3)(C). Pub. L. 111–175, §104(c)(3)(D), (g)(2), substituted "Any such" for "any such" and "non-network" for "nonnetwork".

Subsec. (d)(4). Pub. L. 111–175, §104(c)(4), inserted heading.

Subsec. (d)(5) to (7). Pub. L. 111–175, §104(c)(5), added pars. (5) to (7).

Subsec. (e)(1). Pub. L. 111–175, §104(g)(3), substituted "subsection (f)(2)" for "second paragraph of subsection (f)" in introductory provisions.

Subsec. (e)(1)(A) to (C). Pub. L. 111–175, §104(g)(4)(A)–(C), struck out "and" at end.

Subsec. (e)(1)(C)(iv). Pub. L. 111–175, §104(g)(1)(A), substituted "paragraph" for "clause".

Subsec. (e)(1)(D). Pub. L. 111–175, §104(g)(4)(D), struck out "and" at end.

Subsec. (e)(1)(D)(ii), (E). Pub. L. 111–175, §104(g)(1)(A), substituted "paragraph" for "clause".

Subsec. (e)(1)(F). Pub. L. 111–175, §104(g)(1)(C), substituted "subparagraph" for "subclause".

Subsec. (e)(2). Pub. L. 111–175, §104(g)(1)(A), (6), in introductory provisions, substituted "paragraph" for "clause" and "five entities" for "three territories".

Subsec. (e)(2)(A). Pub. L. 111–175, §104(g)(4)(E), struck out "and" at end.

Subsec. (e)(2)(B), (C). Pub. L. 111–175, §104(g)(1)(A), substituted "paragraph" for "clause".

Subsec. (e)(4). Pub. L. 111–175, §104(g)(5)(A), struck out ", and each of its variant forms," before "means the reproduction".

Subsec. (f). Pub. L. 111–175, §104(g)(5)(B), struck out "and their variant forms" after "terms" in introductory provisions.

Pub. L. 111–175, §104(e)(5) to (8), designated undesignated par. which defined "distant signal equivalent" as par. (5), inserted par. (5) heading, and amended text generally, added pars. (6) to (8), and struck out last three undesignated pars. which defined "network station", "independent station", and "noncommercial educational station", respectively.

Pub. L. 111–175, §104(e)(4)(C), which directed amendment of "the fourth undesignated paragraph, in the first sentence" by striking out "as defined by the rules and regulations of the Federal Communications Commission,", was executed by striking out such phrase after "television station," in the second sentence of par. (4), to reflect the probable intent of Congress.

Pub. L. 111–175, §104(e)(1) to (4)(B), added par. (1) and struck out first undesignated par. which defined "primary transmission", designated second undesignated par. as par. (2), inserted par. (2) heading, and substituted "a cable system" for "a 'cable system'", designated third undesignated par. as par. (3), inserted par. (3) heading, and substituted "territory, trust territory, or possession of the United States" for "Territory, Trust Territory, or Possession", and designated fourth undesignated par. as par. (4), inserted par. (4) heading, and substituted "The 'local service area of a primary transmitter', in the case of both the primary stream and any multicast streams transmitted by a primary transmitter that is a television broadcast station, comprises the area where such primary transmitter could have insisted" for "The 'local service area of a primary transmitter', in the case of a television broadcast station, comprises the area in which such station is entitled to insist" and "76.59 of title 47, Code of Federal Regulations, or within the noise-limited contour as defined in 73.622(e)(1) of title 47, Code of Federal Regulations" for "76.59 of title 47 of the Code of Federal Regulations".

Subsec. (f)(9) to (13). Pub. L. 111–175, §104(e)(9), added pars. (9) to (13).

2008—Subsec. (b). Pub. L. 110–403, §209(a)(2)(A), struck out "and 509" after "506" in introductory provisions.

Subsec. (c)(2). Pub. L. 110–403, §209(a)(2)(B)(i), struck out "and 509" after "506" in introductory provisions.

Subsec. (c)(3). Pub. L. 110–403, §209(a)(2)(B)(ii), substituted "section 510" for "sections 509 and 510".

Subsec. (c)(4). Pub. L. 110–403, §209(a)(2)(B)(iii), struck out "and section 509" after "506".

Subsec. (e)(1). Pub. L. 110–403, §209(a)(2)(C)(i), substituted "section 510" for "sections 509 and 510" in introductory provisions.

Subsec. (e)(2). Pub. L. 110–403, §209(a)(2)(C)(ii), struck out "and 509" after "506" in introductory provisions.

Pub. L. 110–229 substituted "the Federated States of Micronesia, the Republic of Palau, or the Republic of the Marshall Islands" for "or the Trust Territory of the Pacific Islands" in introductory provisions.

2006—Subsec. (d)(2). Pub. L. 109–303, §4(a)(1), substituted "upon authorization by the Copyright Royalty Judges." for "in the event no controversy over distribution exists, or by the Copyright Royalty Judges. in the event a controversy over such distribution exists."

Subsec. (d)(4)(B). Pub. L. 109–303, §4(a)(2)(A), substituted second sentence for former second sentence which read as follows: "If the Copyright Royalty

Judges determine that no such controversy exists, the Librarian shall, after deducting reasonable administrative costs under this section, distribute such fees to the copyright owners entitled to such fees, or to their designated agents." and "find" for "finds" in last sentence.

Subsec. (d)(4)(C). Pub. L. 109–303, §4(a)(2)(B), added subpar. (C) and struck out former subpar. (C) which read as follows: "During the pendency of any proceeding under this subsection, the Copyright Royalty Judges shall withhold from distribution an amount sufficient to satisfy all claims with respect to which a controversy exists, but shall have discretion to proceed to distribute any amounts that are not in controversy."

2004—Subsec. (a)(4). Pub. L. 108–447 struck out "for private home viewing" after "satellite carrier".

Subsec. (d)(1)(A). Pub. L. 108–447 struck out "for private home viewing" after "secondary transmissions".

Subsec. (d)(2). Pub. L. 108–419, §5(a)(1), substituted "the Copyright Royalty Judges." for "a copyright arbitration royalty panel".

Subsec. (d)(4)(A). Pub. L. 108–419, §5(a)(2)(A), substituted "Copyright Royalty Judges" for "Librarian of Congress" in two places.

Subsec. (d)(4)(B). Pub. L. 108–419, §5(a)(2)(B), substituted, in first sentence, "Copyright Royalty Judges shall" for "Librarian of Congress shall, upon the recommendation of the Register of Copyrights,", in second sentence, "Copyright Royalty Judges determine" for "Librarian determines", and, in third sentence, "Copyright Royalty Judges" for "Librarian" in two places and "conduct a proceeding" for "convene a copyright arbitration royalty panel".

Subsec. (d)(4)(C). Pub. L. 108–419, §5(a)(2)(C), substituted "Copyright Royalty Judges" for "Librarian of Congress".

1999—Subsecs. (a), (b). Pub. L. 106–113, §1000(a)(9) [title I, §1011(b)(1)(A), (B)], substituted "performance or display of a work embodied in a primary transmission" for "primary transmission embodying a performance or display of a work" in introductory provisions.

Subsec. (c)(1). Pub. L. 106–113, §1000(a)(9) [title I, §1011(a)(2), (b)(1)(C)(i)], inserted "a performance or display of a work embodied in" after "by a cable system of", struck out "and embodying a performance or display of a work" after "governmental authority of Canada or Mexico", and substituted "statutory" for "compulsory".

Subsec. (c)(3), (4). Pub. L. 106–113, §1000(a)(9) [title I, §1011(b)(1)(C)(ii)], substituted "a performance or display of a work embodied in a primary transmission" for "a primary transmission" and struck out "and embodying a performance or display of a work" after "governmental authority of Canada or Mexico".

Subsec. (d). Pub. L. 106–113, §1000(a)(9) [title I, §1011(a)(2)], which directed substitution of "statutory" for "compulsory", was executed by substituting "Statutory" for "Compulsory" in heading to reflect probable intent of Congress.

Subsec. (d)(1). Pub. L. 106–113, §1000(a)(9) [title I, §1011(a)(2)], substituted "statutory" for "compulsory" in introductory provisions.

Subsec. (d)(1)(B)(i), (3)(C). Pub. L. 106–113, §1000(a)(9) [title I, §1011(a)(1)], substituted "programming" for "programing".

Subsec. (d)(4)(A). Pub. L. 106–113, §1000(a)(9) [title I, §1011(a)(2)], substituted "statutory" for "compulsory" in two places.

Subsec. (f). Pub. L. 106–113, §1000(a)(9) [title I, §1011(a)(1)], substituted "programming" for "programing" wherever appearing.

1995—Subsec. (c)(1). Pub. L. 104–39 inserted "and section 114(d)" after "of this subsection".

1994—Subsec. (f). Pub. L. 103–369, §3(b), in fourth undesignated par. defining local service area of a primary transmitter, inserted "or such station's television market as defined in section 76.55(e) of title 47, Code of Federal Regulations (as in effect on September 18, 1993), or any modifications to such television market made, on or after September 18, 1993, pursuant to section 76.55(e) or 76.59 of title 47 of the Code of Federal Regulations," after "April 15, 1976,".

Pub. L. 103–369, §3(a), inserted "microwave," after "wires, cables," in third undesignated par., defining cable system.

1993—Subsec. (d)(1). Pub. L. 103–198, §6(a)(1), struck out ", after consultation with the Copyright Royalty Tribunal (if and when the Tribunal has been constituted)," after "Register shall" in introductory provisions.

Subsec. (d)(1)(A). Pub. L. 103–198, §6(a)(2), struck out ", after consultation with the Copyright Royalty Tribunal (if and when the Tribunal has been constituted)," after "Register of Copyrights may".

Subsec. (d)(2). Pub. L. 103–198, §6(a)(3), substituted "All funds held by the Secretary of the Treasury shall be invested in interest-bearing United States securities for later distribution with interest by the Librarian of Congress in the event no controversy over distribution exists, or by a copyright arbitration royalty panel in the event a controversy over such distribution exists." for "All funds held by the Secretary of the Treasury shall be invested in interest-bearing United States securities for later distribution with interest by the Copyright Royalty Tribunal as provided by this title. The Register shall submit to the Copyright Royalty Tribunal, on a semiannual basis, a compilation of all statements of account covering the relevant six-month period provided by clause (1) of this subsection."

Subsec. (d)(4)(A). Pub. L. 103–198, §6(a)(4), substituted "Librarian of Congress" for "Copyright Royalty Tribunal" before "claim with the" and for "Tribunal" before "requirements that the".

Subsec. (d)(4)(B). Pub. L. 103–198, §6(a)(5), amended subpar. (B) generally. Prior to amendment, subpar. (B) read as follows: "After the first day of August of each year, the Copyright Royalty Tribunal shall determine whether there exists a controversy concerning the distribution of royalty fees. If the Tribunal determines that no such controversy exists, it shall, after deducting its reasonable administrative costs under this section, distribute such fees to the copyright owners entitled, or to their designated agents. If the Tribunal finds the existence of a controversy, it shall, pursuant to chapter 8 of this title, conduct a proceeding to determine the distribution of royalty fees."

Subsec. (d)(4)(C). Pub. L. 103–198, §6(a)(6), substituted "Librarian of Congress" for "Copyright Royalty Tribunal".

1990—Subsec. (c)(2)(B). Pub. L. 101–318, §3(a)(1), struck out "recorded the notice specified by subsection (d) and" after "where the cable system has not".

Subsec. (d)(2). Pub. L. 101–318, §3(a)(2)(A), substituted "clause (1)" for "paragraph (1)".

Subsec. (d)(3). Pub. L. 101–318, §3(a)(2)(B), substituted "clause (4)" for "clause (5)" in introductory provisions.

Subsec. (d)(3)(B). Pub. L. 101–318, §3(a)(2)(C), substituted "clause (1)(A)" for "clause (2)(A)".

1988—Subsec. (a)(4), (5). Pub. L. 100–667, §202(1)(A), added par. (4) and redesignated former par. (4) as (5).

Subsec. (d)(1)(A). Pub. L. 100–667, §202(1)(B), inserted provision that determination of total number of subscribers and gross amounts paid to cable system for basic service of providing secondary transmissions of primary broadcast transmitters not include subscribers and amounts collected from subscribers receiving secondary transmissions for private home viewing under section 119.

1986—Subsec. (d). Pub. L. 99–397, §2(a)(1), (4), (5), substituted "paragraph (1)" for "clause (2)" in par. (3), struck out par. (1) which related to recordation of notice with Copyright Office by cable systems in order for secondary transmissions to be subject to compulsory licensing, and redesignated pars. (2) to (5) as (1) to (4), respectively.

Pub. L. 99–397, §2(a)(2), (3), which directed the amendment of subsec. (d) by substituting "paragraph (4)" for "clause (5)" in pars. (2) and (2)(B) could not be executed because pars. (2) and (2)(B) did not contain references to "clause (5)". See 1990 Amendment note above.

Subsec. (f). Pub. L. 99–397, §2(b), substituted "subsection (d)(1)" for "subsection (d)(2)" in third undesignated par., defining a cable system.

Pub. L. 99–397, §1, inserted provision in fourth undesignated par., defining "local service area of a primary transmitter", to cover that term in relation to low power television stations.

EFFECTIVE DATE OF 2010 AMENDMENT

Pub. L. 111–175, title I, §104(d), May 27, 2010, 124 Stat. 1235, provided that: "The royalty fee rates established in section 111(d)(1)(B) of title 17, United States Code, as amended by subsection (c)(1)(C) of this section, shall take effect commencing with the first accounting period occurring in 2010."

Pub. L. 111–175, title I, §104(h), May 27, 2010, 124 Stat. 1238, provided that:

"(1) IN GENERAL.—Subject to paragraphs (2) and (3), the amendments made by this section [amending this section and section 804 of this title], to the extent such amendments assign a distant signal equivalent value to the secondary transmission of the multicast stream of a primary transmitter, shall take effect on the date of the enactment of this Act [deemed to refer to Feb. 27, 2010, see section 307(a) of Pub. L. 111–175, set out as a note below].

"(2) DELAYED APPLICABILITY.—

"(A) SECONDARY TRANSMISSIONS OF A MULTICAST STREAM BEYOND THE LOCAL SERVICE AREA OF ITS PRIMARY TRANSMITTER BEFORE 2010 ACT.—In any case in which a cable system was making secondary transmissions of a multicast stream beyond the local service area of its primary transmitter before the date of the enactment of this Act, a distant signal equivalent value (referred to in paragraph (1)) shall not be assigned to secondary transmissions of such multicast stream that are made on or before June 30, 2010.

"(B) MULTICAST STREAMS SUBJECT TO PREEXISTING WRITTEN AGREEMENTS FOR THE SECONDARY TRANSMISSION OF SUCH STREAMS.—In any case in which the secondary transmission of a multicast stream of a primary transmitter is the subject of a written agreement entered into on or before June 30, 2009, between a cable system or an association representing the cable system and a primary transmitter or an association representing the primary transmitter, a distant signal equivalent value (referred to in paragraph (1)) shall not be assigned to secondary transmissions of such multicast stream beyond the local service area of its primary transmitter that are made on or before the date on which such written agreement expires.

"(C) NO REFUNDS OR OFFSETS FOR PRIOR STATEMENTS OF ACCOUNT.—A cable system that has reported secondary transmissions of a multicast stream beyond the local service area of its primary transmitter on a statement of account deposited under section 111 of title 17, United States Code, before the date of the enactment of this Act shall not be entitled to any refund, or offset, of royalty fees paid on account of such secondary transmissions of such multicast stream.

"(3) DEFINITIONS.—In this subsection, the terms 'cable system', 'secondary transmission', 'multicast stream', and 'local service area of a primary transmitter' have the meanings given those terms in section 111(f) of title 17, United States Code, as amended by this section."

Pub. L. 111–175, title III, §307, May 27, 2010, 124 Stat. 1257, provided that:

"(a) EFFECTIVE DATE.—Unless specifically provided otherwise, this Act [see Short Title of 2010 Amendment note set out under section 101 of this title], and the amendments made by this Act, shall take effect on February 27, 2010, and with the exception of the reference in subsection (b), all references to the date of enactment of this Act shall be deemed to refer to February 27, 2010, unless otherwise specified.

"(b) NONINFRINGEMENT OF COPYRIGHT.—The secondary transmission of a performance or display of a work embodied in a primary transmission is not an infringement of copyright if it was made by a satellite carrier on or after February 27, 2010, and prior to enactment of this Act [May 27, 2010], and was in compliance with the law as in existence on February 27, 2010."

EFFECTIVE DATE OF 2006 AMENDMENT

Pub. L. 109–303, §6, Oct. 6, 2006, 120 Stat. 1483, provided that:

"(a) IN GENERAL.—Except as provided under subsection (b), this Act [see Short Title of 2006 Amendment note set out under section 101 of this title] and the amendments made by this Act shall be effective as if included in the Copyright Royalty and Distribution Reform Act of 2004 [Pub. L. 108–419].

"(b) PARTIAL DISTRIBUTION OF ROYALTY FEES.—Section 5 [amending section 801 of this title] shall take effect on the date of enactment of this Act [Oct. 6, 2006]."

EFFECTIVE DATE OF 2004 AMENDMENT

Amendment by Pub. L. 108–419 effective 6 months after Nov. 30, 2004, subject to transition provisions, see section 6 of Pub. L. 108–419, set out as an Effective Date; Transition Provisions note under section 801 of this title.

EFFECTIVE DATE OF 1995 AMENDMENT

Amendment by Pub. L. 104–39 effective 3 months after Nov. 1, 1995, see section 6 of Pub. L. 104–39, set out as a note under section 101 of this title.

EFFECTIVE DATE OF 1994 AMENDMENT

Amendment by section 3(b) of Pub. L. 103–369 effective July 1, 1994, see section 6(d) of Pub. L. 103–369, set out as an Effective and Termination Dates of 1994 Amendment note under section 119 of this title.

EFFECTIVE DATE OF 1993 AMENDMENT

Pub. L. 103–198, §7, Dec. 17, 1993, 107 Stat. 2313, provided that:

"(a) IN GENERAL.—This Act [see Short Title of 1993 Amendment note set out under section 101 of this title] and the amendments made by this Act shall take effect on the date of the enactment of this Act [Dec. 17, 1993].

"(b) EFFECTIVENESS OF EXISTING RATES AND DISTRIBUTIONS.—All royalty rates and all determinations with respect to the proportionate division of compulsory license fees among copyright claimants, whether made by the Copyright Royalty Tribunal, or by voluntary agreement, before the effective date set forth in subsection (a) shall remain in effect until modified by voluntary agreement or pursuant to the amendments made by this Act.

"(c) TRANSFER OF APPROPRIATIONS.—All unexpended balances of appropriations made to the Copyright Royalty Tribunal, as of the effective date of this Act, are transferred on such effective date to the Copyright Office for use by the Copyright Office for the purposes for which such appropriations were made."

EFFECTIVE DATE OF 1990 AMENDMENT

Section 3(e)(1) of Pub. L. 101–318 provided that: "The amendments made by subsections (a) and (b) [amending this section and section 801 of this title] shall be effective as of August 27, 1986."

EFFECTIVE DATE OF 1988 AMENDMENT

Amendment by Pub. L. 100–667 effective Jan. 1, 1989, see section 206 of Pub. L. 100–667, set out as an Effective Date note under section 119 of this title.

SAVINGS PROVISION

Pub. L. 111–175, title III, §306, May 27, 2010, 124 Stat. 1257, provided that:

"(a) IN GENERAL.—Nothing in this Act [see Short Title of 2010 Amendment note set out under section 101 of this title], title 17, United States Code, the Communications Act of 1934 [47 U.S.C. 151 et seq.], regulations promulgated by the Register of Copyrights under this title or title 17, United States Code, or regulations promulgated by the Federal Communications Commission under this Act or the Communications Act of 1934 shall be construed to prevent a multichannel video programming distributor from retransmitting a performance or display of a work pursuant to an authorization granted by the copyright owner or, if within the scope of its authorization, its licensee.

"(b) LIMITATION.—Nothing in subsection (a) shall be construed to affect any obligation of a multichannel video programming distributor under section 325(b) of the Communications Act of 1934 [47 U.S.C. 325(b)] to obtain the authority of a television broadcast station before retransmitting that station's signal."

SEVERABILITY

Pub. L. 111–175, title IV, § 401, May 27, 2010, 124 Stat. 1258, provided that: "If any provision of this Act [see Short Title of 2010 Amendment note set out under section 101 of this title], an amendment made by this Act, or the application of such provision or amendment to any person or circumstance is held to be unconstitutional, the remainder of this Act, the amendments made by this Act, and the application of such provision or amendment to any person or circumstance shall not be affected thereby."

CONSTRUCTION

Pub. L. 111–175, title I, § 108, May 27, 2010, 124 Stat. 1245, provided that: "Nothing in section 111, 119, or 122 of title 17, United States Code, including the amendments made to such sections by this title, shall be construed to affect the meaning of any terms under the Communications Act of 1934 [47 U.S.C. 151 et seq.], except to the extent that such sections are specifically cross-referenced in such Act or the regulations issued thereunder."

§ 112. Limitations on exclusive rights: Ephemeral recordings

(a)(1) Notwithstanding the provisions of section 106, and except in the case of a motion picture or other audiovisual work, it is not an infringement of copyright for a transmitting organization entitled to transmit to the public a performance or display of a work, under a license, including a statutory license under section 114(f), or transfer of the copyright or under the limitations on exclusive rights in sound recordings specified by section 114(a), or for a transmitting organization that is a broadcast radio or television station licensed as such by the Federal Communications Commission and that makes a broadcast transmission of a performance of a sound recording in a digital format on a nonsubscription basis, to make no more than one copy or phonorecord of a particular transmission program embodying the performance or display, if—

(A) the copy or phonorecord is retained and used solely by the transmitting organization that made it, and no further copies or phonorecords are reproduced from it; and

(B) the copy or phonorecord is used solely for the transmitting organization's own transmissions within its local service area, or for purposes of archival preservation or security; and

(C) unless preserved exclusively for archival purposes, the copy or phonorecord is destroyed within six months from the date the transmission program was first transmitted to the public.

(2) In a case in which a transmitting organization entitled to make a copy or phonorecord under paragraph (1) in connection with the transmission to the public of a performance or display of a work is prevented from making such copy or phonorecord by reason of the application by the copyright owner of technical measures that prevent the reproduction of the work, the copyright owner shall make available to the transmitting organization the necessary means for permitting the making of such copy or phonorecord as permitted under that paragraph, if it is technologically feasible and economically reasonable for the copyright owner to do so. If the copyright owner fails to do so in a timely manner in light of the transmitting organization's reasonable business requirements, the transmitting organization shall not be liable for a violation of section 1201(a)(1) of this title for engaging in such activities as are necessary to make such copies or phonorecords as permitted under paragraph (1) of this subsection.

(b) Notwithstanding the provisions of section 106, it is not an infringement of copyright for a governmental body or other nonprofit organization entitled to transmit a performance or display of a work, under section 110(2) or under the limitations on exclusive rights in sound recordings specified by section 114(a), to make no more than thirty copies or phonorecords of a particular transmission program embodying the performance or display, if—

(1) no further copies or phonorecords are reproduced from the copies or phonorecords made under this clause; and

(2) except for one copy or phonorecord that may be preserved exclusively for archival purposes, the copies or phonorecords are destroyed within seven years from the date the transmission program was first transmitted to the public.

(c) Notwithstanding the provisions of section 106, it is not an infringement of copyright for a governmental body or other nonprofit organization to make for distribution no more than one copy or phonorecord, for each transmitting organization specified in clause (2) of this subsection, of a particular transmission program embodying a performance of a nondramatic musical work of a religious nature, or of a sound recording of such a musical work, if—

(1) there is no direct or indirect charge for making or distributing any such copies or phonorecords; and

(2) none of such copies or phonorecords is used for any performance other than a single transmission to the public by a transmitting organization entitled to transmit to the public a performance of the work under a license or transfer of the copyright; and

(3) except for one copy or phonorecord that may be preserved exclusively for archival purposes, the copies or phonorecords are all destroyed within one year from the date the transmission program was first transmitted to the public.

(d) Notwithstanding the provisions of section 106, it is not an infringement of copyright for a governmental body or other nonprofit organization entitled to transmit a performance of a work under section 110(8) to make no more than ten copies or phonorecords embodying the performance, or to permit the use of any such copy or phonorecord by any governmental body or nonprofit organization entitled to transmit a performance of a work under section 110(8), if—

(1) any such copy or phonorecord is retained and used solely by the organization that made it, or by a governmental body or nonprofit organization entitled to transmit a performance of a work under section 110(8), and no further copies or phonorecords are reproduced from it; and

(2) any such copy or phonorecord is used solely for transmissions authorized under section 110(8), or for purposes of archival preservation or security; and

(3) the governmental body or nonprofit organization permitting any use of any such copy or phonorecord by any governmental body or nonprofit organization under this subsection does not make any charge for such use.

(e) STATUTORY LICENSE.—(1) A transmitting organization entitled to transmit to the public a performance of a sound recording under the limitation on exclusive rights specified by section 114(d)(1)(C)(iv) or under a statutory license in accordance with section 114(f) is entitled to a statutory license, under the conditions specified by this subsection, to make no more than 1 phonorecord of the sound recording (unless the terms and conditions of the statutory license allow for more), if the following conditions are satisfied:

(A) The phonorecord is retained and used solely by the transmitting organization that made it, and no further phonorecords are reproduced from it.

(B) The phonorecord is used solely for the transmitting organization's own transmissions originating in the United States under a statutory license in accordance with section 114(f) or the limitation on exclusive rights specified by section 114(d)(1)(C)(iv).

(C) Unless preserved exclusively for purposes of archival preservation, the phonorecord is destroyed within 6 months from the date the sound recording was first transmitted to the public using the phonorecord.

(D) Phonorecords of the sound recording have been distributed to the public under the authority of the copyright owner or the copyright owner authorizes the transmitting entity to transmit the sound recording, and the transmitting entity makes the phonorecord under this subsection from a phonorecord lawfully made and acquired under the authority of the copyright owner.

(2) Notwithstanding any provision of the antitrust laws, any copyright owners of sound recordings and any transmitting organizations entitled to a statutory license under this subsection may negotiate and agree upon royalty rates and license terms and conditions for making phonorecords of such sound recordings under this section and the proportionate division of fees paid among copyright owners, and may designate common agents to negotiate, agree to, pay, or receive such royalty payments.

(3) Proceedings under chapter 8 shall determine reasonable rates and terms of royalty payments for the activities specified by paragraph

(1) during the 5-year period beginning on January 1 of the second year following the year in which the proceedings are to be commenced, or such other period as the parties may agree. Such rates shall include a minimum fee for each type of service offered by transmitting organizations. Any copyright owners of sound recordings or any transmitting organizations entitled to a statutory license under this subsection may submit to the Copyright Royalty Judges licenses covering such activities with respect to such sound recordings. The parties to each proceeding shall bear their own costs.

(4) The schedule of reasonable rates and terms determined by the Copyright Royalty Judges shall, subject to paragraph (5), be binding on all copyright owners of sound recordings and transmitting organizations entitled to a statutory license under this subsection during the 5-year period specified in paragraph (3), or such other period as the parties may agree. Such rates shall include a minimum fee for each type of service offered by transmitting organizations. The Copyright Royalty Judges shall establish rates that most clearly represent the fees that would have been negotiated in the marketplace between a willing buyer and a willing seller. In determining such rates and terms, the Copyright Royalty Judges shall base their decision on economic, competitive, and programming information presented by the parties, including—

(A) whether use of the service may substitute for or may promote the sales of phonorecords or otherwise interferes with or enhances the copyright owner's traditional streams of revenue; and

(B) the relative roles of the copyright owner and the transmitting organization in the copyrighted work and the service made available to the public with respect to relative creative contribution, technological contribution, capital investment, cost, and risk.

In establishing such rates and terms, the Copyright Royalty Judges may consider the rates and terms under voluntary license agreements described in paragraphs (2) and (3). The Copyright Royalty Judges shall also establish requirements by which copyright owners may receive reasonable notice of the use of their sound recordings under this section, and under which records of such use shall be kept and made available by transmitting organizations entitled to obtain a statutory license under this subsection.

(5) License agreements voluntarily negotiated at any time between 1 or more copyright owners of sound recordings and 1 or more transmitting organizations entitled to obtain a statutory license under this subsection shall be given effect in lieu of any decision by the Librarian of Congress or determination by the Copyright Royalty Judges.

(6)(A) Any person who wishes to make a phonorecord of a sound recording under a statutory license in accordance with this subsection may do so without infringing the exclusive right of the copyright owner of the sound recording under section 106(1)—

(i) by complying with such notice requirements as the Copyright Royalty Judges shall prescribe by regulation and by paying royalty fees in accordance with this subsection; or

(ii) if such royalty fees have not been set, by agreeing to pay such royalty fees as shall be determined in accordance with this subsection.

(B) Any royalty payments in arrears shall be made on or before the 20th day of the month next succeeding the month in which the royalty fees are set.

(7) If a transmitting organization entitled to make a phonorecord under this subsection is prevented from making such phonorecord by reason of the application by the copyright owner of technical measures that prevent the reproduction of the sound recording, the copyright owner shall make available to the transmitting organization the necessary means for permitting the making of such phonorecord as permitted under this subsection, if it is technologically feasible and economically reasonable for the copyright owner to do so. If the copyright owner fails to do so in a timely manner in light of the transmitting organization's reasonable business requirements, the transmitting organization shall not be liable for a violation of section 1201(a)(1) of this title for engaging in such activities as are necessary to make such phonorecords as permitted under this subsection.

(8) Nothing in this subsection annuls, limits, impairs, or otherwise affects in any way the existence or value of any of the exclusive rights of the copyright owners in a sound recording, except as otherwise provided in this subsection, or in a musical work, including the exclusive rights to reproduce and distribute a sound recording or musical work, including by means of a digital phonorecord delivery, under sections 106(1), 106(3), and 115, and the right to perform publicly a sound recording or musical work, including by means of a digital audio transmission, under sections 106(4) and 106(6).

(f)(1) Notwithstanding the provisions of section 106, and without limiting the application of subsection (b), it is not an infringement of copyright for a governmental body or other nonprofit educational institution entitled under section 110(2) to transmit a performance or display to make copies or phonorecords of a work that is in digital form and, solely to the extent permitted in paragraph (2), of a work that is in analog form, embodying the performance or display to be used for making transmissions authorized under section 110(2), if—

(A) such copies or phonorecords are retained and used solely by the body or institution that made them, and no further copies or phonorecords are reproduced from them, except as authorized under section 110(2); and

(B) such copies or phonorecords are used solely for transmissions authorized under section 110(2).

(2) This subsection does not authorize the conversion of print or other analog versions of works into digital formats, except that such conversion is permitted hereunder, only with respect to the amount of such works authorized to be performed or displayed under section 110(2), if—

(A) no digital version of the work is available to the institution; or

(B) the digital version of the work that is available to the institution is subject to tech-

nological protection measures that prevent its use for section 110(2).

(g) The transmission program embodied in a copy or phonorecord made under this section is not subject to protection as a derivative work under this title except with the express consent of the owners of copyright in the preexisting works employed in the program.

(Pub. L. 94–553, title I, § 101, Oct. 19, 1976, 90 Stat. 2558; Pub. L. 105–304, title IV, §§ 402, 405(b), Oct. 28, 1998, 112 Stat. 2888, 2899; Pub. L. 106–44, § 1(b), Aug. 5, 1999, 113 Stat. 221; Pub. L. 107–273, div. C, title III, § 13301(c)(1), Nov. 2, 2002, 116 Stat. 1912; Pub. L. 108–419, § 5(b), Nov. 30, 2004, 118 Stat. 2361.)

HISTORICAL AND REVISION NOTES

HOUSE REPORT NO. 94–1476

Section 112 of the bill concerns itself with a special problem that is not dealt with in the present statutes but is the subject of provisions in a number of foreign statutes and in the revisions of the Berne Convention since 1948. This is the problem of what are commonly called "ephemeral recordings": copies or phonorecords of a work made for purposes of later transmission by a broadcasting organization legally entitled to transmit the work. In other words, where a broadcaster has the privilege of performing or displaying a work either because he is licensed or because the performance or display is exempted under the statute, the question is whether he should be given the additional privilege of recording the performance or display to facilitate its transmission. The need for a limited exemption in these cases because of the practical exigencies of broadcasting has been generally recognized, but the scope of the exemption has been a controversial issue.

Recordings for Licensed Transmissions. Under subsection (a) of section 112, an organization that has acquired the right to transmit any work (other than a motion picture or other audiovisual work), or that is free to transmit a sound recording under section 114, may make a single copy or phonorecord of a particular program embodying the work, if the copy or phonorecord is used solely for the organization's own transmissions within its own area; after 6 months it must be destroyed or preserved solely for archival purposes.

Organizations Covered.—The ephemeral recording privilege is given by subsection (a) to "a transmitting organization entitled to transmit to the public a performance or display of a work." Assuming that the transmission meets the other conditions of the provision, it makes no difference what type of public transmission the organization is making: commercial radio and television broadcasts, public radio and television broadcasts not exempted by section 110(2), pay-TV, closed circuit, background music, and so forth. However, to come within the scope of subsection (a), the organization must have the right to make the transmission "under a license or transfer of the copyright or under the limitations on exclusive rights in sound recordings specified by section 114(a)." Thus, except in the case of copyrighted sound recordings (which have no exclusive performing rights under the bill), the organization must be a transferee or licensee (including compulsory licensee) of performing rights in the work in order to make an ephemeral recording of it.

Some concern has been expressed by authors and publishers lest the term "organization" be construed to include a number of affiliated broadcasters who could exchange the recording without restrictions. The term is intended to cover a broadcasting network, or a local broadcaster or individual transmitter; but, under clauses (1) and (2) of the subsection, the ephemeral recording must be "retained and used solely by the transmitting organization that made it," and must be used solely for that organization's own transmissions within its own area. Thus, an ephemeral recording made by one transmitter, whether it be a network or local broadcaster, could not be made available for use by another transmitter. Likewise, this subsection does not apply to those nonsimultaneous transmissions by cable systems not located within a boundary of the forty-eight contiguous States that are granted a compulsory license under section 111.

Scope of the Privilege.—Subsection (a) permits the transmitting organization to make "no more than one copy or phonorecord of a particular transmission program embodying the performance or display." A "transmission program" is defined in section 101 as a body of material produced for the sole purpose of transmission as a unit. Thus, under section 112(a), a transmitter could make only one copy or phonorecord of a particular "transmission program" containing a copyrighted work, but would not be limited as to the number of times the work itself could be duplicated as part of other "transmission programs."

Three specific limitations on the scope of the ephemeral recording privilege are set out in subsection (a), and unless all are met the making of an "ephemeral recording" becomes fully actionable as an infringement. The first requires that the copy or phonorecord be "retained and used solely by the transmitting organization that made it," and that "no further copies or phonorecords are reproduced from it." This means that a transmitting organization would have no privilege of exchanging ephemeral recordings with other transmitters or of allowing them to duplicate their own ephemeral recordings from the copy or phonorecord it has made. There is nothing in the provision to prevent a transmitting organization from having an ephemeral recording made by means of facilities other than its own, although it would not be permissible for a person or organization other than a transmitting organization to make a recording on its own initiative for possible sale or lease to a broadcaster. The ephemeral recording privilege would extend to copies or phonorecords made in advance for later broadcast, as well as recordings of a program that are made while it is being transmitted and are intended for deferred transmission or preservation.

Clause (2) of section 112(a) provides that, to be exempt from copyright, the copy or phonorecord must be "used solely for the transmitting organization's own transmissions within its local service area, or for purposes of archival preservation or security". The term "local service area" is defined in section 111(f).

Clause (3) of section 112(a) provides that, unless preserved exclusively for archival purposes, the copy or phonorecord of a transmission program must be destroyed within six months from the date the transmission program was first transmitted to the public.

Recordings for Instructional Transmissions. Section 112(b) represents a response to the arguments of instructional broadcasters and other educational groups for special recording privileges, although it does not go as far as these groups requested. In general, it permits a nonprofit organization that is free to transmit a performance or display of a work, under section 110(2) or under the limitations on exclusive rights in sound recordings specified by section 114(a), to make not more than thirty copies or phonorecords and to use the ephemeral recordings for transmitting purposes for not more than seven years after the initial transmission.

Organizations Covered.—The privilege of making ephemeral recordings under section 112(b) extends to a "governmental body or other nonprofit organization entitled to transmit a performance or display of a work under section 110(2) or under the limitations on exclusive rights in sound recordings specified by section 114(a)." Aside from phonorecords of copyrighted sound recordings, the ephemeral recordings made by an instructional broadcaster under subsection (b) must embody a performance or display that meets all of the qualifications for exemption under section 110(2). Copies or phonorecords made for educational broadcasts of a general cultural nature, or for transmission as part of

an information storage and retrieval system, would not be exempted from copyright protection under section 112(b).

Motion Pictures and Other Audiovisual Works.—Since the performance exemption provided by section 110(2) applies only to nondramatic literary and musical works, there was no need to exclude motion pictures and other audiovisual works explicitly from the scope of section 112(b). Another point stressed by the producers of educational films in this connection, however, was that ephemeral recordings made by instructional broadcasters are in fact audiovisual works that often compete for exactly the same market. They argued that it is unfair to allow instructional broadcasters to reproduce multiple copies of films and tapes, and to exchange them with other broadcasters, without paying any copyright royalties, thereby directly injuring the market of producers of audiovisual works who now pay substantial fees to authors for the same uses. These arguments are persuasive and justify the placing of reasonable limits on the recording privilege.

Scope of the Privilege.—Under subsection (b) an instructional broadcaster may make "no more than thirty copies or phonorecords of a particular transmission program embodying the performance or display." No further copies or phonorecords can be reproduced from those made under section 112(b), either by the nonprofit organization that made them or by anyone else.

On the other hand, if the nonprofit organization does nothing directly or indirectly to authorize, induce, or encourage others to duplicate additional copies or phonorecords of an ephemeral recording in excess of the limit of thirty, it would not be held responsible as participating in the infringement in such a case, and the unauthorized copies would not be counted against the organization's total of thirty.

Unlike ephemeral recordings made under subsection (a), exchanges of recordings among instructional broadcasters are permitted. An organization that has made copies or phonorecords under subsection (b) may use one of them for purposes of its own transmissions that are exempted by section 110(2), and it may also transfer the other 29 copies to other instructional broadcasters for use in the same way.

As in the case of ephemeral recordings made under section 112(a), a copy or phonorecord made for instructional broadcasting could be reused in any number of transmissions within the time limits specified in the provision. Because of the special problems of instructional broadcasters resulting from the scheduling of courses and the need to prerecord well in advance of transmission, the period of use has been extended to seven years from the date the transmission program was first transmitted to the public.

Religious Broadcasts.—Section 112(c) provides that it is not an infringement of copyright for certain nonprofit organizations to make no more than one copy for each transmitting organization of a broadcast program embodying a performance of a nondramatic musical work of a religious nature or of a sound recording of such a musical work. In order for this exception to be applicable there must be no charge for the distribution of the copies, none of the copies may be used for any performance other than a single transmission by an organization possessing a license to transmit a copyrighted work, and, other than for one copy that may be preserved for archival purposes, the remaining copies must be destroyed within one year from the date the program was first transmitted to the public.

Despite objections by music copyright owners, the Committee found this exemption to be justified by the special circumstances under which many religious programs are broadcast. These programs are produced on tape or disk for distribution by mail of one copy only to each broadcast station carrying the program. None of the programs are prepared for profit, and the program producer either pays the station to carry the program or furnishes it free of charge. The stations have performing licenses, so the copyright owners receive compensation. Following the performance, the tape is returned or the disk destroyed. It seems likely that, as has been alleged, to require a second payment for the mechanical reproduction under these circumstances would simply have the effect of driving some of the copyrighted music off the air.

Ephemeral Recordings for Transmissions to Handicapped Audiences. As a counterpart to its amendment of section 110(8), the Committee adopted a new provision, subsection (d) of section 112, to provide an ephemeral recording exemption in the case of transmissions to the blind and deaf. New subsection would permit the making of one recording of a performance exempted under section 110(8), and its retention for an unlimited period. It would not permit the making of further reproductions or their exchange with other organizations.

Copyright Status of Ephemeral Recordings. A program reproduced in an ephemeral recording made under section 112 in many cases will constitute a motion picture, a sound recording, or some other kind of derivative work, and will thus be potentially copyrightable under section 103. In section 112(e) it is provided that ephemeral recordings are not to be copyrightable as derivative works except with the consent of the owners of the copyrighted material employed in them.

AMENDMENTS

2004—Subsec. (e)(3). Pub. L. 108–419, §5(b)(1), substituted first sentence for former first sentence which read: "No later than 30 days after the date of the enactment of the Digital Millennium Copyright Act, the Librarian of Congress shall cause notice to be published in the Federal Register of the initiation of voluntary negotiation proceedings for the purpose of determining reasonable terms and rates of royalty payments for the activities specified by paragraph (1) of this subsection during the period beginning on the date of the enactment of such Act and ending on December 31, 2000, or such other date as the parties may agree.", substituted "Copyright Royalty Judges licenses" for "Librarian of Congress licenses" in third sentence, and struck out "negotiation" before "proceeding" in last sentence.

Subsec. (e)(4). Pub. L. 108–419, §5(b)(2), substituted first sentence for former first sentence which read: "In the absence of license agreements negotiated under paragraph (2), during the 60-day period commencing 6 months after publication of the notice specified in paragraph (3), and upon the filing of a petition in accordance with section 803(a)(1), the Librarian of Congress shall, pursuant to chapter 8, convene a copyright arbitration royalty panel to determine and publish in the Federal Register a schedule of reasonable rates and terms which, subject to paragraph (5), shall be binding on all copyright owners of sound recordings and transmitting organizations entitled to a statutory license under this subsection during the period beginning on the date of the enactment of the Digital Millennium Copyright Act and ending on December 31, 2000, or such other date as the parties may agree.", and substituted "Copyright Royalty Judges" for "copyright arbitration royalty panel" in third and fourth sentences and in concluding provisions, "their decision" for "its decision", "described" for "negotiated as provided", and "Copyright Royalty Judges shall also establish" for "Librarian of Congress shall also establish".

Subsec. (e)(5). Pub. L. 108–419, §5(b)(3), substituted "decision by the Librarian of Congress or determination by the Copyright Royalty Judges" for "determination by a copyright arbitration royalty panel or decision by the Librarian of Congress".

Subsec. (e)(6). Pub. L. 108–419, §5(b)(4), redesignated par. (7) as (6) and struck out former par. (6) which related to publication of notice of the initiation of voluntary negotiation proceedings as specified in par. (3).

Subsec. (e)(6)(A)(i). Pub. L. 108–419, §5(b)(5), substituted "Copyright Royalty Judges" for "Librarian of Congress".

Subsec. (e)(7) to (9). Pub. L. 108–419, §5(b)(4), redesignated pars. (8) and (9) as (7) and (8), respectively. Former par. (7) redesignated (6).

2002—Subsecs. (f), (g). Pub. L. 107–273 added subsec. (f) and redesignated former subsec. (f) as (g).

1999—Subsec. (e)(2). Pub. L. 106–44, §1(b)(1), redesignated par. (3) as (2).

Subsec. (e)(3). Pub. L. 106–44, §1(b)(1), (2), redesignated par. (4) as (3) and substituted "(1)" for "(2)" in first sentence. Former par. (3) redesignated (2).

Subsec. (e)(4). Pub. L. 106–44, §1(b)(1), (3), redesignated par. (5) as (4), substituted "(2)" for "(3)", "(3)" for "(4)", and "(5)" for "(6)" in first sentence, and substituted "(2) and (3)" for "(3) and (4)" in penultimate sentence of concluding provisions. Former par. (4) redesignated (3).

Subsec. (e)(5). Pub. L. 106–44, §1(b)(1), redesignated par. (6) as (5). Former par. (5) redesignated (4).

Subsec. (e)(6). Pub. L. 106–44, §1(b)(1), (4), redesignated par. (7) as (6), substituted "(3)" for "(4)" wherever appearing, and substituted "(4)" for "(5)" in two places. Former par. (6) redesignated (5).

Subsec. (e)(7) to (10). Pub. L. 106–44, §1(b)(1), redesignated pars. (8) to (10) as (7) to (9), respectively. Former par. (7) redesignated (6).

1998—Subsec. (a). Pub. L. 105–304, §402, designated existing provisions as par. (1), in introductory provisions inserted ", including a statutory license under section 114(f)," after "under a license" and "or for a transmitting organization that is a broadcast radio or television station licensed as such by the Federal Communications Commission and that makes a broadcast transmission of a performance of a sound recording in a digital format on a nonsubscription basis," after "114(a),", redesignated former pars. (1) to (3) as subpars. (A) to (C), respectively, and added par. (2).

Subsecs. (e), (f). Pub. L. 105–304, §405(b), added subsec. (e) and redesignated former subsec. (e) as (f).

EFFECTIVE DATE OF 2004 AMENDMENT

Amendment by Pub. L. 108–419 effective 6 months after Nov. 30, 2004, subject to transition provisions, see section 6 of Pub. L. 108–419, set out as an Effective Date; Transition Provisions note under section 801 of this title.

CONSTRUCTION OF 1998 AMENDMENT

Pub. L. 105–304, title IV, §405(c), Oct. 28, 1998, 112 Stat. 2902, provided that: "Nothing in this section [amending this section and sections 114 and 801 to 803 of this title and enacting provisions set out as notes under section 114 of this title] or the amendments made by this section shall affect the scope of section 112(a) of title 17, United States Code, or the entitlement of any person to an exemption thereunder."

§ 113. Scope of exclusive rights in pictorial, graphic, and sculptural works

(a) Subject to the provisions of subsections (b) and (c) of this section, the exclusive right to reproduce a copyrighted pictorial, graphic, or sculptural work in copies under section 106 includes the right to reproduce the work in or on any kind of article, whether useful or otherwise.

(b) This title does not afford, to the owner of copyright in a work that portrays a useful article as such, any greater or lesser rights with respect to the making, distribution, or display of the useful article so portrayed than those afforded to such works under the law, whether title 17 or the common law or statutes of a State, in effect on December 31, 1977, as held applicable and construed by a court in an action brought under this title.

(c) In the case of a work lawfully reproduced in useful articles that have been offered for sale or other distribution to the public, copyright does not include any right to prevent the making, distribution, or display of pictures or photographs of such articles in connection with advertisements or commentaries related to the distribution or display of such articles, or in connection with news reports.

(d)(1) In a case in which—

(A) a work of visual art has been incorporated in or made part of a building in such a way that removing the work from the building will cause the destruction, distortion, mutilation, or other modification of the work as described in section 106A(a)(3), and

(B) the author consented to the installation of the work in the building either before the effective date set forth in section 610(a) of the Visual Artists Rights Act of 1990, or in a written instrument executed on or after such effective date that is signed by the owner of the building and the author and that specifies that installation of the work may subject the work to destruction, distortion, mutilation, or other modification, by reason of its removal,

then the rights conferred by paragraphs (2) and (3) of section 106A(a) shall not apply.

(2) If the owner of a building wishes to remove a work of visual art which is a part of such building and which can be removed from the building without the destruction, distortion, mutilation, or other modification of the work as described in section 106A(a)(3), the author's rights under paragraphs (2) and (3) of section 106A(a) shall apply unless—

(A) the owner has made a diligent, good faith attempt without success to notify the author of the owner's intended action affecting the work of visual art, or

(B) the owner did provide such notice in writing and the person so notified failed, within 90 days after receiving such notice, either to remove the work or to pay for its removal.

For purposes of subparagraph (A), an owner shall be presumed to have made a diligent, good faith attempt to send notice if the owner sent such notice by registered mail to the author at the most recent address of the author that was recorded with the Register of Copyrights pursuant to paragraph (3). If the work is removed at the expense of the author, title to that copy of the work shall be deemed to be in the author.

(3) The Register of Copyrights shall establish a system of records whereby any author of a work of visual art that has been incorporated in or made part of a building, may record his or her identity and address with the Copyright Office. The Register shall also establish procedures under which any such author may update the information so recorded, and procedures under which owners of buildings may record with the Copyright Office evidence of their efforts to comply with this subsection.

(Pub. L. 94–553, title I, §101, Oct. 19, 1976, 90 Stat. 2560; Pub. L. 101–650, title VI, §604, Dec. 1, 1990, 104 Stat. 5130.)

HISTORICAL AND REVISION NOTES

HOUSE REPORT NO. 94–1476

Section 113 deals with the extent of copyright protection in "works of applied art." The section takes as its starting point the Supreme Court's decision in *Mazer v. Stein*, 347 U.S. 201 (1954) [74 S.Ct. 460, 98 L.Ed. 630, rehearing denied 74 S.Ct. 637, 347 U.S. 949, 98 L.Ed. 1096],

and the first sentence of subsection (a) restates the basic principle established by that decision. The rule of *Mazer*, as affirmed by the bill, is that copyright in a pictorial, graphic, or sculptural work will not be affected if the work is employed as the design of a useful article, and will afford protection to the copyright owner against the unauthorized reproduction of his work in useful as well as nonuseful articles. The terms "pictorial, graphic, and sculptural works" and "useful article" are defined in section 101, and these definitions are discussed above in connection with section 102.

The broad language of section 106(1) and of subsection (a) of section 113 raises questions as to the extent of copyright protection for a pictorial, graphic, or sculptural work that portrays, depicts, or represents an image of a useful article in such a way that the utilitarian nature of the article can be seen. To take the example usually cited, would copyright in a drawing or model of an automobile give the artist the exclusive right to make automobiles of the same design?

The 1961 Report of the Register of Copyrights stated, on the basis of judicial precedent, that "copyright in a pictorial, graphic, or sculptural work, portraying a useful article as such, does not extend to the manufacture of the useful article itself," and recommended specifically that "the distinctions drawn in this area by existing court decisions" not be altered by the statute. The Register's Supplementary Report, at page 48, cited a number of these decisions, and explained the insuperable difficulty of finding "any statutory formulation that would express the distinction satisfactorily." Section 113(b) reflects the Register's conclusion that "the real need is to make clear that there is no intention to change the present law with respect to the scope of protection in a work portraying a useful article as such."

Section 113(c) provides that it would not be an infringement of copyright, where a copyright work has been lawfully published as the design of useful articles, to make, distribute or display pictures of the articles in advertising, in feature stories about the articles, or in the news reports.

In conformity with its deletion from the bill of Title II, relating to the protection of ornamental designs of useful articles, the Committee has deleted subsections (b), (c), and (d) of section 113 of S. 22 as adopted by the Senate, since they are no longer relevant.

REFERENCES IN TEXT

Section 610(a) of the Visual Artists Rights Act of 1990 [Pub. L. 101–650], referred to in subsec. (d)(1)(B), is set out as an Effective Date note under section 106A of this title.

AMENDMENTS

1990—Subsec. (d). Pub. L. 101–650 added subsec. (d).

EFFECTIVE DATE OF 1990 AMENDMENT

Amendment by Pub. L. 101–650 effective 6 months after Dec. 1, 1990, see section 610 of Pub. L. 101–650, set out as an Effective Date note under section 106A of this title.

§ 114. Scope of exclusive rights in sound recordings

(a) The exclusive rights of the owner of copyright in a sound recording are limited to the rights specified by clauses (1), (2), (3) and (6) of section 106, and do not include any right of performance under section 106(4).

(b) The exclusive right of the owner of copyright in a sound recording under clause (1) of section 106 is limited to the right to duplicate the sound recording in the form of phonorecords or copies that directly or indirectly recapture the actual sounds fixed in the recording. The exclusive right of the owner of copyright in a sound recording under clause (2) of section 106 is limited to the right to prepare a derivative work in which the actual sounds fixed in the sound recording are rearranged, remixed, or otherwise altered in sequence or quality. The exclusive rights of the owner of copyright in a sound recording under clauses (1) and (2) of section 106 do not extend to the making or duplication of another sound recording that consists entirely of an independent fixation of other sounds, even though such sounds imitate or simulate those in the copyrighted sound recording. The exclusive rights of the owner of copyright in a sound recording under clauses (1), (2), and (3) of section 106 do not apply to sound recordings included in educational television and radio programs (as defined in section 397 of title 47) distributed or transmitted by or through public broadcasting entities (as defined by section 118(f)): *Provided*, That copies or phonorecords of said programs are not commercially distributed by or through public broadcasting entities to the general public.

(c) This section does not limit or impair the exclusive right to perform publicly, by means of a phonorecord, any of the works specified by section 106(4).

(d) LIMITATIONS ON EXCLUSIVE RIGHT.—Notwithstanding the provisions of section 106(6)—

(1) EXEMPT TRANSMISSIONS AND RETRANSMISSIONS.—The performance of a sound recording publicly by means of a digital audio transmission, other than as a part of an interactive service, is not an infringement of section 106(6) if the performance is part of—

(A) a nonsubscription broadcast transmission;

(B) a retransmission of a nonsubscription broadcast transmission: *Provided*, That, in the case of a retransmission of a radio station's broadcast transmission—

(i) the radio station's broadcast transmission is not willfully or repeatedly retransmitted more than a radius of 150 miles from the site of the radio broadcast transmitter, however—

(I) the 150 mile limitation under this clause shall not apply when a nonsubscription broadcast transmission by a radio station licensed by the Federal Communications Commission is retransmitted on a nonsubscription basis by a terrestrial broadcast station, terrestrial translator, or terrestrial repeater licensed by the Federal Communications Commission; and

(II) in the case of a subscription retransmission of a nonsubscription broadcast retransmission covered by subclause (I), the 150 mile radius shall be measured from the transmitter site of such broadcast retransmitter;

(ii) the retransmission is of radio station broadcast transmissions that are—

(I) obtained by the retransmitter over the air;

(II) not electronically processed by the retransmitter to deliver separate and discrete signals; and

(III) retransmitted only within the local communities served by the retransmitter;

(iii) the radio station's broadcast transmission was being retransmitted to cable systems (as defined in section 111(f)) by a satellite carrier on January 1, 1995, and that retransmission was being retransmitted by cable systems as a separate and discrete signal, and the satellite carrier obtains the radio station's broadcast transmission in an analog format: *Provided*, That the broadcast transmission being retransmitted may embody the programming of no more than one radio station; or

(iv) the radio station's broadcast transmission is made by a noncommercial educational broadcast station funded on or after January 1, 1995, under section 396(k) of the Communications Act of 1934 (47 U.S.C. 396(k)), consists solely of noncommercial educational and cultural radio programs, and the retransmission, whether or not simultaneous, is a nonsubscription terrestrial broadcast retransmission; or

(C) a transmission that comes within any of the following categories—

(i) a prior or simultaneous transmission incidental to an exempt transmission, such as a feed received by and then retransmitted by an exempt transmitter: *Provided*, That such incidental transmissions do not include any subscription transmission directly for reception by members of the public;

(ii) a transmission within a business establishment, confined to its premises or the immediately surrounding vicinity;

(iii) a retransmission by any retransmitter, including a multichannel video programming distributor as defined in section 602(12)[1] of the Communications Act of 1934 (47 U.S.C. 522(12)), of a transmission by a transmitter licensed to publicly perform the sound recording as a part of that transmission, if the retransmission is simultaneous with the licensed transmission and authorized by the transmitter; or

(iv) a transmission to a business establishment for use in the ordinary course of its business: *Provided*, That the business recipient does not retransmit the transmission outside of its premises or the immediately surrounding vicinity, and that the transmission does not exceed the sound recording performance complement. Nothing in this clause shall limit the scope of the exemption in clause (ii).

(2) STATUTORY LICENSING OF CERTAIN TRANSMISSIONS.—The performance of a sound recording publicly by means of a subscription digital audio transmission not exempt under paragraph (1), an eligible nonsubscription transmission, or a transmission not exempt under paragraph (1) that is made by a preexisting satellite digital audio radio service shall be subject to statutory licensing, in accordance with subsection (f) if—

(A)(i) the transmission is not part of an interactive service;

(ii) except in the case of a transmission to a business establishment, the transmitting

---

entity does not automatically and intentionally cause any device receiving the transmission to switch from one program channel to another; and

(iii) except as provided in section 1002(e), the transmission of the sound recording is accompanied, if technically feasible, by the information encoded in that sound recording, if any, by or under the authority of the copyright owner of that sound recording, that identifies the title of the sound recording, the featured recording artist who performs on the sound recording, and related information, including information concerning the underlying musical work and its writer;

(B) in the case of a subscription transmission not exempt under paragraph (1) that is made by a preexisting subscription service in the same transmission medium used by such service on July 31, 1998, or in the case of a transmission not exempt under paragraph (1) that is made by a preexisting satellite digital audio radio service—

(i) the transmission does not exceed the sound recording performance complement; and

(ii) the transmitting entity does not cause to be published by means of an advance program schedule or prior announcement the titles of the specific sound recordings or phonorecords embodying such sound recordings to be transmitted; and

(C) in the case of an eligible nonsubscription transmission or a subscription transmission not exempt under paragraph (1) that is made by a new subscription service or by a preexisting subscription service other than in the same transmission medium used by such service on July 31, 1998—

(i) the transmission does not exceed the sound recording performance complement, except that this requirement shall not apply in the case of a retransmission of a broadcast transmission if the retransmission is made by a transmitting entity that does not have the right or ability to control the programming of the broadcast station making the broadcast transmission, unless—

(I) the broadcast station makes broadcast transmissions—

(aa) in digital format that regularly exceed the sound recording performance complement; or

(bb) in analog format, a substantial portion of which, on a weekly basis, exceed the sound recording performance complement; and

(II) the sound recording copyright owner or its representative has notified the transmitting entity in writing that broadcast transmissions of the copyright owner's sound recordings exceed the sound recording performance complement as provided in this clause;

(ii) the transmitting entity does not cause to be published, or induce or facilitate the publication, by means of an advance program schedule or prior announcement, the titles of the specific sound recordings to be transmitted, the phonorecords embodying such sound recordings, or, other than for illustrative purposes, the names of the featured recording artists, except that this clause does not disqualify a transmitting entity that makes a prior announcement that a particular artist will be featured within an unspecified future time period, and in the case of a retransmission of a broadcast transmission by a transmitting entity that does not have the right or ability to control the programming of the broadcast transmission, the requirement of this clause shall not apply to a prior oral announcement by the broadcast station, or to an advance program schedule published, induced, or facilitated by the broadcast station, if the transmitting entity does not have actual knowledge and has not received written notice from the copyright owner or its representative that the broadcast station publishes or induces or facilitates the publication of such advance program schedule, or if such advance program schedule is a schedule of classical music programming published by the broadcast station in the same manner as published by that broadcast station on or before September 30, 1998;

(iii) the transmission—

(I) is not part of an archived program of less than 5 hours duration;

(II) is not part of an archived program of 5 hours or greater in duration that is made available for a period exceeding 2 weeks;

(III) is not part of a continuous program which is of less than 3 hours duration; or

(IV) is not part of an identifiable program in which performances of sound recordings are rendered in a predetermined order, other than an archived or continuous program, that is transmitted at—

(aa) more than 3 times in any 2-week period that have been publicly announced in advance, in the case of a program of less than 1 hour in duration, or

(bb) more than 4 times in any 2-week period that have been publicly announced in advance, in the case of a program of 1 hour or more in duration,

except that the requirement of this subclause shall not apply in the case of a retransmission of a broadcast transmission by a transmitting entity that does not have the right or ability to control the programming of the broadcast transmission, unless the transmitting entity is given notice in writing by the copyright owner of the sound recording that the broadcast station makes broadcast transmissions that regularly violate such requirement;

(iv) the transmitting entity does not knowingly perform the sound recording, as part of a service that offers transmissions of visual images contemporaneously with transmissions of sound recordings, in a manner that is likely to cause confusion, to cause mistake, or to deceive, as to the affiliation, connection, or association of the copyright owner or featured recording artist with the transmitting entity or a particular product or service advertised by the transmitting entity, or as to the origin, sponsorship, or approval by the copyright owner or featured recording artist of the activities of the transmitting entity other than the performance of the sound recording itself;

(v) the transmitting entity cooperates to prevent, to the extent feasible without imposing substantial costs or burdens, a transmission recipient or any other person or entity from automatically scanning the transmitting entity's transmissions alone or together with transmissions by other transmitting entities in order to select a particular sound recording to be transmitted to the transmission recipient, except that the requirement of this clause shall not apply to a satellite digital audio service that is in operation, or that is licensed by the Federal Communications Commission, on or before July 31, 1998;

(vi) the transmitting entity takes no affirmative steps to cause or induce the making of a phonorecord by the transmission recipient, and if the technology used by the transmitting entity enables the transmitting entity to limit the making by the transmission recipient of phonorecords of the transmission directly in a digital format, the transmitting entity sets such technology to limit such making of phonorecords to the extent permitted by such technology;

(vii) phonorecords of the sound recording have been distributed to the public under the authority of the copyright owner or the copyright owner authorizes the transmitting entity to transmit the sound recording, and the transmitting entity makes the transmission from a phonorecord lawfully made under the authority of the copyright owner, except that the requirement of this clause shall not apply to a retransmission of a broadcast transmission by a transmitting entity that does not have the right or ability to control the programming of the broadcast transmission, unless the transmitting entity is given notice in writing by the copyright owner of the sound recording that the broadcast station makes broadcast transmissions that regularly violate such requirement;

(viii) the transmitting entity accommodates and does not interfere with the transmission of technical measures that are widely used by sound recording copyright owners to identify or protect copyrighted works, and that are technically feasible of being transmitted by the transmitting entity without imposing substantial costs on the transmitting entity or resulting in perceptible aural or visual degradation of the digital signal, except that

the requirement of this clause shall not apply to a satellite digital audio service that is in operation, or that is licensed under the authority of the Federal Communications Commission, on or before July 31, 1998, to the extent that such service has designed, developed, or made commitments to procure equipment or technology that is not compatible with such technical measures before such technical measures are widely adopted by sound recording copyright owners; and

(ix) the transmitting entity identifies in textual data the sound recording during, but not before, the time it is performed, including the title of the sound recording, the title of the phonorecord embodying such sound recording, if any, and the featured recording artist, in a manner to permit it to be displayed to the transmission recipient by the device or technology intended for receiving the service provided by the transmitting entity, except that the obligation in this clause shall not take effect until 1 year after the date of the enactment of the Digital Millennium Copyright Act and shall not apply in the case of a retransmission of a broadcast transmission by a transmitting entity that does not have the right or ability to control the programming of the broadcast transmission, or in the case in which devices or technology intended for receiving the service provided by the transmitting entity that have the capability to display such textual data are not common in the marketplace.

(3) LICENSES FOR TRANSMISSIONS BY INTERACTIVE SERVICES.—

(A) No interactive service shall be granted an exclusive license under section 106(6) for the performance of a sound recording publicly by means of digital audio transmission for a period in excess of 12 months, except that with respect to an exclusive license granted to an interactive service by a licensor that holds the copyright to 1,000 or fewer sound recordings, the period of such license shall not exceed 24 months: *Provided, however*, That the grantee of such exclusive license shall be ineligible to receive another exclusive license for the performance of that sound recording for a period of 13 months from the expiration of the prior exclusive license.

(B) The limitation set forth in subparagraph (A) of this paragraph shall not apply if—

(i) the licensor has granted and there remain in effect licenses under section 106(6) for the public performance of sound recordings by means of digital audio transmission by at least 5 different interactive services: *Provided, however*, That each such license must be for a minimum of 10 percent of the copyrighted sound recordings owned by the licensor that have been licensed to interactive services, but in no event less than 50 sound recordings; or

(ii) the exclusive license is granted to perform publicly up to 45 seconds of a sound recording and the sole purpose of the performance is to promote the distribution or performance of that sound recording.

(C) Notwithstanding the grant of an exclusive or nonexclusive license of the right of public performance under section 106(6), an interactive service may not publicly perform a sound recording unless a license has been granted for the public performance of any copyrighted musical work contained in the sound recording: *Provided,* That such license to publicly perform the copyrighted musical work may be granted either by a performing rights society representing the copyright owner or by the copyright owner.

(D) The performance of a sound recording by means of a retransmission of a digital audio transmission is not an infringement of section 106(6) if—

(i) the retransmission is of a transmission by an interactive service licensed to publicly perform the sound recording to a particular member of the public as part of that transmission; and

(ii) the retransmission is simultaneous with the licensed transmission, authorized by the transmitter, and limited to that particular member of the public intended by the interactive service to be the recipient of the transmission.

(E) For the purposes of this paragraph—

(i) a "licensor" shall include the licensing entity and any other entity under any material degree of common ownership, management, or control that owns copyrights in sound recordings; and

(ii) a "performing rights society" is an association or corporation that licenses the public performance of nondramatic musical works on behalf of the copyright owner, such as the American Society of Composers, Authors and Publishers, Broadcast Music, Inc., and SESAC, Inc.

(4) RIGHTS NOT OTHERWISE LIMITED.—

(A) Except as expressly provided in this section, this section does not limit or impair the exclusive right to perform a sound recording publicly by means of a digital audio transmission under section 106(6).

(B) Nothing in this section annuls or limits in any way—

(i) the exclusive right to publicly perform a musical work, including by means of a digital audio transmission, under section 106(4);

(ii) the exclusive rights in a sound recording or the musical work embodied therein under sections 106(1), 106(2) and 106(3); or

(iii) any other rights under any other clause of section 106, or remedies available under this title, as such rights or remedies exist either before or after the date of enactment of the Digital Performance Right in Sound Recordings Act of 1995.

(C) Any limitations in this section on the exclusive right under section 106(6) apply only to the exclusive right under section 106(6) and not to any other exclusive rights under section 106. Nothing in this section shall be construed to annul, limit, impair or otherwise affect in any way the ability of the owner of a copyright in a sound recording to exercise the rights under sections 106(1), 106(2) and 106(3), or to obtain the remedies available under this title pursuant to such rights, as such rights and remedies exist either before or after the date of enactment of the Digital Performance Right in Sound Recordings Act of 1995.

(e) AUTHORITY FOR NEGOTIATIONS.—

(1) Notwithstanding any provision of the antitrust laws, in negotiating statutory licenses in accordance with subsection (f), any copyright owners of sound recordings and any entities performing sound recordings affected by this section may negotiate and agree upon the royalty rates and license terms and conditions for the performance of such sound recordings and the proportionate division of fees paid among copyright owners, and may designate common agents on a nonexclusive basis to negotiate, agree to, pay, or receive payments.

(2) For licenses granted under section 106(6), other than statutory licenses, such as for performances by interactive services or performances that exceed the sound recording performance complement—

(A) copyright owners of sound recordings affected by this section may designate common agents to act on their behalf to grant licenses and receive and remit royalty payments: *Provided,* That each copyright owner shall establish the royalty rates and material license terms and conditions unilaterally, that is, not in agreement, combination, or concert with other copyright owners of sound recordings; and

(B) entities performing sound recordings affected by this section may designate common agents to act on their behalf to obtain licenses and collect and pay royalty fees: *Provided,* That each entity performing sound recordings shall determine the royalty rates and material license terms and conditions unilaterally, that is, not in agreement, combination, or concert with other entities performing sound recordings.

(f) LICENSES FOR CERTAIN NONEXEMPT TRANSMISSIONS.—

(1)(A) Proceedings under chapter 8 shall determine reasonable rates and terms of royalty payments for subscription transmissions by preexisting subscription services and transmissions by preexisting satellite digital audio radio services specified by subsection (d)(2) during the 5-year period beginning on January 1 of the second year following the year in which the proceedings are to be commenced, except in the case of a different transitional period provided under section 6(b)(3) of the Copyright Royalty and Distribution Reform Act of 2004, or such other period as the parties may agree. Such terms and rates shall distinguish among the different types of digital audio transmission services then in operation. Any copyright owners of sound recordings, preexisting subscription services, or preexisting satellite digital audio radio services may submit to the Copyright Royalty Judges licenses covering such subscription transmissions with respect to such sound recordings. The parties to each proceeding shall bear their own costs.

(B) The schedule of reasonable rates and terms determined by the Copyright Royalty Judges shall, subject to paragraph (3), be binding on all copyright owners of sound recordings and entities performing sound recordings affected by this paragraph during the 5-year period specified in subparagraph (A), a transitional period provided under section 6(b)(3) of the Copyright Royalty and Distribution Reform Act of 2004, or such other period as the parties may agree. In establishing rates and terms for preexisting subscription services and preexisting satellite digital audio radio services, in addition to the objectives set forth in section 801(b)(1), the Copyright Royalty Judges may consider the rates and terms for comparable types of subscription digital audio transmission services and comparable circumstances under voluntary license agreements described in subparagraph (A).

(C) The procedures under subparagraphs (A) and (B) also shall be initiated pursuant to a petition filed by any copyright owners of sound recordings, any preexisting subscription services, or any preexisting satellite digital audio radio services indicating that a new type of subscription digital audio transmission service on which sound recordings are performed is or is about to become operational, for the purpose of determining reasonable terms and rates of royalty payments with respect to such new type of transmission service for the period beginning with the inception of such new type of service and ending on the date on which the royalty rates and terms for subscription digital audio transmission services most recently determined under subparagraph (A) or (B) and chapter 8 expire, or such other period as the parties may agree.

(2)(A) Proceedings under chapter 8 shall determine reasonable rates and terms of royalty payments for public performances of sound recordings by means of eligible nonsubscription transmission services and new subscription services specified by subsection (d)(2) during the 5-year period beginning on January 1 of the second year following the year in which the proceedings are to be commenced, except in the case of a different transitional period provided under section 6(b)(3) of the Copyright Royalty and Distribution Reform Act of 2004, or such other period as the parties may agree. Such rates and terms shall distinguish among the different types of eligible nonsubscription transmission services and new subscription services then in operation and shall include a minimum fee for each such type of service. Any copyright owners of sound recordings or any entities performing sound recordings affected by this paragraph may submit to the Copyright Royalty Judges licenses covering such eligible nonsubscription transmissions and new subscription services with respect to such sound recordings. The parties to each proceeding shall bear their own costs.

(B) The schedule of reasonable rates and terms determined by the Copyright Royalty Judges shall, subject to paragraph (3), be binding on all copyright owners of sound recordings and entities performing sound recordings affected by this paragraph during the 5-year period specified in subparagraph (A), a transitional period provided under section 6(b)(3) of the Copyright Royalty and Distribution[2] Act of 2004, or such other period as the parties may agree. Such rates and terms shall distinguish among the different types of eligible nonsubscription transmission services then in operation and shall include a minimum fee for each such type of service, such differences to be based on criteria including, but not limited to, the quantity and nature of the use of sound recordings and the degree to which use of the service may substitute for or may promote the purchase of phonorecords by consumers. In establishing rates and terms for transmissions by eligible nonsubscription services and new subscription services, the Copyright Royalty Judges shall establish rates and terms that most clearly represent the rates and terms that would have been negotiated in the marketplace between a willing buyer and a willing seller. In determining such rates and terms, the Copyright Royalty Judges shall base their decision on economic, competitive and programming information presented by the parties, including—

(i) whether use of the service may substitute for or may promote the sales of phonorecords or otherwise may interfere with or may enhance the sound recording copyright owner's other streams of revenue from its sound recordings; and

(ii) the relative roles of the copyright owner and the transmitting entity in the copyrighted work and the service made available to the public with respect to relative creative contribution, technological contribution, capital investment, cost, and risk.

In establishing such rates and terms, the Copyright Royalty Judges may consider the rates and terms for comparable types of digital audio transmission services and comparable circumstances under voluntary license agreements described in subparagraph (A).

(C) The procedures under subparagraphs (A) and (B) shall also be initiated pursuant to a petition filed by any copyright owners of sound recordings or any eligible nonsubscription service or new subscription service indicating that a new type of eligible nonsubscription service or new subscription service on which sound recordings are performed is or is about to become operational, for the purpose of determining reasonable terms and rates of royalty payments with respect to such new type of service for the period beginning with the inception of such new type of service and ending on the date on which the royalty rates and terms for eligible nonsubscription services and new subscription services, as the case may be, most recently determined under subpara-

---

[2] So in original. Probably should be followed by "Reform".

graph (A) or (B) and chapter 8 expire, or such other period as the parties may agree.

(3) License agreements voluntarily negotiated at any time between 1 or more copyright owners of sound recordings and 1 or more entities performing sound recordings shall be given effect in lieu of any decision by the Librarian of Congress or determination by the Copyright Royalty Judges.

(4)(A) The Copyright Royalty Judges shall also establish requirements by which copyright owners may receive reasonable notice of the use of their sound recordings under this section, and under which records of such use shall be kept and made available by entities performing sound recordings. The notice and recordkeeping rules in effect on the day before the effective date of the Copyright Royalty and Distribution Reform Act of 2004 shall remain in effect unless and until new regulations are promulgated by the Copyright Royalty Judges. If new regulations are promulgated under this subparagraph, the Copyright Royalty Judges shall take into account the substance and effect of the rules in effect on the day before the effective date of the Copyright Royalty and Distribution Reform Act of 2004 and shall, to the extent practicable, avoid significant disruption of the functions of any designated agent authorized to collect and distribute royalty fees.

(B) Any person who wishes to perform a sound recording publicly by means of a transmission eligible for statutory licensing under this subsection may do so without infringing the exclusive right of the copyright owner of the sound recording—

(i) by complying with such notice requirements as the Copyright Royalty Judges shall prescribe by regulation and by paying royalty fees in accordance with this subsection; or

(ii) if such royalty fees have not been set, by agreeing to pay such royalty fees as shall be determined in accordance with this subsection.

(C) Any royalty payments in arrears shall be made on or before the twentieth day of the month next succeeding the month in which the royalty fees are set.

(5)(A) Notwithstanding section 112(e) and the other provisions of this subsection, the receiving agent may enter into agreements for the reproduction and performance of sound recordings under section 112(e) and this section by any 1 or more commercial webcasters or noncommercial webcasters for a period of not more than 11 years beginning on January 1, 2005, that, once published in the Federal Register pursuant to subparagraph (B), shall be binding on all copyright owners of sound recordings and other persons entitled to payment under this section, in lieu of any determination by the Copyright Royalty Judges. Any such agreement for commercial webcasters may include provisions for payment of royalties on the basis of a percentage of revenue or expenses, or both, and include a minimum fee. Any such agreement may include other terms and conditions, including requirements by which copyright owners may

receive notice of the use of their sound recordings and under which records of such use shall be kept and made available by commercial webcasters or noncommercial webcasters. The receiving agent shall be under no obligation to negotiate any such agreement. The receiving agent shall have no obligation to any copyright owner of sound recordings or any other person entitled to payment under this section in negotiating any such agreement, and no liability to any copyright owner of sound recordings or any other person entitled to payment under this section for having entered into such agreement.

(B) The Copyright Office shall cause to be published in the Federal Register any agreement entered into pursuant to subparagraph (A). Such publication shall include a statement containing the substance of subparagraph (C). Such agreements shall not be included in the Code of Federal Regulations. Thereafter, the terms of such agreement shall be available, as an option, to any commercial webcaster or noncommercial webcaster meeting the eligibility conditions of such agreement.

(C) Neither subparagraph (A) nor any provisions of any agreement entered into pursuant to subparagraph (A), including any rate structure, fees, terms, conditions, or notice and recordkeeping requirements set forth therein, shall be admissible as evidence or otherwise taken into account in any administrative, judicial, or other government proceeding involving the setting or adjustment of the royalties payable for the public performance or reproduction in ephemeral phonorecords or copies of sound recordings, the determination of terms or conditions related thereto, or the establishment of notice or recordkeeping requirements by the Copyright Royalty Judges under paragraph (4) or section 112(e)(4). It is the intent of Congress that any royalty rates, rate structure, definitions, terms, conditions, or notice and recordkeeping requirements, included in such agreements shall be considered as a compromise motivated by the unique business, economic and political circumstances of webcasters, copyright owners, and performers rather than as matters that would have been negotiated in the marketplace between a willing buyer and a willing seller, or otherwise meet the objectives set forth in section 801(b). This subparagraph shall not apply to the extent that the receiving agent and a webcaster that is party to an agreement entered into pursuant to subparagraph (A) expressly authorize the submission of the agreement in a proceeding under this subsection.

(D) Nothing in the Webcaster Settlement Act of 2008, the Webcaster Settlement Act of 2009, or any agreement entered into pursuant to subparagraph (A) shall be taken into account by the United States Court of Appeals for the District of Columbia Circuit in its review of the determination by the Copyright Royalty Judges of May 1, 2007, of rates and terms for the digital performance of sound recordings and ephemeral recordings, pursuant to sections 112 and 114.

(E) As used in this paragraph—

(i) the term "noncommercial webcaster" means a webcaster that—

(I) is exempt from taxation under section 501 of the Internal Revenue Code of 1986 (26 U.S.C. 501);

(II) has applied in good faith to the Internal Revenue Service for exemption from taxation under section 501 of the Internal Revenue Code and has a commercially reasonable expectation that such exemption shall be granted; or

(III) is operated by a State or possession or any governmental entity or subordinate thereof, or by the United States or District of Columbia, for exclusively public purposes;

(ii) the term "receiving agent" shall have the meaning given that term in section 261.2 of title 37, Code of Federal Regulations, as published in the Federal Register on July 8, 2002; and

(iii) the term "webcaster" means a person or entity that has obtained a compulsory license under section 112 or 114 and the implementing regulations therefor.

(F) The authority to make settlements pursuant to subparagraph (A) shall expire at 11:59 p.m. Eastern time on the 30th day after the date of the enactment of the Webcaster Settlement Act of 2009.

(g) PROCEEDS FROM LICENSING OF TRANSMISSIONS.—

(1) Except in the case of a transmission licensed under a statutory license in accordance with subsection (f) of this section—

(A) a featured recording artist who performs on a sound recording that has been licensed for a transmission shall be entitled to receive payments from the copyright owner of the sound recording in accordance with the terms of the artist's contract; and

(B) a nonfeatured recording artist who performs on a sound recording that has been licensed for a transmission shall be entitled to receive payments from the copyright owner of the sound recording in accordance with the terms of the nonfeatured recording artist's applicable contract or other applicable agreement.

(2) An agent designated to distribute receipts from the licensing of transmissions in accordance with subsection (f) shall distribute such receipts as follows:

(A) 50 percent of the receipts shall be paid to the copyright owner of the exclusive right under section 106(6) of this title to publicly perform a sound recording by means of a digital audio transmission.

(B) 2½ percent of the receipts shall be deposited in an escrow account managed by an independent administrator jointly appointed by copyright owners of sound recordings and the American Federation of Musicians (or any successor entity) to be distributed to nonfeatured musicians (whether or not members of the American Federation of Musicians) who have performed on sound recordings.

(C) 2½ percent of the receipts shall be deposited in an escrow account managed by an independent administrator jointly appointed by copyright owners of sound recordings and the American Federation of Television and Radio Artists (or any successor entity) to be distributed to nonfeatured vocalists (whether or not members of the American Federation of Television and Radio Artists) who have performed on sound recordings.

(D) 45 percent of the receipts shall be paid, on a per sound recording basis, to the recording artist or artists featured on such sound recording (or the persons conveying rights in the artists' performance in the sound recordings).

(3) A nonprofit agent designated to distribute receipts from the licensing of transmissions in accordance with subsection (f) may deduct from any of its receipts, prior to the distribution of such receipts to any person or entity entitled thereto other than copyright owners and performers who have elected to receive royalties from another designated agent and have notified such nonprofit agent in writing of such election, the reasonable costs of such agent incurred after November 1, 1995, in—

(A) the administration of the collection, distribution, and calculation of the royalties;

(B) the settlement of disputes relating to the collection and calculation of the royalties; and

(C) the licensing and enforcement of rights with respect to the making of ephemeral recordings and performances subject to licensing under section 112 and this section, including those incurred in participating in negotiations or arbitration proceedings under section 112 and this section, except that all costs incurred relating to the section 112 ephemeral recordings right may only be deducted from the royalties received pursuant to section 112.

(4) Notwithstanding paragraph (3), any designated agent designated to distribute receipts from the licensing of transmissions in accordance with subsection (f) may deduct from any of its receipts, prior to the distribution of such receipts, the reasonable costs identified in paragraph (3) of such agent incurred after November 1, 1995, with respect to such copyright owners and performers who have entered with such agent a contractual relationship that specifies that such costs may be deducted from such royalty receipts.

(h) LICENSING TO AFFILIATES.—

(1) If the copyright owner of a sound recording licenses an affiliated entity the right to publicly perform a sound recording by means of a digital audio transmission under section 106(6), the copyright owner shall make the licensed sound recording available under section 106(6) on no less favorable terms and conditions to all bona fide entities that offer similar services, except that, if there are material differences in the scope of the requested license with respect to the type of service, the particular sound recordings licensed, the frequency of use, the number of subscribers served, or the duration, then the copyright

owner may establish different terms and conditions for such other services.

(2) The limitation set forth in paragraph (1) of this subsection shall not apply in the case where the copyright owner of a sound recording licenses—

(A) an interactive service; or

(B) an entity to perform publicly up to 45 seconds of the sound recording and the sole purpose of the performance is to promote the distribution or performance of that sound recording.

(i) NO EFFECT ON ROYALTIES FOR UNDERLYING WORKS.—License fees payable for the public performance of sound recordings under section 106(6) shall not be taken into account in any administrative, judicial, or other governmental proceeding to set or adjust the royalties payable to copyright owners of musical works for the public performance of their works. It is the intent of Congress that royalties payable to copyright owners of musical works for the public performance of their works shall not be diminished in any respect as a result of the rights granted by section 106(6).

(j) DEFINITIONS.—As used in this section, the following terms have the following meanings:

(1) An "affiliated entity" is an entity engaging in digital audio transmissions covered by section 106(6), other than an interactive service, in which the licensor has any direct or indirect partnership or any ownership interest amounting to 5 percent or more of the outstanding voting or non-voting stock.

(2) An "archived program" is a predetermined program that is available repeatedly on the demand of the transmission recipient and that is performed in the same order from the beginning, except that an archived program shall not include a recorded event or broadcast transmission that makes no more than an incidental use of sound recordings, as long as such recorded event or broadcast transmission does not contain an entire sound recording or feature a particular sound recording.

(3) A "broadcast" transmission is a transmission made by a terrestrial broadcast station licensed as such by the Federal Communications Commission.

(4) A "continuous program" is a predetermined program that is continuously performed in the same order and that is accessed at a point in the program that is beyond the control of the transmission recipient.

(5) A "digital audio transmission" is a digital transmission as defined in section 101, that embodies the transmission of a sound recording. This term does not include the transmission of any audiovisual work.

(6) An "eligible nonsubscription transmission" is a noninteractive nonsubscription digital audio transmission not exempt under subsection (d)(1) that is made as part of a service that provides audio programming consisting, in whole or in part, of performances of sound recordings, including retransmissions of broadcast transmissions, if the primary purpose of the service is to provide to the public such audio or other entertainment programming, and the primary purpose of the service is not to sell, advertise, or promote particular products or services other than sound recordings, live concerts, or other music-related events.

(7) An "interactive service" is one that enables a member of the public to receive a transmission of a program specially created for the recipient, or on request, a transmission of a particular sound recording, whether or not as part of a program, which is selected by or on behalf of the recipient. The ability of individuals to request that particular sound recordings be performed for reception by the public at large, or in the case of a subscription service, by all subscribers of the service, does not make a service interactive, if the programming on each channel of the service does not substantially consist of sound recordings that are performed within 1 hour of the request or at a time designated by either the transmitting entity or the individual making such request. If an entity offers both interactive and noninteractive services (either concurrently or at different times), the noninteractive component shall not be treated as part of an interactive service.

(8) A "new subscription service" is a service that performs sound recordings by means of noninteractive subscription digital audio transmissions and that is not a preexisting subscription service or a preexisting satellite digital audio radio service.

(9) A "nonsubscription" transmission is any transmission that is not a subscription transmission.

(10) A "preexisting satellite digital audio radio service" is a subscription satellite digital audio radio service provided pursuant to a satellite digital audio radio service license issued by the Federal Communications Commission on or before July 31, 1998, and any renewal of such license to the extent of the scope of the original license, and may include a limited number of sample channels representative of the subscription service that are made available on a nonsubscription basis in order to promote the subscription service.

(11) A "preexisting subscription service" is a service that performs sound recordings by means of noninteractive audio-only subscription digital audio transmissions, which was in existence and was making such transmissions to the public for a fee on or before July 31, 1998, and may include a limited number of sample channels representative of the subscription service that are made available on a nonsubscription basis in order to promote the subscription service.

(12) A "retransmission" is a further transmission of an initial transmission, and includes any further retransmission of the same transmission. Except as provided in this section, a transmission qualifies as a "retransmission" only if it is simultaneous with the initial transmission. Nothing in this definition shall be construed to exempt a transmission that fails to satisfy a separate element required to qualify for an exemption under section 114(d)(1).

(13) The "sound recording performance complement" is the transmission during any 3-hour period, on a particular channel used by a transmitting entity, of no more than—

(A) 3 different selections of sound recordings from any one phonorecord lawfully distributed for public performance or sale in the United States, if no more than 2 such selections are transmitted consecutively; or

(B) 4 different selections of sound recordings—

(i) by the same featured recording artist; or

(ii) from any set or compilation of phonorecords lawfully distributed together as a unit for public performance or sale in the United States,

if no more than three such selections are transmitted consecutively:

Provided, That the transmission of selections in excess of the numerical limits provided for in clauses (A) and (B) from multiple phonorecords shall nonetheless qualify as a sound recording performance complement if the programming of the multiple phonorecords was not willfully intended to avoid the numerical limitations prescribed in such clauses.

(14) A "subscription" transmission is a transmission that is controlled and limited to particular recipients, and for which consideration is required to be paid or otherwise given by or on behalf of the recipient to receive the transmission or a package of transmissions including the transmission.

(15) A "transmission" is either an initial transmission or a retransmission.

(Pub. L. 94–553, title I, § 101, Oct. 19, 1976, 90 Stat. 2560; Pub. L. 104–39, § 3, Nov. 1, 1995, 109 Stat. 336; Pub. L. 105–80, § 3, Nov. 13, 1997, 111 Stat. 1531; Pub. L. 105–304, title IV, § 405(a)(1)–(4), Oct. 28, 1998, 112 Stat. 2890–2897; Pub. L. 107–321, §§ 4, 5(b), (c), Dec. 4, 2002, 116 Stat. 2781, 2784; Pub. L. 108–419, § 5(c), Nov. 30, 2004, 118 Stat. 2362; Pub. L. 109–303, § 4(b), Oct. 6, 2006, 120 Stat. 1481; Pub. L. 110–435, § 2, Oct. 16, 2008, 122 Stat. 4974; Pub. L. 111–36, § 2, June 30, 2009, 123 Stat. 1926; Pub. L. 111–295, §§ 5(c), 6(b), (f)(1), Dec. 9, 2010, 124 Stat. 3181.)

HISTORICAL AND REVISION NOTES

HOUSE REPORT NO. 94–1476

Subsection (a) of Section 114 specified that the exclusive rights of the owner of copyright in a sound recording are limited to the rights to reproduce the sound recording in copies or phonorecords, to prepare derivative works based on the copyrighted sound recording, and to distribute copies or phonorecords of the sound recording to the public. Subsection (a) states explicitly that the owner's rights "do not include any right of performance under section 106(4)." The Committee considered at length the arguments in favor of establishing a limited performance right, in the form of a compulsory license, for copyrighted sound recordings, but concluded that the problem requires further study. It therefore added a new subsection (d) to the bill requiring the Register of Copyrights to submit to Congress, on January 3, 1978, "a report setting forth recommendations as to whether this section should be amended to provide for performers and copyright owners * * * any performance rights" in copyrighted sound recordings. Under the new subsection, the report "should describe the status of such rights in foreign countries, the views of major interested parties, and specific legislative or other recommendations, if any."

Subsection (b) of section 114 makes clear that statutory protection for sound recordings extends only to the particular sounds of which the recording consists, and would not prevent a separate recording of another performance in which those sounds are imitated. Thus, infringement takes place whenever all or any substantial portion of the actual sounds that go to make up a copyrighted sound recording are reproduced in phonorecords by repressing, transcribing, recapturing off the air, or any other method, or by reproducing them in the soundtrack or audio portion of a motion picture or other audiovisual work. Mere imitation of a recorded performance would not constitute a copyright infringement even where one performer deliberately sets out to simulate another's performance as exactly as possible.

Under section 114, the exclusive right of owner of copyright in a sound recording to prepare derivative works based on the copyrighted sound recording is recognized. However, in view of the expressed intention not to give exclusive rights against imitative or simulated performances and recordings, the Committee adopted an amendment to make clear the scope of rights under section 106(2) in this context. Section 114(b) provides that the "exclusive right of the owner of copyright in a sound recording under clause (2) of section 106 is limited to the right to prepare a derivative work in which the actual sounds fixed in the sound recording are rearranged, remixed, or otherwise altered in sequence or quality."

Another amendment deals with the use of copyrighted sound recordings "included in educational television and radio programs * * * distributed or transmitted by or through public broadcasting entities." This use of recordings is permissible without authorization from the owner of copyright in the sound recording, as long as "copies or phonorecords of said programs are not commercially distributed by or through public broadcasting entities to the general public."

During the 1975 hearings, the Register of Copyrights expressed some concern that an invaluable segment of this country's musical heritage—in the form of sound recordings—had become inaccessible to musicologists and to others for scholarly purposes. Several of the major recording companies have responded to the Register's concern by granting blanket licenses to the Library of Congress to permit it to make single copy duplications of sound recordings maintained in the Library's archives for research purposes. Moreover, steps are being taken to determine the feasibility of additional licensing arrangements as a means of satisfying the needs of key regional music libraries across the country. The Register has agreed to report to Congress if further legislative consideration should be undertaken.

Section 114(c) states explicitly that nothing in the provisions of section 114 should be construed to "limit or impair the exclusive right to perform publicly, by means of a phonorecord, any of the works specified by section 106(4)." This principle is already implicit in the bill, but it is restated to avoid the danger of confusion between rights in a sound recording and rights in the musical composition or other work embodied in the recording.

REFERENCES IN TEXT

Section 602(12) of the Communications Act of 1934, referred to in subsec. (d)(1)(C)(iii), was subsequently amended, and section 602(12) no longer defines "multichannel video programming distributor". However, such term is defined elsewhere in that section.

The date of the enactment of the Digital Millennium Copyright Act, referred to in subsec. (d)(2)(C)(ix), is the date of enactment of Pub. L. 105–304, which was approved Oct. 28, 1998.

The date of enactment of the Digital Performance Right in Sound Recordings Act of 1995, referred to in subsec. (d)(4)(B)(iii), (C), is the date of enactment of Pub. L. 104–39, which was approved Nov. 1, 1995.

Section 6(b)(3) of the Copyright Royalty and Distribution Reform Act of 2004, referred to in subsec. (f)(1)(A), (B), (2)(A), (B), is section 6(b)(3) of Pub. L. 108–419, which is set out as a note under section 801 of this title.

The effective date of the Copyright Royalty and Distribution Reform Act of 2004, referred to in subsec. (f)(4)(A), is the effective date of Pub. L. 108–419, which is 6 months after Nov. 30, 2004, subject to transition provisions, see section 6 of Pub. L. 108–419, set out as an Effective Date; Transition Provisions note under section 801 of this title.

The Webcaster Settlement Act of 2008, referred to in subsec. (f)(5)(D), is Pub. L. 110–435, Oct. 16, 2008, 122 Stat. 4974, which amended this section and enacted provisions set out as a note under section 101 of this title. For complete classification of this Act to the Code, see Short Title of 2008 Amendment note set out under section 101 of this title and Tables.

The Webcaster Settlement Act of 2009, referred to in subsec. (f)(5)(D), is Pub. L. 111–36, June 30, 2009, 123 Stat. 1926, which amended this section and enacted provisions set out as a note under section 101 of this title. For complete classification of this Act to the Code, see Short Title of 2009 Amendment note set out under section 101 of this title and Tables.

The date of the enactment of the Webcaster Settlement Act of 2009, referred to in subsec. (f)(5)(F), is the date of the enactment of Pub. L. 111–36, which was approved June 30, 2009.

AMENDMENTS

2010—Subsec. (b). Pub. L. 111–295, §6(f)(1), substituted "118(f)" for "118(g)".

Subsec. (f)(2)(B). Pub. L. 111–295, §6(b), substituted "Judges shall base their decision" for "Judges shall base its decision" in introductory provisions.

Subsec. (f)(2)(C). Pub. L. 111–295, §5(c), substituted "eligible nonsubscription services and new subscription services" for "preexisting subscription digital audio transmission services or preexisting satellite digital radio audio services".

2009—Subsec. (f)(5)(D). Pub. L. 111–36, §2(1), substituted "2008, the Webcaster Settlement Act of 2009," for "2008".

Subsec. (f)(5)(E)(iii). Pub. L. 111–36, §2(2), struck out "to make eligible nonsubscription transmissions and ephemeral recordings" after "therefor".

Subsec. (f)(5)(F). Pub. L. 111–36, §2(3), substituted "at 11:59 p.m. Eastern time on the 30th day after the date of the enactment of the Webcaster Settlement Act of 2009" for "February 15, 2009".

2008—Subsec. (f)(5)(A). Pub. L. 110–435, §2(1), substituted "commercial" for "small commercial" wherever appearing, in first sentence substituted "for a period of not more than 11 years beginning on January 1, 2005" for "during the period beginning on October 28, 1998, and ending on December 31, 2004" and "the Copyright Royalty Judges" for "a copyright arbitration royalty panel or decision by the Librarian of Congress", and in second sentence substituted "webcasters may include" for "webcasters shall include".

Subsec. (f)(5)(B). Pub. L. 110–435, §2(2), substituted "commercial" for "small commercial".

Subsec. (f)(5)(C). Pub. L. 110–435, §2(3), substituted "Copyright Royalty Judges" for "Librarian of Congress" and "webcasters" for "small webcasters" and inserted at end "This subparagraph shall not apply to the extent that the receiving agent and a webcaster that is party to an agreement entered into pursuant to subparagraph (A) expressly authorize the submission of the agreement in a proceeding under this subsection."

Subsec. (f)(5)(D). Pub. L. 110–435, §2(4)(B), substituted "Copyright Royalty Judges of May 1, 2007" for "Librarian of Congress of July 8, 2002".

Pub. L. 110–435, §2(4)(A), which directed substitution of "the Webcaster Settlement Act of 2008" for "the Small Webcasters Settlement Act of 2002", was executed by making the substitution for "the Small Webcaster Settlement Act of 2002", to reflect the probable intent of Congress.

Subsec. (f)(5)(F). Pub. L. 110–435, §2(5), substituted "February 15, 2009" for "December 15, 2002, except with respect to noncommercial webcasters for whom the authority shall expire May 31, 2003".

2006—Subsec. (f)(1)(A). Pub. L. 109–303, §4(b)(1), substituted "except in the case of a different transitional period provided under section 6(b)(3) of the Copyright Royalty and Distribution Reform Act of 2004, or such other period as the parties may agree." for "except where a different transitional period is provided under section 6(b)(3) of the Copyright Royalty and Distribution Reform Act of 2004 or such other period."

Subsec. (f)(2)(A). Pub. L. 109–303, §4(b)(2), amended subpar. (A) generally. Prior to amendment, subpar. (A) related to rates and terms of royalty payments for subscription transmissions by eligible nonsubscription transmission services and new subscription services.

Subsec. (f)(2)(B). Pub. L. 109–303, §4(b)(3), substituted "described in" for "negotiated under" in concluding provisions.

2004—Subsec. (f)(1)(A). Pub. L. 108–419, §5(c)(1)(A), substituted first sentence for former first sentence which read: "No later than 30 days after the enactment of the Digital Performance Right in Sound Recordings Act of 1995, the Librarian of Congress shall cause notice to be published in the Federal Register of the initiation of voluntary negotiation proceedings for the purpose of determining reasonable terms and rates of royalty payments for subscription transmissions by preexisting subscription services and transmissions by preexisting satellite digital audio radio services specified by subsection (d)(2) of this section during the period beginning on the effective date of such Act and ending on December 31, 2001, or, if a copyright arbitration royalty panel is convened, ending 30 days after the Librarian issues and publishes in the Federal Register an order adopting the determination of the copyright arbitration royalty panel or an order setting the terms and rates (if the Librarian rejects the panel's determination).", substituted "Copyright Royalty Judges" for "Librarian of Congress" in third sentence, and struck out "negotiation" before "proceeding" in fourth sentence.

Subsec. (f)(1)(B). Pub. L. 108–419, §5(c)(1)(B), substituted first sentence for former first sentence which read: "In the absence of license agreements negotiated under subparagraph (A), during the 60-day period commencing 6 months after publication of the notice specified in subparagraph (A), and upon the filing of a petition in accordance with section 803(a)(1), the Librarian of Congress shall, pursuant to chapter 8, convene a copyright arbitration royalty panel to determine and publish in the Federal Register a schedule of rates and terms which, subject to paragraph (3), shall be binding on all copyright owners of sound recordings and entities performing sound recordings affected by this paragraph." and, in second sentence, substituted "Copyright Royalty Judges may consider" for "copyright arbitration royalty panel may consider" and "described" for "negotiated as provided".

Subsec. (f)(1)(C). Pub. L. 108–419, §5(c)(1)(C), amended subpar. (C) generally. Prior to amendment, subpar. (C) related to repetition of publication of notices of the initiation of voluntary negotiation proceedings as specified in subpar. (A) and repetition of the procedures specified in subpar. (B).

Subsec. (f)(2)(A). Pub. L. 108–419, §5(c)(2)(A)(ii), (iii), substituted "Copyright Royalty Judges" for "Librarian of Congress" in third sentence and struck out "negotiation" after "parties to each" in fourth sentence.

Pub. L. 108–419, §5(c)(2)(A)(i), which directed the general amendment of the first paragraph, was executed by making the amendment to first sentence of subpar. (A) to reflect the probable intent of Congress. Prior to amendment, first sentence read as follows: "No later than 30 days after the date of the enactment of the Digital Millennium Copyright Act, the Librarian of Congress shall cause notice to be published in the Federal Register of the initiation of voluntary negotiation proceedings for the purpose of determining reasonable terms and rates of royalty payments for public performances of sound recordings by means of eligible nonsubscription transmissions and transmissions by new subscription services specified by subsection (d)(2) during the period beginning on the date of the enactment of such Act and ending on December 31, 2000, or such other date as the parties may agree.''

Subsec. (f)(2)(B). Pub. L. 108–419, § 5(c)(2)(B)(iii), which directed substitution of ''described in'' for ''negotiated as provided'' in last sentence, could not be executed because ''negotiated as provided'' does not appear in text.

Pub. L. 108–419, § 5(c)(2)(B)(ii), substituted ''Copyright Royalty Judges'' for ''copyright arbitration royalty panel'' wherever appearing after first sentence.

Pub. L. 108–419, § 5(c)(2)(B)(i), substituted first sentence for former first sentence which read: ''In the absence of license agreements negotiated under subparagraph (A), during the 60-day period commencing 6 months after publication of the notice specified in subparagraph (A), and upon the filing of a petition in accordance with section 803(a)(1), the Librarian of Congress shall, pursuant to chapter 8, convene a copyright arbitration royalty panel to determine and publish in the Federal Register a schedule of rates and terms which, subject to paragraph (3), shall be binding on all copyright owners of sound recordings and entities performing sound recordings affected by this paragraph during the period beginning on the date of the enactment of the Digital Millennium Copyright Act and ending on December 31, 2000, or such other date as the parties may agree.''

Subsec. (f)(2)(C). Pub. L. 108–419, § 5(c)(2)(C), amended subpar. (C) generally. Prior to amendment, subpar. (C) related to repetition of publication of notices of the initiation of voluntary negotiation proceedings as specified in subpar. (A) and repetition of the procedures specified in subpar. (B).

Subsec. (f)(3). Pub. L. 108–419, § 5(c)(3), substituted ''decision by the Librarian of Congress or determination by the Copyright Royalty Judges'' for ''determination by a copyright arbitration royalty panel or decision by the Librarian of Congress''.

Subsec. (f)(4). Pub. L. 108–419, § 5(c)(4), substituted ''Copyright Royalty Judges'' for ''Librarian of Congress'' in two places and inserted after first sentence in subpar. (A) ''The notice and recordkeeping rules in effect on the day before the effective date of the Copyright Royalty and Distribution Reform Act of 2004 shall remain in effect unless and until new regulations are promulgated by the Copyright Royalty Judges. If new regulations are promulgated under this subparagraph, the Copyright Royalty Judges shall take into account the substance and effect of the rules in effect on the day before the effective date of the Copyright Royalty and Distribution Reform Act of 2004 and shall, to the extent practicable, avoid significant disruption of the functions of any designated agent authorized to collect and distribute royalty fees.''

2002—Subsec. (f)(5). Pub. L. 107–321, § 4, added par. (5).

Subsec. (g)(2). Pub. L. 107–321, § 5(c), amended par. (2) generally. Prior to amendment, par. (2) read as follows: ''The copyright owner of the exclusive right under section 106(6) of this title to publicly perform a sound recording by means of a digital audio transmission shall allocate to recording artists in the following manner its receipts from the statutory licensing of transmission performances of the sound recording in accordance with subsection (f) of this section:

''(A) 2½ percent of the receipts shall be deposited in an escrow account managed by an independent administrator jointly appointed by copyright owners of sound recordings and the American Federation of Musicians (or any successor entity) to be distributed to nonfeatured musicians (whether or not members of the American Federation of Musicians) who have performed on sound recordings.

''(B) 2½ percent of the receipts shall be deposited in an escrow account managed by an independent administrator jointly appointed by copyright owners of sound recordings and the American Federation of Television and Radio Artists (or any successor entity) to be distributed to nonfeatured vocalists (whether or not members of the American Federation of Television and Radio Artists) who have performed on sound recordings.

''(C) 45 percent of the receipts shall be allocated, on a per sound recording basis, to the recording artist or artists featured on such sound recording (or the persons conveying rights in the artists' performance in the sound recordings).''

Subsec. (g)(3), (4). Pub. L. 107–321, § 5(b), added pars. (3) and (4).

1998—Subsec. (d)(1)(A). Pub. L. 105–304, § 405(a)(1)(A), added subpar. (A) and struck out former subpar. (A) which read as follows:

''(A)(i) a nonsubscription transmission other than a retransmission;

''(ii) an initial nonsubscription retransmission made for direct reception by members of the public of a prior or simultaneous incidental transmission that is not made for direct reception by members of the public; or

''(iii) a nonsubscription broadcast transmission;''.

Subsec. (d)(2). Pub. L. 105–304, § 405(a)(1)(B), amended heading and text of par. (2) generally. Prior to amendment, text read as follows: ''In the case of a subscription transmission not exempt under subsection (d)(1), the performance of a sound recording publicly by means of a digital audio transmission shall be subject to statutory licensing, in accordance with subsection (f) of this section, if—

''(A) the transmission is not part of an interactive service;

''(B) the transmission does not exceed the sound recording performance complement;

''(C) the transmitting entity does not cause to be published by means of an advance program schedule or prior announcement the titles of the specific sound recordings or phonorecords embodying such sound recordings to be transmitted;

''(D) except in the case of transmission to a business establishment, the transmitting entity does not automatically and intentionally cause any device receiving the transmission to switch from one program channel to another; and

''(E) except as provided in section 1002(e) of this title, the transmission of the sound recording is accompanied by the information encoded in that sound recording, if any, by or under the authority of the copyright owner of that sound recording, that identifies the title of the sound recording, the featured recording artist who performs on the sound recording, and related information, including information concerning the underlying musical work and its writer.''

Subsec. (f). Pub. L. 105–304, § 405(a)(2)(A), substituted ''Certain Nonexempt'' for ''Nonexempt Subscription'' in heading.

Subsec. (f)(1)(A). Pub. L. 105–304, § 405(a)(2)(B), designated existing provisions as subpar. (A), in first sentence, substituted ''subscription transmissions by preexisting subscription services and transmissions by preexisting satellite digital audio radio services'' for ''the activities'' and ''2001'' for ''2000'', and amended third sentence generally. Prior to amendment, third sentence read as follows: ''Any copyright owners of sound recordings or any entities performing sound recordings affected by this section may submit to the Librarian of Congress licenses covering such activities with respect to such sound recordings.''

Subsec. (f)(1)(B), (C). Pub. L. 105–304, § 405(a)(2)(C), added subpars. (B) and (C).

Subsec. (f)(2) to (5). Pub. L. 105–304, § 405(a)(2)(C), added pars. (2) to (4) and struck out former pars. (2) to (5), which provided: in par. (2) that Librarian of Congress would convene a copyright arbitration royalty panel to determine schedule of rates and terms, that panel could consider rates and terms for comparable types of services under voluntary license agreements, and that requirements would be established by which copyright owners would receive notice of use of their recordings; in par. (3) that voluntarily negotiated license agreements would be given effect in lieu of determination by panel or decision by Librarian; in par. (4) that publication of notice of negotiations would be repeated no later than 30 days after petition was filed, in the first week of January, 2000, and at 5-year intervals thereafter, and that par. (2) procedures would be repeated upon filing of petition during a 60-day period commencing six months after publication of notice or on July 1, 2000 and at 5-year intervals thereafter; and in par. (5) that performance by non-exempt subscription transmission without infringing copyright was permissible by compliance with notice requirements and payment of royalty fees or agreement to pay such fees.

Subsec. (g). Pub. L. 105–304, §405(a)(3)(A), struck out "Subscription" before "Transmissions" in heading.

Subsec. (g)(1). Pub. L. 105–304, §405(a)(3)(B), substituted "transmission licensed under a statutory license" for "subscription transmission licensed" in introductory provisions.

Subsec. (g)(1)(A), (B). Pub. L. 105–304, §405(a)(3)(C), struck out "subscription" before "transmission".

Subsec. (g)(2). Pub. L. 105–304, §405(a)(3)(D), struck out "subscription" before "transmission performances" in introductory provisions.

Subsec. (j)(2), (3). Pub. L. 105–304, §405(a)(4)(A), (B), added par. (2) and redesignated former par. (2) as (3). Former par. (3) redesignated (5).

Subsec. (j)(4). Pub. L. 105–304, §405(a)(4)(A), (C), added par. (4) and struck out former par. (4) which read as follows: "An 'interactive service' is one that enables a member of the public to receive, on request, a transmission of a particular sound recording chosen by or on behalf of the recipient. The ability of individuals to request that particular sound recordings be performed for reception by the public at large does not make a service interactive. If an entity offers both interactive and non-interactive services (either concurrently or at different times), the non-interactive component shall not be treated as part of an interactive service."

Subsec. (j)(5). Pub. L. 105–304, §405(a)(4)(A), redesignated par. (3) as (5). Former par. (5) redesignated (9).

Subsec. (j)(6) to (8). Pub. L. 105–304, §405(a)(4)(A), (D), added pars. (6) to (8). Former pars. (6) to (8) redesignated (12) to (14), respectively.

Subsec. (j)(9). Pub. L. 105–304, §405(a)(4)(A), redesignated par. (5) as (9) and struck out former par. (9) which read as follows: "A 'transmission' includes both an initial transmission and a retransmission."

Subsec. (j)(10), (11). Pub. L. 105–304, §405(a)(4)(E), added pars. (10) and (11).

Subsec. (j)(12) to (14). Pub. L. 105–304, §405(a)(4)(A), redesignated pars. (6) to (8) as (12) to (14), respectively.

Subsec. (j)(15). Pub. L. 105–304, §405(a)(4)(F), added par. (15).

1997—Subsec. (f)(1). Pub. L. 105–80, §3(1), inserted ", or, if a copyright arbitration royalty panel is convened, ending 30 days after the Librarian issues and publishes in the Federal Register an order adopting the determination of the copyright arbitration royalty panel or an order setting the terms and rates (if the Librarian rejects the panel's determination)" after "December 31, 2000".

Subsec. (f)(2). Pub. L. 105–80, §3(2), struck out "and publish in the Federal Register" before "a schedule of rates and terms".

1995—Subsec. (a). Pub. L. 104–39, §3(1), substituted "(3) and (6) of section 106" for "and (3) of section 106".

Subsec. (b). Pub. L. 104–39, §3(2), substituted "phonorecords or copies" for "phonorecords, or of copies of motion pictures and other audiovisual works," in first sentence.

Subsec. (d). Pub. L. 104–39, §3(3), added subsec. (d) and struck out former subsec. (d), which read as follows: "On January 3, 1978, the Register of Copyrights, after consulting with representatives of owners of copyrighted materials, representatives of the broadcasting, recording, motion picture, entertainment industries, and arts organizations, representatives of organized labor and performers of copyrighted materials, shall submit to the Congress a report setting forth recommendations as to whether this section should be amended to provide for performers and copyright owners of copyrighted material any performance rights in such material. The report should describe the status of such rights in foreign countries, the views of major in-

terested parties, and specific legislative or other recommendations, if any."

Subsecs. (e) to (j). Pub. L. 104–39, §3(4), added subsecs. (e) to (j).

EFFECTIVE DATE OF 2006 AMENDMENT

Amendment by Pub. L. 109–303 effective as if included in the Copyright Royalty and Distribution Reform Act of 2004, Pub. L. 108–419, see section 6 of Pub. L. 109–303, set out as a note under section 111 of this title.

EFFECTIVE DATE OF 2004 AMENDMENT

Amendment by Pub. L. 108–419 effective 6 months after Nov. 30, 2004, subject to transition provisions, see section 6 of Pub. L. 108–419, set out as an Effective Date; Transition Provisions note under section 801 of this title.

EFFECTIVE DATE OF 1998 AMENDMENT

Amendment by section 405(a)(1), (2)(A), (B)(i)(I), (II), (ii), (3), (4) of Pub. L. 105–304 effective Oct. 28, 1998, except as otherwise provided, see section 407 of Pub. L. 105–304, set out as a note under section 108 of this title.

Pub. L. 105–304, title IV, §405(a)(5), Oct. 28, 1998, 112 Stat. 2899, provided that: "The amendment made by paragraph (2)(B)(i)(III) of this subsection [amending this section] shall be deemed to have been enacted as part of the Digital Performance Right in Sound Recordings Act of 1995 [Pub. L. 104–39], and the publication of notice of proceedings under section 114(f)(1) of title 17, United States Code, as in effect upon the effective date of that Act [see Effective Date of 1995 Amendment note set out under section 101 of this title], for the determination of royalty payments shall be deemed to have been made for the period beginning on the effective date of that Act and ending on December 1, 2001."

EFFECTIVE DATE OF 1995 AMENDMENT

Amendment by Pub. L. 104–39 effective 3 months after Nov. 1, 1995, except that provisions of subsecs. (e) and (f) of this section effective Nov. 1, 1995, see section 6 of Pub. L. 104–39, set out as a note under section 101 of this title.

CONSTRUCTION OF 1998 AMENDMENT

Pub. L. 105–304, title IV, §405(a)(6), Oct. 28, 1998, 112 Stat. 2899, provided that: "The amendments made by this subsection [amending this section] do not annul, limit, or otherwise impair the rights that are preserved by section 114 of title 17, United States Code, including the rights preserved by subsections (c), (d)(4), and (i) of such section."

FINDINGS RELATING TO PUB. L. 107–321

Pub. L. 107–321, §2, Dec. 4, 2002, 116 Stat. 2780, provided that: "Congress finds the following:

"(1) Some small webcasters who did not participate in the copyright arbitration royalty panel proceeding leading to the July 8, 2002 order of the Librarian of Congress establishing rates and terms for certain digital performances and ephemeral reproductions of sound recordings, as provided in part 261 of the Code of Federal Regulations (published in the Federal Register on July 8, 2002) (referred to in this section as 'small webcasters'), have expressed reservations about the fee structure set forth in such order, and have expressed their desire for a fee based on a percentage of revenue.

"(2) Congress has strongly encouraged representatives of copyright owners of sound recordings and representatives of the small webcasters to engage in negotiations to arrive at an agreement that would include a fee based on a percentage of revenue.

"(3) The representatives have arrived at an agreement that they can accept in the extraordinary and unique circumstances here presented, specifically as to the small webcasters, their belief in their inability to pay the fees due pursuant to the July 8 order, and as to the copyright owners of sound recordings and performers, the strong encouragement of Congress to reach an accommodation with the small webcasters on an expedited basis.

"(4) The representatives have indicated that they do not believe the agreement provides for or in any way approximates fair or reasonable royalty rates and terms, or rates and terms that would have been negotiated in the marketplace between a willing buyer and a willing seller.

"(5) Congress has made no determination as to whether the agreement provides for or in any way approximates fair or reasonable fees and terms, or rates and terms that would have been negotiated in the marketplace between a willing buyer and a willing seller.

"(6) Congress likewise has made no determination as to whether the July 8 order is reasonable or arbitrary, and nothing in this Act [amending this section and enacting provisions set out as notes under this section and section 101 of this title] shall be taken into account by the United States Court of Appeals for the District of Columbia Circuit in its review of such order.

"(7) It is, nevertheless, in the public interest for the parties to be able to enter into such an agreement without fear of liability for deviating from the fees and terms of the July 8 order, if it is clear that the agreement will not be admissible as evidence or otherwise taken into account in any government proceeding involving the setting or adjustment of the royalties payable to copyright owners of sound recordings for the public performance or reproduction in ephemeral phonorecords or copies of such works, the determination of terms or conditions related thereto, or the establishment of notice or record-keeping requirements."

Pub. L. 107–321, §5(a), Dec. 4, 2002, 116 Stat. 2783, provided that: "Congress finds that—

"(1) in the case of royalty payments from the licensing of digital transmissions of sound recordings under subsection (f) of section 114 of title 17, United States Code, the parties have voluntarily negotiated arrangements under which payments shall be made directly to featured recording artists and the administrators of the accounts provided in subsection (g)(2) of that section;

"(2) such voluntarily negotiated payment arrangements have been codified in regulations issued by the Librarian of Congress, currently found in section 261.4 of title 37, Code of Federal Regulations, as published in the Federal Register on July 8, 2002;

"(3) other regulations issued by the Librarian of Congress were inconsistent with the voluntarily negotiated arrangements by such parties concerning the deductibility of certain costs incurred for licensing and arbitration, and Congress is therefore restoring those terms as originally negotiated among the parties; and

"(4) in light of the special circumstances described in this subsection, the uncertainty created by the regulations issued by the Librarian of Congress, and the fact that all of the interested parties have reached agreement, the voluntarily negotiated arrangements agreed to among the parties are being codified."

SUSPENSION OF CERTAIN PAYMENTS

Pub. L. 107–321, §3, Dec. 4, 2002, 116 Stat. 2781, provided that:

"(a) NONCOMMERCIAL WEBCASTERS.—

"(1) IN GENERAL.—The payments to be made by noncommercial webcasters for the digital performance of sound recordings under section 114 of title 17, United States Code, and the making of ephemeral phonorecords under section 112 of title 17, United States Code, during the period beginning on October 28, 1998, and ending on May 31, 2003, which have not already been paid, shall not be due until June 20, 2003.

"(2) DEFINITION.—In this subsection, the term 'noncommercial webcaster' has the meaning given that term in section 114(f)(5)(E)(i) of title 17, United States Code, as added by section 4 of this Act.

"(b) SMALL COMMERCIAL WEBCASTERS.—

"(1) IN GENERAL.—The receiving agent may, in a writing signed by an authorized representative thereof, delay the obligation of any 1 or more small commercial webcasters to make payments pursuant to sections 112 and 114 of title 17, United States Code, for a period determined by such entity to allow negotiations as permitted in section 4 of this Act [amending this section], except that any such period shall end no later than December 15, 2002. The duration and terms of any such delay shall be as set forth in such writing.

"(2) DEFINITIONS.—In this subsection—

"(A) the term 'webcaster' has the meaning given that term in section 114(f)(5)(E)(iii) of title 17, United States Code, as added by section 4 of this Act; and

"(B) the term 'receiving agent' shall have the meaning given that term in section 261.2 of title 37, Code of Federal Regulations, as published in the Federal Register on July 8, 2002."

REPORT TO CONGRESS

Pub. L. 107–321, §6, Dec. 4, 2002, 116 Stat. 2785, provided that: "By not later than June 1, 2004, the Comptroller General of the United States, in consultation with the Register of Copyrights, shall conduct and submit to the Committee on the Judiciary of the House of Representatives and the Committee on the Judiciary of the Senate a study concerning the economic arrangements among small commercial webcasters covered by agreements entered into pursuant to section 114(f)(5)(A) of title 17, United States Code, as added by section 4 of this Act, and third parties, and the effect of those arrangements on royalty fees payable on a percentage of revenue or expense basis."

§ 115. Scope of exclusive rights in nondramatic musical works: Compulsory license for making and distributing phonorecords

In the case of nondramatic musical works, the exclusive rights provided by clauses (1) and (3) of section 106, to make and to distribute phonorecords of such works, are subject to compulsory licensing under the conditions specified by this section.

(a) AVAILABILITY AND SCOPE OF COMPULSORY LICENSE.—

(1) When phonorecords of a nondramatic musical work have been distributed to the public in the United States under the authority of the copyright owner, any other person, including those who make phonorecords or digital phonorecord deliveries, may, by complying with the provisions of this section, obtain a compulsory license to make and distribute phonorecords of the work. A person may obtain a compulsory license only if his or her primary purpose in making phonorecords is to distribute them to the public for private use, including by means of a digital phonorecord delivery. A person may not obtain a compulsory license for use of the work in the making of phonorecords duplicating a sound recording fixed by another, unless: (i) such sound recording was fixed lawfully; and (ii) the making of the phonorecords was authorized by the owner of copyright in the sound recording or, if the sound recording was fixed before February 15, 1972, by any person who fixed the sound recording pursuant to an express license from the owner of the copyright in the musical work or pursuant to a valid compulsory li-

cense for use of such work in a sound recording.

(2) A compulsory license includes the privilege of making a musical arrangement of the work to the extent necessary to conform it to the style or manner of interpretation of the performance involved, but the arrangement shall not change the basic melody or fundamental character of the work, and shall not be subject to protection as a derivative work under this title, except with the express consent of the copyright owner.

(b) NOTICE OF INTENTION TO OBTAIN COMPULSORY LICENSE.—

(1) Any person who wishes to obtain a compulsory license under this section shall, before or within thirty days after making, and before distributing any phonorecords of the work, serve notice of intention to do so on the copyright owner. If the registration or other public records of the Copyright Office do not identify the copyright owner and include an address at which notice can be served, it shall be sufficient to file the notice of intention in the Copyright Office. The notice shall comply, in form, content, and manner of service, with requirements that the Register of Copyrights shall prescribe by regulation.

(2) Failure to serve or file the notice required by clause (1) forecloses the possibility of a compulsory license and, in the absence of a negotiated license, renders the making and distribution of phonorecords actionable as acts of infringement under section 501 and fully subject to the remedies provided by sections 502 through 506 and 509.

(c) ROYALTY PAYABLE UNDER COMPULSORY LICENSE.—

(1) To be entitled to receive royalties under a compulsory license, the copyright owner must be identified in the registration or other public records of the Copyright Office. The owner is entitled to royalties for phonorecords made and distributed after being so identified, but is not entitled to recover for any phonorecords previously made and distributed.

(2) Except as provided by clause (1), the royalty under a compulsory license shall be payable for every phonorecord made and distributed in accordance with the license. For this purpose, and other than as provided in paragraph (3), a phonorecord is considered "distributed" if the person exercising the compulsory license has voluntarily and permanently parted with its possession. With respect to each work embodied in the phonorecord, the royalty shall be either two and three-fourths cents, or one-half of one cent per minute of playing time or fraction thereof, whichever amount is larger.

(3)(A) A compulsory license under this section includes the right of the compulsory licensee to distribute or authorize the distribution of a phonorecord of a nondramatic musical work by means of a digital transmission which constitutes a digital phonorecord delivery, regardless of whether the digital transmission is also a public performance of the sound recording under section 106(6) of this title or of any nondramatic musical work embodied therein under section 106(4) of this title. For every digital phonorecord delivery by or under the authority of the compulsory licensee—

(i) on or before December 31, 1997, the royalty payable by the compulsory licensee shall be the royalty prescribed under paragraph (2) and chapter 8 of this title; and

(ii) on or after January 1, 1998, the royalty payable by the compulsory licensee shall be the royalty prescribed under subparagraphs (B) through (E) and chapter 8 of this title.

(B) Notwithstanding any provision of the antitrust laws, any copyright owners of nondramatic musical works and any persons entitled to obtain a compulsory license under subsection (a)(1) may negotiate and agree upon the terms and rates of royalty payments under this section and the proportionate division of fees paid among copyright owners, and may designate common agents on a nonexclusive basis to negotiate, agree to, pay or receive such royalty payments. Such authority to negotiate the terms and rates of royalty payments includes, but is not limited to, the authority to negotiate the year during which the royalty rates prescribed under this subparagraph and subparagraphs (C) through (E) and chapter 8 of this title shall next be determined.

(C) Proceedings under chapter 8 shall determine reasonable rates and terms of royalty payments for the activities specified by this section during the period beginning with the effective date of such rates and terms, but not earlier than January 1 of the second year following the year in which the petition requesting the proceeding is filed, and ending on the effective date of successor rates and terms, or such other period as the parties may agree. Such terms and rates shall distinguish between (i) digital phonorecord deliveries where the reproduction or distribution of a phonorecord is incidental to the transmission which constitutes the digital phonorecord delivery, and (ii) digital phonorecord deliveries in general. Any copyright owners of nondramatic musical works and any persons entitled to obtain a compulsory license under subsection (a)(1) may submit to the Copyright Royalty Judges licenses covering such activities. The parties to each proceeding shall bear their own costs.

(D) The schedule of reasonable rates and terms determined by the Copyright Royalty Judges shall, subject to subparagraph (E), be binding on all copyright owners of nondramatic musical works and persons entitled to obtain a compulsory license under subsection (a)(1) during the period specified in subparagraph (C), such other period as may be determined pursuant to subparagraphs (B) and (C), or such other period as the parties may agree. Such terms and rates shall distinguish between (i) digital phonorecord deliveries where the reproduction or distribution of a phonorecord is incidental to the transmission which constitutes the digital phonorecord delivery, and (ii) digital phonorecord deliveries in general. In addition to the objectives set forth in section 801(b)(1), in establishing such rates and terms, the Copyright Royalty Judges may consider rates and terms under voluntary license agreements described in subparagraphs (B) and (C). The royalty rates payable for a compulsory license for a digital phonorecord delivery under this section shall be established de novo and no precedential effect shall be given to the amount of the royalty payable by a compulsory licensee for digital phonorecord deliveries on or before December 31, 1997. The Copyright Royalty Judges shall also establish requirements by which copyright owners may receive reasonable notice of the use of their works under this section, and under which records of such use shall be kept and made available by persons making digital phonorecord deliveries.

(E)(i) License agreements voluntarily negotiated at any time between one or more copyright owners of nondramatic musical works and one or more persons entitled to obtain a compulsory license under subsection (a)(1) shall be given effect in lieu of any determination by the Librarian of Congress and Copyright Royalty Judges. Subject to clause (ii), the royalty rates determined pursuant to subparagraph[1] (C) and (D) shall be given effect as to digital phonorecord deliveries in lieu of any contrary royalty rates specified in a contract pursuant to which a recording artist who is the author of a nondramatic musical work grants a license under that person's exclusive rights in the musical work under paragraphs (1) and (3) of section 106 or commits another person to grant a license in that musical work under paragraphs (1) and (3) of section 106, to a person desiring to fix in a tangible medium of expression a sound recording embodying the musical work.

(ii) The second sentence of clause (i) shall not apply to—

(I) a contract entered into on or before June 22, 1995, and not modified thereafter for the purpose of reducing the royalty rates determined pursuant to subparagraph[1] (C) and (D) or of increasing the number of musical works within the scope of the contract covered by the reduced rates, except if a contract entered into on or before June 22, 1995, is modified thereafter for the purpose of increasing the number of musical works within the scope of the contract, any contrary royalty rates specified in the contract shall be given effect in lieu of royalty rates determined pursuant to subparagraph[1] (C) and (D) for the number of musical works within the scope of the contract as of June 22, 1995; and

(II) a contract entered into after the date that the sound recording is fixed in a tangible medium of expression substantially in a form intended for commercial release, if at the time the contract is entered into, the recording artist retains the right to grant licenses as to the musical work under paragraphs (1) and (3) of section 106.

(F) Except as provided in section 1002(e) of this title, a digital phonorecord delivery licensed under this paragraph shall be accompanied by the information encoded in the sound recording, if any, by or under the authority of the copyright owner of that sound recording, that identifies the title of the sound recording, the featured recording artist who performs on the sound recording, and related information, including information concerning the underlying musical work and its writer.

(G)(i) A digital phonorecord delivery of a sound recording is actionable as an act of infringement under section 501, and is fully subject to the remedies provided by sections 502 through 506, unless—

(I) the digital phonorecord delivery has been authorized by the copyright owner of the sound recording; and

(II) the owner of the copyright in the sound recording or the entity making the digital phonorecord delivery has obtained a compulsory license under this section or has otherwise been authorized by the copyright owner of the musical work to distribute or authorize the distribution, by means of a digital phonorecord delivery, of each musical work embodied in the sound recording.

(ii) Any cause of action under this subparagraph shall be in addition to those available to the owner of the copyright in the nondramatic musical work under subsection (c)(6) and section 106(4) and the owner of the copyright in the sound recording under section 106(6).

(H) The liability of the copyright owner of a sound recording for infringement of the copyright in a nondramatic musical work embodied in the sound recording shall be determined in accordance with applicable law, except that the owner of a copyright in a sound recording shall not be liable for a digital phonorecord delivery by a third party if the owner of the copyright in the sound recording does not license the distribution of a phonorecord of the nondramatic musical work.

(I) Nothing in section 1008 shall be construed to prevent the exercise of the rights and remedies allowed by this paragraph, paragraph (6), and chapter 5 in the event of a digital phonorecord delivery, except that no action alleging infringement of copyright may be brought under this title against a manufacturer, importer or distributor of a digital audio recording device, a digital audio recording medium, an analog recording device, or an analog recording medium, or against a consumer, based on the actions described in such section.

(J) Nothing in this section annuls or limits (i) the exclusive right to publicly perform a sound recording or the musical work embodied therein, including by means of a digital transmission, under sections 106(4) and 106(6), (ii) except for compulsory licensing under the conditions specified by this section, the exclusive rights to reproduce and distribute the sound recording and the musical work embodied therein under sections 106(1) and 106(3), including by means of a digital phonorecord delivery, or (iii) any other rights under any other provision of section 106, or remedies available under this title, as such rights or remedies exist either before or after the date of enactment of the Digital Performance Right in Sound Recordings Act of 1995.

(K) The provisions of this section concerning digital phonorecord deliveries shall not apply

---

[1] So in original. Probably should be "subparagraphs".

to any exempt transmissions or retransmissions under section 114(d)(1). The exemptions created in section 114(d)(1) do not expand or reduce the rights of copyright owners under section 106(1) through (5) with respect to such transmissions and retransmissions.

(4) A compulsory license under this section includes the right of the maker of a phonorecord of a nondramatic musical work under subsection (a)(1) to distribute or authorize distribution of such phonorecord by rental, lease, or lending (or by acts or practices in the nature of rental, lease, or lending). In addition to any royalty payable under clause (2) and chapter 8 of this title, a royalty shall be payable by the compulsory licensee for every act of distribution of a phonorecord by or in the nature of rental, lease, or lending, by or under the authority of the compulsory licensee. With respect to each nondramatic musical work embodied in the phonorecord, the royalty shall be a proportion of the revenue received by the compulsory licensee from every such act of distribution of the phonorecord under this clause equal to the proportion of the revenue received by the compulsory licensee from distribution of the phonorecord under clause (2) that is payable by a compulsory licensee under that clause and under chapter 8. The Register of Copyrights shall issue regulations to carry out the purpose of this clause.

(5) Royalty payments shall be made on or before the twentieth day of each month and shall include all royalties for the month next preceding. Each monthly payment shall be made under oath and shall comply with requirements that the Register of Copyrights shall prescribe by regulation. The Register shall also prescribe regulations under which detailed cumulative annual statements of account, certified by a certified public accountant, shall be filed for every compulsory license under this section. The regulations covering both the monthly and the annual statements of account shall prescribe the form, content, and manner of certification with respect to the number of records made and the number of records distributed.

(6) If the copyright owner does not receive the monthly payment and the monthly and annual statements of account when due, the owner may give written notice to the licensee that, unless the default is remedied within thirty days from the date of the notice, the compulsory license will be automatically terminated. Such termination renders either the making or the distribution, or both, of all phonorecords for which the royalty has not been paid, actionable as acts of infringement under section 501 and fully subject to the remedies provided by sections 502 through 506.

(d) DEFINITION.—As used in this section, the following term has the following meaning: A "digital phonorecord delivery" is each individual delivery of a phonorecord by digital transmission of a sound recording which results in a specifically identifiable reproduction by or for any transmission recipient of a phonorecord of that sound recording, regardless of whether the digital transmission is also a public performance of the sound recording or any nondramatic musical work embodied therein. A digital phonorecord delivery does not result from a real-time, non-interactive subscription transmission of a sound recording where no reproduction of the sound recording or the musical work embodied therein is made from the inception of the transmission through to its receipt by the transmission recipient in order to make the sound recording audible.

(Pub. L. 94–553, title I, § 101, Oct. 19, 1976, 90 Stat. 2561; Pub. L. 98–450, § 3, Oct. 4, 1984, 98 Stat. 1727; Pub. L. 104–39, § 4, Nov. 1, 1995, 109 Stat. 344; Pub. L. 105–80, §§ 4, 10, 12(a)(7), Nov. 13, 1997, 111 Stat. 1531, 1534; Pub. L. 108–419, § 5(d), Nov. 30, 2004, 118 Stat. 2364; Pub. L. 109–303, § 4(c), Oct. 6, 2006, 120 Stat. 1482; Pub. L. 110–403, title II, § 209(a)(3), Oct. 13, 2008, 122 Stat. 4264; Pub. L. 111–295, § 6(g), Dec. 9, 2010, 124 Stat. 3181.)

HISTORICAL AND REVISION NOTES

HOUSE REPORT NO. 94–1476

The provisions of section 1(e) and 101(e) of the present law [sections 1(e) and 101(e) of former title 17], establishing a system of compulsory licensing for the making and distribution of phonorecords of copyrighted music, are retained with a number of modifications and clarifications in section 115 of the bill. Under these provisions, which represented a compromise of the most controversial issue of the 1909 act, a musical composition that has been reproduced in phonorecords with the permission of the copyright owner may generally be reproduced in phonorecords by another person, if that person notifies the copyright owner and pays a specified royalty.

The fundamental question of whether to retain the compulsory license or to do away with it altogether was a major issue during earlier stages of the program for general revision of the copyright law. At the hearings it was apparent that the argument on this point had shifted, and the real issue was not whether to retain the compulsory license but how much the royalty rate under it should be. The arguments for and against retention of the compulsory license are outlined at pages 66–67 of this Committee's 1967 report (H. Rept. No. 83, 90th Cong., 1st Sess.). The Committee's conclusion on this point remains the same as in 1967: "that a compulsory licensing system is still warranted as a condition for the rights of reproducing and distributing phonorecords of copyrighted music," but "that the present system is unfair and unnecessarily burdensome on copyright owners, and that the present statutory rate is too low."

Availability and Scope of Compulsory License. Subsection (a) of section 115 deals with three doubtful questions under the present law: (1) the nature of the original recording that will make the work available to others for recording under a compulsory license; (2) the nature of the sound recording that can be made under a compulsory license; and (3) the extent to which someone acting under a compulsory license can depart from the work as written or recorded without violating the copyright owner's right to make an "arrangement" or other derivative work. The first two of these questions are answered in clause (1) of section 115(a), and the third is the subject of clause (2).

The present law, though not altogether clear, apparently bases compulsory licensing on the making or licensing of the first recording, even if no authorized records are distributed to the public. The first sentence of section 115(a)(1) would change the basis for compulsory licensing to authorized public distribution of phonorecords (including disks and audio tapes but not the sound tracks or other sound records accompanying a motion picture or other audiovisual work). Under the clause, a compulsory license would be available to anyone as soon as "phonorecords of a nondramatic musical work have been distributed to the public in the United States under the authority of the copyright owner."

The second sentence of clause (1), which has been the subject of some debate, provides that "a person may obtain a compulsory license only if his or her primary purpose in making phonorecords is to distribute them to the public for private use." This provision was criticized as being discriminatory against background music systems, since it would prevent a background music producer from making recordings without the express consent of the copyright owner; it was argued that this could put the producer at a great competitive disadvantage with performing rights societies, allow discrimination, and destroy or prevent entry of businesses. The committee concluded, however, that the purpose of the compulsory license does not extend to manufacturers of phonorecords that are intended primarily for commercial use, including not only broadcasters and jukebox operators but also background music services.

The final sentence of clause (1) provides that a person may not obtain a compulsory license for use of the work in the duplication of a sound recording made by another, unless the sound recording being duplicated was itself fixed lawfully and the making of phonorecords duplicated from it was authorized by the owner of copyright in the sound recording (or, if the recording was fixed before February 15, 1972, by the voluntary or compulsory licensee of the music used in the recording). The basic intent of this sentence is to make clear that a person is not entitled to a compulsory license of copyrighted musical works for the purpose of making an unauthorized duplication of a musical sound recording originally developed and produced by another. It is the view of the Committee that such was the original intent of the Congress in enacting the 1909 Copyright Act, and it has been so construed by the 3d, 5th, 9th and 10th Circuits in the following cases: *Duchess Music Corp. v. Stern*, 458 F.2d 1305 (9th Cir.), cert. denied, 409 U.S. 847 (1972) [93 S.Ct. 52, 34 L.Ed.2d 88]; *Edward B. Marks Music Corp. v. Colorado Magnetics, Inc.*, 497 F.2d 285, aff'd on rehearing en banc, 497 F.2d 292 (10th Cir. 1974), cert. denied, 419 U.S. 1120 (1975) [95 S.Ct. 801, 42 L.Ed.2d 819]; *Jondora Music Publishing Co. v. Melody Recordings, Inc.*, 506 F.2d 392 (3d Cir. 1974, as amended 1975), cert. denied, 421 U.S. 1012 (1975) [95 S.Ct. 2417, 44 L.Ed.2d 680]; and *Fame Publishing Co. v. Alabama Custom Tape, Inc.*, 507 F.2d 667 (5th Cir.), cert. denied, 423 U.S. 841 (1975) [96 S.Ct. 73, 46 L.Ed.2d 61].

Under this provision, it would be possible to obtain a compulsory license for the use of copyrighted music under section 115 if the owner of the sound recording being duplicated authorizes its duplication. This does not, however, in any way require the owner of the original sound recording to grant a license to duplicate the original sound recording. It is not intended that copyright protection for sound recordings be circumscribed by requiring the owners of sound recordings to grant a compulsory license to unauthorized duplicators or others.

The second clause of subsection (a) is intended to recognize the practical need for a limited privilege to make arrangements of music being used under a compulsory license, but without allowing the music to be perverted, distorted, or travestied. Clause (2) permits arrangements of a work "to the extent necessary to conform it to the style or manner of interpretation of the performance involved," so long as it does not "change the basic melody or fundamental character of the work." The provision also prohibits the compulsory licensee from claiming an independent copyright in his arrangement as a "derivative work" without the express consent of the copyright owner.

Procedure for Obtaining Compulsory License. Section 115(b)(1) requires anyone who wishes to take advantage of the compulsory licensing provisions to serve a "notice of intention to obtain a compulsory license," which is much like the "notice of intention to use" required by the present law. Under section 115, the notice must be served before any phonorecords are distrib-

uted, but service can take place "before or within 30 days after making" any phonorecords. The notice is to be served on the copyright owner, but if the owner is not identified in the Copyright Office records, "it shall be sufficient to file the notice of intention in the Copyright Office."

The Committee deleted clause (2) of section 115(b) of S. 22 as adopted by the Senate. The provision was a vestige of jukebox provisions in earlier bills, and its requirements no longer served any useful purpose.

Clause (2) [formerly clause (3)] of section 115(b) [cl. (2) of subsec. (b) of this section] provides that "failure to serve or file the notice required by clause (1) * * * forecloses the possibility of a compulsory license and, in the absence of a negotiated license, renders the making and distribution of phonorecords actionable as acts of infringement under section 501 and fully subject to the remedies provided by sections 502 through 506." The remedies provided in section 501 are those applicable to infringements generally.

Royalty Payable Under Compulsory License. *Identification of Copyright Owner.*—Under the present law a copyright owner is obliged to file a "notice of use" in the Copyright Office, stating that the initial recording of the copyrighted work has been made or licensed, in order to recover against an unauthorized record manufacturer. This requirement has resulted in a technical loss of rights in some cases, and serves little or no purpose where the registration and assignment records of the Copyright Office already show the facts of ownership. Section 115(c)(1) therefore drops any formal "notice of use" requirements and merely provides that, "to be entitled to receive royalties under a compulsory license, the copyright owner must be identified in the registration or other public records of the Copyright Office." On the other hand, since proper identification is an important precondition of recovery, the bill further provides that "the owner is entitled to royalties for phonorecords manufactured and distributed after being so identified, but is not entitled to recover for any phonorecords previously made and distributed."

Basis of Royalty.—Under the present statute the specified royalty is payable "on each such part manufactured," regardless of how many "parts" (i.e., records) are sold. This basis for calculating the royalty has been revised in section 115(c)(2) to provide that "the royalty under a compulsory license shall be payable for every phonorecord made and distributed in accordance with the license." This basis is more compatible with the general practice in negotiated licenses today. It is unjustified to require a compulsory licensee to pay license fees on records which merely go into inventory, which may later be destroyed, and from which the record producer gains no economic benefit.

It is intended that the Register of Copyrights will prescribe regulations insuring that copyright owners will receive full and prompt payment for all phonorecords made and distributed. Section 115(c)(2) states that "a phonorecord is considered 'distributed' if the person exercising the compulsory license has voluntarily and permanently parted with its possession." For this purpose, the concept of "distribution" comprises any act by which the person exercising the compulsory license voluntarily relinquishes possession of a phonorecord (considered as a fungible unit), regardless of whether the distribution is to the public, passes title, constitutes a gift, or is sold, rented, leased, or loaned, unless it is actually returned and the transaction cancelled. Neither involuntary relinquishment, as through theft or fire, nor the destruction of unwanted records, would constitute "distribution."

The term "made" is intended to be broader than "manufactured," and to include within its scope every possible manufacturing or other process capable of reproducing a sound recording in phonorecords. The use of the phrase "made and distributed" establishes the basis upon which the royalty rate for compulsory licensing under section 115 is to be calculated, but it is in no way intended to weaken the liability of record pressers and other manufacturers and makers of phonorecords for copyright infringement where the compulsory licensing requirements have not been met. As under the present law, even if a presser, manufacturer, or other maker had no role in the distribution process, that person would be regarded as jointly and severally liable in a case where the court finds that infringement has taken place because of failure to comply with the provisions of section 115.

Under existing practices in the record industry, phonorecords are distributed to wholesalers and retailers with the privilege of returning unsold copies for credit or exchange. As a result, the number of recordings that have been "permanently" distributed will not usually be known until some time—six or seven months on the average—after the initial distribution. In recognition of this problem, it has become a well-established industry practice, under negotiated licenses, for record companies to maintain reasonable reserves of the mechanical royalties due the copyright owners, against which royalties on the returns can be offset. The Committee recognizes that this practice may be consistent with the statutory requirements for monthly compulsory license accounting reports, but recognizes the possibility that, without proper safeguards, the maintenance of such reserves could be manipulated to avoid making payments of the full amounts owing to copyright owners. Under these circumstances, the regulations prescribed by the Register of Copyrights should contain detailed provisions ensuring that the ultimate disposition of every phonorecord made under a compulsory license is accounted for, and that payment is made for every phonorecord "voluntarily and permanently" distributed. In particular, the Register should prescribe a point in time when, for accounting purposes under section 115, a phonorecord will be considered "permanently distributed," and should prescribe the situations in which a compulsory licensee is barred from maintaining reserves (e.g., situations in which the compulsory licensee has frequently failed to make payments in the past.)

Rate of Royalty.—A large preponderance of the extensive testimony presented to the Committee on section 115 was devoted to the question of the amount of the statutory royalty rate. An extensive review and analysis of the testimony and arguments received on this question appear in the 1974 Senate report (S. Rep. No. 94–473) at page 71–94.

While upon initial review it might be assumed that the rate established in 1909 would not be reasonable at the present time, the committee believes that an increase in the mechanical royalty rate must be justified on the basis of existing economic conditions and not on the mere passage of 67 years. Following a thorough analysis of the problem, the Committee considers that an increase of the present two-cent royalty to a rate of 2¾ cents (or .6 of one cent per minute or fraction of playing time) is justified. This rate will be subject to review by the Copyright Royalty Commission, as provided by section 801, in 1980 and at 10-year intervals thereafter.

Accounting and Payment of Royalties; Effect of Default. Clause (3) of Section 115(c) provides that royalty payments are to be made on a monthly basis, in accordance with requirements that the Register of Copyrights shall prescribe by regulation. In order to increase the protection of copyright proprietors against economic harm from companies which might refuse or fail to pay their just obligations, compulsory licensees will also be required to make a detailed cumulative annual statement of account, certified by a Certified Public Accountant.

A source of criticism with respect to the compulsory licensing provisions of the present statute has been the rather ineffective sanctions against default by compulsory licensees. Clause (4) of section 115(c) corrects this defect by permitting the copyright owner to serve written notice on a defaulting licensee, and by providing for termination of the compulsory license if the default is not remedied within 30 days after notice is given. Termination under this clause "renders either the making

or the distribution, or both, of all phonorecords for which the royalty had not been paid, actionable as acts of infringement under section 501 and fully subject to the remedies provided by sections 502 through 506."

REFERENCES IN TEXT

The date of enactment of the Digital Performance Right in Sound Recordings Act of 1995, referred to in subsec. (c)(3)(J), is the date of enactment of Pub. L. 104–39, which was approved Nov. 1, 1995.

AMENDMENTS

2010—Subsec. (c)(3)(G)(i). Pub. L. 111–295 made technical correction to directory language of Pub. L. 110–403, §209(a)(3)(A). See 2008 Amendment note below.

2008—Subsec. (c)(3)(G)(i). Pub. L. 110–403, §209(a)(3)(A), as amended by Pub. L. 111–295 struck out "and section 509" after "506" in introductory provisions.

Subsec. (c)(6). Pub. L. 110–403, §209(a)(3)(B), struck out "and 509" before period at end.

2006—Subsec. (c)(3)(B). Pub. L. 109–303, §4(c)(1), substituted "this subparagraph and subparagraphs (C) through (E)" for "subparagraphs (B) through (F)".

Subsec. (c)(3)(D). Pub. L. 109–303, §4(c)(2), inserted "in subparagraphs (B) and (C)" after "described" in third sentence.

Subsec. (c)(3)(E)(i), (ii)(I). Pub. L. 109–303, §4(c)(3), substituted "(C) and (D)" for "(C) or (D)" wherever appearing.

2004—Subsec. (c)(3)(A)(ii). Pub. L. 108–419, §5(d)(1), substituted "(E)" for "(F)".

Subsec. (c)(3)(B). Pub. L. 108–419, §5(d)(2)(C), which directed substitution of "this subparagraph and subparagraphs (C) through (E)" for "subparagraphs (C) through (F)", could not be executed because "subparagraphs (C) through (F)" does not appear in text.

Pub. L. 108–419, §5(d)(2)(A), (B), substituted "under this section" for "under this paragraph" and inserted "on a nonexclusive basis" after "common agents".

Subsec. (c)(3)(C). Pub. L. 108–419, §5(d)(3), substituted first sentence for former first sentence which read: "During the period of June 30, 1996, through December 31, 1996, the Librarian of Congress shall cause notice to be published in the Federal Register of the initiation of voluntary negotiation proceedings for the purpose of determining reasonable terms and rates of royalty payments for the activities specified by subparagraph (A) during the period beginning January 1, 1998, and ending on the effective date of any new terms and rates established pursuant to subparagraph (C), (D) or (F), or such other date (regarding digital phonorecord deliveries) as the parties may agree.", substituted "Copyright Royalty Judges" for "Librarian of Congress" in third sentence, and struck out "negotiation" before "proceeding" in last sentence.

Subsec. (c)(3)(D). Pub. L. 108–419, §5(d)(4), substituted first sentence for former first sentence which read: "In the absence of license agreements negotiated under subparagraphs (B) and (C), upon the filing of a petition in accordance with section 803(a)(1), the Librarian of Congress shall, pursuant to chapter 8, convene a copyright arbitration royalty panel to determine a schedule of rates and terms which, subject to subparagraph (E), shall be binding on all copyright owners of nondramatic musical works and persons entitled to obtain a compulsory license under subsection (a)(1) during the period beginning January 1, 1998, and ending on the effective date of any new terms and rates established pursuant to subparagraph (C), (D) or (F), or such other date (regarding digital phonorecord deliveries) as may be determined pursuant to subparagraphs (B) and (C).", substituted "Copyright Royalty Judges may consider" for "copyright arbitration royalty panel may consider" and "described" for "negotiated as provided in subparagraphs (B) and (C)" in third sentence, and "Copyright Royalty Judges shall also establish" for "Librarian of Congress shall also establish" in last sentence.

Subsec. (c)(3)(E)(i). Pub. L. 108–419, §5(d)(5)(A), substituted "Librarian of Congress and Copyright Royalty

Judges'' for "Librarian of Congress" in first sentence and "(C) or (D) shall be given effect as to digital phonorecord deliveries" for "(C), (D) or (F) shall be given effect" in second sentence.

Subsec. (c)(3)(E)(ii)(I). Pub. L. 108–419, §5(d)(5)(B), substituted "(C) or (D)'' for "(C), (D) or (F)'' in two places.

Subsec. (c)(3)(F) to (L). Pub. L. 108–419, §5(d)(6), redesignated subpars. (G) to (L) as (F) to (K), respectively, and struck out former subpar. (F), which read as follows: "The procedures specified in subparagraphs (C) and (D) shall be repeated and concluded, in accordance with regulations that the Librarian of Congress shall prescribe, in each fifth calendar year after 1997, except to the extent that different years for the repeating and concluding of such proceedings may be determined in accordance with subparagraphs (B) and (C).''

1997—Subsec. (c)(3)(D). Pub. L. 105–80, §4, struck out "and publish in the Federal Register" before "a schedule of rates and terms''.

Subsec. (c)(3)(E)(i). Pub. L. 105–80, §12(a)(7)(A), substituted "paragraphs (1) and (3) of section 106" for "sections 106(1) and (3)'' in two places.

Subsec. (c)(3)(E)(ii)(II). Pub. L. 105–80, §12(a)(7)(A), substituted "paragraphs (1) and (3) of section 106" for "sections 106(1) and 106(3)''.

Subsec. (d). Pub. L. 105–80, §10, amended directory language of Pub. L. 104–39, §4. See 1995 Amendment note below.

1995—Subsec. (a)(1). Pub. L. 104–39, §4(1), substituted "any other person, including those who make phonorecords or digital phonorecord deliveries," for "any other person" in first sentence and inserted before period at end of second sentence ", including by means of a digital phonorecord delivery''.

Subsec. (c)(2). Pub. L. 104–39, §4(2), inserted "and other than as provided in paragraph (3)," after "For this purpose," in second sentence.

Subsec. (c)(3) to (6). Pub. L. 104–39, §4(3), added par. (3) and redesignated former pars. (3) to (5) as (4) to (6), respectively.

Subsec. (d). Pub. L. 104–39, §4(4), as renumbered by Pub. L. 105–80, §10, added subsec. (d).

1984—Subsec. (c)(3) to (5). Pub. L. 98–450 added par. (3) and redesignated existing pars. (3) and (4) as (4) and (5), respectively.

EFFECTIVE DATE OF 2006 AMENDMENT

Amendment by Pub. L. 109–303 effective as if included in the Copyright Royalty and Distribution Reform Act of 2004, Pub. L. 108–419, see section 6 of Pub. L. 109–303, set out as a note under section 111 of this title.

EFFECTIVE DATE OF 2004 AMENDMENT

Amendment by Pub. L. 108–419 effective 6 months after Nov. 30, 2004, subject to transition provisions, see section 6 of Pub. L. 108–419, set out as an Effective Date; Transition Provisions note under section 801 of this title.

EFFECTIVE DATE OF 1995 AMENDMENT

Amendment by Pub. L. 104–39 effective 3 months after Nov. 1, 1995, see section 6 of Pub. L. 104–39, set out as a note under section 101 of this title.

PERSONS OPERATING UNDER PREDECESSOR COMPULSORY LICENSING PROVISIONS

Section 106 of Pub. L. 94–553 provided that: "In any case where, before January 1, 1978, a person has lawfully made parts of instruments serving to reproduce mechanically a copyrighted work under the compulsory license provisions of section 1(e) of title 17 as it existed on December 31, 1977, such person may continue to make and distribute such parts embodying the same mechanical reproduction without obtaining a new compulsory license under the terms of section 115 of title 17 as amended by the first section of this Act [this section]. However, such parts made on or after January 1, 1978, constitute phonorecords and are otherwise subject to the provisions of said section 115 [this section].''

§ 116. Negotiated licenses for public performances by means of coin-operated phonorecord players

(a) APPLICABILITY OF SECTION.—This section applies to any nondramatic musical work embodied in a phonorecord.

(b) NEGOTIATED LICENSES.—

(1) AUTHORITY FOR NEGOTIATIONS.—Any owners of copyright in works to which this section applies and any operators of coin-operated phonorecord players may negotiate and agree upon the terms and rates of royalty payments for the performance of such works and the proportionate division of fees paid among copyright owners, and may designate common agents to negotiate, agree to, pay, or receive such royalty payments.

(2) CHAPTER 8 PROCEEDING.—Parties not subject to such a negotiation may have the terms and rates and the division of fees described in paragraph (1) determined in a proceeding in accordance with the provisions of chapter 8.

(c) LICENSE AGREEMENTS SUPERIOR TO DETERMINATIONS BY COPYRIGHT ROYALTY JUDGES.—License agreements between one or more copyright owners and one or more operators of coin-operated phonorecord players, which are negotiated in accordance with subsection (b), shall be given effect in lieu of any otherwise applicable determination by the Copyright Royalty Judges.

(d) DEFINITIONS.—As used in this section, the following terms mean the following:

(1) A "coin-operated phonorecord player" is a machine or device that—

(A) is employed solely for the performance of nondramatic musical works by means of phonorecords upon being activated by the insertion of coins, currency, tokens, or other monetary units or their equivalent;

(B) is located in an establishment making no direct or indirect charge for admission;

(C) is accompanied by a list which is comprised of the titles of all the musical works available for performance on it, and is affixed to the phonorecord player or posted in the establishment in a prominent position where it can be readily examined by the public; and

(D) affords a choice of works available for performance and permits the choice to be made by the patrons of the establishment in which it is located.

(2) An "operator" is any person who, alone or jointly with others—

(A) owns a coin-operated phonorecord player;

(B) has the power to make a coin-operated phonorecord player available for placement in an establishment for purposes of public performance; or

(C) has the power to exercise primary control over the selection of the musical works made available for public performance on a coin-operated phonorecord player.

(Added Pub. L. 100–568, §4(a)(4), Oct. 31, 1988, 102 Stat. 2855, §116A; renumbered §116 and amended Pub. L. 103–198, §3(b)(1), Dec. 17, 1993, 107 Stat. 2309; Pub. L. 105–80, §5, Nov. 13, 1997, 111 Stat.

1531; Pub. L. 108–419, §5(e), Nov. 30, 2004, 118 Stat. 2365.)

PRIOR PROVISIONS

A prior section 116, Pub. L. 94–553, title I, §101, Oct. 19, 1976, 90 Stat. 2562; Pub. L. 100–568, §4(b)(1), Oct. 31, 1988, 102 Stat. 2857, related to scope of exclusive rights in nondramatic musical works and compulsory licenses for public performances by means of coin-operated phonorecord players, prior to repeal by Pub. L. 103–198, §3(a), Dec. 17, 1993, 107 Stat. 2309.

AMENDMENTS

2004—Subsec. (b)(2). Pub. L. 108–419, §5(e)(1), amended heading and text of par. (2) generally. Prior to amendment, text read as follows: "Parties not subject to such a negotiation may determine, by arbitration in accordance with the provisions of chapter 8, the terms and rates and the division of fees described in paragraph (1)."

Subsec. (c). Pub. L. 108–419, §5(e)(2), substituted "Determinations by Copyright Royalty Judges" for "Copyright Arbitration Royalty Panel Determinations" in heading and "the Copyright Royalty Judges" for "a copyright arbitration royalty panel" in text.

1997—Subsec. (b)(2). Pub. L. 105–80, §5(1), amended par. (2) generally. Prior to amendment, par. (2) read as follows:

"(2) ARBITRATION.—Parties to such a negotiation, within such time as may be specified by the Librarian of Congress by regulation, may determine the result of the negotiation by arbitration. Such arbitration shall be governed by the provisions of title 9, to the extent such title is not inconsistent with this section. The parties shall give notice to the Librarian of Congress of any determination reached by arbitration and any such determination shall, as between the parties to the arbitration, be dispositive of the issues to which it relates."

Subsec. (d). Pub. L. 105–80, §5(2), added subsec. (d).

1993—Pub. L. 103–198, §3(b)(1)(A), renumbered section 116A of this title as this section.

Subsec. (b). Pub. L. 103–198, §3(b)(1)(B), (C), redesignated subsec. (c) as (b), substituted "Librarian of Congress" for "Copyright Royalty Tribunal" in two places in par. (2), and struck out former subsec. (b) which related to limitation on exclusive right if licenses not negotiated.

Subsec. (c). Pub. L. 103–198, §3(b)(1)(B), (D), redesignated subsec. (d) as (c), in heading substituted "Arbitration Royalty Panel" for "Royalty Tribunal", and in text substituted "subsection (b)" for "subsection (c)" and "a copyright arbitration royalty panel" for "the Copyright Royalty Tribunal".

Subsecs. (d) to (g). Pub. L. 103–198, §3(b)(1)(B), (E), redesignated subsec. (d) as (c) and struck out subsecs. (e) to (g) which provided, in subsec. (e), for a schedule for negotiation of licenses, in subsec. (f), for a suspension of various ratemaking activities by the Copyright Royalty Tribunal, and in subsec. (g), for transition provisions and retention of Copyright Royalty Tribunal jurisdiction.

EFFECTIVE DATE OF 2004 AMENDMENT

Amendment by Pub. L. 108–419 effective 6 months after Nov. 30, 2004, subject to transition provisions, see section 6 of Pub. L. 108–419, set out as an Effective Date; Transition Provisions note under section 801 of this title.

EFFECTIVE DATE

Section effective Mar. 1, 1989, with any cause of action arising under this title before such date being governed by provisions as in effect when cause of action arose, see section 13 of Pub. L. 100–568, set out as an Effective Date of 1988 Amendment note under section 101 of this title.

[§116A. Renumbered §116]

§117. Limitations on exclusive rights: Computer programs

(a) MAKING OF ADDITIONAL COPY OR ADAPTATION BY OWNER OF COPY.—Notwithstanding the provisions of section 106, it is not an infringement for the owner of a copy of a computer program to make or authorize the making of another copy or adaptation of that computer program provided:

(1) that such a new copy or adaptation is created as an essential step in the utilization of the computer program in conjunction with a machine and that it is used in no other manner, or

(2) that such new copy or adaptation is for archival purposes only and that all archival copies are destroyed in the event that continued possession of the computer program should cease to be rightful.

(b) LEASE, SALE, OR OTHER TRANSFER OF ADDITIONAL COPY OR ADAPTATION.—Any exact copies prepared in accordance with the provisions of this section may be leased, sold, or otherwise transferred, along with the copy from which such copies were prepared, only as part of the lease, sale, or other transfer of all rights in the program. Adaptations so prepared may be transferred only with the authorization of the copyright owner.

(c) MACHINE MAINTENANCE OR REPAIR.—Notwithstanding the provisions of section 106, it is not an infringement for the owner or lessee of a machine to make or authorize the making of a copy of a computer program if such copy is made solely by virtue of the activation of a machine that lawfully contains an authorized copy of the computer program, for purposes only of maintenance or repair of that machine, if—

(1) such new copy is used in no other manner and is destroyed immediately after the maintenance or repair is completed; and

(2) with respect to any computer program or part thereof that is not necessary for that machine to be activated, such program or part thereof is not accessed or used other than to make such new copy by virtue of the activation of the machine.

(d) DEFINITIONS.—For purposes of this section—

(1) the "maintenance" of a machine is the servicing of the machine in order to make it work in accordance with its original specifications and any changes to those specifications authorized for that machine; and

(2) the "repair" of a machine is the restoring of the machine to the state of working in accordance with its original specifications and any changes to those specifications authorized for that machine.

(Pub. L. 94–553, title I, §101, Oct. 19, 1976, 90 Stat. 2565; Pub. L. 96–517, §10(b), Dec. 12, 1980, 94 Stat. 3028; Pub. L. 105–304, title III, §302, Oct. 28, 1998, 112 Stat. 2887.)

HISTORICAL AND REVISION NOTES

HOUSE REPORT NO. 94–1476

As the program for general revision of the copyright law has evolved, it has become increasingly apparent that in one major area the problems are not sufficiently developed for a definitive legislative solution. This is the area of computer uses of copyrighted works: the use of a work "in conjunction with automatic systems capable of storing, processing, retrieving, or transferring information." The Commission on New Technological Uses is, among other things, now engaged in making a thorough study of the emerging patterns in this field and it will, on the basis of its findings, recommend definitive copyright provisions to deal with the situation.

Since it would be premature to change existing law on computer uses at present, the purpose of section 117 is to preserve the status quo. It is intended neither to cut off any rights that may now exist, nor to create new rights that might be denied under the Act of 1909 or under common law principles currently applicable.

The provision deals only with the exclusive rights of a copyright owner with respect to computer uses, that is, the bundle of rights specified for other types of uses in section 106 and qualified in sections 107 through 116 and 118. With respect to the copyright-ability of computer programs, the ownership of copyrights in them, the term of protection, and the formal requirements of the remainder of the bill, the new statute would apply.

Under section 117, an action for infringement of a copyrighted work by means of a computer would necessarily be a federal action brought under the new title 17. The court, in deciding the scope of exclusive rights in the computer area, would first need to determine the applicable law, whether State statutory or common law or the Act of 1909. Having determined what law was applicable, its decision would depend upon its interpretation of what that law was on the point on the day before the effective date of the new statute.

AMENDMENTS

1998—Pub. L. 105–304 designated existing provisions as subsecs. (a) and (b), inserted headings, and added subsecs. (c) and (d).

1980—Pub. L. 96–517 substituted provision respecting limitations on exclusive rights in connection with computer programs for prior provision enunciating scope of exclusive rights and use of the work in conjunction with computers and similar information systems and declaring owner of copyright in a work without any greater or lesser rights with respect to the use of the work in conjunction with automatic systems capable of storing, processing, retrieving, or transferring information, or in conjunction with any similar device, machine, or process, than those afforded to works under the law, whether this title or the common law or statutes of a State, in effect on Dec. 31, 1977, as held applicable and construed by the court in an action brought under this title.

§ 118. Scope of exclusive rights: Use of certain works in connection with noncommercial broadcasting

(a) The exclusive rights provided by section 106 shall, with respect to the works specified by subsection (b) and the activities specified by subsection (d),[1] be subject to the conditions and limitations prescribed by this section.

(b) Notwithstanding any provision of the antitrust laws, any owners of copyright in published nondramatic musical works and published pictorial, graphic, and sculptural works and any public broadcasting entities, respectively, may negotiate and agree upon the terms and rates of royalty payments and the proportionate division of fees paid among various copyright owners, and may designate common agents to negotiate, agree to, pay, or receive payments.

---

[1] See References in Text note below.

(1) Any owner of copyright in a work specified in this subsection or any public broadcasting entity may submit to the Copyright Royalty Judges proposed licenses covering such activities with respect to such works.

(2) License agreements voluntarily negotiated at any time between one or more copyright owners and one or more public broadcasting entities shall be given effect in lieu of any determination by the Librarian of Congress or the Copyright Royalty Judges, if copies of such agreements are filed with the Copyright Royalty Judges within 30 days of execution in accordance with regulations that the Copyright Royalty Judges shall issue.

(3) Voluntary negotiation proceedings initiated pursuant to a petition filed under section 804(a) for the purpose of determining a schedule of terms and rates of royalty payments by public broadcasting entities to owners of copyright in works specified by this subsection and the proportionate division of fees paid among various copyright owners shall cover the 5-year period beginning on January 1 of the second year following the year in which the petition is filed. The parties to each negotiation proceeding shall bear their own costs.

(4) In the absence of license agreements negotiated under paragraph (2) or (3), the Copyright Royalty Judges shall, pursuant to chapter 8, conduct a proceeding to determine and publish in the Federal Register a schedule of rates and terms which, subject to paragraph (2), shall be binding on all owners of copyright in works specified by this subsection and public broadcasting entities, regardless of whether such copyright owners have submitted proposals to the Copyright Royalty Judges. In establishing such rates and terms the Copyright Royalty Judges may consider the rates for comparable circumstances under voluntary license agreements negotiated as provided in paragraph (2) or (3). The Copyright Royalty Judges shall also establish requirements by which copyright owners may receive reasonable notice of the use of their works under this section, and under which records of such use shall be kept by public broadcasting entities.

(c) Subject to the terms of any voluntary license agreements that have been negotiated as provided by subsection (b)(2) or (3), a public broadcasting entity may, upon compliance with the provisions of this section, including the rates and terms established by the Copyright Royalty Judges under subsection (b)(4), engage in the following activities with respect to published nondramatic musical works and published pictorial, graphic, and sculptural works:

(1) performance or display of a work by or in the course of a transmission made by a noncommercial educational broadcast station referred to in subsection (f); and

(2) production of a transmission program, reproduction of copies or phonorecords of such a transmission program, and distribution of such copies or phonorecords, where such production, reproduction, or distribution is made by a nonprofit institution or organization solely for the purpose of transmissions specified in paragraph (1); and

(3) the making of reproductions by a governmental body or a nonprofit institution of a

transmission program simultaneously with its transmission as specified in paragraph (1), and the performance or display of the contents of such program under the conditions specified by paragraph (1) of section 110, but only if the reproductions are used for performances or displays for a period of no more than seven days from the date of the transmission specified in paragraph (1), and are destroyed before or at the end of such period. No person supplying, in accordance with paragraph (2), a reproduction of a transmission program to governmental bodies or nonprofit institutions under this paragraph shall have any liability as a result of failure of such body or institution to destroy such reproduction: *Provided,* That it shall have notified such body or institution of the requirement for such destruction pursuant to this paragraph: *And provided further,* That if such body or institution itself fails to destroy such reproduction it shall be deemed to have infringed.

(d) Except as expressly provided in this subsection, this section shall have no applicability to works other than those specified in subsection (b). Owners of copyright in nondramatic literary works and public broadcasting entities may, during the course of voluntary negotiations, agree among themselves, respectively, as to the terms and rates of royalty payments without liability under the antitrust laws. Any such terms and rates of royalty payments shall be effective upon filing with the Copyright Royalty Judges, in accordance with regulations that the Copyright Royalty Judges shall prescribe as provided in section 803(b)(6).

(e) Nothing in this section shall be construed to permit, beyond the limits of fair use as provided by section 107, the unauthorized dramatization of a nondramatic musical work, the production of a transmission program drawn to any substantial extent from a published compilation of pictorial, graphic, or sculptural works, or the unauthorized use of any portion of an audiovisual work.

(f) As used in this section, the term "public broadcasting entity" means a noncommercial educational broadcast station as defined in section 397 of title 47 and any nonprofit institution or organization engaged in the activities described in paragraph (2) of subsection (c).

(Pub. L. 94–553, title I, §101, Oct. 19, 1976, 90 Stat. 2565; Pub. L. 103–198, §4, Dec. 17, 1993, 107 Stat. 2309; Pub. L. 106–44, §1(g)(3), Aug. 5, 1999, 113 Stat. 222; Pub. L. 107–273, div. C, title III, §13210(7), Nov. 2, 2002, 116 Stat. 1909; Pub. L. 108–419, §5(f), Nov. 30, 2004, 118 Stat. 2365; Pub. L. 109–303, §4(d), Oct. 6, 2006, 120 Stat. 1482.)

HISTORICAL AND REVISION NOTES

HOUSE REPORT NO. 94–1476

General Background. During its consideration of revision legislation in 1975, the Senate Judiciary Committee adopted an amendment offered by Senator Charles McC. Mathias. The amendment, now section 118 of the Senate bill [this section], grants to public broadcasting a compulsory license for use of nondramatic literary and musical works, as well as pictorial, graphic, and sculptural works, subject to payment of reasonable royalty fees to be set by the Copyright Royalty Tribunal established by that bill. The Mathias amendment

requires that public broadcasters, at periodic intervals, file a notice with the Copyright Office containing information required by the Register of Copyrights and deposit a statement of account and the total royalty fees for the period covered by the statement. In July of each year all persons having a claim to such fees are to file their claims with the Register of Copyrights. If no controversy exists, the Register would distribute the royalties to the various copyright owners and their agents after deducting reasonable administrative costs; controversies are to be settled by the Tribunal.

On July 10, 1975, the House Subcommittee heard testimony on the Mathias amendment from representatives of public broadcasters, authors, publishers, and music performing rights societies. The public broadcasters pointed to Congressional concern for the development of their activities as evidenced by the Public Broadcasting Act [47 U.S.C. 390 et seq.]. They urged that a compulsory license was essential to assure public broadcasting broad access to copyrighted materials at reasonable royalties and without administratively cumbersome and costly "clearance" problems that would impair the vitality of their operations. The opponents of the amendment argued that the nature of public broadcasting has changed significantly in the past decade, to the extent that it now competes with commercial broadcasting as a national entertainment and cultural medium. They asserted that the performing rights society arrangements under which copyrighted music is licensed for performance removed any problem in clearing music for broadcasting, and that voluntary agreements could adequately resolve the copyright problems feared by public broadcasters, at less expense and burden than the compulsory license, for synchronization and literary rights. The authors of literary works stressed that a compulsory licensing system would deny them the fundamental right to control the use of their works and protect their reputation in a major communications medium.

General Policy Considerations. The Committee is cognizant of the intent of Congress, in enacting the Public Broadcasting Act on November 7, 1967 [47 U.S.C. 390 et seq.], that encouragement and support of noncommercial broadcasting is in the public interest. It is also aware that public broadcasting may encounter problems not confronted by commercial broadcasting enterprises, due to such factors as the special nature of programming, repeated use of programs, and, of course, limited financial resources. Thus, the Committee determined that the nature of public broadcasting does warrant special treatment in certain areas. However, the Committee did not feel that the broad compulsory license provided in the Senate bill is necessary to the continued successful operation of public broadcasting. In addition, the Committee believes that the system provided in the Senate bill for the deposit of royalty fees with the Copyright Office for distribution to claimants, and the resolution of disputes over such distribution by a statutory tribunal, can be replaced by payments directly between the parties, without the intervention of government machinery and its attendant administrative costs.

In general, the Committee amended the public broadcasting provisions of the Senate bill toward attainment of the objective clearly stated in the Report of the Senate Judiciary Committee, namely, that copyright owners and public broadcasters be encouraged to reach voluntary private agreements.

Procedures. Not later than thirty days following the publication by the President of the notice announcing the initial appointments to the Copyright Royalty Commission (specified in Chapter 8 [§ 801 et seq. of this title]), the Chairman of the Commission is to publish notice in the Federal Register of the initiation of proceedings to determine "reasonable terms and rates" for certain uses of published nondramatic musical works and published pictorial, graphic and sculptural works, during a period ending on December 31, 1982.

Copyright owners and public broadcasting entities that do not reach voluntary agreement are bound by the terms and rates established by the Commission, which are to be published in the Federal Register within six months of the notice of initiation of proceedings. During the period between the effective date of the Act [Jan. 1, 1978] and the publication of the rates and terms, the Committee has preserved the status quo by providing, in section 118(b)(4), that the Act does not afford to copyright owners or public broadcasting entities any greater or lesser rights with respect to the relevant uses of nondramatic musical works and pictorial, graphic, and sculptural works than those afforded under the law in effect on December 31, 1977.

License agreements that have been voluntarily negotiated supersede, as between the parties to the agreement, the terms and rates established by the Commission, provided that copies of the agreements are properly filed with the Copyright Office within 30 days of execution. Under clause (2) of section 118(b), the agreements may be negotiated "at any time"—whether before, during, or after determinations by the Commission.

Under section 118(c), the procedures for the Commission's establishing such rates and terms are to be repeated in the last half of 1982 and every five years thereafter.

Establishment of Reasonable Terms and Rates. In establishing reasonable terms and rates for public broadcasting use of the specified works, the Commission, under clause (b)(1) of section 118 is to consider proposals timely submitted to it, as well as "any other relevant information", including that put forward for its consideration "by any interested party."

The Committee does not intend that owners of copyrighted material be required to subsidize public broadcasting. It is intended that the Commission assure a fair return to copyright owners without unfairly burdening public broadcasters. Section 118(b)(3) provides that "the Commission may consider the rates for comparable circumstances under voluntary license agreements." The Commission is also expected to consider both the general public interest in encouraging the growth and development of public broadcasting, and the "promotion of science and the useful arts" through the encouragement of musical and artistic creation.

The Committee anticipates that the "terms" established by the Commission shall include provisions as to acceptable methods of payment of royalties by public broadcasting entities to copyright owners. For example, where the whereabouts of the copyright owner may not be readily known, the terms should specify the nature of the obligation of the public broadcasting entity to locate the owner, or to set aside or otherwise assure payment of appropriate royalties, should he or she appear and make a claim. Section 118(b)(3) requires the Commission "to establish requirements by which copyright owners may receive reasonable notice of the use of their works." The Committee intends that these requirements shall not impose undue hardships on public broadcasting entities and, in the above illustration, shall provide for the specific termination of any period during which the public broadcasting entity is required to set aside payments. It is expected that, in some cases, especially in the area of pictorial, graphic, and sculptural works, the whereabouts of the owners of copyright may not be known and they may never appear to claim payment of royalties.

The Commission is also to establish record keeping requirements for public broadcasting entities in order to facilitate the identification, calculation, allocation and payment of claims and royalties.

Works Affected. Under sections 118(b) and (e) of the Committee's amendment, the establishment of rates and terms by the Copyright Royalty Commission pertains only to the use of published nondramatic musical works, and published pictorial, graphic, and sculptural works. As under the Senate bill; rights in plays, operas, ballet and other stage presentations, motion pictures, and other audiovisual works are not affected.

Section 118(f) is intended to make clear that this section does not permit unauthorized use, beyond the limits of section 107, of individual frames from a filmstrip or any other portion of any audiovisual work. Additionally, the application of this section to pictorial, graphic, and sculptural works does not extend to the production of transmission programs drawn to any substantial extent from a compilation of such works.

The Committee also concluded that the performance of nondramatic literary works should not be subject to Commission determination. It was particularly concerned that a compulsory license for literary works would result in loss of control by authors over the use of their work in violation of basic principles of artistic and creative freedom. It is recognized that copyright not only provides compensation to authors, but also protection as to how and where their works are used. The Committee was assured by representatives of authors and publishers that licensing arrangements for readings from their books, poems, and other works on public broadcasting programs for reasonable compensation and under reasonable safeguards for authors' rights could be worked out in private negotiation. The Committee strongly urges the parties to work toward mutually acceptable licenses; to facilitate their negotiations and aid in the possible establishment of clearance mechanisms and rates, the Committee's amendment provides the parties, in section 118(e)(1), with an appropriately limited exemption from the antitrust laws [15 U.S.C. 1 et seq.].

The Committee has also provided, in paragraph (2) of clause (e), that on January 3, 1980, the Register of Copyrights, after consultation with the interested parties, shall submit a report to Congress on the extent to which voluntary licensing arrangements have been reached with respect to public broadcast use of nondramatic literary works, and present legislative or other recommendations, if warranted.

The use of copyrighted sound recordings in educational television and radio programs distributed by or through public broadcasting entities is governed by section 114 and is discussed in connection with that section.

Activities Affected. Section 118(d) specifies the activities which may be engaged in by public broadcasting entities under terms and rates established by the Commission. These include the performance or display of published nondramatic musical works, and of published pictorial, graphic, and sculptural works, in the course of transmissions by noncommercial educational broadcast stations; and the production, reproduction, and distribution of transmission programs including such works by nonprofit organizations for the purpose of such transmissions. It is the intent of the Committee that "interconnection" activities serving as a technical adjunct to such transmissions, such as the use of satellites or microwave equipment, be included within the specified activities.

Paragraph (3) of clause (d) also includes the reproduction, simultaneously with transmission, of public broadcasting programs by governmental bodies or nonprofit institutions, and the performance or display of the contents of the reproduction under the conditions of section 110(1). However, the reproduction so made must be destroyed at the end of seven days from the transmission.

This limited provision for unauthorized simultaneous or off-the-air reproduction is limited to nondramatic musical works and pictorial, graphic and sculptural works included in public broadcasting transmissions. It does not extend to other works included in the transmissions, or to the entire transmission program.

It is the intent of the Committee that schools be permitted to engage in off-the-air reproduction to the extent and under the conditions provided in [section] 118(d)(3); however, in the event a public broadcasting station or producer makes the reproduction and distributes a copy to the school, the station or producer will not be held liable for the school's failure to destroy the reproduction, provided it has given notice of the requirement of destruction. In such a case the school itself, although it did not engage in the act of reproduction, is deemed an infringer fully subject to the remedies provided in Chapter 5 of the Act [§501 et seq. of this title]. The establishment of standards for adequate notice under this provision should be considered by the Commission.

Section 118(f) makes it clear that the rights of performance and other activities specified in subsection (d) do not extend to the unauthorized dramatization of a nondramatic musical work.

REFERENCES IN TEXT

Subsection (d), referred to in subsec. (a), was redesignated as subsection (c) of this section by Pub. L. 108–419, §5(f)(2), Nov. 30, 2004, 118 Stat. 2366.

AMENDMENTS

2006—Subsec. (b)(3). Pub. L. 109–303, §4(d)(1), substituted "owners of copyright in works" for "copyright owners in works".

Subsec. (c). Pub. L. 109–303, §4(d)(2), substituted "established by the Copyright Royalty Judges under subsection (b)(4), engage" for "established by the Copyright Royalty Judges under subsection (b)(4), to the extent that they were accepted by the Librarian of Congress, engage" in introductory provisions and "(f)" for "(g)" in par. (1).

2004—Subsec. (b)(1). Pub. L. 108–419, §5(f)(1)(A), substituted "Copyright Royalty Judges" for "Librarian of Congress" in first sentence and struck out at end "The Librarian of Congress shall proceed on the basis of the proposals submitted as well as any other relevant information. The Librarian of Congress shall permit any interested party to submit information relevant to such proceedings."

Subsec. (b)(2). Pub. L. 108–419, §5(f)(1)(B), substituted "Librarian of Congress or the Copyright Royalty Judges, if copies of such agreements are filed with the Copyright Royalty Judges within 30 days of execution in accordance with regulations that the Copyright Royalty Judges shall issue" for "Librarian of Congress: Provided, That copies of such agreements are filed in the Copyright Office within thirty days of execution in accordance with regulations that the Register of Copyrights shall prescribe".

Subsec. (b)(3), (4). Pub. L. 108–419, §5(f)(1)(C), added pars. (3) and (4), redesignated second and third sentences of former par. (3) as second and third sentences of par. (4), substituted "Copyright Royalty Judges" for "copyright arbitration royalty panel" and "paragraph (2) or (3)" for "paragraph (2)" in second sentence of par. (4), substituted "Copyright Royalty Judges" for "Librarian of Congress" in last sentence of par. (4), and struck out "(3) In the absence of license agreements negotiated under paragraph (2), the Librarian of Congress shall, pursuant to chapter 8, convene a copyright arbitration royalty panel to determine and publish in the Federal Register a schedule of rates and terms which, subject to paragraph (2), shall be binding on all owners of copyright in works specified by this subsection and public broadcasting entities, regardless of whether such copyright owners have submitted proposals to the Librarian of Congress."

Subsec. (c). Pub. L. 108–419, §5(f)(3)(C), which directed substitution of "the Copyright Royalty Judges under subsection (b)(3), to the extent that they were accepted by the Librarian of Congress" for "a copyright arbitration royalty panel under subsection (b)(3)" in introductory provisions, was executed before the amendment by Pub. L. 108–419, §5(f)(3)(B), to reflect the probable intent of Congress. See below.

Pub. L. 108–419, §5(f)(3)(B), substituted "(b)(4)" for "(b)(3)" in introductory provisions. See above.

Pub. L. 108–419, §5(f)(3)(A), substituted "(b)(2) or (3)" for "(b)(2)" in introductory provisions.

Pub. L. 108–419, §5(f)(2), redesignated subsec. (d) as (c) and struck out former subsec. (c) which read as follows: "The initial procedure specified in subsection (b) shall be repeated and concluded between June 30 and December 31, 1997, and at five-year intervals thereafter, in accordance with regulations that the Librarian of Congress shall prescribe."

Subsec. (d). Pub. L. 108–419, §5(f)(2), (4), redesignated subsec. (e) as (d) and substituted "with the Copyright Royalty Judges" for "in the Copyright Office" and "Copyright Royalty Judges shall prescribe as provided in section 803(b)(6)" for "Register of Copyrights shall prescribe". Former subsec. (d) redesignated (c).

Subsec. (e). Pub. L. 108–419, §5(f)(2), redesignated subsec. (f) as (e). Former subsec. (e) redesignated (d).

Subsec. (f). Pub. L. 108–419, §5(f)(2), (5), redesignated subsec. (g) as (f) and substituted "(c)" for "(d)". Former subsec. (f) redesignated (e).

Subsec. (g). Pub. L. 108–419, §5(f)(2), redesignated subsec. (g) as (f).

2002—Subsec. (b)(1). Pub. L. 107–273 struck out "to it" after "proposals submitted" in second sentence.

1999—Subsec. (e). Pub. L. 106–44 struck out "(1)" before "Owners of" and struck out par. (2) which read as follows: "On January 3, 1980, the Register of Copyrights, after consulting with authors and other owners of copyright in nondramatic literary works and their representatives, and with public broadcasting entities and their representatives, shall submit to the Congress a report setting forth the extent to which voluntary licensing arrangements have been reached with respect to the use of nondramatic literary works by such broadcast stations. The report should also describe any problems that may have arisen, and present legislative or other recommendations, if warranted."

1993—Subsec. (b). Pub. L. 103–198, §4(1)(A), (B), struck out first two sentences which read as follows: "Not later than thirty days after the Copyright Royalty Tribunal has been constituted in accordance with section 802, the Chairman of the Tribunal shall cause notice to be published in the Federal Register of the initiation of proceedings for the purpose of determining reasonable terms and rates of royalty payments for the activities specified by subsection (d) with respect to published nondramatic musical works and published pictorial, graphic, and sculptural works during a period beginning as provided in clause (3) of this subsection and ending on December 31, 1982. Copyright owners and public broadcasting entities shall negotiate in good faith and cooperate fully with the Tribunal in an effort to reach reasonable and expeditious results.", and in third sentence substituted "published nondramatic musical works and published pictorial, graphic, and sculptural works" for "works specified by this subsection".

Subsec. (b)(1). Pub. L. 103–198, §4(1)(C), struck out ", within one hundred and twenty days after publication of the notice specified in this subsection," after "broadcasting entity may" and substituted "Librarian of Congress" for "Copyright Royalty Tribunal" wherever appearing.

Subsec. (b)(2). Pub. L. 103–198, §4(1)(D), substituted "Librarian of Congress" for "Tribunal".

Subsec. (b)(3). Pub. L. 103–198, §4(1)(E)(ii), (iii), in second sentence, substituted "copyright arbitration royalty panel" for "Copyright Royalty Tribunal" and "paragraph (2)" for "clause (2) of this subsection", and in last sentence, substituted "Librarian of Congress" for "Copyright Royalty Tribunal".

Pub. L. 103–198, §4(1)(E)(i), substituted first sentence for former first sentence which read as follows: "Within six months, but not earlier than one hundred and twenty days, from the date of publication of the notice specified in this subsection the Copyright Royalty Tribunal shall make a determination and publish in the Federal Register a schedule of rates and terms which, subject to clause (2) of this subsection, shall be binding on all owners of copyright in works specified by this subsection and public broadcasting entities, regardless of whether or not such copyright owners and public broadcasting entities have submitted proposals to the Tribunal."

Subsec. (b)(4). Pub. L. 103–198, §4(1)(F), struck out par. (4) which read as follows: "With respect to the period beginning on the effective date of this title and ending on the date of publication of such rates and terms, this title shall not afford to owners of copyright or public broadcasting entities any greater or lesser rights with respect to the activities specified in subsection (d) as applied to works specified in this subsection than those afforded under the law in effect on December 31, 1977, as held applicable and construed by a court in an action brought under this title.''

Subsec. (c). Pub. L. 103–198, § 4(2), substituted ''1997'' for ''1982'' and ''Librarian of Congress'' for ''Copyright Royalty Tribunal''.

Subsec. (d). Pub. L. 103–198, § 4(3), in introductory provisions, struck out ''to the transitional provisions of subsection (b)(4), and'' after ''Subject'' and substituted ''a copyright arbitration royalty panel'' for ''the Copyright Royalty Tribunal'', and in pars. (2) and (3), substituted ''paragraph'' for ''clause'' wherever appearing.

Subsec. (g). Pub. L. 103–198, § 4(4), substituted ''paragraph'' for ''clause''.

EFFECTIVE DATE OF 2006 AMENDMENT

Amendment by Pub. L. 109–303 effective as if included in the Copyright Royalty and Distribution Reform Act of 2004, Pub. L. 108–419, see section 6 of Pub. L. 109–303, set out as a note under section 111 of this title.

EFFECTIVE DATE OF 2004 AMENDMENT

Amendment by Pub. L. 108–419 effective 6 months after Nov. 30, 2004, subject to transition provisions, see section 6 of Pub. L. 108–419, set out as an Effective Date; Transition Provisions note under section 801 of this title.

EFFECTIVE DATE

Section effective Oct. 19, 1976, see section 102 of Pub. L. 94–553, set out as a note preceding section 101 of this title.

§ 119. Limitations on exclusive rights: Secondary transmissions of distant television programming by satellite

(a) SECONDARY TRANSMISSIONS BY SATELLITE CARRIERS.—

(1) NON-NETWORK STATIONS.—Subject to the provisions of paragraphs (4), (5), and (7) of this subsection and section 114(d), secondary transmissions of a performance or display of a work embodied in a primary transmission made by a non-network station shall be subject to statutory licensing under this section if the secondary transmission is made by a satellite carrier to the public for private home viewing or for viewing in a commercial establishment, with regard to secondary transmissions the satellite carrier is in compliance with the rules, regulations, or authorizations of the Federal Communications Commission governing the carriage of television broadcast station signals, and the carrier makes a direct or indirect charge for each retransmission service to each subscriber receiving the secondary transmission or to a distributor that has contracted with the carrier for direct or indirect delivery of the secondary transmission to the public for private home viewing or for viewing in a commercial establishment.

(2) NETWORK STATIONS.—

(A) IN GENERAL.—Subject to the provisions of subparagraph (B) of this paragraph and paragraphs (4), (5), (6), and (7) of this subsection and section 114(d), secondary transmissions of a performance or display of a work embodied in a primary transmission made by a network station shall be subject to statutory licensing under this section if the secondary transmission is made by a satellite carrier to the public for private home viewing, with regard to secondary transmissions the satellite carrier is in compliance with the rules, regulations, or authorizations of the Federal Communications Commission governing the carriage of television broadcast station signals, and the carrier makes a direct or indirect charge for such retransmission service to each subscriber receiving the secondary transmission.

(B) SECONDARY TRANSMISSIONS TO UNSERVED HOUSEHOLDS.—

(i) IN GENERAL.—The statutory license provided for in subparagraph (A) shall be limited to secondary transmissions of the signals of no more than two network stations in a single day for each television network to persons who reside in unserved households.

(ii) ACCURATE DETERMINATIONS OF ELIGIBILITY.—

(I) ACCURATE PREDICTIVE MODEL.—In determining presumptively whether a person resides in an unserved household under subsection (d)(10)(A), a court shall rely on the Individual Location Longley-Rice model set forth by the Federal Communications Commission in Docket No. 98–201, as that model may be amended by the Commission over time under section 339(c)(3) of the Communications Act of 1934 to increase the accuracy of that model.

(II) ACCURATE MEASUREMENTS.—For purposes of site measurements to determine whether a person resides in an unserved household under subsection (d)(10)(A), a court shall rely on section 339(c)(4) of the Communications Act of 1934.

(III) ACCURATE PREDICTIVE MODEL WITH RESPECT TO DIGITAL SIGNALS.—Notwithstanding subclause (I), in determining presumptively whether a person resides in an unserved household under subsection (d)(10)(A) with respect to digital signals, a court shall rely on a predictive model set forth by the Federal Communications Commission pursuant to a rulemaking as provided in section 339(c)(3) of the Communications Act of 1934 (47 U.S.C. 339(c)(3)), as that model may be amended by the Commission over time under such section to increase the accuracy of that model. Until such time as the Commission sets forth such model, a court shall rely on the predictive model as recommended by the Commission with respect to digital signals in its Report to Congress in ET Docket No. 05–182, FCC 05–199 (released December 9, 2005).

(iii) C-BAND EXEMPTION TO UNSERVED HOUSEHOLDS.—

(I) IN GENERAL.—The limitations of clause (i) shall not apply to any secondary transmissions by C-band services of network stations that a subscriber to C-band service received before any termination of such secondary transmissions before October 31, 1999.

(II) DEFINITION.—In this clause, the term "C-band service" means a service that is licensed by the Federal Communications Commission and operates in the Fixed Satellite Service under part 25 of title 47, Code of Federal Regulations.

(C) SUBMISSION OF SUBSCRIBER LISTS TO NETWORKS.—

(i) INITIAL LISTS.—A satellite carrier that makes secondary transmissions of a primary transmission made by a network station pursuant to subparagraph (A) shall, not later than 90 days after commencing such secondary transmissions, submit to the network that owns or is affiliated with the network station a list identifying (by name and address, including street or rural route number, city, State, and 9-digit zip code) all subscribers to which the satellite carrier makes secondary transmissions of that primary transmission to subscribers in unserved households.

(ii) MONTHLY LISTS.—After the submission of the initial lists under clause (i), the satellite carrier shall, not later than the 15th of each month, submit to the network a list, aggregated by designated market area, identifying (by name and address, including street or rural route number, city, State, and 9-digit zip code) any persons who have been added or dropped as subscribers under clause (i) since the last submission under this subparagraph.

(iii) USE OF SUBSCRIBER INFORMATION.— Subscriber information submitted by a satellite carrier under this subparagraph may be used only for purposes of monitoring compliance by the satellite carrier with this subsection.

(iv) APPLICABILITY.—The submission requirements of this subparagraph shall apply to a satellite carrier only if the network to which the submissions are to be made places on file with the Register of Copyrights a document identifying the name and address of the person to whom such submissions are to be made. The Register shall maintain for public inspection a file of all such documents.

(3) STATUTORY LICENSE WHERE RETRANSMISSIONS INTO LOCAL MARKET AVAILABLE.—

(A) RULES FOR SUBSCRIBERS TO SIGNALS UNDER SUBSECTION (e).—

(i) FOR THOSE RECEIVING DISTANT SIGNALS.—In the case of a subscriber of a satellite carrier who is eligible to receive the secondary transmission of the primary transmission of a network station solely by reason of subsection (e) (in this subparagraph referred to as a "distant signal"), and who, as of October 1, 2004, is receiving the distant signal of that network station, the following shall apply:

(I) In a case in which the satellite carrier makes available to the subscriber the secondary transmission of the primary transmission of a local network station affiliated with the same tele-

vision network pursuant to the statutory license under section 122, the statutory license under paragraph (2) shall apply only to secondary transmissions by that satellite carrier to that subscriber of the distant signal of a station affiliated with the same television network—

(aa) if, within 60 days after receiving the notice of the satellite carrier under section 338(h)(1) of the Communications Act of 1934, the subscriber elects to retain the distant signal; but

(bb) only until such time as the subscriber elects to receive such local signal.

(II) Notwithstanding subclause (I), the statutory license under paragraph (2) shall not apply with respect to any subscriber who is eligible to receive the distant signal of a television network station solely by reason of subsection (e), unless the satellite carrier, within 60 days after the date of the enactment of the Satellite Home Viewer Extension and Reauthorization Act of 2004, submits to that television network a list, aggregated by designated market area (as defined in section 122(j)(2)(C)), that—

(aa) identifies that subscriber by name and address (street or rural route number, city, State, and zip code) and specifies the distant signals received by the subscriber; and

(bb) states, to the best of the satellite carrier's knowledge and belief, after having made diligent and good faith inquiries, that the subscriber is eligible under subsection (e) to receive the distant signals.

(ii) FOR THOSE NOT RECEIVING DISTANT SIGNALS.—In the case of any subscriber of a satellite carrier who is eligible to receive the distant signal of a network station solely by reason of subsection (e) and who did not receive a distant signal of a station affiliated with the same network on October 1, 2004, the statutory license under paragraph (2) shall not apply to secondary transmissions by that satellite carrier to that subscriber of the distant signal of a station affiliated with the same network.

(B) RULES FOR LAWFUL SUBSCRIBERS AS OF DATE OF ENACTMENT OF 2010 ACT.—In the case of a subscriber of a satellite carrier who, on the day before the date of the enactment of the Satellite Television Extension and Localism Act of 2010, was lawfully receiving the secondary transmission of the primary transmission of a network station under the statutory license under paragraph (2) (in this subparagraph referred to as the "distant signal"), other than subscribers to whom subparagraph (A) applies, the statutory license under paragraph (2) shall apply to secondary transmissions by that satellite carrier to that subscriber of the distant signal of a station affiliated with the same television network, and the subscriber's household shall continue to be considered to be an unserved household with respect to such network, until such time as the subscriber elects to terminate such secondary transmissions, whether or not the subscriber elects to subscribe to receive the secondary transmission of the primary transmission of a local network station affiliated with the same network pursuant to the statutory license under section 122.

(C) FUTURE APPLICABILITY.—

(i) WHEN LOCAL SIGNAL AVAILABLE AT TIME OF SUBSCRIPTION.—The statutory license under paragraph (2) shall not apply to the secondary transmission by a satellite carrier of the primary transmission of a network station to a person who is not a subscriber lawfully receiving such secondary transmission as of the date of the enactment of the Satellite Television Extension and Localism Act of 2010 and, at the time such person seeks to subscribe to receive such secondary transmission, resides in a local market where the satellite carrier makes available to that person the secondary transmission of the primary transmission of a local network station affiliated with the same network pursuant to the statutory license under section 122.

(ii) WHEN LOCAL SIGNAL AVAILABLE AFTER SUBSCRIPTION.—In the case of a subscriber who lawfully subscribes to and receives the secondary transmission by a satellite carrier of the primary transmission of a network station under the statutory license under paragraph (2) (in this clause referred to as the "distant signal") on or after the date of the enactment of the Satellite Television Extension and Localism Act of 2010, the statutory license under paragraph (2) shall apply to secondary transmissions by that satellite carrier to that subscriber of the distant signal of a station affiliated with the same television network, and the subscriber's household shall continue to be considered to be an unserved household with respect to such network, until such time as the subscriber elects to terminate such secondary transmissions, but only if such subscriber subscribes to the secondary transmission of the primary transmission of a local network station affiliated with the same network within 60 days after the satellite carrier makes available to the subscriber such secondary transmission of the primary transmission of such local network station.

(D) OTHER PROVISIONS NOT AFFECTED.—This paragraph shall not affect the applicability of the statutory license to secondary transmissions to unserved households included under paragraph (11).

(E) WAIVER.—A subscriber who is denied the secondary transmission of a network station under subparagraph (B) or (C) may request a waiver from such denial by submitting a request, through the subscriber's satellite carrier, to the network station in the local market affiliated with the same network where the subscriber is located. The network station shall accept or reject the subscriber's request for a waiver within 30 days after receipt of the request. If the network station fails to accept or reject the subscriber's request for a waiver within that 30-day period, that network station shall be deemed to agree to the waiver request. Unless specifically stated by the network station, a waiver that was granted before the date of the enactment of the Satellite Home Viewer Extension and Reauthorization Act of 2004 under section 339(c)(2) of the Communications Act of 1934 shall not constitute a waiver for purposes of this subparagraph.

(F) AVAILABLE DEFINED.—For purposes of this paragraph, a satellite carrier makes available a secondary transmission of the primary transmission of a local station to a subscriber or person if the satellite carrier offers that secondary transmission to other subscribers who reside in the same 9-digit zip code as that subscriber or person.

(4) NONCOMPLIANCE WITH REPORTING AND PAYMENT REQUIREMENTS.—Notwithstanding the provisions of paragraphs (1) and (2), the willful or repeated secondary transmission to the public by a satellite carrier of a primary transmission made by a non-network station or a network station and embodying a performance or display of a work is actionable as an act of infringement under section 501, and is fully subject to the remedies provided by sections 502 through 506, where the satellite carrier has not deposited the statement of account and royalty fee required by subsection (b), or has failed to make the submissions to networks required by paragraph (2)(C).

(5) WILLFUL ALTERATIONS.—Notwithstanding the provisions of paragraphs (1) and (2), the secondary transmission to the public by a satellite carrier of a performance or display of a work embodied in a primary transmission made by a non-network station or a network station is actionable as an act of infringement under section 501, and is fully subject to the remedies provided by sections 502 through 506 and section 510, if the content of the particular program in which the performance or display is embodied, or any commercial advertising or station announcement transmitted by the primary transmitter during, or immediately before or after, the transmission of such program, is in any way willfully altered by the satellite carrier through changes, deletions, or additions, or is combined with programming from any other broadcast signal.

(6) VIOLATION OF TERRITORIAL RESTRICTIONS ON STATUTORY LICENSE FOR NETWORK STATIONS.—

(A) INDIVIDUAL VIOLATIONS.—The willful or repeated secondary transmission by a satellite carrier of a primary transmission made by a network station and embodying a performance or display of a work to a subscriber who is not eligible to receive the transmission under this section is actionable as an act of infringement under section 501 and is fully subject to the remedies provided by sections 502 through 506, except that—

(i) no damages shall be awarded for such act of infringement if the satellite carrier took corrective action by promptly withdrawing service from the ineligible subscriber, and

(ii) any statutory damages shall not exceed $250 for such subscriber for each month during which the violation occurred.

(B) PATTERN OF VIOLATIONS.—If a satellite carrier engages in a willful or repeated pattern or practice of delivering a primary transmission made by a network station and embodying a performance or display of a work to subscribers who are not eligible to receive the transmission under this section, then in addition to the remedies set forth in subparagraph (A)—

(i) if the pattern or practice has been carried out on a substantially nationwide basis, the court shall order a permanent injunction barring the secondary transmission by the satellite carrier, for private home viewing, of the primary transmissions of any primary network station affiliated with the same network, and the court may order statutory damages of not to exceed $2,500,000 for each 3-month period during which the pattern or practice was carried out; and

(ii) if the pattern or practice has been carried out on a local or regional basis, the court shall order a permanent injunction barring the secondary transmission, for private home viewing in that locality or region, by the satellite carrier of the primary transmissions of any primary network station affiliated with the same network, and the court may order statutory damages of not to exceed $2,500,000 for each 6-month period during which the pattern or practice was carried out.

(C) PREVIOUS SUBSCRIBERS EXCLUDED.—Subparagraphs (A) and (B) do not apply to secondary transmissions by a satellite carrier to persons who subscribed to receive such secondary transmissions from the satellite carrier or a distributor before November 16, 1988.

(D) BURDEN OF PROOF.—In any action brought under this paragraph, the satellite carrier shall have the burden of proving that its secondary transmission of a primary transmission by a network station is to a subscriber who is eligible to receive the secondary transmission under this section.

(E) EXCEPTION.—The secondary transmission by a satellite carrier of a performance or display of a work embodied in a primary transmission made by a network station to subscribers who do not reside in unserved households shall not be an act of infringement if—

(i) the station on May 1, 1991, was retransmitted by a satellite carrier and was not on that date owned or operated by or affiliated with a television network that offered interconnected program service on a regular basis for 15 or more hours per week to at least 25 affiliated television licensees in 10 or more States;

(ii) as of July 1, 1998, such station was retransmitted by a satellite carrier under the statutory license of this section; and

(iii) the station is not owned or operated by or affiliated with a television network that, as of January 1, 1995, offered interconnected program service on a regular basis for 15 or more hours per week to at least 25 affiliated television licensees in 10 or more States.

The court shall direct one half of any statutory damages ordered under clause (i)[1] to be deposited with the Register of Copyrights for distribution to copyright owners pursuant to subsection (b). The Copyright Royalty Judges shall issue regulations establishing procedures for distributing such funds, on a proportional basis, to copyright owners whose works were included in the secondary transmissions that were the subject of the statutory damages.

(7) DISCRIMINATION BY A SATELLITE CARRIER.—Notwithstanding the provisions of paragraph (1), the willful or repeated secondary transmission to the public by a satellite carrier of a performance or display of a work embodied in a primary transmission made by a non-network station or a network station is actionable as an act of infringement under section 501, and is fully subject to the remedies provided by sections 502 through 506, if the satellite carrier unlawfully discriminates against a distributor.

(8) GEOGRAPHIC LIMITATION ON SECONDARY TRANSMISSIONS.—The statutory license created by this section shall apply only to secondary transmissions to households located in the United States.

(9) LOSER PAYS FOR SIGNAL INTENSITY MEASUREMENT; RECOVERY OF MEASUREMENT COSTS IN A CIVIL ACTION.—In any civil action filed relating to the eligibility of subscribing households as unserved households—

(A) a network station challenging such eligibility shall, within 60 days after receipt of the measurement results and a statement of such costs, reimburse the satellite carrier for any signal intensity measurement that is conducted by that carrier in response to a challenge by the network station and that establishes the household is an unserved household; and

(B) a satellite carrier shall, within 60 days after receipt of the measurement results and a statement of such costs, reimburse the network station challenging such eligibility for any signal intensity measurement that is conducted by that station and that establishes the household is not an unserved household.

(10) INABILITY TO CONDUCT MEASUREMENT.—If a network station makes a reasonable attempt to conduct a site measurement of its signal at a subscriber's household and is denied access for the purpose of conducting the measurement, and is otherwise unable to conduct a measurement, the satellite carrier shall within 60 days notice thereof, terminate service of the station's network to that household.

(11) SERVICE TO RECREATIONAL VEHICLES AND COMMERCIAL TRUCKS.—

(A) EXEMPTION.—

----

[1] So in original. Probably means subpar. (B)(i).

(i) IN GENERAL.—For purposes of this subsection, and subject to clauses (ii) and (iii), the term "unserved household" shall include—

(I) recreational vehicles as defined in regulations of the Secretary of Housing and Urban Development under section 3282.8 of title 24, Code of Federal Regulations; and

(II) commercial trucks that qualify as commercial motor vehicles under regulations of the Secretary of Transportation under section 383.5 of title 49, Code of Federal Regulations.

(ii) LIMITATION.—Clause (i) shall apply only to a recreational vehicle or commercial truck if any satellite carrier that proposes to make a secondary transmission of a network station to the operator of such a recreational vehicle or commercial truck complies with the documentation requirements under subparagraphs (B) and (C).

(iii) EXCLUSION.—For purposes of this subparagraph, the terms "recreational vehicle" and "commercial truck" shall not include any fixed dwelling, whether a mobile home or otherwise.

(B) DOCUMENTATION REQUIREMENTS.—A recreational vehicle or commercial truck shall be deemed to be an unserved household beginning 10 days after the relevant satellite carrier provides to the network that owns or is affiliated with the network station that will be secondarily transmitted to the recreational vehicle or commercial truck the following documents:

(i) DECLARATION.—A signed declaration by the operator of the recreational vehicle or commercial truck that the satellite dish is permanently attached to the recreational vehicle or commercial truck, and will not be used to receive satellite programming at any fixed dwelling.

(ii) REGISTRATION.—In the case of a recreational vehicle, a copy of the current State vehicle registration for the recreational vehicle.

(iii) REGISTRATION AND LICENSE.—In the case of a commercial truck, a copy of—

(I) the current State vehicle registration for the truck; and

(II) a copy of a valid, current commercial driver's license, as defined in regulations of the Secretary of Transportation under section 383 of title 49, Code of Federal Regulations, issued to the operator.

(C) UPDATED DOCUMENTATION REQUIREMENTS.—If a satellite carrier wishes to continue to make secondary transmissions to a recreational vehicle or commercial truck for more than a 2-year period, that carrier shall provide each network, upon request, with updated documentation in the form described under subparagraph (B) during the 90 days before expiration of that 2-year period.

(12) STATUTORY LICENSE CONTINGENT ON COMPLIANCE WITH FCC RULES AND REMEDIAL STEPS.—Notwithstanding any other provision of this section, the willful or repeated secondary transmission to the public by a satellite carrier of a primary transmission embodying a performance or display of a work made by a broadcast station licensed by the Federal Communications Commission is actionable as an act of infringement under section 501, and is fully subject to the remedies provided by sections 502 through 506, if, at the time of such transmission, the satellite carrier is not in compliance with the rules, regulations, and authorizations of the Federal Communications Commission concerning the carriage of television broadcast station signals.

(13) WAIVERS.—A subscriber who is denied the secondary transmission of a signal of a network station under subsection (a)(2)(B) may request a waiver from such denial by submitting a request, through the subscriber's satellite carrier, to the network station asserting that the secondary transmission is prohibited. The network station shall accept or reject a subscriber's request for a waiver within 30 days after receipt of the request. If a television network station fails to accept or reject a subscriber's request for a waiver within the 30-day period after receipt of the request, that station shall be deemed to agree to the waiver request and have filed such written waiver. Unless specifically stated by the network station, a waiver that was granted before the date of the enactment of the Satellite Home Viewer Extension and Reauthorization Act of 2004 under section 339(c)(2) of the Communications Act of 1934, and that was in effect on such date of enactment, shall constitute a waiver for purposes of this paragraph.

(14) RESTRICTED TRANSMISSION OF OUT-OF-STATE DISTANT NETWORK SIGNALS INTO CERTAIN MARKETS.—

(A) OUT-OF-STATE NETWORK AFFILIATES.—Notwithstanding any other provision of this title, the statutory license in this subsection and subsection (b) shall not apply to any secondary transmission of the primary transmission of a network station located outside of the State of Alaska to any subscriber in that State to whom the secondary transmission of the primary transmission of a television station located in that State is made available by the satellite carrier pursuant to section 122.

(B) EXCEPTION.—The limitation in subparagraph (A) shall not apply to the secondary transmission of the primary transmission of a digital signal of a network station located outside of the State of Alaska if at the time that the secondary transmission is made, no television station licensed to a community in the State and affiliated with the same network makes primary transmissions of a digital signal.

(b) DEPOSIT OF STATEMENTS AND FEES; VERIFICATION PROCEDURES.—

(1) DEPOSITS WITH THE REGISTER OF COPYRIGHTS.—A satellite carrier whose secondary transmissions are subject to statutory licensing under subsection (a) shall, on a semiannual basis, deposit with the Register of Copyrights, in accordance with requirements that the Register shall prescribe by regulation—

(A) a statement of account, covering the preceding 6-month period, specifying the names and locations of all non-network stations and network stations whose signals were retransmitted, at any time during that period, to subscribers as described in subsections (a)(1) and (a)(2), the total number of subscribers that received such retransmissions, and such other data as the Register of Copyrights may from time to time prescribe by regulation;

(B) a royalty fee payable to copyright owners pursuant to paragraph (4) for that 6-month period, computed by multiplying the total number of subscribers receiving each secondary transmission of a primary stream or multicast stream of each non-network station or network station during each calendar year month by the appropriate rate in effect under this subsection; and

(C) a filing fee, as determined by the Register of Copyrights pursuant to section 708(a).

(2) VERIFICATION OF ACCOUNTS AND FEE PAYMENTS.—The Register of Copyrights shall issue regulations to permit interested parties to verify and audit the statements of account and royalty fees submitted by satellite carriers under this subsection.

(3) INVESTMENT OF FEES.—The Register of Copyrights shall receive all fees (including the filing fee specified in paragraph (1)(C)) deposited under this section and, after deducting the reasonable costs incurred by the Copyright Office under this section (other than the costs deducted under paragraph (5)), shall deposit the balance in the Treasury of the United States, in such manner as the Secretary of the Treasury directs. All funds held by the Secretary of the Treasury shall be invested in interest-bearing securities of the United States for later distribution with interest by the Librarian of Congress as provided by this title.

(4) PERSONS TO WHOM FEES ARE DISTRIBUTED.—The royalty fees deposited under paragraph (3) shall, in accordance with the procedures provided by paragraph (5), be distributed to those copyright owners whose works were included in a secondary transmission made by a satellite carrier during the applicable 6-month accounting period and who file a claim with the Copyright Royalty Judges under paragraph (5).

(5) PROCEDURES FOR DISTRIBUTION.—The royalty fees deposited under paragraph (3) shall be distributed in accordance with the following procedures:

(A) FILING OF CLAIMS FOR FEES.—During the month of July in each year, each person claiming to be entitled to statutory license fees for secondary transmissions shall file a claim with the Copyright Royalty Judges, in accordance with requirements that the Copyright Royalty Judges shall prescribe by regulation. For purposes of this paragraph, any claimants may agree among themselves as to the proportionate division of statutory license fees among them, may lump their claims together and file them jointly or as a single claim, or may designate a common agent to receive payment on their behalf.

(B) DETERMINATION OF CONTROVERSY; DISTRIBUTIONS.—After the first day of August of each year, the Copyright Royalty Judges shall determine whether there exists a controversy concerning the distribution of royalty fees. If the Copyright Royalty Judges determine that no such controversy exists, the Copyright Royalty Judges shall authorize the Librarian of Congress to proceed to distribute such fees to the copyright owners entitled to receive them, or to their designated agents, subject to the deduction of reasonable administrative costs under this section. If the Copyright Royalty Judges find the existence of a controversy, the Copyright Royalty Judges shall, pursuant to chapter 8 of this title, conduct a proceeding to determine the distribution of royalty fees.

(C) WITHHOLDING OF FEES DURING CONTROVERSY.—During the pendency of any proceeding under this subsection, the Copyright Royalty Judges shall have the discretion to authorize the Librarian of Congress to proceed to distribute any amounts that are not in controversy.

(c) ADJUSTMENT OF ROYALTY FEES.—

(1) APPLICABILITY AND DETERMINATION OF ROYALTY FEES FOR SIGNALS.—

(A) INITIAL FEE.—The appropriate fee for purposes of determining the royalty fee under subsection (b)(1)(B) for the secondary transmission of the primary transmissions of network stations and non-network stations shall be the appropriate fee set forth in part 258 of title 37, Code of Federal Regulations, as in effect on July 1, 2009, as modified under this paragraph.

(B) FEE SET BY VOLUNTARY NEGOTIATION.—On or before June 1, 2010, the Copyright Royalty Judges shall cause to be published in the Federal Register of the initiation of voluntary negotiation proceedings for the purpose of determining the royalty fee to be paid by satellite carriers for the secondary transmission of the primary transmissions of network stations and non-network stations under subsection (b)(1)(B).

(C) NEGOTIATIONS.—Satellite carriers, distributors, and copyright owners entitled to royalty fees under this section shall negotiate in good faith in an effort to reach a voluntary agreement or agreements for the payment of royalty fees. Any such satellite carriers, distributors and copyright owners may at any time negotiate and agree to the royalty fee, and may designate common agents to negotiate, agree to, or pay such fees. If the parties fail to identify common agents, the Copyright Royalty Judges shall do so, after requesting recommendations from the parties to the negotiation proceeding. The parties to each negotiation proceeding shall bear the cost thereof.

(D) AGREEMENTS BINDING ON PARTIES; FILING OF AGREEMENTS; PUBLIC NOTICE.—

(i) VOLUNTARY AGREEMENTS; FILING.—Voluntary agreements negotiated at any time in accordance with this paragraph shall be binding upon all satellite carriers, distributors, and copyright owners that are parties thereto. Copies of such agreements shall be filed with the Copyright Office within 30 days after execution in accordance with regulations that the Register of Copyrights shall prescribe.

(ii) PROCEDURE FOR ADOPTION OF FEES.—

(I) PUBLICATION OF NOTICE.—Within 10 days after publication in the Federal Register of a notice of the initiation of voluntary negotiation proceedings, parties who have reached a voluntary agreement may request that the royalty fees in that agreement be applied to all satellite carriers, distributors, and copyright owners without convening a proceeding under subparagraph (F).

(II) PUBLIC NOTICE OF FEES.—Upon receiving a request under subclause (I), the Copyright Royalty Judges shall immediately provide public notice of the royalty fees from the voluntary agreement and afford parties an opportunity to state that they object to those fees.

(III) ADOPTION OF FEES.—The Copyright Royalty Judges shall adopt the royalty fees from the voluntary agreement for all satellite carriers, distributors, and copyright owners without convening the proceeding under subparagraph (F) unless a party with an intent to participate in that proceeding and a significant interest in the outcome of that proceeding objects under subclause (II).

(E) PERIOD AGREEMENT IS IN EFFECT.—The obligation to pay the royalty fees established under a voluntary agreement which has been filed with the Copyright Royalty Judges in accordance with this paragraph shall become effective on the date specified in the agreement, and shall remain in effect until December 31, 2014, or in accordance with the terms of the agreement, whichever is later.

(F) FEE SET BY COPYRIGHT ROYALTY JUDGES PROCEEDING.—

(i) NOTICE OF INITIATION OF THE PROCEEDING.—On or before September 1, 2010, the Copyright Royalty Judges shall cause notice to be published in the Federal Register of the initiation of a proceeding for the purpose of determining the royalty fees to be paid for the secondary transmission of the primary transmissions of network stations and non-network stations under subsection (b)(1)(B) by satellite carriers and distributors—

(I) in the absence of a voluntary agreement filed in accordance with subparagraph (D) that establishes royalty fees to be paid by all satellite carriers and distributors; or

(II) if an objection to the fees from a voluntary agreement submitted for adoption by the Copyright Royalty Judges to apply to all satellite carriers, distributors, and copyright owners is received under subparagraph (D) from a party with an intent to participate in the proceeding and a significant interest in the outcome of that proceeding.

Such proceeding shall be conducted under chapter 8.

(ii) ESTABLISHMENT OF ROYALTY FEES.—In determining royalty fees under this subparagraph, the Copyright Royalty Judges shall establish fees for the secondary transmissions of the primary transmissions of network stations and non-network stations that most clearly represent the fair market value of secondary transmissions, except that the Copyright Royalty Judges shall adjust royalty fees to account for the obligations of the parties under any applicable voluntary agreement filed with the Copyright Royalty Judges in accordance with subparagraph (D). In determining the fair market value, the Judges shall base their decision on economic, competitive, and programming information presented by the parties, including—

(I) the competitive environment in which such programming is distributed, the cost of similar signals in similar private and compulsory license marketplaces, and any special features and conditions of the retransmission marketplace;

(II) the economic impact of such fees on copyright owners and satellite carriers; and

(III) the impact on the continued availability of secondary transmissions to the public.

(iii) EFFECTIVE DATE FOR DECISION OF COPYRIGHT ROYALTY JUDGES.—The obligation to pay the royalty fees established under a determination that is made by the Copyright Royalty Judges in a proceeding under this paragraph shall be effective as of January 1, 2010.

(iv) PERSONS SUBJECT TO ROYALTY FEES.—The royalty fees referred to in clause (iii) shall be binding on all satellite carriers, distributors and copyright owners, who are not party to a voluntary agreement filed with the Copyright Office under subparagraph (D).

(2) ANNUAL ROYALTY FEE ADJUSTMENT.—Effective January 1 of each year, the royalty fee payable under subsection (b)(1)(B) for the secondary transmission of the primary transmissions of network stations and non-network stations shall be adjusted by the Copyright Royalty Judges to reflect any changes occurring in the cost of living as determined by the most recent Consumer Price Index (for all consumers and for all items) published by the Secretary of Labor before December 1 of the preceding year. Notification of the adjusted fees shall be published in the Federal Register at least 25 days before January 1.

(d) DEFINITIONS.—As used in this section—

(1) DISTRIBUTOR.—The term "distributor" means an entity that contracts to distribute secondary transmissions from a satellite carrier and, either as a single channel or in a package with other programming, provides the secondary transmission either directly to individual subscribers or indirectly through other

program distribution entities in accordance with the provisions of this section.

(2) NETWORK STATION.—The term "network station" means—

(A) a television station licensed by the Federal Communications Commission, including any translator station or terrestrial satellite station that rebroadcasts all or substantially all of the programming broadcast by a network station, that is owned or operated by, or affiliated with, one or more of the television networks in the United States that offer an interconnected program service on a regular basis for 15 or more hours per week to at least 25 of its affiliated television licensees in 10 or more States; or

(B) a noncommercial educational broadcast station (as defined in section 397 of the Communications Act of 1934);

except that the term does not include the signal of the Alaska Rural Communications Service, or any successor entity to that service.

(3) PRIMARY NETWORK STATION.—The term "primary network station" means a network station that broadcasts or rebroadcasts the basic programming service of a particular national network.

(4) PRIMARY TRANSMISSION.—The term "primary transmission" has the meaning given that term in section 111(f) of this title.

(5) PRIVATE HOME VIEWING.—The term "private home viewing" means the viewing, for private use in a household by means of satellite reception equipment that is operated by an individual in that household and that serves only such household, of a secondary transmission delivered by a satellite carrier of a primary transmission of a television station licensed by the Federal Communications Commission.

(6) SATELLITE CARRIER.—The term "satellite carrier" means an entity that uses the facilities of a satellite or satellite service licensed by the Federal Communications Commission and operates in the Fixed-Satellite Service under part 25 of title 47, Code of Federal Regulations, or the Direct Broadcast Satellite Service under part 100 of title 47, Code of Federal Regulations, to establish and operate a channel of communications for point-to-multipoint distribution of television station signals, and that owns or leases a capacity or service on a satellite in order to provide such point-to-multipoint distribution, except to the extent that such entity provides such distribution pursuant to tariff under the Communications Act of 1934, other than for private home viewing pursuant to this section.

(7) SECONDARY TRANSMISSION.—The term "secondary transmission" has the meaning given that term in section 111(f) of this title.

(8) SUBSCRIBER; SUBSCRIBE.—

(A) SUBSCRIBER.—The term "subscriber" means a person or entity that receives a secondary transmission service from a satellite carrier and pays a fee for the service, directly or indirectly, to the satellite carrier or to a distributor.

(B) SUBSCRIBE.—The term "subscribe" means to elect to become a subscriber.

(9) NON-NETWORK STATION.—The term "non-network station" means a television station, other than a network station, licensed by the Federal Communications Commission, that is secondarily transmitted by a satellite carrier.

(10) UNSERVED HOUSEHOLD.—The term "unserved household", with respect to a particular television network, means a household that—

(A) cannot receive, through the use of an antenna, an over-the-air signal containing the primary stream, or, on or after the qualifying date, the multicast stream, originating in that household's local market and affiliated with that network of—

(i) if the signal originates as an analog signal, Grade B intensity as defined by the Federal Communications Commission in section 73.683(a) of title 47, Code of Federal Regulations, as in effect on January 1, 1999; or

(ii) if the signal originates as a digital signal, intensity defined in the values for the digital television noise-limited service contour, as defined in regulations issued by the Federal Communications Commission (section 73.622(e) of title 47, Code of Federal Regulations), as such regulations may be amended from time to time;

(B) is subject to a waiver that meets the standards of subsection (a)(13), whether or not the waiver was granted before the date of the enactment of the Satellite Television Extension and Localism Act of 2010;

(C) is a subscriber to whom subsection (e) applies;

(D) is a subscriber to whom subsection (a)(11) applies; or

(E) is a subscriber to whom the exemption under subsection (a)(2)(B)(iii) applies.

(11) LOCAL MARKET.—The term "local market" has the meaning given such term under section 122(j).

(12) COMMERCIAL ESTABLISHMENT.—The term "commercial establishment"—

(A) means an establishment used for commercial purposes, such as a bar, restaurant, private office, fitness club, oil rig, retail store, bank or other financial institution, supermarket, automobile or boat dealership, or any other establishment with a common business area; and

(B) does not include a multi-unit permanent or temporary dwelling where private home viewing occurs, such as a hotel, dormitory, hospital, apartment, condominium, or prison.

(13) QUALIFYING DATE.—The term "qualifying date", for purposes of paragraph (10)(A), means—

(A) October 1, 2010, for multicast streams that exist on March 31, 2010; and

(B) January 1, 2011, for all other multicast streams.

(14) MULTICAST STREAM.—The term "multicast stream" means a digital stream containing programming and program-related material affiliated with a television network, other than the primary stream.

(15) PRIMARY STREAM.—The term "primary stream" means—

(A) the single digital stream of programming as to which a television broadcast station has the right to mandatory carriage with a satellite carrier under the rules of the Federal Communications Commission in effect on July 1, 2009; or

(B) if there is no stream described in subparagraph (A), then either—

(i) the single digital stream of programming associated with the network last transmitted by the station as an analog signal; or

(ii) if there is no stream described in clause (i), then the single digital stream of programming affiliated with the network that, as of July 1, 2009, had been offered by the television broadcast station for the longest period of time.

(e) MORATORIUM ON COPYRIGHT LIABILITY.—Until December 31, 2014, a subscriber who does not receive a signal of Grade A intensity (as defined in the regulations of the Federal Communications Commission under section 73.683(a) of title 47, Code of Federal Regulations, as in effect on January 1, 1999, or predicted by the Federal Communications Commission using the Individual Location Longley-Rice methodology described by the Federal Communications Commission in Docket No. 98–201) of a local network television broadcast station shall remain eligible to receive signals of network stations affiliated with the same network, if that subscriber had satellite service of such network signal terminated after July 11, 1998, and before October 31, 1999, as required by this section, or received such service on October 31, 1999.

(f) EXPEDITED CONSIDERATION BY JUSTICE DEPARTMENT OF VOLUNTARY AGREEMENTS TO PROVIDE SATELLITE SECONDARY TRANSMISSIONS TO LOCAL MARKETS.—

(1) IN GENERAL.—In a case in which no satellite carrier makes available, to subscribers located in a local market, as defined in section 122(j)(2), the secondary transmission into that market of a primary transmission of one or more television broadcast stations licensed by the Federal Communications Commission, and two or more satellite carriers request a business review letter in accordance with section 50.6 of title 28, Code of Federal Regulations (as in effect on July 7, 2004), in order to assess the legality under the antitrust laws of proposed business conduct to make or carry out an agreement to provide such secondary transmission into such local market, the appropriate official of the Department of Justice shall respond to the request no later than 90 days after the date on which the request is received.

(2) DEFINITION.—For purposes of this subsection, the term "antitrust laws"—

(A) has the meaning given that term in subsection (a) of the first section of the Clayton Act (15 U.S.C. 12(a)), except that such term includes section 5 of the Federal Trade Commission Act (15 U.S.C. 45) to the extent such section 5 applies to unfair methods of competition; and

(B) includes any State law similar to the laws referred to in paragraph (1).

(g) CERTAIN WAIVERS GRANTED TO PROVIDERS OF LOCAL-INTO-LOCAL SERVICE TO ALL DMAS.—

(1) INJUNCTION WAIVER.—A court that issued an injunction pursuant to subsection (a)(7)(B) before the date of the enactment of this subsection shall waive such injunction if the court recognizes the entity against which the injunction was issued as a qualified carrier.

(2) LIMITED TEMPORARY WAIVER.—

(A) IN GENERAL.—Upon a request made by a satellite carrier, a court that issued an injunction against such carrier under subsection (a)(7)(B) before the date of the enactment of this subsection shall waive such injunction with respect to the statutory license provided under subsection (a)(2) to the extent necessary to allow such carrier to make secondary transmissions of primary transmissions made by a network station to unserved households located in short markets in which such carrier was not providing local service pursuant to the license under section 122 as of December 31, 2009.

(B) EXPIRATION OF TEMPORARY WAIVER.—A temporary waiver of an injunction under subparagraph (A) shall expire after the end of the 120-day period beginning on the date such temporary waiver is issued unless extended for good cause by the court making the temporary waiver.

(C) FAILURE TO PROVIDE LOCAL-INTO-LOCAL SERVICE TO ALL DMAS.—

(i) FAILURE TO ACT REASONABLY AND IN GOOD FAITH.—If the court issuing a temporary waiver under subparagraph (A) determines that the satellite carrier that made the request for such waiver has failed to act reasonably or has failed to make a good faith effort to provide local-into-local service to all DMAs, such failure—

(I) is actionable as an act of infringement under section 501 and the court may in its discretion impose the remedies provided for in sections 502 through 506 and subsection (a)(6)(B) of this section; and

(II) shall result in the termination of the waiver issued under subparagraph (A).

(ii) FAILURE TO PROVIDE LOCAL-INTO-LOCAL SERVICE.—If the court issuing a temporary waiver under subparagraph (A) determines that the satellite carrier that made the request for such waiver has failed to provide local-into-local service to all DMAs, but determines that the carrier acted reasonably and in good faith, the court may in its discretion impose financial penalties that reflect—

(I) the degree of control the carrier had over the circumstances that resulted in the failure;

(II) the quality of the carrier's efforts to remedy the failure; and

(III) the severity and duration of any service interruption.

(D) SINGLE TEMPORARY WAIVER AVAILABLE.—An entity may only receive one temporary waiver under this paragraph.

(E) SHORT MARKET DEFINED.—For purposes of this paragraph, the term "short market" means a local market in which programming of one or more of the four most widely viewed television networks nationwide as measured on the date of the enactment of this subsection is not offered on the primary stream transmitted by any local television broadcast station.

(3) ESTABLISHMENT OF QUALIFIED CARRIER RECOGNITION.—

(A) STATEMENT OF ELIGIBILITY.—An entity seeking to be recognized as a qualified carrier under this subsection shall file a statement of eligibility with the court that imposed the injunction. A statement of eligibility must include—

(i) an affidavit that the entity is providing local-into-local service to all DMAs;

(ii) a motion for a waiver of the injunction;

(iii) a motion that the court appoint a special master under Rule 53 of the Federal Rules of Civil Procedure;

(iv) an agreement by the carrier to pay all expenses incurred by the special master under paragraph (4)(B)(ii); and

(v) a certification issued pursuant to section 342(a) of Communications Act of 1934.

(B) GRANT OF RECOGNITION AS A QUALIFIED CARRIER.—Upon receipt of a statement of eligibility, the court shall recognize the entity as a qualified carrier and issue the waiver under paragraph (1). Upon motion pursuant to subparagraph (A)(iii), the court shall appoint a special master to conduct the examination and provide a report to the court as provided in paragraph (4)(B).

(C) VOLUNTARY TERMINATION.—At any time, an entity recognized as a qualified carrier may file a statement of voluntary termination with the court certifying that it no longer wishes to be recognized as a qualified carrier. Upon receipt of such statement, the court shall reinstate the injunction waived under paragraph (1).

(D) LOSS OF RECOGNITION PREVENTS FUTURE RECOGNITION.—No entity may be recognized as a qualified carrier if such entity had previously been recognized as a qualified carrier and subsequently lost such recognition or voluntarily terminated such recognition under subparagraph (C).

(4) QUALIFIED CARRIER OBLIGATIONS AND COMPLIANCE.—

(A) CONTINUING OBLIGATIONS.—

(i) IN GENERAL.—An entity recognized as a qualified carrier shall continue to provide local-into-local service to all DMAs.

(ii) COOPERATION WITH COMPLIANCE EXAMINATION.—An entity recognized as a qualified carrier shall fully cooperate with the special master appointed by the court under paragraph (3)(B) in an examination set forth in subparagraph (B).

(B) QUALIFIED CARRIER COMPLIANCE EXAMINATION.—

(i) EXAMINATION AND REPORT.—A special master appointed by the court under paragraph (3)(B) shall conduct an examination of, and file a report on, the qualified carrier's compliance with the royalty payment and household eligibility requirements of the license under this section. The report shall address the qualified carrier's conduct during the period beginning on the date on which the qualified carrier is recognized as such under paragraph (3)(B) and ending on April 30, 2012.

(ii) RECORDS OF QUALIFIED CARRIER.—Beginning on the date that is one year after the date on which the qualified carrier is recognized as such under paragraph (3)(B), but not later than December 1, 2011, the qualified carrier shall provide the special master with all records that the special master considers to be directly pertinent to the following requirements under this section:

(I) Proper calculation and payment of royalties under the statutory license under this section.

(II) Provision of service under this license to eligible subscribers only.

(iii) SUBMISSION OF REPORT.—The special master shall file the report required by clause (i) not later than July 24, 2012, with the court referred to in paragraph (1) that issued the injunction, and the court shall transmit a copy of the report to the Register of Copyrights, the Committees on the Judiciary and on Energy and Commerce of the House of Representatives, and the Committees on the Judiciary and on Commerce, Science, and Transportation of the Senate.

(iv) EVIDENCE OF INFRINGEMENT.—The special master shall include in the report a statement of whether the examination by the special master indicated that there is substantial evidence that a copyright holder could bring a successful action under this section against the qualified carrier for infringement.

(v) SUBSEQUENT EXAMINATION.—If the special master's report includes a statement that its examination indicated the existence of substantial evidence that a copyright holder could bring a successful action under this section against the qualified carrier for infringement, the special master shall, not later than 6 months after the report under clause (i) is filed, initiate another examination of the qualified carrier's compliance with the royalty payment and household eligibility requirements of the license under this section since the last report was filed under clause (iii). The special master shall file a report on the results of the examination conducted under this clause with the court referred to in paragraph (1) that issued the injunction, and the court shall transmit a copy to the Register of Copyrights, the Committees on the Judiciary and on Energy and Commerce of the House of Representatives, and the Committees on the Judiciary and on Commerce, Science, and Transportation of the Senate. The report shall include a statement described in clause (iv).

(vi) COMPLIANCE.—Upon motion filed by an aggrieved copyright owner, the court recognizing an entity as a qualified carrier shall terminate such designation upon finding that the entity has failed to cooperate with an examination required by this subparagraph.

(vii) OVERSIGHT.—During the period of time that the special master is conducting an examination under this subparagraph, the Comptroller General shall monitor the degree to which the entity seeking to be recognized or recognized as a qualified carrier under paragraph (3) is complying with the special master's examination. The qualified carrier shall make available to the Comptroller General all records and individuals that the Comptroller General considers necessary to meet the Comptroller General's obligations under this clause. The Comptroller General shall report the results of the monitoring required by this clause to the Committees on the Judiciary and on Energy and Commerce of the House of Representatives and the Committees on the Judiciary and on Commerce, Science, and Transportation of the Senate at intervals of not less than six months during such period.

(C) AFFIRMATION.—A qualified carrier shall file an affidavit with the district court and the Register of Copyrights 30 months after such status was granted stating that, to the best of the affiant's knowledge, it is in compliance with the requirements for a qualified carrier. The qualified carrier shall attach to its affidavit copies of all reports or orders issued by the court, the special master, and the Comptroller General.

(D) COMPLIANCE DETERMINATION.—Upon the motion of an aggrieved television broadcast station, the court recognizing an entity as a qualified carrier may make a determination of whether the entity is providing local-into-local service to all DMAs.

(E) PLEADING REQUIREMENT.—In any motion brought under subparagraph (D), the party making such motion shall specify one or more designated market areas (as such term is defined in section 122(j)(2)(C)) for which the failure to provide service is being alleged, and, for each such designated market area, shall plead with particularity the circumstances of the alleged failure.

(F) BURDEN OF PROOF.—In any proceeding to make a determination under subparagraph (D), and with respect to a designated market area for which failure to provide service is alleged, the entity recognized as a qualified carrier shall have the burden of proving that the entity provided local-into-local service with a good quality satellite signal to at least 90 percent of the households in such designated market area (based on the most recent census data released by the United States Census Bureau) at the time and place alleged.

(5) FAILURE TO PROVIDE SERVICE.—

(A) PENALTIES.—If the court recognizing an entity as a qualified carrier finds that such entity has willfully failed to provide local-into-local service to all DMAs, such finding shall result in the loss of recognition of the entity as a qualified carrier and the termination of the waiver provided under paragraph (1), and the court may, in its discretion—

(i) treat such failure as an act of infringement under section 501, and subject such infringement to the remedies provided for in sections 502 through 506 and subsection (a)(6)(B) of this section; and

(ii) impose a fine of not less than $250,000 and not more than $5,000,000.

(B) EXCEPTION FOR NONWILLFUL VIOLATION.—If the court determines that the failure to provide local-into-local service to all DMAs is nonwillful, the court may in its discretion impose financial penalties for noncompliance that reflect—

(i) the degree of control the entity had over the circumstances that resulted in the failure;

(ii) the quality of the entity's efforts to remedy the failure and restore service; and

(iii) the severity and duration of any service interruption.

(6) PENALTIES FOR VIOLATIONS OF LICENSE.—A court that finds, under subsection (a)(6)(A), that an entity recognized as a qualified carrier has willfully made a secondary transmission of a primary transmission made by a network station and embodying a performance or display of a work to a subscriber who is not eligible to receive the transmission under this section shall reinstate the injunction waived under paragraph (1), and the court may order statutory damages of not more than $2,500,000.

(7) LOCAL-INTO-LOCAL SERVICE TO ALL DMAS DEFINED.—For purposes of this subsection:

(A) IN GENERAL.—An entity provides "local-into-local service to all DMAs" if the entity provides local service in all designated market areas (as such term is defined in section 122(j)(2)(C)) pursuant to the license under section 122.

(B) HOUSEHOLD COVERAGE.—For purposes of subparagraph (A), an entity that makes available local-into-local service with a good quality satellite signal to at least 90 percent of the households in a designated market area based on the most recent census data released by the United States Census Bureau shall be considered to be providing local service to such designated market area.

(C) GOOD QUALITY SATELLITE SIGNAL DEFINED.—The term "good quality satellite signal" has the meaning given such term under section 342(e)(2) of Communications[2] Act of 1934.

(Added Pub. L. 100–667, title II, § 202(2), Nov. 16, 1988, 102 Stat. 3949; amended Pub. L. 103–198, § 5, Dec. 17, 1993, 107 Stat. 2310; Pub. L. 103–369, § 2, Oct. 18, 1994, 108 Stat. 3477; Pub. L. 104–39, § 5(c), Nov. 1, 1995, 109 Stat. 348; Pub. L. 105–80, §§ 1, 12(a)(8), Nov. 13, 1997, 111 Stat. 1529, 1535; Pub. L. 106–44, § 1(g)(4), Aug. 5, 1999, 113 Stat. 222; Pub. L. 106–113, div. B, § 1000(a)(9) [title I, §§ 1004–1007,

---

[2] So in original. Probably should be preceded by "the".

1008(b), 1011(b)(2), (c)], Nov. 29, 1999, 113 Stat. 1536, 1501A–527 to 1501A–531, 1501A–537, 1501A–543, 1501A–544; Pub. L. 107–273, div. C, title III, §§ 13209, 13210(1), (8), Nov. 2, 2002, 116 Stat. 1908, 1909; Pub. L. 108–419, § 5(g), (h), Nov. 30, 2004, 118 Stat. 2367; Pub. L. 108–447, div. J, title IX [title I, §§ 101(b)–105, 107(a), 108, 111(a)], Dec. 8, 2004, 118 Stat. 3394–3408; Pub. L. 109–303, § 4(e), (g), Oct. 6, 2006, 120 Stat. 1482, 1483; Pub. L. 110–403, title II, § 209(a)(4), Oct. 13, 2008, 122 Stat. 4264; Pub. L. 111–118, div. B, § 1003(a)(1), Dec. 19, 2009, 123 Stat. 3469; Pub. L. 111–144, § 10(a)(1), Mar. 2, 2010, 124 Stat. 47; Pub. L. 111–151, § 2(a)(1), Mar. 26, 2010, 124 Stat. 1027; Pub. L. 111–157, § 9(a)(1), Apr. 15, 2010, 124 Stat. 1118; Pub. L. 111–175, title I, §§ 102(a)(1), (b)–(k), 105, May 27, 2010, 124 Stat. 1219–1226, 1239; Pub. L. 111–295, § 6(c), Dec. 9, 2010, 124 Stat. 3181.)

TERMINATION OF SECTION

For termination of section by section 107(a) of Pub. L. 111–175, see Termination of Section note below.

REFERENCES IN TEXT

The date of the enactment of the Satellite Home Viewer Extension and Reauthorization Act of 2004, referred to in subsec. (a)(3)(A)(i)(II), (E), (13), is the date of the enactment of Pub. L. 108–447, which was approved Dec. 8, 2004.

The date of the enactment of the Satellite Television Extension and Localism Act of 2010, referred to in subsecs. (a)(3)(B), (C) and (d)(10)(B), is the date of enactment of Pub. L. 111–175, which shall be deemed to refer to Feb. 27, 2010, see section 307(a) of Pub. L. 111–175, set out as an Effective Date of 2010 Amendment note under section 111 of this title.

The Communications Act of 1934, referred to in subsec. (d)(6), is act June 19, 1934, ch. 652, 48 Stat. 1064, which is classified principally to chapter 5 (§ 151 et seq.) of Title 47, Telegraphs, Telephones, and Radiotelegraphs. Sections 338, 339, 342, and 397 of the Act are classified to sections 338, 339, 342, and 397, respectively, of Title 47. For complete classification of this Act to the Code, see section 609 of Title 47 and Tables.

The date of the enactment of this subsection, referred to in subsec. (g)(1), (2)(A), (E), is the date of enactment of Pub. L. 111–175, which shall be deemed to refer to Feb. 27, 2010. See section 307(a) of Pub. L. 111–175, set out as an Effective Date of 2010 Amendment note under section 111 of this title.

The Federal Rules of Civil Procedure, referred to in subsec. (g)(3)(A)(iii), are set out in the Appendix to Title 28, Judiciary and Judicial Procedure.

AMENDMENTS

2010—Pub. L. 111–175, § 102(a)(1), substituted "distant television programming by satellite" for "superstations and network stations for private home viewing" in section catchline.

Subsec. (a). Pub. L. 111–175, § 102(h)(1)(B), (C), redesignated pars. (4) to (14) and (16) as (3) to (13) and (14), respectively, and struck out former pars. (3) and (15) which related to secondary transmissions of significantly viewed signals and carriage of low power television stations, respectively.

Subsec. (a)(1). Pub. L. 111–175, § 102(h)(2)(A)(i), substituted "(4), (5), and (7)" for "(5), (6), and (8)".

Pub. L. 111–175, § 102(g)(2), which directed amendment of section by substituting "non-network stations" for "superstations" wherever appearing in headings, was executed by substituting "NON-NETWORK STATIONS" for "SUPERSTATIONS" in par. (1) heading, to reflect the probable intent of Congress.

Pub. L. 111–175, § 102(g)(1), substituted "non-network station" for "superstation".

Subsec. (a)(2)(A). Pub. L. 111–175, § 102(h)(2)(A)(ii)(I), substituted "subparagraph (B) of this paragraph and paragraphs (4), (5), (6), and (7)" for "subparagraphs (B) and (C) of this paragraph and paragraphs (5), (6), (7), and (8)".

Subsec. (a)(2)(B)(i). Pub. L. 111–175, § 102(h)(2)(A)(ii)(II), struck out "The limitation in this clause shall not apply to secondary transmissions under paragraph (3)." at end.

Subsec. (a)(2)(B)(ii)(III). Pub. L. 111–175, § 102(i)(1), added subcl. (III).

Subsec. (a)(2)(B)(iii)(II). Pub. L. 111–175, § 102(i)(5), (k)(1), substituted "In this clause," for "In this clause" and ", Code of Federal Regulations" for "of the Code of Federal Regulations".

Subsec. (a)(2)(C). Pub. L. 111–175, § 102(h)(1)(A), redesignated subpar. (D) as (C) and struck out former subpar. (C), which related to exceptions.

Subsec. (a)(2)(C)(i), (ii). Pub. L. 111–175, § 102(h)(2)(A)(ii)(III), added cls. (i) and (ii) and struck out former cls. (i) and (ii) which related to initial lists and monthly lists, respectively.

Subsec. (a)(2)(D). Pub. L. 111–175, § 102(h)(1)(A), redesignated subpar. (D) as (C).

Subsec. (a)(3)(A). Pub. L. 111–175, § 102(i)(2)(A), struck out "analog" after "subscribers to" in subpar. heading, substituted "distant" for "distant analog" and "primary" for "primary analog" wherever appearing in headings and text, and struck out "analog" after "receive such local" in cl. (i)(I)(bb).

Subsec. (a)(3)(B), (C). Pub. L. 111–175, § 102(i)(2)(B), added subpars. (B) and (C) and struck out former subpars. (B) and (C) which related to rules for other subscribers and future applicability, respectively.

Subsec. (a)(3)(D). Pub. L. 111–175, § 102(i)(2)(B), (C), redesignated subpar. (E) as (D) and struck out former subpar. (D) which related to special rules for distant digital signals.

Subsec. (a)(3)(E). Pub. L. 111–175, § 102(i)(2)(C), (D), redesignated subpar. (F) as (E) and substituted "(B) or (C)" for "(C) or (D)". Former subpar. (E) redesignated (D).

Pub. L. 111–175, § 102(h)(2)(A)(iii), struck out "under paragraph (3) or" after "transmissions" and substituted "paragraph (11)" for "paragraph (12)".

Subsec. (a)(3)(F), (G). Pub. L. 111–175, § 102(i)(2)(C), (E), redesignated subpar. (G) as (F) and inserted "9-digit" before "zip code". Former subpar. (F) redesignated (E).

Subsec. (a)(4). Pub. L. 111–175, § 102(i)(4), struck out "and 509" after "506".

Subsec. (a)(5). Pub. L. 111–175, § 102(g)(1), substituted "non-network station" for "superstation".

Subsec. (a)(6). Pub. L. 111–175, § 102(i)(3)(C), inserted concluding provisions.

Pub. L. 111–175, § 102(g)(1), substituted "non-network station" for "superstation".

Subsec. (a)(6)(A)(ii). Pub. L. 111–175, § 102(i)(3)(A), substituted "$250" for "$5".

Subsec. (a)(6)(B)(i). Pub. L. 111–175, § 102(i)(3)(B)(i), substituted "$2,500,000 for each 3-month period" for "$250,000 for each 6-month period".

Subsec. (a)(6)(B)(ii). Pub. L. 111–175, § 102(i)(3)(B)(ii), substituted "$2,500,000" for "$250,000".

Subsec. (a)(8). Pub. L. 111–175, § 102(g)(1), substituted "non-network station" for "superstation".

Subsec. (a)(11)(A)(i)(I), (II), (B)(iii)(II). Pub. L. 111–175, § 102(k)(1), substituted ", Code of Federal Regulations" for "of the Code of Federal Regulations".

Subsec. (b). Pub. L. 111–175, § 102(d)(1), amended heading generally. Prior to amendment, heading read as follows: "STATUTORY LICENSE FOR SECONDARY TRANSMISSIONS FOR PRIVATE HOME VIEWING.—".

Subsec. (b)(1). Pub. L. 111–175, § 102(h)(2)(B), struck out concluding provisions which read as follows: "Notwithstanding the provisions of subparagraph (B), a satellite carrier whose secondary transmissions are subject to statutory licensing under paragraph (1) or (2) of subsection (a) shall have no royalty obligation for secondary transmissions to a subscriber under paragraph (3) of such subsection."

Subsec. (b)(1)(A). Pub. L. 111–175, § 102(g)(2), substituted "non-network stations" for "superstations".

Subsec. (b)(1)(B). Pub. L. 111–175, § 102(d)(2), added subpar. (B) and struck out former subpar. (B) which read as follows: "a royalty fee for that 6-month period, computed by multiplying the total number of subscribers receiving each secondary transmission of each superstation or network station during each calendar month by the appropriate rate in effect under this section; and".

Subsec. (b)(1)(C). Pub. L. 111–175, § 102(c), added subpar. (C).

Subsec. (b)(2). Pub. L. 111–175, § 102(d)(4), added par. (2). Former par. (2) redesignated (3).

Subsec. (b)(3). Pub. L. 111–175, § 102(d)(3), (5), redesignated par. (2) as (3), inserted "(including the filing fee specified in paragraph (1)(C))" after "shall receive all fees", and substituted "paragraph (5)" for "paragraph (4)". Former par. (3) redesignated (4).

Subsec. (b)(4). Pub. L. 111–175, § 102(d)(3), (6), redesignated par. (3) as (4), substituted "paragraph (3)" for "paragraph (2)", and substituted "paragraph (5)" for "paragraph (4)" in two places. Former par. (4) redesignated (5).

Subsec. (b)(5). Pub. L. 111–175, § 102(d)(3), (7), redesignated par. (4) as (5) and substituted "paragraph (3)" for "paragraph (2)" in introductory provisions.

Subsec. (c)(1). Pub. L. 111–175, § 102(e)(1)(A), struck out "analog" after "fees for" in heading.

Subsec. (c)(1)(A). Pub. L. 111–175, § 102(e)(1)(B), (g)(2), substituted "primary transmissions" for "primary analog transmissions", "non-network stations" for "superstations", and "July 1, 2009" for "July 1, 2004".

Subsec. (c)(1)(B). Pub. L. 111–175, § 102(e)(1)(C), (g)(2), substituted "June 1, 2010, the Copyright Royalty Judges" for "January 2, 2005, the Librarian of Congress", "primary transmissions" for "primary analog transmission", and "non-network stations" for "superstations".

Subsec. (c)(1)(C). Pub. L. 111–175, § 102(e)(1)(D), substituted "Copyright Royalty Judges" for "Librarian of Congress".

Subsec. (c)(1)(D)(i). Pub. L. 111–175, § 102(e)(1)(E)(i), inserted heading and substituted "that are parties" for "that a parties".

Subsec. (c)(1)(D)(ii). Pub. L. 111–175, § 102(e)(1)(E)(ii)(I), inserted heading.

Subsec. (c)(1)(D)(ii)(I). Pub. L. 111–175, § 102(e)(1)(E)(ii)(I), (II), inserted heading and substituted "a proceeding under subparagraph (F)" for "an arbitration proceeding pursuant to subparagraph (E)".

Subsec. (c)(1)(D)(ii)(II). Pub. L. 111–175, § 102(e)(1)(E)(ii)(III), inserted heading and substituted "Upon receiving a request under subclause (I), the Copyright Royalty Judges" for "Upon receiving a request under subclause (I), the Librarian of Congress".

Subsec. (c)(1)(D)(ii)(III). Pub. L. 111–175, § 102(e)(1)(E)(ii)(IV), inserted heading and substituted "The Copyright Royalty Judges" for "The Librarian", "the proceeding under subparagraph (F)" for "an arbitration proceeding", and "that proceeding" for "the arbitration proceeding".

Subsec. (c)(1)(E). Pub. L. 111–175, § 102(e)(1)(F), substituted "Copyright Royalty Judges" for "Copyright Office" and "December 31, 2014" for "May 31, 2010".

Pub. L. 111–157, § 9(a)(1)(A), substituted "May 31, 2010" for "April 30, 2010".

Pub. L. 111–151, § 2(a)(1)(A), substituted "April 30, 2010" for "March 28, 2010".

Pub. L. 111–144, § 10(a)(1)(A), substituted "March 28, 2010" for "February 28, 2010".

Subsec. (c)(1)(F). Pub. L. 111–175, § 102(e)(1)(G)(i), substituted "copyright royalty judges proceeding" for "compulsory arbitration" in heading.

Subsec. (c)(1)(F)(i). Pub. L. 111–175, § 102(e)(1)(G)(ii)(I), (II), (IV), (g)(2), in heading, substituted "the proceeding" for "proceedings", in introductory provisions, substituted "September 1, 2010, the Copyright Royalty Judges" for "May 1, 2005, the Librarian of Congress", "a proceeding" for "arbitration proceedings", "fees to be paid" for "fee to be paid", "the primary transmissions" for "primary analog transmission", "non-

network stations" for "superstations", and "distributors—" for "distributors", and amended concluding provisions generally. Prior to amendment, concluding provisions read as follows: "Such arbitration proceeding shall be conducted under chapter 8 as in effect on the day before the date of the enactment of the Copyright Royalty and Distribution Act of 2004."

Subsec. (c)(1)(F)(i)(II). Pub. L. 111–175, § 102(e)(1)(G)(ii)(III), substituted "Copyright Royalty Judges" for "Librarian of Congress" and struck out "arbitration" after "participate in the".

Subsec. (c)(1)(F)(ii). Pub. L. 111–175, § 102(e)(1)(G)(iii), amended introductory provisions generally. Prior to amendment, introductory provisions read as follows: "In determining royalty fees under this subparagraph, the copyright arbitration royalty panel appointed under chapter 8, as in effect on the day before the date of the enactment of the Copyright Royalty and Distribution Act of 2004 shall establish fees for the secondary transmissions of the primary analog transmission of network stations and superstations that most clearly represent the fair market value of secondary transmissions, except that the Librarian of Congress and any copyright arbitration royalty panel shall adjust those fees to account for the obligations of the parties under any applicable voluntary agreement filed with the Copyright Office pursuant to subparagraph (D). In determining the fair market value, the panel shall base its decision on economic, competitive, and programming information presented by the parties, including—".

Subsec. (c)(1)(F)(iii). Pub. L. 111–175, § 102(e)(1)(G)(iv), amended cl. (iii) generally. Prior to amendment, text read as follows: "The obligation to pay the royalty fee established under a determination which—

"(I) is made by a copyright arbitration royalty panel in an arbitration proceeding under this paragraph and is adopted by the Librarian of Congress under section 802(f), as in effect on the day before the date of the enactment of the Copyright Royalty and Distribution Act of 2004; or

"(II) is established by the Librarian under section 802(f) as in effect on the day before such date of enactment shall be effective as of January 1, 2005."

Subsec. (c)(1)(F)(iv). Pub. L. 111–175, § 102(e)(1)(G)(v), substituted "fees" for "fee" in heading and substituted "fees referred to in clause (iii)" for "fee referred to in (iii)" in text.

Subsec. (c)(2). Pub. L. 111–175, § 102(e)(2), amended par. (2) generally. Prior to amendment, par. (2) related to applicability and determination of royalty fees for digital signals.

Subsec. (d)(1). Pub. L. 111–175, § 102(f)(6), substituted "that contracts" for "which contracts".

Subsec. (d)(2)(A). Pub. L. 111–175, § 102(f)(6), substituted "that offer" for "which offer".

Subsec. (d)(5). Pub. L. 111–175, § 102(f)(6), substituted "that is operated" for "which is operated" and "that serves" for "which serves".

Subsec. (d)(6). Pub. L. 111–175, § 102(k), substituted ", Code of Federal Regulations, or the Direct Broadcast Satellite Service under part 100 of title 47, Code of Federal Regulations" for "of the Code of Federal Regulations or the Direct Broadcast Satellite Service under part 100 of title 47 of the Code of Federal Regulations".

Subsec. (d)(8). Pub. L. 111–175, § 102(f)(1), amended par. (8) generally. Prior to amendment, text read as follows: "The term 'subscriber' means an individual or entity that receives a secondary transmission service by means of a secondary transmission from a satellite carrier and pays a fee for the service, directly or indirectly, to the satellite carrier or to a distributor in accordance with the provisions of this section."

Subsec. (d)(9). Pub. L. 111–175, § 102(g)(1), which directed amendment of section by substituting "non-network station" for "superstation" wherever appearing in headings, was executed by substituting "NON-NETWORK STATION" for "SUPERSTATION" in par. (9) heading, to reflect the probable intent of Congress.

Pub. L. 111–175, § 102(g)(1), substituted "non-network station" for "superstation".

Subsec. (d)(10)(A). Pub. L. 111–175, §102(b)(1)(A), added subpar. (A) and struck out former subpar. (A) which read as follows: "cannot receive, through the use of a conventional, stationary, outdoor rooftop receiving antenna, an over-the-air signal of a primary network station affiliated with that network of Grade B intensity as defined by the Federal Communications Commission under section 73.683(a) of title 47 of the Code of Federal Regulations, as in effect on January 1, 1999;".

Subsec. (d)(10)(B). Pub. L. 111–175, §102(b)(1)(B), substituted "subsection (a)(13)," for "subsection (a)(14)" and "Satellite Television Extension and Localism Act of 2010" for "Satellite Home Viewer Extension and Reauthorization Act of 2004".

Subsec. (d)(10)(D). Pub. L. 111–175, §102(b)(1)(C), substituted "(a)(11)" for "(a)(12)".

Subsec. (d)(11). Pub. L. 111–175, §102(f)(2), amended par. (11) generally. Prior to amendment, text read as follows: "The term 'local market' has the meaning given such term under section 122(j), except that with respect to a low power television station, the term 'local market' means the designated market area in which the station is located."

Subsec. (d)(12), (13). Pub. L. 111–175, §102(f)(3), redesignated pars. (13) and (14) as (12) and (13), respectively, and struck out former par. (12). Text read as follows: "The term 'low power television station' means a low power television as defined under section 74.701(f) of title 47, Code of Federal Regulations, as in effect on June 1, 2004. For purposes of this paragraph, the term 'low power television station' includes a low power television station that has been accorded primary status as a Class A television licensee under section 73.6001(a) of title 47, Code of Federal Regulations."

Subsec. (d)(14). Pub. L. 111–175, §102(f)(4), added par. (14). Former par. (14) redesignated (13).

Pub. L. 111–175, §102(b)(2), added par. (14).

Subsec. (d)(15). Pub. L. 111–175, §102(f)(5), added par. (15).

Subsec. (e). Pub. L. 111–175, §102(j), (k)(1), substituted "December 31, 2014" for "May 31, 2010" and ", Code of Federal Regulations" for "of the Code of Federal Regulations".

Pub. L. 111–157, §9(a)(1)(B), substituted "May 31, 2010" for "April 30, 2010".

Pub. L. 111–151, §2(a)(1)(B), substituted "April 30, 2010" for "March 28, 2010".

Pub. L. 111–144, §10(a)(1)(B), substituted "March 28, 2010" for "February 28, 2010".

Subsec. (g). Pub. L. 111–175, §105, added subsec. (g).

Subsec. (g)(4)(B)(vi). Pub. L. 111–295 substituted "an examination" for "the examinations".

2009—Subsecs. (c)(1)(E), (e). Pub. L. 111–118 substituted "February 28, 2010" for "December 31, 2009".

2008—Subsec. (a)(6). Pub. L. 110–403, §209(a)(4)(A), substituted "section 510" for "sections 509 and 510".

Subsec. (a)(7)(A). Pub. L. 110–403, §209(a)(4)(B), struck out "and 509" after "506" in introductory provisions.

Subsec. (a)(8), (13). Pub. L. 110–403, §209(a)(4)(C), (D), struck out "and 509" after "506".

2006—Subsec. (b)(4)(B). Pub. L. 109–303, §4(e)(1)(A), substituted second sentence for former second sentence which read as follows: "If the Copyright Royalty Judges determine that no such controversy exists, the Librarian of Congress shall, after deducting reasonable administrative costs under this paragraph, distribute such fees to the copyright owners entitled to receive them, or to their designated agents."

Subsec. (b)(4)(C). Pub. L. 109–303, §4(e)(1)(B), amended subpar. (C) generally. Prior to amendment, text of subpar. (C) read as follows: "During the pendency of any proceeding under this subsection, the Copyright Royalty Judges shall withhold from distribution an amount sufficient to satisfy all claims with respect to which a controversy exists, but shall have the discretion to proceed to distribute any amounts that are not in controversy."

Subsec. (c). Pub. L. 109–303, §4(g), deemed amendment by Pub. L. 108–419, §5(h), never to have been enacted. See 2004 Amendment note below.

Subsec. (c)(1)(F)(i). Pub. L. 109–303, §4(e)(2), substituted "arbitration" for "arbitrary" in concluding provisions.

2004—Subsec. (a)(1). Pub. L. 108–447, §107(a)(1), inserted "or for viewing in a commercial establishment" after "for private home viewing" in two places and substituted "subscriber" for "household".

Pub. L. 108–447, §102(1), struck out "and pbs satellite feed" after "Superstations" in heading, substituted "paragraphs (5), (6), and (8)" for "paragraphs (3), (4), and (6)" and struck out "or by the Public Broadcasting Service satellite feed" after "primary transmission made by a superstation" in first sentence, and struck out at end "In the case of the Public Broadcasting Service satellite feed, the statutory license shall be effective until January 1, 2002."

Subsec. (a)(2)(A). Pub. L. 108–447, §102(2)(A), substituted "paragraphs (5), (6), (7), and (8)" for "paragraphs (3), (4), (5), and (6)".

Subsec. (a)(2)(B)(i). Pub. L. 108–447, §102(7), inserted at end "The limitation in this clause shall not apply to secondary transmissions under paragraph (3)."

Subsec. (a)(2)(C), (D). Pub. L. 108–447, §102(2)(B), added subpars. (C) and (D) and struck out heading and text of former subpar. (C). Text read as follows: "A satellite carrier that makes secondary transmissions of a primary transmission made by a network station pursuant to subparagraph (A) shall, 90 days after commencing such secondary transmissions, submit to the network that owns or is affiliated with the network station a list identifying (by name and street address, including county and zip code) all subscribers to which the satellite carrier makes secondary transmissions of that primary transmission. Thereafter, on the 15th of each month, the satellite carrier shall submit to the network a list identifying (by name and street address, including county and zip code) any persons who have been added or dropped as such subscribers since the last submission under this subparagraph. Such subscriber information submitted by a satellite carrier may be used only for purposes of monitoring compliance by the satellite carrier with this subsection. The submission requirements of this subparagraph shall apply to a satellite carrier only if the network to whom the submissions are to be made places on file with the Register of Copyrights a document identifying the name and address of the person to whom such submissions are to be made. The Register shall maintain for public inspection a file of all such documents."

Subsec. (a)(3) to (6). Pub. L. 108–447, §§102(5), (6), 103(1), added pars. (3) and (4) and redesignated former pars. (3) and (4) as (5) and (6), respectively. Former pars. (5) and (6) redesignated (7) and (8), respectively.

Subsec. (a)(7). Pub. L. 108–447, §102(5), redesignated par. (5) as (7). Former par. (7) redesignated (9).

Subsec. (a)(7)(A). Pub. L. 108–447, §103(6)(A), substituted "who is not eligible to receive the transmission under this section" for "who does not reside in an unserved household" in introductory provisions.

Subsec. (a)(7)(B). Pub. L. 108–447, §103(6)(B), substituted "who are not eligible to receive the transmission under this section" for "who do not reside in unserved households" in introductory provisions.

Subsec. (a)(7)(D). Pub. L. 108–447, §103(6)(C), substituted "is to a subscriber who is eligible to receive the secondary transmission under this section" for "is for private home viewing to an unserved household".

Subsec. (a)(8). Pub. L. 108–447, §102(3), (5), redesignated par. (6) as (8) and struck out former par. (8) which related to transitional signal intensity measurement procedures.

Subsec. (a)(9) to (13). Pub. L. 108–447, §102(4), (5), redesignated pars. (7) and (9) to (12) as (9) and (10) to (13), respectively.

Subsec. (a)(14). Pub. L. 108–447, §103(2), added par. (14).

Subsec. (a)(15). Pub. L. 108–447, §104, added par. (15).

Subsec. (a)(16). Pub. L. 108–447, §111(a), added par. (16).

Subsec. (b)(1). Pub. L. 108–447, §103(4), inserted at end: "Notwithstanding the provisions of subparagraph (B), a satellite carrier whose secondary transmissions are subject to statutory licensing under paragraph (1) or (2) of subsection (a) shall have no royalty obligation for secondary transmissions to a subscriber under paragraph (3) of such subsection.''

Subsec. (b)(1)(A). Pub. L. 108–447, § 107(a)(2), struck out "for private home viewing" after "to subscribers".

Subsec. (b)(1)(B). Pub. L. 108–447, § 103(3), added subpar. (B) and struck out former subpar. (B) which read as follows: "a royalty fee for that 6-month period, computed by—

"(i) multiplying the total number of subscribers receiving each secondary transmission of a superstation during each calendar month by 17.5 cents per subscriber in the case of superstations that as retransmitted by the satellite carrier include any program which, if delivered by any cable system in the United States, would be subject to the syndicated exclusivity rules of the Federal Communications Commission, and 14 cents per subscriber in the case of superstations that are syndex-proof as defined in section 258.2 of title 37, Code of Federal Regulations;

"(ii) multiplying the number of subscribers receiving each secondary transmission of a network station or the Public Broadcasting Service satellite feed during each calendar month by 6 cents; and

"(iii) adding together the totals computed under clauses (i) and (ii)."

Subsec. (b)(3). Pub. L. 108–447, § 107(a)(2), struck out "for private home viewing" after "secondary transmission".

Pub. L. 108–419, § 5(g)(1), substituted "Copyright Royalty Judges" for "Librarian of Congress".

Subsec. (b)(4)(A). Pub. L. 108–447, § 107(a)(2), struck out "for private home viewing" after "secondary transmissions".

Pub. L. 108–419, § 5(g)(2)(A), substituted "Copyright Royalty Judges" for "Librarian of Congress" in two places.

Subsec. (b)(4)(B), (C). Pub. L. 108–419, § 5(g)(2)(B), reenacted headings without change and amended text generally, substituting provisions relating to duties of Copyright Royalty Judges concerning determination of royalty fee controversies and distribution of royalty fees for provisions relating to duties of Librarian of Congress relating to such determination and distribution.

Subsec. (c). Pub. L. 108–447, § 103(5), amended heading and text of subsec. (c) generally. Prior to amendment, text related to adjustment, determination, arbitration, and reduction of royalty fees.

Pub. L. 108–419, § 5(h), which directed amendment of subsec. (c) by substituting "Copyright Royalty Judges" for "Librarian of Congress" in par. (2)(B), "Copyright Royalty Judges shall prescribe as provided in section 803(b)(6)" for "Register of Copyrights shall prescribe" in par. (2)(C), "proceedings" for "arbitration proceedings" and for "arbitration proceeding" in par. (3)(A), "Copyright Royalty Judges" for "copyright arbitration royalty panel appointed under chapter 8" and "Copyright Royalty Judges shall base their determination" for "panel shall base its decision" in par. (3)(B), "determination under chapter 8" for "decision of arbitration panel or order of librarian" in heading of par. (3)(C), and "(i) is made by the Copyright Royalty Judges pursuant to this paragraph and becomes final, or" and "(ii) is made by the court on appeal under section 803(d)(3)," for cls. (i) and (ii), respectively, of par. (3)(C), was deemed never to have been enacted by Pub L. 109–303, § 4(g). See Removal of Inconsistent Provisions note below.

Subsec. (d)(1). Pub. L. 108–447, § 107(a)(3), struck out "for private home viewing" after "individual subscribers" and inserted "in accordance with the provisions of this section" before the period at end.

Subsec. (d)(2)(A). Pub. L. 108–447, § 105(1), substituted "a television station licensed by the Federal Communications Commission" for "a television broadcast station".

Subsec. (d)(6). Pub. L. 108–447, § 107(a)(4), inserted "pursuant to this section" before period at end.

Subsec. (d)(8). Pub. L. 108–447, § 107(a)(5), substituted "or entity that" for "who", struck out "for private home viewing" after "transmission service", and inserted "in accordance with the provisions of this section" before period at end.

Subsec. (d)(9). Pub. L. 108–447, § 105(2), amended heading and text of par. (9) generally. Prior to amendment, text read as follows: "The term 'superstation'—

"(A) means a television broadcast station, other than a network station, licensed by the Federal Communications Commission that is secondarily transmitted by a satellite carrier; and

"(B) except for purposes of computing the royalty fee, includes the Public Broadcasting Service satellite feed."

Subsec. (d)(10)(B). Pub. L. 108–447, § 105(3)(A), substituted "that meets the standards of subsection (a)(14) whether or not the waiver was granted before the date of the enactment of the Satellite Home Viewer Extension and Reauthorization Act of 2004" for "granted under regulations established under section 339(c)(2) of the Communications Act of 1934".

Subsec. (d)(10)(D). Pub. L. 108–447, § 105(3)(B), substituted "(a)(12)" for "(a)(11)".

Subsec. (d)(11) to (13). Pub. L. 108–447, § 105(4), added pars. (11) to (13) and struck out former pars. (11) and (12) which read as follows:

"(11) LOCAL MARKET.—The term 'local market' has the meaning given such term under section 122(j).

"(12) PUBLIC BROADCASTING SERVICE SATELLITE FEED.— The term 'Public Broadcasting Service satellite feed' means the national satellite feed distributed and designated for purposes of this section by the Public Broadcasting Service consisting of educational and informational programming intended for private home viewing, to which the Public Broadcasting Service holds national terrestrial broadcast rights."

Subsec. (e). Pub. L. 108–447, § 101(b), substituted "December 31, 2009" for "December 31, 2004".

Subsec. (f). Pub. L. 108–447, § 108, added subsec. (f).

2002—Subsec. (a)(1). Pub. L. 107–273, § 13209(3)(B), amended Pub. L. 106–113, § 1000(a)(9) [title I, § 1011(b)(2)(A)]. See 1999 Amendment note below.

Pub. L. 107–273, § 13209(3)(A), amended Pub. L. 106–113, § 1000(a)(9) [title I, § 1006(a)]. See 1999 Amendment note below.

Subsec. (a)(2)(A). Pub. L. 107–273, § 13209(1)(A), made technical correction to directory language of Pub. L. 106–113, § 1000(a)(9) [title I, § 1007(2)]. See 1999 Amendment note below.

Subsec. (a)(6). Pub. L. 107–273, § 13210(1), substituted "of a performance" for "of performance".

Subsec. (a)(12). Pub. L. 107–273, § 13209(1)(B), made technical correction to directory language of Pub. L. 106–113, § 1000(a)(9) [title I, § 1007(3)]. See 1999 Amendment note below.

Subsec. (b)(1)(A). Pub. L. 107–273, § 13210(8), substituted "retransmitted" for "transmitted" and "retransmissions" for "transmissions".

Subsec. (b)(1)(B)(ii). Pub. L. 107–273, § 13209(2), made technical correction to directory language of Pub. L. 106–113, § 1000(a)(9) [title I, § 1006(b)]. See 1999 Amendment note below.

1999—Subsec. (a)(1). Pub. L. 106–113, § 1000(a)(9) [title I, § 1011(b)(2)(A)], as amended by Pub. L. 107–273, § 13209(3)(B), substituted "performance or display of a work embodied in a primary transmission made by a superstation or by the Public Broadcasting Service satellite feed" for "primary transmission made by a superstation and embodying a performance or display of a work".

Pub. L. 106–113, § 1000(a)(9) [title I, § 1007(1)], inserted "with regard to secondary transmissions the satellite carrier is in compliance with the rules, regulations, or authorizations of the Federal Communications Commission governing the carriage of television broadcast station signals," after "satellite carrier to the public for private home viewing,".

Pub. L. 106–113, § 1000(a)(9) [title I, § 1006(a)], as amended by Pub. L. 107–273, § 13209(3)(A), in heading substituted "Superstations and pbs satellite feed" for "Superstations" and in text inserted "In the case of the Public Broadcasting Service satellite feed, the statutory license shall be effective until January 1, 2002." at end. Pub. L. 107–273, § 13209(3)(A)(ii), which repealed Pub. L. 106–113, § 1000(a)(9) [title I, § 1006(a)(2)], was executed by striking out "or by the Public Broadcasting Service satellite feed" which had been inserted by section 1006(a)(2) after "of a primary transmission made by a superstation", to reflect the probable intent of Congress.

Subsec. (a)(2)(A). Pub. L. 106–113, § 1000(a)(9) [title I, § 1011(b)(2)(A)], substituted "a performance or display of a work embodied in a primary transmission made by a network station" for "programming contained in a primary transmission made by a network station and embodying a performance or display of a work".

Pub. L. 106–113, § 1000(a)(9) [title I, § 1007(2)], as amended by Pub. L. 107–273, § 13209(1)(A), inserted "with regard to secondary transmissions the satellite carrier is in compliance with the rules, regulations, or authorizations of the Federal Communications Commission governing the carriage of television broadcast station signals," after "satellite carrier to the public for private home viewing,".

Subsec. (a)(2)(B). Pub. L. 106–113, § 1000(a)(9) [title I, § 1005(a)(2)], reenacted heading without change and amended text generally. Prior to amendment, text read as follows: "The statutory license provided for in subparagraph (A) shall be limited to secondary transmissions to persons who reside in unserved households."

Subsec. (a)(2)(C). Pub. L. 106–113, § 1000(a)(9) [title I, § 1011(c)], struck out "currently" after "all subscribers to which the satellite carrier" in first sentence.

Subsec. (a)(4). Pub. L. 106–113, § 1000(a)(9) [title I, § 1011(b)(2)(C)], inserted "a performance or display of a work embodied in" after "by a satellite carrier of" and struck out "and embodying a performance or display of a work" after "network station".

Subsec. (a)(5)(E). Pub. L. 106–113, § 1000(a)(9) [title I, § 1005(b)], added subpar. (E).

Subsec. (a)(6). Pub. L. 106–113, § 1000(a)(9) [title I, § 1011(b)(2)(D)], inserted "performance or display of a work embodied in" after "by a satellite carrier of" and struck out "and embodying a performance or display of a work" after "network station".

Subsec. (a)(8)(C)(ii). Pub. L. 106–44 substituted "within the network station's" for "within the network's station" in first sentence.

Subsec. (a)(11). Pub. L. 106–113, § 1000(a)(9) [title I, § 1005(d)], added par. (11).

Subsec. (a)(12). Pub. L. 106–113, § 1000(a)(9) [title I, § 1007(3)], as amended by Pub. L. 107–273, § 13209(1)(B), added par. (12).

Subsec. (b)(1)(B)(ii). Pub. L. 106–113, § 1000(a)(9) [title I, § 1006(b)], as amended by Pub. L. 107–273, § 13209(2), inserted "or the Public Broadcasting Service satellite feed" after "network station".

Subsec. (c)(4), (5). Pub. L. 106–113, § 1000(a)(9) [title I, § 1004], added pars. (4) and (5).

Subsec. (d)(2). Pub. L. 106–113, § 1000(a)(9) [title I, § 1008(b)], substituted a semicolon for the period at end of subpar. (B) and inserted concluding provisions.

Subsec. (d)(9). Pub. L. 106–113, § 1000(a)(9) [title I, § 1006(c)(1)], reenacted heading without change and amended text generally. Prior to amendment, text read as follows: "The term 'superstation' means a television broadcast station, other than a network station, licensed by the Federal Communications Commission that is secondarily transmitted by a satellite carrier."

Subsec. (d)(10). Pub. L. 106–113, § 1000(a)(9) [title I, § 1005(a)(1)], added par. (10) and struck out heading and text of former par. (10). Text read as follows: "The term 'unserved household', with respect to a particular television network, means a household that—

"(A) cannot receive, through the use of a conventional outdoor rooftop receiving antenna, an over-the-air signal of grade B intensity (as defined by the Federal Communications Commission) of a primary network station affiliated with that network, and

"(B) has not, within 90 days before the date on which that household subscribes, either initially or on renewal, to receive secondary transmissions by a satellite carrier of a network station affiliated with that network, subscribed to a cable system that provides the signal of a primary network station affiliated with that network."

Subsec. (d)(11). Pub. L. 106–113, § 1000(a)(9) [title I, § 1005(e)], reenacted heading without change and amended text generally. Prior to amendment, text read as follows: "The term 'local market' means the area encompassed within a network station's predicted Grade B contour as that contour is defined by the Federal Communications Commission."

Subsec. (d)(12). Pub. L. 106–113, § 1000(a)(9) [title I, § 1006(c)(2)], added par. (12).

Subsec. (e). Pub. L. 106–113, § 1000(a)(9) [title I, § 1005(c)], amended heading and text of subsec. (e) generally. Prior to amendment, text read as follows: "No provision of section 111 of this title or any other law (other than this section) shall be construed to contain any authorization, exemption, or license through which secondary transmissions by satellite carrier for private home viewing of programming contained in a primary transmission made by a superstation or a network station may be made without obtaining the consent of the copyright owner."

1997—Subsec. (a)(5)(C). Pub. L. 105–80, § 1(3), amended Pub. L. 103–369, § 2(5)(A). See 1994 Amendment note below.

Subsec. (b)(1)(B)(i). Pub. L. 105–80, § 1(1), amended Pub. L. 103–369, § 2(3)(A). See 1994 Amendment note below.

Subsec. (c)(1). Pub. L. 105–80, § 12(a)(8), which directed substitution of "unless" for "until unless" before "a royalty fee", could not be executed because "until" did not appear subsequent to amendment by Pub. L. 103–369, § 2(4)(A), as amended by Pub. L. 105–80, § 1(2). See 1994 Amendment note below.

Pub. L. 105–80, § 1(2), amended Pub. L. 103–369, § 2(4)(A). See 1994 Amendment note below.

Subsec. (c)(2)(A), (D), (3)(A)–(C). Pub. L. 105–80, § 1(2), amended Pub. L. 103–369, § 2(4). See 1994 Amendment notes below.

1995—Subsec. (a)(1), (2)(A). Pub. L. 104–39 inserted "and section 114(d)" after "of this subsection".

1994—Subsec. (a)(2)(C). Pub. L. 103–369, § 2(1), struck out "90 days after the effective date of the Satellite Home Viewer Act of 1988, or" before "90 days after commencing", "whichever is later," before "submit to the network that owns", and ", on or after the effective date of the Satellite Home Viewer Act of 1988," after "Register of Copyrights", and inserted "name and" after "identifying (by" in two places.

Subsec. (a)(5)(C). Pub. L. 103–369, § 2(5)(A), as amended by Pub. L. 105–80, § 1(3), substituted "November 16, 1988" for "the date of the enactment of the Satellite Home Viewer Act of 1988".

Subsec. (a)(5)(D). Pub. L. 103–369, § 2(2), added subpar. (D).

Subsec. (a)(8) to (10). Pub. L. 103–369, § 2(5)(B), added pars. (8) to (10).

Subsec. (b)(1)(B)(i). Pub. L. 103–369, § 2(3)(A), as amended by Pub. L. 105–80, § 1(1), substituted "17.5 cents per subscriber in the case of superstations that as retransmitted by the satellite carrier include any program which, if delivered by any cable system in the United States, would be subject to the syndicated exclusivity rules of the Federal Communications Commission, and 14 cents per subscriber in the case of superstations that are syndex-proof as defined in section 258.2 of title 37, Code of Federal Regulations" for "12 cents".

Subsec. (b)(1)(B)(ii). Pub. L. 103–369, § 2(3)(B), substituted "6 cents" for "3 cents".

Subsec. (c)(1). Pub. L. 103–369, § 2(4)(A), as amended by Pub. L. 105–80, § 1(2), struck out "until December 31, 1992," before "unless a royalty fee", substituted "paragraph (2) or (3) of this subsection" for "paragraph (2), (3), or (4) of this subsection", and struck out at end

"After that date, the fee shall be determined either in accordance with the voluntary negotiation procedure specified in paragraph (2) or in accordance with the compulsory arbitration procedure specified in paragraphs (3) and (4)."

Subsec. (c)(2)(A). Pub. L. 103–369, § 2(4)(B)(i), as amended by Pub. L. 105–80, § 1(2), substituted "July 1, 1996" for "July 1, 1991".

Subsec. (c)(2)(D). Pub. L. 103–369, § 2(4)(B)(ii), as amended by Pub. L. 105–80, § 1(2), substituted "December 31, 1999, or in accordance with the terms of the agreement, whichever is later" for "December 31, 1994".

Subsec. (c)(3)(A). Pub. L. 103–369, § 2(4)(C)(i), as amended by Pub. L. 105–80, § 1(2), substituted "January 1, 1997" for "December 31, 1991".

Subsec. (c)(3)(B). Pub. L. 103–369, § 2(4)(C)(ii), as amended by Pub. L. 105–80, § 1(2), amended subpar. (B) generally. Prior to amendment, subpar. (B) read as follows:

"(B) FACTORS FOR DETERMINING ROYALTY FEES.—In determining royalty fees under this paragraph, the copyright arbitration royalty panel appointed under chapter 8 shall consider the approximate average cost to a cable system for the right to secondarily transmit to the public a primary transmission made by a broadcast station, the fee established under any voluntary agreement filed with the Copyright Office in accordance with paragraph (2), and the last fee proposed by the parties, before proceedings under this paragraph, for the secondary transmission of superstations or network stations for private home viewing. The fee shall also be calculated to achieve the following objectives:

"(i) To maximize the availability of creative works to the public.

"(ii) To afford the copyright owner a fair return for his or her creative work and the copyright user a fair income under existing economic conditions.

"(iii) To reflect the relative roles of the copyright owner and the copyright user in the product made available to the public with respect to relative creative contribution, technological contribution, capital investment, cost, risk, and contribution to the opening of new markets for creative expression and media for their communication.

"(iv) To minimize any disruptive impact on the structure of the industries involved and on generally prevailing industry practices."

Subsec. (c)(3)(C). Pub. L. 103–369, § 2(4)(C)(iii), as amended by Pub. L. 105–80, § 1(2), inserted before period at end "or July 1, 1997, whichever is later".

Subsec. (d)(2). Pub. L. 103–369, § 2(6)(A), amended par. (2) generally. Prior to amendment, par. (2) read as follows:

"(2) NETWORK STATION.—The term 'network station' has the meaning given that term in section 111(f) of this title, and includes any translator station or terrestrial satellite station that rebroadcasts all or substantially all of the programming broadcast by a network station."

Subsec. (d)(6). Pub. L. 103–369, § 2(6)(B), inserted "and operates in the Fixed-Satellite Service under part 25 of title 47 of the Code of Federal Regulations or the Direct Broadcast Satellite Service under part 100 of title 47 of the Code of Federal Regulations" after "Federal Communications Commission".

Subsec. (d)(11). Pub. L. 103–369, § 2(6)(C), added par. (11).

1993—Subsec. (b)(1). Pub. L. 103–198, § 5(1)(A), struck out ", after consultation with the Copyright Royalty Tribunal," in introductory provisions after "Register shall" and in subpar. (A) after "Copyrights may".

Subsec. (b)(2), (3). Pub. L. 103–198, § 5(1)(B), (C), substituted "Librarian of Congress" for "Copyright Royalty Tribunal".

Subsec. (b)(4). Pub. L. 103–198, § 5(1)(D), in subpar. (A), substituted "Librarian of Congress" for "Copyright Royalty Tribunal" after "claim with the" and for "Tribunal" after "requirements that the", in subpar. (B), substituted "Librarian of Congress" for "Copyright Royalty Tribunal" before "shall determine" and for

"Tribunal" wherever else appearing, and substituted "convene a copyright arbitration royalty panel" for "conduct a proceeding", and in subpar. (C), substituted "Librarian of Congress" for "Copyright Royalty Tribunal".

Subsec. (c). Pub. L. 103–198, § 5(2)(A), substituted "Adjustment" for "Determination" in heading.

Subsec. (c)(2). Pub. L. 103–198, § 5(2)(B), substituted "Librarian of Congress" for "Copyright Royalty Tribunal" in subpars. (A) and (B).

Subsec. (c)(3)(A). Pub. L. 103–198, § 5(2)(C)(i), substituted "Librarian of Congress" for "Copyright Royalty Tribunal" and substituted last sentence for former last sentence which read as follows: "Such notice shall include the names and qualifications of potential arbitrators chosen by the Tribunal from a list of available arbitrators obtained from the American Arbitration Association or such similar organization as the Tribunal shall select."

Subsec. (c)(3)(B). Pub. L. 103–198, § 5(2)(C)(ii), (iii), redesignated subpar. (D) as (B), substituted "copyright arbitration royalty panel appointed under chapter 8" for "Arbitration Panel" in introductory provisions, and struck out former subpar. (B) which provided for the selection of an Arbitration Panel.

Subsec. (c)(3)(C). Pub. L. 103–198, § 5(2)(C)(ii), (v), redesignated subpar. (G) as (C), amended subpar. generally, substituting provisions relating to period during which decision of arbitration panel or order of Librarian of Congress becomes effective for provisions relating to period during which decision of Arbitration Panel or order of Copyright Royalty Tribunal became effective, and struck out former subpar. (C) which related to proceedings in arbitration.

Subsec. (c)(3)(D). Pub. L. 103–198, § 5(2)(C)(vi), redesignated subpar. (H) as (D) and substituted "referred to in subparagraph (C)" for "adopted or ordered under subparagraph (F)". Former subpar. (D) redesignated (B).

Subsec. (c)(3)(E) to (H). Pub. L. 103–198, § 5(2)(C)(iv)–(vi)(I), struck out subpar. (E) which required the Arbitration Panel to report to the Copyright Royalty Tribunal not later than 60 days after publication of notice initiating an arbitration proceeding, struck out subpar. (F) which required action by the Tribunal within 60 days after receiving the report by the Panel, and redesignated subpars. (G) and (H) as (C) and (D), respectively.

Subsec. (c)(4). Pub. L. 103–198, § 5(2)(D), struck out par. (4) which established procedures for judicial review of decisions of the Copyright Royalty Tribunal.

EFFECTIVE DATE OF 2010 AMENDMENT

Amendment by Pub. L. 111–175 effective Feb. 27, 2010, see section 307(a) of Pub. L. 111–175, set out as a note under section 111 of this title.

EFFECTIVE DATE OF 2006 AMENDMENT

Amendment by Pub. L. 109–303 effective as if included in the Copyright Royalty and Distribution Reform Act of 2004, Pub. L. 108–419, see section 6 of Pub. L. 109–303, set out as a note under section 111 of this title.

EFFECTIVE DATE OF 2004 AMENDMENT

Amendment by Pub. L. 108–419 effective 6 months after Nov. 30, 2004, subject to transition provisions, see section 6 of Pub. L. 108–419, set out as an Effective Date; Transition Provisions note under section 801 of this title.

EFFECTIVE DATE OF 1999 AMENDMENT

Amendment by section 1000(a)(9) [title I, §§ 1004, 1006] of Pub. L. 106–113 effective July 1, 1999, and amendment by section 1000(a)(9) [title I, §§ 1005, 1007, 1008(b), 1011(b)(2), (c)] of Pub. L. 106–113 effective Nov. 29, 1999, see section 1000(a)(9) [title I, § 1012] of Pub. L. 106–113, set out as a note under section 101 of this title.

EFFECTIVE DATE OF 1997 AMENDMENT

Section 13 of Pub. L. 105–80 provided that:

"(a) IN GENERAL.—Except as provided in subsections (b) and (c), the amendments made by this Act [amending this section, sections 101, 104A, 108 to 110, 114 to 116, 303, 304, 405, 407, 411, 504, 509, 601, 708, 801 to 803, 909, 910, 1006, and 1007 of this title, and section 2319 of Title 18, Crimes and Criminal Procedure, and amending provisions set out as a note under section 914 of this title] shall take effect on the date of the enactment of this Act [Nov. 13, 1997].

"(b) SATELLITE HOME VIEWER ACT.—The amendments made by section 1 [amending this section] shall be effective as if enacted as part of the Satellite Home Viewer Act of 1994 (Public Law 103–369).

"(c) TECHNICAL AMENDMENT.—The amendment made by section 12(b)(1) [amending provisions set out as a note under section 914 of this title] shall be effective as if enacted on November 9, 1987."

EFFECTIVE DATE OF 1995 AMENDMENT

Amendment by Pub. L. 104–39 effective 3 months after Nov. 1, 1995, see section 6 of Pub. L. 104–39, set out as a note under section 101 of this title.

EFFECTIVE AND TERMINATION DATES OF 1994 AMENDMENT

Pub. L. 103–369, § 6, Oct. 18, 1994, 108 Stat. 3481, provided that:

"(a) IN GENERAL.—Except as provided in subsections (b) and (d), this Act [amending this section and section 111 of this title, enacting provisions set out as notes under this section and section 101 of this title, and repealing provisions set out as a note under this section] and the amendments made by this Act take effect on the date of the enactment of this Act [Oct. 18, 1994].

"(b) BURDEN OF PROOF PROVISIONS.—The provisions of section 119(a)(5)(D) [now section 119(a)(6)(D)] of title 17, United States Code (as added by section 2(2) of this Act) relating to the burden of proof of satellite carriers, shall take effect on January 1, 1997, with respect to civil actions relating to the eligibility of subscribers who subscribed to service as an unserved household before the date of the enactment of this Act.

"(c) TRANSITIONAL SIGNAL INTENSITY MEASUREMENT PROCEDURES.—The provisions of [former] section 119(a)(8) of title 17, United States Code (as added by section 2(5) of this Act), relating to transitional signal intensity measurements, shall cease to be effective on December 31, 1996.

"(d) LOCAL SERVICE AREA OF A PRIMARY TRANSMITTER.—The amendment made by section 3(b) [amending section 111 of this title], relating to the definition of the local service area of a primary transmitter, shall take effect on July 1, 1994."

EFFECTIVE DATE

Section 206 of title II of Pub. L. 100–667 provided that: "This title and the amendments made by this title [enacting this section and sections 612 and 613 of Title 47, Telegraphs, Telephones, and Radiotelegraphs, amending sections 111, 501, 801, and 804 of this title and section 605 of Title 47, and enacting provisions set out as notes under this section and section 101 of this title] take effect on January 1, 1989, except that the authority of the Register of Copyrights to issue regulations pursuant to section 119(b)(1) of title 17, United States Code, as added by section 202 of this Act, takes effect on the date of the enactment of this Act [Nov. 16, 1988]."

Section 207 of title II of Pub. L. 100–667 provided that this title and the amendments made by this title (other than the amendments made by section 205 [amending section 605 of Title 47]) cease to be effective on Dec. 31, 1994, prior to repeal by Pub. L. 103–369, § 4(b), Oct. 18, 1994, 108 Stat. 3481.

TERMINATION OF SECTION

Pub. L. 111–175, title I, § 107(a), May 27, 2010, 124 Stat. 1245, provided that: "Section 119 of title 17, United States Code, as amended by this Act, shall cease to be effective on December 31, 2014."

Pub. L. 111–118, div. B, § 1003(a)(2)(A), Dec. 19, 2009, 123 Stat. 3469, as amended by Pub. L. 111–144, § 10(a)(2), Mar. 2, 2010, 124 Stat. 47; Pub. L. 111–151, § 2(a)(2), Mar. 26, 2010, 124 Stat. 1027; Pub. L. 111–157, § 9(a)(2), Apr. 15, 2010, 124 Stat. 1119, which provided that this section would cease to be effective on May 31, 2010, was repealed by Pub. L. 111–175, title I, § 107(b), May 27, 2010, 124 Stat. 1245.

Pub. L. 103–369, § 4(a), Oct. 18, 1994, 108 Stat. 3481, as amended by Pub. L. 106–113, div. B, § 1000(a)(9) [title I, § 1003], Nov. 29, 1999, 113 Stat. 1536, 1501A–527; Pub. L. 108–447, div. J, title IX [title I, § 101(a)], Dec. 8, 2004, 118 Stat. 3394, which provided that this section would cease to be effective on Dec. 31, 2009, was repealed by Pub. L. 111–118, div. B, § 1003(a)(2)(B), Dec. 19, 2009, 123 Stat. 3469.

REMOVAL OF INCONSISTENT PROVISIONS

Pub. L. 109–303, § 4(g), Oct. 6, 2006, 120 Stat. 1483, provided that: "The amendments contained in subsection (h) of section 5 of the Copyright Royalty and Distribution Reform Act of 2004 [Pub. L. 108–419, amending this section] shall be deemed never to have been enacted."

EFFECT ON CERTAIN PROCEEDINGS

Pub. L. 108–447, div. J, title IX [title I, § 106], Dec. 8, 2004, 118 Stat. 3406, provided that: "Nothing in this title [see Short Title of 2004 Amendment note set out under section 101 of this title] shall modify any remedy imposed on a party that is required by the judgment of a court in any action that was brought before May 1, 2004, against that party for a violation of section 119 of title 17, United States Code."

APPLICABILITY OF 1994 AMENDMENT

Section 5 of Pub. L. 103–369 provided that: "The amendments made by this section apply only to section 119 of title 17, United States Code."

§ 120. Scope of exclusive rights in architectural works

(a) PICTORIAL REPRESENTATIONS PERMITTED.—The copyright in an architectural work that has been constructed does not include the right to prevent the making, distributing, or public display of pictures, paintings, photographs, or other pictorial representations of the work, if the building in which the work is embodied is located in or ordinarily visible from a public place.

(b) ALTERATIONS TO AND DESTRUCTION OF BUILDINGS.—Notwithstanding the provisions of section 106(2), the owners of a building embodying an architectural work may, without the consent of the author or copyright owner of the architectural work, make or authorize the making of alterations to such building, and destroy or authorize the destruction of such building.

(Added Pub. L. 101–650, title VII, § 704(a), Dec. 1, 1990, 104 Stat. 5133.)

EFFECTIVE DATE

Section applicable to any architectural work created on or after Dec. 1, 1990, and any architectural work, that, on Dec. 1, 1990, is unconstructed and embodied in unpublished plans or drawings, except that protection for such architectural work under this title terminates on Dec. 31, 2002, unless the work is constructed by that date, see section 706 of Pub. L. 101–650, set out as an Effective Date of 1990 Amendment note under section 101 of this title.

§ 121. Limitations on exclusive rights: Reproduction for blind or other people with disabilities

(a) Notwithstanding the provisions of section 106, it is not an infringement of copyright for an authorized entity to reproduce or to distribute copies or phonorecords of a previously published, nondramatic literary work if such copies or phonorecords are reproduced or distributed in specialized formats exclusively for use by blind or other persons with disabilities.

(b)(1) Copies or phonorecords to which this section applies shall—

(A) not be reproduced or distributed in a format other than a specialized format exclusively for use by blind or other persons with disabilities;

(B) bear a notice that any further reproduction or distribution in a format other than a specialized format is an infringement; and

(C) include a copyright notice identifying the copyright owner and the date of the original publication.

(2) The provisions of this subsection shall not apply to standardized, secure, or norm-referenced tests and related testing material, or to computer programs, except the portions thereof that are in conventional human language (including descriptions of pictorial works) and displayed to users in the ordinary course of using the computer programs.

(c) Notwithstanding the provisions of section 106, it is not an infringement of copyright for a publisher of print instructional materials for use in elementary or secondary schools to create and distribute to the National Instructional Materials Access Center copies of the electronic files described in sections 612(a)(23)(C), 613(a)(6), and section 674(e) of the Individuals with Disabilities Education Act that contain the contents of print instructional materials using the National Instructional Material Accessibility Standard (as defined in section 674(e)(3) of that Act), if—

(1) the inclusion of the contents of such print instructional materials is required by any State educational agency or local educational agency;

(2) the publisher had the right to publish such print instructional materials in print formats; and

(3) such copies are used solely for reproduction or distribution of the contents of such print instructional materials in specialized formats.

(d) For purposes of this section, the term—

(1) "authorized entity" means a nonprofit organization or a governmental agency that has a primary mission to provide specialized services relating to training, education, or adaptive reading or information access needs of blind or other persons with disabilities;

(2) "blind or other persons with disabilities" means individuals who are eligible or who may qualify in accordance with the Act entitled "An Act to provide books for the adult blind", approved March 3, 1931 (2 U.S.C. 135a; 46 Stat. 1487) to receive books and other publications produced in specialized formats;

(3) "print instructional materials" has the meaning given under section 674(e)(3)(C) of the Individuals with Disabilities Education Act; and

(4) "specialized formats" means—

(A) braille, audio, or digital text which is exclusively for use by blind or other persons with disabilities; and

(B) with respect to print instructional materials, includes large print formats when such materials are distributed exclusively for use by blind or other persons with disabilities.

(Added Pub. L. 104–197, title III, §316(a), Sept. 16, 1996, 110 Stat. 2416; amended Pub. L. 106–379, §3(b), Oct. 27, 2000, 114 Stat. 1445; Pub. L. 107–273, div. C, title III, §13210(3)(A), Nov. 2, 2002, 116 Stat. 1909; Pub. L. 108–446, title III, §306, Dec. 3, 2004, 118 Stat. 2807.)

REFERENCES IN TEXT

Sections 612, 613, and 674 of the Individuals with Disabilities Education Act, referred to in subsecs. (c) and (d)(3), are classified to sections 1412, 1413, and 1474, respectively, of Title 20, Education.

The Act approved March 3, 1931, referred to in subsec. (d)(2), is act Mar. 3, 1931, ch. 400, 46 Stat. 1487, as amended, which is classified generally to sections 135a and 135b of Title 2, The Congress. For complete classification of this Act to the Code, see Tables.

AMENDMENTS

2004—Subsec. (c). Pub. L. 108–446, §306(2), added subsec. (c). Former subsec. (c) redesignated (d).

Subsec. (d). Pub. L. 108–446, §306(1), redesignated subsec. (c) as (d).

Subsec. (d)(3), (4). Pub. L. 108–446, §306(3), added pars. (3) and (4) and struck out former par. (3) which read as follows: " 'specialized formats' means braille, audio, or digital text which is exclusively for use by blind or other persons with disabilities."

2002—Pub. L. 107–273 substituted "Reproduction" for "reproduction" in section catchline.

2000—Subsec. (a). Pub. L. 106–379 substituted "section 106" for "sections 106 and 710".

§ 122. Limitations on exclusive rights: Secondary transmissions of local television programming by satellite

(a) SECONDARY TRANSMISSIONS INTO LOCAL MARKETS.—

(1) SECONDARY TRANSMISSIONS OF TELEVISION BROADCAST STATIONS WITHIN A LOCAL MARKET.—A secondary transmission of a performance or display of a work embodied in a primary transmission of a television broadcast station into the station's local market shall be subject to statutory licensing under this section if—

(A) the secondary transmission is made by a satellite carrier to the public;

(B) with regard to secondary transmissions, the satellite carrier is in compliance with the rules, regulations, or authorizations of the Federal Communications Commission governing the carriage of television broadcast station signals; and

(C) the satellite carrier makes a direct or indirect charge for the secondary transmission to—

(i) each subscriber receiving the secondary transmission; or

(ii) a distributor that has contracted with the satellite carrier for direct or indirect delivery of the secondary transmission to the public.

(2) SIGNIFICANTLY VIEWED STATIONS.—

(A) IN GENERAL.—A secondary transmission of a performance or display of a work embodied in a primary transmission of a television broadcast station to subscribers who receive secondary transmissions of primary transmissions under paragraph (1) shall be subject to statutory licensing under this paragraph if the secondary transmission is of the primary transmission of a network station or a non-network station to a subscriber who resides outside the station's local market but within a community in which the signal has been determined by the Federal Communications Commission to be significantly viewed in such community, pursuant to the rules, regulations, and authorizations of the Federal Communications Commission in effect on April 15, 1976, applicable to determining with respect to a cable system whether signals are significantly viewed in a community.

(B) WAIVER.—A subscriber who is denied the secondary transmission of the primary transmission of a network station or a non-network station under subparagraph (A) may request a waiver from such denial by submitting a request, through the subscriber's satellite carrier, to the network station or non-network station in the local market affiliated with the same network or non-network where the subscriber is located. The network station or non-network station shall accept or reject the subscriber's request for a waiver within 30 days after receipt of the request. If the network station or non-network station fails to accept or reject the subscriber's request for a waiver within that 30-day period, that network station or non-network station shall be deemed to agree to the waiver request.

(3) SECONDARY TRANSMISSION OF LOW POWER PROGRAMMING.—

(A) IN GENERAL.—Subject to subparagraphs (B) and (C), a secondary transmission of a performance or display of a work embodied in a primary transmission of a television broadcast station to subscribers who receive secondary transmissions of primary transmissions under paragraph (1) shall be subject to statutory licensing under this paragraph if the secondary transmission is of the primary transmission of a television broadcast station that is licensed as a low power television station, to a subscriber who resides within the same designated market area as the station that originates the transmission.

(B) NO APPLICABILITY TO REPEATERS AND TRANSLATORS.—Secondary transmissions provided for in subparagraph (A) shall not apply to any low power television station that retransmits the programs and signals of another television station for more than 2 hours each day.

(C) NO IMPACT ON OTHER SECONDARY TRANSMISSIONS OBLIGATIONS.—A satellite carrier that makes secondary transmissions of a primary transmission of a low power television station under a statutory license provided under this section is not required, by reason of such secondary transmissions, to make any other secondary transmissions.

(4) SPECIAL EXCEPTIONS.—A secondary transmission of a performance or display of a work embodied in a primary transmission of a television broadcast station to subscribers who receive secondary transmissions of primary transmissions under paragraph (1) shall, if the secondary transmission is made by a satellite carrier that complies with the requirements of paragraph (1), be subject to statutory licensing under this paragraph as follows:

(A) STATES WITH SINGLE FULL-POWER NETWORK STATION.—In a State in which there is licensed by the Federal Communications Commission a single full-power station that was a network station on January 1, 1995, the statutory license provided for in this paragraph shall apply to the secondary transmission by a satellite carrier of the primary transmission of that station to any subscriber in a community that is located within that State and that is not within the first 50 television markets as listed in the regulations of the Commission as in effect on such date (47 C.F.R. 76.51).

(B) STATES WITH ALL NETWORK STATIONS AND NON-NETWORK STATIONS IN SAME LOCAL MARKET.—In a State in which all network stations and non-network stations licensed by the Federal Communications Commission within that State as of January 1, 1995, are assigned to the same local market and that local market does not encompass all counties of that State, the statutory license provided under this paragraph shall apply to the secondary transmission by a satellite carrier of the primary transmissions of such station to all subscribers in the State who reside in a local market that is within the first 50 major television markets as listed in the regulations of the Commission as in effect on such date (section 76.51 of title 47, Code of Federal Regulations).

(C) ADDITIONAL STATIONS.—In the case of that State in which are located 4 counties that—

(i) on January 1, 2004, were in local markets principally comprised of counties in another State, and

(ii) had a combined total of 41,340 television households, according to the U.S. Television Household Estimates by Nielsen Media Research for 2004,

the statutory license provided under this paragraph shall apply to secondary transmissions by a satellite carrier to subscribers in any such county of the primary transmissions of any network station located in that State, if the satellite carrier was making such secondary transmissions to any subscribers in that county on January 1, 2004.

(D) CERTAIN ADDITIONAL STATIONS.—If 2 adjacent counties in a single State are in a local market comprised principally of counties located in another State, the statutory license provided for in this paragraph shall apply to the secondary transmission by a satellite carrier to subscribers in those 2 counties of the primary transmissions of any network station located in the capital of the State in which such 2 counties are located, if—

(i) the 2 counties are located in a local market that is in the top 100 markets for the year 2003 according to Nielsen Media Research; and

(ii) the total number of television households in the 2 counties combined did not exceed 10,000 for the year 2003 according to Nielsen Media Research.

(E) NETWORKS OF NONCOMMERCIAL EDUCATIONAL BROADCAST STATIONS.—In the case of a system of three or more noncommercial educational broadcast stations licensed to a single State, public agency, or political, educational, or special purpose subdivision of a State, the statutory license provided for in this paragraph shall apply to the secondary transmission of the primary transmission of such system to any subscriber in any county or county equivalent within such State, if such subscriber is located in a designated market area that is not otherwise eligible to receive the secondary transmission of the primary transmission of a noncommercial educational broadcast station located within the State pursuant to paragraph (1).

(5) APPLICABILITY OF ROYALTY RATES AND PROCEDURES.—The royalty rates and procedures under section 119(b) shall apply to the secondary transmissions to which the statutory license under paragraph (4) applies.

(b) REPORTING REQUIREMENTS.—

(1) INITIAL LISTS.—A satellite carrier that makes secondary transmissions of a primary transmission made by a network station under subsection (a) shall, within 90 days after commencing such secondary transmissions, submit to the network that owns or is affiliated with the network station—

(A) a list identifying (by name in alphabetical order and street address, including county and 9-digit zip code) all subscribers to which the satellite carrier makes secondary transmissions of that primary transmission under subsection (a); and

(B) a separate list, aggregated by designated market area (by name and address, including street or rural route number, city, State, and 9-digit zip code), which shall indicate those subscribers being served pursuant to paragraph (2) of subsection (a).

(2) SUBSEQUENT LISTS.—After the list is submitted under paragraph (1), the satellite carrier shall, on the 15th of each month, submit to the network—

(A) a list identifying (by name in alphabetical order and street address, including county and 9-digit zip code) any subscribers who have been added or dropped as subscribers since the last submission under this subsection; and

(B) a separate list, aggregated by designated market area (by name and street address, including street or rural route number, city, State, and 9-digit zip code), identifying those subscribers whose service pursuant to paragraph (2) of subsection (a) has been added or dropped since the last submission under this subsection.

(3) USE OF SUBSCRIBER INFORMATION.—Subscriber information submitted by a satellite carrier under this subsection may be used only for the purposes of monitoring compliance by the satellite carrier with this section.

(4) REQUIREMENTS OF NETWORKS.—The submission requirements of this subsection shall apply to a satellite carrier only if the network to which the submissions are to be made places on file with the Register of Copyrights a document identifying the name and address of the person to whom such submissions are to be made. The Register of Copyrights shall maintain for public inspection a file of all such documents.

(c) NO ROYALTY FEE REQUIRED FOR CERTAIN SECONDARY TRANSMISSIONS.—A satellite carrier whose secondary transmissions are subject to statutory licensing under paragraphs (1), (2), and (3) of subsection (a) shall have no royalty obligation for such secondary transmissions.

(d) NONCOMPLIANCE WITH REPORTING AND REGULATORY REQUIREMENTS.—Notwithstanding subsection (a), the willful or repeated secondary transmission to the public by a satellite carrier into the local market of a television broadcast station of a primary transmission embodying a performance or display of a work made by that television broadcast station is actionable as an act of infringement under section 501, and is fully subject to the remedies provided under sections 502 through 506, if the satellite carrier has not complied with the reporting requirements of subsection (b) or with the rules, regulations, and authorizations of the Federal Communications Commission concerning the carriage of television broadcast signals.

(e) WILLFUL ALTERATIONS.—Notwithstanding subsection (a), the secondary transmission to the public by a satellite carrier into the local market of a television broadcast station of a performance or display of a work embodied in a primary transmission made by that television broadcast station is actionable as an act of infringement under section 501, and is fully subject to the remedies provided by sections 502 through 506 and section 510, if the content of the particular program in which the performance or display is embodied, or any commercial advertising or station announcement transmitted by the primary transmitter during, or immediately before or after, the transmission of such program, is in any way willfully altered by the satellite carrier through changes, deletions, or additions, or is combined with programming from any other broadcast signal.

(f) VIOLATION OF TERRITORIAL RESTRICTIONS ON STATUTORY LICENSE FOR TELEVISION BROADCAST STATIONS.—

(1) INDIVIDUAL VIOLATIONS.—The willful or repeated secondary transmission to the public by a satellite carrier of a primary transmission embodying a performance or display of a work made by a television broadcast station to a subscriber who does not reside in that station's local market, and is not subject to statutory licensing under section 119, subject to statutory licensing by reason of paragraph (2)(A), (3), or (4) of subsection (a), or subject to a private licensing agreement, is actionable as an act of infringement under section 501 and is fully subject to the remedies provided by sections 502 through 506, except that—

(A) no damages shall be awarded for such act of infringement if the satellite carrier took corrective action by promptly withdrawing service from the ineligible subscriber; and

(B) any statutory damages shall not exceed $250 for such subscriber for each month during which the violation occurred.

(2) PATTERN OF VIOLATIONS.—If a satellite carrier engages in a willful or repeated pattern or practice of secondarily transmitting to the public a primary transmission embodying a performance or display of a work made by a television broadcast station to subscribers who do not reside in that station's local market, and are not subject to statutory licensing under section 119, subject to statutory licensing by reason of paragraph (2)(A), (3), or (4) of subsection (a), or subject to a private licensing agreement, then in addition to the remedies under paragraph (1)—

(A) if the pattern or practice has been carried out on a substantially nationwide basis, the court—

(i) shall order a permanent injunction barring the secondary transmission by the satellite carrier of the primary transmissions of that television broadcast station (and if such television broadcast station is a network station, all other television broadcast stations affiliated with such network); and

(ii) may order statutory damages not exceeding $2,500,000 for each 6-month period during which the pattern or practice was carried out; and

(B) if the pattern or practice has been carried out on a local or regional basis with respect to more than one television broadcast station, the court—

(i) shall order a permanent injunction barring the secondary transmission in that locality or region by the satellite carrier of the primary transmissions of any television broadcast station; and

(ii) may order statutory damages not exceeding $2,500,000 for each 6-month period during which the pattern or practice was carried out.

(g) BURDEN OF PROOF.—In any action brought under subsection (f), the satellite carrier shall have the burden of proving that its secondary transmission of a primary transmission by a television broadcast station is made only to subscribers located within that station's local market or subscribers being served in compliance with section 119, paragraph (2)(A), (3), or (4) of subsection (a), or a private licensing agreement.

(h) GEOGRAPHIC LIMITATIONS ON SECONDARY TRANSMISSIONS.—The statutory license created by this section shall apply to secondary transmissions to locations in the United States.

(i) EXCLUSIVITY WITH RESPECT TO SECONDARY TRANSMISSIONS OF BROADCAST STATIONS BY SATELLITE TO MEMBERS OF THE PUBLIC.—No provision of section 111 or any other law (other than this section and section 119) shall be construed to contain any authorization, exemption, or license through which secondary transmissions by satellite carriers of programming contained in a primary transmission made by a television broadcast station may be made without obtaining the consent of the copyright owner.

(j) DEFINITIONS.—In this section—

(1) DISTRIBUTOR.—The term "distributor" means an entity that contracts to distribute secondary transmissions from a satellite carrier and, either as a single channel or in a package with other programming, provides the secondary transmission either directly to individual subscribers or indirectly through other program distribution entities.

(2) LOCAL MARKET.—

(A) IN GENERAL.—The term "local market", in the case of both commercial and noncommercial television broadcast stations, means the designated market area in which a station is located, and—

(i) in the case of a commercial television broadcast station, all commercial television broadcast stations licensed to a community within the same designated market area are within the same local market; and

(ii) in the case of a noncommercial educational television broadcast station, the market includes any station that is licensed to a community within the same designated market area as the noncommercial educational television broadcast station.

(B) COUNTY OF LICENSE.—In addition to the area described in subparagraph (A), a station's local market includes the county in which the station's community of license is located.

(C) DESIGNATED MARKET AREA.—For purposes of subparagraph (A), the term "designated market area" means a designated market area, as determined by Nielsen Media Research and published in the 1999–2000 Nielsen Station Index Directory and Nielsen Station Index United States Television Household Estimates or any successor publication.

(D) CERTAIN AREAS OUTSIDE OF ANY DESIGNATED MARKET AREA.—Any census area, borough, or other area in the State of Alaska that is outside of a designated market area, as determined by Nielsen Media Research, shall be deemed to be part of one of the local markets in the State of Alaska. A satellite carrier may determine which local market in the State of Alaska will be deemed to be the relevant local market in connection with each subscriber in such census area, borough, or other area.

(3) LOW POWER TELEVISION STATION.—The term "low power television station" means a low power TV station as defined in section 74.701(f) of title 47, Code of Federal Regulations, as in effect on June 1, 2004. For purposes of this paragraph, the term "low power television station" includes a low power television station that has been accorded primary status as a Class A television licensee under section 73.6001(a) of title 47, Code of Federal Regulations.

(4) NETWORK STATION; NON-NETWORK STATION; SATELLITE CARRIER; SECONDARY TRANS-

MISSION.—The terms "network station", "non-network station", "satellite carrier", and "secondary transmission" have the meanings given such terms under section 119(d).

(5) NONCOMMERCIAL EDUCATIONAL BROADCAST STATION.—The term "noncommercial educational broadcast station" means a television broadcast station that is a noncommercial educational broadcast station as defined in section 397 of the Communications Act of 1934, as in effect on the date of the enactment of the Satellite Television Extension and Localism Act of 2010.

(6) SUBSCRIBER.—The term "subscriber" means a person or entity that receives a secondary transmission service from a satellite carrier and pays a fee for the service, directly or indirectly, to the satellite carrier or to a distributor.

(7) TELEVISION BROADCAST STATION.—The term "television broadcast station"—

(A) means an over-the-air, commercial or noncommercial television broadcast station licensed by the Federal Communications Commission under subpart E of part 73 of title 47, Code of Federal Regulations, except that such term does not include a low-power or translator television station; and

(B) includes a television broadcast station licensed by an appropriate governmental authority of Canada or Mexico if the station broadcasts primarily in the English language and is a network station as defined in section 119(d)(2)(A).

(Added Pub. L. 106–113, div. B, § 1000(a)(9) [title I, § 1002(a)], Nov. 29, 1999, 113 Stat. 1536, 1501A–523; amended Pub. L. 107–273, div. C, title III, § 13210(2)(A), Nov. 2, 2002, 116 Stat. 1909; Pub. L. 108–447, div. J, title IX [title I, § 111(b)], Dec. 8, 2004, 118 Stat. 3409; Pub. L. 110–403, title II, § 209(a)(5), Oct. 13, 2008, 122 Stat. 4264; Pub. L. 111–175, title I, § 103(a)(1), (b)–(f), May 27, 2010, 124 Stat. 1227–1230.)

REFERENCES IN TEXT

Section 397 of the Communications Act of 1934, referred to in subsec. (j)(5), is classified to section 397 of Title 47, Telegraphs, Telephones, and Radiotelegraphs.

The date of the enactment of the Satellite Television Extension and Localism Act of 2010, referred to in subsec. (j)(5), is the date of enactment of Pub. L. 111–175, which shall be deemed to refer to Feb. 27, 2010, see section 307(a) of Pub. L. 111–175, set out as an Effective Date of 2010 Amendment note under section 111 of this title.

AMENDMENTS

2010—Pub. L. 111–175, § 103(a)(1), substituted "of local television programming by satellite" for "by satellite carriers within local markets" in section catchline.

Subsec. (a). Pub. L. 111–175, § 103(b), amended subsec. (a) generally. Prior to amendment, subsec. (a) related to secondary transmissions of television broadcast stations by satellite carriers.

Subsec. (b)(1). Pub. L. 111–175, § 103(c)(1), substituted "station—" for "station a list identifying (by name in alphabetical order and street address, including county and zip code) all subscribers to which the satellite carrier makes secondary transmissions of that primary transmission under subsection (a)." and added subpars. (A) and (B).

Subsec. (b)(2). Pub. L. 111–175, § 103(c)(2), substituted "network—" for "network a list identifying (by name in alphabetical order and street address, including county and zip code) any subscribers who have been added or dropped as subscribers since the last submission under this subsection." and added subpars. (A) and (B).

Subsec. (c). Pub. L. 111–175, § 103(d), inserted "for Certain Secondary Transmissions" after "Required" in heading and substituted "paragraphs (1), (2), and (3) of subsection (a)" for "subsection (a)" in text.

Subsec. (f)(1). Pub. L. 111–175, § 103(e)(2)(A), substituted "section 119, subject to statutory licensing by reason of paragraph (2)(A), (3), or (4) of subsection (a), or subject to" for "section 119 or" in introductory provisions.

Subsec. (f)(1)(B). Pub. L. 111–175, § 103(e)(1)(A), substituted "$250" for "$5".

Subsec. (f)(2). Pub. L. 111–175, § 103(e)(2)(A), substituted "section 119, subject to statutory licensing by reason of paragraph (2)(A), (3), or (4) of subsection (a), or subject to" for "section 119 or" in introductory provisions.

Subsec. (f)(2)(A)(ii), (B)(ii). Pub. L. 111–175, § 103(e)(1)(B), substituted "$2,500,000" for "$250,000".

Subsec. (g). Pub. L. 111–175, § 103(e)(2)(B), substituted "section 119, paragraph (2)(A), (3), or (4) of subsection (a), or" for "section 119 or".

Subsec. (j)(1). Pub. L. 111–175, § 103(f)(1), substituted "that contracts" for "which contracts".

Subsec. (j)(3). Pub. L. 111–175, § 103(f)(4), added par. (3). Former par. (3) redesignated (4).

Subsec. (j)(4). Pub. L. 111–175, § 103(f)(3), redesignated par. (3) as (4) and inserted "non-network station;" after "Network station;" in heading and "'non-network station'," after "'network station'," in text. Former par. (4) redesignated (6).

Subsec. (j)(5). Pub. L. 111–175, § 103(f)(5), added par. (5). Former par. (5) redesignated (7).

Subsec. (j)(6). Pub. L. 111–175, § 103(f)(6), amended par. (6) generally. Prior to amendment, text read as follows: "The term 'subscriber' means a person who receives a secondary transmission service from a satellite carrier and pays a fee for the service, directly or indirectly, to the satellite carrier or to a distributor."

Pub. L. 111–175, § 103(f)(2), redesignated par. (4) as (6).

Subsec. (j)(7). Pub. L. 111–175, § 103(f)(2), redesignated par. (5) as (7).

2008—Subsec. (d). Pub. L. 110–403, § 209(a)(5)(A), struck out "and 509" after "506".

Subsec. (e). Pub. L. 110–403, § 209(a)(5)(B), substituted "section 510" for "sections 509 and 510".

Subsec. (f)(1). Pub. L. 110–403, § 209(a)(5)(C), struck out "and 509" after "506" in introductory provisions.

2004—Subsec. (j)(2)(D). Pub. L. 108–447 added subpar. (D).

2002—Pub. L. 107–273 substituted "rights: Secondary" for "rights; secondary" in section catchline.

EFFECTIVE DATE OF 2010 AMENDMENT

Amendment by Pub. L. 111–175 effective Feb. 27, 2010, see section 307(a) of Pub. L. 111–175, set out as a note under section 111 of this title.

EFFECTIVE DATE

Section effective July 1, 1999, see section 1000(a)(9) [title I, § 1012] of Pub. L. 106–113, set out as an Effective Date of 1999 Amendment note under section 101 of this title.

CHAPTER 2—COPYRIGHT OWNERSHIP AND TRANSFER

§ 201. Ownership of copyright

(a) INITIAL OWNERSHIP.—Copyright in a work protected under this title vests initially in the author or authors of the work. The authors of a joint work are coowners of copyright in the work.

(b) WORKS MADE FOR HIRE.—In the case of a work made for hire, the employer or other person for whom the work was prepared is considered the author for purposes of this title, and, unless the parties have expressly agreed otherwise in a written instrument signed by them, owns all of the rights comprised in the copyright.

(c) CONTRIBUTIONS TO COLLECTIVE WORKS.— Copyright in each separate contribution to a collective work is distinct from copyright in the collective work as a whole, and vests initially in the author of the contribution. In the absence of an express transfer of the copyright or of any rights under it, the owner of copyright in the collective work is presumed to have acquired only the privilege of reproducing and distributing the contribution as part of that particular collective work, any revision of that collective work, and any later collective work in the same series.

(d) TRANSFER OF OWNERSHIP.—

(1) The ownership of a copyright may be transferred in whole or in part by any means of conveyance or by operation of law, and may be bequeathed by will or pass as personal property by the applicable laws of intestate succession.

(2) Any of the exclusive rights comprised in a copyright, including any subdivision of any of the rights specified by section 106, may be transferred as provided by clause (1) and owned separately. The owner of any particular exclusive right is entitled, to the extent of that right, to all of the protection and remedies accorded to the copyright owner by this title.

(e) INVOLUNTARY TRANSFER.—When an individual author's ownership of a copyright, or of any of the exclusive rights under a copyright, has not previously been transferred voluntarily by that individual author, no action by any governmental body or other official or organization purporting to seize, expropriate, transfer, or exercise rights of ownership with respect to the copyright, or any of the exclusive rights under a copyright, shall be given effect under this title, except as provided under title 11.

(Pub. L. 94–553, title I, § 101, Oct. 19, 1976, 90 Stat. 2568; Pub. L. 95–598, title III, § 313, Nov. 6, 1978, 92 Stat. 2676.)

HISTORICAL AND REVISION NOTES

HOUSE REPORT NO. 94–1476

Initial Ownership. Two basic and well-established principles of copyright law are restated in section 201(a): that the source of copyright ownership is the author of the work, and that, in the case of a "joint work," the coauthors of the work are likewise coowners of the copyright. Under the definition of section 101, a work is "joint" if the authors collaborated with each other, or if each of the authors prepared his or her contribution with the knowledge and intention that it would be merged with the contributions of other authors as "inseparable or interdependent parts of a unitary whole." The touchstone here is the intention, at the time the writing is done, that the parts be absorbed or combined into an integrated unit, although the parts themselves may be either "inseparable" (as the case of a novel or painting) or "interdependent" (as in the case of a motion picture, opera, or the words and music of a song). The definition of "joint work" is to be contrasted with the definition of "collective work," also in section 101, in which the elements of merger and unity are lacking; there the key elements are assemblage or gathering of "separate and independent works * * * into a collective whole."

The definition of "joint works" has prompted some concern lest it be construed as converting the authors of previously written works, such as plays, novels, and music, into coauthors of a motion picture in which their work is incorporated. It is true that a motion picture would normally be a joint rather than a collective work with respect to those authors who actually work on the film, although their usual status as employees for hire would keep the question of coownership from coming up. On the other hand, although a novelist, playwright, or songwriter may write a work with the hope or expectation that it will be used in a motion picture, this is clearly a case of separate or independent authorship rather than one where the basic intention behind the writing of the work was for motion picture use. In this case, the motion picture is a derivative work within the definition of that term, and section 103 makes plain that copyright in a derivative work is independent of, and does not enlarge the scope of rights in, any preexisting material incorporated in it. There is thus no need to spell this conclusion out in the definition of "joint work."

There is also no need for a specific statutory provision concerning the rights and duties of the coowners of a work; court-made law on this point is left undisturbed. Under the bill, as under the present law, coowners of a copyright would be treated generally as tenants in common, with each coowner having an independent right to use or license the use of a work, subject to a duty of accounting to the other coowners for any profits.

Works Made for Hire. Section 201(b) of the bill adopts one of the basic principles of the present law: that in the case of works made for hire the employer is considered the author of the work, and is regarded as the initial owner of copyright unless there has been an agreement otherwise. The subsection also requires that any agreement under which the employee is to own rights be in writing and signed by the parties.

The work-made-for-hire provisions of this bill represent a carefully balanced compromise, and as such they do not incorporate the amendments proposed by screenwriters and composers for motion pictures. Their proposal was for the recognition of something similar to the "shop right" doctrine of patent law: with some exceptions, the employer would acquire the right to use the employee's work to the extent needed for purposes of his regular business, but the employee would retain all other rights as long as he or she refrained from the authorizing of competing uses. However, while this change might theoretically improve the bargaining position of screenwriters and others as a group, the practical benefits that individual authors would receive are highly conjectural. The presumption that initial ownership rights vest in the employer for hire is well established in American copyright law, and to exchange that for the uncertainties of the shop right doctrine would not only be of dubious value to employers and employees alike, but might also reopen a number of other issues.

The status of works prepared on special order or commission was a major issue in the development of the definition of "works made for hire" in section 101, which has undergone extensive revision during the legislative process. The basic problem is how to draw a statutory line between those works written on special order or commission that should be considered as "works made for hire," and those that should not. The definition now provided by the bill represents a compromise which, in effect, spells out those specific categories of commissioned works that can be considered "works made for hire" under certain circumstances.

Of these, one of the most important categories is that of "instructional texts." This term is given its own definition in the bill: "a literary, pictorial, or graphic work prepared for publication with the purpose of use in systematic instructional activities." The concept is intended to include what might be loosely called "textbook material," whether or not in book form or prepared in the form of text matter. The basic characteristic of "instructional texts" is the purpose of their preparation for "use in systematic instructional activities," and they are to be distinguished from works prepared for use by a general readership.

Contributions to Collective Works. Subsection (c) of section 201 deals with the troublesome problem of ownership of copyright in contributions to collective works, and the relationship between copyright ownership in a contribution and in the collective work in which it appears. The first sentence establishes the basic principle that copyright in the individual contribution and copyright in the collective work as a whole are separate and distinct, and that the author of the contribution is, as in every other case, the first owner of copyright in it. Under the definitions in section 101, a "collective work" is a species of "compilation" and, by its nature, must involve the selection, assembly, and arrangement of "a number of contributions." Examples of "collective works" would ordinarily include periodical issues, anthologies, symposia, and collections of the discrete writings of the same authors, but not cases, such as a composition consisting of words and music, a work published with illustrations or front matter, or three one-act plays, where relatively few separate elements have been brought together. Unlike the contents of other types of "compilations," each of the contributions incorporated in a "collective work" must itself constitute a "separate and independent" work, therefore ruling out compilations of information or other uncopyrightable material and works published with editorial revisions or annotations. Moreover, as noted above, there is a basic distinction between a "joint work," where the separate elements merge into a unified whole, and a "collective work," where they remain unintegrated and disparate.

The bill does nothing to change the rights of the owner of copyright in a collective work under the present law. These exclusive rights extend to the elements of compilation and editing that went into the collective work as a whole, as well as the contributions that were written for hire by employees of the owner of the collective work, and those copyrighted contributions that have been transferred in writing to the owner by their authors. However, one of the most significant aims of the bill is to clarify and improve the present confused and frequently unfair legal situation with respect to rights in contributions.

The second sentence of section 201(c), in conjunction with the provisions of section 404 dealing with copyright notice, will preserve the author's copyright in a contribution even if the contribution does not bear a separate notice in the author's name, and without requiring any unqualified transfer of rights to the owner of the collective work. This is coupled with a presumption that, unless there has been an express transfer of more, the owner of the collective work acquires, "only the privilege of reproducing and distributing the contribution as part of that particular collective work, any revision of that collective work, and any later collective work in the same series."

The basic presumption of section 201(c) is fully consistent with present law and practice, and represents a fair balancing of equities. At the same time, the last clause of the subsection, under which the privilege of republishing the contribution under certain limited circumstances would be presumed, is an essential counterpart of the basic presumption. Under the language of this clause a publishing company could reprint a contribution from one issue in a later issue of its magazine, and could reprint an article from a 1980 edition of an encyclopedia in a 1990 revision of it; the publisher could not revise the contribution itself or include it in a new anthology or an entirely different magazine or other collective work.

Transfer of Ownership. The principle of unlimited alienability of copyright is stated in clause (1) of section 201(d). Under that provision the ownership of a copyright, or of any part of it, may be transferred by any means of conveyance or by operation of law, and is to be treated as personal property upon the death of the owner. The term "transfer of copyright ownership" is defined in section 101 to cover any "conveyance, alienation, or hypothecation," including assignments, mortgages, and exclusive licenses, but not including nonexclusive licenses. Representatives of motion picture producers have argued that foreclosures of copyright mortgages should not be left to varying State laws, and that the statute should establish a Federal foreclosure system. However, the benefits of such a system would be of very limited application, and would not justify the complicated statutory and procedural requirements that would have to be established.

Clause (2) of subsection (d) contains the first explicit statutory recognition of the principle of divisibility of copyright in our law. This provision, which has long been sought by authors and their representatives, and which has attracted wide support from other groups, means that any of the exclusive rights that go to make up a copyright, including those enumerated in section 106 and any subdivision of them, can be transferred and owned separately. The definition of "transfer of copyright ownership" in section 101 makes clear that the principle of divisibility applies whether or not the transfer is "limited in time or place of effect," and another definition in the same section provides that the term "copyright owner," with respect to any one exclusive right, refers to the owner of that particular right. The last sentence of section 201(d)(2) adds that the owner, with respect to the particular exclusive right he or she owns, is entitled "to all of the protection and remedies accorded to the copyright owner by this title." It is thus clear, for example, that a local broadcasting station holding an exclusive license to transmit a particular work within a particular geographic area and for a particular period of time, could sue, in its own name as copyright owner, someone who infringed that particular exclusive right.

Subsection (e) provides that when an individual author's ownership of a copyright, or of any of the exclusive rights under a copyright, have not previously been voluntarily transferred, no action by any governmental body or other official or organization purporting to seize, expropriate, transfer, or exercise rights of ownership with respect to the copyright, or any of the exclusive rights under a copyright, shall be given effect under this title.

The purpose of this subsection is to reaffirm the basic principle that the United States copyright of an individual author shall be secured to that author, and cannot be taken away by any involuntary transfer. It is the intent of the subsection that the author be entitled, despite any purported expropriation or involuntary transfer, to continue exercising all rights under the United States statute, and that the governmental body or organization may not enforce or exercise any rights under this title in that situation.

It may sometimes be difficult to ascertain whether a transfer of copyright is voluntary or is coerced by covert pressure. But subsection (e) would protect foreign authors against laws and decrees purporting to divest them of their rights under the United States copyright statute, and would protect authors within the foreign country who choose to resist such covert pressures.

Traditional legal actions that may involve transfer of ownership, such as bankruptcy proceedings and mortgage foreclosures, are not within the scope of this subsection; the authors in such cases have voluntarily consented to these legal processes by their overt actions—for example, by filing in bankruptcy or by hypothecating a copyright.

AMENDMENTS

1978—Subsec. (e). Pub. L. 95–598 inserted ", except as provided under title 11".

EFFECTIVE DATE OF 1978 AMENDMENT

Amendment effective Oct. 1, 1979, see section 402(a) of Pub. L. 95–598 set out as an Effective Date note preceding section 101 of Title 11, Bankruptcy.

§ 202. Ownership of copyright as distinct from ownership of material object

Ownership of a copyright, or of any of the exclusive rights under a copyright, is distinct from ownership of any material object in which the work is embodied. Transfer of ownership of any material object, including the copy or phonorecord in which the work is first fixed, does not of itself convey any rights in the copyrighted work embodied in the object; nor, in the absence of an agreement, does transfer of ownership of a copyright or of any exclusive rights under a copyright convey property rights in any material object.

(Pub. L. 94–553, title I, § 101, Oct. 19, 1976, 90 Stat. 2568.)

HISTORICAL AND REVISION NOTES

HOUSE REPORT NO. 94–1476

The principle restated in section 202 is a fundamental and important one: that copyright ownership and ownership of a material object in which the copyrighted work is embodied are entirely separate things. Thus, transfer of a material object does not of itself carry any rights under the copyright, and this includes transfer of the copy or phonorecord—the original manuscript, the photographic negative, the unique painting or statue, the master tape recording, etc.—in which the work was first fixed. Conversely, transfer of a copyright does not necessarily require the conveyance of any material object.

As a result of the interaction of this section and the provisions of section 204(a) and 301, the bill would change a common law doctrine exemplified by the decision in *Pushman v. New York Graphic Society, Inc.*, 287 N.Y. 302, 39 N.E.2d 249 (1942). Under that doctrine, authors or artists are generally presumed to transfer common law literary property rights when they sell their manuscript or work of art, unless those rights are specifically reserved. This presumption would be reversed under the bill, since a specific written conveyance of rights would be required in order for a sale of any material object to carry with it a transfer of copyright.

§ 203. Termination of transfers and licenses granted by the author

(a) CONDITIONS FOR TERMINATION.—In the case of any work other than a work made for hire, the exclusive or nonexclusive grant of a transfer or license of copyright or of any right under a copyright, executed by the author on or after January 1, 1978, otherwise than by will, is subject to termination under the following conditions:

(1) In the case of a grant executed by one author, termination of the grant may be effected by that author or, if the author is dead, by the person or persons who, under clause (2) of this subsection, own and are entitled to exercise a total of more than one-half of that author's termination interest. In the case of a grant executed by two or more authors of a joint work, termination of the grant may be effected by a majority of the authors who executed it; if any of such authors is dead, the termination interest of any such author may be exercised as a unit by the person or persons who, under clause (2) of this subsection, own and are entitled to exercise a total of more than one-half of that author's interest.

(2) Where an author is dead, his or her termination interest is owned, and may be exercised, as follows:

(A) The widow or widower owns the author's entire termination interest unless there are any surviving children or grandchildren of the author, in which case the widow or widower owns one-half of the author's interest.

(B) The author's surviving children, and the surviving children of any dead child of the author, own the author's entire termination interest unless there is a widow or widower, in which case the ownership of one-half of the author's interest is divided among them.

(C) The rights of the author's children and grandchildren are in all cases divided among them and exercised on a per stirpes basis according to the number of such author's children represented; the share of the children of a dead child in a termination interest can be exercised only by the action of a majority of them.

(D) In the event that the author's widow or widower, children, and grandchildren are not living, the author's executor, administrator, personal representative, or trustee shall own the author's entire termination interest.

(3) Termination of the grant may be effected at any time during a period of five years beginning at the end of thirty-five years from the date of execution of the grant; or, if the grant covers the right of publication of the work, the period begins at the end of thirty-five years from the date of publication of the work under the grant or at the end of forty years from the date of execution of the grant, whichever term ends earlier.

(4) The termination shall be effected by serving an advance notice in writing, signed by the number and proportion of owners of termination interests required under clauses (1) and (2) of this subsection, or by their duly authorized agents, upon the grantee or the grantee's successor in title.

(A) The notice shall state the effective date of the termination, which shall fall within the five-year period specified by clause (3) of this subsection, and the notice shall be served not less than two or more than ten years before that date. A copy of the notice shall be recorded in the Copyright Office before the effective date of termination, as a condition to its taking effect.

(B) The notice shall comply, in form, content, and manner of service, with requirements that the Register of Copyrights shall prescribe by regulation.

(5) Termination of the grant may be effected notwithstanding any agreement to the contrary, including an agreement to make a will or to make any future grant.

(b) EFFECT OF TERMINATION.—Upon the effective date of termination, all rights under this title that were covered by the terminated grants revert to the author, authors, and other persons owning termination interests under clauses (1) and (2) of subsection (a), including those owners who did not join in signing the notice of termination under clause (4) of subsection (a), but with the following limitations:

(1) A derivative work prepared under authority of the grant before its termination may continue to be utilized under the terms of the grant after its termination, but this privilege does not extend to the preparation after the termination of other derivative works based upon the copyrighted work covered by the terminated grant.

(2) The future rights that will revert upon termination of the grant become vested on the date the notice of termination has been served as provided by clause (4) of subsection (a). The rights vest in the author, authors, and other persons named in, and in the proportionate shares provided by, clauses (1) and (2) of subsection (a).

(3) Subject to the provisions of clause (4) of this subsection, a further grant, or agreement to make a further grant, of any right covered by a terminated grant is valid only if it is signed by the same number and proportion of the owners, in whom the right has vested under clause (2) of this subsection, as are required to terminate the grant under clauses (1) and (2) of subsection (a). Such further grant or agreement is effective with respect to all of the persons in whom the right it covers has vested under clause (2) of this subsection, including those who did not join in signing it. If any person dies after rights under a terminated grant have vested in him or her, that person's legal representatives, legatees, or heirs at law represent him or her for purposes of this clause.

(4) A further grant, or agreement to make a further grant, of any right covered by a terminated grant is valid only if it is made after the effective date of the termination. As an exception, however, an agreement for such a further grant may be made between the persons provided by clause (3) of this subsection and the original grantee or such grantee's successor in title, after the notice of termination has been served as provided by clause (4) of subsection (a).

(5) Termination of a grant under this section affects only those rights covered by the grants that arise under this title, and in no way affects rights arising under any other Federal, State, or foreign laws.

(6) Unless and until termination is effected under this section, the grant, if it does not provide otherwise, continues in effect for the term of copyright provided by this title.

(Pub. L. 94–553, title I, § 101, Oct. 19, 1976, 90 Stat. 2569; Pub. L. 105–298, title I, § 103, Oct. 27, 1998, 112 Stat. 2829; Pub. L. 107–273, div. C, title III, § 13210(9), Nov. 2, 2002, 116 Stat. 1909.)

HISTORICAL AND REVISION NOTES

HOUSE REPORT NO. 94–1476

The Problem in General. The provisions of section 203 are based on the premise that the reversionary provisions of the present section on copyright renewal (17 U.S.C. sec. 24 [section 24 of former title 17]) should be eliminated, and that the proposed law should substitute for them a provision safeguarding authors against unremunerative transfers. A provision of this sort is needed because of the unequal bargaining position of authors, resulting in part from the impossibility of determining a work's value until it has been exploited. Section 203 reflects a practical compromise that will further the objectives of the copyright law while recognizing the problems and legitimate needs of all interests involved.

Scope of the Provision. Instead of being automatic, as is theoretically the case under the present renewal provision, the termination of a transfer or license under section 203 would require the serving of an advance notice within specified time limits and under specified conditions. However, although affirmative action is needed to effect a termination, the right to take this action cannot be waived in advance or contracted away. Under section 203(a) the right of termination would apply only to transfers and licenses executed after the effective date of the new statute [Jan. 1, 1978], and would have no retroactive effect.

The right of termination would be confined to inter vivos transfers or licenses executed by the author, and would not apply to transfers by the author's successors in interest or to the author's own bequests. The scope of the right would extend not only to any "transfer of copyright ownership," as defined in section 101, but also to nonexclusive licenses. The right of termination would not apply to "works made for hire," which is one of the principal reasons the definition of that term assumed importance in the development of the bill.

Who Can Terminate a Grant. Two issues emerged from the disputes over section 203 as to the persons empowered to terminate a grant: (1) the specific classes of beneficiaries in the case of joint works; and (2) whether anything less than unanimous consent of all those entitled to terminate should be required to make a termination effective. The bill to some extent reflects a compromise on these points, including a recognition of the dangers of one or more beneficiaries being induced to "hold out" and of unknown children or grandchildren being discovered later. The provision can be summarized as follows:

1. In the case of a work of joint authorship, where the grant was signed by two or more of the authors, majority action by those who signed the grant, or by their interests, would be required to terminate it.

2. There are three different situations in which the shares of joint authors, or of a dead author's widow or widower, children, and grandchildren, must be divided under the statute: (1) The right to effect a termination; (2) the ownership of the terminated rights; and (3) the right to make further grants of reverted rights. The respective shares of the authors, and of a dead author's widow or widower, children, and grandchildren, would be divided in exactly the same way in each of these situations. The terms "widow," "widower," and "children" are defined in section 101 in an effort to avoid problems and uncertainties that have arisen under the present renewal section.

3. The principle of per stirpes representation would also be applied in exactly the same way in all three situations. Take for example, a case where a dead author left a widow, two living children, and three grandchildren by a third child who is dead. The widow will own half of the reverted interests, the two children will each own 16⅔ percent, and the three grandchildren will each own a share of roughly 5½ percent. But who can exercise the right of termi-

nation? Obviously, since she owns 50 percent, the widow is an essential party, but suppose neither of the two surviving children is willing to join her in the termination; is it enough that she gets one of the children of the dead child to join, or can the dead child's interest be exercised only by the action of a majority of his children? Consistent with the per stirpes principle, the interest of a dead child can be exercised only as a unit by majority action of his surviving children. Thus, even though the widow and one grandchild would own 55½ percent of the reverted copyright, they would have to be joined by another child or grandchild in order to effect a termination or a further transfer of reverted rights. This principle also applies where, for example, two joint authors executed a grant and one of them is dead; in order to effect a termination, the living author must be joined by a per stirpes majority of the dead author's beneficiaries. The notice of termination may be signed by the specified owners of termination interests or by "their duly authorized agents," which would include the legally appointed guardians or committees of persons incompetent to sign because of age or mental disability.

When a Grant Can be Terminated. Section 203 draws a distinction between the date when a termination becomes effective and the earlier date when the advance notice of termination is served. With respect to the ultimate effective date, section 203(a)(3) provides, as a general rule, that a grant may be terminated during the 5 years following the expiration of a period of 35 years from the execution of the grant. As an exception to this basic 35-year rule, the bill also provides that "if the grant covers the right of publication of the work, the period begins at the end of 35 years from the date of publication of the work under the grant or at the end of 40 years from the date of execution of the grant, whichever term ends earlier." This alternative method of computation is intended to cover cases where years elapse between the signing of a publication contract and the eventual publication of the work.

The effective date of termination, which must be stated in the advance notice, is required to fall within the 5 years following the end of the applicable 35- or 40-year period, but the advance notice itself must be served earlier. Under section 203(a)(4)(A), the notice must be served "not less than two or more than ten years" before the effective date stated in it.

As an example of how these time-limit requirements would operate in practice, we suggest two typical contract situations:

Case 1: Contract for theatrical production signed on September 2, 1987. Termination of grant can be made to take effect between September 2, 2022 (35 years from execution) and September 1, 2027 (end of 5 year termination period). Assuming that the author decides to terminate on September 1, 2022 (the earliest possible date) the advance notice must be filed between September 1, 2012, and September 1, 2020.

Case 2: Contract for book publication executed on April 10, 1980; book finally published on August 23, 1987. Since contract covers the right of publication, the 5-year termination period would begin on April 10, 2020 (40 years from execution) rather than April 10, 2015 (35 years from execution) or August 23, 2022 (35 years from publication). Assuming that the author decides to make the termination effective on January 1, 2024, the advance notice would have to be served between January 1, 2014, and January 1, 2022.

Effect of Termination. Section 203(b) makes clear that, unless effectively terminated within the applicable 5-year period, all rights covered by an existing grant will continue unchanged, and that rights under other Federal, State, or foreign laws are unaffected. However, assuming that a copyright transfer or license is terminated under section 203, who are bound by the termination and how are they affected?

Under the bill, termination means that ownership of the rights covered by the terminated grant reverts to everyone who owns termination interests on the date the notice of termination was served, whether they joined in signing the notice or not. In other words, if a person could have signed the notice, that person is bound by the action of the majority who did; the termination of the grant will be effective as to that person, and a proportionate share of the reverted rights automatically vests in that person. Ownership is divided proportionately on the same per stirpes basis as that provided for the right to effect termination under section 203(a) and, since the reverted rights vest on the date notice is served, the heirs of a dead beneficiary would inherit his or her share.

Under clause (3) of subsection (b), majority action is required to make a further grant of reverted rights. A problem here, of course, is that years may have passed between the time the reverted rights vested and the time the new owners want to make a further transfer; people may have died and children may have been born in the interim. To deal with this problem, the bill looks back to the date of vesting; out of the group in whom rights vested on that date, it requires the further transfer or license to be signed by "the same number and proportion of the owners" (though not necessarily the same individuals) as were then required to terminate the grant under subsection (a). If some of those in whom the rights originally vested have died, their "legal representatives, legatees, or heirs at law" may represent them for this purpose and, as in the case of the termination itself, any one of the minority who does not join in the further grant is nevertheless bound by it.

An important limitation on the rights of a copyright owner under a terminated grant is specified in section 203(b)(1). This clause provides that, notwithstanding a termination, a derivative work prepared earlier may "continue to be utilized" under the conditions of the terminated grant; the clause adds, however, that this privilege is not broad enough to permit the preparation of other derivative works. In other words, a film made from a play could continue to be licensed for performance after the motion picture contract had been terminated but any remake rights covered by the contract would be cut off. For this purpose, a motion picture would be considered as a "derivative work" with respect to every "preexisting work" incorporated in it, whether the preexisting work was created independently or was prepared expressly for the motion picture.

Section 203 would not prevent the parties to a transfer or license from voluntarily agreeing at any time to terminate an existing grant and negotiating a new one, thereby causing another 35-year period to start running. However, the bill seeks to avoid the situation that has arisen under the present renewal provision, in which third parties have bought up contingent future interests as a form of speculation. Section 203(b)(4) would make a further grant of rights that revert under a terminated grant valid "only if it is made after the effective date of the termination." An exception, in the nature of a right of "first refusal," would permit the original grantee or a successor of such grantee to negotiate a new agreement with the persons effecting the termination at any time after the notice of termination has been served.

Nothing contained in this section or elsewhere in this legislation is intended to extend the duration of any license, transfer or assignment made for a period of less than thirty-five years. If, for example, an agreement provides an earlier termination date or lesser duration, or if it allows the author the right of cancelling or terminating the agreement under certain circumstances, the duration is governed by the agreement. Likewise, nothing in this section or legislation is intended to change the existing state of the law of contracts concerning the circumstances in which an author may cancel or terminate a license, transfer, or assignment.

Section 203(b)(6) provides that, unless and until termination is effected under this section, the grant, "if it does not provide otherwise," continues for the term of copyright. This section means that, if the agreement does not contain provisions specifying its term or duration, and the author has not terminated the agreement under this section, the agreement continues for the term of the copyright, subject to any right of termination under circumstances which may be specified therein. If, however, an agreement does contain provisions governing its duration—for example, a term of fifty years—and the author has not exercised his or her right of termination under the statute, the agreement will continue according to its terms—in this example, for only fifty years. The quoted language is not to be construed as requiring agreements to reserve the right of termination.

AMENDMENTS

2002—Subsec. (a)(2)(A) to (C). Pub. L. 107–273, in subpars. (A) to (C), substituted "The" for "the" and, in subpars. (A) and (B), substituted period for semicolon at end.

1998—Subsec. (a)(2). Pub. L. 105–298, §103(1), struck out "by his widow or her widower and his or her children or grandchildren" after "exercised," in introductory provisions.

Subsec. (a)(2)(D). Pub. L. 105–298, §103(2), added subpar. (D).

§ 204. Execution of transfers of copyright ownership

(a) A transfer of copyright ownership, other than by operation of law, is not valid unless an instrument of conveyance, or a note or memorandum of the transfer, is in writing and signed by the owner of the rights conveyed or such owner's duly authorized agent.

(b) A certificate of acknowledgement is not required for the validity of a transfer, but is prima facie evidence of the execution of the transfer if—

(1) in the case of a transfer executed in the United States, the certificate is issued by a person authorized to administer oaths within the United States; or

(2) in the case of a transfer executed in a foreign country, the certificate is issued by a diplomatic or consular officer of the United States, or by a person authorized to administer oaths whose authority is proved by a certificate of such an officer.

(Pub. L. 94–553, title I, §101, Oct. 19, 1976, 90 Stat. 2570.)

HISTORICAL AND REVISION NOTES

HOUSE REPORT NO. 94–1476

Section 204 is a somewhat broadened and liberalized counterpart of sections 28 and 29 of the present statute [sections 28 and 29 of former title 17]. Under subsection (a), a transfer of copyright ownership (other than one brought about by operation of law) is valid only if there exists an instrument of conveyance, or alternatively a "note or memorandum of the transfer," which is in writing and signed by the copyright owner "or such owner's duly authorized agent." Subsection (b) makes clear that a notarial or consular acknowledgment is not essential to the validity of any transfer, whether executed in the United States or abroad. However, the subsection would liberalize the conditions under which certificates of acknowledgment of documents executed abroad are to be accorded prima facie weight, and would give the same weight to domestic acknowledgments under appropriate circumstances.

§ 205. Recordation of transfers and other documents

(a) CONDITIONS FOR RECORDATION.—Any transfer of copyright ownership or other document

pertaining to a copyright may be recorded in the Copyright Office if the document filed for recordation bears the actual signature of the person who executed it, or if it is accompanied by a sworn or official certification that it is a true copy of the original, signed document. A sworn or official certification may be submitted to the Copyright Office electronically, pursuant to regulations established by the Register of Copyrights.

(b) CERTIFICATE OF RECORDATION.—The Register of Copyrights shall, upon receipt of a document as provided by subsection (a) and of the fee provided by section 708, record the document and return it with a certificate of recordation.

(c) RECORDATION AS CONSTRUCTIVE NOTICE.—Recordation of a document in the Copyright Office gives all persons constructive notice of the facts stated in the recorded document, but only if—

(1) the document, or material attached to it, specifically identifies the work to which it pertains so that, after the document is indexed by the Register of Copyrights, it would be revealed by a reasonable search under the title or registration number of the work; and

(2) registration has been made for the work.

(d) PRIORITY BETWEEN CONFLICTING TRANSFERS.—As between two conflicting transfers, the one executed first prevails if it is recorded, in the manner required to give constructive notice under subsection (c), within one month after its execution in the United States or within two months after its execution outside the United States, or at any time before recordation in such manner of the later transfer. Otherwise the later transfer prevails if recorded first in such manner, and if taken in good faith, for valuable consideration or on the basis of a binding promise to pay royalties, and without notice of the earlier transfer.

(e) PRIORITY BETWEEN CONFLICTING TRANSFER OF OWNERSHIP AND NONEXCLUSIVE LICENSE.—A nonexclusive license, whether recorded or not, prevails over a conflicting transfer of copyright ownership if the license is evidenced by a written instrument signed by the owner of the rights licensed or such owner's duly authorized agent, and if—

(1) the license was taken before execution of the transfer; or

(2) the license was taken in good faith before recordation of the transfer and without notice of it.

(Pub. L. 94–553, title I, §101, Oct. 19, 1976, 90 Stat. 2571; Pub. L. 100–568, §5, Oct. 31, 1988, 102 Stat. 2857; Pub. L. 111–295, §3(b), Dec. 9, 2010, 124 Stat. 3180.)

HISTORICAL AND REVISION NOTES

HOUSE REPORT NO. 94–1476

The recording and priority provisions of section 205 are intended to clear up a number of uncertainties arising from sections 30 and 31 of the present law [sections 30 and 31 of former title 17] and to make them more effective and practical in operation. Any "document pertaining to a copyright" may be recorded under subsection (a) if it "bears that actual signature of the person who executed it," or if it is appropriately certified as a true copy. However, subsection (c) makes clear that the recorded document will give constructive notice of its contents only if two conditions are met: (1) the document or attached material specifically identifies the work to which it pertains so that a reasonable search under the title or registration number would reveal it, and (2) registration has been made for the work. Moreover, even though the Register of Copyrights may be compelled to accept for recordation documents that on their face appear self-serving or colorable, the Register should take care that their nature is not concealed from the public in the Copyright Office's indexing and search reports.

The provisions of subsection (d), requiring recordation of transfers as a prerequisite to the institution of an infringement suit, represent a desirable change in the law. The one- and three-month grace periods provided in subsection (e) are a reasonable compromise between those who want a longer hiatus and those who argue that any grace period makes it impossible for a bona fide transferee to rely on the record at any particular time.

Under subsection (f) of section 205, a nonexclusive license in writing and signed, whether recorded or not, would be valid against a later transfer, and would also prevail as against a prior unrecorded transfer if taken in good faith and without notice. Objections were raised by motion picture producers, particularly to the provision allowing unrecorded nonexclusive licenses to prevail over subsequent transfers, on the ground that a nonexclusive license can have drastic effects on the value of a copyright. On the other hand, the impracticalities and burdens that would accompany any requirement of recordation of nonexclusive licenses outweigh the limited advantages of a statutory recordation system for them.

AMENDMENTS

2010—Subsec. (a). Pub. L. 111–295 inserted at end "A sworn or official certification may be submitted to the Copyright Office electronically, pursuant to regulations established by the Register of Copyrights."

1988—Subsecs. (d) to (f). Pub. L. 100–568 redesignated subsecs. (e) and (f) as (d) and (e), respectively, and struck out former subsec. (d), which read as follows: "No person claiming by virtue of a transfer to be the owner of copyright or of any exclusive right under a copyright is entitled to institute an infringement action under this title until the instrument of transfer under which such person claims has been recorded in the Copyright Office, but suit may be instituted after such recordation on a cause of action that arose before recordation."

EFFECTIVE DATE OF 1988 AMENDMENT

Amendment by Pub. L. 100–568 effective Mar. 1, 1989, with any cause of action arising under this title before such date being governed by provisions in effect when cause of action arose, see section 13 of Pub. L. 100–568, set out as a note under section 101 of this title.

RECORDATION OF SHAREWARE

Pub. L. 101–650, title VIII, § 805, Dec. 1, 1990, 104 Stat. 5136, provided that:

"(a) IN GENERAL.—The Register of Copyrights is authorized, upon receipt of any document designated as pertaining to computer shareware and the fee prescribed by section 708 of title 17, United States Code, to record the document and return it with a certificate of recordation.

"(b) MAINTENANCE OF RECORDS; PUBLICATION OF INFORMATION.—The Register of Copyrights is authorized to maintain current, separate records relating to the recordation of documents under subsection (a), and to compile and publish at periodic intervals information relating to such recordations. Such publications shall be offered for sale to the public at prices based on the cost of reproduction and distribution.

"(c) DEPOSIT OF COPIES IN LIBRARY OF CONGRESS.—In the case of public domain computer software, at the election of the person recording a document under subsection (a), 2 complete copies of the best edition (as defined in section 101 of title 17, United States Code) of the computer software as embodied in machine-readable form may be deposited for the benefit of the Machine-Readable Collections Reading Room of the Library of Congress.

"(d) REGULATIONS.—The Register of Copyrights is authorized to establish regulations not inconsistent with law for the administration of the functions of the Register under this section. All regulations established by the Register are subject to the approval of the Librarian of Congress."

REGISTRATION OF CLAIMS TO COPYRIGHTS AND RECORDATION OF ASSIGNMENTS OF COPYRIGHTS AND OTHER INSTRUMENTS UNDER PREDECESSOR PROVISIONS

Recordation of assignments of copyrights or other instruments received in the Copyright Office before Jan. 1, 1978, to be made in accordance with this title as it existed on Dec. 31, 1977, see section 109 of Pub. L. 94–553, set out as a note under section 410 of this title.

CHAPTER 3—DURATION OF COPYRIGHT

§ 301. Preemption with respect to other laws

(a) On and after January 1, 1978, all legal or equitable rights that are equivalent to any of the exclusive rights within the general scope of copyright as specified by section 106 in works of authorship that are fixed in a tangible medium of expression and come within the subject matter of copyright as specified by sections 102 and 103, whether created before or after that date and whether published or unpublished, are governed exclusively by this title. Thereafter, no person is entitled to any such right or equivalent right in any such work under the common law or statutes of any State.

(b) Nothing in this title annuls or limits any rights or remedies under the common law or statutes of any State with respect to—

(1) subject matter that does not come within the subject matter of copyright as specified by sections 102 and 103, including works of authorship not fixed in any tangible medium of expression; or

(2) any cause of action arising from undertakings commenced before January 1, 1978;

(3) activities violating legal or equitable rights that are not equivalent to any of the exclusive rights within the general scope of copyright as specified by section 106; or

(4) State and local landmarks, historic preservation, zoning, or building codes, relating to architectural works protected under section 102(a)(8).

(c) With respect to sound recordings fixed before February 15, 1972, any rights or remedies under the common law or statutes of any State shall not be annulled or limited by this title until February 15, 2067. The preemptive provisions of subsection (a) shall apply to any such rights and remedies pertaining to any cause of action arising from undertakings commenced on and after February 15, 2067. Notwithstanding the provisions of section 303, no sound recording fixed before February 15, 1972, shall be subject to copyright under this title before, on, or after February 15, 2067.

(d) Nothing in this title annuls or limits any rights or remedies under any other Federal statute.

(e) The scope of Federal preemption under this section is not affected by the adherence of the United States to the Berne Convention or the satisfaction of obligations of the United States thereunder.

(f)(1) On or after the effective date set forth in section 610(a) of the Visual Artists Rights Act of 1990, all legal or equitable rights that are equivalent to any of the rights conferred by section 106A with respect to works of visual art to which the rights conferred by section 106A apply are governed exclusively by section 106A and section 113(d) and the provisions of this title relating to such sections. Thereafter, no person is entitled to any such right or equivalent right in any work of visual art under the common law or statutes of any State.

(2) Nothing in paragraph (1) annuls or limits any rights or remedies under the common law or statutes of any State with respect to—

(A) any cause of action from undertakings commenced before the effective date set forth in section 610(a) of the Visual Artists Rights Act of 1990;

(B) activities violating legal or equitable rights that are not equivalent to any of the rights conferred by section 106A with respect to works of visual art; or

(C) activities violating legal or equitable rights which extend beyond the life of the author.

(Pub. L. 94–553, title I, § 101, Oct. 19, 1976, 90 Stat. 2572; Pub. L. 100–568, § 6, Oct. 31, 1988, 102 Stat. 2857; Pub. L. 101–650, title VI, § 605, title VII, § 705, Dec. 1, 1990, 104 Stat. 5131, 5134; Pub. L. 105–298, title I, § 102(a), Oct. 27, 1998, 112 Stat. 2827.)

HISTORICAL AND REVISION NOTES

HOUSE REPORT NO. 94–1476

Single Federal System. Section 301, one of the bedrock provisions of the bill, would accomplish a fundamental and significant change in the present law. Instead of a dual system of "common law copyright" for unpublished works and statutory copyright for published works, which has been the system in effect in the United States since the first copyright statute in 1790, the bill adopts a single system of Federal statutory copyright from creation. Under section 301 a work would obtain statutory protection as soon as it is "created" or, as that term is defined in section 101 when it is "fixed in a copy or phonorecord for the first time." Common law copyright protection for works coming within the scope of the statute would be abrogated, and the concept of publication would lose its all-embracing importance as a dividing line between common law and statutory protection and between both of these forms of legal protection and the public domain.

By substituting a single Federal system for the present anachronistic, uncertain, impractical, and highly complicated dual system, the bill would greatly improve the operation of the copyright law and would be much more effective in carrying out the basic constitutional aims of uniformity and the promotion of writing and scholarship. The main arguments in favor of a single Federal system can be summarized as follows:

1. One of the fundamental purposes behind the copyright clause of the Constitution, as shown in Madison's comments in The Federalist, was to promote national uniformity and to avoid the practical difficulties of determining and enforcing an author's rights under the differing laws and in the separate courts of the various States. Today when the methods for dissemination of an author's work are incomparably broader and faster than they were in 1789, national uniformity in copyright protection is even more essential than it was then to carry out the constitutional intent.

2. "Publication," perhaps the most important single concept under the present law, also represents its most serious defect. Although at one time when works were disseminated almost exclusively through printed copies, "publication" could serve as a practical dividing line between common law and statutory protection, this is no longer true. With the development of the 20th-century communications revolution, the concept of publication has become increasingly artificial and obscure. To cope with the legal consequences of an established concept that has lost much of its meaning and justification, the courts have given "publication" a number of diverse interpretations, some of them radically different. Not unexpectedly, the results in individual cases have become unpredictable and often unfair. A single Federal system would help to clear up this chaotic situation.

3. Enactment of section 301 would also implement the "limited times" provision of the Constitution [Const. Art. I, § 8, cl. 8], which has become distorted under the traditional concept of "publication." Common law protection in "unpublished" works is now perpetual, no matter how widely they may be disseminated by means other than "publication"; the bill would place a time limit on the duration of exclusive rights in them. The provision would also aid scholarship and the dissemination of historical materials by making unpublished, undisseminated manuscripts available for publication after a reasonable period.

4. Adoption of a uniform national copyright system would greatly improve international dealings in copyrighted material. No other country has anything like our present dual system. In an era when copyrighted works can be disseminated instantaneously to every country on the globe, the need for effective international copyright relations, and the concomitant need for national uniformity, assume ever greater importance.

Under section 301, the statute would apply to all works created after its effective date [Jan 1, 1978], whether or not they are ever published or disseminated. With respect to works created before the effective date of the statute [Jan. 1, 1978] and still under common law protection, section 303 of the statute would provide protection from that date on, and would guarantee a minimum period of statutory copyright.

Preemption of State Law. The intention of section 301 is to preempt and abolish any rights under the common law or statutes of a State that are equivalent to copyright and that extend to works coming within the scope of the Federal copyright law. The declaration of this principle in section 301 is intended to be stated in the clearest and most unequivocal language possible, so as to foreclose any conceivable misinterpretation of its unqualified intention that Congress shall act preemptively, and to avoid the development of any vague borderline areas between State and Federal protection.

Under section 301(a) all "legal or equitable rights that are equivalent to any of the exclusive rights within the general scope of copyright as specified by section 106" are governed exclusively by the Federal copyright statute if the works involved are "works of authorship that are fixed in a tangible medium of expression and come within the subject matter of copyright as specified by sections 102 and 103." All corresponding State laws, whether common law or statutory, are preempted and abrogated. Regardless of when the work was created and whether it is published or unpublished, disseminated or undisseminated, in the public domain or copyrighted under the Federal statute, the States cannot offer it protection equivalent to copyright. Section 1338 of title 28, United States Code, also makes clear that any action involving rights under the Federal copyright law would come within the exclusive jurisdiction of the Federal courts. The preemptive effect of section 301 is limited to State laws; as stated expressly in subsection (d) of section 301, there is no intention to deal with the question of whether Congress can or should offer the equivalent of copyright protection under some constitutional provision other than the patent-copyright clause of article 1, section 8 [Const. Art. I, §8, cl. 8].

As long as a work fits within one of the general subject matter categories of sections 102 and 103, the bill prevents the States from protecting it even if it fails to achieve Federal statutory copyright because it is too minimal or lacking in originality to qualify, or because it has fallen into the public domain. On the other hand section 301(b) explicitly preserves common law copyright protection for one important class of works: works that have not been "fixed in any tangible medium of expression." Examples would include choreography that has never been filmed or notated, an extemporaneous speech, "original works of authorship" communicated solely through conversations or live broadcasts, and a dramatic sketch or musical composition improvised or developed from memory and without being recorded or written down. As mentioned above in connection with section 102, unfixed works are not included in the specified "subject matter of copyright." They are therefore not affected by the preemption of section 301, and would continue to be subject to protection under State statute or common law until fixed in tangible form.

The preemption of rights under State law is complete with respect to any work coming within the scope of the bill, even though the scope of exclusive rights given the work under the bill is narrower than the scope of common law rights in the work might have been.

Representatives of printers, while not opposed to the principle of section 301, expressed concern about its potential impact on protection of preliminary advertising copy and layouts prepared by printers. They argued that this material is frequently "pirated" by competitors, and that it would be a substantial burden if, in order to obtain full protection, the printer would have to make registrations and bear the expense and bother of suing in Federal rather than State courts. On the other hand, these practical problems are essentially procedural rather than substantive, and the proposal for a special exemption to preserve common law rights equivalent to copyright in unpublished advertising material cannot be justified. Moreover, subsection (b), discussed below, will preserve other legal grounds on which the printers can protect themselves against "pirates" under State laws.

In a general way subsection (b) of section 301 represents the obverse of subsection (a). It sets out, in broad terms and without necessarily being exhaustive, some of the principal areas of protection that preemption would not prevent the States from protecting. Its purpose is to make clear, consistent with the 1964 Supreme Court decisions in *Sears, Roebuck & Co., v. Stiffel Co.*, 376 U.S. 225 [84 S.Ct. 784, 11 L.Ed.2d 661, rehearing denied 84 S.Ct. 1131, 376 U.S. 973, 12 L.Ed.2d 87], and *Compco Corp. v. Day-Brite Lighting, Inc.*, 376 U.S. 234 [84 S.Ct. 779, 11 L.Ed.2d 669, rehearing denied 84 S.Ct. 1162, 377 U.S. 913, 12 L.Ed.2d 183], that preemption does not extend to causes of action, or subject matter outside the scope of the revised Federal copyright statute.

The numbered clauses of subsection (b) list three general areas left unaffected by the preemption: (1) subject matter that does not come within the subject matter of copyright; (2) causes of action arising under State law before the effective date of the statute [Jan. 1, 1978];

and (3) violations of rights that are not equivalent to any of the exclusive rights under copyright.

The examples in clause (3), while not exhaustive, are intended to illustrate rights and remedies that are different in nature from the rights comprised in a copyright and that may continue to be protected under State common law or statute. The evolving common law rights of "privacy," "publicity," and trade secrets, and the general laws of defamation and fraud, would remain unaffected as long as the causes of action contain elements, such as an invasion of personal rights or a breach of trust or confidentiality, that are different in kind from copyright infringement. Nothing in the bill derogates from the rights of parties to contract with each other and to sue for breaches of contract; however, to the extent that the unfair competition concept known as "interference with contract relations" is merely the equivalent of copyright protection, it would be preempted.

The last example listed in clause (3)—"deceptive trade practices such as passing off and false representation"—represents an effort to distinguish between those causes of action known as "unfair competition" that the copyright statute is not intended to preempt and those that it is. Section 301 is not intended to preempt common law protection in cases involving activities such as false labeling, fraudulent representation, and passing off even where the subject matter involved comes within the scope of the copyright statute.

"Misappropriation" is not necessarily synonymous with copyright infringement, and thus a cause of action labeled as "misappropriation" is not preempted if it is fact based neither on a right within the general scope of copyright as specified by section 106 nor on a right equivalent thereto. For example, state law should have the flexibility to afford a remedy (under traditional principles of equity) against a consistent pattern of unauthorized appropriation by a competitor of the facts (i.e., not the literary expression) constituting "hot" news, whether in the traditional mold of *International News Service v. Associated Press*, 248 U.S. 215 (1918) [39 S.Ct. 68, 63 L.Ed. 211], or in the newer form of data updates from scientific, business, or financial data bases. Likewise, a person having no trust or other relationship with the proprietor of a computerized data base should not be immunized from sanctions against electronically or cryptographically breaching the proprietor's security arrangements and accessing the proprietor's data. The unauthorized data access which should be remediable might also be achieved by the intentional interception of data transmissions by wire, microwave or laser transmissions, or by the common unintentional means of "crossed" telephone lines occasioned by errors in switching.

The proprietor of data displayed on the cathode ray tube of a computer terminal should be afforded protection against unauthorized printouts by third parties (with or without improper access), even if the data are not copyrightable. For example, the data may not be copyrighted because they are not fixed in a tangible medium of expression (i.e., the data are not displayed for a period or not more than transitory duration).

Nothing contained in section 301 precludes the owner of a material embodiment of a copy or a phonorecord from enforcing a claim of conversion against one who takes possession of the copy or phonorecord without consent.

A unique and difficult problem is presented with respect to the status of sound recordings fixed before February 12, 1972, the effective date of the amendment bringing recordings fixed after that date under Federal copyright protection. In its testimony during the 1975 hearings, the Department of Justice pointed out that, under section 301 as then written:

> This language could be read as abrogating the anti-piracy laws now existing in 29 states relating to pre-February 15, 1972, sound recordings on the grounds that these statutes proscribe activities violating rights equivalent to * * * the exclusive rights within the general scope of copyright. * * * Certainly such a

result cannot have been intended for it would likely effect the immediate resurgence of piracy of pre-February 15, 1972, sound recordings.

The Department recommended that section 301(b) be amended to exclude sound recordings fixed prior to February 15, 1972 from the effect of the preemption.

The Senate adopted this suggestion when it passed S. 22. The result of the Senate amendment would be to leave pre-1972 sound recordings as entitled to perpetual protection under State law, while post-1972 recordings would eventually fall into the public domain as provided in the bill.

The Committee recognizes that, under recent court decisions, pre-1972 recordings are protected by State statute or common law, and that should not all be thrown into the public domain instantly upon the coming into effect of the new law. However, it cannot agree that they should in effect be accorded perpetual protection, as under the Senate amendment, and it has therefore revised clause (4) to establish a future date for the pre-emption to take effect. The date chosen is February 15, 2047 which is 75 years from the effective date of the statute extending Federal protection to recordings.

Subsection (c) makes clear that nothing contained in Title 17 annuls or limits any rights or remedies under any other Federal statute.

REFERENCES IN TEXT

Section 610(a) of the Visual Artists Rights Act of 1990 [Pub. L. 101–650], referred to in subsec. (f)(1), (2)(A), is set out as an Effective Date note under section 106A of this title.

AMENDMENTS

1998—Subsec. (c). Pub. L. 105–298 substituted "2067" for "2047" wherever appearing.

1990—Subsec. (b)(4). Pub. L. 101–650, §705, added par. (4).

Subsec. (f). Pub. L. 101–650, §605, added subsec. (f).

1988—Subsec. (e). Pub. L. 100–568 added subsec. (e).

EFFECTIVE DATE OF 1990 AMENDMENT

Amendment by section 605 of Pub. L. 101–650 effective 6 months after Dec. 1, 1990, see section 610 of Pub. L. 101–650, set out as an Effective Date note under section 106A of this title.

Amendment by section 705 Pub. L. 101–650 applicable to any architectural work created on or after Dec. 1, 1990, and any architectural work, that, on Dec. 1, 1990, is unconstructed and embodied in unpublished plans or drawings, except that protection for such architectural work under this title terminates on Dec. 31, 2002, unless the work is constructed by that date, see section 706 of Pub. L. 101–650, set out as a note under section 101 of this title.

EFFECTIVE DATE OF 1988 AMENDMENT

Amendment by Pub. L. 100–568 effective Mar. 1, 1989, with any cause of action arising under this title before such date being governed by provisions in effect when cause of action arose, see section 13 of Pub. L. 100–568, set out as a note under section 101 of this title.

§ 302. Duration of copyright: Works created on or after January 1, 1978

(a) IN GENERAL.—Copyright in a work created on or after January 1, 1978, subsists from its creation and, except as provided by the following subsections, endures for a term consisting of the life of the author and 70 years after the author's death.

(b) JOINT WORKS.—In the case of a joint work prepared by two or more authors who did not work for hire, the copyright endures for a term consisting of the life of the last surviving author and 70 years after such last surviving author's death.

(c) ANONYMOUS WORKS, PSEUDONYMOUS WORKS, AND WORKS MADE FOR HIRE.—In the case of an anonymous work, a pseudonymous work, or a work made for hire, the copyright endures for a term of 95 years from the year of its first publication, or a term of 120 years from the year of its creation, whichever expires first. If, before the end of such term, the identity of one or more of the authors of an anonymous or pseudonymous work is revealed in the records of a registration made for that work under subsections (a) or (d) of section 408, or in the records provided by this subsection, the copyright in the work endures for the term specified by subsection (a) or (b), based on the life of the author or authors whose identity has been revealed. Any person having an interest in the copyright in an anonymous or pseudonymous work may at any time record, in records to be maintained by the Copyright Office for that purpose, a statement identifying one or more authors of the work; the statement shall also identify the person filing it, the nature of that person's interest, the source of the information recorded, and the particular work affected, and shall comply in form and content with requirements that the Register of Copyrights shall prescribe by regulation.

(d) RECORDS RELATING TO DEATH OF AUTHORS.—Any person having an interest in a copyright may at any time record in the Copyright Office a statement of the date of death of the author of the copyrighted work, or a statement that the author is still living on a particular date. The statement shall identify the person filing it, the nature of that person's interest, and the source of the information recorded, and shall comply in form and content with requirements that the Register of Copyrights shall prescribe by regulation. The Register shall maintain current records of information relating to the death of authors of copyrighted works, based on such recorded statements and, to the extent the Register considers practicable, on data contained in any of the records of the Copyright Office or in other reference sources.

(e) PRESUMPTION AS TO AUTHOR'S DEATH.—After a period of 95 years from the year of first publication of a work, or a period of 120 years from the year of its creation, whichever expires first, any person who obtains from the Copyright Office a certified report that the records provided by subsection (d) disclose nothing to indicate that the author of the work is living, or died less than 70 years before, is entitled to the benefits of a presumption that the author has been dead for at least 70 years. Reliance in good faith upon this presumption shall be a complete defense to any action for infringement under this title.

(Pub. L. 94–553, title I, §101, Oct. 19, 1976, 90 Stat. 2572; Pub. L. 105–298, title I, §102(b), Oct. 27, 1998, 112 Stat. 2827.)

HISTORICAL AND REVISION NOTES

HOUSE REPORT NO. 94–1476

In General. The debate over how long a copyright should last is as old as the oldest copyright statute and will doubtless continue as long as there is a copyright law. With certain exceptions, there appears to be strong support for the principle, as embodied in the bill, of a copyright term consisting of the life of the author and 50 years after his death. In particular, the authors and their representatives stressed that the adoption of a life-plus-50 term was by far their most important legislative goal in copyright law revision. The Register of Copyrights now regards a life-plus-50 term as the foundation of the entire bill.

Under the present law statutory copyright protection begins on the date of publication (or on the date of registration in unpublished form) and continues for 28 years from that date; it may be renewed for a second 28 years, making a total potential term of 56 years in all cases. [Under Public Laws 87–668, 89–142, 90–141, 90–416, 91–147, 91–555, 92–170, 92–566, and 93–573, copyrights that were subsisting in their renewal term on September 19, 1962, and that were scheduled to expire before Dec. 31, 1976, have been extended to that later date, in anticipation that general revision legislation extending their terms still further will be enacted by then.] The principal elements of this system—a definite number of years, computed from either publication or registration, with a renewal feature—have been a part of the U.S. copyright law since the first statute in 1790. The arguments for changing this system to one based on the life of the author can be summarized as follows:

1. The present 56-year term is not long enough to insure an author and his dependents the fair economic benefits from his works. Life expectancy has increased substantially, and more and more authors are seeing their works fall into the public domain during their lifetimes, forcing later works to compete with their own early works in which copyright has expired.

2. The tremendous growth in communications media has substantially lengthened the commercial life of a great many works. A short term is particularly discriminatory against serious works of music, literature, and art, whose value may not be recognized until after many years.

3. Although limitations on the term of copyright are obviously necessary, too short a term harms the author without giving any substantial benefit to the public. The public frequently pays the same for works in the public domain as it does for copyrighted works, and the only result is a commercial windfall to certain users at the author's expense. In some cases the lack of copyright protection actually restrains dissemination of the work, since publishers and other users cannot risk investing in the work unless assured of exclusive rights.

4. A system based on the life of the author would go a long way toward clearing up the confusion and uncertainty involved in the vague concept of "publication," and would provide a much simpler, clearer method for computing the term. The death of the author is a definite, determinable event, and it would be the only date that a potential user would have to worry about. All of a particular author's works, including successive revisions of them, would fall into the public domain at the same time, thus avoiding the present problems of determining a multitude of publication dates and of distinguishing "old" and "new" matter in later editions. The bill answers the problems of determining when relatively obscure authors died, by establishing a registry of death dates and a system of presumptions.

5. One of the worst features of the present copyright law is the provision for renewal of copyright. A substantial burden and expense, this unclear and highly technical requirement results in incalculable amounts of unproductive work. In a number of cases it is the cause of inadvertent and unjust loss of copyright. Under a life-plus-50 system the renewal device would be inappropriate and unnecessary.

6. Under the preemption provisions of section 301 and the single Federal system they would establish, authors will be giving up perpetual, unlimited exclusive common law rights in their unpublished works, including works that have been widely disseminated by means other than publication. A statutory term of life-plus-50 years is no more than a fair recompense for the loss of these perpetual rights.

7. A very large majority of the world's countries have adopted a copyright term of the life of the author and 50 years after the author's death. Since American authors are frequently protected longer in foreign countries than in the United States, the disparity in the duration of copyright has provoked considerable resentment and some proposals for retaliatory legislation. Copyrighted works move across national borders faster and more easily than virtually any other economic commodity, and with the techniques now in common use this movement has in many cases become instantaneous and effortless. The need to conform the duration of U.S. copyright to that prevalent throughout the rest of the world is increasingly pressing in order to provide certainty and simplicity in international business dealings. Even more important, a change in the basis of our copyright term would place the United States in the forefront of the international copyright community. Without this change, the possibility of future United States adherence to the Berne Copyright Union would evaporate, but with it would come a great and immediate improvement in our copyright relations. All of these benefits would accrue directly to American and foreign authors alike.

The need for a longer total term of copyright has been conclusively demonstrated. It is true that a major reason for the striking statistical increase in life expectancy since 1909 is the reduction in infant mortality, but this does not mean that the increase can be discounted. Although not nearly as great as the total increase in life expectancy, there has been a marked increase in longevity, and with medical discoveries and health programs for the elderly this trend shows every indication of continuing. If life expectancy in 1909, which was in the neighborhood of 56 years, offered a rough guide to the length of copyright protection, then life expectancy in the 1970's which is well over 70 years, should offer a similar guide; the Register's 1961 Report included statistics indicating that something between 70 and 76 years was then the average equivalent of life-plus-50 years. A copyright should extend beyond the author's lifetime, and judged by this standard the present term of 56 years is too short.

The arguments as to the benefits of uniformity with foreign laws, and the advantages of international comity that would result from adoption of a life-plus-50 term, are also highly significant. The system has worked well in other countries, and on the whole it would appear to make computation of terms considerably simpler and easier. The registry of death dates and the system of presumptions established in section 302 would solve most of the problems in determining when an individual author died.

No country in the world has provisions on the duration of copyright like ours. Virtually every other copyright law in the world bases the term of protection for works by natural persons on the life of the author, and a substantial majority of these accord protection for 50 years after the author's death. This term is required for adherence to the Berne Convention. It is worth noting that the 1965 revision of the copyright law of the Federal Republic of Germany adopted a term of life plus 70 years.

A point that has concerned some educational groups arose from the possibility that, since a large majority (now about 85 percent) of all copyrighted works are not renewed, a life-plus-50 year term would tie up a substantial body of material that is probably of no commercial interest but that would be more readily available for scholarly use if free of copyright restrictions. A statistical study of renewal registrations made by the Copyright Office in 1966 supports the generalization that most material which is considered to be of continuing or potential commercial value is renewed. Of the remainder, a certain proportion is of practically no value to anyone, but there are a large number of unrenewed works that have scholarly value to historians, archivists, and specialists in a variety of fields. This consideration lay behind the proposals for retaining the renewal device or for limiting the term for unpublished or unregistered works.

It is true that today's ephemera represent tomorrow's social history, and that works of scholarly value, which are now falling into the public domain after 28 years, would be protected much longer under the bill. Balanced against this are the burdens and expenses of renewals, the near impossibility of distinguishing between types of works in fixing a statutory term, and the extremely strong case in favor of a life-plus-50 system. Moreover, it is important to realize that the bill would not restrain scholars from using any work as source material or from making "fair use" of it; the restrictions would extend only to the unauthorized reproduction or distribution of copies of the work, its public performance, or some other use that would actually infringe the copyright owner's exclusive rights. The advantages of a basic term of copyright enduring for the life of the author and for 50 years after the author's death outweigh any possible disadvantages.

Basic Copyright Term. Under subsection (a) of section 302, a work "created" on or after the effective date of the revised statute [Jan. 1, 1978] would be protected by statutory copyright "from its creation" and, with exceptions to be noted below, "endures for a term consisting of the life of the author and 50 years after the author's death."

Under this provision, as a general rule, the life-plus-50 term would apply equally to unpublished works, to works published during the author's lifetime, and to works published posthumously.

The definition of "created" in section 101, which will be discussed in more detail in connection with section 302(c) below, makes clear that "creation" for this purpose means the first time the work is fixed in a copy or phonorecord; up to that point the work is not "created," and is subject to common law protection, even though it may exist in someone's mind and may have been communicated to others in unfixed form.

Joint Works. Since by definition a "joint work" has two or more authors, a statute basing the term of copyright on the life of the author must provide a special method of computing the term of "joint works." Under the system in effect in many foreign countries, the term of copyright is measured from the death of the last survivor of a group of joint authors, no matter how many there are. The bill adopts this system as the simplest and fairest of the alternatives for dealing with the problem.

Anonymous Works, Pseudonymous Works, and Works Made for Hire. Computing the term from the author's death also requires special provisions to deal with cases where the authorship is not revealed or where the "author" is not an individual. Section 302(c) therefore provides a special term for anonymous works, pseudonymous works, and works made for hire: 75 years from publication or 100 years from creation, whichever is shorter. The definitions in section 101 make the status of anonymous and pseudonymous works depend on what is revealed on the copies or phonorecords of a work; a work is "anonymous" if "no natural person is identified as author," and is "pseudonymous" if "the author is identified under a fictitious name."

Section 302(c) provides that the 75- and 100-year terms for an anonymous or pseudonymous work can be converted to the ordinary life-plus-50 term if "the identity of one or more authors * * * is revealed" in special records maintained for this purpose in the Copyright Office. The term in such cases would be "based on the life of the author or authors whose identity has been revealed." Instead of forcing a user to search through countless Copyright Office records to determine if an author's identity has been revealed, the bill sets up a special registry for the purpose, with requirements concerning the filing of identifying statements that parallel those of the following subsection (d) with respect to statements of the date of an author's death.

The alternative terms established in section 302(c)—75 years from publication or 100 years from creation, whichever expires first—are necessary to set a time limit on protection of unpublished material. For example, copyright in a work created in 1978 and published in 1988 would expire in 2063 (75 years from publication). A question arises as to when the copyright should expire if the work is never published. Both the Constitution and the underlying purposes of the bill require the establishment of an alternative term for unpublished work and the only practicable basis for this alternative is "creation." Under the bill a work created in 1980 but not published until after 2005 (or never published) would fall into the public domain in 2080 (100 years after creation).

The definition in section 101 provides that "creation" takes place when a work "is fixed in a copy or phonorecord for the first time." Although the concept of "creation" is inherently lacking in precision, its adoption in the bill would, for example, enable a scholar to use an unpublished manuscript written anonymously, pseudonymously, or for hire, if he determines on the basis of internal or external evidence that the manuscript is at least 100 years old. In the case of works written over a period of time or in successive revised versions, the definition provides that the portion of the work "that has been fixed at any particular time constitutes the work as of that time," and that, "where the work has been prepared in different versions, each version constitutes a separate work." Thus, a scholar or other user, in attempting to determine whether a particular work is in the public domain, needs to look no further than the particular version he wishes to use.

Although "publication" would no longer play the central role assigned to it under the present law, the concept would still have substantial significance under provisions throughout the bill, including those on Federal preemption and duration. Under the definition in section 101, a work is "published" if one or more copies or phonorecords embodying it are distributed to the public—that is, generally to persons under no explicit or implicit restrictions with respect to disclosure of its contents—without regard to the manner in which the copies or phonorecords changed hands. The definition clears up the question of whether the sale of phonorecords constitutes publication, and it also makes plain that any form or dissemination in which a material object does not change hands—performances or displays on television, for example—is not a publication no matter how many people are exposed to the work. On the other hand, the definition also makes clear that, when copies or phonorecords are offered to a group of wholesalers, broadcasters, motion picture theaters, etc., publication takes place if the purpose is "further distribution, public performance, or public display."

Although the periods of 75 or 100 years for anonymous and pseudonymous works and works made for hire seem to be longer than the equivalent term provided by foreign laws and the Berne Conventions, this difference is more apparent than real. In general, the terms in these special cases approximate, on the average, the term of the life of the author plus 50 years established for other works. The 100-year maximum term for unpublished works, although much more limited than the perpetual term now available under common law in the United States and under statute in some foreign countries, is sufficient to guard against unjustified invasions of privacy and to fulfill our obligations under the Universal Copyright Convention.

Records and Presumption as to Author's Death. Subsections (d) and (e) of section 302 together furnish an answer to the practical problems of how to discover the death dates of obscure or unknown authors. Subsection (d) provides a procedure for recording statements that an author died, or that he was still living, on a particular date, and also requires the Register of Copyrights to maintain obituary records on a current basis. Under subsection (e) anyone who, after a specified period, obtains certification from the Copyright Office that its records show nothing to indicate that the author is living or died less than 50 years before, is entitled to rely upon a presumption that the author has been dead for more than 50 years. The period specified in subsection (e)—75 years from publication or 100 years from creation—is purposely uniform with the special term provided in subsection (c).

AMENDMENTS

1998—Subsecs. (a), (b). Pub. L. 105–298, § 102(b)(1), (2), substituted "70" for "fifty".

Subsec. (c). Pub. L. 105–298, § 102(b)(3), in first sentence, substituted "95" for "seventy-five" and "120" for "one hundred".

Subsec. (e). Pub. L. 105–298, § 102(b)(4), in first sentence, substituted "95" for "seventy-five", "120" for "one hundred", and "70" for "fifty" in two places.

§ 303. Duration of copyright: Works created but not published or copyrighted before January 1, 1978

(a) Copyright in a work created before January 1, 1978, but not theretofore in the public domain or copyrighted, subsists from January 1, 1978, and endures for the term provided by section 302. In no case, however, shall the term of copyright in such a work expire before December 31, 2002; and, if the work is published on or before December 31, 2002, the term of copyright shall not expire before December 31, 2047.

(b) The distribution before January 1, 1978, of a phonorecord shall not for any purpose constitute a publication of any musical work, dramatic work, or literary work embodied therein.

(Pub. L. 94–553, title I, § 101, Oct. 19, 1976, 90 Stat. 2573; Pub. L. 105–80, § 11, Nov. 13, 1997, 111 Stat. 1534; Pub. L. 105–298, title I, § 102(c), Oct. 27, 1998, 112 Stat. 2827; Pub. L. 111–295, § 5(a), Dec. 9, 2010, 124 Stat. 3181.)

HISTORICAL AND REVISION NOTES

HOUSE REPORT NO. 94–1476

Theoretically, at least, the legal impact of section 303 would be far reaching. Under it, every "original work of authorship" fixed in tangible form that is in existence would be given statutory copyright protection as long as the work is not in the public domain in this country. The vast majority of these works consist of private material that no one is interested in protecting or infringing, but section 303 would still have practical effects for a prodigious body of material already in existence.

Looked at another way, however, section 303 would have a genuinely restrictive effect. Its basic purpose is to substitute statutory for common law copyright for everything now protected at common law, and to substitute reasonable time limits for the perpetual protection now available. In general, the substituted time limits are those applicable to works created after the effective date of the law [Jan. 1, 1978]; for example, an unpublished work written in 1945 whose author dies in 1980 would be protected under the statute from the effective date [Jan. 1, 1978] through 2030 (50 years after the author's death).

A special problem under this provision is what to do with works whose ordinary statutory terms will have expired or will be nearing expiration on the effective date [Jan. 1, 1978]. The committee believes that a provision taking away subsisting common law rights and substituting statutory rights for a reasonable period is fully in harmony with the constitutional requirements of due process, but it is necessary to fix a "reasonable period" for this purpose. Section 303 provides that under no circumstances would copyright protection expire before December 31, 2002, and also attempts to encourage publication by providing 25 years more protection (through 2027) if the work were published before the end of 2002.

AMENDMENTS

2010—Subsec. (b). Pub. L. 111–295 substituted "any musical work, dramatic work, or literary work" for "the musical work".

1998—Subsec. (a). Pub. L. 105–298 substituted "December 31, 2047" for "December 31, 2027" in second sentence.

1997—Pub. L. 105–80 designated existing provisions as subsec. (a) and added subsec. (b).

§ 304. Duration of copyright: Subsisting copyrights

(a) COPYRIGHTS IN THEIR FIRST TERM ON JANUARY 1, 1978.—(1)(A) Any copyright, the first term of which is subsisting on January 1, 1978, shall endure for 28 years from the date it was originally secured.

(B) In the case of—

(i) any posthumous work or of any periodical, cyclopedic, or other composite work upon which the copyright was originally secured by the proprietor thereof, or

(ii) any work copyrighted by a corporate body (otherwise than as assignee or licensee of the individual author) or by an employer for whom such work is made for hire,

the proprietor of such copyright shall be entitled to a renewal and extension of the copyright in such work for the further term of 67 years.

(C) In the case of any other copyrighted work, including a contribution by an individual author to a periodical or to a cyclopedic or other composite work—

(i) the author of such work, if the author is still living,

(ii) the widow, widower, or children of the author, if the author is not living,

(iii) the author's executors, if such author, widow, widower, or children are not living, or

(iv) the author's next of kin, in the absence of a will of the author,

shall be entitled to a renewal and extension of the copyright in such work for a further term of 67 years.

(2)(A) At the expiration of the original term of copyright in a work specified in paragraph (1)(B) of this subsection, the copyright shall endure for a renewed and extended further term of 67 years, which—

(i) if an application to register a claim to such further term has been made to the Copyright Office within 1 year before the expiration of the original term of copyright, and the claim is registered, shall vest, upon the beginning of such further term, in the proprietor of the copyright who is entitled to claim the renewal of copyright at the time the application is made; or

(ii) if no such application is made or the claim pursuant to such application is not registered, shall vest, upon the beginning of such further term, in the person or entity that was the proprietor of the copyright as of the last day of the original term of copyright.

(B) At the expiration of the original term of copyright in a work specified in paragraph (1)(C) of this subsection, the copyright shall endure for a renewed and extended further term of 67 years, which—

(i) if an application to register a claim to such further term has been made to the Copyright Office within 1 year before the expiration of the original term of copyright, and the claim is registered, shall vest, upon the beginning of such further term, in any person who is entitled under paragraph (1)(C) to the renewal and extension of the copyright at the time the application is made; or

(ii) if no such application is made or the claim pursuant to such application is not registered, shall vest, upon the beginning of such further term, in any person entitled under paragraph (1)(C), as of the last day of the original term of copyright, to the renewal and extension of the copyright.

(3)(A) An application to register a claim to the renewed and extended term of copyright in a work may be made to the Copyright Office—

(i) within 1 year before the expiration of the original term of copyright by any person entitled under paragraph (1)(B) or (C) to such further term of 67 years; and

(ii) at any time during the renewed and extended term by any person in whom such further term vested, under paragraph (2)(A) or (B), or by any successor or assign of such person, if the application is made in the name of such person.

(B) Such an application is not a condition of the renewal and extension of the copyright in a work for a further term of 67 years.

(4)(A) If an application to register a claim to the renewed and extended term of copyright in a work is not made within 1 year before the expiration of the original term of copyright in a work, or if the claim pursuant to such application is not registered, then a derivative work prepared under authority of a grant of a transfer or license of the copyright that is made before the expiration of the original term of copyright may continue to be used under the terms of the grant during the renewed and extended term of copyright without infringing the copyright, except that such use does not extend to the preparation during such renewed and extended term of other derivative works based upon the copyrighted work covered by such grant.

(B) If an application to register a claim to the renewed and extended term of copyright in a work is made within 1 year before its expiration, and the claim is registered, the certificate of such registration shall constitute prima facie evidence as to the validity of the copyright during its renewed and extended term and of the facts stated in the certificate. The evidentiary weight to be accorded the certificates of a registration of a renewed and extended term of copyright made after the end of that 1-year period shall be within the discretion of the court.

(b) COPYRIGHTS IN THEIR RENEWAL TERM AT THE TIME OF THE EFFECTIVE DATE OF THE SONNY BONO COPYRIGHT TERM EXTENSION ACT.—Any copyright still in its renewal term at the time that the Sonny Bono Copyright Term Extension Act becomes effective shall have a copyright term of 95 years from the date copyright was originally secured.

(c) TERMINATION OF TRANSFERS AND LICENSES COVERING EXTENDED RENEWAL TERM.—In the case of any copyright subsisting in either its first or renewal term on January 1, 1978, other than a copyright in a work made for hire, the exclusive or nonexclusive grant of a transfer or license of the renewal copyright or any right under it, executed before January 1, 1978, by any of the persons designated by subsection (a)(1)(C) of this section, otherwise than by will, is subject to termination under the following conditions:

(1) In the case of a grant executed by a person or persons other than the author, termination of the grant may be effected by the surviving person or persons who executed it. In the case of a grant executed by one or more of the authors of the work, termination of the grant may be effected, to the extent of a particular author's share in the ownership of the renewal copyright, by the author who executed it or, if such author is dead, by the person or persons who, under clause (2) of this subsection, own and are entitled to exercise a total of more than one-half of that author's termination interest.

(2) Where an author is dead, his or her termination interest is owned, and may be exercised, as follows:

(A) The widow or widower owns the author's entire termination interest unless there are any surviving children or grandchildren of the author, in which case the widow or widower owns one-half of the author's interest.

(B) The author's surviving children, and the surviving children of any dead child of the author, own the author's entire termination interest unless there is a widow or widower, in which case the ownership of one-half of the author's interest is divided among them.

(C) The rights of the author's children and grandchildren are in all cases divided among them and exercised on a per stirpes basis according to the number of such author's children represented; the share of the children of a dead child in a termination interest can be exercised only by the action of a majority of them.

(D) In the event that the author's widow or widower, children, and grandchildren are not living, the author's executor, administrator, personal representative, or trustee shall own the author's entire termination interest.

(3) Termination of the grant may be effected at any time during a period of five years beginning at the end of fifty-six years from the date copyright was originally secured, or beginning on January 1, 1978, whichever is later.

(4) The termination shall be effected by serving an advance notice in writing upon the grantee or the grantee's successor in title. In the case of a grant executed by a person or persons other than the author, the notice shall be signed by all of those entitled to terminate the grant under clause (1) of this subsection, or by their duly authorized agents. In the case of a grant executed by one or more of the authors of the work, the notice as to any one author's share shall be signed by that author or his or her duly authorized agent or, if that author is dead, by the number and proportion of the owners of his or her termination interest required under clauses (1) and (2) of this subsection, or by their duly authorized agents.

(A) The notice shall state the effective date of the termination, which shall fall within the five-year period specified by clause (3) of this subsection, or, in the case of a termination under subsection (d), within the five-year period specified by subsection (d)(2), and the notice shall be served not less than two or more than ten years before that date. A copy of the notice shall be recorded in the Copyright Office before the effective date of termination, as a condition to its taking effect.

(B) The notice shall comply, in form, content, and manner of service, with requirements that the Register of Copyrights shall prescribe by regulation.

(5) Termination of the grant may be effected notwithstanding any agreement to the contrary, including an agreement to make a will or to make any future grant.

(6) In the case of a grant executed by a person or persons other than the author, all rights under this title that were covered by the terminated grant revert, upon the effective date of termination, to all of those entitled to terminate the grant under clause (1) of this subsection. In the case of a grant executed by one or more of the authors of the work, all of a particular author's rights under this title that were covered by the terminated grant revert, upon the effective date of termination, to that author or, if that author is dead, to the persons owning his or her termination interest under clause (2) of this subsection, including those owners who did not join in signing the notice of termination under clause (4) of this subsection. In all cases the reversion of rights is subject to the following limitations:

(A) A derivative work prepared under authority of the grant before its termination may continue to be utilized under the terms of the grant after its termination, but this privilege does not extend to the preparation after the termination of other derivative works based upon the copyrighted work covered by the terminated grant.

(B) The future rights that will revert upon termination of the grant become vested on the date the notice of termination has been served as provided by clause (4) of this subsection.

(C) Where the author's rights revert to two or more persons under clause (2) of this subsection, they shall vest in those persons in the proportionate shares provided by that clause. In such a case, and subject to the provisions of subclause (D) of this clause, a further grant, or agreement to make a further grant, of a particular author's share with respect to any right covered by a terminated grant is valid only if it is signed by the same number and proportion of the owners, in whom the right has vested under this clause, as are required to terminate the grant under clause (2) of this subsection. Such further grant or agreement is effective with respect to all of the persons in whom the right it covers has vested under this subclause, including those who did not join in signing it. If any person dies after rights under a terminated grant have vested in him

or her, that person's legal representatives, legatees, or heirs at law represent him or her for purposes of this subclause.

(D) A further grant, or agreement to make a further grant, of any right covered by a terminated grant is valid only if it is made after the effective date of the termination. As an exception, however, an agreement for such a further grant may be made between the author or any of the persons provided by the first sentence of clause (6) of this subsection, or between the persons provided by subclause (C) of this clause, and the original grantee or such grantee's successor in title, after the notice of termination has been served as provided by clause (4) of this subsection.

(E) Termination of a grant under this subsection affects only those rights covered by the grant that arise under this title, and in no way affects rights arising under any other Federal, State, or foreign laws.

(F) Unless and until termination is effected under this subsection, the grant, if it does not provide otherwise, continues in effect for the remainder of the extended renewal term.

(d) Termination Rights Provided in Subsection (c) Which Have Expired on or Before the Effective Date of the Sonny Bono Copyright Term Extension Act.—In the case of any copyright other than a work made for hire, subsisting in its renewal term on the effective date of the Sonny Bono Copyright Term Extension Act for which the termination right provided in subsection (c) has expired by such date, where the author or owner of the termination right has not previously exercised such termination right, the exclusive or nonexclusive grant of a transfer or license of the renewal copyright or any right under it, executed before January 1, 1978, by any of the persons designated in subsection (a)(1)(C) of this section, other than by will, is subject to termination under the following conditions:

(1) The conditions specified in subsections (c)(1), (2), (4), (5), and (6) of this section apply to terminations of the last 20 years of copyright term as provided by the amendments made by the Sonny Bono Copyright Term Extension Act.

(2) Termination of the grant may be effected at any time during a period of 5 years beginning at the end of 75 years from the date copyright was originally secured.

(Pub. L. 94–553, title I, § 101, Oct. 19, 1976, 90 Stat. 2573; Pub. L. 102–307, title I, § 102(a), (d), June 26, 1992, 106 Stat. 264, 266; Pub. L. 105–80, § 12(a)(9), Nov. 13, 1997, 111 Stat. 1535; Pub. L. 105–298, title I, §§ 102(d)(1), 103, Oct. 27, 1998, 112 Stat. 2827, 2829; Pub. L. 107–273, div. C, title III, § 13210(10), Nov. 2, 2002, 116 Stat. 1910.)

Historical and Revision Notes

House Report No. 94–1476

The arguments in favor of lengthening the duration of copyright apply to subsisting as well as future copyrights. The bill's basic approach is to increase the present 56-year term to 75 years in the case of copyrights subsisting in both their first and their renewal terms.

Copyrights in Their First Term. Subsection (a) of section 304 reenacts and preserves the renewal provision, now in Section 24 of the statute [section 24 of former title 17], for all of the works presently in their first 28-year term. A great many of the present expectancies in these cases are the subject of existing contracts, and it would be unfair and immensely confusing to cut off or alter these interests. Renewal registration will be required during the 28th year of the copyright but the length of the renewal term will be increased from 28 to 47 years.

Although the bill preserves the language of the present renewal provision without any change in substance, the Committee intends that the reference to a "posthumous work" in this section has the meaning given to it in *Bartok v. Boosey & Hawkes, Inc.*, 523 F.2d 941 (2d Cir. 1975)—one as to which no copyright assignment or other contract for exploitation of the work has occurred during an author's lifetime, rather than one which is simply first published after the author's death.

Copyrights in Their Renewal Term. Renewed copyrights that are subsisting in their second term at any time during the period between December 31, 1976, and December 31, 1977, inclusive, would be extended under section 304(b) to run for a total of 75 years. This provision would add another 19 years to the duration of any renewed copyright whose second term started during the 28 years immediately preceding the effective date of the act (January 1, 1978). In addition, it would extend by varying lesser amounts the duration of renewal copyrights already extended under Public Laws 87–668, 89–142, 90–141, 90–416, 91–147, 91–555, 92–170, 92–566, and 93–573, all of which would otherwise expire on December 31, 1976. The subsection would also extend the duration of renewal copyrights whose second 28-year term is scheduled to expire during 1977. In none of these cases, however, would the total terms of copyright for the work be longer than 75 years.

Subsection (b) also covers the special situation of a subsisting first-term copyright that becomes eligible for renewal registration during the year before the act comes into effect. If a renewal registration is not made before the effective date [Jan. 1, 1978], the case is governed by the provisions of section 304(a) [subsec. (a) of this section]. If a renewal registration is made during the year before the new law takes effect, however, the copyright would be treated as if it were already subsisting in its second term and would be extended to the full period of 75 years without the need for further renewal.

Termination of Grants Covering Extended Term. An issue underlying the 19-year extension of renewal terms under both subsections (a) and (b) of section 304 [subsecs. (a) and (b) of this section] is whether, in a case where their rights have already been transferred, the author or the dependents of the author should be given a chance to benefit from the extended term. The arguments for granting rights of termination are even more persuasive under section 304 than they are under section 203; the extended term represents a completely new property right, and there are strong reasons for giving the author, who is the fundamental beneficiary of copyright under the Constitution, an opportunity to share in it.

Subsection (c) of section 304 is a close but not exact counterpart of section 203. In the case of either a first-term or renewal copyright already subsisting when the new statute becomes effective [Jan. 1, 1978], any grant of rights covering the renewal copyright in the work, executed before the effective date [Jan. 1, 1978], may be terminated under conditions and limitations similar to those provided in section 203. Except for transfers and licenses covering renewal copyrights already extended under Public Laws 87–668, 89–142, 90–141, 90–416, 91–147, 91–555, 92–170, 92–566, and 93–573, which would become subject to termination immediately upon the coming into effect of the revised law, the 5-year period during which termination could be made effective would start 56 years after copyright was originally secured.

The bill distinguishes between the persons who can terminate a grant under section 203 and those entitled to terminate a grant covering an extended term under section 304. Instead of being limited to transfers and licenses executed by the author, the right of termination under section 304(c) also extends to grants executed by those beneficiaries of the author who can claim renewal under the present law: his or her widow or widower, children, executors, or next of kin.

There is good reason for this difference. Under section 203, an author's widow or widower and children are given rights of termination if the author is dead, but these rights apply only to grants by the author, and any effort by a widow, widower, or child to transfer contingent future interests under a termination would be ineffective. In contrast, under the present renewal provisions, any statutory beneficiary of the author can make a valid transfer or license of future renewal rights, which is completely binding if the author is dead and the person who executed the grant turns out to be the proper renewal claimant. Because of this, a great many contingent transfers of future renewal rights have been obtained from widows, widowers, children, and next of kin, and a substantial number of these will be binding. After the present 28-year renewal period has ended, a statutory beneficiary who has signed a disadvantageous grant of this sort should have the opportunity to reclaim the extended term.

As explained above in connection with section 203, the bill adopts the principle that, where a transfer or license by the author is involved, termination may be effected by a per stirpes majority of those entitled to terminate, and this principle also applies to the ownership of rights under a termination and to the making of further grants of reverted rights. In general, this principle has also been adopted with respect to the termination of rights under an extended renewal copyright in section 304, but with several differences made necessary by the differences between the legal status of transfers and licenses made after the effective date of the new law [Jan. 1, 1978] (governed by section 203) and that of grants of renewal rights made earlier and governed by section 304(c). The following are the most important distinctions between the termination rights under the two sections:

1. Joint Authorship.—Under section 304, a grant of renewal rights executed by joint authors during the first term of copyright would be effective only as to those who were living at the time of renewal; where any of them are dead, their statutory beneficiaries are entitled to claim the renewal independently as a new estate. It would therefore be inappropriate to impose a requirement of majority action with respect to transfers executed by two or more joint authors.

2. Grants Not Executed by Author.—Section 304(c) adopts the majority principle underlying the amendments of section 203 [section 203 of this title] with respect to the termination rights of a dead author's widow or widower and children. There is much less reason, as a matter of policy, to apply this principle in the case of transfers and licenses of renewal rights executed under the present law by the author's widow, widower, children, executors, or next of kin, and the practical arguments against doing so are conclusive. It is not clear how the shares of a class of renewal beneficiaries are to be divided under the existing law, and greater difficulties would be presented if any attempt were made to apply the majority principle to further beneficiaries in cases where one or more of the renewal beneficiaries are dead. Therefore, where the grant was executed by a person or persons other than the author, termination can be effected only by the unanimous action of the survivors of those who executed it.

3. Further Grants.—The reason against adopting a principle of majority action with respect to the right to terminate grants by joint authors and grants not executed by the author apply equally with respect to the right to make further grants under section 304(c). The requirement for majority action in clause (6)(C) is therefore confined to cases where the rights under a grant by the author have reverted to his or her widow or widower, or children, or both. Where the extended term reverts to joint authors or to a class of renewal beneficiaries who have joined in executing a grant, their rights would be governed by the general rules of tenancy in common; each coowner would have an independent right to sell his share, or to use or license the work subject to an accounting.

Nothing contained in this section or elsewhere in this legislation is intended to extend the duration of any license, transfer, or assignment made for a period of less than fifty-six years. If, for example, an agreement provides an earlier termination date or lesser duration, or if it allows the author the right of cancelling or terminating the agreement under certain circumstances, the duration is governed by the agreement. Likewise, nothing in this section or legislation is intended to change the existing state of the law of contracts concerning the circumstances in which an author may terminate a license, transfer or assignment.

Section 304(c)(6)(E) provides that, unless and until termination is effected under this section, the grant, "if it does not provide otherwise," continues for the term of copyright. This section means that, if the agreement does not contain provisions specifying its term or duration, and the author has not terminated the agreement under this section, the agreement continues for the term of the copyright, subject to any right of termination under circumstances which may be specified therein. If, however, an agreement does contain provisions governing its duration—for example, a term of sixty years—and the author has not exercised his or her right of termination under the statute, the agreement will continue according to its terms—in this example, for only sixty years. The quoted language is not to be construed as requiring agreements to reserve the right of termination.

REFERENCES IN TEXT

The Sonny Bono Copyright Term Extension Act, referred to in subsecs. (b) and (d), is title I of Pub. L. 105–298, Oct. 27, 1998, 112 Stat. 2827. The effective date of the Act is the date of enactment of Pub. L. 105–298, which was approved Oct. 27, 1998. For complete classification of this Act to the Code, see Short Title of 1998 Amendments note set out under section 101 of this title and Tables.

AMENDMENTS

2002—Subsec. (c)(2)(A) to (C). Pub. L. 107–273, in subpars. (A) to (C), substituted "The" for "the" and, in subpars. (A) and (B), substituted period for semicolon at end.

1998—Subsec. (a)(1)(B), (C). Pub. L. 105–298, §102(d)(1)(A)(i), substituted "67" for "47" in concluding provisions.

Subsec. (a)(2)(A), (B). Pub. L. 105–298, §102(d)(1)(A)(ii), substituted "67" for "47" in introductory provisions.

Subsec. (a)(3)(A)(i), (B). Pub. L. 105–298, §102(d)(1)(A)(iii), substituted "67" for "47".

Subsec. (b). Pub. L. 105–298, §102(d)(1)(B), amended heading and text of subsec. (b) generally. Prior to amendment, text read as follows: "The duration of any copyright, the renewal term of which is subsisting at any time between December 31, 1976, and December 31, 1977, inclusive, or for which renewal registration is made between December 31, 1976, and December 31, 1977, inclusive, is extended to endure for a term of seventy-five years from the date copyright was originally secured."

Subsec. (c)(2). Pub. L. 105–298, §103(1), struck out "by his widow or her widower and his or her children or grandchildren" after "exercised," in introductory provisions.

Subsec. (c)(2)(D). Pub. L. 105–298, §103(2), added subpar. (D).

Subsec. (c)(4)(A). Pub. L. 105–298, §102(d)(1)(C), inserted "or, in the case of a termination under subsection (d), within the five-year period specified by subsection (d)(2)," before "and the notice".

Subsec. (d). Pub. L. 105–298, §102(d)(1)(D), added subsec. (d).

1997—Subsec. (c). Pub. L. 105–80 substituted "subsection (a)(1)(C)" for "the subsection (a)(1)(C)" in introductory provisions.

1992—Subsec. (a). Pub. L. 102–307, §102(a), amended subsec. (a) generally. Prior to amendment, subsec. (a) read as follows: "COPYRIGHTS IN THEIR FIRST TERM ON JANUARY 1, 1978.—Any copyright, the first term of which is subsisting on January 1, 1978, shall endure for twenty-eight years from the date it was originally secured: *Provided*, That in the case of any posthumous work or of any periodical, cyclopedic, or other composite work upon which the copyright was originally secured by the proprietor thereof, or of any work copyrighted by a corporate body (otherwise than as assignee or licensee of the individual author) or by an employer for whom such work is made for hire, the proprietor of such copyright shall be entitled to a renewal and extension of the copyright in such work for the further term of forty-seven years when application for such renewal and extension shall have been made to the Copyright Office and duly registered therein within one year prior to the expiration of the original term of copyright: *And provided further*, That in the case of any other copyrighted work, including a contribution by an individual author to a periodical or to a cyclopedic or other composite work, the author of such work, if still living, or the widow, widower, or children of the author, if the author be not living, or if such author, widow, widower, or children be not living, then the author's executors, or in the absence of a will, his or her next of kin shall be entitled to a renewal and extension of the copyright in such work for a further term of forty-seven years when application for such renewal and extension shall have been made to the Copyright Office and duly registered therein within one year prior to the expiration of the original term of copyright: *And provided further*, That in default of the registration of such application for renewal and extension, the copyright in any work shall terminate at the expiration of twenty-eight years from the date copyright was originally secured."

Subsec. (c). Pub. L. 102–307, §102(d), substituted "subsection (a)(1)(C)" for "second proviso of subsection (a)" in introductory provisions.

EFFECTIVE DATE OF 1992 AMENDMENT

Amendment by Pub. L. 102–307 effective June 26, 1992, but applicable only to copyrights secured between January 1, 1964, and December 31, 1977, and not affecting court proceedings pending on June 26, 1992, with copyrights secured before January 1, 1964, governed by section 304(a) of this title as in effect on the day before June 26, 1992, except each reference to forty-seven years in such provisions deemed to be 67 years, see section 102(g) of Pub. L. 102–307, as amended, set out as a note under section 101 of this title.

EFFECTIVE DATE

Subsec. (b) of this section effective Oct. 19, 1976, see section 102 of Pub. L. 94–553, set out as a note preceding section 101 of this title.

LEGAL EFFECT OF RENEWAL OF COPYRIGHT UNCHANGED

Section 102(c) of Pub. L. 102–307, as amended by Pub. L. 105–298, title I, §102(d)(2)(A), Oct. 27, 1998, 112 Stat. 2828, provided that: "The renewal and extension of a copyright for a further term of 67 years provided for under paragraphs (1) and (2) of section 304(a) of title 17, United States Code[,] shall have the same effect with respect to any grant, before the effective date of the Sonny Bono Copyright Term Extension Act [Oct. 27, 1998], of a transfer or license of the further term as did the renewal of a copyright before the effective date of the Sonny Bono Copyright Term Extension Act under the law in effect at the time of such grant."

AD INTERIM COPYRIGHTS SUBSISTING OR CAPABLE OF
BEING SECURED UNDER PREDECESSOR PROVISIONS

Section 107 of Pub. L. 94–553 provided that: "In the case of any work in which an ad interim copyright is subsisting or is capable of being secured on December 31, 1977, under section 22 of title 17 as it existed on that date, copyright protection is hereby extended to endure for the term or terms provided by section 304 of title 17 as amended by the first section of this Act [this section]."

COPYRIGHT GRANTED TO "SCIENCE AND HEALTH WITH KEY TO THE SCRIPTURES" FOR TERM OF 75 YEARS

Private Law 92–60, Dec. 15, 1971, 85 Stat. 857, provided: "That, any provision of law to the contrary notwithstanding, copyright is hereby granted to the trustees under the will of Mary Baker Eddy, their successors, and assigns, in the work 'Science and Health with Key to the Scriptures' (entitled also in some editions 'Science and Health' or 'Science and Health; with a Key to the Scriptures'), by Mary Baker Eddy, including all editions thereof in English and translation heretofore published, or hereafter published by or on behalf of said trustees, their successors or assigns, for a term of seventy-five years from the effective date of this Act [Dec. 15, 1971] or from the date of first publication, whichever is later. All copies of the protected work hereafter published are to bear notice of copyright, and all new editions hereafter published are to be registered in the Copyright Office, in accordance with the provisions of title 17 of the United States Code or any revision or recodification thereof. The copyright owner shall be entitled to all rights and remedies provided to copyright owners generally by law: *Provided, however*, That no liability shall attach under this Act for lawful uses made or acts done prior to the effective date of this Act in connection with said work, or in respect to the continuance for one year subsequent to such date of any business undertaking or enterprise lawfully undertaken prior to such date involving expenditure or contractual obligation in connection with the exploitation, production, reproduction or circulation of said work. This Act shall be effective upon enactment."

EXTENSION OF RENEWAL TERMS UNDER PRIOR LAW

Pub. L. 93–573, title I, § 104, Dec. 31, 1974, 88 Stat. 1873, provided that in any case in which the renewal term of a copyright subsisting in any work on Dec. 31, 1974, or the term thereof as extended by Public Law 87–668, by Public Law 89–142, by Public Law 90–141, by Public Law 90–416, by Public Law 91–417, by Public Law 91–555, by Public Law 92–170, or by Public Law 92–556 (or by all or certain of said laws) [set out below], would expire prior to Dec. 31, 1976, such term was continued until Dec. 31, 1976.

Pub. L. 92–566, Oct. 25, 1972, 86 Stat. 1181, provided that in any case in which the renewal term of a copyright subsisting in any work on Oct. 25, 1972, or the term thereof as extended by Public Law 87–668, by Public Law 89–142, by Public Law 90–141, by Public Law 90–416, by Public Law 91–147, by Public Law 91–555, or by Public Law 92–170 (or by all or certain of said laws) [set out below], would expire prior to Dec. 31, 1974, such term was continued until Dec. 31, 1974.

Pub. L. 92–170, Nov. 24, 1971, 85 Stat. 490, provided that in any case in which the renewal term of a copyright subsisting in any work on Nov. 24, 1971, or the term thereof as extended by Public Law 87–668, by Public Law 89–142, by Public Law 90–141, by Public Law 90–416, by Public Law 91–147, or by Public Law 91–555 (or by all or certain of said laws), would expire prior to Dec. 31, 1972, such term was continued until Dec. 31, 1972.

Pub. L. 91–555, Dec. 17, 1970, 84 Stat. 1441, provided that in any case in which the renewal term of a copyright subsisting in any work on Dec. 17, 1970, or the term thereof as extended by Public Law 87–668, by Public Law 89–442 [89–142], by Public Law 90–141, by Public Law 90–416, or by Public Law 91–147 (or by all or certain of said laws) [set out below], would expire prior to Dec. 31, 1971, such term was continued until Dec. 31, 1971.

Pub. L. 91–147, Dec. 16, 1969, 83 Stat. 360, provided that in any case in which the renewal term of a copyright subsisting in any work on Dec. 16, 1969, or the term

thereof as extended by Public Law 87–668, by Public Law 89–142, by Public Law 90–141, or by Public Law 90–416 (or by all or certain of said laws) [set out below], would expire prior to Dec. 31, 1970, such term was continued until Dec. 31, 1970.

Pub. L. 90–416, July 23, 1968, 82 Stat. 397, provided that in any case in which the renewal term of a copyright subsisting in any work on July 23, 1968, or the term thereof as extended by Public Law 87–668, by Public Law 89–142, or by Public Law 90–141 (or by all or certain of said laws) [set out below], would expire prior to Dec. 31, 1969, such term was continued until Dec. 31, 1969.

Pub. L. 90–141, Nov. 16, 1967, 81 Stat. 464, provided that in any case in which the renewal term of a copyright subsisting in any work on Nov. 16, 1967, or the term thereof as extended by Public Law 87–668, or by Public Law 89–142 (or by either or both of said laws) [set out below], would expire prior to Dec. 31, 1968, such term was continued until Dec. 31, 1968.

Pub. L. 89–142, Aug. 28, 1965, 79 Stat. 581, provided that in any case in which the renewal term of a copyright subsisting in any work on Aug. 28, 1965, or the term thereof as extended by Public Law 87–668 [set out below], would expire prior to Dec. 31, 1967, such term was continued until Dec. 31, 1967.

Pub. L. 87–668, Sept. 19, 1962, 76 Stat. 555, provided that in any case in which the renewal term of a copyright subsisting in any work on Sept. 19, 1962, would expire prior to Dec. 31, 1965, such term was continued until Dec. 31, 1965.

§ 305. Duration of copyright: Terminal date

All terms of copyright provided by sections 302 through 304 run to the end of the calendar year in which they would otherwise expire.

(Pub. L. 94–553, title I, § 101, Oct. 19, 1976, 90 Stat. 2576.)

HISTORICAL AND REVISION NOTES

HOUSE REPORT NO. 94–1476

Under section 305, which has its counterpart in the laws of most foreign countries, the term of copyright protection for a work extends through December 31 of the year in which the term would otherwise have expired. This will make the duration of copyright much easier to compute, since it will be enough to determine the year, rather than the exact date, of the event from which the term is based.

Section 305 applies only to "terms of copyright provided by sections 302 through 304," which are the sections dealing with duration of copyright. It therefore has no effect on the other time periods specified in the bill; and, since they do not involve "terms of copyright," the periods provided in section 304(c) with respect to termination of grants are not affected by section 305.

The terminal date section would change the duration of subsisting copyrights under section 304 by extending the total terms of protection under subsections (a) and (b) to the end of the 75th year from the date copyright was secured. A copyright subsisting in its first term on the effective date of the act [Jan. 1, 1978] would run through December 31 of the 28th year and would then expire unless renewed. Since all copyright terms under the bill expire on December 31, and since section 304(a) requires that renewal be made "within one year prior to the expiration of the original term of copyright," the period for renewal registration in all cases will run from December 31 through December 31.

A special situation arises with respect to subsisting copyrights whose first 28-year term expires during the first year after the act comes into effect. As already explained in connection with section 304(b), if a renewal registration for a copyright of this sort is made before the effective date [Jan. 1, 1978], the total term is extended to 75 years without the need for a further renewal registration. But, if renewal has not yet been made when the act becomes effective [Jan. 1, 1978], the period for renewal registration may in some cases be extended. If, as the bill provides, the act becomes effective on January 1, 1978, a copyright that was originally secured on September 1, 1950, could have been renewed by virtue of the present statute between September 1, 1977, and December 31, 1977; if not, it can still be renewed under section 304(a) of the new act between January 1, 1978, and December 31, 1978.

CHAPTER 4—COPYRIGHT NOTICE, DEPOSIT, AND REGISTRATION

AMENDMENTS

2008—Pub. L. 110–403, title I, §101(b)(2), Oct. 13, 2008, 122 Stat. 4258, inserted "civil" before "infringement" in item 411.

1988—Pub. L. 100–568, §§7(g), 9(b)(2), Oct. 31, 1988, 102 Stat. 2859, inserted in items 405 and 406 "on certain copies and phonorecords" and substituted in item 411 "Registration and infringement actions" for "Registration as prerequisite to infringement suit".

§ 401. Notice of copyright: Visually perceptible copies

(a) GENERAL PROVISIONS.—Whenever a work protected under this title is published in the United States or elsewhere by authority of the copyright owner, a notice of copyright as provided by this section may be placed on publicly distributed copies from which the work can be visually perceived, either directly or with the aid of a machine or device.

(b) FORM OF NOTICE.—If a notice appears on the copies, it shall consist of the following three elements:

(1) the symbol © (the letter C in a circle), or the word "Copyright", or the abbreviation "Copr."; and

(2) the year of first publication of the work; in the case of compilations, or derivative works incorporating previously published material, the year date of first publication of the compilation or derivative work is sufficient. The year date may be omitted where a pictorial, graphic, or sculptural work, with accompanying text matter, if any, is reproduced in or on greeting cards, postcards, stationery, jewelry, dolls, toys, or any useful articles; and

(3) the name of the owner of copyright in the work, or an abbreviation by which the name can be recognized, or a generally known alternative designation of the owner.

(c) POSITION OF NOTICE.—The notice shall be affixed to the copies in such manner and location as to give reasonable notice of the claim of copyright. The Register of Copyrights shall prescribe by regulation, as examples, specific methods of affixation and positions of the notice on various types of works that will satisfy this requirement, but these specifications shall not be considered exhaustive.

(d) EVIDENTIARY WEIGHT OF NOTICE.—If a notice of copyright in the form and position specified by this section appears on the published copy or copies to which a defendant in a copyright infringement suit had access, then no weight shall be given to such a defendant's interposition of a defense based on innocent infringement in mitigation of actual or statutory damages, except as provided in the last sentence of section 504(c)(2).

(Pub. L. 94–553, title I, §101, Oct. 19, 1976, 90 Stat. 2576; Pub. L. 100–568, §7(a), Oct. 31, 1988, 102 Stat. 2857.)

HISTORICAL AND REVISION NOTES

HOUSE REPORT NO. 94–1476

A requirement that the public be given formal notice of every work in which copyright is claimed was a part of the first U.S. copyright statute enacted in 1790, and since 1802 our copyright laws have always provided that the published copies of copyrighted works must bear a specified notice as a condition of protection. Under the present law the copyright notice serves four principal functions:

(1) It has the effect of placing in the public domain a substantial body of published material that no one is interested in copyrighting;

(2) It informs the public as to whether a particular work is copyrighted;

(3) It identifies the copyright owner; and

(4) It shows the date of publication.

Ranged against these values of a notice requirement are its burdens and unfairness to copyright owners. One of the strongest arguments for revision of the present statute has been the need to avoid the arbitrary and unjust forfeitures now resulting from unintentional or relatively unimportant omissions or errors in the copyright notice. It has been contended that the disadvantages of the notice requirement outweigh its values and that it should therefore be eliminated or substantially liberalized.

The fundamental principle underlying the notice provisions of the bill is that the copyright notice has real values which should be preserved, and that this should be done by inducing use of notice without causing outright forfeiture for errors or omissions. Subject to certain safeguards for innocent infringers, protection would not be lost by the complete omission of copyright notice from large numbers of copies or from a whole edition, if registration for the work is made before or within 5 years after publication. Errors in the name or date in the notice could be corrected without forfeiture of copyright.

Sections 401 and 402 set out the basic notice requirements of the bill, the former dealing with "copies from which the work can be visually perceived," and the latter covering "phonorecords" of a "sound recording." The notice requirements established by these parallel provisions apply only when copies or phonorecords of the work are "publicly distributed." No copyright notice would be required in connection with the public display of a copy by any means, including projectors, television, or cathode ray tubes connected with information storage and retrieval systems, or in connection with the public performance of a work by means of copies or phonorecords, whether in the presence of an audience or through television, radio, computer transmission, or any other process.

It should be noted that, under the definition of "publication" in section 101, there would no longer be any basis for holding, as a few court decisions have done in the past, that the public display of a work of art under some conditions (e.g., without restriction against its reproduction) would constitute publication of the work. And, as indicated above, the public display of a work of art would not require that a copyright notice be placed on the copy displayed.

Subsections (a) of both section 401 and section 402 require that a notice be used whenever the work "is published in the United States or elsewhere by authority of the copyright owner." The phrase "or elsewhere," which does not appear in the present law, makes the notice requirements applicable to copies or phonorecords distributed to the public anywhere in the world, regardless of where and when the work was first published. The values of notice are fully applicable to foreign editions of works copyrighted in the United States, especially with the increased flow of intellectual materials across national boundaries, and the gains in the use of notice on editions published abroad under the Universal Copyright Convention should not be wiped out. The consequences of omissions or mistakes with respect to the notice are far less serious under the bill than under the present law, and section 405(a) makes doubly clear that a copyright owner may guard himself against errors or omissions by others if he makes use of the prescribed notice an express condition of his publishing licenses.

Subsection (b) of section 401, which sets out the form of notice to appear on visually-perceptible copies, retains the basic elements of the notice under the present law: the word "Copyright", the abbreviation "Copr.", or the symbol "©"; the year of first publication; and the name of the copyright owner. The year of publication, which is still significant in computing the term and determining the status of a work, is required for all categories of copyrightable works. Clause (2) of subsection (b) makes clear that, in the case of a derivative work or compilation, it is not necessary to list the dates of publication of all preexisting material incorporated in the work; however, as noted below in connection with section 409, the application for registration covering a compilation or derivative work must identify "any preexisting work or works that it is based on or incorporates." Clause (3) establishes that a recognizable abbreviation or a generally known alternative designation may be used instead of the full name of the copyright owner.

By providing simply that the notice "shall be affixed to the copies in such manner and location as to give reasonable notice of the claim of copyright," subsection (c) follows the flexible approach of the Universal Copyright Convention. The further provision empowering the Register of Copyrights to set forth in regulations a list of examples of "specific methods of affixation and positions of the notice on various types of works that will satisfy this requirement" will offer substantial guidance and avoid a good deal of uncertainty. A notice placed or affixed in accordance with the regulations would clearly meet the requirements but, since the Register's specifications are not to "be considered exhaustive," a notice placed or affixed in some other way might also comply with the law if it were found to "give reasonable notice" of the copyright claim.

AMENDMENTS

1988—Subsec. (a). Pub. L. 100–568, § 7(a)(1), (2), substituted "General provisions" for "General requirement" in heading, and "may be placed on" for "shall be placed on all" in text.

Subsec. (b). Pub. L. 100–568, § 7(a)(3), substituted "If a notice appears on the copies, it" for "The notice appearing on the copies".

Subsec. (d). Pub. L. 100–568, § 7(a)(4), added subsec. (d).

EFFECTIVE DATE OF 1988 AMENDMENT

Amendment by Pub. L. 100–568 effective Mar. 1, 1989, with any cause of action arising under this title before such date being governed by provisions in effect when cause of action arose, see section 13 of Pub. L. 100–568, set out as a note under section 101 of this title.

COMPLIANCE WITH PREDECESSOR NOTICE PROVISIONS; COPIES DISTRIBUTED AFTER DEC. 31, 1977

Section 108 of Pub. L. 94–553 provided that: "The notice provisions of sections 401 through 403 of title 17 as amended by the first section of this Act [sections 401 through 403 of this title] apply to all copies or phonorecords publicly distributed on or after January 1, 1978. However, in the case of a work published before January 1, 1978, compliance with the notice provisions of title 17 either as it existed on December 31, 1977, or as amended by the first section of this Act, is adequate with respect to copies publicly distributed after December 31, 1977."

§ 402. Notice of copyright: Phonorecords of sound recordings

(a) GENERAL PROVISIONS.—Whenever a sound recording protected under this title is published in the United States or elsewhere by authority of the copyright owner, a notice of copyright as provided by this section may be placed on publicly distributed phonorecords of the sound recording.

(b) FORM OF NOTICE.—If a notice appears on the phonorecords, it shall consist of the following three elements:

(1) the symbol Ⓟ (the letter P in a circle); and

(2) the year of first publication of the sound recording; and

(3) the name of the owner of copyright in the sound recording, or an abbreviation by which the name can be recognized, or a generally known alternative designation of the owner; if the producer of the sound recording is named on the phonorecord labels or containers, and if no other name appears in conjunction with the notice, the producer's name shall be considered a part of the notice.

(c) POSITION OF NOTICE.—The notice shall be placed on the surface of the phonorecord, or on the phonorecord label or container, in such manner and location as to give reasonable notice of the claim of copyright.

(d) EVIDENTIARY WEIGHT OF NOTICE.—If a notice of copyright in the form and position specified by this section appears on the published phonorecord or phonorecords to which a defendant in a copyright infringement suit had access, then no weight shall be given to such a defendant's interposition of a defense based on innocent infringement in mitigation of actual or statutory damages, except as provided in the last sentence of section 504(c)(2).

(Pub. L. 94–553, title I, § 101, Oct. 19, 1976, 90 Stat. 2577; Pub. L. 100–568, § 7(b), Oct. 31, 1988, 102 Stat. 2857.)

HISTORICAL AND REVISION NOTES

HOUSE REPORT NO. 94-1476

A special notice requirement, applicable only to the subject matter of sound recordings, is established by section 402. Since the bill protects sound recordings as separate works, independent of protection for any literary or musical works embodied in them, there would be a likelihood of confusion if the same notice requirements applied to sound recordings and to the works they incorporate. Like the present law, therefore, section 402 thus sets forth requirements for a notice to appear on the "phonorecords" of "sound recordings" that are different from the notice requirements established by section 401 for the "copies" of all other types of copyrightable works. Since "phonorecords" are not "copies," there is no need to place a section 401 notice on "phonorecords" to protect the literary or musical works embodied in the records.

In general, the form of the notice specified by section 402(b) consists of the symbol "Ⓟ"; the year of first publication of the sound recording; and the name of the copyright owner or an admissible variant. Where the record producer's name appears on the record label, album, sleeve, jacket, or other container, it will be considered a part of the notice if no other name appears in conjunction with it. Under subsection (c), the notice for a copyrighted sound recording may be affixed to the surface, label, or container of the phonorecord "in such manner and location as to give reasonable notice of the claim of copyright."

There are at least three reasons for prescribing use of the symbol "Ⓟ" rather than "©" in the notice to appear on phonorecords of sound recordings. Aside from the need to avoid confusion between claims to copyright in the sound recording and in the musical or literary work embodied in it, there is also a necessity for distinguishing between copyright claims in the sound recording and in the printed text or art work appearing on the record label, album cover, liner notes, et cetera. The symbol "©" has also been adopted as the international symbol for the protection of sound recordings by the "Phonograms Convention" (the Convention for the Protection of Producers of Phonograms Against Unauthorized Duplication of Their Phonograms, done at Geneva October 29, 1971), to which the United States is a party.

1988—Subsec. (a). Pub. L. 100–568, § 7(b)(1), (2), substituted "General provisions" for "General requirement" in heading, and "may be placed on" for "shall be placed on all" in text.

Subsec. (b). Pub. L. 100–568, § 7(b)(3), substituted "If a notice appears on the phonorecords, it" for "The notice appearing on the phonorecords".

Subsec. (d). Pub. L. 100–568, § 7(b)(4), added subsec. (d).

Amendment by Pub. L. 100–568 effective Mar. 1, 1989, with any cause of action arising under this title before such date being governed by provisions in effect when cause of action arose, see section 13 of Pub. L. 100–568, set out as a note under section 101 of this title.

§ 403. Notice of copyright: Publications incorporating United States Government works

Sections 401(d) and 402(d) shall not apply to a work published in copies or phonorecords consisting predominantly of one or more works of the United States Government unless the notice of copyright appearing on the published copies or phonorecords to which a defendant in the copyright infringement suit had access includes a statement identifying, either affirmatively or negatively, those portions of the copies or phonorecords embodying any work or works protected under this title.

(Pub. L. 94–553, title I, § 101, Oct. 19, 1976, 90 Stat. 2577; Pub. L. 100–568, § 7(c), Oct. 31, 1988, 102 Stat. 2858.)

Section 403 is aimed at a publishing practice that, while technically justified under the present law, has been the object of considerable criticism. In cases where a Government work is published or republished commercially, it has frequently been the practice to add some "new matter" in the form of an introduction, editing, illustrations, etc., and to include a general copyright notice in the name of the commercial publisher. This in no way suggests to the public that the bulk of the work is uncopyrightable and therefore free for use.

To make the notice meaningful rather than misleading, section 403 requires that, when the copies or phonorecords consist "preponderantly of one or more works of the United States Government," the copyright notice (if any) identify those parts of the work in which copyright is claimed. A failure to meet this requirement would be treated as an omission of the notice, subject to the provisions of section 405.

1988—Pub. L. 100–568 amended section generally. Prior to amendment, section read as follows: "Whenever a work is published in copies or phonorecords consisting preponderantly of one or more works of the United States Government, the notice of copyright provided by sections 401 or 402 shall also include a statement identifying, either affirmatively or negatively, those portions of the copies or phonorecords embodying any work or works protected under this title."

Amendment by Pub. L. 100–568 effective Mar. 1, 1989, with any cause of action arising under this title before such date being governed by provisions in effect when cause of action arose, see section 13 of Pub. L. 100–568, set out as a note under section 101 of this title.

§ 404. Notice of copyright: Contributions to collective works

(a) A separate contribution to a collective work may bear its own notice of copyright, as provided by sections 401 through 403. However, a single notice applicable to the collective work as a whole is sufficient to invoke the provisions of section 401(d) or 402(d), as applicable with respect to the separate contributions it contains (not including advertisements inserted on behalf of persons other than the owner of copyright in the collective work), regardless of the ownership of copyright in the contributions and whether or not they have been previously published.

(b) With respect to copies and phonorecords publicly distributed by authority of the copyright owner before the effective date of the Berne Convention Implementation Act of 1988, where the person named in a single notice applicable to a collective work as a whole is not the owner of copyright in a separate contribution that does not bear its own notice, the case is governed by the provisions of section 406(a).

(Pub. L. 94–553, title I, § 101, Oct. 19, 1976, 90 Stat. 2577; Pub. L. 100–568, § 7(d), Oct. 31, 1988, 102 Stat. 2858.)

In conjunction with the provisions of section 201(c), section 404 deals with a troublesome problem under the present law: the notice requirements applicable to contributions published in periodicals and other collective works. The basic approach of the section is threefold:

(1) To permit but not require a separate contribution to bear its own notice;

(2) To make a single notice, covering the collective work as a whole, sufficient to satisfy the notice re-

quirement for the separate contributions it contains, even if they have been previously published or their ownership is different; and

(3) To protect the interests of an innocent infringer of copyright in a contribution that does not bear its own notice, who has dealt in good faith with the person named in the notice covering the collective work as a whole.

As a general rule, under this section, the rights in an individual contribution to a collective work would not be affected by the lack of a separate copyright notice, as long as the collective work as a whole bears a notice. One exception to this rule would apply to "advertisements inserted on behalf of persons other than the owner of copyright in the collective work." Collective works, notably newspapers and magazines, are major advertising media, and it is common for the same advertisement to be published in a number of different periodicals. The general copyright notice in a particular issue would not ordinarily protect the advertisements inserted in it, and relatively little advertising matter today is published with a separate copyright notice. The exception in section 404(a), under which separate notices would be required for most advertisements published in collective works, would impose no undue burdens on copyright owners and is justified by the special circumstances.

Under section 404(b) a separate contribution that does not bear its own notice, and that is published in a collective work with a general notice containing the name of someone other than the copyright owner of the contribution, is treated as if it has been published with the wrong name in the notice. The case is governed by section 406(a), which means that an innocent infringer who in good faith took a license from the person named in the general notice would be shielded from liability to some extent.

REFERENCES IN TEXT

The effective date of the Berne Convention Implementation Act of 1988, referred to in subsec. (b), is Mar. 1, 1989, see section 13 of Pub. L. 100–568, set out as an Effective Date of 1988 Amendment note under section 101 of this title.

AMENDMENTS

1988—Subsec. (a). Pub. L. 100–568, § 7(d)(1), substituted "to invoke the provisions of section 401(d) or 402(d), as applicable" for "to satisfy the requirements of sections 401 through 403".

Subsec. (b). Pub. L. 100–568, § 7(d)(2), substituted "With respect to copies and phonorecords publicly distributed by authority of the copyright owner before the effective date of the Berne Convention Implementation Act of 1988, where" for "Where".

EFFECTIVE DATE OF 1988 AMENDMENT

Amendment by Pub. L. 100–568 effective Mar. 1, 1989, with any cause of action arising under this title before such date being governed by provisions in effect when cause of action arose, see section 13 of Pub. L. 100–568, set out as a note under section 101 of this title.

§ 405. Notice of copyright: Omission of notice on certain copies and phonorecords

(a) EFFECT OF OMISSION ON COPYRIGHT.—With respect to copies and phonorecords publicly distributed by authority of the copyright owner before the effective date of the Berne Convention Implementation Act of 1988, the omission of the copyright notice described in sections 401 through 403 from copies or phonorecords publicly distributed by authority of the copyright owner does not invalidate the copyright in a work if—

(1) the notice has been omitted from no more than a relatively small number of copies or phonorecords distributed to the public; or

(2) registration for the work has been made before or is made within five years after the publication without notice, and a reasonable effort is made to add notice to all copies or phonorecords that are distributed to the public in the United States after the omission has been discovered; or

(3) the notice has been omitted in violation of an express requirement in writing that, as a condition of the copyright owner's authorization of the public distribution of copies or phonorecords, they bear the prescribed notice.

(b) EFFECT OF OMISSION ON INNOCENT INFRINGERS.—Any person who innocently infringes a copyright, in reliance upon an authorized copy or phonorecord from which the copyright notice has been omitted and which was publicly distributed by authority of the copyright owner before the effective date of the Berne Convention Implementation Act of 1988, incurs no liability for actual or statutory damages under section 504 for any infringing acts committed before receiving actual notice that registration for the work has been made under section 408, if such person proves that he or she was misled by the omission of notice. In a suit for infringement in such a case the court may allow or disallow recovery of any of the infringer's profits attributable to the infringement, and may enjoin the continuation of the infringing undertaking or may require, as a condition for permitting the continuation of the infringing undertaking, that the infringer pay the copyright owner a reasonable license fee in an amount and on terms fixed by the court.

(c) REMOVAL OF NOTICE.—Protection under this title is not affected by the removal, destruction, or obliteration of the notice, without the authorization of the copyright owner, from any publicly distributed copies or phonorecords.

(Pub. L. 94–553, title I, § 101, Oct. 19, 1976, 90 Stat. 2578; Pub. L. 100–568, § 7(e), Oct. 31, 1988, 102 Stat. 2858; Pub. L. 105–80, § 12(a)(10), Nov. 13, 1997, 111 Stat. 1535.)

HISTORICAL AND REVISION NOTES

HOUSE REPORT NO. 94–1476

Effect of Omission on Copyright Protection. The provisions of section 405(a) make clear that the notice requirements of sections 401, 402, and 403 are not absolute and that, unlike the law now in effect, the outright omission of a copyright notice does not automatically forfeit protection and throw the work into the public domain. This not only represents a major change in the theoretical framework of American copyright law, but it also seems certain to have immediate practical consequences in a great many individual cases. Under the proposed law a work published without any copyright notice will still be subject to statutory protection for at least 5 years, whether the omission was partial or total, unintentional or deliberate.

Under the general scheme of the bill, statutory copyright protection is secured automatically when a work is created, and is not lost when the work is published, even if the copyright notice is omitted entirely. Subsection (a) of section 405 provides that omission of notice, whether intentional or unintentional, does not invalidate the copyright if either of two conditions is met:

(1) if "no more than a relatively small number" of copies or phonorecords have been publicly distributed without notice; or

(2) if registration for the work has already been made, or is made within 5 years after the publication without notice, and a reasonable effort is made to add notice to copies or phonorecords publicly distributed in the United States after the omission is discovered.

Thus, if notice is omitted from more than a "relatively small number" of copies or phonorecords, copyright is not lost immediately, but the work will go into the public domain if no effort is made to correct the error or if the work is not registered within 5 years.

Section 405(a) takes a middle-ground approach in an effort to encourage use of a copyright notice without causing unfair and unjustifiable forfeitures on technical grounds. Clause (1) provides that, as long as the omission is from "no more than a relatively small number of copies or phonorecords," there is no effect upon the copyright owner's rights except in the case of an innocent infringement covered by section 405(b); there is no need for registration or for efforts to correct the error if this clause is applicable. The phrase "relatively small number" is intended to be less restrictive than the phrase "a particular copy or copies" now in section 21 of the present law [section 21 of former title 21].

Under clause (2) of subsection (a), the first condition for curing an omission from a larger number of copies is that registration be made before the end of 5 years from the defective publication. This registration may have been made before the omission took place or before the work had been published in any form and, since the reasons for the omission have no bearing on the validity of copyright, there would be no need for the application to refer to them. Some time limit for registration is essential and the 5-year period is reasonable and consistent with the period provided in section 410(c).

The second condition established by clause (2) is that the copyright owner make a "reasonable effort," after discovering his error, to add the notice to copies or phonorecords distributed thereafter. This condition is specifically limited to copies or phonorecords publicly distributed in the United States, since it would be burdensome and impractical to require an American copyright owner to police the activities of foreign licensees in this situation.

The basic notice requirements set forth in sections 401(a) and 402(a) are limited to cases where a work is published "by authority of the copyright owner" and, in prescribing the effect of omission of notice, section 405(a) refers only to omission "from copies or phonorecords publicly distributed by authority of the copyright owner." The intention behind this language is that, where the copyright owner authorized publication of the work, the notice requirements would not be met if copies or phonorecords are publicly distributed without a notice, even if he expected a notice to be used. However, if the copyright owner authorized publication only on the express condition that all copies or phonorecords bear a prescribed notice, the provisions of section 401 or 402 and of section 405 would not apply since the publication itself would not be authorized. This principle is stated directly in section 405(a)(3).

Effect of Omission on Innocent Infringers. In addition to the possibility that copyright protection will be forfeited under section 405(a)(2) if the notice is omitted, a second major inducement to use of the notice is found in subsection (b) of section 405. That provision, which limits the rights of a copyright owner against innocent infringers under certain circumstances, would be applicable whether the notice has been omitted from a large number or from a "relatively small number" of copies. The general postulates underlying the provision are that a person acting in good faith and with no reason to think otherwise should ordinarily be able to assume that a work is in the public domain if there is no notice on an authorized copy or phonorecord and that, if he relies on this assumption, he should be shielded from unreasonable liability.

Under section 405(b) an innocent infringer who acts "in reliance upon an authorized copy or phonorecord from which the copyright notice has been omitted", and who proves that he was misled by the omission, is shielded from liability for actual or statutory damages with respect to "any infringing acts committed before receiving actual notice" of registration. Thus, where the infringement is completed before actual notice has been served—as would be the usual case with respect to relatively minor infringements by teachers, librarians, journalists, and the like—liability, if any, would be limited to the profits the infringer realized from the act of infringement. On the other hand, where the infringing enterprise is one running over a period of time, the copyright owner would be able to seek an injunction against continuation of the infringement, and to obtain full monetary recovery for all infringing acts committed after he had served notice of registration. Persons who undertake major enterprises of this sort should check the Copyright Office registration records before starting, even where copies have been published without notice.

The purpose of the second sentence of subsection (b) is to give the courts broad discretion to balance the equities within the framework of section 405 [this section]. Where an infringer made profits from infringing acts committed innocently before receiving notice from the copyright owner, the court may allow or withhold their recovery in light of the circumstances. The court may enjoin an infringement or may permit its continuation on condition that the copyright owner be paid a reasonable license fee.

Removal of Notice by Others. Subsection (c) of section 405 involves the situation arising when, following an authorized publication with notice, someone further down the chain of commerce removes, destroys, or obliterates the notice. The courts dealing with this problem under the present law, especially in connection with copyright notices on the selvage of textile fabrics, have generally upheld the validity of a notice that was securely attached to the copies when they left the control of the copyright owner, even though removal of the notice at some later stage was likely. This conclusion is incorporated in subsection (c).

REFERENCES IN TEXT

The effective date of the Berne Convention Implementation Act of 1988, referred to in subsecs. (a) and (b), is Mar. 1, 1989, see section 13 of Pub. L. 100–568, set out as an Effective Date of 1988 Amendment note under section 101 of this title.

AMENDMENTS

1997—Subsec. (b). Pub. L. 105–80 substituted "condition for permitting the continuation" for "condition or permitting the continuation".

1988—Pub. L. 100–568, §7(e)(3), substituted "notice on certain copies and phonorecords" for "notice" in section catchline.

Subsec. (a). Pub. L. 100–568, §7(e)(1), substituted "With respect to copies and phonorecords publicly distributed by authority of the copyright owner before the effective date of the Berne Convention Implementation Act of 1988, the omission of the copyright notice described in" for "The omission of the copyright notice prescribed by".

Subsec. (b). Pub. L. 100–568, §7(e)(2), substituted "omitted and which was publicly distributed by authority of the copyright owner before the effective date of the Berne Convention Implementation Act of 1988," for "omitted,".

EFFECTIVE DATE OF 1988 AMENDMENT

Amendment by Pub. L. 100–568 effective Mar. 1, 1989, with any cause of action arising under this title before such date being governed by provisions in effect when cause of action arose, see section 13 of Pub. L. 100–568, set out as a note under section 101 of this title.

§ 406. Notice of copyright: Error in name or date on certain copies and phonorecords

(a) ERROR IN NAME.—With respect to copies and phonorecords publicly distributed by authority of the copyright owner before the effective date of the Berne Convention Implementation Act of 1988, where the person named in the copyright notice on copies or phonorecords publicly distributed by authority of the copyright owner is not the owner of copyright, the validity and ownership of the copyright are not affected. In such a case, however, any person who innocently begins an undertaking that infringes the copyright has a complete defense to any action for such infringement if such person proves that he or she was misled by the notice and began the undertaking in good faith under a purported transfer or license from the person named therein, unless before the undertaking was begun—

(1) registration for the work had been made in the name of the owner of copyright; or

(2) a document executed by the person named in the notice and showing the ownership of the copyright had been recorded.

The person named in the notice is liable to account to the copyright owner for all receipts from transfers or licenses purportedly made under the copyright by the person named in the notice.

(b) ERROR IN DATE.—When the year date in the notice on copies or phonorecords distributed before the effective date of the Berne Convention Implementation Act of 1988 by authority of the copyright owner is earlier than the year in which publication first occurred, any period computed from the year of first publication under section 302 is to be computed from the year in the notice. Where the year date is more than one year later than the year in which publication first occurred, the work is considered to have been published without any notice and is governed by the provisions of section 405.

(c) OMISSION OF NAME OR DATE.—Where copies or phonorecords publicly distributed before the effective date of the Berne Convention Implementation Act of 1988 by authority of the copyright owner contain no name or no date that could reasonably be considered a part of the notice, the work is considered to have been published without any notice and is governed by the provisions of section 405 as in effect on the day before the effective date of the Berne Convention Implementation Act of 1988.

(Pub. L. 94–553, title I, § 101, Oct. 19, 1976, 90 Stat. 2578; Pub. L. 100–568, § 7(f), Oct. 31, 1988, 102 Stat. 2858.)

HISTORICAL AND REVISION NOTES

HOUSE REPORT NO. 94–1476

In addition to cases where notice has been omitted entirely, it is common under the present law for a copyright notice to be fatally defective because the name or date has been omitted or wrongly stated. Section 406 is intended to avoid technical forfeitures in these cases, while at the same time inducing use of the correct name and date and protecting users who rely on erroneous information.

Error in Name. Section 406(a) begins with a statement that the use of the wrong name in the notice will not affect the validity or ownership of the copyright, and then deals with situations where someone acting innocently and in good faith infringes a copyright by relying on a purported transfer or license from the person erroneously named in the notice. In such a case the innocent infringer is given a complete defense unless a search of the Copyright Office records would have shown that the owner was someone other than the person named in the notice. Use of the wrong name in the notice is no defense if, at the time infringement was begun, registration had been made in the name of the true owner, or if "a document executed by the person named in the notice and showing the ownership of the copyright had been recorded."

The situation dealt with in section 406(a) presupposes a contractual relation between the copyright owner and the person named in the notice. The copies or phonorecords bearing the defective notice have been "distributed by authority of the copyright owner" and, unless the publication can be considered unauthorized because of breach of an express condition in the contract or other reasons, the owner must be presumed to have acquiesced in the use of the wrong name. If the person named in the notice grants a license for use of the work in good faith or under a misapprehension, that person should not be liable as a copyright infringer, but the last sentence of section 406(a) would make the person named in the notice liable to account to the copyright owner for "all receipts, from transfers or licenses purportedly made under the copyright" by that person.

Error in Date. The familiar problems of antedated and postdated notices are dealt with in subsection (b) of section 406. In the case of an antedated notice, where the year in the notice is earlier than the year of first publication, the bill adopts the established judicial principle that any statutory term measured from the year of publication will be computed from the year given in the notice. This provision would apply not only to the copyright terms of anonymous works, pseudonymous works, and works made for hire under section 302(c), but also to the presumptive periods set forth in section 302(e).

As for postdated notices, subsection (b) provides that, where the year in the notice is more than one year later than the year of first publication the case is treated as if the notice had been omitted and is governed by section 405. Notices postdated by one year are quite common on works published near the end of a year, and it would be unnecessarily strict to equate cases of that sort with works published without notice of any sort.

Omission of Name or Date. Section 406(c) provides that, if the copies or phonorecords "contain no name or no date that could reasonably be considered a part of the notice," the result is the same as if the notice had been omitted entirely, and section 405 controls. Unlike the present law, the bill contains no provision requiring the elements of the copyright notice to "accompany" each other, and under section 406(c) a name or date that could reasonably be read with the other elements may satisfy the requirements even if somewhat separated from them. Direct contiguity or juxtaposition of the elements is no longer necessary; but if the elements are too widely separated for their relation to be apparent, or if uncertainty is created by the presence of other names or dates, the case would have to be treated as if the name or date, and hence the notice itself had been omitted altogether.

REFERENCES IN TEXT

The effective date of the Berne Convention Implementation Act of 1988, referred to in text, is Mar. 1, 1989, see section 13 of Pub. L. 100–568, set out as an Effective Date of 1988 Amendment note under section 101 of this title.

AMENDMENTS

1988—Pub. L. 100–568, § 7(f)(4), substituted "date on certain copies and phonorecords" for "date" in section catchline.

Subsec. (a). Pub. L. 100–568, § 7(f)(1), substituted "With respect to copies and phonorecords publicly distributed by authority of the copyright owner before the effective date of the Berne Convention Implementation Act of 1988, where" for "Where".

Subsec. (b). Pub. L. 100–568, § 7(f)(2), inserted "before the effective date of the Berne Convention Implementation Act of 1988" after "distributed".

Subsec. (c). Pub. L. 100–568, § 7(f)(3), inserted "before the effective date of the Berne Convention Implementation Act of 1988" after "publicly distributed" and "as in effect on the day before the effective date of the Berne Convention Implementation Act of 1988" after "section 405".

EFFECTIVE DATE OF 1988 AMENDMENT

Amendment by Pub. L. 100–568 effective Mar. 1, 1989, with any cause of action arising under this title before such date being governed by provisions in effect when cause of action arose, see section 13 of Pub. L. 100–568, set out as a note under section 101 of this title.

§ 407. Deposit of copies or phonorecords for Library of Congress

(a) Except as provided by subsection (c), and subject to the provisions of subsection (e), the owner of copyright or of the exclusive right of publication in a work published in the United States shall deposit, within three months after the date of such publication—

(1) two complete copies of the best edition; or

(2) if the work is a sound recording, two complete phonorecords of the best edition, together with any printed or other visually perceptible material published with such phonorecords.

Neither the deposit requirements of this subsection nor the acquisition provisions of subsection (e) are conditions of copyright protection.

(b) The required copies or phonorecords shall be deposited in the Copyright Office for the use or disposition of the Library of Congress. The Register of Copyrights shall, when requested by the depositor and upon payment of the fee prescribed by section 708, issue a receipt for the deposit.

(c) The Register of Copyrights may by regulation exempt any categories of material from the deposit requirements of this section, or require deposit of only one copy or phonorecord with respect to any categories. Such regulations shall provide either for complete exemption from the deposit requirements of this section, or for alternative forms of deposit aimed at providing a satisfactory archival record of a work without imposing practical or financial hardships on the depositor, where the individual author is the owner of copyright in a pictorial, graphic, or sculptural work and (i) less than five copies of the work have been published, or (ii) the work has been published in a limited edition consisting of numbered copies, the monetary value of which would make the mandatory deposit of two copies of the best edition of the work burdensome, unfair, or unreasonable.

(d) At any time after publication of a work as provided by subsection (a), the Register of Copyrights may make written demand for the required deposit on any of the persons obligated to make the deposit under subsection (a). Unless deposit is made within three months after the demand is received, the person or persons on whom the demand was made are liable—

(1) to a fine of not more than $250 for each work; and

(2) to pay into a specially designated fund in the Library of Congress the total retail price of the copies or phonorecords demanded, or, if no retail price has been fixed, the reasonable cost to the Library of Congress of acquiring them; and

(3) to pay a fine of $2,500, in addition to any fine or liability imposed under clauses (1) and (2), if such person willfully or repeatedly fails or refuses to comply with such a demand.

(e) With respect to transmission programs that have been fixed and transmitted to the public in the United States but have not been published, the Register of Copyrights shall, after consulting with the Librarian of Congress and other interested organizations and officials, establish regulations governing the acquisition, through deposit or otherwise, of copies or phonorecords of such programs for the collections of the Library of Congress.

(1) The Librarian of Congress shall be permitted, under the standards and conditions set forth in such regulations, to make a fixation of a transmission program directly from a transmission to the public, and to reproduce one copy or phonorecord from such fixation for archival purposes.

(2) Such regulations shall also provide standards and procedures by which the Register of Copyrights may make written demand, upon the owner of the right of transmission in the United States, for the deposit of a copy or phonorecord of a specific transmission program. Such deposit may, at the option of the owner of the right of transmission in the United States, be accomplished by gift, by loan for purposes of reproduction, or by sale at a price not to exceed the cost of reproducing and supplying the copy or phonorecord. The regulations established under this clause shall provide reasonable periods of not less than three months for compliance with a demand, and shall allow for extensions of such periods and adjustments in the scope of the demand or the methods for fulfilling it, as reasonably warranted by the circumstances. Willful failure or refusal to comply with the conditions prescribed by such regulations shall subject the owner of the right of transmission in the United States to liability for an amount, not to exceed the cost of reproducing and supplying the copy or phonorecord in question, to be paid into a specially designated fund in the Library of Congress.

(3) Nothing in this subsection shall be construed to require the making or retention, for purposes of deposit, of any copy or phonorecord of an unpublished transmission program, the transmission of which occurs before the receipt of a specific written demand as provided by clause (2).

(4) No activity undertaken in compliance with regulations prescribed under clauses (1) or (2) of this subsection shall result in liability if intended solely to assist in the acquisition of copies or phonorecords under this subsection.

(Pub. L. 94–553, title I, § 101, Oct. 19, 1976, 90 Stat. 2579; Pub. L. 100–568, § 8, Oct. 31, 1988, 102 Stat. 2859; Pub. L. 105–80, § 12(a)(11), Nov. 13, 1997, 111 Stat. 1535.)

HISTORICAL AND REVISION NOTES

HOUSE REPORT NO. 94–1476

The provisions of sections 407 through 411 of the bill mark another departure from the present law. Under the 1909 statute, deposit of copies for the collections of the Library of Congress and deposit of copies for purposes of copyright registration have been treated as the same thing. The bill's basic approach is to regard deposit and registration as separate though closely related: deposit of copies or phonorecords for the Library of Congress is mandatory, but exceptions can be made for material the Library neither needs nor wants; copyright registration is not generally mandatory, but is a condition of certain remedies for copyright infringement. Deposit for the Library of Congress can be, and in the bulk of cases undoubtedly will be, combined with copyright registration.

The basic requirement of the deposit provision, section 407, is that within 3 months after a work has been published with notice of copyright in the United States, the "owner of copyright or of the exclusive right of publication" must deposit two copies or phonorecords of the work in the Copyright Office. The Register of Copyrights is authorized to exempt any category of material from the deposit requirements. Where the category is not exempted and deposit is not made, the Register may demand it; failure to comply would be penalized by a fine.

Under the present law deposits for the Library of Congress must be combined with copyright registration, and failure to comply with a formal demand for deposit and registration results in complete loss of copyright. Under section 407 of the bill, the deposit requirements can be satisfied without ever making registration, and subsection (a) makes clear that deposit "is not a condition of copyright protection." A realistic fine, coupled with the increased inducements for voluntary registration and deposit under other sections of the bill, seems likely to produce a more effective deposit system than the present one. The bill's approach will also avoid the danger that, under a divisible copyright, one copyright owner's rights could be destroyed by another owner's failure to deposit.

Although the basic deposit requirements are limited to works "published with notice of copyright in the United States," they would become applicable as soon as a work first published abroad is published in this country through the distribution of copies or phonorecords that are either imported or are part of an American edition. With respect to all types or works other than sound recordings, the basic obligation is to deposit "two complete copies of the best edition"; the term "best edition," as defined in section 101, makes clear that the Library of Congress is entitled to receive copies of phonorecords from the edition it believes best suits its needs regardless of the quantity or quality of other U.S. editions that may also have been published before the time of deposit. Once the deposit requirements for a particular work have been satisfied under section 407, however, the Library cannot claim deposit of future editions unless they represent newly copyrightable works under section 103.

The deposit requirement for sound recordings includes "two complete phonorecords of the best edition" and any other visually-perceptible material published with the phonorecords. The reference here is to the text or pictorial matter appearing on record sleeves and album covers or embodied in separate leaflets or booklets included in a sleeve, album, or other container. The required deposit in the case of a sound recording would extend to the entire "package" and not just to the disk, tape, or other phonorecord included as part of it.

Deposits under section 407, although made in the Copyright Office, are "for the use or disposition of the Library of Congress." Thus, the fundamental criteria governing regulations issued under section 407(c), which allows exemptions from the deposit requirements for certain categories of works, would be the needs and wants of the Library. The purpose of this provision is to make the deposit requirements as flexible as possible, so that there will be no obligation to make deposits where it serves no purpose, so that only one copy or phonorecord may be deposited where two are not needed, and so that reasonable adjustments can be made to meet practical needs in special cases. The regulations, in establishing special categories for these purposes, would necessarily balance the value of the copies or phonorecords to the collections of the Library of Congress against the burdens and costs to the copyright owner of providing them.

The Committee adopted an amendment to subsection (c) of section 407, aimed at meeting the concerns expressed by representatives of various artists' groups concerning the deposit of expensive art works and graphics published in limited editions. Under the present law, optional deposit of photographs is permitted for various classes of works, but not for fine prints, and this has resulted in many artists choosing to forfeit copyright protection rather than bear the expense of depositing "two copies of the best edition." To avoid this unfair result, the last sentence of subsection (c) would require the Register to issue regulations under which such works would either be exempted entirely from the mandatory deposit or would be subject to an appropriate alternative form of deposit.

If, within three months after the Register of Copyrights has made a formal demand for deposit in accordance with section 407(d), the person on whom the demand was made has not complied, that person becomes liable to a fine up to $250 for each work, plus the "total retail price of the copies or phonorecords demanded." If no retail price has been fixed, clause (2) of subsection (d) establishes the additional amount as "the reasonable cost to the Library of Congress of acquiring them." Thus, where the copies or phonorecords are not available for sale through normal trade channels—as would be true of many motion picture films, video tapes, and computer tapes, for example—the item of cost to be included in the fine would be equal to the basic expense of duplicating the copies or phonorecords plus a reasonable amount representing what it would have cost the Library to obtain them under its normal acquisitions procedures, if they had been available.

There have been cases under the present law in which the mandatory deposit provisions have been deliberately and repeatedly ignored, presumably on the assumption that the Library is unlikely to enforce them. In addition to the penalties provided in the current bill, the last clause of subsection (d) would add a fine of $2,500 for willful or repeated failure or refusal to deposit upon demand.

The Committee also amended section 407 [this section] by adding a new subsection (e), with conforming amendments of sections 407(a) and 408(b). These amendments are intended to provide a basis for the Library of Congress to acquire, as a part of the copyright deposit system, copies or recordings of non-syndicated radio and television programs, without imposing any hardships on broadcasters. Under subsection (e) the Library is authorized to tape programs off the air in all cases and may "demand" that the broadcaster supply the Library with a copy or phonorecord of a particular program. However, this "demand" authority is extremely limited: (1) The broadcaster is not required to retain any recording of a program after it has been transmitted unless a demand has already been received; (2) the demand would cover only a particular program; "blanket" demands would not be permitted; (3) the broadcaster would have the option of supplying the demand by gift, by loan for purposes of reproduction, or by sale at cost; and (4) the penalty for willful failure or refusal to comply with a demand is limited to the cost of reproducing and supplying the copy or phonorecord in question.

AMENDMENTS

1997—Subsec. (d)(2). Pub. L. 105–80 substituted "cost to the Library of Congress" for "cost of the Library of Congress".

1988—Subsec. (a). Pub. L. 100–568 struck out "with notice of copyright" before "in the United States".

EFFECTIVE DATE OF 1988 AMENDMENT

Amendment by Pub. L. 100–568 effective Mar. 1, 1989, with any cause of action arising under this title before such date being governed by provisions in effect when cause of action arose, see section 13 of Pub. L. 100–568, set out as a note under section 101 of this title.

DEPOSITS AND REGISTRATIONS MADE AFTER DECEMBER 31, 1977, IN RESPONSE TO DEMAND UNDER PREDECESSOR DEMAND AND PENALTY PROVISIONS

Section 110 of Pub. L. 94–553 provided that: "The demand and penalty provisions of section 14 of title 17 as it existed on December 31, 1977, apply to any work in which copyright has been secured by publication with notice of copyright on or before that date, but any deposit and registration made after that date in response to a demand under that section shall be made in accordance with the provisions of title 17 as amended by the first section of this Act."

§ 408. Copyright registration in general

(a) REGISTRATION PERMISSIVE.—At any time during the subsistence of the first term of copyright in any published or unpublished work in which the copyright was secured before January 1, 1978, and during the subsistence of any copyright secured on or after that date, the owner of copyright or of any exclusive right in the work may obtain registration of the copyright claim by delivering to the Copyright Office the deposit specified by this section, together with the application and fee specified by sections 409 and 708. Such registration is not a condition of copyright protection.

(b) DEPOSIT FOR COPYRIGHT REGISTRATION.— Except as provided by subsection (c), the material deposited for registration shall include—

(1) in the case of an unpublished work, one complete copy or phonorecord;

(2) in the case of a published work, two complete copies or phonorecords of the best edition;

(3) in the case of a work first published outside the United States, one complete copy or phonorecord as so published;

(4) in the case of a contribution to a collective work, one complete copy or phonorecord of the best edition of the collective work.

Copies or phonorecords deposited for the Library of Congress under section 407 may be used to satisfy the deposit provisions of this section, if they are accompanied by the prescribed application and fee, and by any additional identifying material that the Register may, by regulation, require. The Register shall also prescribe regulations establishing requirements under which copies or phonorecords acquired for the Library of Congress under subsection (e) of section 407, otherwise than by deposit, may be used to satisfy the deposit provisions of this section.

(c) ADMINISTRATIVE CLASSIFICATION AND OPTIONAL DEPOSIT.—

(1) The Register of Copyrights is authorized to specify by regulation the administrative classes into which works are to be placed for purposes of deposit and registration, and the nature of the copies or phonorecords to be deposited in the various classes specified. The regulations may require or permit, for particular classes, the deposit of identifying material instead of copies or phonorecords, the deposit of only one copy or phonorecord where two would normally be required, or a single registration for a group of related works. This administrative classification of works has no significance with respect to the subject matter of copyright or the exclusive rights provided by this title.

(2) Without prejudice to the general authority provided under clause (1), the Register of Copyrights shall establish regulations specifically permitting a single registration for a group of works by the same individual author, all first published as contributions to periodicals, including newspapers, within a twelve-month period, on the basis of a single deposit, application, and registration fee, under the following conditions:

(A) if the deposit consists of one copy of the entire issue of the periodical, or of the entire section in the case of a newspaper, in which each contribution was first published; and

(B) if the application identifies each work separately, including the periodical containing it and its date of first publication.

(3) As an alternative to separate renewal registrations under subsection (a) of section 304, a single renewal registration may be made for a group of works by the same individual author, all first published as contributions to periodicals, including newspapers, upon the filing of a single application and fee, under all of the following conditions:

(A) the renewal claimant or claimants, and the basis of claim or claims under section 304(a), is the same for each of the works; and

(B) the works were all copyrighted upon their first publication, either through separate copyright notice and registration or by virtue of a general copyright notice in the periodical issue as a whole; and

(C) the renewal application and fee are received not more than twenty-eight or less than twenty-seven years after the thirty-first day of December of the calendar year in which all of the works were first published; and

(D) the renewal application identifies each work separately, including the periodical containing it and its date of first publication.

(d) CORRECTIONS AND AMPLIFICATIONS.—The Register may also establish, by regulation, formal procedures for the filing of an application for supplementary registration, to correct an error in a copyright registration or to amplify the information given in a registration. Such application shall be accompanied by the fee provided by section 708, and shall clearly identify the registration to be corrected or amplified. The information contained in a supplementary registration augments but does not supersede that contained in the earlier registration.

(e) PUBLISHED EDITION OF PREVIOUSLY REGISTERED WORK.—Registration for the first published edition of a work previously registered in unpublished form may be made even though the work as published is substantially the same as the unpublished version.

(f) PREREGISTRATION OF WORKS BEING PREPARED FOR COMMERCIAL DISTRIBUTION.—

(1) RULEMAKING.—Not later than 180 days after the date of enactment of this subsection, the Register of Copyrights shall issue regulations to establish procedures for preregistration of a work that is being prepared for commercial distribution and has not been published.

(2) CLASS OF WORKS.—The regulations established under paragraph (1) shall permit preregistration for any work that is in a class of works that the Register determines has had a history of infringement prior to authorized commercial distribution.

(3) APPLICATION FOR REGISTRATION.—Not later than 3 months after the first publication of a work preregistered under this subsection, the applicant shall submit to the Copyright Office—

(A) an application for registration of the work;

(B) a deposit; and

(C) the applicable fee.

(4) EFFECT OF UNTIMELY APPLICATION.—An action under this chapter for infringement of a work preregistered under this subsection, in a case in which the infringement commenced no later than 2 months after the first publication of the work, shall be dismissed if the items described in paragraph (3) are not submitted to the Copyright Office in proper form within the earlier of—

(A) 3 months after the first publication of the work; or

(B) 1 month after the copyright owner has learned of the infringement.

(Pub. L. 94–553, title I, § 101, Oct. 19, 1976, 90 Stat. 2580; Pub. L. 100–568, § 9(a), Oct. 31, 1988, 102 Stat. 2859; Pub. L. 102–307, title I, § 102(e), June 26, 1992, 106 Stat. 266; Pub. L. 109–9, title I, § 104(a), Apr. 27, 2005, 119 Stat. 221.)

HISTORICAL AND REVISION NOTES

HOUSE REPORT NO. 94–1476

Permissive Registration. Under section 408(a), registration of a claim to copyright in any work whether published or unpublished, can be made voluntarily by "the owner of copyright or of any exclusive right in the work" at any time during the copyright term. The claim may be registered in the Copyright Office by depositing the copies, phonorecords, or other material specified by subsection (b) and (c), together with an application and fee. Except where, under section 405(a), registration is made to preserve a copyright that would otherwise be invalidated because of omission of the notice, registration is not a condition of copyright protection.

Deposit for Purpose of Copyright Registration. In general, and subject to various exceptions, the material to be deposited for copyright registration consists of one complete copy or phonorecord of an unpublished work, and two complete copies or phonorecords of the best edition in the case of a published work. Section 408(b) provides special deposit requirements in the case of a work first published abroad ("one complete copy or phonorecord as so published") and in the case of a contribution to a collective work ("one complete copy or phonorecord of the best edition of the collective work"). As a general rule the deposit of more than a tear sheet or similar fraction of a collective work is needed to identify the contribution properly and to show the form in which it was published. Where appropriate as in the case of collective works such as multivolume encyclopedias, multipart newspaper editions, and works that are rare or out of print, the regulations issued by the Register under section 408(c) can be expected to make exceptions or special provisions.

With respect to works published in the United States, a single deposit could be used to satisfy the deposit requirements of section 407 and the registration requirements of section 408, if the application and fee for registration are submitted at the same time and are accompanied by "any additional identifying material" required by regulations. To serve this dual purpose the deposit and registration would have to be made simultaneously; if a deposit under section 407 had already been made, an additional deposit would be required under section 408. In addition, since deposit for the Library of Congress and registration of a claim to copyright serve essentially different functions, section 408(b) authorizes the Register of Copyrights to issue regulations under which deposit of additional material, needed for identification of the work in which copyright is claimed, could be required in certain cases.

Administrative Classification. It is important that the statutory provisions setting forth the subject matter of copyright be kept entirely separate from any classification of copyrightable works for practical administrative purposes. Section 408(c)(1) thus leaves it to the Register of Copyrights to specify "the administrative classes into which works are to be placed for purposes of deposit and registration," and makes clear that this administrative classification "has no significance with respect to the subject matter of copyright or the exclusive rights provided by this title."

Optional Deposit. Consistent with the principle of administrative flexibility underlying all of the deposit and registration provisions, subsection (c) of section 408 also gives the Register latitude in adjusting the type of material deposited to the needs of the registration system. The Register is authorized to issue regulations specifying "the nature of the copies of phonorecords to be deposited in the various classes" and, for particular classes, to require or permit deposit of identifying material rather than copies or phonorecords, deposit of one copy or phonorecord rather than two, or, in the case of a group of related works, a single rather than a number of separate registrations. Under this provision the Register could, where appropriate, permit deposit of phonorecords rather than notated copies of musical compositions, allow or require deposit of printouts of computer programs under certain circumstances, or permit deposit of one volume of an encyclopedia for purposes of registration of a single contribution.

Where the copies or phonorecords are bulky, unwieldy, easily broken, or otherwise impractical to file and retain as records identifying the work registered, the Register would be able to require or permit the substitute deposit of material that would better serve the purpose of identification. Cases of this sort might include, for example, billboard posters, toys and dolls, ceramics and glassware, costume jewelry, and a wide range of three-dimensional objects embodying copyrighted material. The Register's authority would also extend to rare or extremely valuable copies which would be burdensome or impossible to deposit. Deposit of one copy or phonorecord rather than two would probably be justifiable in the case of most motion pictures, and in any case where the Library of Congress has no need for the deposit and its only purpose is identification.

The provision empowering the Register to allow a number of related works to be registered together as a group represents a needed and important liberalization of the law now in effect. At present the requirement for separate registrations where related works or parts of a work are published separately has created administrative problems and has resulted in unnecessary burdens and expenses on authors and other copyright owners. In a number of cases the technical necessity for separate applications and fees has caused copyright owners to forego copyright altogether. Examples of cases where these undesirable and unnecessary results could be avoided by allowing a single registration include the various editions or issues of a daily newspaper, a work published in serial installments, a group of related jewelry designs, a group of photographs by one photographer, a series of greeting cards related to each other in some way, or a group of poems by a single author.

Single Registration. Section 408(c)(2) directs the Register of Copyrights to establish regulations permitting under certain conditions a single registration for a group of works by the same individual author, all first published as contributions to periodicals, including newspapers, within a twelve-month period, on the basis of a single deposit, application, and registration fee. It is required that each of the works as first published have a separate copyright notice, and that the name of the owner of copyright in the work, (or an abbreviation by which the name can be recognized, or a generally known alternative designation of the owner) is the same in each notice. It is further required that the deposit consist of one copy of the entire issue of the periodical, or of the entire section in the case of a newspaper, in which each contribution is first published. Finally, the application shall identify each work separately, including the periodical containing it and its date of first publication.

Section 408(c)(3) provides under certain conditions an alternative to the separate renewal registrations of subsection (a). If the specified conditions are met, a single renewal registration may be made for a group of works by the same individual author, all first published as contributions to periodicals, including newspapers, upon the filing of a single application and fee. It is required that the renewal claimant or claimants, and the basis of claim or claims under section 304(a), is the same for each of the works; that the works were all copyrighted upon their first publication, either through separate copyright notice and registration or by virtue of a general copyright notice in the periodical issue as a whole; that the renewal application and fee are received not more than twenty-eight or less than twenty-seven years after December 31 of the calendar year in which all of the works were first published; and that the renewal application identifies each work separately, including the periodical containing it and its date of first publication.

Corrections and Amplifications. Another unsatisfactory aspect of the present law is the lack of any provision for correcting or amplifying the information given in a completed registration. Subsection (d) of section 408 would remedy this by authorizing the Register to establish "formal procedures for the filing of an application for supplementary registration," in order to correct an error or amplify the information in a copyright registration. The "error" to be corrected under subsection (d) is an error by the applicant that the Copyright Office could not have been expected to note during its examination of the claim; where the error in a registration is the result of the Copyright Office's own mistake or oversight, the Office can make the correction on its own initiative and without recourse to the "supplementary registration" procedure.

Under subsection (d), a supplementary registration is subject to payment of a separate fee and would be maintained as an independent record, separate and apart from the record of the earlier registration it is intended to supplement. However, it would be required to identify clearly "the registration to be corrected or amplified" so that the two registrations could be tied together by appropriate means in the Copyright Office records. The original registration would not be ex-

punged or cancelled; as stated in the subsection: "The information contained in a supplementary registration augments but does not supersede that contained in the earlier registration."

Published Edition of Previously Registered Work. The present statute requires that, where a work is registered in unpublished form, it must be registered again when it is published, whether or not the published edition contains any new copyrightable material. Under the bill there would be no need to make a second registration for the published edition unless it contains sufficient added material to be considered a "derivative work" or "compilation" under section 103.

On the other hand, there will be a number of cases where the copyright owner, although not required to do so, would like to have registration made for the published edition of the work, especially since the owner will still be obliged to deposit copies or phonorecords of it in the Copyright Office under section 407. From the point of view of the public there are advantages in allowing the owner to do so, since registration for the published edition will put on record the facts about the work in the form in which it is actually distributed to the public. Accordingly, section 408(e), which is intended to accomplish this result, makes an exception to the general rule against allowing more than one registration for the same work.

REFERENCES IN TEXT

The date of enactment of this subsection, referred to in subsec. (f)(1), is the date of enactment of Pub. L. 109–9, which was approved Apr. 27, 2005.

AMENDMENTS

2005—Subsec. (f). Pub. L. 109–9 added subsec. (f).

1992—Subsec. (a). Pub. L. 102–307 substituted "At any time during the subsistence of the first term of copyright in any published or unpublished work in which the copyright was secured before January 1, 1978, and during the subsistence of any copyright secured on or after that date," for "At any time during the subsistence of copyright in any published or unpublished work,".

1988—Subsec. (a). Pub. L. 100–568, §9(a)(1), substituted "Such" for "Subject to the provisions of section 405(a), such".

Subsec. (c)(2). Pub. L. 100–568, §9(a)(2), substituted "the following conditions:" for "all of the following conditions—", struck out subpar. (A) which read "if each of the works as first published bore a separate copyright notice, and the name of the owner of copyright in the work, or an abbreviation by which the name can be recognized, or a generally known alternative designation of the owner was the same in each notice; and", and redesignated subpars. (B) and (C) as (A) and (B), respectively.

EFFECTIVE DATE OF 1992 AMENDMENT

Amendment by Pub. L. 102–307 effective June 26, 1992, but applicable only to copyrights secured between January 1, 1964, and December 31, 1977, and not affecting court proceedings pending on June 26, 1992, with copyrights secured before January 1, 1964, governed by section 304(a) of this title as in effect on the day before June 26, 1992, except each reference to forty-seven years in such provisions deemed to be 67 years, see section 102(g) of Pub. L. 102–307, as amended, set out as a note under section 101 of this title.

EFFECTIVE DATE OF 1988 AMENDMENT

Amendment by Pub. L. 100–568 effective Mar. 1, 1989, with any cause of action arising under this title before such date being governed by provisions in effect when cause of action arose, see section 13 of Pub. L. 100–568, set out as a note under section 101 of this title.

§ 409. Application for copyright registration

The application for copyright registration shall be made on a form prescribed by the Register of Copyrights and shall include—

(1) the name and address of the copyright claimant;

(2) in the case of a work other than an anonymous or pseudonymous work, the name and nationality or domicile of the author or authors, and, if one or more of the authors is dead, the dates of their deaths;

(3) if the work is anonymous or pseudonymous, the nationality or domicile of the author or authors;

(4) in the case of a work made for hire, a statement to this effect;

(5) if the copyright claimant is not the author, a brief statement of how the claimant obtained ownership of the copyright;

(6) the title of the work, together with any previous or alternative titles under which the work can be identified;

(7) the year in which creation of the work was completed;

(8) if the work has been published, the date and nation of its first publication;

(9) in the case of a compilation or derivative work, an identification of any preexisting work or works that it is based on or incorporates, and a brief, general statement of the additional material covered by the copyright claim being registered; and

(10) any other information regarded by the Register of Copyrights as bearing upon the preparation or identification of the work or the existence, ownership, or duration of the copyright.

If an application is submitted for the renewed and extended term provided for in section 304(a)(3)(A) and an original term registration has not been made, the Register may request information with respect to the existence, ownership, or duration of the copyright for the original term.

(Pub. L. 94–553, title I, § 101, Oct. 19, 1976, 90 Stat. 2582; Pub. L. 102–307, title I, § 102(b)(1), June 26, 1992, 106 Stat. 266; Pub. L. 111–295, § 4(b)(2), Dec. 9, 2010, 124 Stat. 3180.)

HISTORICAL AND REVISION NOTES

HOUSE REPORT NO. 94–1476

The various clauses of section 409, which specify the information to be included in an application for copyright registration, are intended to give the Register of Copyrights authority to elicit all of the information needed to examine the application and to make a meaningful record of registration. The list of enumerated items was not exhaustive; under the last clause of the section the application may also include "any other information regarded by the Register of Copyrights as bearing upon the preparation or identification of the work or the existence, ownership, or duration of the copyright."

Among the enumerated items there are several that are not now included in the Copyright Office's application forms, but will become significant under the life-plus-50 term and other provisions of the bill. Clause (5), reflecting the increased importance of the interrelationship between registration of copyright claims and recordation of transfers of ownership, requires a statement of how a claimant who is not the author acquired ownership of the copyright. Clause (9) requires that, "in the case of a compilation or derivative work" the application include "an identification of any preexisting work or works that it is based on or incorporates, and a brief, general statement of the addi-

tional material covered by the copyright claim being registered." It is intended that, under this requirement, the application covering a collection such as a song-book or hymnal would clearly reveal any works in the collection that are in the public domain, and the copyright status of all other previously-published compositions. This information will be readily available in the Copyright Office.

The catch-all clause at the end of the section will enable the Register to obtain more specialized information, such as that bearing on whether the work contains material that is a "work of the United States Government." In the case of works subject to the manufacturing requirement, the application must also include information about the manufacture of the copies.

AMENDMENTS

2010—Par. (9) to (11). Pub. L. 111–295 inserted "and" after semicolon at end of par. (9), redesignated par. (11) as (10), and struck out former par. (10) which read as follows: "in the case of a published work containing material of which copies are required by section 601 to be manufactured in the United States, the names of the persons or organizations who performed the processes specified by subsection (c) of section 601 with respect to that material, and the places where those processes were performed; and".

1992—Pub. L. 102–307 inserted at end "If an application is submitted for the renewed and extended term provided for in section 304(a)(3)(A) and an original term registration has not been made, the Register may request information with respect to the existence, ownership, or duration of the copyright for the original term."

EFFECTIVE DATE OF 1992 AMENDMENT

Amendment by Pub. L. 102–307 effective June 26, 1992, but applicable only to copyrights secured between January 1, 1964, and December 31, 1977, and not affecting court proceedings pending on June 26, 1992, with copyrights secured before January 1, 1964, governed by section 304(a) of this title as in effect on the day before June 26, 1992, except each reference to forty-seven years in such provisions deemed to be 67 years, see section 102(g) of Pub. L. 102–307, as amended, set out as a note under section 101 of this title.

§ 410. Registration of claim and issuance of certificate

(a) When, after examination, the Register of Copyrights determines that, in accordance with the provisions of this title, the material deposited constitutes copyrightable subject matter and that the other legal and formal requirements of this title have been met, the Register shall register the claim and issue to the applicant a certificate of registration under the seal of the Copyright Office. The certificate shall contain the information given in the application, together with the number and effective date of the registration.

(b) In any case in which the Register of Copyrights determines that, in accordance with the provisions of this title, the material deposited does not constitute copyrightable subject matter or that the claim is invalid for any other reason, the Register shall refuse registration and shall notify the applicant in writing of the reasons for such refusal.

(c) In any judicial proceedings the certificate of a registration made before or within five years after first publication of the work shall constitute prima facie evidence of the validity of the copyright and of the facts stated in the certificate. The evidentiary weight to be accorded the certificate of a registration made thereafter shall be within the discretion of the court.

(d) The effective date of a copyright registration is the day on which an application, deposit, and fee, which are later determined by the Register of Copyrights or by a court of competent jurisdiction to be acceptable for registration, have all been received in the Copyright Office.

(Pub. L. 94–553, title I, §101, Oct. 19, 1976, 90 Stat. 2582.)

HISTORICAL AND REVISION NOTES

HOUSE REPORT NO. 94–1476

The first two subsections of section 410 set forth the two basic duties of the Register of Copyrights with respect to copyright registration: (1) to register the claim and issue a certificate if the Register determines that "the material deposited constitutes copyrightable subject matter and that the other legal and formal requirements of this title have been met," and (2) to refuse registration and notify the applicant if the Register determines that "the material deposited does not constitute copyrightable subject matter or that the claim is invalid for any other reason."

Subsection (c) deals with the probative effect of a certificate of registration issued by the Register under subsection (a). Under its provisions, a certificate is required to be given prima facie weight in any judicial proceedings if the registration it covers was made "before or within five years after first publication of the work"; thereafter the court is given discretion to decide what evidentiary weight the certificate should be accorded. This five-year period is based on a recognition that the longer the lapse of time between publication and registration the less likely to be reliable are the facts stated in the certificate.

Under section 410(c), a certificate is to "constitute prima facie evidence of the validity of the copyright and of the facts stated in the certificate." The principle that a certificate represents prima facie evidence of copyright validity has been established in a long line of court decisions, and it is a sound one. It is true that, unlike a patent claim, a claim to copyright is not examined for basic validity before a certificate is issued. On the other hand, endowing a copyright claimant who has obtained a certificate with a rebuttable presumption of the validity of the copyright does not deprive the defendant in an infringement suit of any rights, it merely orders the burdens of proof. The plaintiff should not ordinarily be forced in the first instance to prove all of the multitude of facts that underline the validity of the copyright unless the defendant, by effectively challenging them, shifts the burden of doing so to the plaintiff.

Section 410(d), which is in accord with the present practice of the Copyright Office, makes the effective date of registration the day when an application, deposit, and fee "which are later determined by the Register of Copyrights or by a court of competent jurisdiction to be acceptable for registration" have all been received. Where the three necessary elements are received at different times the date of receipt of the last of them is controlling, regardless of when the Copyright Office acts on the claim. The provision not only takes account of the inevitable timelag between receipt of the application and other material and the issuance of the certificate, but it also recognizes the possibility that a court might later find the Register wrong in refusing registration.

REGISTRATION OF CLAIMS TO COPYRIGHTS AND RECORDATION OF ASSIGNMENTS OF COPYRIGHTS AND OTHER INSTRUMENTS UNDER PREDECESSOR PROVISIONS

Section 109 of Pub. L. 94–553 provided that: "The registration of claims to copyright for which the required deposit, application, and fee were received in the Copyright Office before January 1, 1978, and the recordation of assignments of copyright or other instruments received in the Copyright Office before January 1, 1978, shall be made in accordance with title 17 as it existed on December 31, 1977."

§411. Registration and civil infringement actions

(a) Except for an action brought for a violation of the rights of the author under section 106A(a), and subject to the provisions of subsection (b),[1] no civil action for infringement of the copyright in any United States work shall be instituted until preregistration or registration of the copyright claim has been made in accordance with this title. In any case, however, where the deposit, application, and fee required for registration have been delivered to the Copyright Office in proper form and registration has been refused, the applicant is entitled to institute a civil action for infringement if notice thereof, with a copy of the complaint, is served on the Register of Copyrights. The Register may, at his or her option, become a party to the action with respect to the issue of registrability of the copyright claim by entering an appearance within sixty days after such service, but the Register's failure to become a party shall not deprive the court of jurisdiction to determine that issue.

(b)(1) A certificate of registration satisfies the requirements of this section and section 412, regardless of whether the certificate contains any inaccurate information, unless—

(A) the inaccurate information was included on the application for copyright registration with knowledge that it was inaccurate; and

(B) the inaccuracy of the information, if known, would have caused the Register of Copyrights to refuse registration.

(2) In any case in which inaccurate information described under paragraph (1) is alleged, the court shall request the Register of Copyrights to advise the court whether the inaccurate information, if known, would have caused the Register of Copyrights to refuse registration.

(3) Nothing in this subsection shall affect any rights, obligations, or requirements of a person related to information contained in a registration certificate, except for the institution of and remedies in infringement actions under this section and section 412.

(c) In the case of a work consisting of sounds, images, or both, the first fixation of which is made simultaneously with its transmission, the copyright owner may, either before or after such fixation takes place, institute an action for infringement under section 501, fully subject to the remedies provided by sections 502 through 505 and section 510, if, in accordance with requirements that the Register of Copyrights shall prescribe by regulation, the copyright owner—

(1) serves notice upon the infringer, not less than 48 hours before such fixation, identifying the work and the specific time and source of its first transmission, and declaring an intention to secure copyright in the work; and

(2) makes registration for the work, if required by subsection (a), within three months after its first transmission.

---

[1] See References in Text note below.

(Pub. L. 94–553, title I, § 101, Oct. 19, 1976, 90 Stat. 2583; Pub. L. 100–568, § 9(b)(1), Oct. 31, 1988, 102 Stat. 2859; Pub. L. 101–650, title VI, § 606(c)(1), Dec. 1, 1990, 104 Stat. 5131; Pub. L. 105–80, § 6, Nov. 13, 1997, 111 Stat. 1532; Pub. L. 105–304, title I, § 102(d), Oct. 28, 1998, 112 Stat. 2863; Pub. L. 109–9, title I, § 104(b), Apr. 27, 2005, 119 Stat. 222; Pub. L. 110–403, title I, § 101(a), title II, § 209(a)(6), Oct. 13, 2008, 122 Stat. 4257, 4264.)

HISTORICAL AND REVISION NOTES

HOUSE REPORT NO. 94–1476

The first sentence of section 411(a) restates the present statutory requirement that registration must be made before a suit for copyright infringement is instituted. Under the bill, as under the law now in effect, a copyright owner who has not registered his claim can have a valid cause of action against someone who has infringed his copyright, but he cannot enforce his rights in the courts until he has made registration.

The second and third sentences of section 411(a) would alter the present law as interpreted in *Vacheron & Constantin-Le Coultre Watches, Inc. v. Benrus Watch Co.*, 260 F.2d 637 (2d Cir. 1958). That case requires an applicant, who has sought registration and has been refused, to bring an action against the Register of Copyrights to compel the issuance of a certificate, before suit can be brought against an infringer. Under section 411, a rejected claimant who has properly applied for registration may maintain an infringement suit if notice of it is served on the Register of Copyrights. The Register is authorized, though not required, to enter the suit within 60 days; the Register would be a party on the issue of registrability only, and a failure by the Register to join the action would "not deprive the court of jurisdiction to determine that issue."

Section 411(b) is intended to deal with the special situation presented by works that are being transmitted "live" at the same time they are being fixed in tangible form for the first time. Under certain circumstances, where the infringer has been given advance notice, an injunction could be obtained to prevent the unauthorized use of the material included in the "live" transmission.

REFERENCES IN TEXT

Subsection (b), referred to in subsec. (a), was redesignated subsec. (c) of this section by Pub. L. 110–403, title I, § 101(a)(3), Oct. 13, 2008, 122 Stat. 4257.

AMENDMENTS

2008—Pub. L. 110–403, § 101(a)(1), inserted "civil" before "infringement" in section catchline.

Subsec. (a). Pub. L. 110–403, § 101(a)(2), substituted "no civil action" for "no action" in first sentence and "a civil action" for "an action" in second sentence.

Subsec. (b). Pub. L. 110–403, § 209(a)(6), which directed amendment of subsec. (b) by substituting "section 510" for "sections 509 and 510", could not be executed because of prior amendment by Pub. L. 110–403, § 101(a)(3), (4). See below.

Pub. L. 110–403, § 101(a)(5), added subsec. (b). Former subsec. (b) redesignated (c).

Subsec. (c). Pub. L. 110–403, § 101(a)(4), substituted "505 and section" for "506 and sections 509 and" in introductory provisions.

Pub. L. 110–403, § 101(a)(3), redesignated subsec. (b) as (c).

2005—Subsec. (a). Pub. L. 109–9 inserted "preregistration or" after "shall be instituted until".

1998—Subsec. (a). Pub. L. 105–304, in first sentence, struck out "actions for infringement of copyright in Berne Convention works whose country of origin is not the United States and" after "Except for" and inserted "United States" after "copyright in any".

1997—Subsec. (b)(1). Pub. L. 105–80 amended par. (1) generally. Prior to amendment, par. (1) read as follows:

"serves notice upon the infringer, not less than ten or more than thirty days before such fixation, identifying the work and the specific time and source of its first transmission, and declaring an intention to secure copyright in the work; and".

1990—Subsec. (a). Pub. L. 101–650 inserted "and an action brought for a violation of the rights of the author under section 106A(a)" after "United States".

1988—Pub. L. 100–568, § 9(b)(1)(A), substituted "Registration and infringement actions" for "Registration as prerequisite to infringement suit" in section catchline.

Subsec. (a). Pub. L. 100–568, § 9(b)(1)(B), substituted "Except for actions for infringement of copyright in Berne Convention works whose country of origin is not the United States, and subject" for "Subject".

Subsec. (b)(2). Pub. L. 100–568, § 9(b)(1)(C), substituted "work, if required by subsection (a)," for "work".

EFFECTIVE DATE OF 1990 AMENDMENT

Amendment by Pub. L. 101–650 effective 6 months after Dec. 1, 1990, see section 610 of Pub. L. 101–650, set out as an Effective Date note under section 106A of this title.

EFFECTIVE DATE OF 1988 AMENDMENT

Amendment by Pub. L. 100–568 effective Mar. 1, 1989, with any cause of action arising under this title before such date being governed by provisions in effect when cause of action arose, see section 13 of Pub. L. 100–568, set out as a note under section 101 of this title.

§ 412. Registration as prerequisite to certain remedies for infringement

In any action under this title, other than an action brought for a violation of the rights of the author under section 106A(a), an action for infringement of the copyright of a work that has been preregistered under section 408(f) before the commencement of the infringement and that has an effective date of registration not later than the earlier of 3 months after the first publication of the work or 1 month after the copyright owner has learned of the infringement, or an action instituted under section 411(c), no award of statutory damages or of attorney's fees, as provided by sections 504 and 505, shall be made for—

(1) any infringement of copyright in an unpublished work commenced before the effective date of its registration; or

(2) any infringement of copyright commenced after first publication of the work and before the effective date of its registration, unless such registration is made within three months after the first publication of the work.

(Pub. L. 94–553, title I, § 101, Oct. 19, 1976, 90 Stat. 2583; Pub. L. 101–650, title VI, § 606(c)(2), Dec. 1, 1990, 104 Stat. 5131; Pub. L. 109–9, title I, § 104(c), Apr. 27, 2005, 119 Stat. 222; Pub. L. 110–403, title I, § 101(b)(1), Oct. 13, 2008, 122 Stat. 4258.)

HISTORICAL AND REVISION NOTES

HOUSE REPORT NO. 94–1476

The need for section 412 arises from two basic changes the bill will make in the present law.

(1) Copyright registration for published works, which is useful and important to users and the public at large, would no longer be compulsory, and should therefore be induced in some practical way.

(2) The great body of unpublished works now protected at common law would automatically be brought under copyright and given statutory protection. The remedies for infringement presently avail-

able at common law should continue to apply to these works under the statute, but they should not be given special statutory remedies unless the owner has, by registration, made a public record of his copyright claim.

Under the general scheme of the bill, a copyright owner whose work has been infringed before registration would be entitled to the remedies ordinarily available in infringement cases: an injunction on terms the court considers fair, and his actual damages plus any applicable profits not used as a measure of damages. However, section 412 would deny any award of the special or "extraordinary" remedies of statutory damages or attorney's fees where infringement of copyright in an unpublished work began before registration or where, in the case of a published work, infringement commenced after publication and before registration (unless registration has been made within a grace period of three months after publication). These provisions would be applicable to works of foreign and domestic origin alike.

In providing that statutory damages and attorney's fees are not recoverable for infringement of unpublished, unregistered works, clause (1) of section 412 in no way narrows the remedies available under the present law. With respect to published works, clause (2) would generally deny an award of those two special remedies where infringement takes place before registration. As an exception, however, the clause provides a grace period of three months after publication during which registration can be made without loss of remedies; full remedies could be recovered for any infringement begun during the three months after publication if registration is made before that period has ended. This exception is needed to take care of newsworthy or suddenly popular works which may be infringed almost as soon as they are published, before the copyright owner has had a reasonable opportunity to register his claim.

AMENDMENTS

2008—Pub. L. 110–403 substituted "section 411(c)" for "section 411(b)" in introductory provisions.

2005—Pub. L. 109–9 inserted ", an action for infringement of the copyright of a work that has been preregistered under section 408(f) before the commencement of the infringement and that has an effective date of registration not later than the earlier of 3 months after the first publication of the work or 1 month after the copyright owner has learned of the infringement," after "section 106A(a)" in introductory provisions.

1990—Pub. L. 101–650 inserted "an action brought for a violation of the rights of the author under section 106A(a) or" after "other than" in introductory provisions.

EFFECTIVE DATE OF 1990 AMENDMENT

Amendment by Pub. L. 101–650 effective 6 months after Dec. 1, 1990, see section 610 of Pub. L. 101–650, set out as an Effective Date note under section 106A of this title.

CHAPTER 5—COPYRIGHT INFRINGEMENT AND REMEDIES

AMENDMENTS

2008—Pub. L. 110–403, title II, §201(b)(2), Oct. 13, 2008, 122 Stat. 4260, struck out item 509 "Seizure and forfeiture."

1999—Pub. L. 106–113, div. B, §1000(a)(9) [title I, §1011(a)(1)], Nov. 29, 1999, 113 Stat. 1536, 1501A–543, substituted "programming" for "programing" in item 510.

Pub. L. 106–44, §1(c)(2), Aug. 5, 1999, 113 Stat. 222, renumbered item 512 "Determination of reasonable license fees for individual proprietors" as 513.

1998—Pub. L. 105–304, title II, §202(b), Oct. 28, 1998, 112 Stat. 2886, added item 512 "Limitations on liability relating to material online".

Pub. L. 105–298, title II, §203(b), Oct. 27, 1998, 112 Stat. 2833, added item 512 "Determination of reasonable license fees for individual proprietors".

1997—Pub. L. 105–80, §12(a)(12), Nov. 13, 1997, 105 Stat. 1535, substituted "Damages" for "Damage" in item 504.

1990—Pub. L. 101–553, §2(a)(3), Nov. 15, 1990, 104 Stat. 2750, added item 511.

§501. Infringement of copyright

(a) Anyone who violates any of the exclusive rights of the copyright owner as provided by sections 106 through 122 or of the author as provided in section 106A(a), or who imports copies or phonorecords into the United States in violation of section 602, is an infringer of the copyright or right of the author, as the case may be. For purposes of this chapter (other than section 506), any reference to copyright shall be deemed to include the rights conferred by section 106A(a). As used in this subsection, the term "anyone" includes any State, any instrumentality of a State, and any officer or employee of a State or instrumentality of a State acting in his or her official capacity. Any State, and any such instrumentality, officer, or employee, shall be subject to the provisions of this title in the same manner and to the same extent as any nongovernmental entity.

(b) The legal or beneficial owner of an exclusive right under a copyright is entitled, subject to the requirements of section 411, to institute an action for any infringement of that particular right committed while he or she is the owner of it. The court may require such owner to serve written notice of the action with a copy of the complaint upon any person shown, by the records of the Copyright Office or otherwise, to have or claim an interest in the copyright, and shall require that such notice be served upon any person whose interest is likely to be affected by a decision in the case. The court may require the joinder, and shall permit the intervention, of any person having or claiming an interest in the copyright.

(c) For any secondary transmission by a cable system that embodies a performance or a display of a work which is actionable as an act of infringement under subsection (c) of section 111, a television broadcast station holding a copyright or other license to transmit or perform the same version of that work shall, for purposes of subsection (b) of this section, be treated as a legal or beneficial owner if such secondary transmission occurs within the local service area of that television station.

(d) For any secondary transmission by a cable system that is actionable as an act of infringement pursuant to section 111(c)(3), the following shall also have standing to sue: (i) the primary transmitter whose transmission has been altered by the cable system; and (ii) any broadcast station within whose local service area the secondary transmission occurs.

(e) With respect to any secondary transmission that is made by a satellite carrier of a performance or display of a work embodied in a primary transmission and is actionable as an act of infringement under section 119(a)(5),[1] a network station holding a copyright or other license to transmit or perform the same version of that work shall, for purposes of subsection (b) of this section, be treated as a legal or beneficial owner if such secondary transmission occurs within the local service area of that station.

(f)(1) With respect to any secondary transmission that is made by a satellite carrier of a performance or display of a work embodied in a primary transmission and is actionable as an act of infringement under section 122, a television broadcast station holding a copyright or other license to transmit or perform the same version of that work shall, for purposes of subsection (b) of this section, be treated as a legal or beneficial owner if such secondary transmission occurs within the local market of that station.

(2) A television broadcast station may file a civil action against any satellite carrier that has refused to carry television broadcast signals, as required under section 122(a)(2), to enforce that television broadcast station's rights under section 338(a) of the Communications Act of 1934.

(Pub. L. 94–553, title I, § 101, Oct. 19, 1976, 90 Stat. 2584; Pub. L. 100–568, § 10(a), Oct. 31, 1988, 102 Stat. 2860; Pub. L. 100–667, title II, § 202(3), Nov. 16, 1988, 102 Stat. 3957; Pub. L. 101–553, § 2(a)(1), Nov. 15, 1990, 104 Stat. 2749; Pub. L. 101–650, title VI, § 606(a), Dec. 1, 1990, 104 Stat. 5131; Pub. L. 106–44, § 1(g)(5), Aug. 5, 1999, 113 Stat. 222; Pub. L. 106–113, div. B, § 1000(a)(9) [title I, §§ 1002(b), 1011(b)(3)], Nov. 29, 1999, 113 Stat. 1536, 1501A–527, 1501A–544; Pub. L. 107–273, div. C, title III, § 13210(4)(B), Nov. 2, 2002, 116 Stat. 1909.)

HISTORICAL AND REVISION NOTES

HOUSE REPORT NO. 94–1476

The bill, unlike the present law, contains a general statement of what constitutes infringement of copyright. Section 501(a) identifies a copyright infringer as someone who "violates any of the exclusive rights of the copyright owner as provided by sections 106 through 118" of the bill, or who imports copies or phonorecords in violation of section 602. Under the latter section an unauthorized importation of copies or phonorecords acquired abroad is an infringement of the exclusive right of distribution under certain circumstances.

The principle of the divisibility of copyright ownership, established by section 201(d), carries with it the

need in infringement actions to safeguard the rights of all copyright owners and to avoid a multiplicity of suits. Subsection (b) of section 501 enables the owner of a particular right to bring an infringement action in that owner's name alone, while at the same time insuring to the extent possible that the other owners whose rights may be affected are notified and given a chance to join the action.

The first sentence of subsection (b) empowers the "legal or beneficial owner of an exclusive right" to bring suit for "any infringement of that particular right committed while he or she is the owner of it." A "beneficial owner" for this purpose would include, for example, an author who had parted with legal title to the copyright in exchange for percentage royalties based on sales or license fees.

The second and third sentences of section 501(b), which supplement the provisions of the Federal Rules of Civil Procedure [Title 28, Judiciary and Judicial Procedure], give the courts discretion to require the plaintiff to serve notice of the plaintiff's suit on "any person shown, by the records of the Copyright Office or otherwise, to have or claim an interest in the copyright"; where a person's interest "is likely to be affected by a decision in the case" a court order requiring service of notice is mandatory. As under the Federal rules, the court has discretion to require joinder of "any person having or claiming an interest in the copyright"; but, if any such person wishes to become a party, the court must permit that person's intervention.

In addition to cases involving divisibility of ownership in the same version of a work, section 501(b) is intended to allow a court to permit or compel joinder of the owners of rights in works upon which a derivative work is based.

Section 501 contains two provisions conferring standing to sue under the statue upon broadcast stations in specific situations involving secondary transmissions by cable systems. Under subsection (c), a local television broadcaster licensed to transmit a work can sue a cable system importing the same version of the work into the broadcaster's local service area in violation of section 111(c). Subsection (d) deals with cases arising under section 111(c)(3), the provision dealing with substitution or alteration by a cable system of commercials or other programming; in such cases standing to sue is also conferred on: (1) the primary transmitter whose transmission has been altered by the cable system, and (2) any broadcast stations within whose local service area the secondary transmission occurs. These provisions are linked to section 509, a new provision on remedies for alteration of programming by cable systems, discussed below.

Vicarious Liability for Infringing Performances. The committee has considered and rejected an amendment to this section intended to exempt the proprietors of an establishment, such as a ballroom or night club, from liability for copyright infringement committed by an independent contractor, such as an orchestra leader. A well-established principle of copyright law is that a person who violates any of the exclusive rights of the copyright owner is an infringer, including persons who can be considered related or vicarious infringers. To be held a related or vicarious infringer in the case of performing rights, a defendant must either actively operate or supervise the operation of the place wherein the performances occur, or control the content of the infringing program, and expect commercial gain from the operation and either direct or indirect benefit from the infringing performance. The committee has decided that no justification exists for changing existing law, and causing a significant erosion of the public performance right.

REFERENCES IN TEXT

Section 119(a)(5) of this title, referred to in subsec. (e), was redesignated as section 119(a)(4) of this title by Pub. L. 111–175, title I, § 102(h)(1)(B), May 27, 2010, 124 Stat. 1224.

Section 338(a) of the Communications Act of 1934, referred to in subsec. (f)(2), is classified to section 338(a)

---

[1] See References in Text note below.

of Title 47, Telegraphs, Telephones, and Radio-telegraphs.

AMENDMENTS

2002—Subsec. (a). Pub. L. 107–273 substituted "122" for "121".

1999—Subsec. (a). Pub. L. 106–44 substituted "121" for "118".

Subsec. (e). Pub. L. 106–113, § 1000(a)(9) [title I, § 1011(b)(3)], substituted "performance or display of a work embodied in a primary transmission" for "primary transmission embodying the performance or display of a work".

Subsec. (f). Pub. L. 106–113, § 1000(a)(9) [title I, § 1002(b)], added subsec. (f).

1990—Subsec. (a). Pub. L. 101–650 inserted "or of the author as provided in section 106A(a)" after "118" and substituted "copyright or right of the author, as the case may be. For purposes of this chapter (other than section 506), any reference to copyright shall be deemed to include the rights conferred by section 106A(a)." for "copyright."

Pub. L. 101–553 inserted sentences at end defining "anyone" and providing that any State and any instrumentality, officer, or employee be subject to the provisions of this title in the same manner and to the same extent as any nongovernmental entity.

1988—Subsec. (b). Pub. L. 100–568 substituted "section 411" for "sections 205(d) and 411".

Subsec. (e). Pub. L. 100–667 added subsec. (e).

EFFECTIVE DATE OF 1999 AMENDMENT

Amendment by section 1000(a)(9) [title I, § 1002(b)] of Pub. L. 106–113 effective July 1, 1999, and amendment by section 1000(a)(9) [title I, § 1011(b)(3)] of Pub. L. 106–113 effective Nov. 29, 1999, see section 1000(a)(9) [title I, § 1012] of Pub. L. 106–113, set out as a note under section 101 of this title.

EFFECTIVE DATE OF 1990 AMENDMENTS

Amendment by Pub. L. 101–650 effective 6 months after Dec. 1, 1990, see section 610 of Pub. L. 101–650, set out as an Effective Date note under section 106A of this title.

Section 3 of Pub. L. 101–553 provided that: "The amendments made by this Act [enacting section 511 of this title and amending this section and sections 910 and 911 of this title] shall take effect with respect to violations that occur on or after the date of the enactment of this Act [Nov. 15, 1990]."

EFFECTIVE DATE OF 1988 AMENDMENTS

Amendment by Pub. L. 100–667 effective Jan. 1, 1989, see section 206 of Pub. L. 100–667, set out as an Effective Date note under section 119 of this title.

Amendment by Pub. L. 100–568 effective Mar. 1, 1989, with any cause of action arising under this title before such date being governed by provisions in effect when cause of action arose, see section 13 of Pub. L. 100–568, set out as a note under section 101 of this title.

CAUSES OF ACTION ARISING UNDER PREDECESSOR PROVISIONS

Section 112 of Pub. L. 94–553 provided that: "All causes of action that arose under title 17 before January 1, 1978, shall be governed by title 17 as it existed when the cause of action arose."

§ 502. Remedies for infringement: Injunctions

(a) Any court having jurisdiction of a civil action arising under this title may, subject to the provisions of section 1498 of title 28, grant temporary and final injunctions on such terms as it may deem reasonable to prevent or restrain infringement of a copyright.

(b) Any such injunction may be served anywhere in the United States on the person enjoined; it shall be operative throughout the United States and shall be enforceable, by proceedings in contempt or otherwise, by any United States court having jurisdiction of that person. The clerk of the court granting the injunction shall, when requested by any other court in which enforcement of the injunction is sought, transmit promptly to the other court a certified copy of all the papers in the case on file in such clerk's office.

(Pub. L. 94–553, title I, § 101, Oct. 19, 1976, 90 Stat. 2584.)

HISTORICAL AND REVISION NOTES

HOUSE REPORT NO. 94–1476

Section 502(a) [subsec. (a) of this section] reasserts the discretionary power of courts to grant injunctions and restraining orders, whether "preliminary," "temporary," "interlocutory," "permanent," or "final," to prevent or stop infringements of copyright. This power is made subject to the provisions of section 1498 of title 28 dealing with infringement actions against the United States. The latter reference in section 502(a) makes it clear that the bill would not permit the granting of an injunction against an infringement for which the Federal Government is liable under section 1498.

Under subsection (b), which is the counterpart of provisions in sections 112 and 113 of the present statute [sections 112 and 113 of former title 17], a copyright owner who has obtained an injunction in one State will be able to enforce it against a defendant located anywhere else in the United States.

§ 503. Remedies for infringement: Impounding and disposition of infringing articles

(a)(1) At any time while an action under this title is pending, the court may order the impounding, on such terms as it may deem reasonable—

(A) of all copies or phonorecords claimed to have been made or used in violation of the exclusive right of the copyright owner;

(B) of all plates, molds, matrices, masters, tapes, film negatives, or other articles by means of which such copies or phonorecords may be reproduced; and

(C) of records documenting the manufacture, sale, or receipt of things involved in any such violation, provided that any records seized under this subparagraph shall be taken into the custody of the court.

(2) For impoundments of records ordered under paragraph (1)(C), the court shall enter an appropriate protective order with respect to discovery and use of any records or information that has been impounded. The protective order shall provide for appropriate procedures to ensure that confidential, private, proprietary, or privileged information contained in such records is not improperly disclosed or used.

(3) The relevant provisions of paragraphs (2) through (11) of section 34(d) of the Trademark Act (15 U.S.C. 1116(d)(2) through (11)) shall extend to any impoundment of records ordered under paragraph (1)(C) that is based upon an ex parte application, notwithstanding the provisions of rule 65 of the Federal Rules of Civil Procedure. Any references in paragraphs (2) through (11) of section 34(d) of the Trademark Act to section 32 of such Act shall be read as references to section 501 of this title, and references to use of

a counterfeit mark in connection with the sale, offering for sale, or distribution of goods or services shall be read as references to infringement of a copyright.

(b) As part of a final judgment or decree, the court may order the destruction or other reasonable disposition of all copies or phonorecords found to have been made or used in violation of the copyright owner's exclusive rights, and of all plates, molds, matrices, masters, tapes, film negatives, or other articles by means of which such copies or phonorecords may be reproduced.

(Pub. L. 94–553, title I, § 101, Oct. 19, 1976, 90 Stat. 2585; Pub. L. 110–403, title I, § 102(a), Oct. 13, 2008, 122 Stat. 4258; Pub. L. 111–295, § 6(d), Dec. 9, 2010, 124 Stat. 3181.)

HISTORICAL AND REVISION NOTES

HOUSE REPORT NO. 94–1476

The two subsections of section 503 deal respectively with the courts' power to impound allegedly infringing articles during the time an action is pending, and to order the destruction or other disposition of articles found to be infringing. In both cases the articles affected include "all copies or phonorecords" which are claimed or found "to have been made or used in violation of the copyright owner's exclusive rights," and also "all plates, molds, matrices, masters, tapes, film negatives, or other articles by means of which such copies of phonorecords may be reproduced." The alternative phrase "made or used" in both subsections enables a court to deal as it sees fit with articles which, though reproduced and acquired lawfully, have been used for infringing purposes such as rentals, performances, and displays.

Articles may be impounded under subsection (a) "at any time while an action under this title is pending," thus permitting seizures of articles alleged to be infringing as soon as suit has been filed and without waiting for an injunction. The same subsection empowers the court to order impounding "on such terms as it may deem reasonable." The present Supreme Court rules with respect to seizure and impounding were issued even though there is no specific provision authorizing them in the copyright statute, and there appears no need for including a special provision on the point in the bill.

Under section 101(d) of the present statute [section 101(d) of former title 17], articles found to be infringing may be ordered to be delivered up for destruction. Section 503(b) of the bill would make this provision more flexible by giving the court discretion to order "destruction or other reasonable disposition" of the articles found to be infringing. Thus, as part of its final judgment or decree, the court could order the infringing articles sold, delivered to the plaintiff, or disposed of in some other way that would avoid needless waste and best serve the ends of justice.

REFERENCES IN TEXT

The Trademark Act, referred to in subsec. (a)(3), probably means the Trademark Act of 1946, act July 5, 1946, ch. 540, 60 Stat. 427, also popularly known as the Lanham Act, which is classified generally to chapter 22 of Title 15, Commerce and Trade. Section 32 of the Act is classified to section 1114 of Title 15. For complete classification of this Act to the Code, see Short Title note set out under section 1051 of Title 15 and Tables.

The Federal Rules of Civil Procedure, referred to in subsec. (a)(3), are set out in the Appendix to Title 28, Judiciary and Judicial Procedure.

AMENDMENTS

2010—Subsec. (a)(1)(B). Pub. L. 111–295 substituted "copies or phonorecords" for "copies of phonorecords".

2008—Subsec. (a). Pub. L. 110–403 amended subsec. (a) generally. Prior to amendment, subsec. (a) read as follows: "At any time while an action under this title is pending, the court may order the impounding, on such terms as it may deem reasonable, of all copies or phonorecords claimed to have been made or used in violation of the copyright owner's exclusive rights, and of all plates, molds, matrices, masters, tapes, film negatives, or other articles by means of which such copies or phonorecords may be reproduced."

§ 504. Remedies for infringement: Damages and profits

(a) IN GENERAL.—Except as otherwise provided by this title, an infringer of copyright is liable for either—

(1) the copyright owner's actual damages and any additional profits of the infringer, as provided by subsection (b); or

(2) statutory damages, as provided by subsection (c).

(b) ACTUAL DAMAGES AND PROFITS.—The copyright owner is entitled to recover the actual damages suffered by him or her as a result of the infringement, and any profits of the infringer that are attributable to the infringement and are not taken into account in computing the actual damages. In establishing the infringer's profits, the copyright owner is required to present proof only of the infringer's gross revenue, and the infringer is required to prove his or her deductible expenses and the elements of profit attributable to factors other than the copyrighted work.

(c) STATUTORY DAMAGES.—

(1) Except as provided by clause (2) of this subsection, the copyright owner may elect, at any time before final judgment is rendered, to recover, instead of actual damages and profits, an award of statutory damages for all infringements involved in the action, with respect to any one work, for which any one infringer is liable individually, or for which any two or more infringers are liable jointly and severally, in a sum of not less than $750 or more than $30,000 as the court considers just. For the purposes of this subsection, all the parts of a compilation or derivative work constitute one work.

(2) In a case where the copyright owner sustains the burden of proving, and the court finds, that infringement was committed willfully, the court in its discretion may increase the award of statutory damages to a sum of not more than $150,000. In a case where the infringer sustains the burden of proving, and the court finds, that such infringer was not aware and had no reason to believe that his or her acts constituted an infringement of copyright, the court in its discretion may reduce the award of statutory damages to a sum of not less than $200. The court shall remit statutory damages in any case where an infringer believed and had reasonable grounds for believing that his or her use of the copyrighted work was a fair use under section 107, if the infringer was: (i) an employee or agent of a nonprofit educational institution, library, or archives acting within the scope of his or her employment who, or such institution, library, or archives itself, which infringed by reproducing the work in copies or phonorecords; or (ii) a public broadcasting entity which or a person

who, as a regular part of the nonprofit activities of a public broadcasting entity (as defined in section 118(f)) infringed by performing a published nondramatic literary work or by reproducing a transmission program embodying a performance of such a work.

(3)(A) In a case of infringement, it shall be a rebuttable presumption that the infringement was committed willfully for purposes of determining relief if the violator, or a person acting in concert with the violator, knowingly provided or knowingly caused to be provided materially false contact information to a domain name registrar, domain name registry, or other domain name registration authority in registering, maintaining, or renewing a domain name used in connection with the infringement.

(B) Nothing in this paragraph limits what may be considered willful infringement under this subsection.

(C) For purposes of this paragraph, the term "domain name" has the meaning given that term in section 45 of the Act entitled "An Act to provide for the registration and protection of trademarks used in commerce, to carry out the provisions of certain international conventions, and for other purposes" approved July 5, 1946 (commonly referred to as the "Trademark Act of 1946"; 15 U.S.C. 1127).

(d) ADDITIONAL DAMAGES IN CERTAIN CASES.— In any case in which the court finds that a defendant proprietor of an establishment who claims as a defense that its activities were exempt under section 110(5) did not have reasonable grounds to believe that its use of a copyrighted work was exempt under such section, the plaintiff shall be entitled to, in addition to any award of damages under this section, an additional award of two times the amount of the license fee that the proprietor of the establishment concerned should have paid the plaintiff for such use during the preceding period of up to 3 years.

(Pub. L. 94–553, title I, § 101, Oct. 19, 1976, 90 Stat. 2585; Pub. L. 100–568, § 10(b), Oct. 31, 1988, 102 Stat. 2860; Pub. L. 105–80, § 12(a)(13), Nov. 13, 1997, 111 Stat. 1535; Pub. L. 105–298, title II, § 204, Oct. 27, 1998, 112 Stat. 2833; Pub. L. 106–160, § 2, Dec. 9, 1999, 113 Stat. 1774; Pub. L. 108–482, title II, § 203, Dec. 23, 2004, 118 Stat. 3916; Pub. L. 111–295, § 6(f)(2), Dec. 9, 2010, 124 Stat. 3181.)

HISTORICAL AND REVISION NOTES

HOUSE REPORT NO. 94–1476

In General. A cornerstone of the remedies sections and of the bill as a whole is section 504, the provision dealing with recovery of actual damages, profits, and statutory damages. The two basic aims of this section are reciprocal and correlative: (1) to give the courts specific unambiguous directions concerning monetary awards, thus avoiding the confusion and uncertainty that have marked the present law on the subject, and, at the same time, (2) to provide the courts with reasonable latitude to adjust recovery to the circumstances of the case, thus avoiding some of the artificial or overly technical awards resulting from the language of the existing statute.

Subsection (a) lays the groundwork for the more detailed provisions of the section by establishing the liability of a copyright infringer for either "the copyright owner's actual damages and any additional profits of the infringer," or statutory damages. Recovery of actual damages and profits under section 504(b) or of statutory damages under section 504(c) is alternative and for the copyright owner to elect; as under the present law, the plaintiff in an infringement suit is not obliged to submit proof of damages and profits and may choose to rely on the provision for minimum statutory damages. However, there is nothing in section 504 to prevent a court from taking account of evidence concerning actual damages and profits in making an award of statutory damages within the range set out in subsection (c).

Actual Damages and Profits. In allowing the plaintiff to recover "the actual damages suffered by him or her as a result of the infringement," plus any of the infringer's profits "that are attributable to the infringement and are not taken into account in computing the actual damages," section 504(b) recognizes the different purposes served by awards of damages and profits. Damages are awarded to compensate the copyright owner for losses from the infringement, and profits are awarded to prevent the infringer from unfairly benefiting from a wrongful act. Where the defendant's profits are nothing more than a measure of the damages suffered by the copyright owner, it would be inappropriate to award damages and profits cumulatively, since in effect they amount to the same thing. However, in cases where the copyright owner has suffered damages not reflected in the infringer's profits, or where there have been profits attributable to the copyrighted work but not used as a measure of damages, subsection (b) authorizes the award of both.

The language of the subsection makes clear that only those profits "attributable to the infringement" are recoverable; where some of the defendant's profits result from the infringement and other profits are caused by different factors, it will be necessary for the court to make an apportionment. However, the burden of proof is on the defendant in these cases; in establishing profits the plaintiff need prove only "the infringer's gross revenue," and the defendant must prove not only "his or her deductible expenses" but also "the element of profit attributable to factors other than the copyrighted work."

Statutory Damages. Subsection (c) of section 504 makes clear that the plaintiff's election to recover statutory damages may take place at any time during the trial before the court has rendered its final judgment. The remainder of clause (1) of the subsection represents a statement of the general rates applicable to awards of statutory damages. Its principal provisions may be summarized as follows:

1. As a general rule, where the plaintiff elects to recover statutory damages, the court is obliged to award between $250 and $10,000. It can exercise discretion in awarding an amount within that range but, unless one of the exceptions provided by clause (2) is applicable, it cannot make an award of less than $250 or of more than $10,000 if the copyright owner has chosen recovery under section 504(c).

2. Although, as explained below, an award of minimum statutory damages may be multiplied if separate works and separately liable infringers are involved in the suit, a single award in the $250 to $10,000 range is to be made "for all infringements involved in the action." A single infringer of a single work is liable for a single amount between $250 and $10,000, no matter how many acts of infringement are involved in the action and regardless of whether the acts were separate, isolated, or occurred in a related series.

3. Where the suit involves infringement of more than one separate and independent work, minimum statutory damages for each work must be awarded. For example, if one defendant has infringed three copyrighted works, the copyright owner is entitled to statutory damages of at least $750 and may be awarded up to $30,000. Subsection (c)(1) makes clear, however, that, although they are regarded as independent works for other purposes, "all the parts of a compila-

tion or derivative work constitute one work" for this purpose. Moreover, although the minimum and maximum amounts are to be multiplied where multiple "works" are involved in the suit, the same is not true with respect to multiple copyrights, multiple owners, multiple exclusive rights, or multiple registrations. This point is especially important since, under a scheme of divisible copyright, it is possible to have the rights of a number of owners of separate "copyrights" in a single "work" infringed by one act of a defendant.

4. Where the infringements of one work were committed by a single infringer acting individually, a single award of statutory damages would be made. Similarly, where the work was infringed by two or more joint tortfeasors, the bill would make them jointly and severally liable for an amount in the $250 to $10,000 range. However, where separate infringements for which two or more defendants are not jointly liable are joined in the same action, separate awards of statutory damages would be appropriate.

Clause (2) of section 504(c) provides for exceptional cases in which the maximum award of statutory damages could be raised from $10,000 to $50,000, and in which the minimum recovery could be reduced from $250 to $100. The basic principle underlying this provision is that the courts should be given discretion to increase statutory damages in cases of willful infringement and to lower the minimum where the infringer is innocent. The language of the clause makes clear that in these situations the burden of proving willfulness rests on the copyright owner and that of proving innocence rests on the infringer, and that the court must make a finding of either willfulness or innocence in order to award the exceptional amounts.

The "innocent infringer" provision of section 504(c)(2) has been the subject of extensive discussion. The exception, which would allow reduction of minimum statutory damages to $100 where the infringer "was not aware and had no reason to believe that his or her acts constituted an infringement of copyright," is sufficient to protect against unwarranted liability in cases of occasional or isolated innocent infringement, and it offers adequate insulation to users, such as broadcasters and newspaper publishers, who are particularly vulnerable to this type of infringement suit. On the other hand, by establishing a realistic floor for liability, the provision preserves its intended deterrent effect; and it would not allow an infringer to escape simply because the plaintiff failed to disprove the defendant's claim of innocence.

In addition to the general "innocent infringer" provision clause (2) deals with the special situation of teachers, librarians, archivists, and public broadcasters, and the nonprofit institutions of which they are a part. Section 504(c)(2) provides that, where such a person or institution infringed copyrighted material in the honest belief that what they were doing constituted fair use, the court is precluded from awarding any statutory damages. It is intended that, in cases involving this provision, the burden of proof with respect to the defendant's good faith should rest on the plaintiff.

AMENDMENTS

2010—Subsec. (c)(2). Pub. L. 111–295 substituted "section 118(f)" for "subsection (g) of section 118".

2004—Subsec. (c)(3). Pub. L. 108–482 added par. (3).

1999—Subsec. (c)(1). Pub. L. 106–160, §2(1), substituted "$750" for "$500" and "$30,000" for "$20,000".

Subsec. (c)(2). Pub. L. 106–160, §2(2), substituted "$150,000" for "$100,000".

1998—Subsec. (d). Pub. L. 105–298 added subsec. (d).

1997—Subsec. (c)(2). Pub. L. 105–80 substituted "the court in its discretion" for "the court it its discretion".

1988—Subsec. (c)(1). Pub. L. 100–568, §10(b)(1), substituted "$500" for "$250" and "$20,000" for "$10,000".

Subsec. (c)(2). Pub. L. 100–568, §10(b)(2), substituted "$100,000" for "$50,000" and "$200" for "$100".

EFFECTIVE DATE OF 1999 AMENDMENT

Pub. L. 106–160, §4, Dec. 9, 1999, 113 Stat. 1774, provided that: "The amendments made by section 2 [amending this section] shall apply to any action brought on or after the date of the enactment of this Act [Dec. 9, 1999], regardless of the date on which the alleged activity that is the basis of the action occurred."

EFFECTIVE DATE OF 1998 AMENDMENT

Amendment by Pub. L. 105–298 effective 90 days after Oct. 27, 1998, see section 207 of Pub. L. 105–298, set out as a note under section 101 of this title.

EFFECTIVE DATE OF 1988 AMENDMENT

Amendment by Pub. L. 100–568 effective Mar. 1, 1989, with any cause of action arising under this title before such date being governed by provisions in effect when cause of action arose, see section 13 of Pub. L. 100–568, set out as a note under section 101 of this title.

§ 505. Remedies for infringement: Costs and attorney's fees

In any civil action under this title, the court in its discretion may allow the recovery of full costs by or against any party other than the United States or an officer thereof. Except as otherwise provided by this title, the court may also award a reasonable attorney's fee to the prevailing party as part of the costs.

(Pub. L. 94–553, title I, §101, Oct. 19, 1976, 90 Stat. 2586.)

HISTORICAL AND REVISION NOTES

HOUSE REPORT NO. 94–1476

Under section 505 the awarding of costs and attorney's fees are left to the court's discretion, and the section also makes clear that neither costs nor attorney's fees can be awarded to or against "the United States or an officer thereof."

§ 506. Criminal offenses

(a) CRIMINAL INFRINGEMENT.—

(1) IN GENERAL.—Any person who willfully infringes a copyright shall be punished as provided under section 2319 of title 18, if the infringement was committed—

(A) for purposes of commercial advantage or private financial gain;

(B) by the reproduction or distribution, including by electronic means, during any 180–day period, of 1 or more copies or phonorecords of 1 or more copyrighted works, which have a total retail value of more than $1,000; or

(C) by the distribution of a work being prepared for commercial distribution, by making it available on a computer network accessible to members of the public, if such person knew or should have known that the work was intended for commercial distribution.

(2) EVIDENCE.—For purposes of this subsection, evidence of reproduction or distribution of a copyrighted work, by itself, shall not be sufficient to establish willful infringement of a copyright.

(3) DEFINITION.—In this subsection, the term "work being prepared for commercial distribution" means—

(A) a computer program, a musical work, a motion picture or other audiovisual work, or a sound recording, if, at the time of unauthorized distribution—

    (i) the copyright owner has a reasonable expectation of commercial distribution; and

    (ii) the copies or phonorecords of the work have not been commercially distributed; or

    (B) a motion picture, if, at the time of unauthorized distribution, the motion picture—

    (i) has been made available for viewing in a motion picture exhibition facility; and

    (ii) has not been made available in copies for sale to the general public in the United States in a format intended to permit viewing outside a motion picture exhibition facility.

(b) FORFEITURE, DESTRUCTION, AND RESTITUTION.—Forfeiture, destruction, and restitution relating to this section shall be subject to section 2323 of title 18, to the extent provided in that section, in addition to any other similar remedies provided by law.

(c) FRAUDULENT COPYRIGHT NOTICE.—Any person who, with fraudulent intent, places on any article a notice of copyright or words of the same purport that such person knows to be false, or who, with fraudulent intent, publicly distributes or imports for public distribution any article bearing such notice or words that such person knows to be false, shall be fined not more than $2,500.

(d) FRAUDULENT REMOVAL OF COPYRIGHT NOTICE.—Any person who, with fraudulent intent, removes or alters any notice of copyright appearing on a copy of a copyrighted work shall be fined not more than $2,500.

(e) FALSE REPRESENTATION.—Any person who knowingly makes a false representation of a material fact in the application for copyright registration provided for by section 409, or in any written statement filed in connection with the application, shall be fined not more than $2,500.

(f) RIGHTS OF ATTRIBUTION AND INTEGRITY.—Nothing in this section applies to infringement of the rights conferred by section 106A(a).

(Pub. L. 94–553, title I, § 101, Oct. 19, 1976, 90 Stat. 2586; Pub. L. 97–180, § 5, May 24, 1982, 96 Stat. 93; Pub. L. 101–650, title VI, § 606(b), Dec. 1, 1990, 104 Stat. 5131; Pub. L. 105–147, § 2(b), Dec. 16, 1997, 111 Stat. 2678; Pub. L. 109–9, title I, § 103(a), Apr. 27, 2005, 119 Stat. 220; Pub. L. 110–403, title II, § 201(a), Oct. 13, 2008, 122 Stat. 4260.)

HISTORICAL AND REVISION NOTES

HOUSE REPORT NO. 94–1476

Four types of criminal offenses actionable under the bill are listed in section 506: willful infringement for profit, fraudulent use of a copyright notice, fraudulent removal of notice, and false representation in connection with a copyright application. The maximum fine on conviction has been increased to $10,000 and, in conformity with the general pattern of the Criminal Code (18 U.S.C.), no minimum fines have been provided. In addition to or instead of a fine, conviction for criminal infringement under section 506(a) can carry with it a sentence of imprisonment of up to one year. Section 506(b) deals with seizure, forfeiture, and destruction of material involved in cases of criminal infringement.

Section 506(a) contains a special provision applying to any person who infringes willfully and for purposes of commercial advantage the copyright in a sound recording or a motion picture. For the first such offense a person shall be fined not more than $25,000 or imprisoned for not more than one year, or both. For any subsequent offense a person shall be fined not more than $50,000 or imprisoned not more than two years, or both.

AMENDMENTS

2008—Subsec. (b). Pub. L. 110–403 amended subsec. (b) generally. Prior to amendment, text read as follows: "When any person is convicted of any violation of subsection (a), the court in its judgment of conviction shall, in addition to the penalty therein prescribed, order the forfeiture and destruction or other disposition of all infringing copies or phonorecords and all implements, devices, or equipment used in the manufacture of such infringing copies or phonorecords."

2005—Subsec. (a). Pub. L. 109–9 reenacted heading without change and amended text generally. Prior to amendment, text read as follows: "Any person who infringes a copyright willfully either—

    "(1) for purposes of commercial advantage or private financial gain, or

    "(2) by the reproduction or distribution, including by electronic means, during any 180-day period, of 1 or more copies or phonorecords of 1 or more copyrighted works, which have a total retail value of more than $1,000,

shall be punished as provided under section 2319 of title 18, United States Code. For purposes of this subsection, evidence of reproduction or distribution of a copyrighted work, by itself, shall not be sufficient to establish willful infringement."

1997—Subsec. (a). Pub. L. 105–147 amended subsec. (a) generally. Prior to amendment, subsec. (a) read as follows:

"(a) CRIMINAL INFRINGEMENT.—Any person who infringes a copyright willfully and for purposes of commercial advantage or private financial gain shall be punished as provided in section 2319 of title 18."

1990—Subsec. (f). Pub. L. 101–650 added subsec. (f).

1982—Subsec. (a). Pub. L. 97–180 substituted "shall be punished as provided in section 2319 of title 18" for "shall be fined not more than $10,000 or imprisoned for not more than one year, or both: *Provided, however,* That any person who infringes willfully and for purposes of commercial advantage or private financial gain the copyright in a sound recording afforded by subsections (1), (2), or (3) of section 106 or the copyright in a motion picture afforded by subsections (1), (3), or (4) of section 106 shall be fined not more than $25,000 or imprisoned for not more than one year, or both, for the first such offense and shall be fined not more than $50,000 or imprisoned for not more than two years, or both, for any subsequent offense".

EFFECTIVE DATE OF 1990 AMENDMENT

Amendment by Pub. L. 101–650 effective 6 months after Dec. 1, 1990, see section 610 of Pub. L. 101–650, set out as an Effective Date note under section 106A of this title.

§ 507. Limitations on actions

(a) CRIMINAL PROCEEDINGS.—Except as expressly provided otherwise in this title, no criminal proceeding shall be maintained under the provisions of this title unless it is commenced within 5 years after the cause of action arose.

(b) CIVIL ACTIONS.—No civil action shall be maintained under the provisions of this title unless it is commenced within three years after the claim accrued.

(Pub. L. 94–553, title I, § 101, Oct. 19, 1976, 90 Stat. 2586; Pub. L. 105–147, § 2(c), Dec. 16, 1997, 111 Stat. 2678; Pub. L. 105–304, title I, § 102(e), Oct. 28, 1998, 112 Stat. 2863.)

Section 507, which is substantially identical with section 115 of the present law [section 115 of former title 17], establishes a three-year statute of limitations for both criminal proceedings and civil actions. The language of this section, which was adopted by the act of September 7, 1957 (71 Stat. 633) [Pub. L. 85–313, § 1, Sept. 7, 1957, 71 Stat. 633], represents a reconciliation of views, and has therefore been left unaltered.

AMENDMENTS

1998—Subsec. (a). Pub. L. 105–304 substituted "Except as expressly provided otherwise in this title, no" for "No".

1997—Subsec. (a). Pub. L. 105–147 substituted "5" for "three".

§ 508. Notification of filing and determination of actions

(a) Within one month after the filing of any action under this title, the clerks of the courts of the United States shall send written notification to the Register of Copyrights setting forth, as far as is shown by the papers filed in the court, the names and addresses of the parties and the title, author, and registration number of each work involved in the action. If any other copyrighted work is later included in the action by amendment, answer, or other pleading, the clerk shall also send a notification concerning it to the Register within one month after the pleading is filed.

(b) Within one month after any final order or judgment is issued in the case, the clerk of the court shall notify the Register of it, sending with the notification a copy of the order or judgment together with the written opinion, if any, of the court.

(c) Upon receiving the notifications specified in this section, the Register shall make them a part of the public records of the Copyright Office.

(Pub. L. 94–553, title I, § 101, Oct. 19, 1976, 90 Stat. 2586.)

Section 508, which corresponds to some extent with a provision in the patent law (35 U.S.C. 290), is intended to establish a method for notifying the Copyright Office and the public of the filing and disposition of copyright cases. The clerks of the Federal courts are to notify the Copyright Office of the filing of any copyright actions and of their final disposition, and the Copyright Office is to make these notifications a part of its public records.

[§ 509. Repealed. Pub. L. 110–403, title II, § 201(b)(1), Oct. 13, 2008, 122 Stat. 4260]

Section, Pub. L. 94–553, title I, § 101, Oct. 19, 1976, 90 Stat. 2587; Pub. L. 105–80, § 12(a)(14), Nov. 13, 1997, 111 Stat. 1535, related to seizure and forfeiture.

§ 510. Remedies for alteration of programming by cable systems

(a) In any action filed pursuant to section 111(c)(3), the following remedies shall be available:

(1) Where an action is brought by a party identified in subsections (b) or (c) of section 501, the remedies provided by sections 502 through 505, and the remedy provided by subsection (b) of this section; and

(2) When an action is brought by a party identified in subsection (d) of section 501, the remedies provided by sections 502 and 505, together with any actual damages suffered by such party as a result of the infringement, and the remedy provided by subsection (b) of this section.

(b) In any action filed pursuant to section 111(c)(3), the court may decree that, for a period not to exceed thirty days, the cable system shall be deprived of the benefit of a statutory license for one or more distant signals carried by such cable system.

(Pub. L. 94–553, title I, § 101, Oct. 19, 1976, 90 Stat. 2587; Pub. L. 106–113, div. B, § 1000(a)(9) [title I, § 1011(a)(1), (3)], Nov. 29, 1999, 113 Stat. 1536, 1501A–543.)

Section 509(b) specifies a new discretionary remedy for alteration of programming by cable systems in violation of section 111(c)(3): the court in such cases may decree that, "for a period not to exceed thirty days, the cable system shall be deprived of the benefit of a compulsory license for one or more distant signals carried by such cable system." The term "distant signals" in this provision is intended to have a meaning consistent with the definition of "distant signal equivalent" in section 111.

Under section 509(a), four types of plaintiffs are entitled to bring an action in cases of alteration of programming by cable systems in violation of section 111(c)(3). For regular copyright owners and local broadcaster-licensees, the full battery of remedies for infringement would be available. The two new classes of potential plaintiffs under section 501(d)—the distant-signal transmitter and other local stations—would be limited to the following remedies: (i) discretionary injunctions; (ii) discretionary costs and attorney's fees; (iii) any actual damages the plaintiff can prove were attributable to the act of altering program content; and (iv) the new discretionary remedy of suspension of compulsory licensing.

AMENDMENTS

1999—Pub. L. 106–113, § 1000(a)(9) [title I, § 1011(a)(1)], substituted "programming" for "programing" in section catchline.

Subsec. (b). Pub. L. 106–113, § 1000(a)(9) [title I, § 1011(a)(3)], substituted "statutory" for "compulsory".

§ 511. Liability of States, instrumentalities of States, and State officials for infringement of copyright

(a) IN GENERAL.—Any State, any instrumentality of a State, and any officer or employee of a State or instrumentality of a State acting in his or her official capacity, shall not be immune, under the Eleventh Amendment of the Constitution of the United States or under any other doctrine of sovereign immunity, from suit in Federal court by any person, including any governmental or nongovernmental entity, for a violation of any of the exclusive rights of a copyright owner provided by sections 106 through 122, for importing copies of phonorecords in violation of section 602, or for any other violation under this title.

(b) REMEDIES.—In a suit described in subsection (a) for a violation described in that subsection, remedies (including remedies both at law and in equity) are available for the violation to the same extent as such remedies are available for such a violation in a suit against any public or private entity other than a State, instrumentality of a State, or officer or employee of a State acting in his or her official capacity. Such remedies include impounding and disposition of infringing articles under section 503, actual damages and profits and statutory damages under section 504, costs and attorney's fees under section 505, and the remedies provided in section 510.

(Added Pub. L. 101–553, §2(a)(2), Nov. 15, 1990, 104 Stat. 2749; amended Pub. L. 106–44, §1(g)(6), Aug. 5, 1999, 113 Stat. 222; Pub. L. 107–273, div. C, title III, §13210(4)(C), Nov. 2, 2002, 116 Stat. 1909.)

AMENDMENTS

2002—Subsec. (a). Pub. L. 107–273 substituted "122" for "121".

1999—Subsec. (a). Pub. L. 106–44 substituted "121" for "119".

EFFECTIVE DATE

Section effective with respect to violations that occur on or after Nov. 15, 1990, see section 3 of Pub. L. 101–553, set out as an Effective Date of 1990 Amendment note under section 501 of this title.

§512. Limitations on liability relating to material online

(a) TRANSITORY DIGITAL NETWORK COMMUNICATIONS.—A service provider shall not be liable for monetary relief, or, except as provided in subsection (j), for injunctive or other equitable relief, for infringement of copyright by reason of the provider's transmitting, routing, or providing connections for, material through a system or network controlled or operated by or for the service provider, or by reason of the intermediate and transient storage of that material in the course of such transmitting, routing, or providing connections, if—

(1) the transmission of the material was initiated by or at the direction of a person other than the service provider;

(2) the transmission, routing, provision of connections, or storage is carried out through an automatic technical process without selection of the material by the service provider;

(3) the service provider does not select the recipients of the material except as an automatic response to the request of another person;

(4) no copy of the material made by the service provider in the course of such intermediate or transient storage is maintained on the system or network in a manner ordinarily accessible to anyone other than anticipated recipients, and no such copy is maintained on the system or network in a manner ordinarily accessible to such anticipated recipients for a longer period than is reasonably necessary for the transmission, routing, or provision of connections; and

(5) the material is transmitted through the system or network without modification of its content.

(b) SYSTEM CACHING.—

(1) LIMITATION ON LIABILITY.—A service provider shall not be liable for monetary relief, or, except as provided in subsection (j), for injunctive or other equitable relief, for infringement of copyright by reason of the intermediate and temporary storage of material on a system or network controlled or operated by or for the service provider in a case in which—

(A) the material is made available online by a person other than the service provider;

(B) the material is transmitted from the person described in subparagraph (A) through the system or network to a person other than the person described in subparagraph (A) at the direction of that other person; and

(C) the storage is carried out through an automatic technical process for the purpose of making the material available to users of the system or network who, after the material is transmitted as described in subparagraph (B), request access to the material from the person described in subparagraph (A),

if the conditions set forth in paragraph (2) are met.

(2) CONDITIONS.—The conditions referred to in paragraph (1) are that—

(A) the material described in paragraph (1) is transmitted to the subsequent users described in paragraph (1)(C) without modification to its content from the manner in which the material was transmitted from the person described in paragraph (1)(A);

(B) the service provider described in paragraph (1) complies with rules concerning the refreshing, reloading, or other updating of the material when specified by the person making the material available online in accordance with a generally accepted industry standard data communications protocol for the system or network through which that person makes the material available, except that this subparagraph applies only if those rules are not used by the person described in paragraph (1)(A) to prevent or unreasonably impair the intermediate storage to which this subsection applies;

(C) the service provider does not interfere with the ability of technology associated with the material to return to the person described in paragraph (1)(A) the information that would have been available to that person if the material had been obtained by the subsequent users described in paragraph (1)(C) directly from that person, except that this subparagraph applies only if that technology—

(i) does not significantly interfere with the performance of the provider's system or network or with the intermediate storage of the material;

(ii) is consistent with generally accepted industry standard communications protocols; and

(iii) does not extract information from the provider's system or network other than the information that would have been available to the person described in paragraph (1)(A) if the subsequent users had gained access to the material directly from that person;

(D) if the person described in paragraph (1)(A) has in effect a condition that a person must meet prior to having access to the material, such as a condition based on payment of a fee or provision of a password or other information, the service provider permits access to the stored material in significant part only to users of its system or network that have met those conditions and only in accordance with those conditions; and

(E) if the person described in paragraph (1)(A) makes that material available online without the authorization of the copyright owner of the material, the service provider responds expeditiously to remove, or disable access to, the material that is claimed to be infringing upon notification of claimed infringement as described in subsection (c)(3), except that this subparagraph applies only if—

(i) the material has previously been removed from the originating site or access to it has been disabled, or a court has ordered that the material be removed from the originating site or that access to the material on the originating site be disabled; and

(ii) the party giving the notification includes in the notification a statement confirming that the material has been removed from the originating site or access to it has been disabled or that a court has ordered that the material be removed from the originating site or that access to the material on the originating site be disabled.

(c) INFORMATION RESIDING ON SYSTEMS OR NETWORKS AT DIRECTION OF USERS.—

(1) IN GENERAL.—A service provider shall not be liable for monetary relief, or, except as provided in subsection (j), for injunctive or other equitable relief, for infringement of copyright by reason of the storage at the direction of a user of material that resides on a system or network controlled or operated by or for the service provider, if the service provider—

(A)(i) does not have actual knowledge that the material or an activity using the material on the system or network is infringing;

(ii) in the absence of such actual knowledge, is not aware of facts or circumstances from which infringing activity is apparent; or

(iii) upon obtaining such knowledge or awareness, acts expeditiously to remove, or disable access to, the material;

(B) does not receive a financial benefit directly attributable to the infringing activity, in a case in which the service provider has the right and ability to control such activity; and

(C) upon notification of claimed infringement as described in paragraph (3), responds expeditiously to remove, or disable access to, the material that is claimed to be infringing or to be the subject of infringing activity.

(2) DESIGNATED AGENT.—The limitations on liability established in this subsection apply to a service provider only if the service provider has designated an agent to receive notifications of claimed infringement described in paragraph (3), by making available through its service, including on its website in a location accessible to the public, and by providing to the Copyright Office, substantially the following information:

(A) the name, address, phone number, and electronic mail address of the agent.

(B) other contact information which the Register of Copyrights may deem appropriate.

The Register of Copyrights shall maintain a current directory of agents available to the public for inspection, including through the Internet, and may require payment of a fee by service providers to cover the costs of maintaining the directory.

(3) ELEMENTS OF NOTIFICATION.—

(A) To be effective under this subsection, a notification of claimed infringement must be a written communication provided to the designated agent of a service provider that includes substantially the following:

(i) A physical or electronic signature of a person authorized to act on behalf of the owner of an exclusive right that is allegedly infringed.

(ii) Identification of the copyrighted work claimed to have been infringed, or, if multiple copyrighted works at a single online site are covered by a single notification, a representative list of such works at that site.

(iii) Identification of the material that is claimed to be infringing or to be the subject of infringing activity and that is to be removed or access to which is to be disabled, and information reasonably sufficient to permit the service provider to locate the material.

(iv) Information reasonably sufficient to permit the service provider to contact the complaining party, such as an address, telephone number, and, if available, an electronic mail address at which the complaining party may be contacted.

(v) A statement that the complaining party has a good faith belief that use of the material in the manner complained of is not authorized by the copyright owner, its agent, or the law.

(vi) A statement that the information in the notification is accurate, and under penalty of perjury, that the complaining party is authorized to act on behalf of the owner of an exclusive right that is allegedly infringed.

(B)(i) Subject to clause (ii), a notification from a copyright owner or from a person authorized to act on behalf of the copyright owner that fails to comply substantially with the provisions of subparagraph (A) shall not be considered under paragraph (1)(A) in determining whether a service provider has actual knowledge or is aware of facts or circumstances from which infringing activity is apparent.

(ii) In a case in which the notification that is provided to the service provider's designated agent fails to comply substantially with all the provisions of subparagraph (A) but substantially complies with clauses (ii), (iii), and (iv) of subparagraph (A), clause (i) of this subparagraph applies only if the service provider promptly attempts to contact the person making the notification or takes other reasonable steps to assist in the receipt of notification that substantially complies with all the provisions of subparagraph (A).

(d) INFORMATION LOCATION TOOLS.—A service provider shall not be liable for monetary relief, or, except as provided in subsection (j), for injunctive or other equitable relief, for infringement of copyright by reason of the provider referring or linking users to an online location containing infringing material or infringing activity, by using information location tools, including a directory, index, reference, pointer, or hypertext link, if the service provider—

(1)(A) does not have actual knowledge that the material or activity is infringing;

(B) in the absence of such actual knowledge, is not aware of facts or circumstances from which infringing activity is apparent; or

(C) upon obtaining such knowledge or awareness, acts expeditiously to remove, or disable access to, the material;

(2) does not receive a financial benefit directly attributable to the infringing activity, in a case in which the service provider has the right and ability to control such activity; and

(3) upon notification of claimed infringement as described in subsection (c)(3), responds expeditiously to remove, or disable access to, the material that is claimed to be infringing or to be the subject of infringing activity, except that, for purposes of this paragraph, the information described in subsection (c)(3)(A)(iii) shall be identification of the reference or link, to material or activity claimed to be infringing, that is to be removed or access to which is to be disabled, and information reasonably sufficient to permit the service provider to locate that reference or link.

(e) LIMITATION ON LIABILITY OF NONPROFIT EDUCATIONAL INSTITUTIONS.—(1) When a public or other nonprofit institution of higher education is a service provider, and when a faculty member or graduate student who is an employee of such institution is performing a teaching or research function, for the purposes of subsections (a) and (b) such faculty member or graduate student shall be considered to be a person other than the institution, and for the purposes of subsections (c) and (d) such faculty member's or graduate student's knowledge or awareness of his or her infringing activities shall not be attributed to the institution, if—

(A) such faculty member's or graduate student's infringing activities do not involve the provision of online access to instructional materials that are or were required or recommended, within the preceding 3-year period, for a course taught at the institution by such faculty member or graduate student;

(B) the institution has not, within the preceding 3-year period, received more than two notifications described in subsection (c)(3) of claimed infringement by such faculty member or graduate student, and such notifications of claimed infringement were not actionable under subsection (f); and

(C) the institution provides to all users of its system or network informational materials that accurately describe, and promote compliance with, the laws of the United States relating to copyright.

(2) For the purposes of this subsection, the limitations on injunctive relief contained in subsections (j)(2) and (j)(3), but not those in (j)(1), shall apply.

(f) MISREPRESENTATIONS.—Any person who knowingly materially misrepresents under this section—

(1) that material or activity is infringing, or

(2) that material or activity was removed or disabled by mistake or misidentification,

shall be liable for any damages, including costs and attorneys' fees, incurred by the alleged infringer, by any copyright owner or copyright owner's authorized licensee, or by a service provider, who is injured by such misrepresentation, as the result of the service provider relying upon such misrepresentation in removing or disabling access to the material or activity claimed to be infringing, or in replacing the removed material or ceasing to disable access to it.

(g) REPLACEMENT OF REMOVED OR DISABLED MATERIAL AND LIMITATION ON OTHER LIABILITY.—

(1) NO LIABILITY FOR TAKING DOWN GENERALLY.—Subject to paragraph (2), a service provider shall not be liable to any person for any claim based on the service provider's good faith disabling of access to, or removal of, material or activity claimed to be infringing or based on facts or circumstances from which infringing activity is apparent, regardless of whether the material or activity is ultimately determined to be infringing.

(2) EXCEPTION.—Paragraph (1) shall not apply with respect to material residing at the direction of a subscriber of the service provider on a system or network controlled or operated by or for the service provider that is removed, or to which access is disabled by the service provider, pursuant to a notice provided under subsection (c)(1)(C), unless the service provider—

(A) takes reasonable steps promptly to notify the subscriber that it has removed or disabled access to the material;

(B) upon receipt of a counter notification described in paragraph (3), promptly provides the person who provided the notification under subsection (c)(1)(C) with a copy of the counter notification, and informs that person that it will replace the removed material or cease disabling access to it in 10 business days; and

(C) replaces the removed material and ceases disabling access to it not less than 10, nor more than 14, business days following receipt of the counter notice, unless its designated agent first receives notice from the person who submitted the notification under subsection (c)(1)(C) that such person has filed an action seeking a court order to restrain the subscriber from engaging in infringing activity relating to the material on the service provider's system or network.

(3) CONTENTS OF COUNTER NOTIFICATION.—To be effective under this subsection, a counter notification must be a written communication provided to the service provider's designated agent that includes substantially the following:

(A) A physical or electronic signature of the subscriber.

(B) Identification of the material that has been removed or to which access has been disabled and the location at which the material appeared before it was removed or access to it was disabled.

(C) A statement under penalty of perjury that the subscriber has a good faith belief that the material was removed or disabled as a result of mistake or misidentification of the material to be removed or disabled.

(D) The subscriber's name, address, and telephone number, and a statement that the subscriber consents to the jurisdiction of Federal District Court for the judicial district in which the address is located, or if the subscriber's address is outside of the United States, for any judicial district in which the service provider may be found, and that the subscriber will accept service of process from the person who provided notification under subsection (c)(1)(C) or an agent of such person.

(4) LIMITATION ON OTHER LIABILITY.—A service provider's compliance with paragraph (2) shall not subject the service provider to liability for copyright infringement with respect to the material identified in the notice provided under subsection (c)(1)(C).

(h) SUBPOENA TO IDENTIFY INFRINGER.—

(1) REQUEST.—A copyright owner or a person authorized to act on the owner's behalf may request the clerk of any United States district court to issue a subpoena to a service provider for identification of an alleged infringer in accordance with this subsection.

(2) CONTENTS OF REQUEST.—The request may be made by filing with the clerk—

(A) a copy of a notification described in subsection (c)(3)(A);

(B) a proposed subpoena; and

(C) a sworn declaration to the effect that the purpose for which the subpoena is sought is to obtain the identity of an alleged infringer and that such information will only be used for the purpose of protecting rights under this title.

(3) CONTENTS OF SUBPOENA.—The subpoena shall authorize and order the service provider receiving the notification and the subpoena to expeditiously disclose to the copyright owner or person authorized by the copyright owner information sufficient to identify the alleged infringer of the material described in the notification to the extent such information is available to the service provider.

(4) BASIS FOR GRANTING SUBPOENA.—If the notification filed satisfies the provisions of subsection (c)(3)(A), the proposed subpoena is in proper form, and the accompanying declaration is properly executed, the clerk shall expeditiously issue and sign the proposed subpoena and return it to the requester for delivery to the service provider.

(5) ACTIONS OF SERVICE PROVIDER RECEIVING SUBPOENA.—Upon receipt of the issued subpoena, either accompanying or subsequent to the receipt of a notification described in subsection (c)(3)(A), the service provider shall expeditiously disclose to the copyright owner or person authorized by the copyright owner the information required by the subpoena, notwithstanding any other provision of law and regardless of whether the service provider responds to the notification.

(6) RULES APPLICABLE TO SUBPOENA.—Unless otherwise provided by this section or by applicable rules of the court, the procedure for issuance and delivery of the subpoena, and the remedies for noncompliance with the subpoena, shall be governed to the greatest extent practicable by those provisions of the Federal Rules of Civil Procedure governing the issuance, service, and enforcement of a subpoena duces tecum.

(i) CONDITIONS FOR ELIGIBILITY.—

(1) ACCOMMODATION OF TECHNOLOGY.—The limitations on liability established by this section shall apply to a service provider only if the service provider—

(A) has adopted and reasonably implemented, and informs subscribers and account holders of the service provider's system or network of, a policy that provides for the termination in appropriate circumstances of subscribers and account holders of the service provider's system or network who are repeat infringers; and

(B) accommodates and does not interfere with standard technical measures.

(2) DEFINITION.—As used in this subsection, the term "standard technical measures" means technical measures that are used by copyright owners to identify or protect copyrighted works and—

(A) have been developed pursuant to a broad consensus of copyright owners and service providers in an open, fair, voluntary, multi-industry standards process;

(B) are available to any person on reasonable and nondiscriminatory terms; and

(C) do not impose substantial costs on service providers or substantial burdens on their systems or networks.

(j) INJUNCTIONS.—The following rules shall apply in the case of any application for an injunction under section 502 against a service provider that is not subject to monetary remedies under this section:

(1) SCOPE OF RELIEF.—(A) With respect to conduct other than that which qualifies for the limitation on remedies set forth in subsection (a), the court may grant injunctive relief with respect to a service provider only in one or more of the following forms:

(i) An order restraining the service provider from providing access to infringing material or activity residing at a particular online site on the provider's system or network.

(ii) An order restraining the service provider from providing access to a subscriber or account holder of the service provider's system or network who is engaging in infringing activity and is identified in the order, by terminating the accounts of the subscriber or account holder that are specified in the order.

(iii) Such other injunctive relief as the court may consider necessary to prevent or restrain infringement of copyrighted material specified in the order of the court at a particular online location, if such relief is the least burdensome to the service provider among the forms of relief comparably effective for that purpose.

(B) If the service provider qualifies for the limitation on remedies described in subsection (a), the court may only grant injunctive relief in one or both of the following forms:

(i) An order restraining the service provider from providing access to a subscriber or account holder of the service provider's system or network who is using the provider's service to engage in infringing activity and is identified in the order, by terminating the accounts of the subscriber or account holder that are specified in the order.

(ii) An order restraining the service provider from providing access, by taking reasonable steps specified in the order to block access, to a specific, identified, online location outside the United States.

(2) CONSIDERATIONS.—The court, in considering the relevant criteria for injunctive relief under applicable law, shall consider—

(A) whether such an injunction, either alone or in combination with other such injunctions issued against the same service provider under this subsection, would significantly burden either the provider or the operation of the provider's system or network;

(B) the magnitude of the harm likely to be suffered by the copyright owner in the digital network environment if steps are not taken to prevent or restrain the infringement;

(C) whether implementation of such an injunction would be technically feasible and effective, and would not interfere with access to noninfringing material at other online locations; and

(D) whether other less burdensome and comparably effective means of preventing or restraining access to the infringing material are available.

(3) NOTICE AND EX PARTE ORDERS.—Injunctive relief under this subsection shall be available only after notice to the service provider and an opportunity for the service provider to appear are provided, except for orders ensuring the preservation of evidence or other orders having no material adverse effect on the operation of the service provider's communications network.

(k) DEFINITIONS.—

(1) SERVICE PROVIDER.—(A) As used in subsection (a), the term "service provider" means an entity offering the transmission, routing, or providing of connections for digital online communications, between or among points specified by a user, of material of the user's choosing, without modification to the content of the material as sent or received.

(B) As used in this section, other than subsection (a), the term "service provider" means a provider of online services or network access, or the operator of facilities therefor, and includes an entity described in subparagraph (A).

(2) MONETARY RELIEF.—As used in this section, the term "monetary relief" means damages, costs, attorneys' fees, and any other form of monetary payment.

(l) OTHER DEFENSES NOT AFFECTED.—The failure of a service provider's conduct to qualify for limitation of liability under this section shall not bear adversely upon the consideration of a defense by the service provider that the service provider's conduct is not infringing under this title or any other defense.

(m) PROTECTION OF PRIVACY.—Nothing in this section shall be construed to condition the applicability of subsections (a) through (d) on—

(1) a service provider monitoring its service or affirmatively seeking facts indicating infringing activity, except to the extent consistent with a standard technical measure complying with the provisions of subsection (i); or

(2) a service provider gaining access to, removing, or disabling access to material in cases in which such conduct is prohibited by law.

(n) CONSTRUCTION.—Subsections (a), (b), (c), and (d) describe separate and distinct functions for purposes of applying this section. Whether a service provider qualifies for the limitation on liability in any one of those subsections shall be based solely on the criteria in that subsection, and shall not affect a determination of whether that service provider qualifies for the limitations on liability under any other such subsection.

(Added Pub. L. 105–304, title II, § 202(a), Oct. 28, 1998, 112 Stat. 2877; amended Pub. L. 106–44, § 1(d), Aug. 5, 1999, 113 Stat. 222; Pub. L. 111–295, § 3(a), Dec. 9, 2010, 124 Stat. 3180.)

REFERENCES IN TEXT

The Federal Rules of Civil Procedure, referred to in subsec. (h)(6), are set out in the Appendix to Title 28, Judiciary and Judicial Procedure.

CODIFICATION

Another section 512 was renumbered section 513 of this title.

AMENDMENTS

2010—Subsec. (c)(2). Pub. L. 111–295 struck out ", in both electronic and hard copy formats" after "Internet" in concluding provisions.

1999—Subsec. (e). Pub. L. 106–44, § 1(d)(1)(A), substituted "Limitation on Liability of Nonprofit Educational Institutions" for "Limitation on liability of nonprofit educational institutions" in heading.

Subsec. (e)(2). Pub. L. 106–44, § 1(d)(1)(B), struck out par. heading "Injunctions".

Subsec. (j)(3). Pub. L. 106–44, § 1(d)(2), substituted "Notice and ex parte orders" for "Notice and Ex Parte Orders" in heading.

Pub. L. 105–304, title II, § 203, Oct. 28, 1998, 112 Stat. 2886, provided that: "This title [enacting this section and provisions set out as a note under section 101 of this title] and the amendments made by this title shall take effect on the date of the enactment of this Act [Oct. 28, 1998]."

§ 513. Determination of reasonable license fees for individual proprietors

In the case of any performing rights society subject to a consent decree which provides for the determination of reasonable license rates or fees to be charged by the performing rights society, notwithstanding the provisions of that consent decree, an individual proprietor who owns or operates fewer than 7 non-publicly traded establishments in which nondramatic musical works are performed publicly and who claims that any license agreement offered by that performing rights society is unreasonable in its license rate or fee as to that individual proprietor, shall be entitled to determination of a reasonable license rate or fee as follows:

(1) The individual proprietor may commence such proceeding for determination of a reasonable license rate or fee by filing an application in the applicable district court under paragraph (2) that a rate disagreement exists and by serving a copy of the application on the performing rights society. Such proceeding shall commence in the applicable district court within 90 days after the service of such copy, except that such 90-day requirement shall be subject to the administrative requirements of the court.

(2) The proceeding under paragraph (1) shall be held, at the individual proprietor's election, in the judicial district of the district court with jurisdiction over the applicable consent decree or in that place of holding court of a district court that is the seat of the Federal circuit (other than the Court of Appeals for the Federal Circuit) in which the proprietor's establishment is located.

(3) Such proceeding shall be held before the judge of the court with jurisdiction over the consent decree governing the performing rights society. At the discretion of the court, the proceeding shall be held before a special master or magistrate judge appointed by such judge. Should that consent decree provide for the appointment of an advisor or advisors to the court for any purpose, any such advisor shall be the special master so named by the court.

(4) In any such proceeding, the industry rate shall be presumed to have been reasonable at the time it was agreed to or determined by the court. Such presumption shall in no way affect a determination of whether the rate is being correctly applied to the individual proprietor.

(5) Pending the completion of such proceeding, the individual proprietor shall have the right to perform publicly the copyrighted musical compositions in the repertoire of the performing rights society by paying an interim license rate or fee into an interest bearing escrow account with the clerk of the court, subject to retroactive adjustment when a final rate or fee has been determined, in an amount equal to the industry rate, or, in the absence of an industry rate, the amount of the most recent license rate or fee agreed to by the parties.

(6) Any decision rendered in such proceeding by a special master or magistrate judge named under paragraph (3) shall be reviewed by the judge of the court with jurisdiction over the consent decree governing the performing rights society. Such proceeding, including such review, shall be concluded within 6 months after its commencement.

(7) Any such final determination shall be binding only as to the individual proprietor commencing the proceeding, and shall not be applicable to any other proprietor or any other performing rights society, and the performing rights society shall be relieved of any obligation of nondiscrimination among similarly situated music users that may be imposed by the consent decree governing its operations.

(8) An individual proprietor may not bring more than one proceeding provided for in this section for the determination of a reasonable license rate or fee under any license agreement with respect to any one performing rights society.

(9) For purposes of this section, the term "industry rate" means the license fee a performing rights society has agreed to with, or which has been determined by the court for, a significant segment of the music user industry to which the individual proprietor belongs.

(Added Pub. L. 105–298, title II, § 203(a), Oct. 27, 1998, 112 Stat. 2831, § 512; renumbered § 513, Pub. L. 106–44, § 1(c)(1), Aug. 5, 1999, 113 Stat. 221.)

1999—Pub. L. 106–44 renumbered section 512 of this title as this section.

Section effective 90 days after Oct. 27, 1998, see section 207 of Pub. L. 105–298, set out as an Effective Date of 1998 Amendments note under section 101 of this title.

CHAPTER 6—IMPORTATION AND EXPORTATION

2010—Pub. L. 111–295, § 4(a), (b)(1)(A), Dec. 9, 2010, 124 Stat. 3180, substituted "IMPORTATION AND EXPORTATION" for "MANUFACTURING REQUIREMENTS, IMPORTATION, AND EXPORTATION" in chapter heading and struck out item 601 "Manufacture, importation, and public distribution of certain copies".

2008—Pub. L. 110–403, title I, § 105(a), Oct. 13, 2008, 122 Stat. 4259, substituted "MANUFACTURING REQUIREMENTS, IMPORTATION, AND EXPORTATION" for "MANUFACTURING REQUIREMENTS AND IMPORTATION" in chapter heading.

---

[1] So in original. Does not conform to section catchline.

[§ 601. Repealed. Pub. L. 111–295, § 4(a), Dec. 9, 2010, 124 Stat. 3180]

Section, Pub. L. 94–553, title I, § 101, Oct. 19, 1976, 90 Stat. 2588; Pub. L. 97–215, July 13, 1982, 96 Stat. 178; Pub. L. 105–80, § 12(a)(15), (16), Nov. 13, 1997, 111 Stat. 1535; Pub. L. 110–403, title I, § 105(c)(2), Oct. 13, 2008, 122 Stat. 4260, related to manufacture, importation, and public distribution of certain copies of nondramatic English-language literary material protected under this title.

§ 602. Infringing importation or exportation of copies or phonorecords

(a) INFRINGING IMPORTATION OR EXPORTATION.—

(1) IMPORTATION.—Importation into the United States, without the authority of the owner of copyright under this title, of copies or phonorecords of a work that have been acquired outside the United States is an infringement of the exclusive right to distribute copies or phonorecords under section 106, actionable under section 501.

(2) IMPORTATION OR EXPORTATION OF INFRINGING ITEMS.—Importation into the United States or exportation from the United States, without the authority of the owner of copyright under this title, of copies or phonorecords, the making of which either constituted an infringement of copyright, or which would have constituted an infringement of copyright if this title had been applicable, is an infringement of the exclusive right to distribute copies or phonorecords under section 106, actionable under sections 501 and 506.

(3) EXCEPTIONS.—This subsection does not apply to—

(A) importation or exportation of copies or phonorecords under the authority or for the use of the Government of the United States or of any State or political subdivision of a State, but not including copies or phonorecords for use in schools, or copies of any audiovisual work imported for purposes other than archival use;

(B) importation or exportation, for the private use of the importer or exporter and not for distribution, by any person with respect to no more than one copy or phonorecord of any one work at any one time, or by any person arriving from outside the United States or departing from the United States with respect to copies or phonorecords forming part of such person's personal baggage; or

(C) importation by or for an organization operated for scholarly, educational, or religious purposes and not for private gain, with respect to no more than one copy of an audiovisual work solely for its archival purposes, and no more than five copies or phonorecords of any other work for its library lending or archival purposes, unless the importation of such copies or phonorecords is part of an activity consisting of systematic reproduction or distribution, engaged in by such organization in violation of the provisions of section 108(g)(2).

(b) IMPORT PROHIBITION.—In a case where the making of the copies or phonorecords would have constituted an infringement of copyright if this title had been applicable, their importation is prohibited. In a case where the copies or phonorecords were lawfully made, United States Customs and Border Protection has no authority to prevent their importation. In either case, the Secretary of the Treasury is authorized to prescribe, by regulation, a procedure under which any person claiming an interest in the copyright in a particular work may, upon payment of a specified fee, be entitled to notification by United States Customs and Border Protection of the importation of articles that appear to be copies or phonorecords of the work.

(Pub. L. 94–553, title I, § 101, Oct. 19, 1976, 90 Stat. 2589; Pub. L. 110–403, title I, § 105(b), (c)(1), Oct. 13, 2008, 122 Stat. 4259, 4260; Pub. L. 111–295, § 4(c), Dec. 9, 2010, 124 Stat. 3181.)

HISTORICAL AND REVISION NOTES

HOUSE REPORT NO. 94–1476

Scope of the Section. Section 602, which has nothing to do with the manufacturing requirements of section 601, deals with two separate situations: importation of "piratical" articles (that is, copies or phonorecords made without any authorization of the copyright owner), and unauthorized importation of copies or phonorecords that were lawfully made. The general approach of section 602 is to make unauthorized importation an act of infringement in both cases, but to permit the United States Customs Service to prohibit importation only of "piratical" articles.

Section 602(a) first states the general rule that unauthorized importation is an infringement merely if the copies or phonorecords "have been acquired outside the United States", but then enumerates three specific exceptions: (1) importation under the authority or for the use of a governmental body, but not including material for use in schools or copies of an audiovisual work imported for any purpose other than archival use; (2) importation for the private use of the importer of no more than one copy or phonorecord of a work at a time, or of articles in the personal baggage of travelers from abroad; or (3) importation by nonprofit organizations "operated for scholarly, educational, or religious purposes" of "no more than one copy of an audiovisual work solely for archival purposes, and no more than five copies or phonorecords of any other work for its library lending or archival purposes." The bill specifies that the third exception does not apply if the importation "is part of an activity consisting of systematic reproduction or distribution, engaged in by such organization in violation of the provisions of section 108(g)(2)."

If none of the three exemptions applies, any unauthorized importer of copies or phonorecords acquired abroad could be sued for damages and enjoined from making any use of them, even before any public distribution in this country has taken place.

Importation of "Piratical" Copies. Section 602(b) retains the present statute's prohibition against importation of "piratical" copies or phonorecords—those whose making "would have constituted an infringement of copyright if this title has been applicable." Thus, the Customs Service could exclude copies or phonorecords that were unlawful in the country where they were made; it could also exclude copies or phonorecords which, although made lawfully under the domestic law of that country, would have been unlawful if the U.S. copyright law could have been applied. A typical example would be a work by an American author which is in the public domain in a foreign country because that country does not have copyright relations with the United States; the making and publication of an authorized edition would be lawful in that country, but the Customs Service could prevent the importation of any copies of that edition.

Importation for Infringing Distribution. The second situation covered by section 602 is that where the copies or phonorecords were lawfully made but their distribution in the United States would infringe the U.S. copyright owner's exclusive rights. As already said, the mere act of importation in this situation would constitute an act of infringement and could be enjoined. However, in cases of this sort it would be impracticable for the United States Customs Service to attempt to enforce the importation prohibition, and section 602(b) provides that, unless a violation of the manufacturing requirements is also involved, the Service has no authority to prevent importation, "where the copies or phonorecords were lawfully made." The subsection would authorize the establishment of a procedure under which copyright owners could arrange for the Customs Service to notify them wherever articles appearing to infringe their works are imported.

AMENDMENTS

2010—Subsec. (b). Pub. L. 111–295 struck out "unless the provisions of section 601 are applicable" after "prevent their importation" in second sentence.

2008—Pub. L. 110–403, § 105(c)(1)(A), inserted "or exportation" after "importation" in section catchline.

Subsec. (a). Pub. L. 110–403, § 105(b), inserted heading, designated introductory provisions as par. (1), struck out "This subsection does not apply to—" at end in par. (1), added par. (2) and par. (3) designation, heading, and introductory provisions, redesignated former pars. (1) to (3) as subpars. (A) to (C) of par. (3), respectively, and realigned margins, inserted "or exportation" after "importation" in par. (3)(A), and substituted "importation or exportation, for the private use of the importer or exporter" for "importation, for the private use of the importer" and inserted "or departing from the United States" after "United States" in par. (3)(B).

Subsec. (b). Pub. L. 110–403, § 105(c)(1)(B), inserted heading and substituted "United States Customs and Border Protection has" for "the United States Customs Service has" and "United States Customs and Border Protection of" for "the Customs Service of".

§ 603. Importation prohibitions: Enforcement and disposition of excluded articles

(a) The Secretary of the Treasury and the United States Postal Service shall separately or jointly make regulations for the enforcement of the provisions of this title prohibiting importation.

(b) These regulations may require, as a condition for the exclusion of articles under section 602—

(1) that the person seeking exclusion obtain a court order enjoining importation of the articles; or

(2) that the person seeking exclusion furnish proof, of a specified nature and in accordance with prescribed procedures, that the copyright in which such person claims an interest is valid and that the importation would violate the prohibition in section 602; the person seeking exclusion may also be required to post a surety bond for any injury that may result if the detention or exclusion of the articles proves to be unjustified.

(c) Articles imported in violation of the importation prohibitions of this title are subject to seizure and forfeiture in the same manner as property imported in violation of the customs revenue laws. Forfeited articles shall be destroyed as directed by the Secretary of the Treasury or the court, as the case may be.

(Pub. L. 94–553, title I, § 101, Oct. 19, 1976, 90 Stat. 2590; Pub. L. 104–153, § 8, July 2, 1996, 110 Stat. 1388.)

HISTORICAL AND REVISION NOTES

HOUSE REPORT NO. 94–1476

The importation prohibitions of both sections 601 and 602 would be enforced under section 603, which is similar to section 109 of the statute now in effect [section 109 of former title 17]. Subsection (a) would authorize the Secretary of the Treasury and the United States Postal Service to make regulations for this purpose, and subsection (c) provides for the disposition of excluded articles.

Subsection (b) of section 603 deals only with the prohibition against importation of "piratical" copies or phonorecords, and is aimed at solving problems that have arisen under the present statute. Since the United States Customs Service is often in no position to make determinations as to whether particular articles are "piratical," section 603(b) would permit the Customs regulations to require the person seeking exclusion either to obtain a court order enjoining importation, or to furnish proof of his claim and to post bond.

AMENDMENTS

1996—Subsec. (c). Pub. L. 104–153 substituted a period at end for "; however, the articles may be returned to the country of export whenever it is shown to the satisfaction of the Secretary of the Treasury that the importer had no reasonable grounds for believing that his or her acts constituted a violation of law."

CHAPTER 7—COPYRIGHT OFFICE

HISTORICAL AND REVISION NOTES

HOUSE REPORT NO. 94–1476

Chapter 7 entitled "Copyright Office," sets forth the administrative and housekeeping provisions of the bill.

Administrative Procedure Act. Under an amendment to section 701 adopted by the Committee, the Copyright Office is made fully subject to the Administrative Procedure Act [5 U.S.C. 551 et seq. and 701 et seq.] with one exception: under section 706(b), reproduction and distribution of copyright deposit copies would be made under the Freedom of Information Act [5 U.S.C. 552] only to the extent permitted by the Copyright Office regulations.

Retention and Disposition of Deposited Articles. A recurring problem in the administration of the copyright law has been the need to reconcile the storage limitations of the Copyright Office with the continued value of deposits in identifying copyrighted works. Aside from its indisputable utility to future historians and scholars, a substantially complete collection of both published and unpublished deposits, other than those selected by the Library of Congress, would avoid the many difficulties encountered when copies needed for identification in connection with litigation or other purposes have been destroyed. The basic policy behind section 704 is that copyright deposits should be retained as long as possible, but that the Register of Copyrights and the Librarian of Congress should be empowered to dispose of them under appropriate safeguards when they decide that it has become necessary to do so.

Under subsection (a) of section 704, any copy, phonorecord, or identifying material deposited for registration, whether registered or not, becomes "the property of the United States Government." This means that the copyright owner or person who made the deposit cannot demand its return as a matter of right, even in rejection cases, although the provisions of section 407 and 408 are flexible enough to allow for special arrangements in exceptional cases. On the other hand, Government ownership of deposited articles under section 704(a) carries with it no privileges under the copyright itself; use of a deposited article in violation of the copyright owner's exclusive rights would be infringement.

With respect to published works, section 704(b) makes all deposits available to the Library of Congress "for its collections, or for exchanges or transfer to any other library"; where the work is unpublished, the Library is authorized to select any deposit for its own collections or for transfer to the National Archives of the United States or to a Federal records center.

Motion picture producers have expressed some concern lest the right to transfer copies of works, such as motion pictures, that have been published under rental, lease, or loan arrangements, might lead to abuse. However, the Library of Congress has not knowingly transferred works of this sort to other libraries in the past, and there is no reason to expect it to do so in the future.

The Committee added a new subsection (c) to section 704, under which the Register is authorized to make microfilm or other record copies of copyright deposits before transferring or otherwise disposing of them.

For deposits not selected by the Library, subsection (d) provides that they, or "identifying portions or reproductions of them," are to be retained under Copyright Office control "for the longest period considered practicable and desirable" by the Register and the Librarian. When and if they ultimately decide that retention of certain deposited articles is no longer "practicable and desirable," the Register and Librarian have joint discretion to order their "destruction or other disposition." Because of the unique value and irreplaceable nature of unpublished deposits, the subsection prohibits their intentional destruction during their copyright term, unless a facsimile reproduction has been made.

Subsection (e) of section 704 establishes a new procedure under which a copyright owner can request retention of deposited material for the full term of copyright. The Register of Copyrights is authorized to issue regulations prescribing the fees for this service and the "conditions under which such requests are to be made and granted."

Catalog of Copyright Entries. Section 707(a) of the bill retains the present statute's basis requirement that the Register compile and publish catalogs of all copyright registrations at periodic intervals, but provides for "discretion to determine, on the basis of practicability and usefulness the form and frequency of publication of each particular part". This provision will in no way diminish the utility or value of the present catalogs, and the flexibility of approach, coupled with use of the new mechanical and electronic devices now becoming available, will avoid waste and result in a better product.

Copyright Office Fees. The schedule of fees set out in section 708 reflects a general increase in the fees of the Copyright Office from those established by the Congress in 1965. The basic fees are $10 for registration, $6 for renewal registration, $10 for recordation of documents and $10 per hour for searching. The section also contains new fee provisions needed because of new requirements or services established under the bill, and subsection (a)(11) authorizes the Register to fix additional fees, on the "basis of the cost of providing the service," "for any other special services requiring a substantial amount of time or expense." Subsection (b) makes clear that, except for the possibility of waivers in "occasional or isolated cases involving relatively small amounts," the Register is to charge fees for services rendered to other Government agencies.

Postal Interruptions. Section 709 authorizes the Register of Copyrights to issue regulation to permit the acceptance by the Copyright Office of documents which are delivered after the close of the prescribed period if the delay was caused by a general disruption or suspension of postal or other transportation or communications services.

Reproductions for the Blind and Handicapped. Section 710 directs the Register of Copyrights to establish by regulation forms and procedures by which the copyright owners of certain categories of works may voluntarily grant to the Library of Congress a license to reproduce and distribute copies or phonorecords of the work solely for the use of the blind and physically handicapped.

AMENDMENTS

2000—Pub. L. 106–379, §3(a)(1), Oct. 27, 2000, 114 Stat. 1445, struck out item 710 "Reproduction for use of the blind and physically handicapped: Voluntary licensing forms and procedures."

1997—Pub. L. 105–80, §12(a)(17), Nov. 13, 1997, 111 Stat. 1535, substituted "Reproduction" for "Reproductions" in item 710.

§ 701. The Copyright Office: General responsibilities and organization

(a) All administrative functions and duties under this title, except as otherwise specified, are the responsibility of the Register of Copyrights as director of the Copyright Office of the Library of Congress. The Register of Copyrights, together with the subordinate officers and employees of the Copyright Office, shall be appointed by the Librarian of Congress, and shall act under the Librarian's general direction and supervision.

(b) In addition to the functions and duties set out elsewhere in this chapter, the Register of Copyrights shall perform the following functions:

(1) Advise Congress on national and international issues relating to copyright, other matters arising under this title, and related matters.

(2) Provide information and assistance to Federal departments and agencies and the Judiciary on national and international issues relating to copyright, other matters arising under this title, and related matters.

(3) Participate in meetings of international intergovernmental organizations and meetings with foreign government officials relating to copyright, other matters arising under this title, and related matters, including as a member of United States delegations as authorized by the appropriate Executive branch authority.

(4) Conduct studies and programs regarding copyright, other matters arising under this title, and related matters, the administration of the Copyright Office, or any function vested in the Copyright Office by law, including educational programs conducted cooperatively with foreign intellectual property offices and international intergovernmental organizations.

(5) Perform such other functions as Congress may direct, or as may be appropriate in furtherance of the functions and duties specifically set forth in this title.

(c) The Register of Copyrights shall adopt a seal to be used on and after January 1, 1978, to authenticate all certified documents issued by the Copyright Office.

(d) The Register of Copyrights shall make an annual report to the Librarian of Congress of the work and accomplishments of the Copyright Office during the previous fiscal year. The annual report of the Register of Copyrights shall be published separately and as a part of the annual report of the Librarian of Congress.

(e) Except as provided by section 706(b) and the regulations issued thereunder, all actions taken by the Register of Copyrights under this title are subject to the provisions of the Administrative Procedure Act of June 11, 1946, as amended (c. 324, 60 Stat. 237, title 5, United States Code, Chapter 5, Subchapter II and Chapter 7).

(f) The Register of Copyrights shall be compensated at the rate of pay in effect for level III of the Executive Schedule under section 5314 of title 5. The Librarian of Congress shall establish not more than four positions for Associate Registers of Copyrights, in accordance with the recommendations of the Register of Copyrights. The Librarian shall make appointments to such positions after consultation with the Register of Copyrights. Each Associate Register of Copyrights shall be paid at a rate not to exceed the maximum annual rate of basic pay payable for GS–18 of the General Schedule under section 5332 of title 5.

(Pub. L. 94–553, title I, § 101, Oct. 19, 1976, 90 Stat. 2591; Pub. L. 101–319, § 2(b), July 3, 1990, 104 Stat. 290; Pub. L. 105–304, title IV, § 401(a)(2), (b), Oct. 28, 1998, 112 Stat. 2887.)

References in Text

The Administrative Procedure Act of June 11, 1946, referred to in subsec. (e), was repealed and the provisions thereof were reenacted as subchapter II of chapter 5, and chapter 7, of Title 5, Government Organization and Employees, by Pub. L. 89–554, Sept. 6, 1966, 80 Stat. 278.

Amendments

1998—Subsecs. (b) to (e). Pub. L. 105–304, § 401(b)(1), added subsec. (b) and redesignated former subsecs. (b) to (d) as (c) to (e), respectively. Former subsec. (e) redesignated (f).

Subsec. (f). Pub. L. 105–304 redesignated subsec. (e) as (f) and substituted "III" for "IV" and "5314" for "5315" in first sentence.

1990—Subsec. (e). Pub. L. 101–319 added subsec. (e).

Effective Date of 1990 Amendment

Section 5 of Pub. L. 101–319 provided that:

"(a) Effective Date.—The amendments made by this Act [amending this section and section 802 of this title and sections 5315 and 5316 of Title 5, Government Organization and Employees, and enacting provisions set out as a note under section 101 of this title] shall take effect on the date of the enactment of this Act [July 3, 1990].

"(b) Budget Act.—Any new spending authority (within the meaning of section 401 of the Congressional Budget Act of 1974 [2 U.S.C. 651]) which is provided under this Act shall be effective for any fiscal year only to the extent or in such amounts as are provided in appropriations Acts."

References in Other Laws to GS–16, 17, or 18 Pay Rates

References in laws to the rates of pay for GS–16, 17, or 18, or to maximum rates of pay under the General Schedule, to be considered references to rates payable under specified sections of Title 5, Government Organization and Employees, see section 529 [title I, § 101(c)(1)] of Pub. L. 101–509, set out in a note under section 5376 of Title 5.

National Commission on New Technological Uses of Copyrighted Works

Pub. L. 93–573, title II, §§ 201–208, Dec. 31, 1974, 88 Stat. 1873–1875, as amended by Pub. L. 94–314, June 21, 1976, 90 Stat. 692; Pub. L. 95–146, Oct. 28, 1977, 91 Stat. 1226, created in the Library of Congress a National Commission on New Technological Uses of Copyrighted Works to study and compile data on (1) the reproduction and use of copyrighted works of authorship (A) in conjunction with automatic systems capable of storing, processing, retrieving, and transferring information, and (B) by various forms of machine reproduction, not including reproduction by or at the request of instructors for use in face-to-face teaching activities, and (2) the creation of new works by the application or intervention of such automatic systems or machine reproduction, required the Commission to submit a final report to the President and Congress on or before July 31, 1978, and provided that the Commission terminated the sixtieth day after submitting the final report.

§ 702. Copyright Office regulations

The Register of Copyrights is authorized to establish regulations not inconsistent with law for the administration of the functions and duties made the responsibility of the Register under this title. All regulations established by the Register under this title are subject to the approval of the Librarian of Congress.

(Pub. L. 94–553, title I, § 101, Oct. 19, 1976, 90 Stat. 2591.)

§ 703. Effective date of actions in Copyright Office

In any case in which time limits are prescribed under this title for the performance of an action in the Copyright Office, and in which the last day of the prescribed period falls on a Saturday, Sunday, holiday, or other nonbusiness day within the District of Columbia or the Federal Government, the action may be taken on the next succeeding business day, and is effective as of the date when the period expired.

(Pub. L. 94–553, title I, § 101, Oct. 19, 1976, 90 Stat. 2591.)

§ 704. Retention and disposition of articles deposited in Copyright Office

(a) Upon their deposit in the Copyright Office under sections 407 and 408, all copies, phonorecords, and identifying material, including those deposited in connection with claims that have been refused registration, are the property of the United States Government.

(b) In the case of published works, all copies, phonorecords, and identifying material deposited are available to the Library of Congress for its collections, or for exchange or transfer to any other library. In the case of unpublished works, the Library is entitled, under regulations that the Register of Copyrights shall prescribe, to select any deposits for its collections or for transfer to the National Archives of the United States or to a Federal records center, as defined in section 2901 of title 44.

(c) The Register of Copyrights is authorized, for specific or general categories of works, to make a facsimile reproduction of all or any part of the material deposited under section 408, and to make such reproduction a part of the Copyright Office records of the registration, before transferring such material to the Library of Congress as provided by subsection (b), or before destroying or otherwise disposing of such material as provided by subsection (d).

(d) Deposits not selected by the Library under subsection (b), or identifying portions or reproductions of them, shall be retained under the control of the Copyright Office, including retention in Government storage facilities, for the longest period considered practicable and desirable by the Register of Copyrights and the Librarian of Congress. After that period it is within the joint discretion of the Register and the Librarian to order their destruction or other disposition; but, in the case of unpublished works, no deposit shall be knowingly or intentionally destroyed or otherwise disposed of during its term of copyright unless a facsimile reproduction of the entire deposit has been made a part of the Copyright Office records as provided by subsection (c).

(e) The depositor of copies, phonorecords, or identifying material under section 408, or the copyright owner of record, may request retention, under the control of the Copyright Office, of one or more of such articles for the full term of copyright in the work. The Register of Copyrights shall prescribe, by regulation, the conditions under which such requests are to be made and granted, and shall fix the fee to be charged under section 708(a) if the request is granted.

(Pub. L. 94–553, title I, §101, Oct. 19, 1976, 90 Stat. 2591; Pub. L. 101–318, §2(c), July 3, 1990, 104 Stat. 288; Pub. L. 111–295, §6(e), Dec. 9, 2010, 124 Stat. 3181.)

AMENDMENTS

2010—Subsec. (e). Pub. L. 111–295 substituted "section 708(a)" for "section 708(a)(10)".
1990—Subsec. (e). Pub. L. 101–318 substituted "708(a)(10)" for "708(a)(11)".

EFFECTIVE DATE OF 1990 AMENDMENT

Amendment by Pub. L. 101–318 effective 6 months after July 3, 1990, and applicable to (A) claims to original, supplementary, and renewal copyright received for registration, and to items received for recordation in Copyright Office, on or after such effective date, and (B) other requests for services received on or after such effective date, or received before such effective date for services not yet rendered as of such date, and with claims to original, supplementary, and renewal copyright received for registration and items received for recordation in acceptable form in Copyright Office before such effective date, and requests for services which are rendered before such effective date, to be governed by section 708 of this title as in effect before such effective date, see section 2(d) of Pub. L. 101–318, set out as a note under section 708 of this title.

§ 705. Copyright Office records: Preparation, maintenance, public inspection, and searching

(a) The Register of Copyrights shall ensure that records of deposits, registrations, recordations, and other actions taken under this title are maintained, and that indexes of such records are prepared.

(b) Such records and indexes, as well as the articles deposited in connection with completed copyright registrations and retained under the control of the Copyright Office, shall be open to public inspection.

(c) Upon request and payment of the fee specified by section 708, the Copyright Office shall make a search of its public records, indexes, and deposits, and shall furnish a report of the information they disclose with respect to any particular deposits, registrations, or recorded documents.

(Pub. L. 94–553, title I, §101, Oct. 19, 1976, 90 Stat. 2592; Pub. L. 106–379, §3(a)(2), Oct. 27, 2000, 114 Stat. 1445.)

AMENDMENTS

2000—Subsec. (a). Pub. L. 106–379 amended subsec. (a) generally. Prior to amendment, subsec. (a) read as follows: "The Register of Copyrights shall provide and keep in the Copyright Office records of all deposits, registrations, recordations, and other actions taken under this title, and shall prepare indexes of all such records."

§ 706. Copies of Copyright Office records

(a) Copies may be made of any public records or indexes of the Copyright Office; additional certificates of copyright registration and copies of any public records or indexes may be furnished upon request and payment of the fees specified by section 708.

(b) Copies or reproductions of deposited articles retained under the control of the Copyright Office shall be authorized or furnished only under the conditions specified by the Copyright Office regulations.

(Pub. L. 94–553, title I, §101, Oct. 19, 1976, 90 Stat. 2592.)

§ 707. Copyright Office forms and publications

(a) CATALOG OF COPYRIGHT ENTRIES.—The Register of Copyrights shall compile and publish at periodic intervals catalogs of all copyright registrations. These catalogs shall be divided into parts in accordance with the various classes of works, and the Register has discretion to determine, on the basis of practicability and usefulness, the form and frequency of publication of each particular part.

(b) OTHER PUBLICATIONS.—The Register shall furnish, free of charge upon request, application forms for copyright registration and general informational material in connection with the functions of the Copyright Office. The Register also has the authority to publish compilations of information, bibliographies, and other material he or she considers to be of value to the public.

(c) DISTRIBUTION OF PUBLICATIONS.—All publications of the Copyright Office shall be furnished to depository libraries as specified under section 1905 of title 44, and, aside from those furnished free of charge, shall be offered for sale to the public at prices based on the cost of reproduction and distribution.

(Pub. L. 94–553, title I, §101, Oct. 19, 1976, 90 Stat. 2592.)

§ 708. Copyright Office fees

(a) FEES.—Fees shall be paid to the Register of Copyrights—

(1) on filing each application under section 408 for registration of a copyright claim or for a supplementary registration, including the issuance of a certificate of registration if registration is made;

(2) on filing each application for registration of a claim for renewal of a subsisting copyright under section 304(a), including the issuance of a certificate of registration if registration is made;

(3) for the issuance of a receipt for a deposit under section 407;

(4) for the recordation, as provided by section 205, of a transfer of copyright ownership or other document;

(5) for the filing, under section 115(b), of a notice of intention to obtain a compulsory license;

(6) for the recordation, under section 302(c), of a statement revealing the identity of an author of an anonymous or pseudonymous work, or for the recordation, under section 302(d), of a statement relating to the death of an author;

(7) for the issuance, under section 706, of an additional certificate of registration;

(8) for the issuance of any other certification;

(9) for the making and reporting of a search as provided by section 705, and for any related services;

(10) on filing a statement of account based on secondary transmissions of primary transmissions pursuant to section 119 or 122; and

(11) on filing a statement of account based on secondary transmissions of primary transmissions pursuant to section 111.

The Register is authorized to fix fees for other services, including the cost of preparing copies of Copyright Office records, whether or not such copies are certified, based on the cost of providing the service. Fees established under paragraphs (10) and (11) shall be reasonable and may not exceed one-half of the cost necessary to cover reasonable expenses incurred by the Copyright Office for the collection and administration of the statements of account and any royalty fees deposited with such statements.

(b) ADJUSTMENT OF FEES.—The Register of Copyrights may, by regulation, adjust the fees for the services specified in paragraphs (1) through (9) of subsection (a) in the following manner:

(1) The Register shall conduct a study of the costs incurred by the Copyright Office for the registration of claims, the recordation of documents, and the provision of services. The study shall also consider the timing of any adjustment in fees and the authority to use such fees consistent with the budget.

(2) The Register may, on the basis of the study under paragraph (1), and subject to paragraph (5), adjust fees to not more than that necessary to cover the reasonable costs incurred by the Copyright Office for the services described in paragraph (1), plus a reasonable inflation adjustment to account for any estimated increase in costs.

(3) Any fee established under paragraph (2) shall be rounded off to the nearest dollar, or for a fee less than $12, rounded off to the nearest 50 cents.

(4) Fees established under this subsection shall be fair and equitable and give due consideration to the objectives of the copyright system.

(5) If the Register determines under paragraph (2) that fees should be adjusted, the Register shall prepare a proposed fee schedule and submit the schedule with the accompanying economic analysis to the Congress. The fees proposed by the Register may be instituted after the end of 120 days after the schedule is submitted to the Congress unless, within that 120-day period, a law is enacted stating in substance that the Congress does not approve the schedule.

(c) The fees prescribed by or under this section are applicable to the United States Government and any of its agencies, employees, or officers, but the Register of Copyrights has discretion to waive the requirement of this subsection in occasional or isolated cases involving relatively small amounts.

(d)(1) Except as provided in paragraph (2), all fees received under this section shall be deposited by the Register of Copyrights in the Treasury of the United States and shall be credited to the appropriations for necessary expenses of the Copyright Office. Such fees that are collected shall remain available until expended. The Register may, in accordance with regulations that he or she shall prescribe, refund any sum paid by mistake or in excess of the fee required by this section.

(2) In the case of fees deposited against future services, the Register of Copyrights shall request the Secretary of the Treasury to invest in interest-bearing securities in the United States Treasury any portion of the fees that, as determined by the Register, is not required to meet current deposit account demands. Funds from such portion of fees shall be invested in securities that permit funds to be available to the Copyright Office at all times if they are determined to be necessary to meet current deposit account demands. Such investments shall be in public debt securities with maturities suitable to the needs of the Copyright Office, as determined by the Register of Copyrights, and bearing interest at rates determined by the Secretary of the Treasury, taking into consideration current market yields on outstanding marketable obligations of the United States of comparable maturities.

(3) The income on such investments shall be deposited in the Treasury of the United States and shall be credited to the appropriations for necessary expenses of the Copyright Office.

(Pub. L. 94–553, title I, § 101, Oct. 19, 1976, 90 Stat. 2593; Pub. L. 95–94, title IV, § 406(b), Aug. 5, 1977, 91 Stat. 682; Pub. L. 97–366, § 1, Oct. 25, 1982, 96 Stat. 1759; Pub. L. 101–318, § 2(a), (b), July 3, 1990, 104 Stat. 287, 288; Pub. L. 102–307, title I, § 102(f), June 26, 1992, 106 Stat. 266; Pub. L. 105–80, § 7, Nov. 13, 1997, 111 Stat. 1532; Pub. L. 106–379, § 3(a)(3), Oct. 27, 2000, 114 Stat. 1445; Pub. L. 111–175, title I, § 106, May 27, 2010, 124 Stat. 1244.)

Amendments

2010—Subsec. (a). Pub. L. 111–175, §106(4), inserted at end of concluding provisions "Fees established under paragraphs (10) and (11) shall be reasonable and may not exceed one-half of the cost necessary to cover reasonable expenses incurred by the Copyright Office for the collection and administration of the statements of account and any royalty fees deposited with such statements."

Subsec. (a)(10), (11). Pub. L. 111–175, §106(1)–(3), added pars. (10) and (11).

2000—Subsec. (a). Pub. L. 106–379, §3(a)(3)(A), amended subsec. (a) generally. Prior to amendment, subsec. (a) read as follows: "The following fees shall be paid to the Register of Copyrights:

"(1) on filing each application under section 408 for registration of a copyright claim or for a supplementary registration, including the issuance of a certificate of registration if registration is made, $20;

"(2) on filing each application for registration of a claim for renewal of a subsisting copyright under section 304(a), including the issuance of a certificate of registration if registration is made, $20;

"(3) for the issuance of a receipt for a deposit under section 407, $4;

"(4) for the recordation, as provided by section 205, of a transfer of copyright ownership or other document covering not more than one title, $20; for additional titles, $10 for each group of not more than 10 titles;

"(5) for the filing, under section 115(b), of a notice of intention to obtain a compulsory license, $12;

"(6) for the recordation, under section 302(c), of a statement revealing the identity of an author of an anonymous or pseudonymous work, or for the recordation, under section 302(d), of a statement relating to the death of an author, $20 for a document covering not more than one title; for each additional title, $2;

"(7) for the issuance, under section 706, of an additional certificate of registration, $8;

"(8) for the issuance of any other certification, $20 for each hour or fraction of an hour consumed with respect thereto;

"(9) for the making and reporting of a search as provided by section 705, and for any related services, $20 for each hour or fraction of an hour consumed with respect thereto; and

"(10) for any other special services requiring a substantial amount of time or expense, such fees as the Register of Copyrights may fix on the basis of the cost of providing the service.

The Register of Copyrights is authorized to fix the fees for preparing copies of Copyright Office records, whether or not such copies are certified, on the basis of the cost of such preparation."

Subsec. (b). Pub. L. 106–379, §3(a)(3)(B)(i), inserted introductory provisions and struck out former introductory provisions which read as follows: "In calendar year 1997 and in any subsequent calendar year, the Register of Copyrights, by regulation, may increase the fees specified in subsection (a) in the following manner:".

Subsec. (b)(1). Pub. L. 106–379, §3(a)(3)(B)(ii), substituted "adjustment" for "increase".

Subsec. (b)(2). Pub. L. 106–379, §3(a)(3)(B)(iii), substituted "adjust fees to not more" for "increase fees to not more".

Subsec. (b)(5). Pub. L. 106–379, §3(a)(3)(B)(iv), substituted "adjusted" for "increased".

1997—Subsec. (b). Pub. L. 105–80, §7(a), amended subsec. (b) generally. Prior to amendment, subsec. (b) read as follows: "In calendar year 1995 and in each subsequent fifth calendar year, the Register of Copyrights, by regulation, may increase the fees specified in subsection (a) by the percent change in the annual average, for the preceding calendar year, of the Consumer Price Index published by the Bureau of Labor Statistics, over the annual average of the Consumer Price Index for the fifth calendar year preceding the calendar year in which such increase is authorized."

Subsec. (d). Pub. L. 105–80, §7(b), amended subsec. (d) generally. Prior to amendment, subsec. (d) read as follows: "All fees received under this section shall be deposited by the Register of Copyrights in the Treasury of the United States and shall be credited to the appropriation for necessary expenses of the Copyright Office. The Register may, in accordance with regulations that he or she shall prescribe, refund any sum paid by mistake or in excess of the fee required by this section."

1992—Subsec. (a)(2). Pub. L. 102–307 struck out "in its first term" after "copyright" and substituted "$20" for "$12".

1990—Subsec. (a). Pub. L. 101–318, §2(a), amended subsec. (a) generally. Prior to amendment, subsec. (a) read as follows: "The following fees shall be paid to the Register of Copyrights:

"(1) on filing each application for registration of a copyright claim or a supplementary registration under section 408, including the issuance of a certificate of registration if registration is made, $10;

"(2) on filing each application for registration of a claim to renewal of a subsisting copyright in its first term under section 304(a), including the issuance of a certificate of registration if registration is made, $6;

"(3) for the issuance of a receipt for a deposit under section 407, $2;

"(4) for the recordation, as provided by section 205, of a transfer of copyright ownership or other document of six pages or less, covering no more than one title, $10; for each page over six and each title over one, 50 cents additional;

"(5) for the filing, under section 115(b), of a notice of intention to make phonorecords, $6;

"(6) for the recordation, under section 302(c), of a statement revealing the identity of an author of an anonymous or pseudonymous work, or for the recordation, under section 302(d), of a statement relating to the death of an author, $10 for a document of six pages or less, covering no more than one title; for each page over six and for each title over one, $1 additional;

"(7) for the issuance, under section 601, of an import statement, $3;

"(8) for the issuance, under section 706, of an additional certificate of registration, $4;

"(9) for the issuance of any other certification, $4; the Register of Copyrights has discretion, on the basis of their cost, to fix the fees for preparing copies of Copyright Office records, whether they are to be certified or not;

"(10) for the making and reporting of a search as provided by section 705, and for any related services, $10 for each hour or fraction of an hour consumed;

"(11) for any other special services requiring a substantial amount of time or expense, such fees as the Register of Copyrights may fix on the basis of the cost of providing the service."

Subsecs. (b) to (d). Pub. L. 101–318, §2(b), added subsec. (b) and redesignated former subsecs. (b) and (c) as (c) and (d), respectively.

1982—Subsec. (a)(1). Pub. L. 97–366, §1(1), substituted provision for a $10 fee on filing each application for registration of a copyright claim or a supplementary registration under section 408, including the issuance of a certificate of registration if registration is made, for provision for a $10 fee for the registration of a copyright claim or a supplementary registration under section 408, including the issuance of a certificate of registration.

Subsec. (a)(2). Pub. L. 97–366, §1(1), substituted provision for a $6 fee on filing each application for registration of a claim to renewal of a subsisting copyright in its first term under section 304(a), including the issuance of a certificate of registration if registration is made, for provision for a $6 fee for the registration of a claim to renewal of a subsisting copyright in its first term under section 304(a), including the issuance of a certificate of registration.

Subsec. (c). Pub. L. 97–366, §1(2), struck out provision that, before making a refund in any case involving a refusal to register a claim under section 410(b), the Register could deduct all or any part of the prescribed registration fee to cover the reasonable administrative costs of processing the claim.

1977—Subsec. (c). Pub. L. 95–94 substituted provisions relating to crediting of all fees received, to the appropriation for necessary expenses of the Copyright Office, for provisions relating to crediting of all fees received in the manner directed by the Secretary of the Treasury.

EFFECTIVE DATE OF 2010 AMENDMENT

Amendment by Pub. L. 111–175 effective Feb. 27, 2010, see section 307(a) of Pub. L. 111–175, set out as a note under section 111 of this title.

EFFECTIVE DATE OF 2000 AMENDMENT

Pub. L. 106–379, §3(c)(1), Oct. 27, 2000, 114 Stat. 1445, provided that: "The amendments made by this section [amending this section and sections 121 and 705 of this title and repealing section 710 of this title] shall take effect on the date of the enactment of this Act [Oct. 27, 2000]."

EFFECTIVE DATE OF 1992 AMENDMENT

Amendment by Pub. L. 102–307 effective June 26, 1992, but applicable only to copyrights secured between January 1, 1964, and December 31, 1977, and not affecting court proceedings pending on June 26, 1992, with copyrights secured before January 1, 1964, governed by section 304(a) of this title as in effect on the day before June 26, 1992, except each reference to forty-seven years in such provisions deemed to be 67 years, see section 102(g) of Pub. L. 102–307, as amended, set out as a note under section 101 of this title.

EFFECTIVE DATE OF 1990 AMENDMENT

Section 2(d) of Pub. L. 101–318 provided that:

"(1) IN GENERAL.—The amendments made by this section [amending this section and section 704 of this title] shall take effect 6 months after the date of the enactment of this Act [July 3, 1990] and shall apply to—

"(A) claims to original, supplementary, and renewal copyright received for registration, and to items received for recordation in the Copyright Office, on or after such effective date, and

"(B) other requests for services received on or after such effective date, or received before such effective date for services not yet rendered as of such date.

"(2) PRIOR CLAIMS.—Claims to original, supplementary, and renewal copyright received for registration and items received for recordation in acceptable form in the Copyright Office before the effective date set forth in paragraph (1), and requests for services which are rendered before such effective date shall be governed by section 708 of title 17, United States Code, as in effect before such effective date."

EFFECTIVE DATE OF 1982 AMENDMENT; TRANSITIONAL RULE

Section 2 of Pub. L. 97–366 provided that: "This Act [amending this section, section 110 of this title, and section 3 of Title 35, Patents] shall take effect thirty days after its enactment [Oct. 25, 1982] and shall apply to claims to original, supplementary, and renewal copyright received for registration in the Copyright Office on or after the effective date. Claims to original, supplementary, and renewal copyright received for registration in acceptable form in the Copyright Office before the effective date shall be governed by the provisions of section 708(a)(1) and (2) in effect prior to this enactment."

EFFECTIVE DATE OF 1977 AMENDMENT

Section 406(b) of Pub. L. 95–94 provided that the amendment made by that section is effective Jan. 1, 1978.

CARRY-OVER OF EXISTING FEES

Pub. L. 106–379, §3(c)(2), Oct. 27, 2000, 114 Stat. 1446, provided that: "The fees under section 708(a) of title 17, United States Code, on the date of the enactment of this Act [Oct. 27, 2000] shall be the fees in effect under section 708(a) of such title on the day before such date of enactment."

§ 709. Delay in delivery caused by disruption of postal or other services

In any case in which the Register of Copyrights determines, on the basis of such evidence as the Register may by regulation require, that a deposit, application, fee, or any other material to be delivered to the Copyright Office by a particular date, would have been received in the Copyright Office in due time except for a general disruption or suspension of postal or other transportation or communications services, the actual receipt of such material in the Copyright Office within one month after the date on which the Register determines that the disruption or suspension of such services has terminated, shall be considered timely.

(Pub. L. 94–553, title I, §101, Oct. 19, 1976, 90 Stat. 2594.)

[§ 710. Repealed. Pub. L. 106–379, §3(a)(1), Oct. 27, 2000, 114 Stat. 1445]

Section, Pub. L. 94–553, title I, §101, Oct. 19, 1976, 90 Stat. 2594, related to forms and procedures for granting the Library of Congress licenses to reproduce works for the blind and physically handicapped.

CHAPTER 8—PROCEEDINGS BY COPYRIGHT ROYALTY JUDGES

PRIOR PROVISIONS

This chapter consisted of sections 801 to 803, related to proceedings by copyright arbitration royalty panels, prior to being amended generally by Pub. L. 108–419.

AMENDMENTS

2004—Pub. L. 108–419, §3(a), Nov. 30, 2004, 118 Stat. 2341, amended chapter heading and analysis generally, substituting chapter heading and items 801 to 805 for chapter heading "COPYRIGHT ARBITRATION ROYALTY PANELS", and items 801 "Copyright arbitration royalty panels: Establishment and purpose", 802 "Membership and proceedings of copyright arbitration royalty panels", and 803 "Institution and conclusion of proceedings".

1997—Pub. L. 105–80, §12(a)(18), Nov. 13, 1997, 111 Stat. 1535, substituted "Establishment" for "establishment" in item 801.

1993—Pub. L. 103–198, §2(f), Dec. 17, 1993, 107 Stat. 2308, amended table of sections generally, substituting chapter heading and items 801 to 803 for chapter heading "COPYRIGHT ROYALTY TRIBUNAL", item 801 "Copyright Royalty Tribunal: Establishment and purpose", item 802 "Membership of the Tribunal", item 804 "Institution and conclusion of proceedings", item 805 "Staff of the Tribunal", item 806 "Administrative support of the Tribunal", item 807 "Deduction of costs of proceedings", item 808 "Reports", item 809 "Effective date of final determinations", and item 810 "Judicial review".

Pub. L. 103–198, §2(c), Dec. 17, 1993, 107 Stat. 2307, struck out item 803 "Procedures of the Tribunal."

§ 801. Copyright Royalty Judges; appointment and functions

(a) APPOINTMENT.—The Librarian of Congress shall appoint 3 full-time Copyright Royalty Judges, and shall appoint 1 of the 3 as the Chief Copyright Royalty Judge. The Librarian shall make appointments to such positions after consultation with the Register of Copyrights.

(b) FUNCTIONS.—Subject to the provisions of this chapter, the functions of the Copyright Royalty Judges shall be as follows:

(1) To make determinations and adjustments of reasonable terms and rates of royalty payments as provided in sections 112(e), 114, 115, 116, 118, 119, and 1004. The rates applicable under sections 114(f)(1)(B), 115, and 116 shall be calculated to achieve the following objectives:

(A) To maximize the availability of creative works to the public.

(B) To afford the copyright owner a fair return for his or her creative work and the copyright user a fair income under existing economic conditions.

(C) To reflect the relative roles of the copyright owner and the copyright user in the product made available to the public with respect to relative creative contribution, technological contribution, capital investment, cost, risk, and contribution to the opening of new markets for creative expression and media for their communication.

(D) To minimize any disruptive impact on the structure of the industries involved and on generally prevailing industry practices.

(2) To make determinations concerning the adjustment of the copyright royalty rates under section 111 solely in accordance with the following provisions:

(A) The rates established by section 111(d)(1)(B) may be adjusted to reflect—

(i) national monetary inflation or deflation; or

(ii) changes in the average rates charged cable subscribers for the basic service of providing secondary transmissions to maintain the real constant dollar level of the royalty fee per subscriber which existed as of the date of October 19, 1976,

except that—

(I) if the average rates charged cable system subscribers for the basic service of providing secondary transmissions are changed so that the average rates exceed national monetary inflation, no change in the rates established by section 111(d)(1)(B) shall be permitted; and

(II) no increase in the royalty fee shall be permitted based on any reduction in the average number of distant signal equivalents per subscriber.

The Copyright Royalty Judges may consider all factors relating to the maintenance of such level of payments, including, as an extenuating factor, whether the industry has been restrained by subscriber rate regulating authorities from increasing the rates for the basic service of providing secondary transmissions.

(B) In the event that the rules and regulations of the Federal Communications Commission are amended at any time after April 15, 1976, to permit the carriage by cable systems of additional television broadcast signals beyond the local service area of the primary transmitters of such signals, the royalty rates established by section 111(d)(1)(B) may be adjusted to ensure that the rates for the additional distant signal equivalents resulting from such carriage are reasonable in the light of the changes effected by the amendment to such rules and regulations. In determining the reasonableness of rates proposed following an amendment of Federal Communications Commission rules and regulations, the Copyright Royalty Judges shall consider, among other factors, the economic impact on copyright owners and users; except that no adjustment in royalty rates shall be made under this subparagraph with respect to any distant signal equivalent or fraction thereof represented by—

(i) carriage of any signal permitted under the rules and regulations of the Federal Communications Commission in effect on April 15, 1976, or the carriage of a signal of the same type (that is, independent, network, or noncommercial educational) substituted for such permitted signal; or

(ii) a television broadcast signal first carried after April 15, 1976, pursuant to an individual waiver of the rules and regulations of the Federal Communications Commission, as such rules and regulations were in effect on April 15, 1976.

(C) In the event of any change in the rules and regulations of the Federal Communications Commission with respect to syndicated and sports program exclusivity after April 15, 1976, the rates established by section 111(d)(1)(B) may be adjusted to assure that such rates are reasonable in light of the changes to such rules and regulations, but any such adjustment shall apply only to the affected television broadcast signals carried on those systems affected by the change.

(D) The gross receipts limitations established by section 111(d)(1)(C) and (D)[1] shall be adjusted to reflect national monetary inflation or deflation or changes in the average rates charged cable system subscribers for the basic service of providing secondary transmissions to maintain the real constant dollar value of the exemption provided by such section, and the royalty rate specified therein shall not be subject to adjustment.

(3)(A) To authorize the distribution, under sections 111, 119, and 1007, of those royalty fees collected under sections 111, 119, and 1005, as the case may be, to the extent that the Copyright Royalty Judges have found that the distribution of such fees is not subject to controversy.

(B) In cases where the Copyright Royalty Judges determine that controversy exists, the Copyright Royalty Judges shall determine the distribution of such fees, including partial dis-

---

[1] See References in Text note below.

tributions, in accordance with section 111, 119, or 1007, as the case may be.

(C) Notwithstanding section 804(b)(8), the Copyright Royalty Judges, at any time after the filing of claims under section 111, 119, or 1007, may, upon motion of one or more of the claimants and after publication in the Federal Register of a request for responses to the motion from interested claimants, make a partial distribution of such fees, if, based upon all responses received during the 30-day period beginning on the date of such publication, the Copyright Royalty Judges conclude that no claimant entitled to receive such fees has stated a reasonable objection to the partial distribution, and all such claimants—

(i) agree to the partial distribution;

(ii) sign an agreement obligating them to return any excess amounts to the extent necessary to comply with the final determination on the distribution of the fees made under subparagraph (B);

(iii) file the agreement with the Copyright Royalty Judges; and

(iv) agree that such funds are available for distribution.

(D) The Copyright Royalty Judges and any other officer or employee acting in good faith in distributing funds under subparagraph (C) shall not be held liable for the payment of any excess fees under subparagraph (C). The Copyright Royalty Judges shall, at the time the final determination is made, calculate any such excess amounts.

(4) To accept or reject royalty claims filed under sections 111, 119, and 1007, on the basis of timeliness or the failure to establish the basis for a claim.

(5) To accept or reject rate adjustment petitions as provided in section 804 and petitions to participate as provided in section 803(b) (1) and (2).

(6) To determine the status of a digital audio recording device or a digital audio interface device under sections 1002 and 1003, as provided in section 1010.

(7)(A) To adopt as a basis for statutory terms and rates or as a basis for the distribution of statutory royalty payments, an agreement concerning such matters reached among some or all of the participants in a proceeding at any time during the proceeding, except that—

(i) the Copyright Royalty Judges shall provide to those that would be bound by the terms, rates, or other determination set by any agreement in a proceeding to determine royalty rates an opportunity to comment on the agreement and shall provide to participants in the proceeding under section 803(b)(2) that would be bound by the terms, rates, or other determination set by the agreement an opportunity to comment on the agreement and object to its adoption as a basis for statutory terms and rates; and

(ii) the Copyright Royalty Judges may decline to adopt the agreement as a basis for statutory terms and rates for participants that are not parties to the agreement, if any participant described in clause (i) objects to the agreement and the Copyright Royalty

Judges conclude, based on the record before them if one exists, that the agreement does not provide a reasonable basis for setting statutory terms or rates.

(B) License agreements voluntarily negotiated pursuant to section 112(e)(5), 114(f)(3), 115(c)(3)(E)(i), 116(c), or 118(b)(2) that do not result in statutory terms and rates shall not be subject to clauses (i) and (ii) of subparagraph (A).

(C) Interested parties may negotiate and agree to, and the Copyright Royalty Judges may adopt, an agreement that specifies as terms notice and recordkeeping requirements that apply in lieu of those that would otherwise apply under regulations.

(8) To perform other duties, as assigned by the Register of Copyrights within the Library of Congress, except as provided in section 802(g), at times when Copyright Royalty Judges are not engaged in performing the other duties set forth in this section.

(c) RULINGS.—The Copyright Royalty Judges may make any necessary procedural or evidentiary rulings in any proceeding under this chapter and may, before commencing a proceeding under this chapter, make any such rulings that would apply to the proceedings conducted by the Copyright Royalty Judges.

(d) ADMINISTRATIVE SUPPORT.—The Librarian of Congress shall provide the Copyright Royalty Judges with the necessary administrative services related to proceedings under this chapter.

(e) LOCATION IN LIBRARY OF CONGRESS.—The offices of the Copyright Royalty Judges and staff shall be in the Library of Congress.

(f) EFFECTIVE DATE OF ACTIONS.—On and after the date of the enactment of the Copyright Royalty and Distribution Reform Act of 2004, in any case in which time limits are prescribed under this title for performance of an action with or by the Copyright Royalty Judges, and in which the last day of the prescribed period falls on a Saturday, Sunday, holiday, or other nonbusiness day within the District of Columbia or the Federal Government, the action may be taken on the next succeeding business day, and is effective as of the date when the period expired.

(Added Pub. L. 108–419, § 3(a), Nov. 30, 2004, 118 Stat. 2341; amended Pub. L. 109–303, §§ 3(1), (2), 5, Oct. 6, 2006, 120 Stat. 1478, 1483.)

REFERENCES IN TEXT

Section 111(d)(1)(D) of this title, referred to in subsec. (b)(2)(D), was amended generally by Pub. L. 111–175, title I, § 104(c)(1)(C), May 27, 2010, 124 Stat. 1232, and, as so amended, no longer relates to gross receipts limitations.

The date of the enactment of the Copyright Royalty and Distribution Reform Act of 2004, referred to in subsec. (f), is the date of the enactment of Pub. L. 108–419, which was approved Nov. 30, 2004.

PRIOR PROVISIONS

A prior section 801, Pub. L. 94–553, title I, § 101, Oct. 19, 1976, 90 Stat. 2594; Pub. L. 99–397, § 2(c), (d), Aug. 27, 1986, 100 Stat. 848; Pub. L. 100–568, § 11(1), Oct. 31, 1988, 102 Stat. 2860; Pub. L. 100–667, title II, § 202(4), Nov. 16, 1988, 102 Stat. 3958; Pub. L. 101–318, § 3(b), July 3, 1990, 104 Stat. 288; Pub. L. 102–563, § 3(a)(1), Oct. 28, 1992, 106 Stat. 4247; Pub. L. 103–198, § 2(a), Dec. 17, 1993, 107 Stat.

2304; Pub. L. 104–39, §5(d)(1), Nov. 1, 1995, 109 Stat. 348; Pub. L. 105–80, §§8(a), 12(a)(19), Nov. 13, 1997, 111 Stat. 1533, 1535; Pub. L. 105–304, title IV, §405(e)(1), Oct. 28, 1998, 112 Stat. 2902, related to the establishment and purpose of copyright arbitration royalty panels, prior to the general amendment of this chapter by Pub. L. 108–419.

AMENDMENTS

2006—Subsec. (b)(1). Pub. L. 109–303, §3(1), substituted "119, and 1004" for "119 and 1004".

Subsec. (b)(3)(C). Pub. L. 109–303, §5(1), added introductory provisions and struck out former introductory provisions which read as follows: "The Copyright Royalty Judges may make a partial distribution of such fees during the pendency of the proceeding under subparagraph (B) if all participants under section 803(b)(2) in the proceeding that are entitled to receive those fees that are to be partially distributed—".

Subsec. (b)(3)(C)(i). Pub. L. 109–303, §5(2), substituted "the" for "such".

Subsec. (f). Pub. L. 109–303, §3(2), added subsec. (f).

EFFECTIVE DATE OF 2006 AMENDMENT

Amendment by section 3 of Pub. L. 109–303 effective as if included in the Copyright Royalty and Distribution Reform Act of 2004, Pub. L. 108–419, and amendment by section 5 of Pub. L. 109–303 effective October 6, 2004, see section 6 of Pub. L. 109–303, set out as a note under section 111 of this title.

EFFECTIVE DATE; TRANSITION PROVISIONS

Pub. L. 108–419, §6, Nov. 30, 2004, 118 Stat. 2369, as amended by Pub. L. 109–303, §4(h), Oct. 6, 2006, 120 Stat. 1483, provided that:

"(a) EFFECTIVE DATE.—This Act [see Short Title of 2004 Amendment note set out under section 101 of this title] and the amendments made by this Act shall take effect 6 months after the date of enactment of this Act [Nov. 30, 2004], except that the Librarian of Congress shall appoint 1 or more interim Copyright Royalty Judges under section 802(d) of title 17, United States Code, as amended by this Act, within 90 days after such date of enactment to carry out the functions of the Copyright Royalty Judges under title 17, United States Code, to the extent that Copyright Royalty Judges provided for in section 801(a) of title 17, United States Code, as amended by this Act, have not been appointed before the end of that 90-day period.

"(b) TRANSITION PROVISIONS.—

"(1) IN GENERAL.—Subject to paragraphs (2) and (3), the amendments made by this Act shall not affect any proceedings commenced, petitions filed, or voluntary agreements entered into before the effective date provided in subsection (a) under the provisions of title 17, United States Code, as amended by this Act, and pending on such effective date. Such proceedings shall continue, determinations made in such proceedings, and appeals taken therefrom, as if this Act had not been enacted, and shall continue in effect until modified under title 17, United States Code, as amended by this Act. Such petitions filed and voluntary agreements entered into shall remain in effect as if this Act had not been enacted. For purposes of this paragraph, the Librarian of Congress may determine whether a proceeding has commenced. The Librarian of Congress may terminate any proceeding commenced before the effective date provided in subsection (a) pursuant to chapter 8 of title 17, United States Code, and any proceeding so terminated shall become null and void. In such cases, the Copyright Royalty Judges may initiate a new proceeding in accordance with regulations adopted pursuant to section 803(b)(6) of title 17, United States Code.

"(2) CERTAIN ROYALTY RATE PROCEEDINGS.—Notwithstanding paragraph (1), the amendments made by this Act shall not affect proceedings to determine royalty rates pursuant to section 119(c) of title 17, United States Code, that are commenced before January 31, 2006.

"(3) PENDING PROCEEDINGS.—Notwithstanding paragraph (1), any proceedings to establish or adjust rates and terms for the statutory licenses under section 114(f)(2) or 112(e) of title 17, United States Code, for a statutory period commencing on or after January 1, 2005, shall be terminated upon the date of enactment of this Act and shall be null and void. The rates and terms in effect under section 114(f)(2) or 112(e) of title 17, United States Code, on December 31, 2004, for new subscription services, eligible nonsubscription services, and services exempt under section 114(d)(1)(C)(iv) of such title, and the rates and terms published in the Federal Register under the authority of the Small Webcaster Settlement Act of 2002 (17 U.S.C. 114 note; Public Law 107–321) (including the amendments made by that Act) for the years 2003 through 2004, as well as any notice and recordkeeping provisions adopted pursuant thereto, shall remain in effect until the later of the first applicable effective date for successor terms and rates specified in section 804(b) (2) or (3)(A) of title 17, United States Code, or such later date as the parties may agree or the Copyright Royalty Judges may establish. For the period commencing January 1, 2005, an eligible small webcaster or a noncommercial webcaster, as defined in the regulations published by the Register of Copyrights pursuant to the Small Webcaster Settlement Act of 2002 (17 U.S.C. 114 note; Public Law 107–321) (including the amendments made by that Act [amending section 114 of this title and enacting provisions set out as notes under sections 101 and 114 of this title], may elect to be subject to the rates and terms published in those regulations by complying with the procedures governing the election process set forth in those regulations not later than the first date on which the webcaster would be obligated to make a royalty payment for such period. Until successor terms and rates have been established for the period commencing January 1, 2006, licensees shall continue to make royalty payments at the rates and on the terms previously in effect, subject to retroactive adjustment when successor rates and terms for such services are established.

"(4) INTERIM PROCEEDINGS.—Notwithstanding subsection (a), as soon as practicable after the date of enactment of this Act, the Copyright Royalty Judges or interim Copyright Royalty Judges shall publish the notice described in section 803(b)(1)(A) of title 17, United States Code, as amended by this Act, to initiate a proceeding to establish or adjust rates and terms for the statutory licenses under section 114(f)(2) or 112(e) of title 17, United States Code, for new subscription services and eligible nonsubscription services for the period commencing January 1, 2006. The Copyright Royalty Judges or Interim Copyright Royalty Judges are authorized to cause that proceeding to take place as provided in subsection (b) of section 803 of that title within the time periods set forth in that subsection. Notwithstanding section 803(c)(1) of that title, the Copyright Royalty Judges shall not be required to issue their determination in that proceeding before the expiration of the statutory rates and terms in effect on December 31, 2004.

"(c) EXISTING APPROPRIATIONS.—Any funds made available in an appropriations Act to carry out chapter 8 of title 17, United States Code, shall be available to the extent necessary to carry out this section."

§ 802. Copyright Royalty Judgeships; staff

(a) QUALIFICATIONS OF COPYRIGHT ROYALTY JUDGES.—

(1) IN GENERAL.—Each Copyright Royalty Judge shall be an attorney who has at least 7 years of legal experience. The Chief Copyright Royalty Judge shall have at least 5 years of experience in adjudications, arbitrations, or court trials. Of the other 2 Copyright Royalty Judges, 1 shall have significant knowledge of

copyright law, and the other shall have significant knowledge of economics. An individual may serve as a Copyright Royalty Judge only if the individual is free of any financial conflict of interest under subsection (h).

(2) DEFINITION.—In this subsection, the term "adjudication" has the meaning given that term in section 551 of title 5, but does not include mediation.

(b) STAFF.—The Chief Copyright Royalty Judge shall hire 3 full-time staff members to assist the Copyright Royalty Judges in performing their functions.

(c) TERMS.—The individual first appointed as the Chief Copyright Royalty Judge shall be appointed to a term of 6 years, and of the remaining individuals first appointed as Copyright Royalty Judges, 1 shall be appointed to a term of 4 years, and the other shall be appointed to a term of 2 years. Thereafter, the terms of succeeding Copyright Royalty Judges shall each be 6 years. An individual serving as a Copyright Royalty Judge may be reappointed to subsequent terms. The term of a Copyright Royalty Judge shall begin when the term of the predecessor of that Copyright Royalty Judge ends. When the term of office of a Copyright Royalty Judge ends, the individual serving that term may continue to serve until a successor is selected.

(d) VACANCIES OR INCAPACITY.—

(1) VACANCIES.—If a vacancy should occur in the position of Copyright Royalty Judge, the Librarian of Congress shall act expeditiously to fill the vacancy, and may appoint an interim Copyright Royalty Judge to serve until another Copyright Royalty Judge is appointed under this section. An individual appointed to fill the vacancy occurring before the expiration of the term for which the predecessor of that individual was appointed shall be appointed for the remainder of that term.

(2) INCAPACITY.—In the case in which a Copyright Royalty Judge is temporarily unable to perform his or her duties, the Librarian of Congress may appoint an interim Copyright Royalty Judge to perform such duties during the period of such incapacity.

(e) COMPENSATION.—

(1) JUDGES.—The Chief Copyright Royalty Judge shall receive compensation at the rate of basic pay payable for level AL–1 for administrative law judges pursuant to section 5372(b) of title 5, and each of the other two Copyright Royalty Judges shall receive compensation at the rate of basic pay payable for level AL–2 for administrative law judges pursuant to such section. The compensation of the Copyright Royalty Judges shall not be subject to any regulations adopted by the Office of Personnel Management pursuant to its authority under section 5376(b)(1) of title 5.

(2) STAFF MEMBERS.—Of the staff members appointed under subsection (b)—

(A) the rate of pay of 1 staff member shall be not more than the basic rate of pay payable for level 10 of GS–15 of the General Schedule;

(B) the rate of pay of 1 staff member shall be not less than the basic rate of pay payable for GS–13 of the General Schedule and not more than the basic rate of pay payable for level 10 of GS–14 of such Schedule; and

(C) the rate of pay for the third staff member shall be not less than the basic rate of pay payable for GS–8 of the General Schedule and not more than the basic rate of pay payable for level 10 of GS–11 of such Schedule.

(3) LOCALITY PAY.—All rates of pay referred to under this subsection shall include locality pay.

(f) INDEPENDENCE OF COPYRIGHT ROYALTY JUDGE.—

(1) IN MAKING DETERMINATIONS.—

(A) IN GENERAL.—(i) Subject to subparagraph (B) and clause (ii) of this subparagraph, the Copyright Royalty Judges shall have full independence in making determinations concerning adjustments and determinations of copyright royalty rates and terms, the distribution of copyright royalties, the acceptance or rejection of royalty claims, rate adjustment petitions, and petitions to participate, and in issuing other rulings under this title, except that the Copyright Royalty Judges may consult with the Register of Copyrights on any matter other than a question of fact.

(ii) One or more Copyright Royalty Judges may, or by motion to the Copyright Royalty Judges, any participant in a proceeding may, request from the Register of Copyrights an interpretation of any material questions of substantive law that relate to the construction of provisions of this title and arise in the course of the proceeding. Any request for a written interpretation shall be in writing and on the record, and reasonable provision shall be made to permit participants in the proceeding to comment on the material questions of substantive law in a manner that minimizes duplication and delay. Except as provided in subparagraph (B), the Register of Copyrights shall deliver to the Copyright Royalty Judges a written response within 14 days after the receipt of all briefs and comments from the participants. The Copyright Royalty Judges shall apply the legal interpretation embodied in the response of the Register of Copyrights if it is timely delivered, and the response shall be included in the record that accompanies the final determination. The authority under this clause shall not be construed to authorize the Register of Copyrights to provide an interpretation of questions of procedure before the Copyright Royalty Judges, the ultimate adjustments and determinations of copyright royalty rates and terms, the ultimate distribution of copyright royalties, or the acceptance or rejection of royalty claims, rate adjustment petitions, or petitions to participate in a proceeding.

(B) NOVEL QUESTIONS.—(i) In any case in which a novel material question of substantive law concerning an interpretation of those provisions of this title that are the subject of the proceeding is presented, the Copyright Royalty Judges shall request a decision of the Register of Copyrights, in writing, to resolve such novel question. Reasonable provision shall be made for comment on such request by the participants in the proceeding, in such a way as to minimize duplication and delay. The Register of Copyrights shall transmit his or her decision to the Copyright Royalty Judges within 30 days after the Register of Copyrights receives all of the briefs or comments of the participants. Such decision shall be in writing and included by the Copyright Royalty Judges in the record that accompanies their final determination. If such a decision is timely delivered to the Copyright Royalty Judges, the Copyright Royalty Judges shall apply the legal determinations embodied in the decision of the Register of Copyrights in resolving material questions of substantive law.

(ii) In clause (i), a "novel question of law" is a question of law that has not been determined in prior decisions, determinations, and rulings described in section 803(a).

(C) CONSULTATION.—Notwithstanding the provisions of subparagraph (A), the Copyright Royalty Judges shall consult with the Register of Copyrights with respect to any determination or ruling that would require that any act be performed by the Copyright Office, and any such determination or ruling shall not be binding upon the Register of Copyrights.

(D) REVIEW OF LEGAL CONCLUSIONS BY THE REGISTER OF COPYRIGHTS.—The Register of Copyrights may review for legal error the resolution by the Copyright Royalty Judges of a material question of substantive law under this title that underlies or is contained in a final determination of the Copyright Royalty Judges. If the Register of Copyrights concludes, after taking into consideration the views of the participants in the proceeding, that any resolution reached by the Copyright Royalty Judges was in material error, the Register of Copyrights shall issue a written decision correcting such legal error, which shall be made part of the record of the proceeding. The Register of Copyrights shall issue such written decision not later than 60 days after the date on which the final determination by the Copyright Royalty Judges is issued. Additionally, the Register of Copyrights shall cause to be published in the Federal Register such written decision, together with a specific identification of the legal conclusion of the Copyright Royalty Judges that is determined to be erroneous. As to conclusions of substantive law involving an interpretation of the statutory provisions of this title, the decision of the Register of Copyrights shall be binding as precedent upon the Copyright Royalty Judges in subsequent proceedings under this chapter. When a decision has been rendered pursuant to this subparagraph, the Register of Copyrights may, on the basis of and in accordance with such decision, intervene as of right in any appeal of a final determination of the Copyright Royalty Judges pursuant to section 803(d) in the United States Court of Appeals for the Dis-

trict of Columbia Circuit. If, prior to intervening in such an appeal, the Register of Copyrights gives notification to, and undertakes to consult with, the Attorney General with respect to such intervention, and the Attorney General fails, within a reasonable period after receiving such notification, to intervene in such appeal, the Register of Copyrights may intervene in such appeal in his or her own name by any attorney designated by the Register of Copyrights for such purpose. Intervention by the Register of Copyrights in his or her own name shall not preclude the Attorney General from intervening on behalf of the United States in such an appeal as may be otherwise provided or required by law.

(E) EFFECT ON JUDICIAL REVIEW.—Nothing in this section shall be interpreted to alter the standard applied by a court in reviewing legal determinations involving an interpretation or construction of the provisions of this title or to affect the extent to which any construction or interpretation of the provisions of this title shall be accorded deference by a reviewing court.

(2) PERFORMANCE APPRAISALS.—

(A) IN GENERAL.—Notwithstanding any other provision of law or any regulation of the Library of Congress, and subject to subparagraph (B), the Copyright Royalty Judges shall not receive performance appraisals.

(B) RELATING TO SANCTION OR REMOVAL.— To the extent that the Librarian of Congress adopts regulations under subsection (h) relating to the sanction or removal of a Copyright Royalty Judge and such regulations require documentation to establish the cause of such sanction or removal, the Copyright Royalty Judge may receive an appraisal related specifically to the cause of the sanction or removal.

(g) INCONSISTENT DUTIES BARRED.—No Copyright Royalty Judge may undertake duties that conflict with his or her duties and responsibilities as a Copyright Royalty Judge.

(h) STANDARDS OF CONDUCT.—The Librarian of Congress shall adopt regulations regarding the standards of conduct, including financial conflict of interest and restrictions against ex parte communications, which shall govern the Copyright Royalty Judges and the proceedings under this chapter.

(i) REMOVAL OR SANCTION.—The Librarian of Congress may sanction or remove a Copyright Royalty Judge for violation of the standards of conduct adopted under subsection (h), misconduct, neglect of duty, or any disqualifying physical or mental disability. Any such sanction or removal may be made only after notice and opportunity for a hearing, but the Librarian of Congress may suspend the Copyright Royalty Judge during the pendency of such hearing. The Librarian shall appoint an interim Copyright Royalty Judge during the period of any such suspension.

(Added Pub. L. 108–419, §3(a), Nov. 30, 2004, 118 Stat. 2345; amended Pub. L. 109–303, §3(3), (4), Oct. 6, 2006, 120 Stat. 1478, 1479.)

The General Schedule, referred to in subsec. (e)(2), is set out under section 5332 of Title 5, Government Organization and Employees.

A prior section 802, Pub. L. 94–553, title I, §101, Oct. 19, 1976, 90 Stat. 2596; Pub. L. 101–319, §2(a), July 3, 1990, 104 Stat. 290; Pub. L. 103–198, §2(b), Dec. 17, 1993, 107 Stat. 2305; Pub. L. 104–39, §5(d)(2)–(4), Nov. 1, 1995, 109 Stat. 349; Pub. L. 105–80, §8(b), Nov. 13, 1997, 111 Stat. 1533; Pub. L. 105–304, title IV, §405(d), (e)(2)–(4), Oct. 28, 1998, 112 Stat. 2902; Pub. L. 107–273, div. C, title III, §13301(c)(2), Nov. 2, 2002, 116 Stat. 1912, related to membership and proceedings of copyright arbitration royalty panels, prior to the general amendment of this chapter by Pub. L. 108–419.

2006—Subsec. (f)(1)(A)(i). Pub. L. 109–303, §3(3)(A), substituted "subparagraph (B) and clause (ii) of this subparagraph" for "clause (ii) of this subparagraph and subparagraph (B)".

Subsec. (f)(1)(A)(ii). Pub. L. 109–303, §3(3)(B), added cl. (ii) and struck out former cl. (ii) which related to request for interpretation by the Register of Copyrights of material question of substantive law concerning construction of provisions of this title that are the subject of the proceeding.

Subsec. (f)(1)(D). Pub. L. 109–303, §3(4), inserted a comma after "undertakes to consult with".

Amendment by Pub. L. 109–303 effective as if included in the Copyright Royalty and Distribution Reform Act of 2004, Pub. L. 108–419, see section 6 of Pub. L. 109–303, set out as a note under section 111 of this title.

§ 803. Proceedings of Copyright Royalty Judges

(a) PROCEEDINGS.—

(1) IN GENERAL.—The Copyright Royalty Judges shall act in accordance with this title, and to the extent not inconsistent with this title, in accordance with subchapter II of chapter 5 of title 5, in carrying out the purposes set forth in section 801. The Copyright Royalty Judges shall act in accordance with regulations issued by the Copyright Royalty Judges and the Librarian of Congress, and on the basis of a written record, prior determinations and interpretations of the Copyright Royalty Tribunal, Librarian of Congress, the Register of Copyrights, copyright arbitration royalty panels (to the extent those determinations are not inconsistent with a decision of the Librarian of Congress or the Register of Copyrights), and the Copyright Royalty Judges (to the extent those determinations are not inconsistent with a decision of the Register of Copyrights that was timely delivered to the Copyright Royalty Judges pursuant to section 802(f)(1)(A) or (B), or with a decision of the Register of Copyrights pursuant to section 802(f)(1)(D)), under this chapter, and decisions of the court of appeals under this chapter before, on, or after the effective date of the Copyright Royalty and Distribution Reform Act of 2004.

(2) JUDGES ACTING AS PANEL AND INDIVIDUALLY.—The Copyright Royalty Judges shall preside over hearings in proceedings under this chapter en banc. The Chief Copyright Royalty Judge may designate a Copyright Royalty Judge to preside individually over

such collateral and administrative proceedings, and over such proceedings under paragraphs (1) through (5) of subsection (b), as the Chief Judge considers appropriate.

(3) DETERMINATIONS.—Final determinations of the Copyright Royalty Judges in proceedings under this chapter shall be made by majority vote. A Copyright Royalty Judge dissenting from the majority on any determination under this chapter may issue his or her dissenting opinion, which shall be included with the determination.

(b) PROCEDURES.—

(1) INITIATION.—

(A) CALL FOR PETITIONS TO PARTICIPATE.—

(i) The Copyright Royalty Judges shall cause to be published in the Federal Register notice of commencement of proceedings under this chapter, calling for the filing of petitions to participate in a proceeding under this chapter for the purpose of making the relevant determination under section 111, 112, 114, 115, 116, 118, 119, 1004, or 1007, as the case may be—

(I) promptly upon a determination made under section 804(a);

(II) by no later than January 5 of a year specified in paragraph (2) of section 804(b) for the commencement of proceedings;

(III) by no later than January 5 of a year specified in subparagraph (A) or (B) of paragraph (3) of section 804(b) for the commencement of proceedings, or as otherwise provided in subparagraph (A) or (C) of such paragraph for the commencement of proceedings;

(IV) as provided under section 804(b)(8); or

(V) by no later than January 5 of a year specified in any other provision of section 804(b) for the filing of petitions for the commencement of proceedings, if a petition has not been filed by that date, except that the publication of notice requirement shall not apply in the case of proceedings under section 111 that are scheduled to commence in 2005.

(ii) Petitions to participate shall be filed by no later than 30 days after publication of notice of commencement of a proceeding under clause (i), except that the Copyright Royalty Judges may, for substantial good cause shown and if there is no prejudice to the participants that have already filed petitions, accept late petitions to participate at any time up to the date that is 90 days before the date on which participants in the proceeding are to file their written direct statements. Notwithstanding the preceding sentence, petitioners whose petitions are filed more than 30 days after publication of notice of commencement of a proceeding are not eligible to object to a settlement reached during the voluntary negotiation period under paragraph (3), and any objection filed by such a petitioner shall not be taken into account by the Copyright Royalty Judges.

(B) PETITIONS TO PARTICIPATE.—Each petition to participate in a proceeding shall describe the petitioner's interest in the subject matter of the proceeding. Parties with similar interests may file a single petition to participate.

(2) PARTICIPATION IN GENERAL.—Subject to paragraph (4), a person may participate in a proceeding under this chapter, including through the submission of briefs or other information, only if—

(A) that person has filed a petition to participate in accordance with paragraph (1) (either individually or as a group under paragraph (1)(B));

(B) the Copyright Royalty Judges have not determined that the petition to participate is facially invalid;

(C) the Copyright Royalty Judges have not determined, sua sponte or on the motion of another participant in the proceeding, that the person lacks a significant interest in the proceeding; and

(D) the petition to participate is accompanied by either—

(i) in a proceeding to determine royalty rates, a filing fee of $150; or

(ii) in a proceeding to determine distribution of royalty fees—

(I) a filing fee of $150; or

(II) a statement that the petitioner (individually or as a group) will not seek a distribution of more than $1000, in which case the amount distributed to the petitioner shall not exceed $1000.

(3) VOLUNTARY NEGOTIATION PERIOD.—

(A) COMMENCEMENT OF PROCEEDINGS.—

(i) RATE ADJUSTMENT PROCEEDING.— Promptly after the date for filing of petitions to participate in a proceeding, the Copyright Royalty Judges shall make available to all participants in the proceeding a list of such participants and shall initiate a voluntary negotiation period among the participants.

(ii) DISTRIBUTION PROCEEDING.—Promptly after the date for filing of petitions to participate in a proceeding to determine the distribution of royalties, the Copyright Royalty Judges shall make available to all participants in the proceeding a list of such participants. The initiation of a voluntary negotiation period among the participants shall be set at a time determined by the Copyright Royalty Judges.

(B) LENGTH OF PROCEEDINGS.—The voluntary negotiation period initiated under subparagraph (A) shall be 3 months.

(C) DETERMINATION OF SUBSEQUENT PROCEEDINGS.—At the close of the voluntary negotiation proceedings, the Copyright Royalty Judges shall, if further proceedings under this chapter are necessary, determine whether and to what extent paragraphs (4) and (5) will apply to the parties.

(4) SMALL CLAIMS PROCEDURE IN DISTRIBUTION PROCEEDINGS.—

(A) IN GENERAL.—If, in a proceeding under this chapter to determine the distribution of royalties, the contested amount of a claim is $10,000 or less, the Copyright Royalty Judges shall decide the controversy on the basis of the filing of the written direct statement by the participant, the response by any opposing participant, and 1 additional response by each such party.

(B) BAD FAITH INFLATION OF CLAIM.—If the Copyright Royalty Judges determine that a participant asserts in bad faith an amount in controversy in excess of $10,000 for the purpose of avoiding a determination under the procedure set forth in subparagraph (A), the Copyright Royalty Judges shall impose a fine on that participant in an amount not to exceed the difference between the actual amount distributed and the amount asserted by the participant.

(5) PAPER PROCEEDINGS.—The Copyright Royalty Judges in proceedings under this chapter may decide, sua sponte or upon motion of a participant, to determine issues on the basis of the filing of the written direct statement by the participant, the response by any opposing participant, and one additional response by each such participant. Prior to making such decision to proceed on such a paper record only, the Copyright Royalty Judges shall offer to all parties to the proceeding the opportunity to comment on the decision. The procedure under this paragraph—

(A) shall be applied in cases in which there is no genuine issue of material fact, there is no need for evidentiary hearings, and all participants in the proceeding agree in writing to the procedure; and

(B) may be applied under such other circumstances as the Copyright Royalty Judges consider appropriate.

(6) REGULATIONS.—

(A) IN GENERAL.—The Copyright Royalty Judges may issue regulations to carry out their functions under this title. All regulations issued by the Copyright Royalty Judges are subject to the approval of the Librarian of Congress and are subject to judicial review pursuant to chapter 7 of title 5, except as set forth in subsection (d). Not later than 120 days after Copyright Royalty Judges or interim Copyright Royalty Judges, as the case may be, are first appointed after the enactment of the Copyright Royalty and Distribution Reform Act of 2004, such judges shall issue regulations to govern proceedings under this chapter.

(B) INTERIM REGULATIONS.—Until regulations are adopted under subparagraph (A), the Copyright Royalty Judges shall apply the regulations in effect under this chapter on the day before the effective date of the Copyright Royalty and Distribution Reform Act of 2004, to the extent such regulations are not inconsistent with this chapter, except that functions carried out under such regulations by the Librarian of Congress, the Register of Copyrights, or copyright arbitration royalty panels that, as of such date of enactment, are to be carried out by the Copyright Royalty Judges under this chapter, shall be carried out by the Copyright Royalty Judges under such regulations.

(C) REQUIREMENTS.—Regulations issued under subparagraph (A) shall include the following:

(i) The written direct statements and written rebuttal statements of all participants in a proceeding under paragraph (2) shall be filed by a date specified by the Copyright Royalty Judges, which, in the case of written direct statements, may be not earlier than 4 months, and not later than 5 months, after the end of the voluntary negotiation period under paragraph (3). Notwithstanding the preceding sentence, the Copyright Royalty Judges may allow a participant in a proceeding to file an amended written direct statement based on new information received during the discovery process, within 15 days after the end of the discovery period specified in clause (iv).

(ii)(I) Following the submission to the Copyright Royalty Judges of written direct statements and written rebuttal statements by the participants in a proceeding under paragraph (2), the Copyright Royalty Judges, after taking into consideration the views of the participants in the proceeding, shall determine a schedule for conducting and completing discovery.

(II) In this chapter, the term "written direct statements" means witness statements, testimony, and exhibits to be presented in the proceedings, and such other information that is necessary to establish terms and rates, or the distribution of royalty payments, as the case may be, as set forth in regulations issued by the Copyright Royalty Judges.

(iii) Hearsay may be admitted in proceedings under this chapter to the extent deemed appropriate by the Copyright Royalty Judges.

(iv) Discovery in connection with written direct statements shall be permitted for a period of 60 days, except for discovery ordered by the Copyright Royalty Judges in connection with the resolution of motions, orders, and disputes pending at the end of such period. The Copyright Royalty Judges may order a discovery schedule in connection with written rebuttal statements.

(v) Any participant under paragraph (2) in a proceeding under this chapter to determine royalty rates may request of an opposing participant nonprivileged documents directly related to the written direct statement or written rebuttal statement of that participant. Any objection to such a request shall be resolved by a motion or request to compel production made to the Copyright Royalty Judges in accordance with regulations adopted by the Copyright Royalty Judges. Each motion or request to compel discovery shall be determined by the Copyright Royalty Judges, or by a Copyright Royalty Judge when permitted under subsection (a)(2). Upon such motion, the Copyright Royalty Judges may order discovery pursuant to regulations established under this paragraph.

(vi)(I) Any participant under paragraph (2) in a proceeding under this chapter to determine royalty rates may, by means of written motion or on the record, request of an opposing participant or witness other relevant information and materials if, absent the discovery sought, the Copyright Royalty Judges' resolution of the proceeding would be substantially impaired. In determining whether discovery will be granted under this clause, the Copyright Royalty Judges may consider—

(aa) whether the burden or expense of producing the requested information or materials outweighs the likely benefit, taking into account the needs and resources of the participants, the importance of the issues at stake, and the probative value of the requested information or materials in resolving such issues;

(bb) whether the requested information or materials would be unreasonably cumulative or duplicative, or are obtainable from another source that is more convenient, less burdensome, or less expensive; and

(cc) whether the participant seeking discovery has had ample opportunity by discovery in the proceeding or by other means to obtain the information sought.

(II) This clause shall not apply to any proceeding scheduled to commence after December 31, 2010.

(vii) In a proceeding under this chapter to determine royalty rates, the participants entitled to receive royalties shall collectively be permitted to take no more than 10 depositions and secure responses to no more than 25 interrogatories, and the participants obligated to pay royalties shall collectively be permitted to take no more than 10 depositions and secure responses to no more than 25 interrogatories. The Copyright Royalty Judges shall resolve any disputes among similarly aligned participants to allocate the number of depositions or interrogatories permitted under this clause.

(viii) The rules and practices in effect on the day before the effective date of the Copyright Royalty and Distribution Reform Act of 2004, relating to discovery in proceedings under this chapter to determine the distribution of royalty fees, shall continue to apply to such proceedings on and after such effective date.

(ix) In proceedings to determine royalty rates, the Copyright Royalty Judges may issue a subpoena commanding a participant or witness to appear and give testimony, or to produce and permit inspection of documents or tangible things, if the Copyright Royalty Judges' resolution of the proceeding would be substantially impaired by the absence of such testimony or production of documents or tangible things. Such subpoena shall specify with reasonable particularity the materials to be produced or the scope and nature of the required testimony. Nothing in this clause shall preclude the Copyright Royalty Judges from requesting the production by a nonparticipant of information or materials relevant to the resolution by the Copyright Royalty Judges of a material issue of fact.

(x) The Copyright Royalty Judges shall order a settlement conference among the participants in the proceeding to facilitate the presentation of offers of settlement among the participants. The settlement conference shall be held during a 21-day period following the 60-day discovery period specified in clause (iv) and shall take place outside the presence of the Copyright Royalty Judges.

(xi) No evidence, including exhibits, may be submitted in the written direct statement or written rebuttal statement of a participant without a sponsoring witness, except where the Copyright Royalty Judges have taken official notice, or in the case of incorporation by reference of past records, or for good cause shown.

(c) DETERMINATION OF COPYRIGHT ROYALTY JUDGES.—

(1) TIMING.—The Copyright Royalty Judges shall issue their determination in a proceeding not later than 11 months after the conclusion of the 21-day settlement conference period under subsection (b)(6)(C)(x), but, in the case of a proceeding to determine successors to rates or terms that expire on a specified date, in no event later than 15 days before the expiration of the then current statutory rates and terms.

(2) REHEARINGS.—

(A) IN GENERAL.—The Copyright Royalty Judges may, in exceptional cases, upon motion of a participant in a proceeding under subsection (b)(2), order a rehearing, after the determination in the proceeding is issued under paragraph (1), on such matters as the Copyright Royalty Judges determine to be appropriate.

(B) TIMING FOR FILING MOTION.—Any motion for a rehearing under subparagraph (A) may only be filed within 15 days after the date on which the Copyright Royalty Judges deliver to the participants in the proceeding their initial determination.

(C) PARTICIPATION BY OPPOSING PARTY NOT REQUIRED.—In any case in which a rehearing is ordered, any opposing party shall not be required to participate in the rehearing, except that nonparticipation may give rise to the limitations with respect to judicial review provided for in subsection (d)(1).

(D) NO NEGATIVE INFERENCE.—No negative inference shall be drawn from lack of participation in a rehearing.

(E) CONTINUITY OF RATES AND TERMS.—(i) If the decision of the Copyright Royalty Judges on any motion for a rehearing is not rendered before the expiration of the statutory rates and terms that were previously in effect, in the case of a proceeding to determine successors to rates and terms that expire on a specified date, then—

(I) the initial determination of the Copyright Royalty Judges that is the subject of the rehearing motion shall be effective as of the day following the date on which the rates and terms that were previously in effect expire; and

(II) in the case of a proceeding under section 114(f)(1)(C) or 114(f)(2)(C), royalty rates and terms shall, for purposes of section 114(f)(4)(B), be deemed to have been set at those rates and terms contained in the initial determination of the Copyright Royalty Judges that is the subject of the rehearing motion, as of the date of that determination.

(ii) The pendency of a motion for a rehearing under this paragraph shall not relieve persons obligated to make royalty payments who would be affected by the determination on that motion from providing the statements of account and any reports of use, to the extent required, and paying the royalties required under the relevant determination or regulations.

(iii) Notwithstanding clause (ii), whenever royalties described in clause (ii) are paid to a person other than the Copyright Office, the entity designated by the Copyright Royalty Judges to which such royalties are paid by the copyright user (and any successor thereto) shall, within 60 days after the motion for rehearing is resolved or, if the motion is granted, within 60 days after the rehearing is concluded, return any excess amounts previously paid to the extent necessary to comply with the final determination of royalty rates by the Copyright Royalty Judges. Any underpayment of royalties resulting from a rehearing shall be paid within the same period.

(3) CONTENTS OF DETERMINATION.—A determination of the Copyright Royalty Judges shall be supported by the written record and shall set forth the findings of fact relied on by the Copyright Royalty Judges. Among other terms adopted in a determination, the Copyright Royalty Judges may specify notice and recordkeeping requirements of users of the copyrights at issue that apply in lieu of those that would otherwise apply under regulations.

(4) CONTINUING JURISDICTION.—The Copyright Royalty Judges may issue an amendment to a written determination to correct any technical or clerical errors in the determination or to modify the terms, but not the rates, of royalty payments in response to unforeseen circumstances that would frustrate the proper implementation of such determination. Such amendment shall be set forth in a written addendum to the determination that shall be distributed to the participants of the proceeding and shall be published in the Federal Register.

(5) PROTECTIVE ORDER.—The Copyright Royalty Judges may issue such orders as may be appropriate to protect confidential information, including orders excluding confidential information from the record of the determination that is published or made available to the public, except that any terms or rates of royalty payments or distributions may not be excluded.

(6) PUBLICATION OF DETERMINATION.—By no later than the end of the 60-day period pro-

vided in section 802(f)(1)(D), the Librarian of Congress shall cause the determination, and any corrections thereto, to be published in the Federal Register. The Librarian of Congress shall also publicize the determination and corrections in such other manner as the Librarian considers appropriate, including, but not limited to, publication on the Internet. The Librarian of Congress shall also make the determination, corrections, and the accompanying record available for public inspection and copying.

(7) LATE PAYMENT.—A determination of the Copyright Royalty Judges may include terms with respect to late payment, but in no way shall such terms prevent the copyright holder from asserting other rights or remedies provided under this title.

(d) JUDICIAL REVIEW.—

(1) APPEAL.—Any determination of the Copyright Royalty Judges under subsection (c) may, within 30 days after the publication of the determination in the Federal Register, be appealed, to the United States Court of Appeals for the District of Columbia Circuit, by any aggrieved participant in the proceeding under subsection (b)(2) who fully participated in the proceeding and who would be bound by the determination. Any participant that did not participate in a rehearing may not raise any issue that was the subject of that rehearing at any stage of judicial review of the hearing determination. If no appeal is brought within that 30-day period, the determination of the Copyright Royalty Judges shall be final, and the royalty fee or determination with respect to the distribution of fees, as the case may be, shall take effect as set forth in paragraph (2).

(2) EFFECT OF RATES.—

(A) EXPIRATION ON SPECIFIED DATE.—When this title provides that the royalty rates and terms that were previously in effect are to expire on a specified date, any adjustment or determination by the Copyright Royalty Judges of successor rates and terms for an ensuing statutory license period shall be effective as of the day following the date of expiration of the rates and terms that were previously in effect, even if the determination of the Copyright Royalty Judges is rendered on a later date. A licensee shall be obligated to continue making payments under the rates and terms previously in effect until such time as rates and terms for the successor period are established. Whenever royalties pursuant to this section are paid to a person other than the Copyright Office, the entity designated by the Copyright Royalty Judges to which such royalties are paid by the copyright user (and any successor thereto) shall, within 60 days after the final determination of the Copyright Royalty Judges establishing rates and terms for a successor period or the exhaustion of all rehearings or appeals of such determination, if any, return any excess amounts previously paid to the extent necessary to comply with the final determination of royalty rates. Any underpayment of royalties by a copyright user shall be paid to the entity designated by the Copyright Royalty Judges within the same period.

(B) OTHER CASES.—In cases where rates and terms have not, prior to the inception of an activity, been established for that particular activity under the relevant license, such rates and terms shall be retroactive to the inception of activity under the relevant license covered by such rates and terms. In other cases where rates and terms do not expire on a specified date, successor rates and terms shall take effect on the first day of the second month that begins after the publication of the determination of the Copyright Royalty Judges in the Federal Register, except as otherwise provided in this title, or by the Copyright Royalty Judges, or as agreed by the participants in a proceeding that would be bound by the rates and terms. Except as otherwise provided in this title, the rates and terms, to the extent applicable, shall remain in effect until such successor rates and terms become effective.

(C) OBLIGATION TO MAKE PAYMENTS.—

(i) The pendency of an appeal under this subsection shall not relieve persons obligated to make royalty payments under section 111, 112, 114, 115, 116, 118, 119, or 1003, who would be affected by the determination on appeal, from—

(I) providing the applicable statements of account and reports of use; and

(II) paying the royalties required under the relevant determination or regulations.

(ii) Notwithstanding clause (i), whenever royalties described in clause (i) are paid to a person other than the Copyright Office, the entity designated by the Copyright Royalty Judges to which such royalties are paid by the copyright user (and any successor thereto) shall, within 60 days after the final resolution of the appeal, return any excess amounts previously paid (and interest thereon, if ordered pursuant to paragraph (3)) to the extent necessary to comply with the final determination of royalty rates on appeal. Any underpayment of royalties resulting from an appeal (and interest thereon, if ordered pursuant to paragraph (3)) shall be paid within the same period.

(3) JURISDICTION OF COURT.—Section 706 of title 5 shall apply with respect to review by the court of appeals under this subsection. If the court modifies or vacates a determination of the Copyright Royalty Judges, the court may enter its own determination with respect to the amount or distribution of royalty fees and costs, and order the repayment of any excess fees, the payment of any underpaid fees, and the payment of interest pertaining respectively thereto, in accordance with its final judgment. The court may also vacate the determination of the Copyright Royalty Judges and remand the case to the Copyright Royalty Judges for further proceedings in accordance with subsection (a).

(e) ADMINISTRATIVE MATTERS.—

(1) DEDUCTION OF COSTS OF LIBRARY OF CONGRESS AND COPYRIGHT OFFICE FROM FILING FEES.—

(A) DEDUCTION FROM FILING FEES.—The Librarian of Congress may, to the extent not otherwise provided under this title, deduct from the filing fees collected under subsection (b) for a particular proceeding under this chapter the reasonable costs incurred by the Librarian of Congress, the Copyright Office, and the Copyright Royalty Judges in conducting that proceeding, other than the salaries of the Copyright Royalty Judges and the 3 staff members appointed under section 802(b).

(B) AUTHORIZATION OF APPROPRIATIONS.— There are authorized to be appropriated such sums as may be necessary to pay the costs incurred under this chapter not covered by the filing fees collected under subsection (b). All funds made available pursuant to this subparagraph shall remain available until expended.

(2) POSITIONS REQUIRED FOR ADMINISTRATION OF COMPULSORY LICENSING.—Section 307 of the Legislative Branch Appropriations Act, 1994, shall not apply to employee positions in the Library of Congress that are required to be filled in order to carry out section 111, 112, 114, 115, 116, 118, or 119 or chapter 10.

(Added Pub. L. 108–419, §3(a), Nov. 30, 2004, 118 Stat. 2348; amended Pub. L. 108–447, div. J, title IX [title I, §112], Dec. 8, 2004, 118 Stat. 3409; Pub. L. 109–303, §3(5)–(11), Oct. 6, 2006, 120 Stat. 1479, 1481; Pub. L. 111–295, §5(b), Dec. 9, 2010, 124 Stat. 3181.)

REFERENCES IN TEXT

The effective date of the Copyright Royalty and Distribution Reform Act of 2004, referred to in subsecs. (a)(1) and (b)(6)(B), (C)(viii), is the effective date of Pub. L. 108–419, which is 6 months after Nov. 30, 2004, subject to transition provisions, see section 6 of Pub. L. 108–419, set out as an Effective Date; Transition Provisions note under section 801 of this title.

The enactment of the Copyright Royalty and Distribution Reform Act of 2004 and such date of enactment, referred to in subsec. (b)(6)(A), (B), probably mean the date of enactment of Pub. L. 108–419, which was approved Nov. 30, 2004.

Section 307 of the Legislative Branch Appropriations Act, 1994, referred to in subsec. (e)(2), is section 307 of Pub. L. 103–69, which is set out as a note under section 60–1 of Title 2, The Congress.

PRIOR PROVISIONS

A prior section 803, Pub. L. 94–553, title I, §101, Oct. 19, 1976, 90 Stat. 2597, §804; Pub. L. 100–568, §11(2), Oct. 31, 1988, 102 Stat. 2860; Pub. L. 100–667, title II, §202(5), Nov. 16, 1988, 102 Stat. 3958; Pub. L. 101–318, §3(c), July 3, 1990, 104 Stat. 288; Pub. L. 102–563, §3(a)(2), Oct. 28, 1992, 106 Stat. 4248; renumbered §803 and amended Pub. L. 103–198, §2(d), Dec. 17, 1993, 107 Stat. 2307; Pub. L. 104–39, §5(d)(5)–(7), Nov. 1, 1995, 109 Stat. 349; Pub. L. 105–80, §12(a)(20), Nov. 13, 1997, 111 Stat. 1535; Pub. L. 105–304, title IV, §405(e)(5), (6), Oct. 28, 1998, 112 Stat. 2902, related to institution and conclusion of proceedings of copyright arbitration royalty panels, prior to the general amendment of this chapter by Pub. L. 108–419.

Another prior section 803, Pub. L. 94–553, title I, §101, Oct. 19, 1976, 90 Stat. 2596, related to procedures of the Copyright Royalty Tribunal, prior to repeal by Pub. L. 103–198, §2(c), Dec. 17, 1993, 107 Stat. 2307.

AMENDMENTS

2010—Subsec. (b)(6)(A). Pub. L. 111–295 substituted "All regulations issued by the Copyright Royalty Judges are subject to the approval of the Librarian of Congress and are subject to judicial review pursuant to chapter 7 of title 5, except as set forth in subsection (d)." for "All regulations issued by the Copyright Royalty Judges are subject to the approval of the Librarian of Congress."

2006—Subsec. (a)(1). Pub. L. 109–303, §3(5), substituted "The Copyright Royalty Judges shall act in accordance with this title, and to the extent not inconsistent with this title, in accordance with subchapter II of chapter 5 of title 5, in carrying out the purposes set forth in section 801. The Copyright" for "The Copyright" and inserted "copyright arbitration royalty panels (to the extent those determinations are not inconsistent with a decision of the Librarian of Congress or the Register of Copyrights)," after "Congress, the Register of Copyrights,".

Subsec. (b)(1)(A)(i)(V). Pub. L. 109–303, §3(6)(A), substituted "the publication of notice requirement shall not apply in the case of" for "in the case of" and struck out ", such notice may not be published." at end.

Subsec. (b)(2). Pub. L. 109–303, §3(6)(B), struck out ", together with a filing fee of $150" before semicolon at end of subpar. (A) and added subpar. (D).

Subsec. (b)(3)(A). Pub. L. 109–303, §3(6)(C), substituted "Commencement of proceedings" for "In general" in heading, designated existing provisions as cl. (i), inserted cl. (i) heading, and added cl. (ii).

Subsec. (b)(4)(A). Pub. L. 109–303, §3(6)(D), struck out last sentence which read as follows: "The participant asserting the claim shall not be required to pay the filing fee under paragraph (2)."

Subsec. (b)(6)(C)(i). Pub. L. 109–303, §3(6)(E)(i), inserted "and written rebuttal statements" after "written direct statements" and substituted "which, in the case of written direct statements, may" for "which may" and "clause (iv)" for "clause (iii)".

Subsec. (b)(6)(C)(ii)(I). Pub. L. 109–303, §3(6)(E)(ii), amended subcl. (I) generally. Prior to amendment, subcl. (I) read as follows: "Following the submission to the Copyright Royalty Judges of written direct statements by the participants in a proceeding under paragraph (2), the judges shall meet with the participants for the purpose of setting a schedule for conducting and completing discovery. Such schedule shall be determined by the Copyright Royalty Judges."

Subsec. (b)(6)(C)(iv). Pub. L. 109–303, §3(6)(E)(iii), amended cl. (iv) generally. Prior to amendment, cl. (iv) read as follows: "Discovery in such proceedings shall be permitted for a period of 60 days, except for discovery ordered by the Copyright Royalty Judges in connection with the resolution of motions, orders, and disputes pending at the end of such period."

Subsec. (b)(6)(C)(x). Pub. L. 109–303, §3(6)(E)(iv), amended cl. (x) generally. Prior to amendment, cl. (x) read as follows: "The Copyright Royalty Judges shall order a settlement conference among the participants in the proceeding to facilitate the presentation of offers of settlement among the participants. The settlement conference shall be held during a 21-day period following the end of the discovery period and shall take place outside the presence of the Copyright Royalty Judges."

Subsec. (c)(2)(B). Pub. L. 109–303, §3(7), struck out "concerning rates and terms" before period at end.

Subsec. (c)(4). Pub. L. 109–303, §3(8), struck out ", with the approval of the Register of Copyrights," before "issue an amendment".

Subsec. (c)(7). Pub. L. 109–303, §3(9), substituted "of the Copyright" for "of Copyright".

Subsec. (d)(2)(C)(i)(I). Pub. L. 109–303, §3(10), substituted "applicable statements of account and reports of use" for "statements of account and any report of use".

Subsec. (d)(3). Pub. L. 109–303, §3(11), substituted "Section 706 of title 5 shall apply with respect to review by the court of appeals under this subsection. If the court modifies'' for ''If the court, pursuant to section 706 of title 5, modifies''.

2004—Subsec. (b)(1)(A)(i)(V). Pub. L. 108–447 inserted '', except that in the case of proceedings under section 111 that are scheduled to commence in 2005, such notice may not be published.'' before period at end.

EFFECTIVE DATE OF 2006 AMENDMENT

Amendment by Pub. L. 109–303 effective as if included in the Copyright Royalty and Distribution Reform Act of 2004, Pub. L. 108–419, see section 6 of Pub. L. 109–303, set out as a note under section 111 of this title.

§ 804. Institution of proceedings

(a) FILING OF PETITION.—With respect to proceedings referred to in paragraphs (1) and (2) of section 801(b) concerning the determination or adjustment of royalty rates as provided in sections 111, 112, 114, 115, 116, 118, 119, and 1004, during the calendar years specified in the schedule set forth in subsection (b), any owner or user of a copyrighted work whose royalty rates are specified by this title, or are established under this chapter before or after the enactment of the Copyright Royalty and Distribution Reform Act of 2004, may file a petition with the Copyright Royalty Judges declaring that the petitioner requests a determination or adjustment of the rate. The Copyright Royalty Judges shall make a determination as to whether the petitioner has such a significant interest in the royalty rate in which a determination or adjustment is requested. If the Copyright Royalty Judges determine that the petitioner has such a significant interest, the Copyright Royalty Judges shall cause notice of this determination, with the reasons for such determination, to be published in the Federal Register, together with the notice of commencement of proceedings under this chapter. With respect to proceedings under paragraph (1) of section 801(b) concerning the determination or adjustment of royalty rates as provided in sections 112 and 114, during the calendar years specified in the schedule set forth in subsection (b), the Copyright Royalty Judges shall cause notice of commencement of proceedings under this chapter to be published in the Federal Register as provided in section 803(b)(1)(A).

(b) TIMING OF PROCEEDINGS.—

(1) SECTION 111 PROCEEDINGS.—(A) A petition described in subsection (a) to initiate proceedings under section 801(b)(2) concerning the adjustment of royalty rates under section 111 to which subparagraph (A) or (D) of section 801(b)(2) applies may be filed during the year 2015 and in each subsequent fifth calendar year.

(B) In order to initiate proceedings under section 801(b)(2) concerning the adjustment of royalty rates under section 111 to which subparagraph (B) or (C) of section 801(b)(2) applies, within 12 months after an event described in either of those subsections, any owner or user of a copyrighted work whose royalty rates are specified by section 111, or by a rate established under this chapter before or after the enactment of the Copyright Royalty and Distribution Reform Act of 2004, may file a petition with the Copyright Royalty Judges declaring that the petitioner requests an ad-

justment of the rate. The Copyright Royalty Judges shall then proceed as set forth in subsection (a) of this section. Any change in royalty rates made under this chapter pursuant to this subparagraph may be reconsidered in the year 2015, and each fifth calendar year thereafter, in accordance with the provisions in section 801(b)(2)(B) or (C), as the case may be. A petition for adjustment of rates established by section 111(d)(1)(B) as a result of a change in the rules and regulations of the Federal Communications Commission shall set forth the change on which the petition is based.

(C) Any adjustment of royalty rates under section 111 shall take effect as of the first accounting period commencing after the publication of the determination of the Copyright Royalty Judges in the Federal Register, or on such other date as is specified in that determination.

(2) CERTAIN SECTION 112 PROCEEDINGS.—Proceedings under this chapter shall be commenced in the year 2007 to determine reasonable terms and rates of royalty payments for the activities described in section 112(e)(1) relating to the limitation on exclusive rights specified by section 114(d)(1)(C)(iv), to become effective on January 1, 2009. Such proceedings shall be repeated in each subsequent fifth calendar year.

(3) SECTION 114 AND CORRESPONDING 112 PROCEEDINGS.—

(A) FOR ELIGIBLE NONSUBSCRIPTION SERVICES AND NEW SUBSCRIPTION SERVICES.—Proceedings under this chapter shall be commenced as soon as practicable after the date of enactment of the Copyright Royalty and Distribution Reform Act of 2004 to determine reasonable terms and rates of royalty payments under sections 114 and 112 for the activities of eligible nonsubscription transmission services and new subscription services, to be effective for the period beginning on January 1, 2006, and ending on December 31, 2010. Such proceedings shall next be commenced in January 2009 to determine reasonable terms and rates of royalty payments, to become effective on January 1, 2011. Thereafter, such proceedings shall be repeated in each subsequent fifth calendar year.

(B) FOR PREEXISTING SUBSCRIPTION AND SATELLITE DIGITAL AUDIO RADIO SERVICES.—Proceedings under this chapter shall be commenced in January 2006 to determine reasonable terms and rates of royalty payments under sections 114 and 112 for the activities of preexisting subscription services, to be effective during the period beginning on January 1, 2008, and ending on December 31, 2012, and preexisting satellite digital audio radio services, to be effective during the period beginning on January 1, 2007, and ending on December 31, 2012. Such proceedings shall next be commenced in 2011 to determine reasonable terms and rates of royalty payments, to become effective on January 1, 2013. Thereafter, such proceedings shall be repeated in each subsequent fifth calendar year.

(C)(i) Notwithstanding any other provision of this chapter, this subparagraph shall govern proceedings commenced pursuant to section 114(f)(1)(C) and 114(f)(2)(C) concerning new types of services.

(ii) Not later than 30 days after a petition to determine rates and terms for a new type of service is filed by any copyright owner of sound recordings, or such new type of service, indicating that such new type of service is or is about to become operational, the Copyright Royalty Judges shall issue a notice for a proceeding to determine rates and terms for such service.

(iii) The proceeding shall follow the schedule set forth in subsections (b), (c), and (d) of section 803, except that—

(I) the determination shall be issued by not later than 24 months after the publication of the notice under clause (ii); and

(II) the decision shall take effect as provided in subsections (c)(2) and (d)(2) of section 803 and section 114(f)(4)(B)(ii) and (C).

(iv) The rates and terms shall remain in effect for the period set forth in section 114(f)(1)(C) or 114(f)(2)(C), as the case may be.

(4) SECTION 115 PROCEEDINGS.—A petition described in subsection (a) to initiate proceedings under section 801(b)(1) concerning the adjustment or determination of royalty rates as provided in section 115 may be filed in the year 2006 and in each subsequent fifth calendar year, or at such other times as the parties have agreed under section 115(c)(3)(B) and (C).

(5) SECTION 116 PROCEEDINGS.—(A) A petition described in subsection (a) to initiate proceedings under section 801(b) concerning the determination of royalty rates and terms as provided in section 116 may be filed at any time within 1 year after negotiated licenses authorized by section 116 are terminated or expire and are not replaced by subsequent agreements.

(B) If a negotiated license authorized by section 116 is terminated or expires and is not replaced by another such license agreement which provides permission to use a quantity of musical works not substantially smaller than the quantity of such works performed on coin-operated phonorecord players during the 1-year period ending March 1, 1989, the Copyright Royalty Judges shall, upon petition filed under paragraph (1) within 1 year after such termination or expiration, commence a proceeding to promptly establish an interim royalty rate or rates for the public performance by means of a coin-operated phonorecord player of nondramatic musical works embodied in phonorecords which had been subject to the terminated or expired negotiated license agreement. Such rate or rates shall be the same as the last such rate or rates and shall remain in force until the conclusion of proceedings by the Copyright Royalty Judges, in accordance with section 803, to adjust the royalty rates applicable to such works, or until superseded by a new negotiated license agreement, as provided in section 116(b).

(6) SECTION 118 PROCEEDINGS.—A petition described in subsection (a) to initiate proceedings under section 801(b)(1) concerning the determination of reasonable terms and rates of royalty payments as provided in section 118 may be filed in the year 2006 and in each subsequent fifth calendar year.

(7) SECTION 1004 PROCEEDINGS.—A petition described in subsection (a) to initiate proceedings under section 801(b)(1) concerning the adjustment of reasonable royalty rates under section 1004 may be filed as provided in section 1004(a)(3).

(8) PROCEEDINGS CONCERNING DISTRIBUTION OF ROYALTY FEES.—With respect to proceedings under section 801(b)(3) concerning the distribution of royalty fees in certain circumstances under section 111, 119, or 1007, the Copyright Royalty Judges shall, upon a determination that a controversy exists concerning such distribution, cause to be published in the Federal Register notice of commencement of proceedings under this chapter.

(Added Pub. L. 108–419, §3(a), Nov. 30, 2004, 118 Stat. 2357; amended Pub. L. 109–303, §3(12), (13), Oct. 6, 2006, 120 Stat. 1481; Pub. L. 111–175, title I, §104(f), May 27, 2010, 124 Stat. 1238.)

REFERENCES IN TEXT

The enactment of and the date of enactment of the Copyright Royalty and Distribution Reform Act of 2004, referred to in subsecs. (a) and (b)(1)(B), (3)(A), mean the date of enactment of Pub. L. 108–419, which was approved Nov. 30, 2004.

PRIOR PROVISIONS

A prior section 804 was renumbered section 803 of this title prior to the general amendment of this chapter by Pub. L. 108–419.

AMENDMENTS

2010—Subsec. (b)(1)(A), (B). Pub. L. 111–175 substituted "2015" for "2005".

2006—Subsec. (b)(1)(B). Pub. L. 109–303, §3(12), substituted "801(b)(2)(B) or (C)" for "801(b)(3)(B) or (C)" and "change in" for "change is".

Subsec. (b)(3)(A). Pub. L. 109–303, §3(13)(A), substituted "date of enactment" for "effective date".

Subsec. (b)(3)(C)(ii). Pub. L. 109–303, §3(13)(B)(i), substituted "is filed" for "that is filed".

Subsec. (b)(3)(C)(iii). Pub. L. 109–303, §3(13)(B)(ii), substituted "subsections (b)" for "such subsections (b)".

EFFECTIVE DATE OF 2010 AMENDMENT

Amendment by Pub. L. 111–175 effective Feb. 27, 2010, see section 307(a) of Pub. L. 111–175, set out as a note under section 111 of this title.

EFFECTIVE DATE OF 2006 AMENDMENT

Amendment by Pub. L. 109–303 effective as if included in the Copyright Royalty and Distribution Reform Act of 2004, Pub. L. 108–419, see section 6 of Pub. L. 109–303, set out as a note under section 111 of this title.

§ 805. General rule for voluntarily negotiated agreements

Any rates or terms under this title that—

(1) are agreed to by participants to a proceeding under section 803(b)(3),

(2) are adopted by the Copyright Royalty Judges as part of a determination under this chapter, and

(3) are in effect for a period shorter than would otherwise apply under a determination pursuant to this chapter,

shall remain in effect for such period of time as would otherwise apply under such determination, except that the Copyright Royalty Judges shall adjust the rates pursuant to the voluntary negotiations to reflect national monetary inflation during the additional period the rates remain in effect.

(Added Pub. L. 108–419, § 3(a), Nov. 30, 2004, 118 Stat. 2360.)

PRIOR PROVISIONS

Prior sections 805 to 810 were repealed by Pub. L. 103–198, § 2(e), Dec. 17, 1993, 107 Stat. 2308.

Section 805, Pub. L. 94–553, title I, § 101, Oct. 19, 1976, 90 Stat. 2598, related to staff of Copyright Royalty Tribunal.

Section 806, Pub. L. 94–553, title I, § 101, Oct. 19, 1976, 90 Stat. 2598, related to administrative support of Tribunal.

Section 807, Pub. L. 94–553, title I, § 101, Oct. 19, 1976, 90 Stat. 2598, related to deduction of costs of proceedings involving distribution of royalty fees.

Section 808, Pub. L. 94–553, title I, § 101, Oct. 19, 1976, 90 Stat. 2598, related to reporting requirements of the Tribunal.

Section 809, Pub. L. 94–553, title I, § 101, Oct. 19, 1976, 90 Stat. 2598, related to effective date of final determinations of Tribunal.

Section 810, Pub. L. 94–553, title I, § 101, Oct. 19, 1976, 90 Stat. 2598, related to judicial review of final decisions of Tribunal.

CHAPTER 9—PROTECTION OF SEMICONDUCTOR CHIP PRODUCTS

AMENDMENTS

2002—Pub. L. 107–273, div. C, title III, § 13210(11), Nov. 2, 2002, 116 Stat. 1910, substituted "licensing" for "licensure" in item 903.

1997—Pub. L. 105–80, § 12(a)(21), Nov. 13, 1997, 111 Stat. 1535, substituted "Ownership, transfer, licensure, and recordation" for "Ownership and transfer" in item 903.

§ 901. Definitions

(a) As used in this chapter—

(1) a "semiconductor chip product" is the final or intermediate form of any product—

(A) having two or more layers of metallic, insulating, or semiconductor material, deposited or otherwise placed on, or etched away or otherwise removed from, a piece of semiconductor material in accordance with a predetermined pattern; and

(B) intended to perform electronic circuitry functions;

(2) a "mask work" is a series of related images, however fixed or encoded—

(A) having or representing the predetermined, three-dimensional pattern of metallic, insulating, or semiconductor material present or removed from the layers of a semiconductor chip product; and

(B) in which series the relation of the images to one another is that each image has the pattern of the surface of one form of the semiconductor chip product;

(3) a mask work is "fixed" in a semiconductor chip product when its embodiment in the product is sufficiently permanent or stable to permit the mask work to be perceived or reproduced from the product for a period of more than transitory duration;

(4) to "distribute" means to sell, or to lease, bail, or otherwise transfer, or to offer to sell, lease, bail, or otherwise transfer;

(5) to "commercially exploit" a mask work is to distribute to the public for commercial purposes a semiconductor chip product embodying the mask work; except that such term includes an offer to sell or transfer a semiconductor chip product only when the offer is in writing and occurs after the mask work is fixed in the semiconductor chip product;

(6) the "owner" of a mask work is the person who created the mask work, the legal representative of that person if that person is deceased or under a legal incapacity, or a party to whom all the rights under this chapter of such person or representative are transferred in accordance with section 903(b); except that, in the case of a work made within the scope of a person's employment, the owner is the employer for whom the person created the mask work or a party to whom all the rights under this chapter of the employer are transferred in accordance with section 903(b);

(7) an "innocent purchaser" is a person who purchases a semiconductor chip product in good faith and without having notice of protection with respect to the semiconductor chip product;

(8) having "notice of protection" means having actual knowledge that, or reasonable grounds to believe that, a mask work is protected under this chapter; and

(9) an "infringing semiconductor chip product" is a semiconductor chip product which is made, imported, or distributed in violation of the exclusive rights of the owner of a mask work under this chapter.

(b) For purposes of this chapter, the distribution or importation of a product incorporating a semiconductor chip product as a part thereof is a distribution or importation of that semiconductor chip product.

(Added Pub. L. 98–620, title III, § 302, Nov. 8, 1984, 98 Stat. 3347.)

AUTHORIZATION OF APPROPRIATIONS

Section 304 of title III of Pub. L. 98–620 provided that: "There are authorized to be appropriated such sums as may be necessary to carry out the purposes of this title and the amendments made by this title [enacting this chapter]."

§ 902. Subject matter of protection

(a)(1) Subject to the provisions of subsection (b), a mask work fixed in a semiconductor chip product, by or under the authority of the owner of the mask work, is eligible for protection under this chapter if—

(A) on the date on which the mask work is registered under section 908, or is first commercially exploited anywhere in the world, whichever occurs first, the owner of the mask work is (i) a national or domiciliary of the United States, (ii) a national, domiciliary, or sovereign authority of a foreign nation that is a party to a treaty affording protection to mask works to which the United States is also a party, or (iii) a stateless person, wherever that person may be domiciled;

(B) the mask work is first commercially exploited in the United States; or

(C) the mask work comes within the scope of a Presidential proclamation issued under paragraph (2).

(2) Whenever the President finds that a foreign nation extends, to mask works of owners who are nationals or domiciliaries of the United States protection (A) on substantially the same basis as that on which the foreign nation extends protection to mask works of its own nationals and domiciliaries and mask works first commercially exploited in that nation, or (B) on substantially the same basis as provided in this chapter, the President may by proclamation extend protection under this chapter to mask works (i) of owners who are, on the date on which the mask works are registered under section 908, or the date on which the mask works are first commercially exploited anywhere in the world, whichever occurs first, nationals, domiciliaries, or sovereign authorities of that nation, or (ii) which are first commercially exploited in that nation. The President may revise, suspend, or revoke any such proclamation or impose any conditions or limitations on protection extended under any such proclamation.

(b) Protection under this chapter shall not be available for a mask work that—

(1) is not original; or

(2) consists of designs that are staple, commonplace, or familiar in the semiconductor industry, or variations of such designs, combined in a way that, considered as a whole, is not original.

(c) In no case does protection under this chapter for a mask work extend to any idea, procedure, process, system, method of operation, concept, principle, or discovery, regardless of the form in which it is described, explained, illustrated, or embodied in such work.

(Added Pub. L. 98–620, title III, §302, Nov. 8, 1984, 98 Stat. 3348; amended Pub. L. 100–159, §3, Nov. 9, 1987, 101 Stat. 900.)

AMENDMENTS

1987—Subsec. (a)(2). Pub. L. 100–159 inserted provision at end permitting the President to revise, suspend, or revoke any such proclamation or impose any conditions or limitations on protection extended under any such proclamation.

EX. ORD. NO. 12504. PROTECTION OF SEMICONDUCTOR CHIP PRODUCTS

Ex. Ord. No. 12504, Jan. 31, 1985, 50 F.R. 4849, provided:
By the authority vested in me as President by the Constitution and laws of the United States of America, including the Semiconductor Chip Protection Act of 1984 (17 U.S.C. 901 *et seq.*) and in order to provide for the orderly implementation of that Act, it is hereby ordered that, subject to the authority of the Director of the Office of Management and Budget under Executive Order No. 11030, as amended [44 U.S.C. 1505 note], requests for issuance by the President of a proclamation extending the protection of Chapter 9 of title 17 of the United States Code against unauthorized duplication of semiconductor chip products to foreign nationals, domiciliaries, and sovereign authorities shall be presented to the President through the Secretary of Commerce in accordance with such regulations as the Secretary may, after consultation with the Secretary of State, prescribe and cause to be published in the Federal Register.

RONALD REAGAN.

§903. Ownership, transfer, licensing, and recordation

(a) The exclusive rights in a mask work subject to protection under this chapter belong to the owner of the mask work.

(b) The owner of the exclusive rights in a mask work may transfer all of those rights, or license all or less than all of those rights, by any written instrument signed by such owner or a duly authorized agent of the owner. Such rights may be transferred or licensed by operation of law, may be bequeathed by will, and may pass as personal property by the applicable laws of intestate succession.

(c)(1) Any document pertaining to a mask work may be recorded in the Copyright Office if the document filed for recordation bears the actual signature of the person who executed it, or if it is accompanied by a sworn or official certification that it is a true copy of the original, signed document. The Register of Copyrights shall, upon receipt of the document and the fee specified pursuant to section 908(d), record the document and return it with a certificate of recordation. The recordation of any transfer or license under this paragraph gives all persons constructive notice of the facts stated in the recorded document concerning the transfer or license.

(2) In any case in which conflicting transfers of the exclusive rights in a mask work are made, the transfer first executed shall be void as against a subsequent transfer which is made for a valuable consideration and without notice of the first transfer, unless the first transfer is recorded in accordance with paragraph (1) within three months after the date on which it is executed, but in no case later than the day before the date of such subsequent transfer.

(d) Mask works prepared by an officer or employee of the United States Government as part of that person's official duties are not protected under this chapter, but the United States Government is not precluded from receiving and holding exclusive rights in mask works transferred to the Government under subsection (b).

(Added Pub. L. 98–620, title III, §302, Nov. 8, 1984, 98 Stat. 3349.)

§904. Duration of protection

(a) The protection provided for a mask work under this chapter shall commence on the date on which the mask work is registered under section 908, or the date on which the mask work is first commercially exploited anywhere in the world, whichever occurs first.

(b) Subject to subsection (c) and the provisions of this chapter, the protection provided under this chapter to a mask work shall end ten years after the date on which such protection commences under subsection (a).

(c) All terms of protection provided in this section shall run to the end of the calendar year in which they would otherwise expire.

(Added Pub. L. 98–620, title III, § 302, Nov. 8, 1984, 98 Stat. 3349.)

§ 905. Exclusive rights in mask works

The owner of a mask work provided protection under this chapter has the exclusive rights to do and to authorize any of the following:

(1) to reproduce the mask work by optical, electronic, or any other means;

(2) to import or distribute a semiconductor chip product in which the mask work is embodied; and

(3) to induce or knowingly to cause another person to do any of the acts described in paragraphs (1) and (2).

(Added Pub. L. 98–620, title III, § 302, Nov. 8, 1984, 98 Stat. 3350.)

§ 906. Limitation on exclusive rights: reverse engineering; first sale

(a) Notwithstanding the provisions of section 905, it is not an infringement of the exclusive rights of the owner of a mask work for—

(1) a person to reproduce the mask work solely for the purpose of teaching, analyzing, or evaluating the concepts or techniques embodied in the mask work or the circuitry, logic flow, or organization of components used in the mask work; or

(2) a person who performs the analysis or evaluation described in paragraph (1) to incorporate the results of such conduct in an original mask work which is made to be distributed.

(b) Notwithstanding the provisions of section 905(2), the owner of a particular semiconductor chip product made by the owner of the mask work, or by any person authorized by the owner of the mask work, may import, distribute, or otherwise dispose of or use, but not reproduce, that particular semiconductor chip product without the authority of the owner of the mask work.

(Added Pub. L. 98–620, title III, § 302, Nov. 8, 1984, 98 Stat. 3350.)

§ 907. Limitation on exclusive rights: innocent infringement

(a) Notwithstanding any other provision of this chapter, an innocent purchaser of an infringing semiconductor chip product—

(1) shall incur no liability under this chapter with respect to the importation or distribution of units of the infringing semiconductor chip product that occurs before the innocent purchaser has notice of protection with respect to the mask work embodied in the semiconductor chip product; and

(2) shall be liable only for a reasonable royalty on each unit of the infringing semiconductor chip product that the innocent purchaser imports or distributes after having notice of protection with respect to the mask work embodied in the semiconductor chip product.

(b) The amount of the royalty referred to in subsection (a)(2) shall be determined by the court in a civil action for infringement unless the parties resolve the issue by voluntary negotiation, mediation, or binding arbitration.

(c) The immunity of an innocent purchaser from liability referred to in subsection (a)(1) and the limitation of remedies with respect to an innocent purchaser referred to in subsection (a)(2) shall extend to any person who directly or indirectly purchases an infringing semiconductor chip product from an innocent purchaser.

(d) The provisions of subsections (a), (b), and (c) apply only with respect to those units of an infringing semiconductor chip product that an innocent purchaser purchased before having notice of protection with respect to the mask work embodied in the semiconductor chip product.

(Added Pub. L. 98–620, title III, § 302, Nov. 8, 1984, 98 Stat. 3350.)

§ 908. Registration of claims of protection

(a) The owner of a mask work may apply to the Register of Copyrights for registration of a claim of protection in a mask work. Protection of a mask work under this chapter shall terminate if application for registration of a claim of protection in the mask work is not made as provided in this chapter within two years after the date on which the mask work is first commercially exploited anywhere in the world.

(b) The Register of Copyrights shall be responsible for all administrative functions and duties under this chapter. Except for section 708, the provisions of chapter 7 of this title relating to the general responsibilities, organization, regulatory authority, actions, records, and publications of the Copyright Office shall apply to this chapter, except that the Register of Copyrights may make such changes as may be necessary in applying those provisions to this chapter.

(c) The application for registration of a mask work shall be made on a form prescribed by the Register of Copyrights. Such form may require any information regarded by the Register as bearing upon the preparation or identification of the mask work, the existence or duration of protection of the mask work under this chapter, or ownership of the mask work. The application shall be accompanied by the fee set pursuant to subsection (d) and the identifying material specified pursuant to such subsection.

(d) The Register of Copyrights shall by regulation set reasonable fees for the filing of applications to register claims of protection in mask works under this chapter, and for other services relating to the administration of this chapter or the rights under this chapter, taking into consideration the cost of providing those services, the benefits of a public record, and statutory fee schedules under this title. The Register shall also specify the identifying material to be deposited in connection with the claim for registration.

(e) If the Register of Copyrights, after examining an application for registration, determines, in accordance with the provisions of this chapter, that the application relates to a mask work which is entitled to protection under this chapter, then the Register shall register the claim of protection and issue to the applicant a certificate of registration of the claim of protection under the seal of the Copyright Office. The effective date of registration of a claim of protection shall be the date on which an application, deposit of identifying material, and fee, which are determined by the Register of Copyrights or by a court of competent jurisdiction to be acceptable for registration of the claim, have all been received in the Copyright Office.

(f) In any action for infringement under this chapter, the certificate of registration of a mask work shall constitute prima facie evidence (1) of the facts stated in the certificate, and (2) that the applicant issued the certificate has met the requirements of this chapter, and the regulations issued under this chapter, with respect to the registration of claims.

(g) Any applicant for registration under this section who is dissatisfied with the refusal of the Register of Copyrights to issue a certificate of registration under this section may seek judicial review of that refusal by bringing an action for such review in an appropriate United States district court not later than sixty days after the refusal. The provisions of chapter 7 of title 5 shall apply to such judicial review. The failure of the Register of Copyrights to issue a certificate of registration within four months after an application for registration is filed shall be deemed to be a refusal to issue a certificate of registration for purposes of this subsection and section 910(b)(2), except that, upon a showing of good cause, the district court may shorten such four-month period.

(Added Pub. L. 98–620, title III, § 302, Nov. 8, 1984, 98 Stat. 3351.)

§ 909. Mask work notice

(a) The owner of a mask work provided protection under this chapter may affix notice to the mask work, and to masks and semiconductor chip products embodying the mask work, in such manner and location as to give reasonable notice of such protection. The Register of Copyrights shall prescribe by regulation, as examples, specific methods of affixation and positions of notice for purposes of this section, but these specifications shall not be considered exhaustive. The affixation of such notice is not a condition of protection under this chapter, but shall constitute prima facie evidence of notice of protection.

(b) The notice referred to in subsection (a) shall consist of—

(1) the words "mask work", the symbol *M*, or the symbol Ⓜ (the letter M in a circle); and
(2) the name of the owner or owners of the mask work or an abbreviation by which the name is recognized or is generally known.

(Added Pub. L. 98–620, title III, § 302, Nov. 8, 1984, 98 Stat. 3352; amended Pub. L. 105–80, § 12(a)(22), Nov. 13, 1997, 111 Stat. 1535.)

AMENDMENTS

1997—Subsec. (b)(1). Pub. L. 105–80 substituted "'mask work', the symbol" for "'mask force', the sumbol".

§ 910. Enforcement of exclusive rights

(a) Except as otherwise provided in this chapter, any person who violates any of the exclusive rights of the owner of a mask work under this chapter, by conduct in or affecting commerce, shall be liable as an infringer of such rights. As used in this subsection, the term "any person" includes any State, any instrumentality of a State, and any officer or employee of a State or instrumentality of a State acting in his or her official capacity. Any State, and any such instrumentality, officer, or employee, shall be subject to the provisions of this chapter in the same manner and to the same extent as any nongovernmental entity.

(b)(1) The owner of a mask work protected under this chapter, or the exclusive licensee of all rights under this chapter with respect to the mask work, shall, after a certificate of registration of a claim of protection in that mask work has been issued under section 908, be entitled to institute a civil action for any infringement with respect to the mask work which is committed after the commencement of protection of the mask work under section 904(a).

(2) In any case in which an application for registration of a claim of protection in a mask work and the required deposit of identifying material and fee have been received in the Copyright Office in proper form and registration of the mask work has been refused, the applicant is entitled to institute a civil action for infringement under this chapter with respect to the mask work if notice of the action, together with a copy of the complaint, is served on the Register of Copyrights, in accordance with the Federal Rules of Civil Procedure. The Register may, at his or her option, become a party to the action with respect to the issue of whether the claim of protection is eligible for registration by entering an appearance within sixty days after such service, but the failure of the Register to become a party to the action shall not deprive the court of jurisdiction to determine that issue.

(c)(1) The Secretary of the Treasury and the United States Postal Service shall separately or jointly issue regulations for the enforcement of the rights set forth in section 905 with respect to importation. These regulations may require, as a condition for the exclusion of articles from the United States, that the person seeking exclusion take any one or more of the following actions:

(A) Obtain a court order enjoining, or an order of the International Trade Commission under section 337 of the Tariff Act of 1930 excluding, importation of the articles.
(B) Furnish proof that the mask work involved is protected under this chapter and that the importation of the articles would infringe the rights in the mask work under this chapter.
(C) Post a surety bond for any injury that may result if the detention or exclusion of the articles proves to be unjustified.

(2) Articles imported in violation of the rights set forth in section 905 are subject to seizure and

forfeiture in the same manner as property imported in violation of the customs laws. Any such forfeited articles shall be destroyed as directed by the Secretary of the Treasury or the court, as the case may be, except that the articles may be returned to the country of export whenever it is shown to the satisfaction of the Secretary of the Treasury that the importer had no reasonable grounds for believing that his or her acts constituted a violation of the law.

(Added Pub. L. 98–620, title III, § 302, Nov. 8, 1984, 98 Stat. 3352; amended Pub. L. 101–553, § 2(b)(1), Nov. 15, 1990, 104 Stat. 2750; Pub. L. 105–80, § 12(a)(23), Nov. 13, 1997, 111 Stat. 1535.)

REFERENCES IN TEXT

The Federal Rules of Civil Procedure, referred to in subsec. (b)(2), are set out in the Appendix to Title 28, Judiciary and Judicial Procedure.

Section 337 of the Tariff Act of 1930, referred to in subsec. (c)(1)(A), is classified to section 1337 of Title 19, Customs Duties.

AMENDMENTS

1997—Subsec. (a). Pub. L. 105–80 substituted "As used" for "as used" in second sentence.

1990—Subsec. (a). Pub. L. 101–553 inserted sentences at end defining "any person" and providing that any State and any instrumentality, officer, or employee be subject to the provisions of this chapter in the same manner and to the same extent as any nongovernmental entity.

EFFECTIVE DATE OF 1990 AMENDMENT

Amendment by Pub. L. 101–553 effective with respect to violations that occur on or after Nov. 15, 1990, see section 3 of Pub. L. 101–553, set out as a note under section 501 of this title.

§ 911. Civil actions

(a) Any court having jurisdiction of a civil action arising under this chapter may grant temporary restraining orders, preliminary injunctions, and permanent injunctions on such terms as the court may deem reasonable to prevent or restrain infringement of the exclusive rights in a mask work under this chapter.

(b) Upon finding an infringer liable, to a person entitled under section 910(b)(1) to institute a civil action, for an infringement of any exclusive right under this chapter, the court shall award such person actual damages suffered by the person as a result of the infringement. The court shall also award such person the infringer's profits that are attributable to the infringement and are not taken into account in computing the award of actual damages. In establishing the infringer's profits, such person is required to present proof only of the infringer's gross revenue, and the infringer is required to prove his or her deductible expenses and the elements of profit attributable to factors other than the mask work.

(c) At any time before final judgment is rendered, a person entitled to institute a civil action for infringement may elect, instead of actual damages and profits as provided by subsection (b), an award of statutory damages for all infringements involved in the action, with respect to any one mask work for which any one infringer is liable individually, or for which any two or more infringers are liable jointly and sev-

erally, in an amount not more than $250,000 as the court considers just.

(d) An action for infringement under this chapter shall be barred unless the action is commenced within three years after the claim accrues.

(e)(1) At any time while an action for infringement of the exclusive rights in a mask work under this chapter is pending, the court may order the impounding, on such terms as it may deem reasonable, of all semiconductor chip products, and any drawings, tapes, masks, or other products by means of which such products may be reproduced, that are claimed to have been made, imported, or used in violation of those exclusive rights. Insofar as practicable, applications for orders under this paragraph shall be heard and determined in the same manner as an application for a temporary restraining order or preliminary injunction.

(2) As part of a final judgment or decree, the court may order the destruction or other disposition of any infringing semiconductor chip products, and any masks, tapes, or other articles by means of which such products may be reproduced.

(f) In any civil action arising under this chapter, the court in its discretion may allow the recovery of full costs, including reasonable attorneys' fees, to the prevailing party.

(g)(1) Any State, any instrumentality of a State, and any officer or employee of a State or instrumentality of a State acting in his or her official capacity, shall not be immune, under the Eleventh Amendment of the Constitution of the United States or under any other doctrine of sovereign immunity, from suit in Federal court by any person, including any governmental or nongovernmental entity, for a violation of any of the exclusive rights of the owner of a mask work under this chapter, or for any other violation under this chapter.

(2) In a suit described in paragraph (1) for a violation described in that paragraph, remedies (including remedies both at law and in equity) are available for the violation to the same extent as such remedies are available for such a violation in a suit against any public or private entity other than a State, instrumentality of a State, or officer or employee of a State acting in his or her official capacity. Such remedies include actual damages and profits under subsection (b), statutory damages under subsection (c), impounding and disposition of infringing articles under subsection (e), and costs and attorney's fees under subsection (f).

(Added Pub. L. 98–620, title III, § 302, Nov. 8, 1984, 98 Stat. 3353; amended Pub. L. 101–553, § 2(b)(2), Nov. 15, 1990, 104 Stat. 2750.)

AMENDMENTS

1990—Subsec. (g). Pub. L. 101–553 added subsec. (g).

EFFECTIVE DATE OF 1990 AMENDMENT

Amendment by Pub. L. 101–553 effective with respect to violations that occur on or after Nov. 15, 1990, see section 3 of Pub. L. 101–553, set out as a note under section 501 of this title.

§ 912. Relation to other laws

(a) Nothing in this chapter shall affect any right or remedy held by any person under chapters 1 through 8 or 10 of this title, or under title 35.

(b) Except as provided in section 908(b) of this title, references to "this title" or "title 17" in chapters 1 through 8 or 10 of this title shall be deemed not to apply to this chapter.

(c) The provisions of this chapter shall preempt the laws of any State to the extent those laws provide any rights or remedies with respect to a mask work which are equivalent to those rights or remedies provided by this chapter, except that such preemption shall be effective only with respect to actions filed on or after January 1, 1986.

(d) Notwithstanding subsection (c), nothing in this chapter shall detract from any rights of a mask work owner, whether under Federal law (exclusive of this chapter) or under the common law or the statutes of a State, heretofore or hereafter declared or enacted, with respect to any mask work first commercially exploited before July 1, 1983.

(Added Pub. L. 98–620, title III, §302, Nov. 8, 1984, 98 Stat. 3354; amended Pub. L. 100–702, title X, §1020(b), Nov. 19, 1988, 102 Stat. 4672; Pub. L. 102–563, §3(c), Oct. 28, 1992, 106 Stat. 4248.)

AMENDMENTS

1992—Subsecs. (a), (b). Pub. L. 102–563 inserted "or 10" after "8".

1988—Subsecs. (d), (e). Pub. L. 100–702 redesignated subsec. (e) as (d) and struck out former subsec. (d) which read as follows: "The provisions of sections 1338, 1400(a), and 1498(b) and (c) of title 28 shall apply with respect to exclusive rights in mask works under this chapter."

§913. Transitional provisions

(a) No application for registration under section 908 may be filed, and no civil action under section 910 or other enforcement proceeding under this chapter may be instituted, until sixty days after the date of the enactment of this chapter.

(b) No monetary relief under section 911 may be granted with respect to any conduct that occurred before the date of the enactment of this chapter, except as provided in subsection (d).

(c) Subject to subsection (a), the provisions of this chapter apply to all mask works that are first commercially exploited or are registered under this chapter, or both, on or after the date of the enactment of this chapter.

(d)(1) Subject to subsection (a), protection is available under this chapter to any mask work that was first commercially exploited on or after July 1, 1983, and before the date of the enactment of this chapter, if a claim of protection in the mask work is registered in the Copyright Office before July 1, 1985, under section 908.

(2) In the case of any mask work described in paragraph (1) that is provided protection under this chapter, infringing semiconductor chip product units manufactured before the date of the enactment of this chapter may, without liability under sections 910 and 911, be imported into or distributed in the United States, or both, until two years after the date of registration of the mask work under section 908, but only if the importer or distributor, as the case may be, first pays or offers to pay the reasonable royalty re-

ferred to in section 907(a)(2) to the mask work owner, on all such units imported or distributed, or both, after the date of the enactment of this chapter.

(3) In the event that a person imports or distributes infringing semiconductor chip product units described in paragraph (2) of this subsection without first paying or offering to pay the reasonable royalty specified in such paragraph, or if the person refuses or fails to make such payment, the mask work owner shall be entitled to the relief provided in sections 910 and 911.

(Added Pub. L. 98–620, title III, §302, Nov. 8, 1984, 98 Stat. 3354.)

REFERENCES IN TEXT

The date of enactment of this chapter, referred to in text, is the date of enactment of Pub. L. 98–620, which was approved Nov. 8, 1984.

§914. International transitional provisions

(a) Notwithstanding the conditions set forth in subparagraphs (A) and (C) of section 902(a)(1) with respect to the availability of protection under this chapter to nationals, domiciliaries, and sovereign authorities of a foreign nation, the Secretary of Commerce may, upon the petition of any person, or upon the Secretary's own motion, issue an order extending protection under this chapter to such foreign nationals, domiciliaries, and sovereign authorities if the Secretary finds—

(1) that the foreign nation is making good faith efforts and reasonable progress toward—

(A) entering into a treaty described in section 902(a)(1)(A); or

(B) enacting or implementing legislation that would be in compliance with subparagraph (A) or (B) of section 902(a)(2); and

(2) that the nationals, domiciliaries, and sovereign authorities of the foreign nation, and persons controlled by them, are not engaged in the misappropriation, or unauthorized distribution or commercial exploitation, of mask works; and

(3) that issuing the order would promote the purposes of this chapter and international comity with respect to the protection of mask works.

(b) While an order under subsection (a) is in effect with respect to a foreign nation, no application for registration of a claim for protection in a mask work under this chapter may be denied solely because the owner of the mask work is a national, domiciliary, or sovereign authority of that foreign nation, or solely because the mask work was first commercially exploited in that foreign nation.

(c) Any order issued by the Secretary of Commerce under subsection (a) shall be effective for such period as the Secretary designates in the order, except that no such order may be effective after the date on which the authority of the Secretary of Commerce terminates under subsection (e). The effective date of any such order shall also be designated in the order. In the case of an order issued upon the petition of a person, such effective date may be no earlier than the date on which the Secretary receives such petition.

(d)(1) Any order issued under this section shall terminate if—

(A) the Secretary of Commerce finds that any of the conditions set forth in paragraphs (1), (2), and (3) of subsection (a) no longer exist; or

(B) mask works of nationals, domiciliaries, and sovereign authorities of that foreign nation or mask works first commercially exploited in that foreign nation become eligible for protection under subparagraph (A) or (C) of section 902(a)(1).

(2) Upon the termination or expiration of an order issued under this section, registrations of claims of protection in mask works made pursuant to that order shall remain valid for the period specified in section 904.

(e) The authority of the Secretary of Commerce under this section shall commence on the date of the enactment of this chapter, and shall terminate on July 1, 1995.

(f)(1) The Secretary of Commerce shall promptly notify the Register of Copyrights and the Committees on the Judiciary of the Senate and the House of Representatives of the issuance or termination of any order under this section, together with a statement of the reasons for such action. The Secretary shall also publish such notification and statement of reasons in the Federal Register.

(2) Two years after the date of the enactment of this chapter, the Secretary of Commerce, in consultation with the Register of Copyrights, shall transmit to the Committees on the Judiciary of the Senate and the House of Representatives a report on the actions taken under this section and on the current status of international recognition of mask work protection. The report shall include such recommendations for modifications of the protection accorded under this chapter to mask works owned by nationals, domiciliaries, or sovereign authorities of foreign nations as the Secretary, in consultation with the Register of Copyrights, considers would promote the purposes of this chapter and international comity with respect to mask work protection. Not later than July 1, 1994, the Secretary of Commerce, in consultation with the Register of Copyrights, shall transmit to the Committees on the Judiciary of the Senate and the House of Representatives a report updating the matters contained in the report transmitted under the preceding sentence.

(Added Pub. L. 98–620, title III, § 302, Nov. 8, 1984, 98 Stat. 3355; amended Pub. L. 100–159, §§ 2, 4, Nov. 9, 1987, 101 Stat. 899, 900; Pub. L. 102–64, §§ 3, 4, June 28, 1991, 105 Stat. 320, 321.)

References in Text

The date of enactment of this chapter, referred to in subsecs. (e) and (f)(2), is the date of enactment of Pub. L. 98–620, which was approved Nov. 8, 1984.

Amendments

1991—Subsec. (a)(1)(B). Pub. L. 102–64, § 3(1), inserted "or implementing" after "enacting".

Subsec. (e). Pub. L. 102–64, § 3(2), substituted "July 1, 1995" for "July 1, 1991".

Subsec. (f)(2). Pub. L. 102–64, § 4, substituted "July 1, 1994" for "July 1, 1990".

1987—Subsec. (e). Pub. L. 100–159, § 2, substituted "on July 1, 1991" for "three years after such date of enactment".

Subsec. (f)(2). Pub. L. 100–159, § 4, which directed the amendment of subsec. (f) by inserting at end "Not later than July 1, 1990, the Secretary of Commerce, in consultation with the Register of Copyrights, shall transmit to the Committees on the Judiciary of the Senate and the House of Representatives a report updating the matters contained in the report transmitted under the preceding sentence.", was executed by inserting new language at end of par. (2) of subsec. (f) as the probable intent of Congress.

Findings and Purposes

Section 2 of Pub. L. 102–64 provided that:

"(a) Findings.—The Congress finds that—

"(1) section 914 of title 17, United States Code, which authorizes the Secretary of Commerce to issue orders extending interim protection under chapter 9 of title 17, United States Code, to mask works fixed in semiconductor chip products and originating in foreign countries that are making good faith efforts and reasonable progress toward providing protection, by treaty or legislation, to mask works of United States nationals, has resulted in substantial and positive legislative developments in foreign countries regarding protection of mask works;

"(2) the Secretary of Commerce has determined that most of the industrialized countries of the world are eligible for orders affording interim protection under section 914 of title 17, United States Code;

"(3) no multilateral treaty recognizing the protection of mask works has come into force, nor has the United States become bound by any multilateral agreement regarding such protection; and

"(4) bilateral and multilateral relationships regarding the protection of mask works should be directed toward the international protection of mask works in an effective, consistent, and harmonious manner, and the existing bilateral authority of the Secretary of Commerce under chapter 9 of title 17, United States Code, should be extended to facilitate the continued development of protection for mask works.

"(b) Purposes.—The purposes of this Act [amending this section and enacting provisions set out as a note under section 901 of this title] are—

"(1) to extend the period within which the Secretary of Commerce may grant interim protection orders under section 914 of title 17, United States Code, to continue the incentive for the bilateral and multilateral protection of mask works; and

"(2) to clarify the Secretary's authority to issue such interim protection orders."

Section 1 of Pub. L. 100–159, as amended by Pub. L. 105–80, § 12(b)(1), Nov. 13, 1997, 111 Stat. 1536, provided that:

"(a) Findings.—The Congress finds that—

"(1) section 914 of title 17, United States Code, which authorizes the Secretary of Commerce to issue orders extending interim protection under chapter 9 of title 17, United States Code, to mask works fixed in semiconductor chip products and originating in foreign countries that are making good faith efforts and reasonable progress toward providing protection, by treaty or legislation, to mask works of United States nationals, has resulted in substantial and positive legislative developments in foreign countries regarding protection of mask works;

"(2) the Secretary of Commerce has determined that most of the industrialized countries of the world are eligible for orders affording interim protection under section 914 of title 17, United States Code;

"(3) the World Intellectual Property Organization has commenced meetings to draft an international convention regarding the protection of integrated electronic circuits;

"(4) these bilateral and multilateral developments are encouraging steps toward improving international protection of mask works in a consistent and harmonious manner; and

"(5) it is inherent in section 902 of title 17, United States Code, that the President has the authority to revise, suspend, or revoke, as well as issue, proclamations extending mask work protection to nationals, domiciliaries, and sovereign authorities of other countries, if conditions warrant.

"(b) PURPOSES.—The purposes of this Act [amending this section and section 902 of this title] are—

"(1) to extend the period within which the Secretary of Commerce may grant interim protective orders under section 914 of title 17, United States Code, to continue this incentive for the bilateral and multilateral protection of mask works; and

"(2) to codify the President's existing authority to revoke, suspend, or limit the protection extended to mask works of foreign entities in nations that extend mask work protection to United States nationals."

CHAPTER 10—DIGITAL AUDIO RECORDING DEVICES AND MEDIA

SUBCHAPTER A—DEFINITIONS

AMENDMENTS

2004—Pub. L. 108–419, §5(i)(4)(B), Nov. 30, 2004, 118 Stat. 2369, substituted "Determination" for "Arbitration" in item 1010.

SUBCHAPTER A—DEFINITIONS

§ 1001. Definitions

As used in this chapter, the following terms have the following meanings:

(1) A "digital audio copied recording" is a reproduction in a digital recording format of a digital musical recording, whether that reproduction is made directly from another digital musical recording or indirectly from a transmission.

(2) A "digital audio interface device" is any machine or device that is designed specifically to communicate digital audio information and related interface data to a digital audio recording device through a nonprofessional interface.

(3) A "digital audio recording device" is any machine or device of a type commonly distributed to individuals for use by individuals, whether or not included with or as part of some other machine or device, the digital recording function of which is designed or marketed for the primary purpose of, and that is capable of, making a digital audio copied recording for private use, except for—

(A) professional model products, and

(B) dictation machines, answering machines, and other audio recording equipment that is designed and marketed primarily for the creation of sound recordings resulting from the fixation of nonmusical sounds.

(4)(A) A "digital audio recording medium" is any material object in a form commonly distributed for use by individuals, that is primarily marketed or most commonly used by consumers for the purpose of making digital audio copied recordings by use of a digital audio recording device.

(B) Such term does not include any material object—

(i) that embodies a sound recording at the time it is first distributed by the importer or manufacturer; or

(ii) that is primarily marketed and most commonly used by consumers either for the purpose of making copies of motion pictures or other audiovisual works or for the purpose of making copies of nonmusical literary works, including computer programs or data bases.

(5)(A) A "digital musical recording" is a material object—

(i) in which are fixed, in a digital recording format, only sounds, and material, statements, or instructions incidental to those fixed sounds, if any, and

(ii) from which the sounds and material can be perceived, reproduced, or otherwise communicated, either directly or with the aid of a machine or device.

(B) A "digital musical recording" does not include a material object—

(i) in which the fixed sounds consist entirely of spoken word recordings, or

(ii) in which one or more computer programs are fixed, except that a digital musical recording may contain statements or instructions constituting the fixed sounds and incidental material, and statements or instructions to be used directly or indirectly in order to bring about the perception, reproduction, or communication of the fixed sounds and incidental material.

(C) For purposes of this paragraph—

(i) a "spoken word recording" is a sound recording in which are fixed only a series of spoken words, except that the spoken words may be accompanied by incidental musical or other sounds, and

(ii) the term "incidental" means related to and relatively minor by comparison.

(6) "Distribute" means to sell, lease, or assign a product to consumers in the United States, or to sell, lease, or assign a product in the United States for ultimate transfer to consumers in the United States.

(7) An "interested copyright party" is—

(A) the owner of the exclusive right under section 106(1) of this title to reproduce a sound recording of a musical work that has been embodied in a digital musical recording or analog musical recording lawfully made under this title that has been distributed;

(B) the legal or beneficial owner of, or the person that controls, the right to reproduce in a digital musical recording or analog musical recording a musical work that has been embodied in a digital musical recording or analog musical recording lawfully made under this title that has been distributed;

(C) a featured recording artist who performs on a sound recording that has been distributed; or

(D) any association or other organization—

(i) representing persons specified in subparagraph (A), (B), or (C), or

(ii) engaged in licensing rights in musical works to music users on behalf of writers and publishers.

(8) To "manufacture" means to produce or assemble a product in the United States. A "manufacturer" is a person who manufactures.

(9) A "music publisher" is a person that is authorized to license the reproduction of a particular musical work in a sound recording.

(10) A "professional model product" is an audio recording device that is designed, manufactured, marketed, and intended for use by recording professionals in the ordinary course of a lawful business, in accordance with such requirements as the Secretary of Commerce shall establish by regulation.

(11) The term "serial copying" means the duplication in a digital format of a copyrighted musical work or sound recording from a digital reproduction of a digital musical recording. The term "digital reproduction of a digital musical recording" does not include a digital musical recording as distributed, by authority of the copyright owner, for ultimate sale to consumers.

(12) The "transfer price" of a digital audio recording device or a digital audio recording medium—

(A) is, subject to subparagraph (B)—

(i) in the case of an imported product, the actual entered value at United States Customs (exclusive of any freight, insurance, and applicable duty), and

(ii) in the case of a domestic product, the manufacturer's transfer price (FOB the manufacturer, and exclusive of any direct sales taxes or excise taxes incurred in connection with the sale); and

(B) shall, in a case in which the transferor and transferee are related entities or within a single entity, not be less than a reasonable arms-length price under the principles of the regulations adopted pursuant to section 482 of the Internal Revenue Code of 1986, or any successor provision to such section.

(13) A "writer" is the composer or lyricist of a particular musical work.

(Added Pub. L. 102–563, § 2, Oct. 28, 1992, 106 Stat. 4237.)

Section 482 of the Internal Revenue Code of 1986, referred to in par. (12)(B), is classified to section 482 of Title 26, Internal Revenue Code.

Pub. L. 102–563, § 4, Oct. 28, 1992, 106 Stat. 4248, provided that: "This Act [see Short Title of 1992 Amendments note set out under section 101 of this title] and the amendments made by this Act shall take effect on the date of the enactment of this Act [Oct. 28, 1992]."

SUBCHAPTER B—COPYING CONTROLS

§ 1002. Incorporation of copying controls

(a) Prohibition on Importation, Manufacture, and Distribution.—No person shall import, manufacture, or distribute any digital audio recording device or digital audio interface device that does not conform to—

(1) the Serial Copy Management System;

(2) a system that has the same functional characteristics as the Serial Copy Management System and requires that copyright and generation status information be accurately sent, received, and acted upon between devices using the system's method of serial copying regulation and devices using the Serial Copy Management System; or

(3) any other system certified by the Secretary of Commerce as prohibiting unauthorized serial copying.

(b) Development of Verification Procedure.—The Secretary of Commerce shall establish a procedure to verify, upon the petition of an interested party, that a system meets the standards set forth in subsection (a)(2).

(c) Prohibition on Circumvention of the System.—No person shall import, manufacture, or distribute any device, or offer or perform any service, the primary purpose or effect of which is to avoid, bypass, remove, deactivate, or otherwise circumvent any program or circuit which implements, in whole or in part, a system described in subsection (a).

(d) Encoding of Information on Digital Musical Recordings.—

(1) Prohibition on Encoding Inaccurate Information.—No person shall encode a digital musical recording of a sound recording with inaccurate information relating to the category code, copyright status, or generation status of the source material for the recording.

(2) Encoding of Copyright Status Not Required.—Nothing in this chapter requires any person engaged in the importation or manufacture of digital musical recordings to encode any such digital musical recording with respect to its copyright status.

(e) Information Accompanying Transmissions in Digital Format.—Any person who transmits or otherwise communicates to the public any sound recording in digital format is not required under this chapter to transmit or otherwise communicate the information relating to the copyright status of the sound recording. Any such person who does transmit or otherwise communicate such copyright status information shall transmit or communicate such information accurately.

(Added Pub. L. 102–563, § 2, Oct. 28, 1992, 106 Stat. 4240.)

SUBCHAPTER C—ROYALTY PAYMENTS

§ 1003. Obligation to make royalty payments

(a) Prohibition on Importation and Manufacture.—No person shall import into and distribute, or manufacture and distribute, any digital audio recording device or digital audio recording medium unless such person records the notice specified by this section and subsequently deposits the statements of account and applicable royalty payments for such device or medium specified in section 1004.

(b) FILING OF NOTICE.—The importer or manufacturer of any digital audio recording device or digital audio recording medium, within a product category or utilizing a technology with respect to which such manufacturer or importer has not previously filed a notice under this subsection, shall file with the Register of Copyrights a notice with respect to such device or medium, in such form and content as the Register shall prescribe by regulation.

(c) FILING OF QUARTERLY AND ANNUAL STATEMENTS OF ACCOUNT.—

(1) GENERALLY.—Any importer or manufacturer that distributes any digital audio recording device or digital audio recording medium that it manufactured or imported shall file with the Register of Copyrights, in such form and content as the Register shall prescribe by regulation, such quarterly and annual statements of account with respect to such distribution as the Register shall prescribe by regulation.

(2) CERTIFICATION, VERIFICATION, AND CONFIDENTIALITY.—Each such statement shall be certified as accurate by an authorized officer or principal of the importer or manufacturer. The Register shall issue regulations to provide for the verification and audit of such statements and to protect the confidentiality of the information contained in such statements. Such regulations shall provide for the disclosure, in confidence, of such statements to interested copyright parties.

(3) ROYALTY PAYMENTS.—Each such statement shall be accompanied by the royalty payments specified in section 1004.

(Added Pub. L. 102–563, § 2, Oct. 28, 1992, 106 Stat. 4240.)

§ 1004. Royalty payments

(a) DIGITAL AUDIO RECORDING DEVICES.—

(1) AMOUNT OF PAYMENT.—The royalty payment due under section 1003 for each digital audio recording device imported into and distributed in the United States, or manufactured and distributed in the United States, shall be 2 percent of the transfer price. Only the first person to manufacture and distribute or import and distribute such device shall be required to pay the royalty with respect to such device.

(2) CALCULATION FOR DEVICES DISTRIBUTED WITH OTHER DEVICES.—With respect to a digital audio recording device first distributed in combination with one or more devices, either as a physically integrated unit or as separate components, the royalty payment shall be calculated as follows:

(A) If the digital audio recording device and such other devices are part of a physically integrated unit, the royalty payment shall be based on the transfer price of the unit, but shall be reduced by any royalty payment made on any digital audio recording device included within the unit that was not first distributed in combination with the unit.

(B) If the digital audio recording device is not part of a physically integrated unit and substantially similar devices have been distributed separately at any time during the preceding 4 calendar quarters, the royalty payment shall be based on the average transfer price of such devices during those 4 quarters.

(C) If the digital audio recording device is not part of a physically integrated unit and substantially similar devices have not been distributed separately at any time during the preceding 4 calendar quarters, the royalty payment shall be based on a constructed price reflecting the proportional value of such device to the combination as a whole.

(3) LIMITS ON ROYALTIES.—Notwithstanding paragraph (1) or (2), the amount of the royalty payment for each digital audio recording device shall not be less than $1 nor more than the royalty maximum. The royalty maximum shall be $8 per device, except that in the case of a physically integrated unit containing more than 1 digital audio recording device, the royalty maximum for such unit shall be $12. During the 6th year after the effective date of this chapter, and not more than once each year thereafter, any interested copyright party may petition the Copyright Royalty Judges to increase the royalty maximum and, if more than 20 percent of the royalty payments are at the relevant royalty maximum, the Copyright Royalty Judges shall prospectively increase such royalty maximum with the goal of having no more than 10 percent of such payments at the new royalty maximum; however the amount of any such increase as a percentage of the royalty maximum shall in no event exceed the percentage increase in the Consumer Price Index during the period under review.

(b) DIGITAL AUDIO RECORDING MEDIA.—The royalty payment due under section 1003 for each digital audio recording medium imported into and distributed in the United States, or manufactured and distributed in the United States, shall be 3 percent of the transfer price. Only the first person to manufacture and distribute or import and distribute such medium shall be required to pay the royalty with respect to such medium.

(Added Pub. L. 102–563, § 2, Oct. 28, 1992, 106 Stat. 4241; amended Pub. L. 103–198, § 6(b)(1), Dec. 17, 1993, 107 Stat. 2312; Pub. L. 108–419, § 5(i)(1), Nov. 30, 2004, 118 Stat. 2368.)

REFERENCES IN TEXT

The effective date of this chapter, referred to in subsec. (a)(3), is Oct. 28, 1992. See Effective Date note set out under section 1001 of this title.

AMENDMENTS

2004—Subsec. (a)(3). Pub. L. 108–419 substituted "Copyright Royalty Judges" for "Librarian of Congress" in two places.

1993—Subsec. (a)(3). Pub. L. 103–198 substituted "Librarian of Congress" for "Copyright Royalty Tribunal" after "may petition the" and for "Tribunal" before "shall prospectively".

EFFECTIVE DATE OF 2004 AMENDMENT

Amendment by Pub. L. 108–419 effective 6 months after Nov. 30, 2004, subject to transition provisions, see section 6 of Pub. L. 108–419, set out as an Effective Date; Transition Provisions note under section 801 of this title.

§ 1005. Deposit of royalty payments and deduction of expenses

The Register of Copyrights shall receive all royalty payments deposited under this chapter and, after deducting the reasonable costs incurred by the Copyright Office under this chapter, shall deposit the balance in the Treasury of the United States as offsetting receipts, in such manner as the Secretary of the Treasury directs. All funds held by the Secretary of the Treasury shall be invested in interest-bearing United States securities for later distribution with interest under section 1007. The Register may, in the Register's discretion, 4 years after the close of any calendar year, close out the royalty payments account for that calendar year, and may treat any funds remaining in such account and any subsequent deposits that would otherwise be attributable to that calendar year as attributable to the succeeding calendar year.

(Added Pub. L. 102–563, § 2, Oct. 28, 1992, 106 Stat. 4242; amended Pub. L. 103–198, § 6(b)(2), Dec. 17, 1993, 107 Stat. 2312.)

AMENDMENTS

1993—Pub. L. 103–198 struck out at end "The Register shall submit to the Copyright Royalty Tribunal, on a monthly basis, a financial statement reporting the amount of royalties under this chapter that are available for distribution."

§ 1006. Entitlement to royalty payments

(a) INTERESTED COPYRIGHT PARTIES.—The royalty payments deposited pursuant to section 1005 shall, in accordance with the procedures specified in section 1007, be distributed to any interested copyright party—

(1) whose musical work or sound recording has been—

(A) embodied in a digital musical recording or an analog musical recording lawfully made under this title that has been distributed, and

(B) distributed in the form of digital musical recordings or analog musical recordings or disseminated to the public in transmissions, during the period to which such payments pertain; and

(2) who has filed a claim under section 1007.

(b) ALLOCATION OF ROYALTY PAYMENTS TO GROUPS.—The royalty payments shall be divided into 2 funds as follows:

(1) THE SOUND RECORDINGS FUND.—66⅔ percent of the royalty payments shall be allocated to the Sound Recordings Fund. 2⅝ percent of the royalty payments allocated to the Sound Recordings Fund shall be placed in an escrow account managed by an independent administrator jointly appointed by the interested copyright parties described in section 1001(7)(A) and the American Federation of Musicians (or any successor entity) to be distributed to nonfeatured musicians (whether or not members of the American Federation of Musicians or any successor entity) who have performed on sound recordings distributed in the United States. 1⅝ percent of the royalty payments allocated to the Sound Recordings Fund shall be placed in an escrow account managed by an independent administrator jointly appointed by the interested copyright parties described in section 1001(7)(A) and the American Federation of Television and Radio Artists (or any successor entity) to be distributed to nonfeatured vocalists (whether or not members of the American Federation of Television and Radio Artists or any successor entity) who have performed on sound recordings distributed in the United States. 40 percent of the remaining royalty payments in the Sound Recordings Fund shall be distributed to the interested copyright parties described in section 1001(7)(C), and 60 percent of such remaining royalty payments shall be distributed to the interested copyright parties described in section 1001(7)(A).

(2) THE MUSICAL WORKS FUND.—

(A) 33⅓ percent of the royalty payments shall be allocated to the Musical Works Fund for distribution to interested copyright parties described in section 1001(7)(B).

(B)(i) Music publishers shall be entitled to 50 percent of the royalty payments allocated to the Musical Works Fund.

(ii) Writers shall be entitled to the other 50 percent of the royalty payments allocated to the Musical Works Fund.

(c) ALLOCATION OF ROYALTY PAYMENTS WITHIN GROUPS.—If all interested copyright parties within a group specified in subsection (b) do not agree on a voluntary proposal for the distribution of the royalty payments within each group, the Copyright Royalty Judges shall, pursuant to the procedures specified under section 1007(c), allocate royalty payments under this section based on the extent to which, during the relevant period—

(1) for the Sound Recordings Fund, each sound recording was distributed in the form of digital musical recordings or analog musical recordings; and

(2) for the Musical Works Fund, each musical work was distributed in the form of digital musical recordings or analog musical recordings or disseminated to the public in transmissions.

(Added Pub. L. 102–563, § 2, Oct. 28, 1992, 106 Stat. 4242; amended Pub. L. 103–198, § 6(b)(3), Dec. 17, 1993, 107 Stat. 2312; Pub. L. 105–80, § 12(a)(24), Nov. 13, 1997, 111 Stat. 1535; Pub. L. 108–419, § 5(i)(2), Nov. 30, 2004, 118 Stat. 2368.)

AMENDMENTS

2004—Subsec. (c). Pub. L. 108–419 substituted "Copyright Royalty Judges" for "Librarian of Congress shall convene a copyright arbitration royalty panel which" in introductory provisions.

1997—Subsec. (b)(1). Pub. L. 105–80 substituted "Federation of Television" for "Federation Television" before "and Radio Artists or any successor entity)".

1993—Subsec. (c). Pub. L. 103–198 substituted "Librarian of Congress shall convene a copyright arbitration royalty panel which" for "Copyright Royalty Tribunal" in introductory provisions.

EFFECTIVE DATE OF 2004 AMENDMENT

Amendment by Pub. L. 108–419 effective 6 months after Nov. 30, 2004, subject to transition provisions, see section 6 of Pub. L. 108–419, set out as an Effective Date; Transition Provisions note under section 801 of this title.

§ 1007. Procedures for distributing royalty payments

(a) FILING OF CLAIMS AND NEGOTIATIONS.—

(1) FILING OF CLAIMS.—During the first 2 months of each calendar year, every interested copyright party seeking to receive royalty payments to which such party is entitled under section 1006 shall file with the Copyright Royalty Judges a claim for payments collected during the preceding year in such form and manner as the Copyright Royalty Judges shall prescribe by regulation.

(2) NEGOTIATIONS.—Notwithstanding any provision of the antitrust laws, for purposes of this section interested copyright parties within each group specified in section 1006(b) may agree among themselves to the proportionate division of royalty payments, may lump their claims together and file them jointly or as a single claim, or may designate a common agent, including any organization described in section 1001(7)(D), to negotiate or receive payment on their behalf; except that no agreement under this subsection may modify the allocation of royalties specified in section 1006(b).

(b) DISTRIBUTION OF PAYMENTS IN THE ABSENCE OF A DISPUTE.—After the period established for the filing of claims under subsection (a), in each year, the Copyright Royalty Judges shall determine whether there exists a controversy concerning the distribution of royalty payments under section 1006(c). If the Copyright Royalty Judges determine that no such controversy exists, the Copyright Royalty Judges shall, within 30 days after such determination, authorize the distribution of the royalty payments as set forth in the agreements regarding the distribution of royalty payments entered into pursuant to subsection (a). The Librarian of Congress shall, before such royalty payments are distributed, deduct the reasonable administrative costs incurred under this section.

(c) RESOLUTION OF DISPUTES.—If the Copyright Royalty Judges find the existence of a controversy, the Copyright Royalty Judges shall, pursuant to chapter 8 of this title, conduct a proceeding to determine the distribution of royalty payments. During the pendency of such a proceeding, the Copyright Royalty Judges shall withhold from distribution an amount sufficient to satisfy all claims with respect to which a controversy exists, but shall, to the extent feasible, authorize the distribution of any amounts that are not in controversy. The Librarian of Congress shall, before such royalty payments are distributed, deduct the reasonable administrative costs incurred under this section.

(Added Pub. L. 102–563, § 2, Oct. 28, 1992, 106 Stat. 4244; amended Pub. L. 103–198, § 6(b)(4), Dec. 17, 1993, 107 Stat. 2312; Pub. L. 105–80, §§ 9, 12(a)(25), Nov. 13, 1997, 111 Stat. 1534, 1535; Pub. L. 108–419, § 5(i)(3), Nov. 30, 2004, 118 Stat. 2368; Pub. L. 109–303, § 4(f), Oct. 6, 2006, 120 Stat. 1483.)

AMENDMENTS

2006—Subsec. (b). Pub. L. 109–303, § 4(f)(1), substituted "Copyright Royalty Judges" for "Librarian of Congress" in second sentence and struck out "by the Librarian" after "administrative costs incurred" in last sentence.

Subsec. (c). Pub. L. 109–303, § 4(f)(2), struck out "by the Librarian" after "administrative costs incurred" in last sentence.

2004—Subsec. (a)(1). Pub. L. 108–419, § 5(i)(3)(A), reenacted heading without change and amended text generally. Prior to amendment, text read as follows: "During the first 2 months of each calendar year after calendar year 1992, every interested copyright party seeking to receive royalty payments to which such party is entitled under section 1006 shall file with the Librarian of Congress a claim for payments collected during the preceding year in such form and manner as the Librarian of Congress shall prescribe by regulation."

Subsec. (b). Pub. L. 108–419, § 5(i)(3)(B), reenacted heading without change and amended text generally. Prior to amendment, text read as follows: "After the period established for the filing of claims under subsection (a), in each year after 1992, the Librarian of Congress shall determine whether there exists a controversy concerning the distribution of royalty payments under section 1006(c). If the Librarian of Congress determines that no such controversy exists, the Librarian of Congress shall, within 30 days after such determination, authorize the distribution of the royalty payments as set forth in the agreements regarding the distribution of royalty payments entered into pursuant to subsection (a), after deducting its reasonable administrative costs under this section."

Subsec. (c). Pub. L. 108–419, § 5(i)(3)(B), reenacted heading without change and amended text generally. Prior to amendment, text read as follows: "If the Librarian of Congress finds the existence of a controversy, the Librarian shall, pursuant to chapter 8 of this title, convene a copyright arbitration royalty panel to determine the distribution of royalty payments. During the pendency of such a proceeding, the Librarian of Congress shall withhold from distribution an amount sufficient to satisfy all claims with respect to which a controversy exists, but shall, to the extent feasible, authorize the distribution of any amounts that are not in controversy. The Librarian of Congress shall, before authorizing the distribution of such royalty payments, deduct the reasonable administrative costs incurred by the Librarian under this section."

1997—Subsec. (a)(1). Pub. L. 105–80, § 12(a)(25)(A), substituted "calendar year 1992" for "the calendar year in which this chapter takes effect".

Subsec. (b). Pub. L. 105–80, §§ 9, 12(a)(25)(B), substituted "After the period established" for "Within 30 days after the period established" and "each year after 1992" for "each year after the year in which this section takes effect".

1993—Subsec. (a)(1). Pub. L. 103–198, § 6(b)(4)(A), substituted "Librarian of Congress" for "Copyright Royalty Tribunal" before "a claim for" and for "Tribunal" before "shall prescribe".

Subsec. (b). Pub. L. 103–198, § 6(b)(4)(B), substituted "Librarian of Congress" for "Copyright Royalty Tribunal" before "shall determine whether" and for "Tribunal" wherever appearing.

Subsec. (c). Pub. L. 103–198, § 6(b)(4)(C), substituted first sentence for "If the Tribunal finds the existence of a controversy, it shall, pursuant to chapter 8 of this title, conduct a proceeding to determine the distribution of royalty payments.", substituted "Librarian of Congress" for "Tribunal" wherever appearing in second and third sentences, and "the reasonable administrative costs incurred by the Librarian" for "its reasonable administrative costs" in last sentence.

EFFECTIVE DATE OF 2006 AMENDMENT

Amendment by Pub. L. 109–303 effective as if included in the Copyright Royalty and Distribution Reform Act of 2004, Pub. L. 108–419, see section 6 of Pub. L. 109–303, set out as a note under section 111 of this title.

EFFECTIVE DATE OF 2004 AMENDMENT

Amendment by Pub. L. 108–419 effective 6 months after Nov. 30, 2004, subject to transition provisions, see section 6 of Pub. L. 108–419, set out as an Effective Date; Transition Provisions note under section 801 of this title.

SUBCHAPTER D—PROHIBITION ON CERTAIN INFRINGEMENT ACTIONS, REMEDIES, AND ARBITRATION

§ 1008. Prohibition on certain infringement actions

No action may be brought under this title alleging infringement of copyright based on the manufacture, importation, or distribution of a digital audio recording device, a digital audio recording medium, an analog recording device, or an analog recording medium, or based on the noncommercial use by a consumer of such a device or medium for making digital musical recordings or analog musical recordings.

(Added Pub. L. 102–563, § 2, Oct. 28, 1992, 106 Stat. 4244.)

§ 1009. Civil remedies

(a) CIVIL ACTIONS.—Any interested copyright party injured by a violation of section 1002 or 1003 may bring a civil action in an appropriate United States district court against any person for such violation.

(b) OTHER CIVIL ACTIONS.—Any person injured by a violation of this chapter may bring a civil action in an appropriate United States district court for actual damages incurred as a result of such violation.

(c) POWERS OF THE COURT.—In an action brought under subsection (a), the court—

(1) may grant temporary and permanent injunctions on such terms as it deems reasonable to prevent or restrain such violation;

(2) in the case of a violation of section 1002, or in the case of an injury resulting from a failure to make royalty payments required by section 1003, shall award damages under subsection (d);

(3) in its discretion may allow the recovery of costs by or against any party other than the United States or an officer thereof; and

(4) in its discretion may award a reasonable attorney's fee to the prevailing party.

(d) AWARD OF DAMAGES.—

(1) DAMAGES FOR SECTION 1002 OR 1003 VIOLATIONS.—

(A) ACTUAL DAMAGES.—(i) In an action brought under subsection (a), if the court finds that a violation of section 1002 or 1003 has occurred, the court shall award to the complaining party its actual damages if the complaining party elects such damages at any time before final judgment is entered.

(ii) In the case of section 1003, actual damages shall constitute the royalty payments that should have been paid under section 1004 and deposited under section 1005. In such a case, the court, in its discretion, may award an additional amount of not to exceed 50 percent of the actual damages.

(B) STATUTORY DAMAGES FOR SECTION 1002 VIOLATIONS.—

(i) DEVICE.—A complaining party may recover an award of statutory damages for each violation of section 1002(a) or (c) in the sum of not more than $2,500 per device involved in such violation or per device on which a service prohibited by section 1002(c) has been performed, as the court considers just.

(ii) DIGITAL MUSICAL RECORDING.—A complaining party may recover an award of statutory damages for each violation of section 1002(d) in the sum of not more than $25 per digital musical recording involved in such violation, as the court considers just.

(iii) TRANSMISSION.—A complaining party may recover an award of damages for each transmission or communication that violates section 1002(e) in the sum of not more than $10,000, as the court considers just.

(2) REPEATED VIOLATIONS.—In any case in which the court finds that a person has violated section 1002 or 1003 within 3 years after a final judgment against that person for another such violation was entered, the court may increase the award of damages to not more than double the amounts that would otherwise be awarded under paragraph (1), as the court considers just.

(3) INNOCENT VIOLATIONS OF SECTION 1002.—The court in its discretion may reduce the total award of damages against a person violating section 1002 to a sum of not less than $250 in any case in which the court finds that the violator was not aware and had no reason to believe that its acts constituted a violation of section 1002.

(e) PAYMENT OF DAMAGES.—Any award of damages under subsection (d) shall be deposited with the Register pursuant to section 1005 for distribution to interested copyright parties as though such funds were royalty payments made pursuant to section 1003.

(f) IMPOUNDING OF ARTICLES.—At any time while an action under subsection (a) is pending, the court may order the impounding, on such terms as it deems reasonable, of any digital audio recording device, digital musical recording, or device specified in section 1002(c) that is in the custody or control of the alleged violator and that the court has reasonable cause to believe does not comply with, or was involved in a violation of, section 1002.

(g) REMEDIAL MODIFICATION AND DESTRUCTION OF ARTICLES.—In an action brought under subsection (a), the court may, as part of a final judgment or decree finding a violation of section 1002, order the remedial modification or the destruction of any digital audio recording device, digital musical recording, or device specified in section 1002(c) that—

(1) does not comply with, or was involved in a violation of, section 1002, and

(2) is in the custody or control of the violator or has been impounded under subsection (f).

(Added Pub. L. 102–563, § 2, Oct. 28, 1992, 106 Stat. 4245.)

§ 1010. Determination of certain disputes

(a) SCOPE OF DETERMINATION.—Before the date of first distribution in the United States of a digital audio recording device or a digital audio interface device, any party manufacturing, importing, or distributing such device, and any interested copyright party may mutually agree to petition the Copyright Royalty Judges to determine whether such device is subject to section 1002, or the basis on which royalty payments for such device are to be made under section 1003.

(b) INITIATION OF PROCEEDINGS.—The parties under subsection (a) shall file the petition with the Copyright Royalty Judges requesting the commencement of a proceeding. Within 2 weeks after receiving such a petition, the Chief Copyright Royalty Judge shall cause notice to be published in the Federal Register of the initiation of the proceeding.

(c) STAY OF JUDICIAL PROCEEDINGS.—Any civil action brought under section 1009 against a party to a proceeding under this section shall, on application of one of the parties to the proceeding, be stayed until completion of the proceeding.

(d) PROCEEDING.—The Copyright Royalty Judges shall conduct a proceeding with respect to the matter concerned, in accordance with such procedures as the Copyright Royalty Judges may adopt. The Copyright Royalty Judges shall act on the basis of a fully documented written record. Any party to the proceeding may submit relevant information and proposals to the Copyright Royalty Judges. The parties to the proceeding shall each bear their respective costs of participation.

(e) JUDICIAL REVIEW.—Any determination of the Copyright Royalty Judges under subsection (d) may be appealed, by a party to the proceeding, in accordance with section 803(d) of this title. The pendency of an appeal under this subsection shall not stay the determination of the Copyright Royalty Judges. If the court modifies the determination of the Copyright Royalty Judges, the court shall have jurisdiction to enter its own decision in accordance with its final judgment. The court may further vacate the determination of the Copyright Royalty Judges and remand the case for proceedings as provided in this section.

(Added Pub. L. 102–563, §2, Oct. 28, 1992, 106 Stat. 4246; amended Pub. L. 103–198, §6(b)(5), Dec. 17, 1993, 107 Stat. 2312; Pub. L. 108–419, §5(i)(4)(A), Nov. 30, 2004, 118 Stat. 2368.)

AMENDMENTS

2004—Pub. L. 108–419 amended section catchline and text generally, substituting provisions relating to determination of certain disputes for provisions relating to arbitration of certain disputes.

1993—Subsec. (b). Pub. L. 103–198, §6(b)(5)(A), substituted "Librarian of Congress" for "Copyright Royalty Tribunal" before "requesting the commencement" and for "Tribunal" wherever appearing.

Subsec. (e). Pub. L. 103–198, §6(b)(5)(B), substituted "Librarian of Congress" for "Copyright Royalty Tribunal" in heading and text.

Subsec. (f). Pub. L. 103–198, §6(b)(5)(C), substituted "Librarian of Congress" for "Copyright Royalty Tribunal" in heading and before "shall adopt or reject" in text, substituted "Librarian of Congress" for "Tribunal" wherever appearing, and substituted "the Librarian's" for "its".

Subsec. (g). Pub. L. 103–198, §6(b)(5)(D), substituted "Librarian of Congress" for "Copyright Royalty Tribunal" after "Any decision of the", "decision of the Librarian of Congress" for "Tribunal's decision" in second sentence, and "Librarian of Congress" for "Tribunal" wherever appearing in third through fifth sentences.

EFFECTIVE DATE OF 2004 AMENDMENT

Amendment by Pub. L. 108–419 effective 6 months after Nov. 30, 2004, subject to transition provisions, see section 6 of Pub. L. 108–419, set out as an Effective Date; Transition Provisions note under section 801 of this title.

CHAPTER 11—SOUND RECORDINGS AND MUSIC VIDEOS

<table>
<tr><td>Sec.</td><td></td></tr>
<tr><td>1101.</td><td>Unauthorized fixation and trafficking in sound recordings and music videos.</td></tr>
</table>

§ 1101. Unauthorized fixation and trafficking in sound recordings and music videos

(a) UNAUTHORIZED ACTS.—Anyone who, without the consent of the performer or performers involved—

(1) fixes the sounds or sounds and images of a live musical performance in a copy or phonorecord, or reproduces copies or phonorecords of such a performance from an unauthorized fixation,

(2) transmits or otherwise communicates to the public the sounds or sounds and images of a live musical performance, or

(3) distributes or offers to distribute, sells or offers to sell, rents or offers to rent, or traffics in any copy or phonorecord fixed as described in paragraph (1), regardless of whether the fixations occurred in the United States,

shall be subject to the remedies provided in sections 502 through 505, to the same extent as an infringer of copyright.

(b) DEFINITION.—In this section, the term "traffic" has the same meaning as in section 2320(e)[1] of title 18.

(c) APPLICABILITY.—This section shall apply to any act or acts that occur on or after the date of the enactment of the Uruguay Round Agreements Act.

(d) STATE LAW NOT PREEMPTED.—Nothing in this section may be construed to annul or limit any rights or remedies under the common law or statutes of any State.

(Added Pub. L. 103–465, title V, §512(a), Dec. 8, 1994, 108 Stat. 4974; amended Pub. L. 109–181, §2(c)(3), Mar. 16, 2006, 120 Stat. 288.)

REFERENCES IN TEXT

Section 2320 of title 18, referred to in subsec. (b), was amended generally by Pub. L. 112–81, div. A, title VIII, §818(h), Dec. 31, 2011, 125 Stat. 1497, and, as so amended, provisions similar to those formerly appearing in subsec. (e) are now contained in subsec. (f).

The date of the enactment of the Uruguay Round Agreements Act, referred to in subsec. (c), is the date of enactment of Pub. L. 103–465, which was approved Dec. 8, 1994.

AMENDMENTS

2006—Subsec. (b). Pub. L. 109–181 added subsec. (b) and struck out heading and text of former subsec. (b). Text

---

[1] See References in Text note below.

read as follows: "As used in this section, the term 'traffic in' means transport, transfer, or otherwise dispose of, to another, as consideration for anything of value, or make or obtain control of with intent to transport, transfer, or dispose of."

CHAPTER 12—COPYRIGHT PROTECTION AND MANAGEMENT SYSTEMS

§ 1201. Circumvention of copyright protection systems

(a) VIOLATIONS REGARDING CIRCUMVENTION OF TECHNOLOGICAL MEASURES.—(1)(A) No person shall circumvent a technological measure that effectively controls access to a work protected under this title. The prohibition contained in the preceding sentence shall take effect at the end of the 2-year period beginning on the date of the enactment of this chapter.

(B) The prohibition contained in subparagraph (A) shall not apply to persons who are users of a copyrighted work which is in a particular class of works, if such persons are, or are likely to be in the succeeding 3-year period, adversely affected by virtue of such prohibition in their ability to make noninfringing uses of that particular class of works under this title, as determined under subparagraph (C).

(C) During the 2-year period described in subparagraph (A), and during each succeeding 3-year period, the Librarian of Congress, upon the recommendation of the Register of Copyrights, who shall consult with the Assistant Secretary for Communications and Information of the Department of Commerce and report and comment on his or her views in making such recommendation, shall make the determination in a rulemaking proceeding for purposes of subparagraph (B) of whether persons who are users of a copyrighted work are, or are likely to be in the succeeding 3-year period, adversely affected by the prohibition under subparagraph (A) in their ability to make noninfringing uses under this title of a particular class of copyrighted works. In conducting such rulemaking, the Librarian shall examine—

(i) the availability for use of copyrighted works;

(ii) the availability for use of works for non-profit archival, preservation, and educational purposes;

(iii) the impact that the prohibition on the circumvention of technological measures applied to copyrighted works has on criticism, comment, news reporting, teaching, scholarship, or research;

(iv) the effect of circumvention of technological measures on the market for or value of copyrighted works; and

(v) such other factors as the Librarian considers appropriate.

(D) The Librarian shall publish any class of copyrighted works for which the Librarian has determined, pursuant to the rulemaking conducted under subparagraph (C), that noninfringing uses by persons who are users of a copyrighted work are, or are likely to be, adversely affected, and the prohibition contained in subparagraph (A) shall not apply to such users with respect to such class of works for the ensuing 3-year period.

(E) Neither the exception under subparagraph (B) from the applicability of the prohibition contained in subparagraph (A), nor any determination made in a rulemaking conducted under subparagraph (C), may be used as a defense in any action to enforce any provision of this title other than this paragraph.

(2) No person shall manufacture, import, offer to the public, provide, or otherwise traffic in any technology, product, service, device, component, or part thereof, that—

(A) is primarily designed or produced for the purpose of circumventing a technological measure that effectively controls access to a work protected under this title;

(B) has only limited commercially significant purpose or use other than to circumvent a technological measure that effectively controls access to a work protected under this title; or

(C) is marketed by that person or another acting in concert with that person with that person's knowledge for use in circumventing a technological measure that effectively controls access to a work protected under this title.

(3) As used in this subsection—

(A) to "circumvent a technological measure" means to descramble a scrambled work, to decrypt an encrypted work, or otherwise to avoid, bypass, remove, deactivate, or impair a technological measure, without the authority of the copyright owner; and

(B) a technological measure "effectively controls access to a work" if the measure, in the ordinary course of its operation, requires the application of information, or a process or a treatment, with the authority of the copyright owner, to gain access to the work.

(b) ADDITIONAL VIOLATIONS.—(1) No person shall manufacture, import, offer to the public, provide, or otherwise traffic in any technology, product, service, device, component, or part thereof, that—

(A) is primarily designed or produced for the purpose of circumventing protection afforded by a technological measure that effectively protects a right of a copyright owner under this title in a work or a portion thereof;

(B) has only limited commercially significant purpose or use other than to circumvent protection afforded by a technological measure that effectively protects a right of a copyright owner under this title in a work or a portion thereof; or

(C) is marketed by that person or another acting in concert with that person with that person's knowledge for use in circumventing protection afforded by a technological measure that effectively protects a right of a copyright owner under this title in a work or a portion thereof.

(2) As used in this subsection—

(A) to "circumvent protection afforded by a technological measure" means avoiding, bypassing, removing, deactivating, or otherwise impairing a technological measure; and

(B) a technological measure "effectively protects a right of a copyright owner under this title" if the measure, in the ordinary course of its operation, prevents, restricts, or otherwise limits the exercise of a right of a copyright owner under this title.

(c) OTHER RIGHTS, ETC., NOT AFFECTED.—(1) Nothing in this section shall affect rights, remedies, limitations, or defenses to copyright infringement, including fair use, under this title.

(2) Nothing in this section shall enlarge or diminish vicarious or contributory liability for copyright infringement in connection with any technology, product, service, device, component, or part thereof.

(3) Nothing in this section shall require that the design of, or design and selection of parts and components for, a consumer electronics, telecommunications, or computing product provide for a response to any particular technological measure, so long as such part or component, or the product in which such part or component is integrated, does not otherwise fall within the prohibitions of subsection (a)(2) or (b)(1).

(4) Nothing in this section shall enlarge or diminish any rights of free speech or the press for activities using consumer electronics, telecommunications, or computing products.

(d) EXEMPTION FOR NONPROFIT LIBRARIES, ARCHIVES, AND EDUCATIONAL INSTITUTIONS.—(1) A nonprofit library, archives, or educational institution which gains access to a commercially exploited copyrighted work solely in order to make a good faith determination of whether to acquire a copy of that work for the sole purpose of engaging in conduct permitted under this title shall not be in violation of subsection (a)(1)(A). A copy of a work to which access has been gained under this paragraph—

(A) may not be retained longer than necessary to make such good faith determination; and

(B) may not be used for any other purpose.

(2) The exemption made available under paragraph (1) shall only apply with respect to a work when an identical copy of that work is not reasonably available in another form.

(3) A nonprofit library, archives, or educational institution that willfully for the purpose of commercial advantage or financial gain violates paragraph (1)—

(A) shall, for the first offense, be subject to the civil remedies under section 1203; and

(B) shall, for repeated or subsequent offenses, in addition to the civil remedies under section 1203, forfeit the exemption provided under paragraph (1).

(4) This subsection may not be used as a defense to a claim under subsection (a)(2) or (b), nor may this subsection permit a nonprofit library, archives, or educational institution to manufacture, import, offer to the public, provide, or otherwise traffic in any technology, product, service, component, or part thereof, which circumvents a technological measure.

(5) In order for a library or archives to qualify for the exemption under this subsection, the collections of that library or archives shall be—

(A) open to the public; or

(B) available not only to researchers affiliated with the library or archives or with the institution of which it is a part, but also to other persons doing research in a specialized field.

(e) LAW ENFORCEMENT, INTELLIGENCE, AND OTHER GOVERNMENT ACTIVITIES.—This section does not prohibit any lawfully authorized investigative, protective, information security, or intelligence activity of an officer, agent, or employee of the United States, a State, or a political subdivision of a State, or a person acting pursuant to a contract with the United States, a State, or a political subdivision of a State. For purposes of this subsection, the term "information security" means activities carried out in order to identify and address the vulnerabilities of a government computer, computer system, or computer network.

(f) REVERSE ENGINEERING.—(1) Notwithstanding the provisions of subsection (a)(1)(A), a person who has lawfully obtained the right to use a copy of a computer program may circumvent a technological measure that effectively controls access to a particular portion of that program for the sole purpose of identifying and analyzing those elements of the program that are necessary to achieve interoperability of an independently created computer program with other programs, and that have not previously been readily available to the person engaging in the circumvention, to the extent any such acts of identification and analysis do not constitute infringement under this title.

(2) Notwithstanding the provisions of subsections (a)(2) and (b), a person may develop and employ technological means to circumvent a technological measure, or to circumvent protection afforded by a technological measure, in order to enable the identification and analysis under paragraph (1), or for the purpose of enabling interoperability of an independently created computer program with other programs, if such means are necessary to achieve such interoperability, to the extent that doing so does not constitute infringement under this title.

(3) The information acquired through the acts permitted under paragraph (1), and the means permitted under paragraph (2), may be made available to others if the person referred to in paragraph (1) or (2), as the case may be, provides such information or means solely for the purpose of enabling interoperability of an independently created computer program with other programs, and to the extent that doing so does not constitute infringement under this title or violate applicable law other than this section.

(4) For purposes of this subsection, the term "interoperability" means the ability of computer programs to exchange information, and of such programs mutually to use the information which has been exchanged.

(g) ENCRYPTION RESEARCH.—

(1) DEFINITIONS.—For purposes of this subsection—

(A) the term "encryption research" means activities necessary to identify and analyze flaws and vulnerabilities of encryption technologies applied to copyrighted works, if these activities are conducted to advance the state of knowledge in the field of encryption technology or to assist in the development of encryption products; and

(B) the term "encryption technology" means the scrambling and descrambling of information using mathematical formulas or algorithms.

(2) PERMISSIBLE ACTS OF ENCRYPTION RESEARCH.—Notwithstanding the provisions of subsection (a)(1)(A), it is not a violation of that subsection for a person to circumvent a technological measure as applied to a copy, phonorecord, performance, or display of a published work in the course of an act of good faith encryption research if—

(A) the person lawfully obtained the encrypted copy, phonorecord, performance, or display of the published work;

(B) such act is necessary to conduct such encryption research;

(C) the person made a good faith effort to obtain authorization before the circumvention; and

(D) such act does not constitute infringement under this title or a violation of applicable law other than this section, including section 1030 of title 18 and those provisions of title 18 amended by the Computer Fraud and Abuse Act of 1986.

(3) FACTORS IN DETERMINING EXEMPTION.—In determining whether a person qualifies for the exemption under paragraph (2), the factors to be considered shall include—

(A) whether the information derived from the encryption research was disseminated, and if so, whether it was disseminated in a manner reasonably calculated to advance the state of knowledge or development of encryption technology, versus whether it was disseminated in a manner that facilitates infringement under this title or a violation of applicable law other than this section, including a violation of privacy or breach of security;

(B) whether the person is engaged in a legitimate course of study, is employed, or is appropriately trained or experienced, in the field of encryption technology; and

(C) whether the person provides the copyright owner of the work to which the technological measure is applied with notice of the findings and documentation of the research, and the time when such notice is provided.

(4) USE OF TECHNOLOGICAL MEANS FOR RESEARCH ACTIVITIES.—Notwithstanding the provisions of subsection (a)(2), it is not a violation of that subsection for a person to—

(A) develop and employ technological means to circumvent a technological measure for the sole purpose of that person performing the acts of good faith encryption research described in paragraph (2); and

(B) provide the technological means to another person with whom he or she is working collaboratively for the purpose of conducting the acts of good faith encryption research described in paragraph (2) or for the purpose of having that other person verify his or her acts of good faith encryption research described in paragraph (2).

(5) REPORT TO CONGRESS.—Not later than 1 year after the date of the enactment of this chapter, the Register of Copyrights and the Assistant Secretary for Communications and Information of the Department of Commerce shall jointly report to the Congress on the effect this subsection has had on—

(A) encryption research and the development of encryption technology;

(B) the adequacy and effectiveness of technological measures designed to protect copyrighted works; and

(C) protection of copyright owners against the unauthorized access to their encrypted copyrighted works.

The report shall include legislative recommendations, if any.

(h) EXCEPTIONS REGARDING MINORS.—In applying subsection (a) to a component or part, the court may consider the necessity for its intended and actual incorporation in a technology, product, service, or device, which—

(1) does not itself violate the provisions of this title; and

(2) has the sole purpose to prevent the access of minors to material on the Internet.

(i) PROTECTION OF PERSONALLY IDENTIFYING INFORMATION.—

(1) CIRCUMVENTION PERMITTED.—Notwithstanding the provisions of subsection (a)(1)(A), it is not a violation of that subsection for a person to circumvent a technological measure that effectively controls access to a work protected under this title, if—

(A) the technological measure, or the work it protects, contains the capability of collecting or disseminating personally identifying information reflecting the online activities of a natural person who seeks to gain access to the work protected;

(B) in the normal course of its operation, the technological measure, or the work it protects, collects or disseminates personally identifying information about the person who seeks to gain access to the work protected, without providing conspicuous notice of such collection or dissemination to such person, and without providing such person with the capability to prevent or restrict such collection or dissemination;

(C) the act of circumvention has the sole effect of identifying and disabling the capability described in subparagraph (A), and has no other effect on the ability of any person to gain access to any work; and

(D) the act of circumvention is carried out solely for the purpose of preventing the collection or dissemination of personally identifying information about a natural person who seeks to gain access to the work protected, and is not in violation of any other law.

(2) INAPPLICABILITY TO CERTAIN TECHNOLOGICAL MEASURES.—This subsection does not apply to a technological measure, or a work it protects, that does not collect or disseminate

personally identifying information and that is disclosed to a user as not having or using such capability.

(j) SECURITY TESTING.—

(1) DEFINITION.—For purposes of this subsection, the term "security testing" means accessing a computer, computer system, or computer network, solely for the purpose of good faith testing, investigating, or correcting, a security flaw or vulnerability, with the authorization of the owner or operator of such computer, computer system, or computer network.

(2) PERMISSIBLE ACTS OF SECURITY TESTING.—Notwithstanding the provisions of subsection (a)(1)(A), it is not a violation of that subsection for a person to engage in an act of security testing, if such act does not constitute infringement under this title or a violation of applicable law other than this section, including section 1030 of title 18 and those provisions of title 18 amended by the Computer Fraud and Abuse Act of 1986.

(3) FACTORS IN DETERMINING EXEMPTION.—In determining whether a person qualifies for the exemption under paragraph (2), the factors to be considered shall include—

(A) whether the information derived from the security testing was used solely to promote the security of the owner or operator of such computer, computer system or computer network, or shared directly with the developer of such computer, computer system, or computer network; and

(B) whether the information derived from the security testing was used or maintained in a manner that does not facilitate infringement under this title or a violation of applicable law other than this section, including a violation of privacy or breach of security.

(4) USE OF TECHNOLOGICAL MEANS FOR SECURITY TESTING.—Notwithstanding the provisions of subsection (a)(2), it is not a violation of that subsection for a person to develop, produce, distribute or employ technological means for the sole purpose of performing the acts of security testing described in subsection (2),[1] provided such technological means does not otherwise violate section[2] (a)(2).

(k) CERTAIN ANALOG DEVICES AND CERTAIN TECHNOLOGICAL MEASURES.—

(1) CERTAIN ANALOG DEVICES.—

(A) Effective 18 months after the date of the enactment of this chapter, no person shall manufacture, import, offer to the public, provide or otherwise traffic in any—

(i) VHS format analog video cassette recorder unless such recorder conforms to the automatic gain control copy control technology;

(ii) 8mm format analog video cassette camcorder unless such camcorder conforms to the automatic gain control technology;

(iii) Beta format analog video cassette recorder, unless such recorder conforms to the automatic gain control copy control technology, except that this requirement shall not apply until there are 1,000 Beta format analog video cassette recorders sold in the United States in any one calendar year after the date of the enactment of this chapter;

(iv) 8mm format analog video cassette recorder that is not an analog video cassette camcorder, unless such recorder conforms to the automatic gain control copy control technology, except that this requirement shall not apply until there are 20,000 such recorders sold in the United States in any one calendar year after the date of the enactment of this chapter; or

(v) analog video cassette recorder that records using an NTSC format video input and that is not otherwise covered under clauses (i) through (iv), unless such device conforms to the automatic gain control copy control technology.

(B) Effective on the date of the enactment of this chapter, no person shall manufacture, import, offer to the public, provide or otherwise traffic in—

(i) any VHS format analog video cassette recorder or any 8mm format analog video cassette recorder if the design of the model of such recorder has been modified after such date of enactment so that a model of recorder that previously conformed to the automatic gain control copy control technology no longer conforms to such technology; or

(ii) any VHS format analog video cassette recorder, or any 8mm format analog video cassette recorder that is not an 8mm analog video cassette camcorder, if the design of the model of such recorder has been modified after such date of enactment so that a model of recorder that previously conformed to the four-line colorstripe copy control technology no longer conforms to such technology.

Manufacturers that have not previously manufactured or sold a VHS format analog video cassette recorder, or an 8mm format analog cassette recorder, shall be required to conform to the four-line colorstripe copy control technology in the initial model of any such recorder manufactured after the date of the enactment of this chapter, and thereafter to continue conforming to the four-line colorstripe copy control technology. For purposes of this subparagraph, an analog video cassette recorder "conforms to" the four-line colorstripe copy control technology if it records a signal that, when played back by the playback function of that recorder in the normal viewing mode, exhibits, on a reference display device, a display containing distracting visible lines through portions of the viewable picture.

(2) CERTAIN ENCODING RESTRICTIONS.—No person shall apply the automatic gain control copy control technology or colorstripe copy control technology to prevent or limit consumer copying except such copying—

(A) of a single transmission, or specified group of transmissions, of live events or of

---

audiovisual works for which a member of the public has exercised choice in selecting the transmissions, including the content of the transmissions or the time of receipt of such transmissions, or both, and as to which such member is charged a separate fee for each such transmission or specified group of transmissions;

(B) from a copy of a transmission of a live event or an audiovisual work if such transmission is provided by a channel or service where payment is made by a member of the public for such channel or service in the form of a subscription fee that entitles the member of the public to receive all of the programming contained in such channel or service;

(C) from a physical medium containing one or more prerecorded audiovisual works; or

(D) from a copy of a transmission described in subparagraph (A) or from a copy made from a physical medium described in subparagraph (C).

In the event that a transmission meets both the conditions set forth in subparagraph (A) and those set forth in subparagraph (B), the transmission shall be treated as a transmission described in subparagraph (A).

(3) INAPPLICABILITY.—This subsection shall not—

(A) require any analog video cassette camcorder to conform to the automatic gain control copy control technology with respect to any video signal received through a camera lens;

(B) apply to the manufacture, importation, offer for sale, provision of, or other trafficking in, any professional analog video cassette recorder; or

(C) apply to the offer for sale or provision of, or other trafficking in, any previously owned analog video cassette recorder, if such recorder was legally manufactured and sold when new and not subsequently modified in violation of paragraph (1)(B).

(4) DEFINITIONS.—For purposes of this subsection:

(A) An "analog video cassette recorder" means a device that records, or a device that includes a function that records, on electromagnetic tape in an analog format the electronic impulses produced by the video and audio portions of a television program, motion picture, or other form of audiovisual work.

(B) An "analog video cassette camcorder" means an analog video cassette recorder that contains a recording function that operates through a camera lens and through a video input that may be connected with a television or other video playback device.

(C) An analog video cassette recorder "conforms" to the automatic gain control copy control technology if it—

(i) detects one or more of the elements of such technology and does not record the motion picture or transmission protected by such technology; or

(ii) records a signal that, when played back, exhibits a meaningfully distorted or degraded display.

(D) The term "professional analog video cassette recorder" means an analog video cassette recorder that is designed, manufactured, marketed, and intended for use by a person who regularly employs such a device for a lawful business or industrial use, including making, performing, displaying, distributing, or transmitting copies of motion pictures on a commercial scale.

(E) The terms "VHS format", "8mm format", "Beta format", "automatic gain control copy control technology", "colorstripe copy control technology", "four-line version of the colorstripe copy control technology", and "NTSC" have the meanings that are commonly understood in the consumer electronics and motion picture industries as of the date of the enactment of this chapter.

(5) VIOLATIONS.—Any violation of paragraph (1) of this subsection shall be treated as a violation of subsection (b)(1) of this section. Any violation of paragraph (2) of this subsection shall be deemed an "act of circumvention" for the purposes of section 1203(c)(3)(A) of this chapter.

(Added Pub. L. 105–304, title I, § 103(a), Oct. 28, 1998, 112 Stat. 2863; amended Pub. L. 106–113, div. B, § 1000(a)(9) [title V, § 5006], Nov. 29, 1999, 113 Stat. 1536, 1501A–594.)

REFERENCES IN TEXT

The date of the enactment of this chapter, referred to in subsecs. (a)(1)(A), (g)(5), and (k)(1), (4)(E), is the date of enactment of Pub. L. 105–304, which was approved Oct. 28, 1998.

The Computer Fraud and Abuse Act of 1986, referred to in subsecs. (g)(2)(D) and (j)(2), is Pub. L. 99–474, Oct. 16, 1986, 100 Stat. 1213, which amended section 1030 of Title 18, Crimes and Criminal Procedure, and enacted provisions set out as a note under section 1001 of Title 18. For complete classification of this Act to the Code, see Short Title of 1986 Amendment note set out under section 1001 of Title 18 and Tables.

AMENDMENTS

1999—Subsec. (a)(1)(C). Pub. L. 106–113 struck out "on the record" after "determination in a rulemaking proceeding" in first sentence.

§ 1202. Integrity of copyright management information

(a) FALSE COPYRIGHT MANAGEMENT INFORMATION.—No person shall knowingly and with the intent to induce, enable, facilitate, or conceal infringement—

(1) provide copyright management information that is false, or

(2) distribute or import for distribution copyright management information that is false.

(b) REMOVAL OR ALTERATION OF COPYRIGHT MANAGEMENT INFORMATION.—No person shall, without the authority of the copyright owner or the law—

(1) intentionally remove or alter any copyright management information,

(2) distribute or import for distribution copyright management information knowing that the copyright management information has been removed or altered without authority of the copyright owner or the law, or

(3) distribute, import for distribution, or publicly perform works, copies of works, or phonorecords, knowing that copyright management information has been removed or altered without authority of the copyright owner or the law,

knowing, or, with respect to civil remedies under section 1203, having reasonable grounds to know, that it will induce, enable, facilitate, or conceal an infringement of any right under this title.

(c) DEFINITION.—As used in this section, the term "copyright management information" means any of the following information conveyed in connection with copies or phonorecords of a work or performances or displays of a work, including in digital form, except that such term does not include any personally identifying information about a user of a work or of a copy, phonorecord, performance, or display of a work:

(1) The title and other information identifying the work, including the information set forth on a notice of copyright.

(2) The name of, and other identifying information about, the author of a work.

(3) The name of, and other identifying information about, the copyright owner of the work, including the information set forth in a notice of copyright.

(4) With the exception of public performances of works by radio and television broadcast stations, the name of, and other identifying information about, a performer whose performance is fixed in a work other than an audiovisual work.

(5) With the exception of public performances of works by radio and television broadcast stations, in the case of an audiovisual work, the name of, and other identifying information about, a writer, performer, or director who is credited in the audiovisual work.

(6) Terms and conditions for use of the work.

(7) Identifying numbers or symbols referring to such information or links to such information.

(8) Such other information as the Register of Copyrights may prescribe by regulation, except that the Register of Copyrights may not require the provision of any information concerning the user of a copyrighted work.

(d) LAW ENFORCEMENT, INTELLIGENCE, AND OTHER GOVERNMENT ACTIVITIES.—This section does not prohibit any lawfully authorized investigative, protective, information security, or intelligence activity of an officer, agent, or employee of the United States, a State, or a political subdivision of a State, or a person acting pursuant to a contract with the United States, a State, or a political subdivision of a State. For purposes of this subsection, the term "information security" means activities carried out in order to identify and address the vulnerabilities of a government computer, computer system, or computer network.

(e) LIMITATIONS ON LIABILITY.—

(1) ANALOG TRANSMISSIONS.—In the case of an analog transmission, a person who is making transmissions in its capacity as a broadcast station, or as a cable system, or someone who provides programming to such station or system, shall not be liable for a violation of subsection (b) if—

(A) avoiding the activity that constitutes such violation is not technically feasible or would create an undue financial hardship on such person; and

(B) such person did not intend, by engaging in such activity, to induce, enable, facilitate, or conceal infringement of a right under this title.

(2) DIGITAL TRANSMISSIONS.—

(A) If a digital transmission standard for the placement of copyright management information for a category of works is set in a voluntary, consensus standard-setting process involving a representative cross-section of broadcast stations or cable systems and copyright owners of a category of works that are intended for public performance by such stations or systems, a person identified in paragraph (1) shall not be liable for a violation of subsection (b) with respect to the particular copyright management information addressed by such standard if—

(i) the placement of such information by someone other than such person is not in accordance with such standard; and

(ii) the activity that constitutes such violation is not intended to induce, enable, facilitate, or conceal infringement of a right under this title.

(B) Until a digital transmission standard has been set pursuant to subparagraph (A) with respect to the placement of copyright management information for a category of works, a person identified in paragraph (1) shall not be liable for a violation of subsection (b) with respect to such copyright management information, if the activity that constitutes such violation is not intended to induce, enable, facilitate, or conceal infringement of a right under this title, and if—

(i) the transmission of such information by such person would result in a perceptible visual or aural degradation of the digital signal; or

(ii) the transmission of such information by such person would conflict with—

(I) an applicable government regulation relating to transmission of information in a digital signal;

(II) an applicable industry-wide standard relating to the transmission of information in a digital signal that was adopted by a voluntary consensus standards body prior to the effective date of this chapter; or

(III) an applicable industry-wide standard relating to the transmission of information in a digital signal that was adopted in a voluntary, consensus standards-setting process open to participation by a representative cross-section of broadcast stations or cable systems and copyright owners of a category of works that are intended for public performance by such stations or systems.

(3) DEFINITIONS.—As used in this subsection—

(A) the term "broadcast station" has the meaning given that term in section 3 of the Communications Act of 1934 (47 U.S.C. 153); and

(B) the term "cable system" has the meaning given that term in section 602 of the Communications Act of 1934 (47 U.S.C. 522).

(Added Pub. L. 105–304, title I, §103(a), Oct. 28, 1998, 112 Stat. 2872; amended Pub. L. 106–44, §1(e), Aug. 5, 1999, 113 Stat. 222.)

REFERENCES IN TEXT

The effective date of this chapter, referred to in subsec. (e)(2)(B)(ii)(II), is Oct. 28, 1998. See section 105 of Pub. L. 105–304, set out as an Effective Date of 1998 Amendment note under section 101 of this title.

AMENDMENTS

1999—Subsec. (e)(2)(B). Pub. L. 106–44 substituted "category of works" for "category or works" in introductory provisions.

§ 1203. Civil remedies

(a) CIVIL ACTIONS.—Any person injured by a violation of section 1201 or 1202 may bring a civil action in an appropriate United States district court for such violation.

(b) POWERS OF THE COURT.—In an action brought under subsection (a), the court—

(1) may grant temporary and permanent injunctions on such terms as it deems reasonable to prevent or restrain a violation, but in no event shall impose a prior restraint on free speech or the press protected under the 1st amendment to the Constitution;

(2) at any time while an action is pending, may order the impounding, on such terms as it deems reasonable, of any device or product that is in the custody or control of the alleged violator and that the court has reasonable cause to believe was involved in a violation;

(3) may award damages under subsection (c);

(4) in its discretion may allow the recovery of costs by or against any party other than the United States or an officer thereof;

(5) in its discretion may award reasonable attorney's fees to the prevailing party; and

(6) may, as part of a final judgment or decree finding a violation, order the remedial modification or the destruction of any device or product involved in the violation that is in the custody or control of the violator or has been impounded under paragraph (2).

(c) AWARD OF DAMAGES.—

(1) IN GENERAL.—Except as otherwise provided in this title, a person committing a violation of section 1201 or 1202 is liable for either—

(A) the actual damages and any additional profits of the violator, as provided in paragraph (2), or

(B) statutory damages, as provided in paragraph (3).

(2) ACTUAL DAMAGES.—The court shall award to the complaining party the actual damages suffered by the party as a result of the violation, and any profits of the violator that are attributable to the violation and are not taken into account in computing the actual damages, if the complaining party elects such damages at any time before final judgment is entered.

(3) STATUTORY DAMAGES.—(A) At any time before final judgment is entered, a complaining party may elect to recover an award of statutory damages for each violation of section 1201 in the sum of not less than $200 or more than $2,500 per act of circumvention, device, product, component, offer, or performance of service, as the court considers just.

(B) At any time before final judgment is entered, a complaining party may elect to recover an award of statutory damages for each violation of section 1202 in the sum of not less than $2,500 or more than $25,000.

(4) REPEATED VIOLATIONS.—In any case in which the injured party sustains the burden of proving, and the court finds, that a person has violated section 1201 or 1202 within 3 years after a final judgment was entered against the person for another such violation, the court may increase the award of damages up to triple the amount that would otherwise be awarded, as the court considers just.

(5) INNOCENT VIOLATIONS.—

(A) IN GENERAL.—The court in its discretion may reduce or remit the total award of damages in any case in which the violator sustains the burden of proving, and the court finds, that the violator was not aware and had no reason to believe that its acts constituted a violation.

(B) NONPROFIT LIBRARY, ARCHIVES, EDUCATIONAL INSTITUTIONS, OR PUBLIC BROADCASTING ENTITIES.—

(i) DEFINITION.—In this subparagraph, the term "public broadcasting entity" has the meaning given such term under section 118(f).

(ii) IN GENERAL.—In the case of a nonprofit library, archives, educational institution, or public broadcasting entity, the court shall remit damages in any case in which the library, archives, educational institution, or public broadcasting entity sustains the burden of proving, and the court finds, that the library, archives, educational institution, or public broadcasting entity was not aware and had no reason to believe that its acts constituted a violation.

(Added Pub. L. 105–304, title I, §103(a), Oct. 28, 1998, 112 Stat. 2874; amended Pub. L. 106–113, div. B, §1000(a)(9) [title V, §5004(a)], Nov. 29, 1999, 113 Stat. 1536, 1501A–593; Pub. L. 111–295, §6(f)(3), Dec. 9, 2010, 124 Stat. 3181.)

AMENDMENTS

2010—Subsec. (c)(5)(B)(i). Pub. L. 111–295 substituted "118(f)" for "118(g)".

1999—Subsec. (c)(5)(B). Pub. L. 106–113 amended heading and text of subpar. (B) generally. Prior to amendment, text read as follows: "In the case of a nonprofit library, archives, or educational institution, the court shall remit damages in any case in which the library, archives, or educational institution sustains the burden of proving, and the court finds, that the library, archives, or educational institution was not aware and had no reason to believe that its acts constituted a violation."

§ 1204. Criminal offenses and penalties

(a) IN GENERAL.—Any person who violates section 1201 or 1202 willfully and for purposes of commercial advantage or private financial gain—

(1) shall be fined not more than $500,000 or imprisoned for not more than 5 years, or both, for the first offense; and

(2) shall be fined not more than $1,000,000 or imprisoned for not more than 10 years, or both, for any subsequent offense.

(b) LIMITATION FOR NONPROFIT LIBRARY, ARCHIVES, EDUCATIONAL INSTITUTION, OR PUBLIC BROADCASTING ENTITY.—Subsection (a) shall not apply to a nonprofit library, archives, educational institution, or public broadcasting entity (as defined under section 118(f)).

(c) STATUTE OF LIMITATIONS.—No criminal proceeding shall be brought under this section unless such proceeding is commenced within 5 years after the cause of action arose.

(Added Pub. L. 105–304, title I, § 103(a), Oct. 28, 1998, 112 Stat. 2876; amended Pub. L. 106–113, div. B, § 1000(a)(9) [title V, § 5004(b)], Nov. 29, 1999, 113 Stat. 1536, 1501A–593; Pub. L. 111–295, § 6(f)(3), Dec. 9, 2010, 124 Stat. 3181.)

AMENDMENTS

2010—Subsec. (b). Pub. L. 111–295 substituted ''118(f)'' for ''118(g)''.

1999—Subsec. (b). Pub. L. 106–113 amended heading and text of subsec. (b) generally. Prior to amendment, text read as follows: ''Subsection (a) shall not apply to a nonprofit library, archives, or educational institution.''

§ 1205. Savings clause

Nothing in this chapter abrogates, diminishes, or weakens the provisions of, nor provides any defense or element of mitigation in a criminal prosecution or civil action under, any Federal or State law that prevents the violation of the privacy of an individual in connection with the individual's use of the Internet.

(Added Pub. L. 105–304, title I, § 103(a), Oct. 28, 1998, 112 Stat. 2876.)

CHAPTER 13—PROTECTION OF ORIGINAL DESIGNS

§ 1301. Designs protected

(a) DESIGNS PROTECTED.—

(1) IN GENERAL.—The designer or other owner of an original design of a useful article which makes the article attractive or distinctive in appearance to the purchasing or using public may secure the protection provided by this chapter upon complying with and subject to this chapter.

(2) VESSEL FEATURES.—The design of a vessel hull, deck, or combination of a hull and deck, including a plug or mold, is subject to protection under this chapter, notwithstanding section 1302(4).

(3) EXCEPTIONS.—Department of Defense rights in a registered design under this chapter, including the right to build to such registered design, shall be determined solely by operation of section 2320 of title 10 or by the instrument under which the design was developed for the United States Government.

(b) DEFINITIONS.—For the purpose of this chapter, the following terms have the following meanings:

(1) A design is ''original'' if it is the result of the designer's creative endeavor that provides a distinguishable variation over prior work pertaining to similar articles which is more than merely trivial and has not been copied from another source.

(2) A ''useful article'' is a vessel hull or deck, including a plug or mold, which in normal use has an intrinsic utilitarian function that is not merely to portray the appearance of the article or to convey information. An article which normally is part of a useful article shall be deemed to be a useful article.

(3) A ''vessel'' is a craft—

(A) that is designed and capable of independently steering a course on or through water through its own means of propulsion; and

(B) that is designed and capable of carrying and transporting one or more passengers.

(4) A ''hull'' is the exterior frame or body of a vessel, exclusive of the deck, superstructure, masts, sails, yards, rigging, hardware, fixtures, and other attachments.

(5) A ''plug'' means a device or model used to make a mold for the purpose of exact duplication, regardless of whether the device or model has an intrinsic utilitarian function that is not only to portray the appearance of the product or to convey information.

(6) A ''mold'' means a matrix or form in which a substance for material is used, regard-

less of whether the matrix or form has an intrinsic utilitarian function that is not only to portray the appearance of the product or to convey information.

(7) A "deck" is the horizontal surface of a vessel that covers the hull, including exterior cabin and cockpit surfaces, and exclusive of masts, sails, yards, rigging, hardware, fixtures, and other attachments.

(Added Pub. L. 105–304, title V, § 502, Oct. 28, 1998, 112 Stat. 2905; amended Pub. L. 106–113, div. B, § 1000(a)(9) [title V, § 5005(a)(3)], Nov. 29, 1999, 113 Stat. 1536, 1501A–593; Pub. L. 110–434, § 1(b)–(d), Oct. 16, 2008, 122 Stat. 4972.)

AMENDMENTS

2008—Subsec. (a)(2). Pub. L. 110–434, § 1(b), added par. (2) and struck out former par. (2). Prior to amendment, text read as follows: "The design of a vessel hull, including a plug or mold, is subject to protection under this chapter, notwithstanding section 1302(4)."

Subsec. (a)(3). Pub. L. 110–434, § 1(c), added par. (3).

Subsec. (b)(2). Pub. L. 110–434, § 1(d)(1), substituted "vessel hull or deck, including a plug or mold," for "vessel hull, including a plug or mold,".

Subsec. (b)(4). Pub. L. 110–434, § 1(d)(2), added par. (4) and struck out former par. (4) which read as follows: "A 'hull' is the frame or body of a vessel, including the deck of a vessel, exclusive of masts, sails, yards, and rigging."

Subsec. (b)(7). Pub. L. 110–434, § 1(d)(3), added par. (7).

1999—Subsec. (b)(3). Pub. L. 106–113 amended par. (3) generally. Prior to amendment, par. (3) read as follows: "A 'vessel' is a craft, especially one larger than a rowboat, designed to navigate on water, but does not include any such craft that exceeds 200 feet in length."

EFFECTIVE DATE

Pub. L. 105–304, title V, § 505, Oct. 28, 1998, 112 Stat. 2918, as amended by Pub. L. 106–113, div. B, § 1000(a)(9) [title V, § 5005(a)(2)], Nov. 29, 1999, 113 Stat. 1536, 1501A–593, provided that: "The amendments made by sections 502 and 503 [enacting this chapter and amending sections 1338, 1400, and 1498 of Title 28, Judiciary and Judicial Procedure] shall take effect on the date of the enactment of this Act [Oct. 28, 1998]."

JOINT STUDY OF EFFECT OF THIS CHAPTER

Pub. L. 105–304, title V, § 504, Oct. 28, 1998, 112 Stat. 2917, as amended by Pub. L. 106–113, div. B, § 1000(a)(9) [title IV, § 4741(b)(1), title V, § 5005(a)(1)], Nov. 29, 1999, 113 Stat. 1536, 1501A–586, 1501A–593, provided that:

"(a) IN GENERAL.—Not later than November 1, 2003, the Register of Copyrights and the Under Secretary of Commerce for Intellectual Property and Director of the United States Patent and Trademark Office shall submit to the Committees on the Judiciary of the Senate and the House of Representatives a joint report evaluating the effect of the amendments made by this title [enacting this chapter and amending sections 1338, 1400, and 1498 of Title 28, Judiciary and Judicial Procedure].

"(b) ELEMENTS FOR CONSIDERATION.—In carrying out subsection (a), the Register of Copyrights and the Under Secretary of Commerce for Intellectual Property and Director of the United States Patent and Trademark Office shall consider—

"(1) the extent to which the amendments made by this title has been effective in suppressing infringement of the design of vessel hulls;

"(2) the extent to which the registration provided for in chapter 13 of title 17, United States Code, as added by this title, has been utilized;

"(3) the extent to which the creation of new designs of vessel hulls have been encouraged by the amendments made by this title;

"(4) the effect, if any, of the amendments made by this title on the price of vessels with hulls protected under such amendments; and

"(5) such other considerations as the Register and the Under Secretary of Commerce for Intellectual Property and Director of the United States Patent and Trademark Office may deem relevant to accomplish the purposes of the evaluation conducted under subsection (a)."

§ 1302. Designs not subject to protection

Protection under this chapter shall not be available for a design that is—

(1) not original;

(2) staple or commonplace, such as a standard geometric figure, a familiar symbol, an emblem, or a motif, or another shape, pattern, or configuration which has become standard, common, prevalent, or ordinary;

(3) different from a design excluded by paragraph (2) only in insignificant details or in elements which are variants commonly used in the relevant trades;

(4) dictated solely by a utilitarian function of the article that embodies it; or

(5) embodied in a useful article that was made public by the designer or owner in the United States or a foreign country more than 2 years before the date of the application for registration under this chapter.

(Added Pub. L. 105–304, title V, § 502, Oct. 28, 1998, 112 Stat. 2906; amended Pub. L. 106–44, § 1(f)(1), Aug. 5, 1999, 113 Stat. 222.)

AMENDMENTS

1999—Par. (5). Pub. L. 106–44 substituted "2 years" for "1 year".

§ 1303. Revisions, adaptations, and rearrangements

Protection for a design under this chapter shall be available notwithstanding the employment in the design of subject matter excluded from protection under section 1302 if the design is a substantial revision, adaptation, or rearrangement of such subject matter. Such protection shall be independent of any subsisting protection in subject matter employed in the design, and shall not be construed as securing any right to subject matter excluded from protection under this chapter or as extending any subsisting protection under this chapter.

(Added Pub. L. 105–304, title V, § 502, Oct. 28, 1998, 112 Stat. 2906.)

§ 1304. Commencement of protection

The protection provided for a design under this chapter shall commence upon the earlier of the date of publication of the registration under section 1313(a) or the date the design is first made public as defined by section 1310(b).

(Added Pub. L. 105–304, title V, § 502, Oct. 28, 1998, 112 Stat. 2907.)

§ 1305. Term of protection

(a) IN GENERAL.—Subject to subsection (b), the protection provided under this chapter for a design shall continue for a term of 10 years beginning on the date of the commencement of protection under section 1304.

(b) EXPIRATION.—All terms of protection provided in this section shall run to the end of the calendar year in which they would otherwise expire.

(c) TERMINATION OF RIGHTS.—Upon expiration or termination of protection in a particular design under this chapter, all rights under this chapter in the design shall terminate, regardless of the number of different articles in which the design may have been used during the term of its protection.

(Added Pub. L. 105–304, title V, §502, Oct. 28, 1998, 112 Stat. 2907.)

§ 1306. Design notice

(a) CONTENTS OF DESIGN NOTICE.—(1) Whenever any design for which protection is sought under this chapter is made public under section 1310(b), the owner of the design shall, subject to the provisions of section 1307, mark it or have it marked legibly with a design notice consisting of—

(A) the words "Protected Design", the abbreviation "Prot'd Des.", or the letter "D" with a circle, or the symbol "*D*";

(B) the year of the date on which protection for the design commenced; and

(C) the name of the owner, an abbreviation by which the name can be recognized, or a generally accepted alternative designation of the owner.

Any distinctive identification of the owner may be used for purposes of subparagraph (C) if it has been recorded by the Administrator before the design marked with such identification is registered.

(2) After registration, the registration number may be used instead of the elements specified in subparagraphs (B) and (C) of paragraph (1).

(b) LOCATION OF NOTICE.—The design notice shall be so located and applied as to give reasonable notice of design protection while the useful article embodying the design is passing through its normal channels of commerce.

(c) SUBSEQUENT REMOVAL OF NOTICE.—When the owner of a design has complied with the provisions of this section, protection under this chapter shall not be affected by the removal, destruction, or obliteration by others of the design notice on an article.

(Added Pub. L. 105–304, title V, §502, Oct. 28, 1998, 112 Stat. 2907.)

§ 1307. Effect of omission of notice

(a) ACTIONS WITH NOTICE.—Except as provided in subsection (b), the omission of the notice prescribed in section 1306 shall not cause loss of the protection under this chapter or prevent recovery for infringement under this chapter against any person who, after receiving written notice of the design protection, begins an undertaking leading to infringement under this chapter.

(b) ACTIONS WITHOUT NOTICE.—The omission of the notice prescribed in section 1306 shall prevent any recovery under section 1323 against a person who began an undertaking leading to infringement under this chapter before receiving written notice of the design protection. No injunction shall be issued under this chapter with respect to such undertaking unless the owner of the design reimburses that person for any rea-

sonable expenditure or contractual obligation in connection with such undertaking that was incurred before receiving written notice of the design protection, as the court in its discretion directs. The burden of providing written notice of design protection shall be on the owner of the design.

(Added Pub. L. 105–304, title V, §502, Oct. 28, 1998, 112 Stat. 2907.)

§ 1308. Exclusive rights

The owner of a design protected under this chapter has the exclusive right to—

(1) make, have made, or import, for sale or for use in trade, any useful article embodying that design; and

(2) sell or distribute for sale or for use in trade any useful article embodying that design.

(Added Pub. L. 105–304, title V, §502, Oct. 28, 1998, 112 Stat. 2908.)

§ 1309. Infringement

(a) ACTS OF INFRINGEMENT.—Except as provided in subsection (b), it shall be infringement of the exclusive rights in a design protected under this chapter for any person, without the consent of the owner of the design, within the United States and during the term of such protection, to—

(1) make, have made, or import, for sale or for use in trade, any infringing article as defined in subsection (e); or

(2) sell or distribute for sale or for use in trade any such infringing article.

(b) ACTS OF SELLERS AND DISTRIBUTORS.—A seller or distributor of an infringing article who did not make or import the article shall be deemed to have infringed on a design protected under this chapter only if that person—

(1) induced or acted in collusion with a manufacturer to make, or an importer to import such article, except that merely purchasing or giving an order to purchase such article in the ordinary course of business shall not of itself constitute such inducement or collusion; or

(2) refused or failed, upon the request of the owner of the design, to make a prompt and full disclosure of that person's source of such article, and that person orders or reorders such article after receiving notice by registered or certified mail of the protection subsisting in the design.

(c) ACTS WITHOUT KNOWLEDGE.—It shall not be infringement under this section to make, have made, import, sell, or distribute, any article embodying a design which was created without knowledge that a design was protected under this chapter and was copied from such protected design.

(d) ACTS IN ORDINARY COURSE OF BUSINESS.—A person who incorporates into that person's product of manufacture an infringing article acquired from others in the ordinary course of business, or who, without knowledge of the protected design embodied in an infringing article, makes or processes the infringing article for the account of another person in the ordinary course of business, shall not be deemed to have infringed the rights in that design under this chapter except under a condition contained in paragraph (1) or (2) of subsection (b). Accepting an order or reorder from the source of the infringing article shall be deemed ordering or reordering within the meaning of subsection (b)(2).

(e) INFRINGING ARTICLE DEFINED.—As used in this section, an "infringing article" is any article the design of which has been copied from a design protected under this chapter, without the consent of the owner of the protected design. An infringing article is not an illustration or picture of a protected design in an advertisement, book, periodical, newspaper, photograph, broadcast, motion picture, or similar medium. A design shall not be deemed to have been copied from a protected design if it is original and not substantially similar in appearance to a protected design.

(f) ESTABLISHING ORIGINALITY.—The party to any action or proceeding under this chapter who alleges rights under this chapter in a design shall have the burden of establishing the design's originality whenever the opposing party introduces an earlier work which is identical to such design, or so similar as to make prima facie showing that such design was copied from such work.

(g) REPRODUCTION FOR TEACHING OR ANALYSIS.—It is not an infringement of the exclusive rights of a design owner for a person to reproduce the design in a useful article or in any other form solely for the purpose of teaching, analyzing, or evaluating the appearance, concepts, or techniques embodied in the design, or the function of the useful article embodying the design.

(Added Pub. L. 105–304, title V, § 502, Oct. 28, 1998, 112 Stat. 2908.)

§ 1310. Application for registration

(a) TIME LIMIT FOR APPLICATION FOR REGISTRATION.—Protection under this chapter shall be lost if application for registration of the design is not made within 2 years after the date on which the design is first made public.

(b) WHEN DESIGN IS MADE PUBLIC.—A design is made public when an existing useful article embodying the design is anywhere publicly exhibited, publicly distributed, or offered for sale or sold to the public by the owner of the design or with the owner's consent.

(c) APPLICATION BY OWNER OF DESIGN.—Application for registration may be made by the owner of the design.

(d) CONTENTS OF APPLICATION.—The application for registration shall be made to the Administrator and shall state—

(1) the name and address of the designer or designers of the design;

(2) the name and address of the owner if different from the designer;

(3) the specific name of the useful article embodying the design;

(4) the date, if any, that the design was first made public, if such date was earlier than the date of the application;

(5) affirmation that the design has been fixed in a useful article; and

(6) such other information as may be required by the Administrator.

The application for registration may include a description setting forth the salient features of the design, but the absence of such a description shall not prevent registration under this chapter.

(e) SWORN STATEMENT.—The application for registration shall be accompanied by a statement under oath by the applicant or the applicant's duly authorized agent or representative, setting forth, to the best of the applicant's knowledge and belief—

(1) that the design is original and was created by the designer or designers named in the application;

(2) that the design has not previously been registered on behalf of the applicant or the applicant's predecessor in title; and

(3) that the applicant is the person entitled to protection and to registration under this chapter.

If the design has been made public with the design notice prescribed in section 1306, the statement shall also describe the exact form and position of the design notice.

(f) EFFECT OF ERRORS.—(1) Error in any statement or assertion as to the utility of the useful article named in the application under this section, the design of which is sought to be registered, shall not affect the protection secured under this chapter.

(2) Errors in omitting a joint designer or in naming an alleged joint designer shall not affect the validity of the registration, or the actual ownership or the protection of the design, unless it is shown that the error occurred with deceptive intent.

(g) DESIGN MADE IN SCOPE OF EMPLOYMENT.—In a case in which the design was made within the regular scope of the designer's employment and individual authorship of the design is difficult or impossible to ascribe and the application so states, the name and address of the employer for whom the design was made may be stated instead of that of the individual designer.

(h) PICTORIAL REPRESENTATION OF DESIGN.—The application for registration shall be accompanied by two copies of a drawing or other pictorial representation of the useful article embodying the design, having one or more views, adequate to show the design, in a form and style suitable for reproduction, which shall be deemed a part of the application.

(i) DESIGN IN MORE THAN ONE USEFUL ARTICLE.—If the distinguishing elements of a design are in substantially the same form in different useful articles, the design shall be protected as to all such useful articles when protected as to one of them, but not more than one registration shall be required for the design.

(j) APPLICATION FOR MORE THAN ONE DESIGN.—More than one design may be included in the same application under such conditions as may be prescribed by the Administrator. For each design included in an application the fee prescribed for a single design shall be paid.

(Added Pub. L. 105–304, title V, § 502, Oct. 28, 1998, 112 Stat. 2909.)

§ 1311. Benefit of earlier filing date in foreign country

An application for registration of a design filed in the United States by any person who has, or whose legal representative or predecessor or successor in title has, previously filed an application for registration of the same design in a foreign country which extends to designs of owners who are citizens of the United States, or to applications filed under this chapter, similar protection to that provided under this chapter shall have that same effect as if filed in the United States on the date on which the application was first filed in such foreign country, if the application in the United States is filed within 6 months after the earliest date on which any such foreign application was filed.

(Added Pub. L. 105–304, title V, § 502, Oct. 28, 1998, 112 Stat. 2910.)

§ 1312. Oaths and acknowledgments

(a) IN GENERAL.—Oaths and acknowledgments required by this chapter—

(1) may be made—

(A) before any person in the United States authorized by law to administer oaths; or

(B) when made in a foreign country, before any diplomatic or consular officer of the United States authorized to administer oaths, or before any official authorized to administer oaths in the foreign country concerned, whose authority shall be proved by a certificate of a diplomatic or consular officer of the United States; and

(2) shall be valid if they comply with the laws of the State or country where made.

(b) WRITTEN DECLARATION IN LIEU OF OATH.— (1) The Administrator may by rule prescribe that any document which is to be filed under this chapter in the Office of the Administrator and which is required by any law, rule, or other regulation to be under oath, may be subscribed to by a written declaration in such form as the Administrator may prescribe, and such declaration shall be in lieu of the oath otherwise required.

(2) Whenever a written declaration under paragraph (1) is used, the document containing the declaration shall state that willful false statements are punishable by fine or imprisonment, or both, pursuant to section 1001 of title 18, and may jeopardize the validity of the application or document or a registration resulting therefrom.

(Added Pub. L. 105–304, title V, § 502, Oct. 28, 1998, 112 Stat. 2911.)

§ 1313. Examination of application and issue or refusal of registration

(a) DETERMINATION OF REGISTRABILITY OF DESIGN; REGISTRATION.—Upon the filing of an application for registration in proper form under section 1310, and upon payment of the fee prescribed under section 1316, the Administrator shall determine whether or not the application relates to a design which on its face appears to be subject to protection under this chapter, and, if so, the Register shall register the design. Registration under this subsection shall be announced by publication. The date of registration shall be the date of publication.

(b) REFUSAL TO REGISTER; RECONSIDERATION.— If, in the judgment of the Administrator, the application for registration relates to a design which on its face is not subject to protection under this chapter, the Administrator shall send to the applicant a notice of refusal to register and the grounds for the refusal. Within 3 months after the date on which the notice of refusal is sent, the applicant may, by written request, seek reconsideration of the application. After consideration of such a request, the Administrator shall either register the design or send to the applicant a notice of final refusal to register.

(c) APPLICATION TO CANCEL REGISTRATION.— Any person who believes he or she is or will be damaged by a registration under this chapter may, upon payment of the prescribed fee, apply to the Administrator at any time to cancel the registration on the ground that the design is not subject to protection under this chapter, stating the reasons for the request. Upon receipt of an application for cancellation, the Administrator shall send to the owner of the design, as shown in the records of the Office of the Administrator, a notice of the application, and the owner shall have a period of 3 months after the date on which such notice is mailed in which to present arguments to the Administrator for support of the validity of the registration. The Administrator shall also have the authority to establish, by regulation, conditions under which the opposing parties may appear and be heard in support of their arguments. If, after the periods provided for the presentation of arguments have expired, the Administrator determines that the applicant for cancellation has established that the design is not subject to protection under this chapter, the Administrator shall order the registration stricken from the record. Cancellation under this subsection shall be announced by publication, and notice of the Administrator's final determination with respect to any application for cancellation shall be sent to the applicant and to the owner of record. Costs of the cancellation procedure under this subsection shall be borne by the nonprevailing party or parties, and the Administrator shall have the authority to assess and collect such costs.

(Added Pub. L. 105–304, title V, § 502, Oct. 28, 1998, 112 Stat. 2911; amended Pub. L. 106–113, div. B, § 1000(a)(9) [title V, § 5005(a)(4)], Nov. 29, 1999, 113 Stat. 1536, 1501A–594.)

AMENDMENTS

1999—Subsec. (c). Pub. L. 106–113 inserted at end "Costs of the cancellation procedure under this subsection shall be borne by the nonprevailing party or parties, and the Administrator shall have the authority to assess and collect such costs."

§ 1314. Certification of registration

Certificates of registration shall be issued in the name of the United States under the seal of the Office of the Administrator and shall be recorded in the official records of the Office. The certificate shall state the name of the useful article, the date of filing of the application, the date of registration, and the date the design was made public, if earlier than the date of filing of the application, and shall contain a reproduction of the drawing or other pictorial representation of the design. If a description of the salient features of the design appears in the application, the description shall also appear in the certificate. A certificate of registration shall be admitted in any court as prima facie evidence of the facts stated in the certificate.

(Added Pub. L. 105–304, title V, § 502, Oct. 28, 1998, 112 Stat. 2912.)

§ 1315. Publication of announcements and indexes

(a) PUBLICATIONS OF THE ADMINISTRATOR.—The Administrator shall publish lists and indexes of registered designs and cancellations of designs and may also publish the drawings or other pictorial representations of registered designs for sale or other distribution.

(b) FILE OF REPRESENTATIVES OF REGISTERED DESIGNS.—The Administrator shall establish and maintain a file of the drawings or other pictorial representations of registered designs. The file shall be available for use by the public under such conditions as the Administrator may prescribe.

(Added Pub. L. 105–304, title V, § 502, Oct. 28, 1998, 112 Stat. 2912.)

§ 1316. Fees

The Administrator shall by regulation set reasonable fees for the filing of applications to register designs under this chapter and for other services relating to the administration of this chapter, taking into consideration the cost of providing these services and the benefit of a public record.

(Added Pub. L. 105–304, title V, § 502, Oct. 28, 1998, 112 Stat. 2912.)

§ 1317. Regulations

The Administrator may establish regulations for the administration of this chapter.

(Added Pub. L. 105–304, title V, § 502, Oct. 28, 1998, 112 Stat. 2912.)

§ 1318. Copies of records

Upon payment of the prescribed fee, any person may obtain a certified copy of any official record of the Office of the Administrator that relates to this chapter. That copy shall be admissible in evidence with the same effect as the original.

(Added Pub. L. 105–304, title V, § 502, Oct. 28, 1998, 112 Stat. 2913.)

§ 1319. Correction of errors in certificates

The Administrator may, by a certificate of correction under seal, correct any error in a registration incurred through the fault of the Office, or, upon payment of the required fee, any error of a clerical or typographical nature occurring in good faith but not through the fault of the Office. Such registration, together with the certificate, shall thereafter have the same effect as if it had been originally issued in such corrected form.

(Added Pub. L. 105–304, title V, § 502, Oct. 28, 1998, 112 Stat. 2913.)

§ 1320. Ownership and transfer

(a) PROPERTY RIGHT IN DESIGN.—The property right in a design subject to protection under this chapter shall vest in the designer, the legal representatives of a deceased designer or of one under legal incapacity, the employer for whom the designer created the design in the case of a design made within the regular scope of the designer's employment, or a person to whom the rights of the designer or of such employer have been transferred. The person in whom the property right is vested shall be considered the owner of the design.

(b) TRANSFER OF PROPERTY RIGHT.—The property right in a registered design, or a design for which an application for registration has been or may be filed, may be assigned, granted, conveyed, or mortgaged by an instrument in writing, signed by the owner, or may be bequeathed by will.

(c) OATH OR ACKNOWLEDGMENT OF TRANSFER.—An oath or acknowledgment under section 1312 shall be prima facie evidence of the execution of an assignment, grant, conveyance, or mortgage under subsection (b).

(d) RECORDATION OF TRANSFER.—An assignment, grant, conveyance, or mortgage under subsection (b) shall be void as against any subsequent purchaser or mortgagee for a valuable consideration, unless it is recorded in the Office of the Administrator within 3 months after its date of execution or before the date of such subsequent purchase or mortgage.

(Added Pub. L. 105–304, title V, § 502, Oct. 28, 1998, 112 Stat. 2913; amended Pub. L. 106–44, § 1(f)(2), Aug. 5, 1999, 113 Stat. 222.)

AMENDMENTS

1999—Subsec. (c). Pub. L. 106–44 substituted "Acknowledgment" for "Acknowledgement" in heading.

§ 1321. Remedy for infringement

(a) IN GENERAL.—The owner of a design is entitled, after issuance of a certificate of registration of the design under this chapter, to institute an action for any infringement of the design.

(b) REVIEW OF REFUSAL TO REGISTER.—(1) Subject to paragraph (2), the owner of a design may seek judicial review of a final refusal of the Administrator to register the design under this chapter by bringing a civil action, and may in the same action, if the court adjudges the design subject to protection under this chapter, enforce the rights in that design under this chapter.

(2) The owner of a design may seek judicial review under this section if—

(A) the owner has previously duly filed and prosecuted to final refusal an application in proper form for registration of the design;

(B) the owner causes a copy of the complaint in the action to be delivered to the Administrator within 10 days after the commencement of the action; and

(C) the defendant has committed acts in respect to the design which would constitute infringement with respect to a design protected under this chapter.

(c) ADMINISTRATOR AS PARTY TO ACTION.—The Administrator may, at the Administrator's option, become a party to the action with respect to the issue of registrability of the design claim by entering an appearance within 60 days after being served with the complaint, but the failure of the Administrator to become a party shall not deprive the court of jurisdiction to determine that issue.

(d) USE OF ARBITRATION TO RESOLVE DISPUTE.—The parties to an infringement dispute under this chapter, within such time as may be specified by the Administrator by regulation, may determine the dispute, or any aspect of the dispute, by arbitration. Arbitration shall be governed by title 9. The parties shall give notice of any arbitration award to the Administrator, and such award shall, as between the parties to which it relates, be dispositive of the issues to which it relates. The arbitration award shall be unenforceable until such notice is given. Nothing in this subsection shall preclude the Administrator from determining whether a design is subject to registration in a cancellation proceeding under section 1313(c).

(Added Pub. L. 105–304, title V, § 502, Oct. 28, 1998, 112 Stat. 2913.)

§ 1322. Injunctions

(a) IN GENERAL.—A court having jurisdiction over actions under this chapter may grant injunctions in accordance with the principles of equity to prevent infringement of a design under this chapter, including, in its discretion, prompt relief by temporary restraining orders and preliminary injunctions.

(b) DAMAGES FOR INJUNCTIVE RELIEF WRONGFULLY OBTAINED.—A seller or distributor who suffers damage by reason of injunctive relief wrongfully obtained under this section has a cause of action against the applicant for such injunctive relief and may recover such relief as may be appropriate, including damages for lost profits, cost of materials, loss of good will, and punitive damages in instances where the injunctive relief was sought in bad faith, and, unless the court finds extenuating circumstances, reasonable attorney's fees.

(Added Pub. L. 105–304, title V, § 502, Oct. 28, 1998, 112 Stat. 2914.)

§ 1323. Recovery for infringement

(a) DAMAGES.—Upon a finding for the claimant in an action for infringement under this chapter, the court shall award the claimant damages adequate to compensate for the infringement. In addition, the court may increase the damages to such amount, not exceeding $50,000 or $1 per copy, whichever is greater, as the court determines to be just. The damages awarded shall constitute compensation and not a penalty. The court may receive expert testimony as an aid to the determination of damages.

(b) INFRINGER'S PROFITS.—As an alternative to the remedies provided in subsection (a), the court may award the claimant the infringer's profits resulting from the sale of the copies if the court finds that the infringer's sales are reasonably related to the use of the claimant's de-

sign. In such a case, the claimant shall be required to prove only the amount of the infringer's sales and the infringer shall be required to prove its expenses against such sales.

(c) STATUTE OF LIMITATIONS.—No recovery under subsection (a) or (b) shall be had for any infringement committed more than 3 years before the date on which the complaint is filed.

(d) ATTORNEY'S FEES.—In an action for infringement under this chapter, the court may award reasonable attorney's fees to the prevailing party.

(e) DISPOSITION OF INFRINGING AND OTHER ARTICLES.—The court may order that all infringing articles, and any plates, molds, patterns, models, or other means specifically adapted for making the articles, be delivered up for destruction or other disposition as the court may direct.

(Added Pub. L. 105–304, title V, § 502, Oct. 28, 1998, 112 Stat. 2914.)

§ 1324. Power of court over registration

In any action involving the protection of a design under this chapter, the court, when appropriate, may order registration of a design under this chapter or the cancellation of such a registration. Any such order shall be certified by the court to the Administrator, who shall make an appropriate entry upon the record.

(Added Pub. L. 105–304, title V, § 502, Oct. 28, 1998, 112 Stat. 2915.)

§ 1325. Liability for action on registration fraudulently obtained

Any person who brings an action for infringement knowing that registration of the design was obtained by a false or fraudulent representation materially affecting the rights under this chapter, shall be liable in the sum of $10,000, or such part of that amount as the court may determine. That amount shall be to compensate the defendant and shall be charged against the plaintiff and paid to the defendant, in addition to such costs and attorney's fees of the defendant as may be assessed by the court.

(Added Pub. L. 105–304, title V, § 502, Oct. 28, 1998, 112 Stat. 2915.)

§ 1326. Penalty for false marking

(a) IN GENERAL.—Whoever, for the purpose of deceiving the public, marks upon, applies to, or uses in advertising in connection with an article made, used, distributed, or sold, a design which is not protected under this chapter, a design notice specified in section 1306, or any other words or symbols importing that the design is protected under this chapter, knowing that the design is not so protected, shall pay a civil fine of not more than $500 for each such offense.

(b) SUIT BY PRIVATE PERSONS.—Any person may sue for the penalty established by subsection (a), in which event one-half of the penalty shall be awarded to the person suing and the remainder shall be awarded to the United States.

(Added Pub. L. 105–304, title V, § 502, Oct. 28, 1998, 112 Stat. 2915.)

§ 1327. Penalty for false representation

Whoever knowingly makes a false representation materially affecting the rights obtainable under this chapter for the purpose of obtaining registration of a design under this chapter shall pay a penalty of not less than $500 and not more than $1,000, and any rights or privileges that individual may have in the design under this chapter shall be forfeited.

(Added Pub. L. 105–304, title V, § 502, Oct. 28, 1998, 112 Stat. 2915.)

§ 1328. Enforcement by Treasury and Postal Service

(a) REGULATIONS.—The Secretary of the Treasury and the United States Postal Service shall separately or jointly issue regulations for the enforcement of the rights set forth in section 1308 with respect to importation. Such regulations may require, as a condition for the exclusion of articles from the United States, that the person seeking exclusion take any one or more of the following actions:

(1) Obtain a court order enjoining, or an order of the International Trade Commission under section 337 of the Tariff Act of 1930 excluding, importation of the articles.

(2) Furnish proof that the design involved is protected under this chapter and that the importation of the articles would infringe the rights in the design under this chapter.

(3) Post a surety bond for any injury that may result if the detention or exclusion of the articles proves to be unjustified.

(b) SEIZURE AND FORFEITURE.—Articles imported in violation of the rights set forth in section 1308 are subject to seizure and forfeiture in the same manner as property imported in violation of the customs laws. Any such forfeited articles shall be destroyed as directed by the Secretary of the Treasury or the court, as the case may be, except that the articles may be returned to the country of export whenever it is shown to the satisfaction of the Secretary of the Treasury that the importer had no reasonable grounds for believing that his or her acts constituted a violation of the law.

(Added Pub. L. 105–304, title V, § 502, Oct. 28, 1998, 112 Stat. 2916.)

§ 1329. Relation to design patent law

The issuance of a design patent under title 35, United States Code, for an original design for an article of manufacture shall terminate any protection of the original design under this chapter.

(Added Pub. L. 105–304, title V, § 502, Oct. 28, 1998, 112 Stat. 2916.)

§ 1330. Common law and other rights unaffected

Nothing in this chapter shall annul or limit—

(1) common law or other rights or remedies, if any, available to or held by any person with respect to a design which has not been registered under this chapter; or

(2) any right under the trademark laws or any right protected against unfair competition.

(Added Pub. L. 105–304, title V, § 502, Oct. 28, 1998, 112 Stat. 2916.)

§ 1331. Administrator; Office of the Administrator

In this chapter, the "Administrator" is the Register of Copyrights, and the "Office of the Administrator" and the "Office" refer to the Copyright Office of the Library of Congress.

(Added Pub. L. 105–304, title V, § 502, Oct. 28, 1998, 112 Stat. 2916.)

§ 1332. No retroactive effect

Protection under this chapter shall not be available for any design that has been made public under section 1310(b) before the effective date of this chapter.

(Added Pub. L. 105–304, title V, § 502, Oct. 28, 1998, 112 Stat. 2916.)